Fodor's 2015

NORTHERN CALIFORNIA

Excerpted from *Fodor's California 2015*

WELCOME TO NORTHERN CALIFORNIA

It's easy to tap into the good life in Northern California. Between rounds of golf at Pebble Beach, winding drives along the iconic Big Sur coast, or scenic treks through Yosemite National Park, you can indulge in a wealth of top-notch outdoor activities. In Napa and Sonoma, eating and drinking are cultivated as high arts. You can sip wine at picturesque vineyards and then dine at stellar locavore restaurants. Urban pleasures await in San Francisco, too, where cable cars zip through vibrant neighborhoods lined with chic boutiques and cutting-edge museums.

TOP REASONS TO GO

★ **San Francisco:** This diverse city beguiles with natural beauty and contagious energy.

★ **Wine Country:** Top-notch whites and reds in Napa, Sonoma, and beyond.

★ **Feasts:** Cutting-edge cuisine, food trucks, fusion flavors, farmers' markets.

★ **Stunning Scenery:** Picture-perfect backdrops from the Golden Gate Bridge to redwoods.

★ **Outdoor Adventures:** National park excursions, hiking, and golfing are all excellent.

★ **Road Trips:** The Pacific Coast Highway offers spectacular views and thrills aplenty.

Fodor's NORTHERN CALIFORNIA 2015

Publisher: Amanda D'Acierno, *Senior Vice President*

Editorial: Arabella Bowen, *Editor in Chief*; Linda Cabasin, *Editorial Director*

Design: Fabrizio La Rocca, *Vice President, Creative Director*; Tina Malaney, *Associate Art Director*; Chie Ushio, *Senior Designer*; Ann McBride, *Production Designer*

Photography: Melanie Marin, *Associate Director of Photography*; Jessica Parkhill and Jennifer Romains, *Researchers*

Maps: Rebecca Baer, *Senior Map Editor*; David Lindroth and Mark Stroud, *Cartographers*

Production: Linda Schmidt, *Managing Editor*; Evangelos Vasilakis, *Associate Managing Editor*; Angela L. McLean, *Senior Production Manager*

Sales: Jacqueline Lebow, *Sales Director*

Marketing & Publicity: Heather Dalton, *Marketing Director*; Katherine Punia, *Senior Publicist*

Business & Operations: Susan Livingston, *Vice President, Strategic Business Planning*; Sue Daulton, *Vice President, Operations*

Fodors.com: Megan Bell, *Executive Director, Revenue & Business Development*; Yasmin Marinaro, *Senior Director, Marketing & Partnerships*

Copyright © 2015 by Fodor's Travel, a division of Random House LLC

Writers: Michele Bigley, Cheryl Crabtree, Denise M. Leto, Daniel Mangin, Jenie Skoy, Christine Vovakes, Sharron Wood, Bobbi Zane

Editors: Luke Epplin *(lead project editor)*, Salwa Jabado

Editorial Contributors: Linda Cabasin, Andrew Collins, Daniel Mangin, Steven Montero, Jacinta O'Halloran, Amanda Sadlowski, Emma Scoble

Production Editor: Evangelos Vasilakis

ISBN 978-0-8041-4281-6

ISSN 1543–1045

SPECIAL SALES

PRINTED IN THE UNITED STATES OF AMERICA

10 9 8 7 6 5 4 3 2 1

CONTENTS

MAPS

ABOUT THIS GUIDE

Fodor's Recommendations

Everything in this guide is worth doing—we don't cover what isn't—but exceptional sights, hotels, and restaurants are recognized with additional accolades. **Fodor's**Choice★ indicates our top recommendations; and **Best Bets** call attention to notable hotels and restaurants in various categories. Care to nominate a new place? Visit Fodors.com/contact-us.

Trip Costs

We list prices wherever possible to help you budget well. Hotel and restaurant price categories from $ to $$$$ are noted alongside each recommendation. For hotels, we include the lowest cost of a standard double room in high season. For restaurants, we cite the average price of a main course at dinner or, if dinner isn't served, at lunch. For attractions, we always list adult admission fees; discounts are usually available for children, students, and senior citizens.

Hotels

Our local writers vet every hotel to recommend the best overnights in each price category, from budget to expensive. Unless otherwise specified, you can expect private bath, phone, and TV in your room. For expanded hotel reviews, facilities, and deals visit Fodors.com.

Restaurants

Unless we state otherwise, restaurants are open for lunch and dinner daily. We mention dress code only when there's a specific requirement and reservations only when they're essential or not accepted. To make restaurant reservations, visit Fodors.com.

Credit Cards

The hotels and restaurants in this guide typically accept credit cards. If not, we'll say so.

Top Picks
★ **Fodor's**Choice

Listings
⊠ Address
⊠ Branch address
☎ Telephone
🖷 Fax
⊕ Website
✉ E-mail
🎫 Admission fee
🕙 Open/closed times
Ⓜ Subway
✛ Directions or Map coordinates

Hotels & Restaurants
🏨 Hotel
🛏 Number of rooms
🍽 Meal plans
✕ Restaurant
🖎 Reservations
👔 Dress code
🚫 No credit cards
$ Price

Other
⇨ See also
☞ Take note
⛳ Golf facilities

EXPERIENCE NORTHERN CALIFORNIA

WHAT'S NEW IN NORTHERN CALIFORNIA

Foodie's Paradise

Great dining is a staple of the California lifestyle, and a new young generation of chefs is challenging old ideas about preparing and presenting great food. Food-truck frenzy has created a movable feast up and down the state. Esteemed chefs and urban foodies follow the trucks on Twitter as they move around cities 24/7 purveying delicious, cheap, fresh meals. California chefs continue to shop locally for produce and farmer-sourced meat. Tender Greens (with locations in Walnut Creek as well as in Southern California) sets the bar high by serving hand-raised produce; grain-fed, hormone-free beef; hand-raised chickens; and line-caught tuna.

Grape Expectations

California wine culture is alive and well and continues to grow beyond the traditional wine country of Napa and Sonoma. Winemaking is expanding in the Central Valley and Shasta Cascade areas. The Truckee River Winery, near Lake Tahoe, claims to be the highest and coldest winery in the nation.

Suite Dreams

Hotels are coming back to life in a big way. Visitors to Yountville in the Napa Valley have another lodging choice, the Bardessono, a LEED-certified hotel that sports an eco spa and an underground geothermal system.

All Aboard

Riding the rails can be a satisfying experience, particularly in California where the distances between destinations sometimes run into the hundreds of miles. The best trip is on the luxuriously appointed Coast Starlight, a long-distance train with sleeping cars that runs between Seattle and Los Angeles, passing some of California's most beautiful coastline as it hugs the beach. For the best surfside viewing, get a seat or a room on the left side of the train and ride south to north from San Diego to Oakland.

Amtrak offers regular service throughout the Northern and Southern regions of the state. These are coach cars, but many of the trains have been upgraded and are comfortable and convenient, especially if you want to get off and on the train at several destinations—ranging from Los Angeles up to Santa Barbara, San Luis Obispo, and Oakland (just a BART ride to San Francisco).

Head for the Hills

Things are looking up for visitors to California's alpine recreation areas, thanks to a host of enhancements. In 2014, Yosemite National Park celebrated the 150th anniversary of the Yosemite Land Grant, which protected the Yosemite Valley and Mariposa Grove and also made the area the first California state park. Yosemite National Park observed its 120th birthday in late 2011 with some new ways to see the park. Yosemite Guide Service offers guided day hikes, customized driving tours, and backpacking trips. You can also take Yosemite Audio Adventures CD tours with you as you explore the park.

Homegrown Hospitality

Agritourism in California isn't new (remember, Knott's Berry Farm once *was* a berry farm), but it is on the rise, with farm tours and agricultural festivals sprouting up everywhere.

Wine country is a particularly fertile area—spurred by the success of vineyards, the area's lavender growers and olive-oil producers have started welcoming visitors. Sonoma Farm Trail Tours include walking the land and a farm-driven dinner with paired wines.

WHEN TO GO

Because it offers activities indoors and out, Northern California rates as an all-season destination. Early spring—when the gray-whale migration overlaps with the end of the elephant-seal breeding season and the start of the bird migration—is the optimal time to visit Point Reyes National Seashore. Yosemite is ideal in the late spring because roads closed in winter are reopened, and the park's waterfalls—swollen with melting snow—run fast. Autumn is "crush time" in all the wine destinations, from Napa/Sonoma in the north to the central coast. Snowfall makes winter peak season for skiers in Mammoth Mountain and Lake Tahoe, where runs typically open around Thanksgiving. (They sometimes remain in operation into June.)

Climate

It's difficult to generalize much about the state's weather beyond saying that precipitation comes in winter and summer is dry in most places. As a rule, inland regions are hotter in summer and colder in winter, compared with coastal areas, which are relatively cool year-round. Fog is a potential hazard any day of the year in coastal regions. As you climb into the mountains, seasonal variations are more apparent: winter brings snow (at elevations above 3,000 feet), autumn is crisp, spring can go either way, and summer is sunny and warm, with only an occasional thundershower in the southern part of the state.

Microclimates

Mountains separate the California coastline from the state's interior, and the weather can sometimes vary dramatically within a 15-minute drive. On a foggy summer day in San Francisco, you'll be grateful for a sweater—but head 50 miles north inland to Napa Valley, and you'll likely be content in short sleeves. Day and nighttime temperatures can also vary greatly. Temperature swings elsewhere can be even more extreme. Take Sacramento: On August afternoons the mercury hits the 90s and occasionally exceeds 100°F. Yet as darkness falls, it sometimes plummets to 40°F.

Forecasts

National Weather Service
⊕ *www.wrh.noaa.gov.*

WHAT'S WHERE

The following numbers refer to chapters.

2 The Central Coast. Three of the state's top stops—swanky Santa Barbara, Hearst Castle, and Big Sur—sit along the scenic 200-mile route.

3 Monterey Bay Area. Postcard-perfect Monterey, Victorian-flavored Pacific Grove, and exclusive Carmel all share this stretch of California coast. To the north, Santa Cruz boasts a board-walk, a UC campus, ethnic clothing shops, and plenty of surfers.

4 San Francisco. To see why so many have left their hearts here, you need to see the city's iconic neighbor-hoods—posh Pacific Heights, the Hispanic Mission, and gay-friendly Castro.

5 The Bay Area. The area that rings San Francisco is nothing like the city—but it is home to some of the nation's great universities, fabulous bay views, Silicon Valley, and Alice Waters' Chez Panisse.

6 The Wine Country. Napa and Sonoma counties retain their title as the California Wine Country, by virtue of award-winning vintages, luxe lodgings, and epicurean eats.

7 The North Coast. The star attractions here are the natural ones, from the secluded beaches and wave-battered bluffs of Point Reyes National Seashore to the towering redwood forests.

8 Redwood National Park. More than 200 miles of trails, ranging from easy to strenuous, allow visitors to see these spectacu-lar trees in their primitive environments.

9 The Southern Sierra. In the Mammoth Lakes region, sawtooth mountains and deep powdery snowdrifts combine to create the state's premier conditions for skiing and snowboarding.

10 Yosemite National Park. The views immortal-ized by photographer Ansel Adams—of towering granite monoliths, verdant glacial valleys, and lofty water-falls—are still camera-ready.

11 Sequoia and Kings Canyon National Parks. The sight of ancient redwoods towering above jagged mountains will take your breath away.

12 Sacramento and the Gold Country. The 1849 gold rush that built San Francisco and Sacramento began here, and the former mining camps strung along 185 miles of Highway 49 replay their past to the hilt.

13 Lake Tahoe. With miles of crystalline water reflect-ing the peaks of the High Sierra, Lake Tahoe is the perfect setting for activi-ties like hiking and golfing in summer and skiing and snowmobiling in winter.

14 The Far North. Califor-nia's far northeast corner is home to snowcapped Mount Shasta, the pristine Trinity Wilderness, and abundant backwoods character that appeals to outdoorsy types.

NORTHERN CALIFORNIA PLANNER

Car Travel

Driving may be a way of life in California, but it isn't cheap (gas prices here are usually among the highest in the nation). It's also not for the fainthearted; you've surely heard horror stories about California's freeways, but even the state's scenic highways and byways have their own hassles. For instance, on the dramatic coastal road between San Simeon and Carmel, twists, turns, and divinely distracting vistas cause frequently slow traffic; in rainy season, mud slides can close the road altogether. ⚠ **Never cross the double line to pass a slower car ahead of you. If you see that cars are backing up behind you, stop at the first available pullout to allow faster drivers to pass.**

On California's notorious freeways, other rules apply. Nervous Nellies must resist the urge to stay in the two slow-moving lanes on the far right, used primarily by trucks. To drive at least the speed limit, get yourself in a middle lane. If you're ready to bend the rules a bit, the second (lanes are numbered from 1 starting at the center) lane moves about 5 mph faster. But avoid the far-left lane (the one next to the carpool lane), where speeds range from 75 mph to 90 mph.

Air Travel

Air travelers beginning or ending their vacation in San Francisco have two main airports to choose from: San Francisco International (SFO) or Oakland International (OAK) across the bay. The former lands you closer to the city core (ground transportation will take about 20 minutes versus 35), but the latter is less heavily trafficked and less prone to pesky fog delays. BART, the Bay Area's affordable rapid-transit system, serves both airports. So your decision will probably rest on which one has the best fares and connections for your particular route.

If your final destination is Monterey or Carmel, San Jose International Airport (SJC), about 40 miles south of San Francisco, is another alternative.

FAQ

I'm not particularly active. Will I still enjoy visiting a national park? Absolutely, the most popular parks have something for everyone. In Yosemite the ultrafit embark on 12-hour trail treks and mere mortals can hike Cook's Meadow—an easy 1-mile loop that's also wheelchair accessible. Or just hop on a free shuttle or drive yourself to sites.

What's the single best place to take the kids? For its sheer smorgasbord of activities, San Francisco is hard to beat. A cable-car ride is a no-brainer—but be sure to also take a spin on the historic F-line trolleys. Other classic kid-friendly SF sights include the Exploratorium, the San Francisco Zoo, Alcatraz, the Ferry Building, and the California Academy of Sciences. Or head to Musée Mécanique to see what kids played way before Nintendo's Wii came out.

California sounds expensive. How can I save on sightseeing? CityPass (☎ 888/330–5008 ⊕ www.citypass.com) includes admission and some upgrades for main attractions in San Francisco. Also, many museums set aside free-admission days. Prefer the great outdoors? An $80 America the Beautiful annual pass (☎ 888/275–8747 ⊕ www.nps.gov) admits you to every site under the National Park Service umbrella. Better yet, depending on the property, passengers in your vehicle get in free, too.

NORTHERN CALIFORNIA'S TOP EXPERIENCES

Hit the Road

Kings Canyon Highway, Redwood Highway, Tioga Pass, 17-Mile Drive, the Lake Tahoe loop: California has some splendid and challenging roads. You'll drive through a tunnel formed by towering redwood trees on the Redwood Highway. If you venture over the Sierras by way of Tioga Pass (through Yosemite in summer only), you'll see emerald green meadows, gray granite monoliths, and pristine blue lakes—and very few people.

Pan for Gold

Though California's gold rush ended more than a hundred years ago, you can still feel the '49er fever on the western face of the Sierra Nevada in Columbia, a well-preserved town populated by costumed interpreters, where you can pan for gold or tour a mine. Or visit Bodie, an eerie ghost town in the eastern Sierra that remains in a state of "arrested decay."

Think Globally, Eat Locally

Over the years California cuisine has evolved from a mere trend into a respected gastronomic tradition: one that pairs local, often organic or sustainable, ingredients with techniques inspired by European, Asian, and, increasingly, Indian and Middle Eastern cookery.

See Eccentric Architecture

California has always drawn creative and, well, eccentric people. And all that quirkiness has left its mark in the form of oddball architecture that makes for some fun sightseeing. Begin by touring Hearst Castle—the beautifully bizarre estate William Randolph Hearst built above San Simeon. And Lake Tahoe's Vikingsholm (a re-created Viking castle) is equally odd.

Be Transported

San Franciscans take cable cars seriously—and riding on one is a must-do. You may even want to visit the (free!) Cable Car Museum to get a handle on the inner workings or just ring a gripman's bell. *(See the Cable Car feature in the San Francisco chapter.)*But, the city's options for vintage public transport doesn't end there: the lesser known F line streetcars are every bit as photogenic, and they have shorter lines.

Go Wild

California communities host hundreds of annual events, but some of the best are organized by Mother Nature. The most famous is the "miracle migration" that sees swallows flock back to Mission San Juan Capistrano in Orange County each March. In Pacific Grove masses of monarch butterflies reliably arrive for their winter vacation every year in October. If you can't make it there, visit the butterfly sanctuary in the California Academy of Sciences in San Francisco.

People-Watch

Opportunities for world-class people-watching abound in California. Just saunter the rainbow-flagged streets of San Francisco's Castro neighborhood or enjoy the century-old boardwalk in time-warped, resiliently boho Santa Cruz.

NORTHERN CALIFORNIA TODAY

The People

California is as much a state of mind as a state in the union—a kind of perpetual promised land that has represented many things to many people. In the 18th century, Spanish missionaries came seeking converts and gold. In the 19th, miners rushed here to search for gold. And, in the years since, a long line of Dust Bowl farmers, land speculators, Haight-Ashbury hippies, migrant workers, dot-commers, real estate speculators, and would-be actors has come chasing their own dreams.

The result is a population that leans toward idealism—without necessarily being as liberal as you might think. (Remember, this is Ronald Reagan's old stomping ground.) And despite the stereotype of the blue-eyed, blond surfer, California's population is not homogeneous either. Ten million people who live here (more than 27% of Californians) are foreign born. Almost half hail from Latin American countries; another third emigrated from Asia, following the waves of Chinese workers who arrived in the 1860s to build the railroads and subsequent waves of Indochinese refugees from the Vietnam War.

The Politics

What's blue and red and green all over? California: a predominantly Democratic state with an aggressive "go green" agenda. Democratic Governor Jerry Brown, who was elected to the office for the second time in 30 years, is moving the progressive agenda ahead with policies that make California the greenest state in the nation supporting more green construction, wind farms, and solar panels.

The Economy

Leading all other states in terms of the income generated by agriculture, tourism, entertainment, and industrial activity, California has the country's most diverse state economy. Moreover, with a gross state product of more than $2 trillion, California would be one of the top 10 economies *in the world* if it were an independent nation. Due to its wealth ($61,400 median household income) and productivity, California took a large hit in the recession that began in 2007, although the state has shown signs of recovery recently.

But the Golden State's economic history is filled with boom and bust cycles—beginning with the mid-19th-century gold rush that started it all. Optimists already have their eyes on the next potential boom: high-tech and bio research, "green companies" focused on alternative energy, renewables, electric cars, and the like.

The Culture

Cultural organizations thrive in California. San Francisco—a city with only about 812,000 residents—has well-regarded ballet, opera, and theater companies, and is home to one of the continent's most noteworthy orchestras. Museums like San Francisco Museum of Modern Art (SFMOMA) and the de Young also represent the city's ongoing commitment to the arts. And now websites are coming to thrive in that creative landscape—Facebook, YouTube, and Google are all California companies.

The Parks and Preserves

Cloud-spearing redwood groves, snow-tipped mountains, canyon-slashed deserts, primordial lava beds, and a seemingly endless coast: California's natural diversity is staggering—and efforts to protect it started early. Yosemite, the first national park, was established here in 1890, and the National Park Service now oversees 30 sites in California (more than in any other state). When you factor in 278 state parks—which encompass underwater preserves, historic sites, wildlife reserves, dune systems, and other sensitive habitats—the number of acres involved is almost as impressive as the topography itself.

Due to encroaching development and pollution, keeping these natural treasures in pristine condition is an ongoing challenge. For instance, Sequoia and Kings Canyon (which is plagued by pesticides and other agricultural pollutants blown in from the San Joaquin Valley) has been named America's "smoggiest park" by the National Parks Conservation Association, and the Environmental Protection Agency has designated it as an "ozone non-attainment area with levels of ozone pollution that threaten human health."

There is no question that Californians love their 278 state parks. Nearly every park has its grass-roots supporters, who volunteer to raise money, volunteer as rangers, and work other jobs to keep the parks open.

The Cuisine

California gave us McDonald's, Denny's, Carl's Jr., Taco Bell, and, of course, In-N-Out Burger. Fortunately for those of us with fast-clogging arteries, the state also kick-started the organic food movement. Back in the 1970s, California-based chefs put American cuisine on the culinary map by focusing on freshly prepared seasonal ingredients.

Today, this focus has spawned the "locavore" or sustainable food movement—followers try to only consume food produced within a 100-mile radius of where they live, since processing and refining food and transporting goods over long distances is bad for both the body and the environment. This isn't much of a restriction in California, where a huge variety of crops grow year-round. Some 350 cities and towns have certified farmers' markets—and their stalls are bursting with a variety of goods. California has been America's top agricultural producer for the last 50 years, growing more fruits and vegetables than any other state. Dairies and ranches also thrive here, and fishing fleets harvest fish and shellfish from the rich waters offshore.

NORTHERN CALIFORNIA TOP ATTRACTIONS

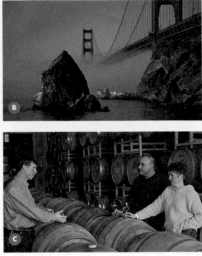

Yosemite National Park

(A) Nature looms large here, both literally and figuratively. In addition to hulking Half Dome, the park is home to El Capitan (the world's largest exposed granite monolith, rising 3,593 feet above the glacier-carved valley floor) and Yosemite Falls (North America's tallest cascade). In Yosemite's signature stand of giant sequoias—the Mariposa Grove—even the trees are Bunyanesque. Needless to say, crowds can be supersized, too.

San Francisco

(B) Population-wise, San Francisco is smaller than Indianapolis. But when it comes to sites (and soul), this city is a giant. Start working through the standard travelers' "to do" list by strolling across the Golden Gate Bridge, taking a ferry to Alcatraz, and hopping on the Powell–Hyde cable car. Just leave enough time to explore the diverse neighborhoods where San Francisco's distinctive

personality—an amalgam of gold-rush history, immigrant traditions, counterculture proclivities, and millennial materialism—is on display.

Wine Country

(C) Although the vineyard-blanketed hills of California's original Wine Country are undeniably scenic, the wine itself (preferably accompanied by the area's famed cuisine) remains the big draw here. Budding oenophiles can educate their palettes on scores of tours and tasting sessions.

Point Reyes National Seashore

(D) Aside from the namesake seashore, this Marin County preserve encompasses ecosystems that range from woodlands and marshlands to heathlike grasslands. The range of wildlife here is equally diverse—depending on when you visit, expect to see gray whales, rare Tule elk, and almost 500 species of birds. December through March, you can also see male elephant seals compete for mates.

Lake Tahoe

(E) Deep, clear, and intensely blue, this forest-rimmed body of water straddling the California–Nevada border is one of the continent's prettiest alpine lakes. That environmental controls can keep it that way is something of a miracle, given Tahoe's popularity. Throngs of outdoor adventurers flock to the California side to ski, hike, bike, and boat. On the Nevada side, where casinos are king, gambling often wins out over fresh-air activities—but natural wonders are never far away.

Gold Country

(F) California's gold rush was one of the most significant events in U.S. history. It saved the Union and helped open the western frontier, when Argonauts flooded a 300-mile-long stretch of the Sierra foothills. Remnants of the gold rush remain to this day in the towns, diggings, trains, museums, and culture that

you'll encounter along historic Highway 49; it runs north to south from Loyalton near the Nevada border to Oakhurst, just south of Yosemite. Towns along the way, mostly updated and renovated, allow you to dig into the past and discover what the excitement was all about.

QUINTESSENTIAL NORTHERN CALIFORNIA

The Wine

If California were a country, it would rank as the world's fourth-largest wine producer, after Italy, France, and Spain. In those countries, where vino is barely considered an alcoholic beverage, wine drinking has evolved into a relaxing ritual best shared with friends and family. A modern, Americanized version of that mentality integrates wine into daily life in California, and there are many places to sample it. The Napa and Sonoma valleys come to mind first. However, there are other destinations for oenophiles who want a vintage vacation. You can find great wineries around Monterey Bay and Gold Country's Amador County, too. All are respected appellations, and their winery tours and tastings will show you what all the buzz is about.

The Beach

California's beach culture is, in a word, legendary. Of course, it only makes sense that folks living in a state with a 1,264-mile coastline (a hefty portion of which sees the sun upward of 300 days a year) would perfect the art of beach-going. True aficionados begin with a reasonably fit physique, plus a stylish wardrobe consisting of flip-flops, bikinis, wet suits, and such. Mastery of at least one beach skill—surfing, boogie boarding, kayaking, Frisbee tossing, or looking fab while catching rays—is also essential. As a visitor, though, you need only a swimsuit and some rented equipment for most sports. You can then hit the beach almost anywhere, thanks to the California belief in coastal access as a birthright. The farther south you go, the wider, sandier, and sunnier the beaches become; moving north they are rockier and foggier, with colder and rougher surf.

Californians live in such a large and splashy state that they sometimes seem to forget about the rest of the country. They've developed a distinctive culture all their own, which you can delve into by doing as the locals do.

The Outdoors

One of California's greatest assets—the mild year-round weather enjoyed by most of the state—inspires residents to spend as much time outside as they possibly can. They have a tremendous enthusiasm for every imaginable outdoor sport, and, up north especially, fresh-air adventures are extremely popular (which may explain why everyone there seems to own at least one pair of hiking boots). But the California-alfresco creed is more broadly interpreted, and the general rule when planning any activity is "if it can happen outside, it will!" *Plein air* vacation opportunities include dining on patios, decks, and wharves; shopping in street markets or elaborate open-air malls; hearing almost any kind of music at moonlight concerts; touring the sculpture gardens that grace major art museums; and celebrating everything from gay pride to garlic at outdoor fairs.

The Automobile

Americans may have a love affair with the automobile, but Californians have an out-and-out obsession. Even when gas prices rev up and freeway traffic slows down, their passion burns as hot as ever. You can witness this ardor any summer weekend at huge classic- and custom-car shows held statewide. Even better, you can feel it yourself by taking the wheel. Trace an old stagecoach route through the mountains above Santa Barbara on Highway 154; track migrating whales up the coast to Big Sur; or take 17-Mile Drive along the precipitous edge of the Monterey Peninsula. Glorious for the most part, but authentically congested in some areas in the south, Highway 1 runs almost the entire length of the state, hugging the coast most of the way.

GREAT ITINERARIES

SIERRA RICHES: YOSEMITE, GOLD COUNTRY, AND TAHOE, 10 DAYS

This tour will show you why Tony Bennett left his heart in San Francisco. It also includes some of the most beautiful places is a very scenic state, plus gold-rush-era history, and a chance to hike a trail or two.

Day 1: San Francisco

Straight from the airport, drop your bags at the lighthearted **Hotel Monaco** near **Union Square** and request a goldfish for your room. A Union Square stroll packs a wallop of people-watching, window-shopping, and architecture viewing. **Chinatown**, chock-full of dim sum shops, storefront temples, and open-air markets, promises unfamiliar tastes for lunch. Catch a Powell Street **cable car** to the end of the line and get off to see the bay views and the antique arcade games at **Musée Mécanique**, the hidden gem of otherwise mindless **Fisherman's Wharf**. No need to go any farther than cosmopolitan North Beach for cocktail hour, dinner, and live music.

Day 2: Golden Gate Park

In **Golden Gate Park**, linger amid the flora of the **Conservatory of Flowers** and the **San Francisco Botanical Garden at Strybing Arboretum**, soak up some art at the **de Young Museum**, and find serene refreshment at the **San Francisco Japanese Tea Garden**. The Pacific surf pounds the cliffs below the **Legion of Honor** art museum, which has an exquisite view of the **Golden Gate Bridge**—when the fog stays away. Sunset cocktails at the circa-1909 **Cliff House** include a prospect over Seal Rock (actually occupied by sea lions). Eat dinner elsewhere: Pacific Heights, the Mission, and SoMa teem with excellent restaurants.

Day 3: Into the High Sierra

First thing in the morning, pick up your rental car and head for the hills. A five-hour drive due east brings you to **Yosemite National Park**, where **Bridalveil Fall** and **El Capitan,** the 350-story granite monolith, greet you on your way to **Yosemite Village**. Ditch the car and pick up information and refreshment before hopping on the year-round shuttle to explore. Justly famous sights cram Yosemite Valley: massive **Half Dome** and **Sentinel Dome**, thundering **Yosemite Falls**, and wispy **Ribbon Fall** and **Nevada Fall**. Invigorating short hikes off the shuttle route lead to numerous vantage points. Celebrate your arrival in one of the world's most sublime spots with dinner in the dramatic **Ahwahnee Hotel Dining Room** and stay the night there (reserve well in advance).

Day 4: Yosemite National Park

Ardent hikers consider **John Muir Trail to Half Dome** a must-do, tackling the rigorous 12-hour round-trip to the top of Half Dome in search of life-changing vistas. The merely mortal hike downhill from Glacier Point on Four-Mile Trail or **Panorama Trail**, the latter an all-day trek past waterfalls. Less demanding still is a drive to Wawona for a stroll in the **Mariposa Grove of Big Trees** and lunch at the 19th-century **Wawona Hotel Dining Room**. In bad weather, take shelter in the Ansel Adams Gallery and Yosemite Museum; in fair conditions, drive up to **Glacier Point** for a breathtaking sunset view.

Day 5: Gold Country South

Highway 49 traces the mother lode that yielded many fortunes in gold in the 1850s and 1860s. Step into a living gold-rush town at **Columbia State Historic Park,**

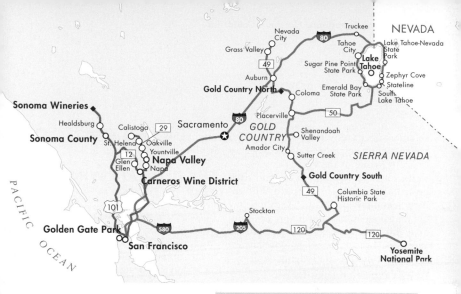

where you can ride a stagecoach and pan for riches. **Sutter Creek's** well-preserved downtown bursts with shopping opportunities, but the vintage goods displayed at **Monteverde Store Museum** are not for sale. A different sort of vintage powers the present-day bonanza of **Shenandoah Valley,** heart of the Sierra Foothills Wine Country. Taste your way through Rhône-style blended Zinfandels and Syrahs at boutique wineries such as **Shenandoah Vineyards** and **Sobon Estate.** Amador City's 1879 **Imperial Hotel** places you firmly in the past for the night.

Day 6: Gold Country North

In **Placerville,** a mineshaft invites investigation at **Hangtown's Gold Bug Mine,** while **Marshall Gold Discovery State Historic Park** encompasses most of **Coloma** and preserves the spot where James Marshall's 1849 find set off the California gold rush. Old Town **Auburn,** with its museums and courthouse, makes a good lunch stop, but if you hold out until you reach Grass Valley you can try authentic miners' pasties. A tour of **Empire Mine State Historic Park** takes you into a mine, and a few miles away horse-drawn carriages ply the narrow, shop-lined streets of downtown **Nevada City.** Both Nevada City and **Grass Valley** hold a collection of

TIPS

Parking in San Francisco is expensive and scarce. When you fly in, take a shuttle or taxi from the airport to the city, and then use the excellent public transportation to get around.

Try to time your trip for late spring or early fall to avoid the worst of the crowds and the road-closing snowfalls in Yosemite and around Lake Tahoe. Yosemite's falls peak in spring and early summer, while fall brings the grape harvest in the Sierra Nevada foothills.

For a visit in any season, reserve your hotel or campground accommodations in Yosemite as far in advance as possible—up to a year ahead.

bed-and-breakfast inns that date back to gold-rush days. For more contemporary accommodations backtrack to Auburn or Placerville.

Day 7: Lake Tahoe

Jewel-like **Lake Tahoe** is a straight shot east of Placerville on Highway 50; stop for picnic provisions in commercial **South Lake Tahoe.** A stroll past the three magnificent estates in **Pope-Baldwin Recreation Area** hints at the sumptuous lakefront summers once enjoyed by the elite. High above a glittering cove, **Emerald Bay State Park** offers one of the best lake views as well as a steep hike down to (and back up from) **Vikingsholm**, a replica 9th-century Scandinavian castle. Another fine, old mansion—plus a nature preserve and many hiking trails—lies in **Sugar Pine Point State Park.** Tahoe City offers more history and ample dining and lodging choices.

Day 8: Exploring Lake Tahoe

The picture-perfect beaches and bays of **Lake Tahoe–Nevada State Park** line the Nevada shoreline, a great place to bask in the sun or go mountain biking. For a different perspective of the lake, get out on the azure water aboard the sternwheeler MS *Dixie II* from **Zephyr Cove.** In South Lake Tahoe, another view unfurls as the **Heavenly Gondola** travels 2½ miles up a mountain. Keep your adrenaline pumping into the evening with some action at the massive casinos clustered in Stateline, Nevada.

Day 9: Return to San Francisco

After a long (five hours) morning of driving, return your rental car in San Francisco and soak up some more urban excitement. Good options include a late lunch at the **Ferry Building,** followed by a visit to the **San Francisco Museum of Modern Art,** or lunch in **Japantown** followed by shopping in **Pacific Heights.** People-watching excels in the late afternoon bustle of the **Castro** and the **Haight.** Say good-bye to Northern California at one of the plush lounges or trendy bars in the downtown hotels.

Day 10: Departure

Check the weather and your flight information before you start out for the airport: Fog sometimes causes delays at SFO. On a clear day, your flight path might give you one last fabulous glimpse of the City by the Bay.

THE ULTIMATE WINE TRIP, 5 DAYS

In these five days of wine tasting, you'll have a chance to see legendary wineries that produce well-known brands, stay in lovely hotels with knowledgeable hosts, and dine at restaurants operated by celebrity chefs.

Day 1: Sonoma County

Begin your wine tour in **Healdsburg,** about 65 miles north of San Francisco on Highway 101. Healdsburg was named one of the Top Small Towns in America by Fodor's editors in 2013 for its charming atmosphere, great restaurants, and lovely B&Bs. The best choices to overnight at are **The Honor Mansion** or **Hotel Healdsburg.** Take your pick of the trendy restaurants that ring the plaza. Stellar choices are **Scopa** and **Spoonbar.** End the day with a stroll around the plaza.

Day 2: Sonoma Wineries

You won't have to travel far to begin your day of wine tasting. Many local wineries have tasting rooms within walking distance of the Healdsburg plaza. You'll find some of the most interesting wineries in the countryside surrounding the town, including **Preston Vineyards, Francis Ford Coppola Winery,** and **Dry Creek Vineyard.** All produce wonderful Cabernet Sauvignon, Chardonnay, and Zinfandel. Most have picnic areas where you can savor a bite while sampling the grape. In the afternoon head south on Highway 101 to scenic Highway 12. Take a break at **Glen Ellen** to visit **Jack London State Historic Park,** the memorabilia-filled home of the famed writer.

Day 3: Napa Valley

Plan to spend two nights in the same lodging in the **Napa Valley,** in the city of **Napa** or a few miles north in **Yountville.** For your Day 3 tasting schedule head north to **Saint Helena,** which has the largest concentration of wineries, like the **Beringer Vineyards, John Phelps Vineyards,** and **Spring Mountain Vineyard,** and most of the well-known names in the region plus the **Culinary Institute of America** and **Wine Spectator Greystone Restaurant.** Yountville has **V Marketplace** where you'll find **Napa-Style,** a luxury food market and deli, and celebrity chef Michael Chiarello's **Bottega** restaurant.

Day 4: North on Hwy 29

After breakfast, head north on Highway 29 to **Oakville,** home of the oldest continually operating grocery store in California, the **Oakville Grocery. Calistoga,** a few miles up the road, dates back more than 100 years and is known for its hot spring spas. Robert Louis Stevenson and his bride spent their honeymoon in 1880 here. Head south for dinner at one of the Napa Valley's celebrity restaurants.

Day 5: Carneros to San Francisco

Your final day in the Wine Country includes a couple of stops in the Carneros Wine District on the way back to San Francisco. Stop at **Domaine Carneros,** a Taittinger brand that creates perfectly dry sparkling wine in the French tradition. The art-stuffed **di Rosa** preserve nearby is worth a stop as well. Give yourself plenty of time to get to your departure airport; traffic is generally heavy as you close in on the Bay Area.

THE ULTIMATE ROAD TRIP

CALIFORNIA'S LEGENDARY HIGHWAY 1

by Cheryl Crabtree

One of the world's most scenic drives, California's State Route 1 (also known as Highway 1, the Pacific Coast Highway, the PCH) stretches along the edge of the state for nearly 660 miles, from Southern California's Dana Point to its northern terminus near Leggett, about 40 miles north of Fort Bragg. As you travel south to north, the water's edge transitions from long, sandy beaches and low-lying bluffs to towering dunes, craggy cliffs, and ancient redwood groves. The ocean changes as well; the relatively tame and surfable swells lapping the Southern California shore give way to the frigid, powerful waves crashing against weatherbeaten rocks in the north.

HIGHWAY 1 TOP 10

- Santa Monica
- Santa Barbara
- Hearst San Simeon State Historical Monument
- Big Sur
- Carmel
- 17–Mile Drive
- Monterey
- San Francisco
- Marin Headlands
- Point Reyes National Seashore

Give yourself lots of extra time to pull off the road and enjoy the scenery

STARTING YOUR JOURNEY

You may decide to drive the road's entire 660-mile route, or bite off a smaller piece. In either case, a Highway 1 road trip allows you to experience California at your own pace, stopping when and where you wish. Hike a beachside trail, dig your toes in the sand, and search for creatures in the tidepools. Buy some artichokes and strawberries from a roadside farmstand. Talk to people along the way (you'll run into everyone from soul-searching meditators, farmers, and beatniks to city-slackers and working-class folks), and take lots of pictures. Don't rush—you could easily spend a lifetime discovering secret spots along this route.

To help you plan your trip, we've broken the road into three regions (Santa Monica to Carmel, Carmel to San Francisco, and San Francisco to Fort Bragg); each region is then broken up into smaller segments—many of which are suitable for a day's drive. If you're pressed for time, you can always tackle a section of Highway 1, and then head inland to U.S. 101 or I-5 to reach your next destination more quickly.

WHAT'S IN A NAME?

Though it's often referred to as the Pacific Coast Highway (or PCH), sections of Highway 1 actually have different names. The southernmost section (Dana Point to Oxnard) is the Pacific Coast Highway. After that, the road becomes the Cabrillo Highway (Las Cruces to Lompoc), the Big Sur Coast Highway (San Luis Obispo County line to Monterey), the North Coast Scenic Byway (San Luis Obispo city limit to the Monterey County line), the Cabrillo Highway again (Santa Cruz County line to Half Moon Bay), and finally the Shoreline Highway (Marin City to Leggett). To make matters more confusing, smaller chunks of the road have additional honorary monikers.

Just follow the green triangular signs that say "California 1."

HIGHWAY 1 DRIVING

- Rent a convertible. (You will not regret it.)
- Begin the drive north from Santa Monica, where congestion and traffic delays pose less of a problem.
- Take advantage of turnouts. Let cars pass you as you take in the ocean view and snap a picture.
- Mind your manners: Don't tailgate or glare at other drivers.
- If you're prone to motion sickness, take the wheel yourself. Focusing on the landscape outside should help you feel less queasy.
- If you're afraid of heights, drive from south to north so you'll be on the mountain rather than the cliff side of the road.
- Driving PCH is glorious during winter, but check weather conditions before you go as landslides are frequent after storms.

HIGHWAY 1: SANTA MONICA TO BIG SUR

Hearst Castle

THE PLAN

Distance: approx. 335 mi

Time: 3-5 days

Good Overnight Options: Malibu, Santa Barbara, Pismo Beach, San Luis Obispo, Cambria, Carmel

For more information on the sights and attractions along this portion of Highway 1, please see the Central Coast chapter

SANTA MONICA TO MALIBU (approx. 26 mi)

Highway 1 begins in Dana point, but it seems more appropriate to begin a PCH adventure in **Santa Monica.** Be sure to experience the beach culture, then balance the tacky pleasures of Santa Monica's amusement pier with a stylish dinner in a neighborhood restaurant.

MALIBU TO SANTA BARBARA (approx. 70 mi)

The PCH follows the curve of Santa Monica Bay all the way to **Malibu** and **Point Mugu,**

near **Oxnard.** Chances are you'll experience *déjà vu* driving this 27-mile stretch: mountains on one side, ocean on the other, opulent homes perched on hillsides; you've seen this piece of coast countless times on TV and film. Be sure to walk out on the **Malibu Pier** for a great photo opp, then check out **Surfrider Beach,** with three famous points where perfect waves ignited a worldwide surfing rage in the 1960s.

After Malibu you'll drive through miles of protected, largely unpopulated coastline. Ride a wave at **Zuma Beach,** scout for offshore whales at **Point Dume State Beach,** or hike the trails at **Point Mugu State Park.** After skirting Point Mugu, Highway 1 merges with U.S. 101 for about 70 mi before reaching **Santa Barbara.** A mini-tour of the city includes a real Mexican lunch at **La Super-Rica,** a visit to the magnificent Spanish **Mission Santa Barbara,** and a walk down hopping **State Street to Stearns Wharf.**

SANTA BARBARA TO SAN SIMEON (approx. 147 mi)

North of Santa Barbara, Highway 1 morphs into the Cabrillo Highway, separating

Santa Barbara

from and then rejoining U.S. 101. The route winds through rolling vineyards and rangeland to **San Luis Obispo,** where any legit road trip includes a photo stop at the quirky **Madonna Inn.** Be sure to also climb the humungous dunes at **Guadalupe-Nipomo Dunes Preserve.**

In downtown San Luis Obispo, the **Mission San Luis Obispo de Tolosa** stands by a tree-shaded creek edged with shops and cafés. Highway 1 continues to **Morro Bay** and up the coast. About 4 mi north of Morro Bay, you'll reach **Cayucos,** a classic old California beach town with an 1875 pier, restaurants, taverns, and shops in historic buildings. The road continues through **Cambria** to solitary **Hearst San Simeon State Historical Monument**—the art-filled pleasure palace at **San Simeon.** Just four miles north of the castle, elephant seals grunt and cavort at the

Santa Monica

Big Sur

TOP 5 PLACES TO LINGER

- Point Dume State Beach
- Santa Barbara
- Hearst San Simeon State Historical Monument
- Big Sur/Julia Pfeiffer Burns State Park
- Carmel

Piedras Blancas Elephant Seal Rookery, just off the side of the road.

SAN SIMEON TO CARMEL (approx. 92 mi) Heading north, you'll drive through **Big Sur,** a place of ancient forests and rugged shoreline stretching 90 mi from San Simeon to **Carmel.** Much of Big Sur lies within several state parks and the 165,000-acre **Ventana Wilderness,** itself part of the **Los Padres National Forest.** This famously scenic stretch of the coastal drive, which twists up and down bluffs above the ocean, can last hours. Take your time.

At **Julia Pfeiffer Burns State Park** one easy but rewarding hike leads to an iconic waterfall off a beach-front cliff. When you reach lovely **Carmel,** stroll around the picture-perfect town's mission, galleries, and shops.

HIGHWAY 1: CARMEL TO SAN FRANCISCO

San Francisco

THE PLAN

Distance: approx. 123 mi

Time: 2-4 days

Good Overnight Options: Carmel, Monterey, Santa Cruz, Half Moon Bay, San Francisco

For more information on the sights and attractions along this portion of Highway 1, please see chapters Monterey Bay, San Francisco, and Bay Area.

CARMEL TO MONTEREY

(approx. 4 mi)

Between **Carmel** and **Monterey,** Highway 1 cuts across the base of the Monterey Peninsula. Pony up the toll and take a brief detour to follow famous **17-Mile Drive,** which traverses a surf-pounded landscape of cypress trees, sea lions, gargantuan estates, and the world famous **Pebble Beach Golf Links.** Take your time here as well, and be sure to allow lots of time for pulling off to enjoy the gorgeous views.

Monterey

If you have the time, spend a day checking out the sights in **Monterey,** especially the kelp forests and bat rays of the **Monterey Bay Aquarium** and the adobes and artifacts of **Monterey State Historic Park.**

MONTEREY TO SANTA CRUZ (approx. 42 mi)

From Monterey the highway rounds the gentle curve of Monterey Bay, passing through sand dunes and artichoke fields on its way to **Moss Landing** and the **Elkhorn Slough National Estuarine Marine Preserve.** Kayak near or walk through the protected wetlands here, or board a pontoon safari boat—don't forget your binoculars. The historic seaside villages of **Aptos, Capitola,** and **Soquel,** just off the highway near the bay's midpoint, are ideal stopovers for beachcombing, antiquing, and hiking through redwoods. In boho **Santa Cruz,** just 7 mi north, walk along the **wharf,** ride the historic roller coaster on the **boardwalk,** and perch on the cliffs to watch surfers peel through tubes at **Steamer Lane.**

SANTA CRUZ TO SAN FRANCISCO

(approx. 77 mi)

Highway 1 hugs the ocean's edge once again as it departs Santa Cruz and runs

Davenport cliffs, Devenport

northward past a string of secluded beaches and small towns. Stop and stretch your legs in the tiny, artsy town of **Davenport,** where you can wander through several galleries and enjoy sumptuous views from the bluffs. At **Año Nuevo State Park,** walk down to the dunes to view gargantuan elephant

FRIGID WATERS

If you're planning to jump in the ocean in Northern California, wear a wetsuit or prepare to shiver. Even in summer, the water temperatures warm up to just barely tolerable. The fog tends to burn off earlier in the day at relatively sheltered beaches near Monterey Bay's midpoint, near Aptos, Capitola and Santa Cruz. These beaches also tend to attract softer waves than those on the bay's outer edges.

Half Moon Bay

TOP 5 PLACES TO LINGER

- 17-Mile Drive
- Monterey
- Santa Cruz
- Año Nuevo State Reserve
- Half Moon Bay

eals lounging on shore, hen break for a meal or nack in **Pescadero** or **Half Moon Bay.**

rom Half Moon Bay to **Daly City,** the road includes a umber of shoulderless wists and turns that de- mand slower speeds and erves of steel. Signs of rban development soon ap- pear: mansions holding fast o Pacific cliffs and then, as he road veers slightly inland o merge with Skyline Boule- ard, boxlike houses sprawl- ing across **Daly City** and outh San Francisco.

Golden Gate Nat'l. Recreation Area

San Francisco

Daly City

Pacifica

South San Francisco

San Francisco Bay

Moss Beach

El Granada

San Mateo

Pillar Point
Half Moon Bay

Half Moon Bay

Belmont

Hayward

San Gregorio

Palo Alto

Pescadero Point

Pescadero

Mountain View

Santa Clara

Bolsa Point

Pigeon Point

San Jose

Año Nuevo State Park

Saratoga

Los Gatos

Point Año Nuevo

Boulder Creek

The Forest of Nisene Marks State Park

Davenport

Santa Cruz

Soquel

Aptos

Capitola

Watsonville

Monterey Bay

Elkhorn Slough National Estuarine Marine Preserve

Moss Landing

Castroville

17-Mile Drive

Pacific Grove

Salinas

Cypress Point

Pebble Beach

Carmel Bay

Monterey

Carmel

Carmel Valley

Point Sur

Big Sur

0   10 mi

0   10 km

HIGHWAY 1: SAN FRANCISCO TO FORT BRAGG

Mendocino Coast Botanical Garden

THE PLAN

Distance: 177 mi

Time: 2-4 days

Good Overnight Options: San Francisco, Olema, Bodega Bay, Gualala, Mendocino, Fort Bragg

For more information on the sights and attractions along this portion of Highway 1, please see San Francisco, Bay Area, and North Coast chapters

SAN FRANCISCO

The official Highway 1 heads straight through **San Francisco** along 19th Avenue through **Golden Gate Park** and the **Presidio** toward the **Golden Gate Bridge.** For a more scenic tour, watch for signs announcing exits for 35 North/Skyline Boulevard, then Ocean Beach/The Great Highway (past Lake Merced). The Great Highway follows the coast along the western border of San Francisco; you'll cruise past entrances to the **San Francisco Zoo, Golden Gate Park,** and the **Cliff**

Golden Gate Bridge

House. Hike out to **Point Lobos** or **Land's End** for awesome vistas, then drive through **Lincoln Park** and the **Palace of the Legion of Honor** and follow El Camino del Mar/Lincoln Boulevard all the way to the Golden Gate Bridge.

The best way to see San Francisco is on foot and public transportation. A **Union Square** stroll—complete with people-watching, window-shopping, and architecture-viewing—is a good first stop. In **Chinatown,** department stores give way to storefront temples, open-air markets, and delightful dim-sum shops. After lunch in one, catch a **Powell Street cable car** to the end of the line and get off to see the bay views and the antique arcade games at **Musée Mécanique** (the gem of otherwise mindless **Fisherman's Wharf**). For dinner and live music, try cosmopolitan **North Beach.**

SAN FRANCISCO TO OLEMA

(approx. 37 mi)

Leaving the city the next day, your drive across the Golden Gate Bridge and a stop at a **Marin Headlands** overlook will yield memorable views (if fog hasn't socked in the bay). So will a hike in **Point Reyes National Seashore,** farther up Highway 1 (now

Point Reyes National Seashore

called Shoreline Highway). On this wild swath of coast you'll likely be able to claim an unspoiled beach for yourself. You should expect company, however, around the lighthouse at the tip of Point Reyes because year-round views—and seasonal elephant seal– and whale-watching—draw crowds. If you have time, poke around tiny **Olema,** which has some excellent restaurants, and is home to the historic Olema Inn & Restaurant.

OLEMA TO MENDOCINO

(approx. 131 mi)

Passing only a few minuscule towns, this next stretch of Highway 1 showcases the northern coast in all its rugged glory. The reconstructed compound of eerily foreign buildings at **Fort Ross State Historic Park** recalls the era of Russian fur trading in California. Pull into **Gualala** for an espresso, a sandwich, and a little human contact

Point Reyes National Seashore

TOP 5 PLACES TO LINGER

- San Francisco
- Marin Headlands
- Point Reyes National Seashore
- Fort Ross State Historic Park
- Mendocino

efore rolling onward. After nother 50 mi of tranquil tate beaches and parks ou'll return to civilization in 1endocino.

MENDOCINO TO ORT BRAGG

approx. 9 mi)

xploring Mendocino you may eel like you've fallen through rabbit hole: the weather creams Northern California, ut the 19th-century build- igs—erected by homesick ankee loggers—definitely ay New England. Once ou've browsed around the rtsy shops, continue on the **Mendocino Coast otanical Gardens;** then avel back in time on the kunk Train, which follows n old logging route from ort Bragg deep into the dwood forest.

Leggett
Rockpoint
Westport
Laytonville
Fort Bragg
Mendocino Coast Botanical Gardens
Caspar
Mendocino
20
Little River
Willits
Albion
Elk
128
Navarro
ANDERSON VALLEY
Calpella
20
Philo
Ukiah
Point Arena
Manchester
Boonville
Point Arena
1
Anchor Bay
Hopland
Gualala
Yorkville
Kelseyville
Pacific Coast Highway
Stewarts Point
Cloverdale
Horseshoe Cove
Salt Point State Park
Geyserville
Fort Ross State Hist. Park
Fort Ross
1
Healdsburg
Jenner
101
Duncan Point
Carmet
116
Santa Rosa
Calistoga
Bodega Bay
Sebastopol
Bodega Head
Bodega Bay
Tomales Point
Tomales
Sonoma
Tomales Bay
Marshall
Inverness
Petaluma
Point Reyes Station
Point Reyes
BOLINAS RIDGE
Drakes Bay
Olema
101
Point Reyes National Seashore
1
San Rafael
Bolinas
80
Bolinas Bay
Mt. Tamalpais
Richmond
Stinson Beach
Muir Beach
Marin Headlands
Golden Gate Nat'l. Rec. Area
Sausalito
Golden Gate Park
San Francisco
FARALLON ISLANDS
PACIFIC OCEAN

0   15 mi
0   15 km

101
280
Oakland

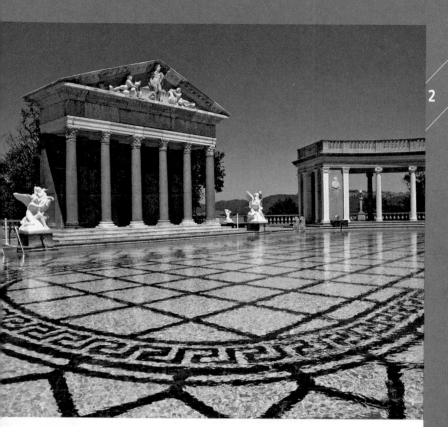

THE CENTRAL COAST

From Ventura to Big Sur

WELCOME TO THE CENTRAL COAST

TOP REASONS TO GO

★ **Incredible nature:** Much of the Central Coast looks as wild and wonderful as it did centuries ago. The area is home to Channel Islands National Park, two national marine sanctuaries, state parks and beaches, and the vast and rugged Los Padres National Forest.

★ **Edible bounty:** Land and sea provide enough fresh regional foods to satisfy even the most sophisticated foodies—grapes, strawberries, seafood, olive oil . . . the list goes on and on. Get your fill at countless farmers' markets, wineries, and restaurants.

★ **Outdoor activities:** Kick back and revel in the casual California lifestyle. Surf, golf, kayak, hike, play tennis—or just hang out and enjoy the gorgeous scenery.

★ **Small-town charm, big-city culture:** Small, friendly, uncrowded towns offer amazing cultural amenities. With all the art and history museums, theater, music, and festivals, you might start thinking you're in L.A. or San Francisco.

1 Ventura County. Ventura is a classic California city with a thriving arts community, miles of beaches, and a vibrant harbor—the gateway to Channel Islands National Park. Eleven miles inland, tiny, artsy Ojai plays host to folks who want to golf, meditate, and commune with tony peers in an idyllic mountain setting.

2 Santa Barbara. Down-home surfers rub elbows with Hollywood celebrities in sunny, well-scrubbed Santa Barbara, 95 miles north of Los Angeles. Its Spanish-Mexican heritage is reflected in the architectural style of its mission, courthouse, and many homes and public buildings.

3 **Santa Barbara County.** Wineries, ranches, and small villages dominate the quintessentially Californian landscape here.

4 **San Luis Obispo County.** Friendly college town San Luis Obispo serves as the hub of a burgeoning wine region that stretches nearly 100 miles from Pismo Beach north to Paso Robles; the 230-plus wineries here have earned reputations for high-quality vintages that rival those of Northern California.

5 **The Big Sur Coastline.** Rugged cliffs meet the Pacific for more than 60 miles—one of the most scenic and dramatic drives in the world.

6 **Channel Islands National Park.** Home to 145 species of plants and animals found nowhere else on Earth, this relatively undiscovered gem of a park encompasses five islands and a mile of surrounding ocean.

GETTING ORIENTED

The Central Coast region begins about 60 miles north of Los Angeles, near the seaside city of Ventura. North along the sinuous coastline from here lie the cities of Santa Barbara and San Luis Obispo, and beyond them the smaller towns of Morro Bay, Cambria, and Big Sur. The nearly 300-mile drive through this region, especially the section of Highway 1 from San Simeon to Big Sur, is one of the most scenic in the state.

2

| 0 | | | 20 miles |
| 0 | | | 30 kilometers |

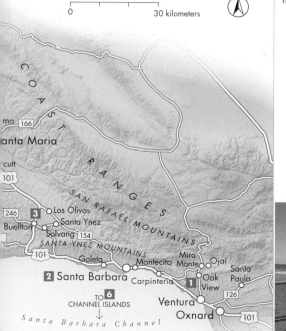

mo 166
anta Maria
cutt
101
246 **3** Los Olivos
Buellton Santa Ynez
Solvang 154
SANTA YNEZ MOUNTAINS
101 Goleta
Montecito Mira Monte Ojai
2 Santa Barbara Carpinteria Oak Santa Paula
View
TO **6** **1** 126
CHANNEL ISLANDS Ventura
Oxnard 101
Santa Barbara Channel

C O A S T
R A N G E S
SAN RAFAEL MOUNTAINS

Updated by Cheryl Crabtree

Balmy weather, glorious beaches, crystal clear air, and serene landscapes have lured people to the Central Coast since prehistoric times. Today it's also known for its farm-fresh bounty, from grapes vintners craft into world-class wines to strawberries and other produce chefs incorporate into distinctive cuisine. The scenic variety along the Pacific coast is equally impressive—you'll see everything from dramatic cliffs and grass-tufted bluffs to wildlife estuaries and miles of dunes. It's an ideal place to relax, slow down, and appreciate the sheer abundance of beauty.

Offshore, a pristine national park and a vast marine sanctuary protect the wild, wonderful underwater resources of this incredible corner of the planet. But not all of the Central Coast's top attractions are natural: Ventura, Santa Barbara, and San Luis Obispo are filled with sparkling examples of Spanish-Mediterranean architecture, bustling shopping districts, and first-rate restaurants showcasing regional foods and wines.

PLANNING

WHEN TO GO

The Central Coast climate is mild year-round. If you like to swim in warmer (if still nippy) ocean waters, July and August are the best months to visit. Be aware that this is also high season. Fog often rolls in along the coastal areas in early summer; you'll need a jacket, especially after sunset, close to the shore. It usually rains from December through March. From April to early June and in early fall the weather is almost as fine as in high season, and the pace is less hectic.

GETTING HERE AND AROUND
AIR TRAVEL
Alaska Air, Frontier, and United, and US Airways fly to Santa Barbara Airport (SBA), 9 miles from downtown. United and US Airways provide service to San Luis Obispo County Regional Airport (SBP), 3 miles from downtown San Luis Obispo.

Santa Barbara Airbus shuttles travelers between Santa Barbara and Los Angeles for $50 one-way and $95 round-trip. The Santa Barbara Metropolitan Transit District Bus 11 ($1.75) runs every 30 minutes from the airport to the downtown transit center. A taxi between the airport and the hotel districts costs between $20 and $38.

Airport Contacts San Luis Obispo County Regional Airport ⊠ *903 Airport Dr., off Hwy. 227, San Luis Obispo* ☎ *805/781–5205* ⊕ *www.sloairport.com.* **Santa Barbara Airport** ⊠ *500 Fowler Rd., off U.S. 101 Exit 104B, Santa Barbara* ☎ *805/683–4011* ⊕ *www.flysba.com.* **Santa Barbara Airbus** ☎ *805/964–7759, 800/423–1618* ⊕ *www.sbairbus.com.* **Santa Barbara Metropolitan Transit District** ☎ *805/963–3366* ⊕ *www.sbmtd.gov.*

BUS TRAVEL
Greyhound provides service from Los Angeles and San Francisco to San Luis Obispo, Ventura, and Santa Barbara. Local transit companies serve these three cities and several smaller towns. Buses can be useful for visiting some urban sights, particularly in Santa Barbara; they're less so for rural ones.

Bus Contact Greyhound ☎ *800/231–2222* ⊕ *www.greyhound.com.*

CAR TRAVEL
Driving is the easiest way to experience the Central Coast. U.S. 101 and Highway 1, which run north–south, are the main routes to and through the Central Coast from Los Angeles and San Francisco. Highly scenic Highway 1 hugs the coast, and U.S. 101 runs inland. Between Ventura County and northern Santa Barbara County, the two highways are the same road. Highway 1 again separates from U.S. 101 north of Gaviota, then rejoins the highway at Pismo Beach. Along any stretch where these two highways are separate, U.S. 101 is the quicker route.

The most dramatic section of the Central Coast is the 70 miles between San Simeon and Big Sur. The road is narrow and twisting, with a single lane in each direction. In fog or rain the drive can be downright nerve-racking; in wet seasons mudslides can close portions of the road.

Other routes into the Central Coast include Highway 46 and Highway 33, which head, respectively, west and south from Interstate 5 near Bakersfield.

Road Conditions Caltrans ☎ *800/427–7623, 888/836–0866 Hwy. 1 Visitor Hotline (Cambria north to Carmel)* ⊕ *www.dot.ca.gov.*

TRAIN TRAVEL
The Amtrak *Coast Starlight,* which runs between Los Angeles and Seattle via Oakland, stops in Paso Robles, San Luis Obispo, Santa Barbara, and Oxnard. Amtrak runs several *Pacific Surfliner* trains and buses daily

between San Luis Obispo, Santa Barbara, Los Angeles, and San Diego. Metrolink Regional Rail Service trains connect Ventura and Oxnard with Los Angeles and points between.

Train Contacts Amtrak ☎ 800/872-7245 ⊕ www.amtrak.com.
Metrolink ☎ 800/371-5465 ⊕ www.metrolinktrains.com.

RESTAURANTS

The cuisine in Ventura and Santa Barbara is every bit as eclectic as it is in California's bigger cities; fresh seafood is a standout. A foodie renaissance has overtaken the entire region from Ventura to Paso Robles, spawning dozens of restaurants touting locavore cuisine made with fresh organic produce and meats. Dining attire on the Central Coast is generally casual, though slightly dressy casual wear is the custom at pricier restaurants.

HOTELS

Expect to pay top dollar for rooms along the shore, especially in summer. Moderately priced hotels and motels do exist—most just a short drive inland from their higher-price counterparts. Make your reservations as early as possible and take advantage of midweek specials to get the best rates. It's common for lodgings to require two-day minimum stays on holidays and some weekends, especially in summer, and to double rates during festivals and other events. *Hotel reviews have been shortened. For full information, visit Fodors.com.*

WHAT IT COSTS			
$	$$	$$$	$$$$
Restaurants	under 16	$16–$22	$23–$30	over $30
Hotels	under $121	$121–$175	$176–$250	over $250

Restaurant prices are the average cost of a main course at dinner or, if dinner is not served, at lunch, excluding sales tax of 8%–8.25% (depending on location). Hotel prices are the lowest cost of a standard double room in high season, excluding service charges and occupancy 9%–12% tax.

TOUR OPTIONS

Many of the tour companies will pick you up at your hotel or central locations; ask about this when booking.

Central Coast Food Tours. Food and wine destinations are the focus of this outfit's walking tours of shops, restaurants, wineries, and other spots in San Luis Obispo, Paso Robles, and elsewhere. ☎ 800/979–3370, 212/209–3370 ⊕ www.centralcoastfoodtours.com ➧ From $69.

Cloud Climbers Jeep and Wine Tours. This outfit conducts trips in open-air, six-passenger jeeps to the Santa Barbara/Santa Ynez mountains and Wine Country. Tour options include wine tasting, mountain, sunset, and a Discovery Adventure for families. The company also offers a four-hour All Around Ojai Tour and arranges horseback-riding and trapshooting tours. ☎ 805/646–3200 ⊕ www.ccjeeps.com ➧ From $89.

The Grapeline Wine Country Shuttle. Wine and vineyard picnic tours in Paso Robles and the Santa Ynez Valley are the Grapeline's specialty. ☎ 888/894–6379, 805/325–0059 ⊕ *www.gogrape.com* ✉ *From $99.*

Santa Barbara Wine Country Cycling Tours. The company leads half- and full-day tours of the Santa Ynez wine region, conducts hiking and cycling tours, and rents bicycles. ✉ *3630 Sagunto St., Santa Ynez* ☎ 888/557–8687, 805/686–9490 ⊕ *www.winecountrycycling.com* ✉ *From $80.*

Spencer's Limousine & Tours. Based in Santa Barbara, Spencer's conducts customized tours of Santa Barbara and the Wine Country via sedan, limousine, or van. ☎ *805/884–9700* ⊕ *www.spencerslimo.com* ✉ *From $90.*

Stagecoach Wine Tours. Locally owned and operated, Stagecoach runs daily wine-tasting excursions through the Santa Ynez Valley in vans, minicoaches, and SUVs. ✉ *Solvang* ☎ *805/686–8347* ⊕ *www. winetourssantaynez.com* ✉ *From $129.*

Sustainable Vine Wine Tours. This green-minded company specializes in eco-friendly Santa Ynez Valley wine tours in nine-passenger Mercedes Sprinter vans. Trips include tastings at limited-production wineries committed to sustainable practices. An organic picnic lunch is served. ☎ *805/698–3911* ⊕ *www.sustainablevine.com* ✉ *$125.*

Wine Edventures. This learning-oriented company conducts Santa Ynez Valley wine tours in vans, minicoaches, and other vehicles. ✉ *Santa Barbara* ☎ *805/965–9463* ⊕ *www.welovewines.com* ✉ *From $105.*

VISITOR INFORMATION

Contact **Central Coast Tourism Council** ⊕ *www.centralcoast-tourism.com.*

VENTURA COUNTY

Ventura County was first settled by the Chumash Indians. Spanish missionaries were the first Europeans to arrive, followed by Americans and other Europeans, who established bustling towns, transportation networks, and highly productive farms. Since the 1920s, agriculture has been steadily replaced as the area's main industry—first by the oil business and more recently by tourism.

VENTURA

60 miles north of Los Angeles.

Like Los Angeles, the city of Ventura enjoys gorgeous weather and sun-kissed beaches—but without the smog and congestion. The miles of beautiful beaches attract athletes—bodysurfers and boogie boarders, runners and bikers—and those who'd rather doze beneath an umbrella all day. Ventura Harbor is home to myriad fishing boats, restaurants, and water-activity centers where you can rent boats and take harbor cruises. Foodies can get their fix all over Ventura—dozens of upscale cafés and wine and tapas bars have opened in recent years. Arts and antiques buffs have long trekked downtown to browse the galleries and shops there.

GETTING HERE AND AROUND

Amtrak and Metrolink trains serve the area from Los Angeles. Greyhound buses stop in Ventura; Gold Coast Transit serves the city and the rest of Ventura County.

U.S. 101 is the north–south main route into town, but for a scenic drive, take Highway 1 north from Santa Monica. The highway merges with U.S. 101 just south of Ventura. ■TIP➜ Traveling north to Ventura from Los Angeles on weekdays it's best to depart before 6 am, between 10 and 2, or after 7, or you'll get caught in the extended rush-hour traffic. Coming south from Santa Barbara, depart before 1 or after 6. On weekends, traffic is generally fine except southbound on U.S. 101 between Santa Barbara and Ventura.

ESSENTIALS

Bus Contact Gold Coast Transit ☎ 805/643–3158 ⊕ www.goldcoasttransit.org.

Visitor Information Ventura Visitors and Convention Bureau ⊠ Downtown Visitor Center, 101 S. California St. ☎ 805/648–2075, 800/483–6214 ⊕ www.ventura-usa.com.

EXPLORING

FAMILY **Lake Casitas Recreation Area.** Lunker largemouth bass, rainbow trout, crappie, redears, and channel catfish live in the waters at this park, one of the country's best bass-fishing areas. Nestled below the Santa Ynez Mountains' Laguna Ridge, Lake Casitas is also a beautiful spot for pitching a tent or having a picnic. The Casitas Water Adventure, which has two water playgrounds and a lazy river for tubing and floating, provides kids with endless diversions in summer. ⊠ 11311 Santa Ana Rd., off Hwy. 33, 13 miles northwest of Ventura ☎ 805/649–2233, 805/649–1122 campground and water park reservations ⊕ www.lakecasitas.info ☎ $10–$15 per vehicle, $13 per boat; Water Adventure $12 ($6 5–7 pm) ☉ Daily.

Mission San Buenaventura. The ninth of the 21 California missions, Mission San Buenaventura was established in 1782 but burned to the ground in the 1790s. It was rebuilt and rededicated in 1809. A self-guided tour takes you through a small museum, a quiet courtyard, and a chapel with 250-year-old paintings. ⊠ 211 E. Main St., at Figueroa St. ☎ 805/643–4318 ⊕ www.sanbuenaventuramission.org ☎ $4 ☉ Weekdays 10–5, Sat. 9–5, Sun. 10–4.

Museum of Ventura County. Exhibits in a contemporary complex of galleries and a sunny courtyard plaza tell the story of Ventura County from prehistoric times to the present. A highlight is the gallery that contains Ojai artist George Stuart's historical figures, dressed in exceptionally detailed, custom-made clothing reflecting their particular eras. In the courtyard, eight panels made with 45,000 pieces of cut glass form a historical timeline. ⊠ 100 E. Main St., at S. Ventura Ave. ☎ 805/653–0323 ⊕ ventura-museum.org ☎ $4, free first Sun. of the month ☉ Tues.–Sun. 11–5.

Ventura Oceanfront. Four miles of gorgeous coastline stretch from the county fairgrounds at the northern border of the city of San Buenaventura, through San Buenaventura State Beach, down to Ventura Harbor in the south. The main attraction here is the San Buenaventura City Pier,

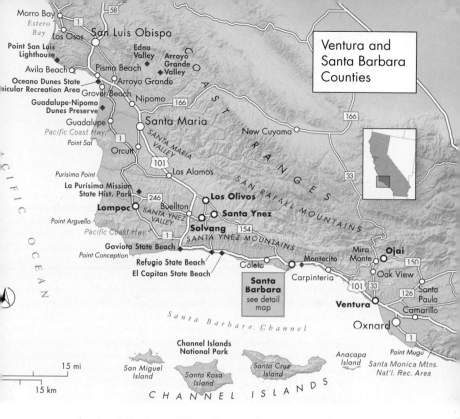

Ventura and
Santa Barbara
Counties

a landmark built in 1872 and restored in 1993. Surfers rip the waves just north of the pier, and sunbathers relax on white-sand beaches on either side. The mile-long promenade and the Omer Rains Bike Trail north of the pier attract scores of joggers, surrey cyclers, and bikers throughout the year. ⊠ *California St., at ocean's edge.*

WHERE TO EAT

$$ ✕ **Brophy Bros.** The Ventura outpost of the wildly popular Santa Barbara
SEAFOOD restaurant provides the same fresh seafood-oriented meals in a spacious second-story setting overlooking the harbor. Feast on everything from fish-and-chips and crab cakes to chowder and delectable fish—often straight from the boats moored below. $ *Average main: $22* ⊠ *1559 Spinnaker Dr., in Ventura Harbor Village* ☎ *805/639–0865* ⊕ *www. brophybros.com* ⊝ *Reservations not accepted.*

$ ✕ **Busy Bee Cafe.** A local favorite for decades, this classic 1950s diner
AMERICAN has a jukebox on every table and serves hearty burgers and comfort food (think meat loaf and mashed potatoes, pot roast, and Cobb salad). For breakfast, tuck into a huge omelet; for a snack or dessert, order a shake or hot fudge sundae from the soda fountain. $ *Average main: $13* ⊠ *478 E. Main St., near S. California St.* ☎ *805/643–4864* ⊕ *www. busybeecafe.biz.*

$ ✕ **Lure Fish House.** Fresh, sustainably caught seafood charbroiled over
SEAFOOD   a mesquite grill, a well-stocked oyster bar, specialty cocktails, and a
wine list heavy on local vintages lure diners into this slick, nautical-
theme space downtown. The menu, which changes daily, centers on
the mostly local catch and organic veggies, and also includes tacos,
sandwiches, and salads. Grilled entrées come with a choice of unusual
farm-to-table sides: quinoa salad, sweet-potato fries, pineapple cole
slaw. The regulars rave about the shrimp-and-chips, cioppino, and
citrus crab-cake salad. $ *Average main: $15* ⊠ *60 S. California St.*
☎ *805/567–4400* ⊕ *www.lurefishhouse.com.*

WHERE TO STAY

$$ ⛫ **Crowne Plaza Ventura Beach.** A 12-story hotel with an enviable location
HOTEL   on the beach and next to a historic pier, the Crowne Plaza is also within
walking distance of downtown restaurants and nightlife. **Pros:** on the
beach; near downtown; steps from waterfront. **Cons:** early-morning
train noise; waterfront crowded in summer; most rooms on the small
side. $ *Rooms from: $169* ⊠ *450 E. Harbor Blvd.* ☎ *800/842–0800,*
805/648–2100 ⊕ *cpventura.com* ⇆ *254 rooms, 4 suites* ⓘⓞⓘ *No meals.*

$$ ⛫ **Four Points by Sheraton Ventura Harbor Resort.** An on-site restaurant,
RESORT   spacious rooms, and a slew of amenities make this 17-acre property—
which includes sister hotel Holiday Inn Express—a popular and
practical choice for Channel Islands visitors. **Pros:** close to island
transportation; mostly quiet; short drive to historic downtown. **Cons:**
not in the heart of downtown; noisy seagulls sometimes congregate
nearby. $ *Rooms from: $160* ⊠ *1050 Schooner Dr.* ☎ *805/658–1212,*
800/368–7764 ⊕ *www.fourpoints.com/ventura* ⇆ *102 rooms, 4 suites*
ⓘⓞⓘ *No meals.*

$$ ⛫ **Holiday Inn Express Ventura Harbor.** A favorite among Channel Islands
HOTEL   visitors, this quiet, comfortable, lodge-inspired property sits right at
the Ventura Harbor entrance. **Pros:** quiet at night; easy access to har-
bor restaurants and activities; five-minute drive to downtown. **Cons:**
busy area on weekends; complaints of erratic service. $ *Rooms from:*
$145 ⊠ *1080 Navigator Dr.* ☎ *805/856–9533, 888/233–9450* ⊕ *www.*
holidayinnexpress.com/venturaca ⇆ *69 rooms* ⓘⓞⓘ *Breakfast.*

$$$ ⛫ **Ventura Beach Marriott.** Spacious, contemporary rooms, a peaceful
HOTEL   location just steps from San Buenaventura State Beach, and easy access
to downtown arts and culture make the Marriott a popular choice.
Pros: walk to beach and biking/jogging trails; a block from historic pier;
great value for location. **Cons:** close to highway; near busy intersection. $ *Rooms from: $189* ⊠ *2055 E. Harbor Blvd.* ☎ *805/643–6000,*
888/236–2427 ⊕ *www.marriottventurabeach.com* ⇆ *270 rooms, 15*
suites ⓘⓞⓘ *No meals.*

$$ ⛫ **Wyndham Garden Ventura Pierpont Inn.** Back in 1910, Josephine Pier-
HOTEL   pont-Ginn built the original Pierpont Inn on a hill overlooking Ventura
Beach. **Pros:** near the beach; lush gardens; Tempur-Pedic mattresses
and pillows. **Cons:** near the freeway and train tracks; difficult to walk
to downtown from here. $ *Rooms from: $129* ⊠ *550 Sanjon Rd.*
☎ *805/643–6144* ⊕ *www.pierpontinn.com* ⇆ *65 rooms, 9 suites, 2*
cottages ⓘⓞⓘ *No meals.*

SPORTS AND THE OUTDOORS

The most popular outdoor activities in Ventura are beachgoing and whale-watching. California gray whales migrate offshore through the Santa Barbara Channel from late December through March; giant blue and humpback whales feed here from mid-June through September. The channel teems with marine life year-round, so tours, which depart from Ventura Harbor, include more than just whale sightings. To learn about the spectacular hiking trails on the five islands that comprise Channel Islands National Park, check out its visitor center, also at the harbor.

Island Packers. A cruise through the Santa Barbara Channel with Island Packers will give you the chance to spot dolphins and seals—and sometimes even whales—throughout the year. ⊠ *Ventura Harbor, 1691 Spinnaker Dr.* ☎ *805/642–1393* ⊕ *www.islandpackers.com.*

OJAI

15 miles north of Ventura.

The Ojai Valley, which director Frank Capra used as a backdrop for his 1936 film *Lost Horizon,* sizzles in the summer when temperatures routinely reach 90°F. The acres of orange and avocado groves here evoke postcard images of long-ago agricultural Southern California. Many artists and celebrities have sought refuge from life in the fast lane in lush Ojai.

GETTING HERE AND AROUND

From northern Ventura, Highway 33 veers east from U.S. 101 and climbs inland to Ojai. From Santa Barbara, exit U.S. 101 at Highway 150 in Carpinteria, then travel east 20 miles on a twisting, two-lane road that is not recommended at night or during poor weather. You can also access Ojai by heading west from Interstate 5 on Highway 126. Exit at Santa Paula and follow Highway 150 north for 16 miles to Ojai. Gold Coast Transit provides service to Ojai from Ventura.

Ojai can be easily explored on foot; you can also hop on the Ojai Trolley ($1, or $2 day pass), which until about 5 pm follows two routes around Ojai and neighboring Miramonte on weekdays and one route on weekends. Tell the driver you're visiting and you'll get an informal guided tour.

ESSENTIALS

Bus Contacts Gold Coast Transit ☎ *805/643-3158* ⊕ *www.goldcoasttransit.org.* **Ojai Trolley** ☎ *805/646-5581* ⊕ *www.ojaitrolley.com.*

Visitor Information Ojai Visitors Bureau ⊠ *206 N. Signal St., Ste. P, at E. Ojai Ave.* ☎ *888/652-4669, 805/640-3606* ⊕ *www.ojaivisitors.com* ☉ *Weekdays 8–5.*

EXPLORING

Ojai Art Center. California's oldest nonprofit, multipurpose arts center exhibits visual art from various disciplines and presents theater, dance, and other performances. ⊠ *113 S. Montgomery St., near E. Ojai Ave.* ☎ *805/646-0117* ⊕ *www.ojaiartcenter.org* ☉ *Tues.–Sun. noon–4.*

Ojai Avenue. The work of local artists is displayed in the Spanish-style shopping arcade along the avenue downtown. Organic and specialty growers sell their produce on Sundays between 9 and 1 at the outdoor market behind the arcade.

Ojai Valley Museum. The museum collects, preserves, and exhibits the art, history, and culture of Ojai and Ojai Valley. Walking tours of Ojai depart from here. ⊠ *130 W. Ojai Ave.* ☎ *805/640–1390* ⊕ *www.ojaivalleymuseum.org* ▭ *Museum $5, walking tour $5 ($15 family)* ☉ *Tues.–Sat. 10–4, Sun. noon–4; tour Oct.–July, Sat. 10:30.*

Ojai Valley Trail. The 18-mile trail is open to pedestrians, joggers, equestrians, bikers, and others on nonmotorized vehicles. You can access it anywhere along its route. ⊠ *Parallel to Hwy. 33 from Soule Park in Ojai to ocean in Ventura* ☎ *888/652–4669* ⊕ *www.ojaivisitors.com.*

WHERE TO EAT

$$$ ✕ **Azu.** Farm-fresh tapas, a full bar, slick furnishings, and piped jazz
MEDITERRANEAN music draw diners to this artsy Mediterranean bistro. You can also order soups, salads, and bistro fare such as steak frites and paella. Save room for the homemade gelato. ⑤ *Average main: $24* ⊠ *457 E. Ojai Ave.* ☎ *805/640–7987* ⊕ *azuojai.com.*

$ ✕ **Boccali's.** Edging a ranch, citrus groves, and a seasonal garden that
ITALIAN provides produce for menu items, the modest but cheery Boccali's attracts many loyal fans. When it's warm, you can dine alfresco in the oak-shaded patio and lawn area and sometimes listen to live music. The family-run operation, best known for hand-rolled pizzas and home-style pastas (don't miss the eggplant lasagna), also serves a popular seasonal strawberry shortcake. ⑤ *Average main: $15* ⊠ *3277 Ojai Ave., about 2 miles east of downtown* ☎ *805/646–6116* ⊕ *www.boccalis.com* ▭ *No credit cards* ☉ *No lunch Mon. and Tues.*

$$$ ✕ **The Ranch House.** This elegant yet laid-back eatery has been around
AMERICAN for decades. Main dishes such as the broiled-and-roasted rack of lamb with pineapple guava chutney and the grilled diver scallops with curried sweet-corn sauce are not to be missed. The verdant patio is a wonderful place to have Sunday brunch. ⑤ *Average main: $29* ⊠ *500 S. Lomita Ave.* ☎ *805/646–2360* ⊕ *www.theranchhouse.com* ☉ *Closed Mon. No lunch.*

$$$ ✕ **Suzanne's Cuisine.** Peppered filet mignon, linguine with steamed
EUROPEAN clams, and pan-roasted salmon with a roasted mango sauce are among the offerings at this European-style restaurant. Game, seafood, and vegetarian dishes dominate the dinner menu, and salads and soups star at lunchtime. All the desserts are made on the premises. ⑤ *Average main: $27* ⊠ *502 W. Ojai Ave.* ☎ *805/640–1961* ⊕ *www.suzannescuisine.com* ☉ *Closed Tues.*

WHERE TO STAY

$$ ⊡ **The Blue Iguana Inn & Suites.** Artists run this Southwestern-style hotel,
B&B/INN and their work (which is for sale) decorates the rooms. **Pros:** colorful art everywhere; secluded. **Cons:** 2 miles from downtown; on a highway; small. ⑤ *Rooms from: $129* ⊠ *11794 N. Ventura Ave.* ☎ *805/646–5277* ⊕ *www.iguanainnsofojai.com* ⇌ *4 rooms, 8 suites, 8 cottages* ⦿| *Breakfast.*

$$$ 🏨 **Oaks at Ojai.** Rejuvenation is the name of the game at this destina-
RESORT tion spa. **Pros:** great place to get fit; peaceful retreat; healthful meals.
Cons: some rooms are basic; on main road through town. ⑤ *Rooms
from: $240* ✉ *122 E. Ojai Ave.* ☎ *805/646–5573, 800/753–6257*
⊕ *www.oaksspa.com* ➥ *44 rooms, 2 suites* �‖ *All meals* ⌁ *2-night
minimum stay.*

$$$$ 🏨 **Ojai Valley Inn & Spa.** This outdoorsy, golf-oriented resort and spa
RESORT is set on beautifully landscaped grounds, with hillside views in nearly
Fodor'sChoice all directions. **Pros:** gorgeous grounds; exceptional outdoor activities;
★ romantic yet kid-friendly. **Cons:** expensive; areas near restaurants can
be noisy. ⑤ *Rooms from: $400* ✉ *905 Country Club Rd.* ☎ *805/646–
1111, 855/697–8780* ⊕ *www.ojairesort.com* ➥ *231 rooms, 77 suites*
�‖ *No meals.*

$$$ 🏨 **Su Nido Inn.** A short walk from downtown Ojai sights and restau-
B&B/INN rants, this posh Mission revival–style inn sits in a quiet neighborhood
a few blocks from Libbey Park. **Pros:** walking distance from downtown; homey feel. **Cons:** no pool; can get hot during summer. ⑤ *Rooms
from: $199* ✉ *301 N. Montgomery St.* ☎ *805/646–7080, 866/646–7080*
⊕ *www.sunidoinn.com* ➥ *3 rooms, 9 suites* �‖ *No meals* ⌁ *2-night
minimum stay on weekends.*

SANTA BARBARA

27 miles northwest of Ventura and 29 miles west of Ojai.

Santa Barbara has long been an oasis for Los Angelenos seeking respite
from big-city life. The attractions begin at the ocean and end in the foothills of the Santa Ynez Mountains. A few miles up the coast east and
west—but still very much a part of Santa Barbara—are the exclusive
residential districts of Montecito and Hope Ranch. Santa Barbara is on
a jog in the coastline, so the ocean is actually to the south, instead of
the west; for this reason, directions can be confusing. "Up" the coast
toward San Francisco is west, "down" toward Los Angeles is east, and
the mountains are north.

GETTING HERE AND AROUND

U.S. 101 is the main route into Santa Barbara. If you're staying in
town, a car is handy but not essential; the beaches and downtown are
easily explored by bicycle or on foot. Visit the Santa Barbara Car Free
website for bike-route and walking-tour maps, suggestions for car-free
vacations, and transportation discounts.

Santa Barbara Metropolitan Transit District's Line 22 bus serves major
tourist sights. Several bus lines connect with the very convenient electric shuttles that cruise the downtown and waterfront every 10 to 15
minutes (50¢ each way).

Santa Barbara Trolley Co. operates a motorized San Francisco–style
cable car that loops past major hotels, shopping areas, and attractions from 10 to 4. Get off whenever you like, and pick up another
trolley (they come every hour) when you're ready to move on. The
fare is $19 for the day.

Continued on page 54

ON A MISSION

Their soul may belong to Spain, their heart to the New World, but the historic missions of California, with their lovely churches, beckon the traveler on a soulful journey back to the very founding of the American West.

by Cheryl Crabtree and Robert I.C. Fisher

California history changed forever in the 18th century when Spanish explorers founded a series of missions along the Pacific coast. Believing they were following God's will, they wanted to spread the gospel and convert as many natives as possible. The process produced a collision between the Hispanic and California Indian cultures, resulting in one of the most striking legacies of Old California: the Spanish mission churches. Rising like mirages in the middle of desert plains and rolling hills, these historic sites transport you back to the days of the Spanish colonial period.

GOD AND MAN IN CALIFORNIA

The Alta California territory came under pressure in the 1760s when Spain feared foreign advances into the territory explorer Juan Rodríguez Cabrillo had claimed for the Spanish crown back in 1542. But how could Spain create a visible and viable presence halfway around the world? They decided to build on the model that had already worked well in Spain's Mexico colony. The plan involved establishing a series of missions, to be operated by the Catholic Church and protected by four of Spain's *presidios* (military outposts). The native Indians— after quick conversion to Christianity—would provide the labor force necessary to build mission towns.

FATHER OF THE MISSIONS

Father Junípero Serra is an icon of the Spanish colonial period. At the behest of the Spanish government, the diminutive padre then well into his fifties, and despite a chronic leg infection— started out on foot from Baja California to search for suitable mission sites, with a goal of reaching Monterey. In 1769 he helped establish Alta California's first mission in San Diego and continued his travels until his death, in 1784, by which time he had founded eight more missions.

The system ended about a decade after the Mexican government took control of Alta California in the early 1820s and began to secularize the missions. The church lost horses and cattle, as well as vast tracts of land, which the Mexican government in turn granted to private individuals. They also lost laborers, as the Indians were for the most part free to find work and a life beyond the missions. In 1848, the Americans assumed control of the territory, and California became part of the United States. Today, these missions stand as extraordinary monuments to their colorful past.

Mission Santa Barbara Museum

MISSION ACCOMPLISHED

California's Mission Trail is the best way to follow in the fathers' footsteps. Here, below, are its 21 settlements, north to south.

Amazingly, all 21 Spanish missions in California are still visible—some in their pristine historic state, others with modifications made over the centuries. Many are found on or near the "King's Road"—El Camino Real—which linked these mission outposts. At the height of the mission system the trail was approximately 600 miles long, eventually extending from San Diego to Sonoma. Today the road is commemorated on portions of routes 101 and 82 in the form of roadside bell markers erected by CalTrans every one to two miles between San Diego and San Francisco.

San Francisco Solano, Sonoma (1823; this was the final California mission constructed.)

San Rafael, San Rafael (1817)

San Francisco de Asís (aka Mission Dolores), San Francisco (1776). Situated in the heart of San Francisco,

Mission Santa Clara de Asís

these mission grounds and nearby Arroyo de los Dolores (Creek of Sorrows) are home to the oldest intact building in the city.

Santa Clara de Asís, Santa Clara (1777). On the campus of Santa Clara University, this beautifully restored mission contains original paintings, statues, a bell, and hundreds of artifacts, as well as a spectacular rose garden.

San José, Fremont (1797)

Santa Cruz, Santa Cruz (1791)

San Juan Bautista, San Juan Bautista (1797). Immortalized in Hitchcock's *Vertigo*, this remarkably preserved pueblo contains the largest church of all the California missions, as well as 18th- and 19th-century buildings and a sprawling plaza.

San Carlos Borromeo del Río Carmelo, Carmel (1770). Carmel Mission was head-

quarters for the California mission system under Father Serra and the Father Presidents who succeeded him; the on-site museum includes Serra's tiny sleeping quarters (where he died in 1784).

Nuestra Señora de la Soledad, Soledad (1791)

San Antonio de Padua, Jolon (1771)

San Miguel Arcángel, San Miguel (1797). San Miguel boasts the only intact original interior wall painting in any of the missions, painted in 1821 by Native American converts under the direction of Spanish artist Esteban Muras.

Painting from 1818, San Juan Bautista.

Mission Santa Inés

San Luis Obispo de Tolosa, San Luis Obispo (1772). Bear meat from grizzlies captured here saved the Spaniards from starving, which helped convince Father Serra to establish a mission.

La Purísima Concepción, Lompoc (1787). La Purísima is the nation's most completely restored mission complex. It is now a living-history museum with a church and nearly forty craft and residence rooms.

Santa Inés, Solvang (1804). Home to one of the most significant pieces of religious art created by a California mission Indian.

Santa Bárbara, Santa Barbara (1786). The "Queen of the Missions" has twin bell towers, gorgeous gardens with heirloom plant varietals, a massive collection of rare artworks and artifacts, and lovely stonework.

San Buenaventura, Ventura (1782). This was the last mission founded by Father Serra; it is still an active parish in the Archdiocese of Los Angeles.

Mission San Fernando Rey de España

San Fernando Rey de España, Mission Hills (1797)

San Gabriel Arcángel, San Gabriel (1771)

San Luis Rey de Francia, Oceanside (1798)

San Juan Capistrano, San Juan Capistrano (1776). This mission is famed for its Saint Joseph's Day (March 19) celebration of the return of swallows in the springtime. The mission's adobe walls enclose acres of lush gardens and historic buildings.

San Diego de Alcalá, San Diego (1769). This was the first California missions constructed, although the original was destroyed in 1775 and rebuilt over a number of years.

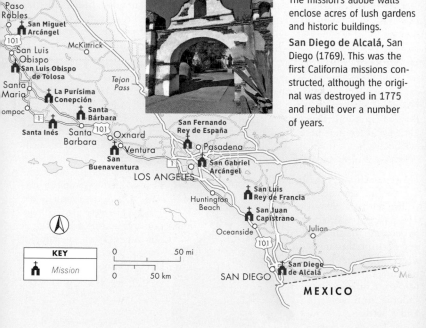

Coalinga

Paso Robles

San Miguel Arcángel

101

San Luis Obispo

San Luis Obispo de Tolosa

McKittrick

Santa Maria

La Purísima Conepción

Tejon Pass

ompoc

Santa Bárbara

Santa Inés   Santa Barbara   101   Oxnard

San Buenaventura   Ventura

LOS ANGELES   1

San Fernando Rey de España

Pasadena

San Gabriel Arcángel

Huntington Beach

San Luis Rey de Francia

San Juan Capistrano

Oceanside   Julian

101

San Diego de Alcalá

SAN DIEGO

Me

MEXICO

KEY	0	50 mi
⛪ Mission	0	50 km

SPANISH MISSION STYLE

(left) Mission San Luis Rey de Francia; (right) Mission San Antonio de Padua

The Spanish mission churches derive much of their strength and enduring power from their extraordinary admixture of styles. They are spectacular examples of the combination of races and cultures that bloomed along Father Serra's road through Alta California.

SPIRIT OF THE PLACE

In building the missions, the Franciscan padres had to rely on available resources. Spanish churches back in Europe boasted marble floors and gilded statues. But here, whitewashed adobe walls gleamed in the sun and floors were often merely packed earth.

However simple the structures, the art within the mission confines continued to glorify the Church. The padres imported much finery to decorate the churches and perform the mass— silver, silk and lovely paintings to teach the life of Christ to the Indians and soldiers and settlers. Serra himself commissioned

fine artists in Mexico to produce custom works using the best materials and according to exact specifications. Sculptures of angels, Mary, Joseph, Jesus and the Franciscan heroes and saints—and of course the Stations of the Cross—adorned all the missions.

AN ENDURING LEGACY

Mission architecture reflects a gorgeous blend of European and New World influences. While naves followed the simple forms of Franciscan Gothic, cloisters (with beautiful arcades) adopted aspects of the Romanesque style, and ornamental touches of the Spanish Renaissance— including red-tiled roofs and wrought-iron grilles—added even more elegance. In the 20th century, the Mission Revival Style had a huge impact on architecture and design in California, as seen in examples ranging from San Diego's Union Station to Stanford University's main quadrangle.

Father Junípero Serra statue at Mission San Gabriel

FOR WHOM THE BELLS TOLLED

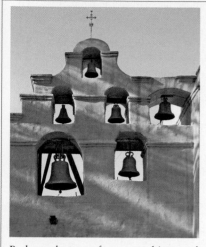

Perhaps the most famous architectural motif of the Spanish Mission churches was the belltower. These took the form of either a campanile—a single tower called a campanario—or, more spectacularly, of an open-work espedaña, a perforated adobe wall housing a series of bells (notable examples of this form are at San Juan Capistrano and San Diego de Alcalá). Bells were essential to maintaining the routines of daily life at the missions.

MISSION LIFE

Morning bells summoned residents to chapel for services; noontime bells introduced the main meal, while the evening bells sounded the alert to gather around 5 pm for mass and dinner. Many of the natives were happy with their new faith, and even enjoyed putting in numerous hours a week working as farmers, soapmakers, weavers, and masons.

Others were less willing to abandon their traditional culture, but were coerced to abide by the new Spanish laws and mission rules. Natives were sometimes mistreated by the friars, who used a system of punishments typical of the times to enforce submission to the new culture.

NATIVE TRAGEDY

In the end, mission life proved extremely destructive to the Native Californian population. European diseases and contaminated water caused the death of nearly a third, with some tribes—notably the Chumash—suffering disproportionately.

Despite these losses, small numbers did survive. After the Mexican government secularized the missions in 1833, a majority of the native population was reduced to poverty. Some stayed at the missions, while others went to live in the pueblos, ranchos, and countryside.

Many Native Californian people today still work and live near the missions that are monuments to their artistry skills.

FOR MORE INFORMATION

California Missions Foundation

✉ 123 E. Canon Perdido St. Santa Barbara, CA 93101

☎ 805/963-1633

⊕ www.california missionsfoundation.org

Top, Mission San Gabriel Arcángel
Bottom, Mission San Miguel Arcángel

TOURS

Land and Sea Tours. This outfit conducts 90-minute narrated tours in an amphibious 49-passenger vehicle nicknamed the Land Shark. The adventure begins with a drive through the city, followed by a plunge into the harbor for a cruise along the coast. ⊠ *10 E. Cabrillo Blvd., at Stearns Wharf* ☎ *805/683–7600* ⊕ *www.out2seesb.com* ⊡ *From $25* ⊙ *Tours May–Oct., daily noon, 2, and 4; Nov.–Apr., daily noon and 2.*

Segway Tours of Santa Barbara. After a brief training session, a guide leads you around town on electric-powered personal balancing transporters. Tour options include the waterfront (1¼ hours), Butterfly Beach and Montecito (2 hours), historic downtown Santa Barbara (2½ hours), and through town to the mission (3 hours). ⊠ *16 Helena Ave., at Cabrillo Blvd.* ☎ *805/963–7672* ⊕ *www.segwayofsb.com* ⊡ *From $75.*

ESSENTIALS

Transportation Contacts Santa Barbara Car Free ☎ *805/696–1100* ⊕ *www.santabarbaracarfree.org.* **Santa Barbara Metropolitan Transit District** ☎ *805/963-3366* ⊕ *www.sbmtd.gov.* **Santa Barbara Trolley Co.** ☎ *805/965-0353* ⊕ *www.sbtrolley.com.*

Visitor Information Outdoors Santa Barbara Visitor Center ⊠ *113 Harbor Way, off Shoreline Dr.* ☎ *805/456–8752* ⊙ *Daily 11–5.*

Santa Barbara Visitor Center ⊠ *1 Garden St., at Cabrillo Blvd.* ☎ *805/965-3021, 805/568-1811* ⊕ *www.sbchamber.org* ⊙ *Feb.–Oct., Mon.–Sat. 9–5, Sun. 10–5; Nov.–Jan., Mon.–Sat. 9–4, Sun. 10–4.* **Visit Santa Barbara** ⊠ *500 E. Montecito St.* ☎ *805/966–9222* ⊕ *www.santabarbaraca.com.*

EXPLORING

Santa Barbara's waterfront is beautiful, with palm-studded promenades and plenty of sand. In the few miles between the beaches and the hills are downtown, the old mission, and the botanic gardens.

TOP ATTRACTIONS

El Presidio State Historic Park. Founded in 1782, El Presidio was one of four military strongholds established by the Spanish along the coast of California. The park encompasses much of the original site in the heart of downtown. El Cuartel, the adobe guardhouse, is the oldest building in Santa Barbara and the second oldest in California. ⊠ *123 E. Canon Perdido St., at Anacapa St.* ☎ *805/965–0093* ⊕ *www.sbthp.org* ⊡ *$5* ⊙ *Daily 10:30–4:30.*

FAMILY
Fodor'sChoice
★

Lotusland. The 37-acre estate called Lotusland once belonged to the Polish opera singer Ganna Walska, who purchased it in the late 1940s and lived here until her death in 1984. Many of the exotic trees and other subtropical flora were planted in 1882 by horticulturist R. Kinton Stevens. On the two-hour guided tour—the only option for visiting unless you're a member; reserve well ahead in summer—you'll see an outdoor theater, a topiary garden, a huge collection of rare cycads (an unusual plant genus that has been around since the time of the dinosaurs), and a lotus pond. ■ TIP→ Child-friendly family tours are available for groups with children under the age of 10; contact Lotusland for scheduling.

2

Santa Barbara

✉ *695 Ashley Rd., off Sycamore Canyon Rd. (Hwy. 192), Montecito* ☎ *805/969–9990* ⊕ *www.lotusland.org* 🖼 *$45* ⊗ *Mid-Feb.–mid-Nov., Wed.–Sat. at 10 and 1:30 by appointment only.*

Fodor's Choice **Mission Santa Barbara.** Widely referred to as the "Queen of Missions,"
★ this is one of the most beautiful and frequently photographed buildings in coastal California. Dating to 1786, the architecture evolved from adobe-brick buildings with thatch roofs to more permanent edifices as the mission's population burgeoned. An earthquake in 1812 destroyed the third church built on the site. Its replacement, the present structure, is still a functioning Catholic church. Mission Santa Barbara has a splendid Spanish/Mexican colonial art collection, as well as Chumash sculptures and the only Native American–made altar and tabernacle left in the California missions. Docents lead 60-minute tours ($8 adult) Thursday and Friday at 11 and Saturday at 10:30. ✉ *2201 Laguna St., at E. Los Olivos St.* ☎ *805/682–4149 gift shop, 805/682–4713* ⊕ *www. santabarbaramission.org* 🖼 *$6* ⊗ *Daily 9–4:15.*

Santa Barbara Botanic Garden. Scenic trails meander through the garden's 78 acres of native plants. The Mission Dam, built in 1806, stands just beyond the redwood grove and above the restored aqueduct that once carried water to Mission Santa Barbara. More than a thousand plant species thrive in various themed sections, including mountains, deserts, meadows, redwoods, and Channel Islands. ✉ *1212 Mission Canyon Rd., north of Foothill Rd. (Hwy. 192)* ☎ *805/682–4726* ⊕ *www.sbbg. org* 🖼 *$10* ⊗ *Mar.–Oct., daily 9–6; Nov.–Feb., daily 9–5. Guided tours weekends at 11 and 2, Mon. at 2.*

Fodor's Choice **Santa Barbara County Courthouse.** Hand-painted tiles and a spiral staircase
★ infuse the courthouse, a national historic landmark, with the grandeur of a Moorish palace. This magnificent building was completed in 1929, part of a rebuilding process after a 1925 earthquake destroyed many downtown structures. At the time, Santa Barbara was also in the midst of a cultural awakening, and the trend was toward an architectural style appropriate to the area's climate and history. The result is the harmonious Mediterranean–Spanish look of much of the downtown area, especially the municipal buildings. An elevator rises to an arched observation area in the courthouse tower that provides a panoramic view of the city. The murals in the ceremonial chambers on the courthouse's second floor were painted by an artist who did backdrops for some of Cecil B. DeMille's films. ✉ *1100 Anacapa St., at E. Anapamu St.* ☎ *805/962–6464* ⊕ *www.santabarbaracourthouse.org* ⊗ *Weekdays 8–4:45, weekends 10–4:30. Free guided tours Mon., Tues., Wed., and Fri. at 10:30, daily at 2.*

QUICK BITES **Jeannine's.** Take a break from State Street shopping at Jeannine's, revered locally for its wholesome sandwiches, salads, and baked goods, made from scratch with organic and natural ingredients. Pick up a turkey cranberry or chicken pesto sandwich to go, and picnic in the courthouse gardens a block away. ✉ *La Arcada, 15 E. Figueroa St., at State St.* ☎ *805/966–1717* ⊕ *jeannines.com/restaurants* ⊗ *Daily 6:30–3.*

Santa Barbara Museum of Art. The highlights of this museum's permanent collection include ancient sculpture, Asian art, impressionist paintings, contemporary art, photography, and American works in several media. ⊠ *1130 State St., at E. Anapamu St.* ☎ *805/963–4364* ⊕ *www.sbma.net* ⊡ *$10, free Thurs. 5–8* ☉ *Tues., Wed., Fri. and weekends 11–5, Thurs. 11–8.*

FAMILY **Santa Barbara Museum of Natural History.** The gigantic skeleton of a blue whale greets you at the entrance of this complex. The major draws include the planetarium, space lab, and a gem and mineral display. A room of dioramas illustrates Chumash Indian history and culture. Startlingly alive-looking stuffed specimens, complete with nests and eggs, roost in the bird hall. Many exhibits have interactive components. Outdoors, nature trails wind through the serene oak-studded grounds. ■TIP→ A Nature Pass, available at the museum and the associated Ty Warner Sea Center, is good for discounted unlimited two-day admission to both facilities. ⊠ *2559 Puesta del Sol Rd., off Mission Canyon Rd.* ☎ *805/682–4711* ⊕ *www.sbnature.org* ⊡ *$13 May–Sept.; $12 Oct.–Apr.; free 3rd Sun. of month Sept.–Apr.* ☉ *Daily 10–5.*

FAMILY **Santa Barbara Zoo.** This compact zoo's grounds are so gorgeous people book weddings here long in advance. The palm-studded lawns on a hilltop overlooking the beach are perfect spots for family picnics. The natural settings of the zoo shelter elephants, gorillas, exotic birds like the California condor, and big cats such as the rare snow leopard, a thick-furred, high-altitude dweller from Asia. For small children, there's a scenic railroad and barnyard petting zoo. Three high-tech dinosaurs perform in live stage shows, daily in summer, on weekends the rest of the year (free with admission). ⊠ *500 Niños Dr., off El Cabrillo Blvd.* ☎ *805/962–5339 main line, 805/962–6310 information* ⊕ *www.santabarbarazoo.org* ⊡ *Zoo $15, parking $6* ☉ *Daily 10–5.*

Stearns Wharf. Built in 1872, Stearns Wharf is Santa Barbara's most visited landmark. Expansive views of the mountains, cityscape, and harbor unfold from every vantage point on the three-block-long pier. Although it's a nice walk from the Cabrillo Boulevard parking areas, you can also park on the pier and then wander through the shops or stop for a meal at one of the wharf's restaurants. ⊠ *Cabrillo Blvd. and State St.* ⊕ *www.stearnswharf.org.*

FAMILY **Ty Warner Sea Center.** A branch of the Santa Barbara Museum of Natural History, the center specializes in Santa Barbara Channel marine life and conservation. Though small compared to aquariums in Monterey and Long Beach, this is a fascinating, hands-on marine science laboratory that lets you participate in experiments, projects, and exhibits, including touch tanks. Two-story glass walls here open to stunning ocean, mountain, and city views. You can purchase a Nature Pass, which includes discounted two-day admission to the natural history museum and the Sea Center. ☒ *211 Stearns Wharf* ☎ *805/962–2526* ⊕ *www.sbnature. org* ☜ *$8* ☉ *Daily 10–5.*

WORTH NOTING

Andree Clark Bird Refuge. This peaceful lagoon and its gardens sit north of East Beach. Bike trails and footpaths, punctuated by signs identifying native and migratory birds, skirt the lagoon. ☒ *1400 E. Cabrillo Blvd., near the zoo* ☜ *Free.*

FAMILY **Carriage and Western Art Museum.** The country's largest collection of old horse-drawn vehicles—painstakingly restored—is exhibited here, everything from polished hearses to police buggies to old stagecoaches and circus vehicles. In August the Old Spanish Days Fiesta borrows many of the vehicles for a jaunt around town. ■TIP→ This is one of the city's hidden gems. ☒ *Pershing Park, 129 Castillo St.* ☎ *805/962–2353* ⊕ *www.carriagemuseum.org* ☜ *Free* ☉ *Weekdays 9–3, 3rd Sun. of month 1–4 for tours.*

Funk Zone. A formerly run-down industrial neighborhood near the waterfront and train station, the Funk Zone has evolved into a hip hangout filled with wine-tasting rooms, arts-and-crafts studios, murals, breweries, restaurants, and small shops. It's fun to poke around the three-square-block district. ■TIP→ Street parking is limited, so leave your car in a nearby city lot and cruise up and down the alleys on foot. ☒ *Between State and Garden Sts. and Cabrillo Blvd. and U.S. 101* ⊕ *funkzone.net.*

Montecito. Since the late 1800s the tree-studded hills and valleys of this town have attracted the rich and famous: Hollywood icons, business tycoons, tech moguls, and old-money families who installed themselves years ago. Shady roads wind through the community, which consists mostly of gated estates. Swank boutiques line **Coast Village Road,** where well-heeled residents such as Oprah Winfrey sometimes browse for truffle oil, picture frames, and designer jeans. Residents also hang out in the Upper Village, a chic shopping area with restaurants and cafés at the intersection of San Ysidro and East Valley roads.

FAMILY **Santa Barbara Maritime Museum.** California's seafaring history is the focus here. High-tech, hands-on exhibits, such as a sportfishing activity that lets participants catch a "big one" and a local surfing history retrospective, make this a fun stop for families. The museum's shining star is an extremely rare, 17-foot-tall First Order Fresnel lens from the historic Point Conception Lighthouse. ☒ *113 Harbor Way, off Shoreline Dr.* ☎ *805/962–8404* ⊕ *www.sbmm.org* ☜ *$7* ☉ *June–Aug., Thurs.–Tues. 10–6; Sept.–May, Thurs.–Tues. 10–5.*

Urban Wine Trail. Nearly two dozen winery tasting rooms form the Urban Wine Trail; most are within walking distance of the waterfront and the lower State Street shopping and restaurant district. **Santa Barbara Winery,** at 202 Anacapa Street, and **Au Bon Climat,** at 813 Anacapa Street, are good places to start your oenological trek. ⊕ *urbanwinetrailsb.com.*

Santa Barbara's downtown is attractive, but be sure also to visit its beautiful—and usually uncrowded—beaches.

BEACHES

Santa Barbara's beaches don't have the big surf of the shoreline farther south, but they also don't have the crowds. You can usually find a solitary spot to swim or sunbathe. In June and July, fog often hugs the coast until about noon.

Arroyo Burro Beach. The beach's usually gentle surf makes it ideal for families with young children. It's a local favorite, since you can walk for miles in both directions when tides are low. Leashed dogs are allowed on the main stretch of beach and westward; they are allowed to romp off-leash east of the slough at the beach entrance. The parking lots fill early on weekends and throughout the summer, but the park is relatively quiet at other times. Walk along the beach just a few hundreds yards away from the main steps at the entrance to escape crowds on warm-weather days. Surfers, swimmers, standup paddlers, and boogie boarders regularly ply the waves, and photographers come often to catch the vivid sunsets. **Amenities:** food and drink; lifeguard in summer; parking; showers, toilets. **Best for:** sunset; surfing; swimming; walking. ⊠ *Cliff Dr. and Las Positas Rd.* ⊕ *www.countyofsb.org/parks.*

FAMILY **East Beach.** The wide swath of sand at the east end of Cabrillo Boulevard is a great spot for people-watching. East Beach has sand volleyball courts, summertime lifeguard and sports competitions, and arts-and-crafts shows on Sunday and holidays. You can use showers, a weight room, and lockers (bring your own towel) and rent umbrellas and boogie boards at the Cabrillo Bathhouse. Next door, there's an elaborate jungle-gym play area for kids. Hotels line the boulevard across from the beach. **Amenities:** food and drink; life-guards in summer; parking (fee); showers; toilets; water sports. **Best for:** walking; swimming; surfing. ⊠ *1118 Cabrillo Blvd., at Ninos Dr.* ☎ *805/897–2680.*

WHERE TO EAT

$$$
JAPANESE
✕ **Arigato Sushi.** You might have to wait for a table at this trendy, two-story restaurant and sushi bar—locals line up early for the wildly creative combination rolls and other delectables. Fans of authentic Japanese food sometimes disagree about the quality of the seafood, but all dishes are fresh and artfully presented. The menu includes traditional dishes as well as innovative creations such as jalapeño yellowtail sashimi and ahi carpaccio. ⑤ *Average main: $25* ⊠ *1225 State St., near W. Victoria St.* ☎ *805/965–6074* ⊕ *www.arigatosantabarbara.com* ⌦ *Reservations not accepted* ⊘ *No lunch.*

$$
SEAFOOD
✕ **Brophy Bros.** The outdoor tables at this casual harborside restaurant have perfect views of the marina and mountains. Staffers serve enormous, exceptionally fresh fish dishes—don't miss the seafood salad and chowder—and provide guests with a pager if there's a long wait for a table. Stroll along the waterfront until the beep lets you know your table's ready. Hugely popular, Brophy Bros. can be crowded and loud, especially on weekend evenings. ⑤ *Average main: $22* ⊠ *119 Harbor Way, off Shoreline Dr.* ☎ *805/966–4418* ⊕ *www.brophy bros.com.*

$
INDIAN
✕ **Flavor of India.** Feast on authentic northern Indian dishes like tandoori chicken, lamb biryani, and a host of curries at this local favorite in a residential neighborhood. Best bets include the combination dinners served in a traditional Indian tray and the all-you-can-eat lunch buffet ($9). ⑤ *Average main: $13* ⊠ *3026 State St., at De La Vina St.* ☎ *805/682–6561* ⊕ *www.flavorofindiasb.com* ⊘ *Closed Sun.*

$$$
SEAFOOD
✕ **The Hungry Cat.** The hip Santa Barbara sibling of a famed Hollywood eatery, run by chefs David Lentz and his wife, Suzanne Goin, dishes up savory seafood in a small but lively nook in the downtown arts district. Feast on sea urchin, addictive peel-and-eat shrimp, and creative cocktails made from farmers' market fruits and veggies. A busy nightspot on weekends, the Cat also awakens for a popular brunch on Sunday. Night or day, come early or be prepared for a wait. ⑤ *Average main: $28* ⊠ *1134 Chapala St., near W. Figueroa St.* ☎ *805/884–4701* ⊕ *www.thehungrycat.com* ⊘ *No lunch Mon. Sept.–Apr.*

$
MEXICAN
✕ **La Super-Rica.** This food stand on the east side of town serves some of the spiciest and most authentic Mexican dishes between Los Angeles and San Francisco. Fans (the late chef Julia Child was one) fill up on the soft tacos served with yummy spicy or mild sauces and legendary beans. Portions are on the small side; order several dishes and share. ⑤ *Average main: $10* ⊠ *622 N. Milpas St., at Alphonse St.* ☎ *805/963–4940* ⊟ *No credit cards* ⊘ *Closed Wed.*

$$$
ITALIAN
✕ **Olio e Limone.** Sophisticated Italian cuisine (with an emphasis on Sicily) is served at this restaurant near the Arlington Center. The juicy veal chop is popular, but surprises abound here; be sure to try unusual dishes such as ribbon pasta with quail and sausage in a mushroom ragout,

or the duck ravioli. Tables are placed close together, so this may not be the best spot for intimate conversations. Next door is the more casual Olio Pizzeria, a combination pizzeria and wine bar, and Olio Crudo, a raw bar. ⑤ *Average main: $30* ✉ *17 W. Victoria St., at State St.* ☎ *805/899–2699* ⊕ *www. olioelimone.com* ☺ *No lunch Sun.*

$$$
SOUTHERN

✕ **Palace Grill.** Mardi Gras energy, team-style service, lively music, and great food have made the Palace a Santa Barbara icon. Acclaimed for its Cajun and creole dishes such as blackened redfish and jambalaya with dirty rice, the Palace also serves Caribbean fare, including a delicious coconut-shrimp dish. If you're spice-phobic, you can choose pasta, soft-shell crab, or filet mignon. Be prepared to wait for a table on Friday and Saturday nights (when reservations are taken for a 5:30 seating only), though the live entertainment and free appetizers, sent out front when the line is long, will whet your appetite for the feast to come. ⑤ *Average main: $29* ✉ *8 E. Cota St., at State St.* ☎ *805/963–5000* ⊕ *palacegrill.com.*

TAKE THE KIDS

Two playful playgrounds provide welcome interludes for the young set. Children love tooling around **Kids' World** (✉ *Garden and Micheltorena Sts.*), a public playground with a castle-shape maze of climbing structures, slides, and tunnels. At **Shipwreck Playground** (✉ *Chase Palm Park, E. Cabrillo Blvd., east of Garden St.*), parents take as much pleasure in the waterfront views as the kids do in the nautical-theme diversions and the antique carousel.

$$
MODERN
AMERICAN

✕ **Roy.** In a low-key room with a loungelike feel, owner-chef Leroy Gandy serves stylish contemporary cuisine and local wines at reasonable prices. Entrées might include sautéed local fish with an almond crust, lemon-butter sauce, and papaya orange salsa, or bacon-wrapped filet mignon. ■**TIP**→ Roy is a favorite spot for late-night dining—it's open until midnight and has a full bar. ⑤ *Average main: $20* ✉ *7 W. Carrillo St., near State St.* ☎ *805/966–5636* ⊕ *www.restaurantroy. com* ☺ *No lunch.*

$$$$
AMERICAN
Fodor's Choice
★

✕ **The Stonehouse.** The elegant Stonehouse is inside a century-old granite former farmhouse at the San Ysidro Ranch resort. Executive chef Matt Johnson creates outstanding regional cuisine centered around herbs and veggies from the on-site garden and top-quality local ingredients. The menu changes constantly but typically includes favorites such as panseared abalone and classic steak Diane flambéed tableside. Dine on the radiant-heated oceanview deck with stone fireplace, next to a fountain under a canopy of loquat trees, or in the romantic, candlelit dining room overlooking a creek. ■**TIP**→ The Plow & Angel pub, downstairs, serves casual bistro fare. ⑤ *Average main: $49* ✉ *900 San Ysidro La., off San Ysidro Rd., Montecito* ☎ *805/565–1700* ⊕ *www.sanysidroranch.com* ⌂ *Reservations essential* ☺ *No lunch Sun.–Tues.*

$$$
AMERICAN

✕ **Wine Cask.** A reinvention of a same-named local favorite that closed a few years back, the Wine Cask serves bistro-style meals—many of them made with ingredients from a nearby farmers' market—in a comfortable and classy dining room. The dishes are paired with wines from Santa Barbara's most extensive wine list. The more casual bar-café, Intermezzo, across the courtyard, serves pizzas, salads, small plates, wines, and cocktails and is open late. $ *Average main: $29* ✉ *El Paseo, 813 Anacapa St., at E. De La Guerra St.* ☎ *805/966–9463* ⊕ *www.winecask.com* ⌂ *Reservations essential.*

WHERE TO STAY

$$$$
RESORT

▨ Bacara Resort & Spa. A luxury resort with four restaurants and a 42,000-square-foot spa and fitness center with 36 treatment rooms, the Bacara provides a gorgeous setting for relaxing retreats. **Pros:** serene natural setting; nature trails; first-rate spa; three zero-edge pools. **Cons:** pricey; not close to downtown; sand on beach not pristine enough for some. $ *Rooms from: $450* ✉ *8301 Hollister Ave., Goleta* ☎ *805/968–0100, 855/817–9782* ⊕ *www.bacararesort.com* ⌁ *306 rooms, 45 suites* �🍽 *No meals.*

$$$$
HOTEL

▨ Canary Hotel. The only full-service hotel in the heart of downtown, this Kimpton property blends a casual, beach-getaway feel with urban sophistication. **Pros:** easy stroll to museums, shopping, dining; friendly, attentive service; adjacent fitness center. **Cons:** across from transit center; some rooms feel cramped. $ *Rooms from: $400* ✉ *31 W. Carrillo St.* ☎ *805/884–0300, 877/468–3515* ⊕ *www.canarysantabarbara.com* ⌁ *77 rooms, 20 suites* ⟨🍽 *No meals.*

$$$$
HOTEL
Fodor'sChoice
★

▨ Belmond El Encanto. Following years of extensive renovations by Orient-Express, this Santa Barbara icon lives on to thrill a new generation of guests with its relaxed-luxe bungalow rooms, lush gardens, and personalized service. **Pros:** revitalized historic landmark; stellar spa facility; drinks and dining with stunning views; friendly and personal service; free use of electric bikes. **Cons:** long walk to downtown; pricey, restaurant menus limited if you are staying for more than a few days. $ *Rooms from: $650* ✉ *800 Alvarado Pl.* ☎ *805/845–5800, 800/393–5315* ⊕ *elencanto.com* ⌁ *70 rooms, 22 suites* ⟨🍽 *No meals.*

$$$$
RESORT
Fodor'sChoice
★

▨ Four Seasons Resort The Biltmore Santa Barbara. Surrounded by lush, perfectly manicured gardens and across from the beach, Santa Barbara's grande dame has long been a favorite for quiet, California-style luxury. **Pros:** first-class resort; historic Santa Barbara character; personal service; steps from the beach. **Cons:** back rooms are close to train tracks; expensive. $ *Rooms from: $425* ✉ *1260 Channel Dr.* ☎ *805/969–2261, 805/332–3442 reservations* ⊕ *www.fourseasons.com/santabarbara* ⌁ *181 rooms, 26 suites* ⟨🍽 *No meals.*

$$
HOTEL

▨ Franciscan Inn. The friendly staff and the range of cheery, spacious beach-theme rooms, from singles to mini- and family suites, at this family-owned Spanish-Mediterranean motel make this a good choice for all types of travelers; its location just a block from the harbor and West Beach is hard to beat. **Pros:** walking distance from waterfront and harbor; family-friendly; great value. **Cons:** busy lobby; pool can be crowded. $ *Rooms from: $145* ✉ *109 Bath St.* ☎ *805/963–8845* ⊕ *www.franciscaninn.com* ⌁ *33 rooms, 20 suites* ⟨🍽 *Breakfast.*

$$$
HOTEL

▨ Hotel Indigo. The closest hotel to the train station, artsy Hotel Indigo (opened in 2012) is a great choice for travelers who appreciate contemporary art and want easy access to dining, nightlife, and the beach. **Pros:** multilingual staff; a block from Stearns Wharf; great value for location. **Cons:** showers only (no bathtubs); train whistles early morning; rooms on small side. ⑤ *Rooms from: $189* ⊠ *121 State St.* ☎ *805/966–6586, 877/270–1392 toll-free* ⊕ *www.indigosanta barbara.com* ⊅ *41 rooms* ❄ *No meals.*

$$$
HOTEL
🛏 **Hyatt Santa Barbara.** A complex of four buildings on three landscaped acres, the Hyatt provides an appealing lodging option in a prime location right across from East Beach. **Pros:** steps from the beach; many room types and rates; walk to the zoo and waterfront shuttle. **Cons:** motelish vibe; busy area in summer. ⑤ *Rooms from: $229* ⊠ *1111 E. Cabrillo Blvd.* ☎ *805/882–1234, 800/643–1994* ⊕ *www.santabarbara.hyatt.com* ⊅ *171 rooms, 3 suites* ❄ *No meals.*

$
HOTEL
🛏 **Motel 6 Santa Barbara Beach.** A half block from East Beach amid fancier hotels sits this basic but comfortable motel—the first Motel 6 in existence and the first in the chain to transform into a contemporary Euro-style abode. **Pros:** very close to zoo and beach; friendly staff; clean. **Cons:** no frills; motel-style rooms; no breakfast. ⑤ *Rooms from: $119* ⊠ *443 Corona Del Mar Dr.* ☎ *805/564–1392, 800/466–8356* ⊕ *www.motel6.com* ⊅ *51 rooms* ❄ *No meals.*

$$$$
RESORT
Fodor's Choice
★
🛏 **San Ysidro Ranch.** At this romantic hideaway on a historic property in the Montecito foothills—where John and Jackie Kennedy spent their honeymoon and Oprah sends her out-of-town visitors—guest cottages are scattered among groves of orange trees and flower beds. **Pros:** ultimate privacy; surrounded by nature; celebrity hangout; pet-friendly. **Cons:** very expensive; too remote for some. ⑤ *Rooms from: $695* ⊠ *900 San Ysidro La., Montecito* ☎ *805/565–1700, 800/368–6788* ⊕ *www.sanysidroranch.com* ⊅ *23 rooms, 4 suites, 14 cottages* ❄ *No meals* ⟳ *2-day minimum stay on weekends, 3 days on holiday weekends.*

$$$$
B&B/INN
Fodor's Choice
★
🛏 **Simpson House Inn.** If you're a fan of traditional B&Bs, this property, with its beautifully appointed Victorian main house and acre of lush gardens, is for you. **Pros:** impeccable landscaping; walking distance from everything downtown; ranked among the nation's top B&Bs. **Cons:** some rooms in main building are small; two-night minimum stay on weekends. ⑤ *Rooms from: $255* ⊠ *121 E. Arrellaga St.* ☎ *805/963–7067, 800/676–1280* ⊕ *www.simpsonhouseinn.com* ⊅ *11 rooms, 4 cottages* ❄ *Breakfast.*

$$$$
B&B/INN
🛏 **Spanish Garden Inn.** A half block from the Presidio in the heart of downtown, this elegant Spanish-Mediterranean retreat celebrates Santa Barbara style, from the tile floors, wrought-iron balconies, and exotic plants, to the original art by local plein-air artists. **Pros:** walking distance from downtown; classic Spanish-Mediterranean style; caring staff. **Cons:** no restaurant. ⑤ *Rooms from: $379* ⊠ *915 Garden St.* ☎ *805/564–4700, 866/564–4700* ⊕ *www.spanishgardeninn.com* ⊅ *23 rooms* ❄ *Breakfast.*

> **BEST VIEWS**
>
> Drive along Alameda Padre Serra, a hillside road that begins near the mission and continues to Montecito, to feast your eyes on spectacular views of the city and the Santa Barbara Channel.

NIGHTLIFE AND THE ARTS

Most major hotels present entertainment nightly during the summer and on weekends all year. The bar, club, and live-music scene centers on lower State Street, between the 300 and 800 blocks. The thriving arts district, with theaters, restaurants, and cafés, starts around the 900 block of State Street and continues north to the Arlington Center for the Performing Arts, in the 1300 block. To see what's scheduled around town, pick up a copy of the free weekly *Santa Barbara Independent* newspaper or visit its website, ⊕ *www.independent.com.*

NIGHTLIFE

Blue Agave. Leather couches, a crackling fire in chilly weather, a cigar balcony, and pool tables draw a fancy crowd here for good food and designer martinis. ⊠ *20 E. Cota St., near State St.* ☎ *805/899–4694* ⊕ *www.blueagavesb.com.*

Dargan's. Lively Dargan's pub has pool tables, great draft beers and Irish whiskeys, and serves a full menu of traditional Irish dishes. ⊠ *18 E. Ortega St., at Anacapa St.* ☎ *805/568–0702* ⊕ *darganssb.com.*

James Joyce. A good place to have a few beers and while away an evening, the James Joyce sometimes hosts folk and rock performers. ⊠ *513 State St., at W. Haley St.* ☎ *805/962–2688* ⊕ *www.sbjamesjoyce.com.*

Joe's Cafe. Steins of beer accompany hearty bar food at Joe's. It's a fun, if occasionally rowdy, collegiate scene. ⊠ *536 State St., at E. Cota St.* ☎ *805/966–4638* ⊕ *www.joescafesb.com.*

Lucky's. A slick sports bar attached to an upscale steak house owned by the maker of Lucky Brand dungarees, this place attracts hip patrons hoping to see and be seen. ⊠ *1279 Coast Village Rd., near Olive Mill Rd., Montecito* ☎ *805/565–7540* ⊕ *www.luckys-steakhouse.com/bar.*

Milk & Honey. Artfully prepared tapas, mango mojitos, and exotic cocktails lure trendy crowds to swank M&H, despite high prices and a reputation for inattentive service. ⊠ *30 W. Anapamu St., at State St.* ☎ *805/275–4232* ⊕ *milknhoneytapas.com.*

SOhO. A hip restaurant, bar, and music club, SOhO books bands, from jazz to blues to rock, nightly. ⊠ *1221 State St., at W. Victoria St.* ☎ *805/962–7776* ⊕ *www.sohosb.com.*

THE ARTS

Arlington Theatre. This Moorish-style auditorium hosts events during the two-week Santa Barbara International Film Festival every winter and presents touring performers and films throughout the year. ⊠ *1317 State St., at Arlington Ave.* ☎ *805/963–4408* ⊕ *www.thearlingtontheatre.com.*

The Granada Theatre. A restored, modernized landmark that dates to 1924, the Granada hosts Broadway touring shows and dance, music, and other cultural events. ⊠ *1214 State St., at E. Anapamu St.* ☎ *805/899–2222 box office* ⊕ *www.granadasb.org.*

Lobero Theatre. A state landmark, the Lobero hosts community theater groups and touring professionals. ⊠ *33 E. Canon Perdido St., at Anacapa St.* ☎ *805/963–0761* ⊕ *www.lobero.com.*

Santa Barbara International Film Festival. The hottest ticket in town in late January, the 11-day festival attracts film enthusiasts and major stars to various downtown venues for screenings, industry panels, and celebrity tributes. ⊕ *sbiff.org.*

SPORTS AND THE OUTDOORS

BIKING

Cabrillo Bike Lane. The level, two-lane, 3-mile Cabrillo Bike Lane passes the Santa Barbara Zoo, the Andree Clark Bird Refuge, beaches, and the harbor. There are restaurants along the way, and you can stop for a picnic along the palm-lined path looking out on the Pacific.

Wheel Fun Rentals. You can rent bikes, quadricycles, and skates here. ⊠ *23 E. Cabrillo Blvd.* ☎ *805/966–2282* ⊕ *www.wheelfunrentalssb.com.*

BOATS AND CHARTERS

Channel Islands Outfitters. A full-service paddle sports center in the harbor, this outfit rents kayaks, stand-up paddleboards, surfboards, boogie boards, and water-sports gear, and conducts guided tours and excursions. Smaller outlets are at Goleta Beach near UC Santa Barbara (year-round) and at West Beach next to Stearns Wharf (summer). ⊠ *117 B Harbor Way, off Shoreline Dr.* ☎ *805/899–4925 tours, 805/617–3425 rentals* ⊕ *www.channelislandso.com.*

Condor Express. From SEA Landing, the *Condor Express*, a 75-foot high-speed catamaran, whisks up to 149 passengers toward the Channel Islands on dinner cruises, whale-watching excursions, and pelagic-bird trips. ⊠ *301 W. Cabrillo Blvd.* ☎ *805/882–0088, 888/779–4253* ⊕ *condorexpress.com.*

Santa Barbara Sailing Center. The center offers sailing instruction; rents and charters sailboats, kayaks, and stand-up paddleboards; and organizes dinner and sunset champagne cruises, island excursions, and whale-watching trips. ⊠ *Santa Barbara Harbor launching ramp* ☎ *805/962–2826* ⊕ *www.sbsail.com.*

FAMILY **Santa Barbara Water Taxi.** Children beg to ride *Lil' Toot*, a cherry yellow water taxi that cruises from the harbor to Stearns Wharf and back again. The fare for kids is $1 each way. ⊠ *Santa Barbara Harbor and Stearns Wharf* ☎ *888/316–9363* ⊕ *sbwatertaxi.com* ⊠ *$4 one-way* ⊙ *June–Aug., daily noon–6, Sept.–May, Fri.–Sun. noon–sunset.*

Truth Aquatics. Truth runs kayaking, paddleboarding, hiking, and scuba excursions to the National Marine Sanctuary and Channel Islands National Park. ⊠ *Departures from SEA Landing, Santa Barbara Harbor* ☎ *805/962–1127* ⊕ *www.truthaquatics.com.*

GOLF

Sandpiper Golf Club. This course sits on the ocean bluffs and combines super-scenic views with a challenging game. ⊠ *7925 Hollister Ave., 14 miles north of downtown off U.S. 101* ☎ *805/968–1541* ⊕ *www.sandpipergolf.com* ⊠ *$140 Mon.–Thurs., $160 Fri.–Sun./holidays* ⅄ *18 holes, 7000 yards, par 72.*

Santa Barbara Golf Club. The well-maintained public club—among the area's most affordable—occupies a hilltop site with sweeping views of mountains, ocean, and islands. Hotel guests receive greens-fee discounts by showing a room key card. ⊠ *3500 McCaw Ave., at Las Positas Rd.* ☎ *805/687–7087* ⊕ *www.thesantabarbaragolfclub.com* ⊠ *Nonresidents $50 weekdays, $60 weekends* ⚑ *18 holes, 6037 yards, par 70.*

TENNIS

Many hotels in Santa Barbara have courts.

City of Santa Barbara Parks and Recreation Department. The City of Santa Barbara Parks and Recreation Department operates public courts with lighted play until 9 pm weekdays. You can purchase day permits ($8) at the courts, or call the department. ☎ *805/564–5573* ⊕ *www. sbparksandrecreation.com.*

Municipal Tennis Center. The center's 12 hard courts include an enclosed stadium court and three that are lighted on weekdays. ⊠ *1414 Park Pl., near Salinas St. and U.S. 101.*

Pershing Park. The eight lighted courts here are available for public play after 5 pm weekdays and all day on weekends and some holidays. ⊠ *100 Castillo St., near Cabrillo Blvd.*

SHOPPING

BOOKS

Book Den. Bibliophiles have browsed for new, used, and out-of-print books at this independent shop since 1933. ⊠ *15 E. Anapamu St., at State St.* ☎ *805/962–3321* ⊕ *www.bookden.com.*

Chaucer's Bookstore. This well-stocked independent shop is a favorite of many locals. ⊠ *Loreto Plaza, 3321 State St., at Los Positas Rd.* ☎ *805/682–6787* ⊕ *www.chaucersbooks.com.*

Granada Books. A nonprofit community bookstore in the arts and culture district, Granada has an excellent collection of local books and regularly hosts lectures and events. ⊠ *1224 State St.* ☎ *805/845–1818* ⊕ *www.sbgranadabooks.com.*

CLOTHING

Diani. This upscale, European-style women's boutique dresses clients in designer clothing from around the world. A sibling shoe shop is nearby. ⊠ *1324 State St., at Arlington Ave.* ☎ *805/966–3114, 805/966–7175 shoe shop* ⊕ *www.dianiboutique.com.*

Surf N Wear's Beach House. This shop carries surf clothing, gear, and collectibles; it's also the home of Santa Barbara Surf Shop and the exclusive local dealer of Surfboards by Yater. ⊠ *10 State St., at Cabrillo Blvd.* ☎ *805/963–1281* ⊕ *surfnwear.com.*

Wendy Foster. This store sells casual-chic women's fashions. ⊠ *833 State St., at W. Canon Perdido St.* ☎ *805/966–2276* ⊕ *www.wendyfoster.com.*

SHOPPING AREAS

Brinkerhoff Avenue. Antiques and gift shops are clustered in restored Victorian buildings on Brinkerhoff Avenue. ⊠ *2 blocks west of State St., at W. Cota St.*

El Paseo. Shops, art galleries, and studios share the courtyard and gardens of El Paseo, a historic arcade. ⊠ *Canon Perdido St., between State and Anacapa Sts.*

State Street. Between Cabrillo Boulevard and Sola Street, State Street is a shopper's paradise. Chic malls, quirky storefronts, antiques emporia, elegant boutiques, and funky thrift shops abound. You can shop on foot or ride a battery-powered trolley (50¢) that runs between the waterfront and the 1300 block. Nordstrom and Macy's anchor **Paseo Nuevo**, an open-air mall in the 700 block. Shops, restaurants, galleries, and fountains line the tiled walkways of **La Arcada,** a small complex of landscaped courtyards in the 1100 block designed by architect Myron Hunt in 1926.

Summerland. Serious antiques hunters head southeast of Santa Barbara to Summerland, which is full of shops and markets. Several good ones are along Lillie Avenue and Ortega Hill Road. ⊠ *Summerland.*

> ## EARTH DAY
>
> In 1969, 200,000 gallons of crude oil spilled into the Santa Barbara Channel, causing an immediate outcry from residents. The day after the spill, Get Oil Out (GOO) was established; the group helped lead the successful fight for legislation to limit and regulate offshore drilling in California. The Santa Barbara spill also spawned Earth Day, which is still celebrated across the nation today.

SANTA BARBARA COUNTY

Residents refer to the glorious 30-mile stretch of coastline from Carpinteria to Gaviota as the South Coast. The Santa Ynez Mountains divide the county geographically; U.S. 101 passes through a mountain tunnel leading inland. Northern Santa Barbara County used to be known for its sprawling ranches and strawberry and broccoli fields. Today its 100-plus wineries and 22,000 acres of vineyards dominate the landscape from the Santa Ynez Valley in the south to Santa Maria in the north. The hit film *Sideways* was filmed almost entirely in the North County Wine Country; when the movie won Golden Globe and Oscar awards in 2005, it sparked national and international interest in visits to the region.

GETTING HERE AND AROUND

Two-lane Highway 154 over San Marcos Pass is the shortest and most scenic route from Santa Barbara into the Santa Ynez Valley. You can also drive along U.S. 101 north 43 miles to Buellton, then 7 miles east through Solvang to Santa Ynez. Santa Ynez Valley Transit shuttle buses serve Santa Ynez, Los Olivos, Ballard, Solvang, and Buellton. COLT Wine Country Express buses connect Lompoc, Buellton, and Solvang on weekdays except holidays.

ESSENTIALS

Bus Contacts COLT Wine Country Express ⊠ *Lompoc* ☎ *805/736–7666* ⊕ *www.cityoflompoc.com/transit.* **Santa Ynez Valley Transit** ☎ *805/688–5452* ⊕ *www.syvt.com.*

Visitor Information **Santa Barbara Wine Country** ☎ *805/688–0881*
⊕ *www.sbcountywines.com.* **Visit Santa Barbara** ⊕ *www.santabarbaraca.com.*
Visit the Santa Ynez Valley ☎ *805/686–0053* ⊕ *www.visitthesantaynezvalley.com.*

SANTA YNEZ

2

31 miles north of Goleta.

Founded in 1882, the tiny town of Santa Ynez still has many of its original frontier buildings. You can walk through the three-block downtown area in a few minutes, shop for antiques, and hang around the old-time saloon. At some of the Santa Ynez Valley's best restaurants, you just might bump into one of the celebrities who own nearby ranches.

GETTING HERE AND AROUND

Take Highway 154 over San Marcos Pass or U.S. 101 north 43 miles to Buellton, then 7 miles east.

WHERE TO EAT AND STAY

$$ ✕**Trattoria Grappolo.** Authentic Italian fare, an open kitchen, and festive,
ITALIAN family-style seating make this trattoria equally popular with celebrities from Hollywood and ranchers from the Santa Ynez Valley. Thin-crust pizza, homemade ravioli, risottos, and seafood linguine are among the menu favorites. The noise level tends to rise in the evening, so this isn't the best spot for a romantic getaway. ⑤ *Average main: $22* ✉ *3687-C Sagunto St.* ☎ *805/688–6899* ⊕ *www.trattoriagrappolo.com* ✆ *No lunch Mon.*

$$$ 🏨 **Santa Ynez Inn.** This posh two-story Victorian inn in downtown
B&B/INN Santa Ynez was built from scratch in 2002, and the owners have furnished all the rooms with authentic historical pieces. **Pros:** near restaurants; unusual antiques; spacious rooms. **Cons:** high price for location; building not historic. ⑤ *Rooms from: $245* ✉ *3627 Sagunto St.* ☎ *805/688–5588, 800/643–5774* ⊕ *www.santaynezinn.com* ✆ *20 rooms* ⏸⃝*Breakfast.*

SPORTS AND THE OUTDOORS

Santa Barbara Soaring. Scenic glider rides operated by this outfit last from 10 to 50 minutes. Options include a basic tour of the Santa Ynez Valley; the coastal mountains and part of the Channel Islands, and a glide-by of celebrities' homes. ✉ *Santa Ynez Airport, 900 Airport Rd.* ☎ *805/688–2517* ⊕ *www.sbsoaring.com* ▱ *$149–$499.*

LOS OLIVOS

4 miles north of Santa Ynez.

This pretty village was once on Spanish-built El Camino Real (Royal Road) and later a stop on major stagecoach and rail routes. Tasting rooms, art galleries, antiques stores, and country markets line Grand Avenue and intersecting streets for several blocks.

GETTING HERE AND AROUND

From U.S. 101 north or south, exit at Highway 154 and drive east about 8 miles. From Santa Barbara, travel 30 miles northwest on Highway 154.

EXPLORING

Carhartt Vineyard Tasting Room. Pinot Noir, Sauvignon Blanc, and Syrah are among the small-lot vintages produced by owner-winemakers Mike and Brooke Carhartt. You'll often find the duo pouring at their intimate tasting room. ⊠ *2990-A Grand Ave.* ☎ *805/693–5100* ⊕ *www.carharttvineyard.com* ☜ *Tasting $10* ☼ *Daily 11–6.*

Daniel Gehrs Tasting Room. Heather Cottage, built in the early 1900s as a doctor's office, houses winemaker Gehrs's tasting room, where you can sample Port, Chardonnay, Gewürztraminer, Riesling, and other small-lot wines. ⊠ *2939 Grand Ave.* ☎ *805/693–9686* ⊕ *www.danielgehrswines.com* ☜ *Tastings $5–$10* ☼ *Sun.–Fri. 11–5, Sat. 11–6.*

Firestone Vineyard. Heirs to the Firestone tire fortune developed (but no longer own) this winery known for Chardonnay, Gewürztraminer, Merlot, Riesling, and Syrah—and for the fantastic valley views from its tasting room and picnic area. The tour here is highly informative. ⊠ *5017 Zaca Station Rd., off U.S. 101* ☎ *805/688–3940* ⊕ *www.firestonewine.com* ☜ *Tastings $10–$15* ☼ *Daily 10–5; tours 11:15, 1:15, and 3:15.*

WHERE TO EAT AND STAY

$$
AMERICAN

✕ **Los Olivos Cafe.** Part wine store and part social hub, this café that appeared in the film *Sideways* focuses on wine-friendly fish, pasta, and meat dishes, plus salads, pizzas, and burgers. Don't miss the homemade muffuletta and olive tapenade spreads. Other house favorites include an artisanal cheese plate, baked Brie with honey-roasted hazelnuts, and braised short ribs with smashed potatoes. ⑤ *Average main: $21* ⊠ *2879 Grand Ave.* ☎ *805/688–7265* ⊕ *www.losolivoscafe.com.*

$$$
AMERICAN

✕ **Sides Hardware & Shoes: A Brothers Restaurant.** After renovating a historic Los Olivos storefront, brothers Matt and Jeff Nichols shuttered their highly popular Brothers restaurant and began serving comfort food prepared with their inimitable panache. The Kobe-style burgers make a great lunch, and the dinner favorites include fried chicken and lamb sirloin with herbed gnocchi. ⑤ *Average main: $24* ⊠ *2375 Alamo Pintado Ave.* ☎ *805/688–4820* ⊕ *www.brothersrestaurant.com.*

$$$$
B&B/INN

▦ **The Ballard Inn & Restaurant.** Set among orchards and vineyards in the tiny town of Ballard, 2 miles south of Los Olivos, this inn makes an elegant Wine Country escape. **Pros:** exceptional food; attentive staff; secluded. **Cons:** some baths could use updating. ⑤ *Rooms from: $265* ⊠ *2436 Baseline Ave., Ballard* ☎ *805/688–7770, 800/638–2466* ⊕ *www.ballardinn.com* ⬎ *15 rooms* ℗ *Breakfast.*

$$$$
B&B/INN

▦ **Fess Parker's Wine Country Inn and Spa.** This luxury inn includes an elegant, tree-shaded French country–style main building and an equally attractive annex across the street with a pool and day spa. **Pros:** convenient wine-touring base; walking distance from restaurants and galleries; well-appointed rooms. **Cons:** pricey; not pet-friendly. ⑤ *Rooms from: $395* ⊠ *2860 Grand Ave.* ☎ *805/688–7788, 800/446–2455* ⊕ *www.fessparkerinn.com* ⬎ *15 rooms, 4 suites* ℗ *Breakfast.*

SOLVANG

5 miles south of Los Olivos.

You'll know you've reached the town of Solvang when the architecture suddenly changes to half-timber buildings and windmills. Danish educators settled the town in 1911—the flatlands and rolling green hills reminded them of home—and even today, more than half the residents are of Danish descent. Although Solvang has attracted tourists for decades, it's lately become more sophisticated, with galleries, upscale restaurants, and wine-tasting rooms. The visitor center on Copenhagen Drive has walking-tour maps (also available online). The Sweet Treats tour covers the town's bakeries, confectionary stores, and ice-cream parlors, all well worth investigating.

GETTING HERE AND AROUND

Highway 246 West (Mission Drive) traverses Solvang, connecting with U.S. 101 to the west and Highway 154 to the east. Alamo Pintado Road connects Solvang with Ballard and Los Olivos to the north. Park your car in one of the free public lots and stroll the town. Or take the bus: Santa Ynez Valley Transit shuttles run between Solvang and nearby towns.

TOURS

Segway Tours of Solvang. After a brief training session, tool around Solvang on a guided tour via electric-powered personal balancing transporters. This company also offers early-evening adventures, and trips high up Figueroa Mountain. ☎ *805/688–8899* ⊕ *www.advoutwest.com* ✉ *$65* ⊙ *Nov.–Mar., tours at 11, 1, and 3; Apr.–Oct., tours at 9, 11, 1, 3, and 5.*

ESSENTIALS

Visitor Information Solvang Conference & Visitors Bureau ✉ *1639 Copenhagen Dr., at 2nd St.* ☎ *805/688–6144* ⊕ *www.solvangusa.com.*

EXPLORING

Alma Rosa Winery. Winemaker Richard Sanford helped put Santa Barbara County on the international wine map with a 1989 Pinot Noir. For Alma Rosa, started in 2005, he crafts wines from grapes grown on 100-plus acres of certified organic vineyards in the Santa Rita Hills. The Pinot Noirs and Chardonnays are exceptional. ✉ *181 C Industrial Way, off Hwy. 246, west of U.S. 101, Buellton* ☎ *805/688–9090* ⊕ *www. almarosawinery.com* ✉ *Tastings $10–$15* ⊙ *Daily 11–4:30.*

Lafond Winery and Vineyards. A rich, concentrated Pinot Noir is the main attention-getter at this winery that also produces noteworthy Chardonnays and Syrahs. Bottles with Lafond's SRH (Santa Rita Hills) label are an especially good value. ✉ *6855 Santa Rosa Rd., west off U.S. 101 Exit 139, Buellton* ☎ *805/688–7921* ⊕ *www.lafondwinery.com* ✉ *Tasting $5 weekdays, $10 weekends (includes logo glass)* ⊙ *Daily 10–5.*

Mission Santa Inés. The mission holds an impressive collection of paintings, statuary, vestments, and Chumash and Spanish artifacts in a serene bluff-top setting. You can tour the museum, sanctuary, and gardens. ✉ *1760 Mission Dr., at Alisal Rd.* ☎ *805/688–4815* ⊕ *www.mission santaines.org* ✉ *$5* ⊙ *Daily 9–4:30.*

Rideau Vineyard. This winery celebrates its locale's rich history—the King of Spain himself once owned this land, and the tasting room occupies a former guest ranch inn—but fully embraces the area's wine-making present. The Rhône varietals Marsanne, Mourvèdre, Roussanne, Syrah, and Viognier are the specialty. ✉ *1562 Alamo Pintado Rd., 2 miles north of Hwy. 246* 🕾 *805/688–0717* ⊕ *www.rideauvineyard.com* 🖪 *Tasting $12* ☉ *Sun.–Fri. 11–4:30, Sat. 11–5.*

WHERE TO EAT

$$$
AMERICAN
✕**The Hitching Post II.** You'll find everything from grilled artichokes to quail at this casual eatery just outside Solvang, but most people come for the smoky Santa Maria–style barbecue. Be sure to try a glass of owner-chef-winemaker Frank Ostini's signature Highliner Pinot Noir, a star in the film *Sideways.* ⑤ *Average main: $29* ✉ *406 E. Hwy. 246, off U.S. 101, Buellton* 🕾 *805/688–0676* ⊕ *www.hitchingpost2.com* ☉ *No lunch.*

$$$
AMERICAN
Fodor'sChoice
★
✕**Root 246.** The chefs at this chic restaurant tap local purveyors and shop for organic ingredients at farmers' markets before deciding on the day's menu. Depending on the season, you might feast on boar sausage and other house-cured meats, swordfish or Santa Maria–style tritip grilled over an oak fire, or smoky lamb shank served with yogurt and harissa. The well-informed waitstaff can recommend regional wines from the restaurant's 1,800-bottle selection. Root 246's gorgeous design incorporates wood, stone, tempered glass, and leather elements in several distinct areas, including the slick dining room, a more casual bar with sofas and chairs, and a hip lounge. ⑤ *Average main: $29* ✉ *Hotel Corque, 420 Alisal Rd., at Molle Way* 🕾 *805/686–8681* ⊕ *www.root-246.com* ☉ *Closed Mon. No lunch Tues.–Sat.*

WHERE TO STAY

$$$$
RESORT
🏨**Alisal Guest Ranch and Resort.** Since 1946 this 10,000-acre ranch has been popular with celebrities and plain folk alike. **Pros:** Old West atmosphere; tons of activities; ultraprivate. **Cons:** isolated; cut off from high-tech world; some units aging. ⑤ *Rooms from: $515* ✉ *1054 Alisal Rd.* 🕾 *805/688–6411, 800/425–4725* ⊕ *www.alisal.com* 🍴 *36 rooms, 37 suites* ⦿ *Some meals.*

$$$
HOTEL
🏨**Hotel Corque.** Sleek, stunning Hotel Corque—the Santa Ynez Valley's largest hotel—provides a full slate of upscale amenities. **Pros:** front desk staff are trained concierges; short walk to shops, tasting rooms and restaurants; smoke-free. **Cons:** no kitchenettes or laundry facilities; pricey. ⑤ *Rooms from: $239* ✉ *400 Alisal Rd.* 🕾 *805/688–8000, 800/624–5572* ⊕ *www.hotelcorque.com* 🍴 *122 rooms, 10 suites* ⦿ *No meals.*

$$$
B&B/INN
🏨**Petersen Village Inn.** The canopy beds here are plush, the bathrooms small but sparkling, and the rates include a European buffet breakfast. **Pros:** in the heart of Solvang; easy parking; comfy beds. **Cons:** on highway; some find atmosphere too traditional. ⑤ *Rooms from: $195* ✉ *1576 Mission Dr.* 🕾 *805/688–3121, 800/321–8985* ⊕ *peterseninn. com* 🍴 *37 rooms, 1 suite* ⦿ *No meals.*

$
B&B/INN
🏨**Solvang Gardens Lodge.** The lush gardens with fountains and waterfalls and the cheery English-country-theme rooms make for a peaceful retreat just a few blocks—but worlds away—from Solvang's main

tourist area. **Pros:** homey; family-friendly; colorful gardens. **Cons:** some rooms tiny; some need upgrades. ⑤ *Rooms from: $119* ⊠ *293 Alisal Rd.* ☏ *805/688–4404, 888/688–4404* ⊕ *www.solvanggardens.com* ⤴ *16 rooms, 8 suites* ⦿ *Breakfast.*

LOMPOC

20 miles west of Solvang.

Known as the flower-seed capital of the world, Lompoc is blanketed with vast fields of brightly colored flowers that bloom from May through August.

GETTING HERE AND AROUND

Driving is the easiest way to get to Lompoc. From Santa Barbara, follow U.S. 101 north to Highway 1 exit off Gaviota Pass, or Highway 246 west at Buellton.

ESSENTIALS

Visitor Information Lompoc Valley Chamber of Commerce & Visitors Bureau ⊠ *111 S. I St., at Hwy. 246* ☏ *805/736–4567, 800/240–0999* ⊕ *www.lompoc.com.*

EXPLORING

FAMILY **La Purísima Mission State Historic Park.** The state's most fully restored mission, founded in 1787, stands in a stark and still remote location that powerfully evokes the lives and isolation of California's Spanish settlers. Docents lead tours every afternoon, and vivid displays illustrate the secular and religious activities that formed mission life. Special events include crafts demonstrations by costumed docents. ⊠ *2295 Purisima Rd., off Hwy. 246* ☏ *805/733–3713* ⊕ *www.lapurisimamission.org* 🎫 *$6 per vehicle* ⊗ *Daily 9–5; tour daily at 1.*

Lompoc Wine Ghetto. Nearly 20 laid-back tasting rooms with premium wines from the surrounding Santa Rita Hills appellation—among them Fiddlehead Cellars and Longoria (both known for stellar Pinot Noirs)—cluster in a downtown industrial park. ⊠ *Take 7th St. north from Hwy. 1/246 and turn east (right), 200 N. 9th St.* ☏ *805/735–8937* ⊕ *www. lompoctrail.com* 🎫 *Tasting fee varies, some free* ⊗ *Most rooms open Thurs.–Sun., 11 or noon until 4 or 5; some also Mon. and by appointment* ⊗ *Closed Tues. and Wed.*

EN ROUTE **Guadalupe-Nipomo Dunes Preserve.** This spectacular preserve straddles the coast for 18 miles between Santa Barbara and San Luis Obispo counties. California's largest and most ecologically diverse dune system, this habitat shelters more than 200 species of birds as well as sea otters, black bears, bobcats, coyotes, and deer. The 1,500-foot Mussel Rock is the highest beach dune in the western states. About two-dozen movies have been filmed here, including Cecil B. DeMille's 1923 silent epic *The Ten Commandments.* At the **Dunes Center** (*1065 Guadalupe St.*) in downtown Guadalupe, you can get nature information and view an exhibit about DeMille's movie set. ⊠ *Hwy. 166/Main St., west 5 miles from Hwy. 1, Guadalupe* ☏ *805/343–2455* ⊕ *www.dunescenter.org* 🎫 *Free ($3 suggested donation)* ⊗ *Dunes daily sunrise–sunset; center Wed.–Sun. 10–4, Mon. and Tues. by appointment.*

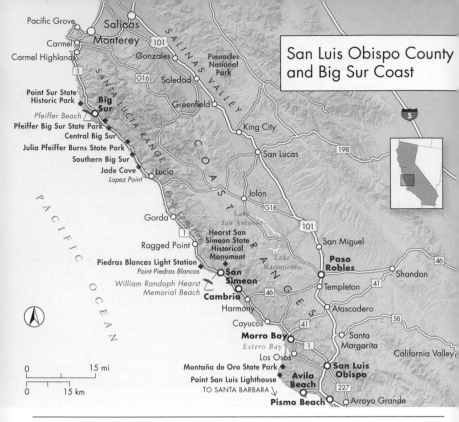

San Luis Obispo County and Big Sur Coast

Pacific Grove
Salinas
Monterey
Carmel
Carmel Highlands
101
Gonzales
Pinnacles National Park
Soledad
G16
Point Sur State Historic Park
Pfeiffer Beach
Pfeiffer Big Sur State Park
Central Big Sur
Julia Pfeiffer Burns State Park
Southern Big Sur
Jade Cove
Lopez Point
Big Sur
Greenfield
King City
San Lucas
198
Jolon
G18
Lake San Antonio
Gorda
Ragged Point
Lake Nacimiento
San Miguel
101
Paso Robles
Shandon
46
Hearst San Simeon State Historical Monument
Piedras Blancas Light Station
Point Piedras Blancas
William Randoph Hearst Memorial Beach
San Simeon
Cambria
Templeton
41
Harmony
46
Atascadero
Cayucos
41
58
Morro Bay
Estero Bay
Los Osos
Santa Margarita
California Valley
Montaña de Oro State Park
Point San Luis Lighthouse
TO SANTA BARBARA
Avila Beach
San Luis Obispo
227
Pismo Beach
Arroyo Grande
Lucia

PACIFIC OCEAN
SANTA LUCIA RANGE
SALINAS VALLEY
COAST RANGE
Pacific Coast Hwy

0   15 mi
0   15 km

5

SAN LUIS OBISPO COUNTY

San Luis Obispo County's pristine landscapes and abundant wildlife areas, especially those around Morro Bay and Montaña de Oro State Park, have long attracted nature lovers. In the south, Pismo Beach and other coastal towns have great sand and surf; inland, a booming wine region stretches from the Edna, Arroyo Grande, and Avila valleys and Nipomo in the south to Paso Robles in the north. With historical attractions, a photogenic downtown, and busy shops and restaurants, the college town of San Luis Obispo is at the heart of the county.

GETTING HERE AND AROUND

San Luis Obispo Regional Transit Authority operates buses in San Luis Obispo and serves Paso Robles as well as Pismo Beach and other coastal towns.

ESSENTIALS

Transportation Contact San Luis Obispo Regional Transit Authority ☎ 805/541–2228 ⊕ www.slorta.org.

Visitor Information Visit San Luis Obispo County ⊠ 835 12th St., Suite 204, Paso Robles ☎ 805/541–8000, 800/634–1414 ⊕ www.visitsanluisobispocounty. com. **WineCoastCountry** ⊠ San Luis Obispo ⊕ winecoastcountry.com.

PISMO BEACH

40 miles north of Lompoc.

About 20 miles of sandy shoreline—nicknamed the Bakersfield Riviera for the throngs of vacationers who come here from the Central Valley—begins at the town of Pismo Beach. The southern end of town runs along sand dunes, some of which are open to cars and off-road vehicles. Sheltered by the dunes, a grove of eucalyptus trees attracts thousands of migrating monarch butterflies from November through February. A long, broad beach fronts the center of town, where a municipal pier extends into the sea at the foot of shop-lined Pomeroy Street. To the north, hotels and homes perch atop chalky oceanfront cliffs. Fewer than 10,000 people live in this quintessential surfer haven, but Pismo Beach has a slew of hotels and restaurants with great views of the Pacific Ocean.

GETTING HERE AND AROUND

Pismo Beach straddles both sides of U.S. 101. If you're coming from the south and have time for a scenic drive, exit U.S. 101 in Santa Maria and take Highway 166 west for 8 miles to Guadalupe and follow Highway 1 north 16 miles to Pismo Beach. South County Area Transit (SCAT; ⊕ *www.slorta.org*) buses run throughout San Luis Obispo and connect the city with nearby towns. On summer weekends, the free Avila Trolley extends service to Pismo Beach.

ESSENTIALS

Visitor Information California Welcome Center ⊠ *333 Five Cities Dr.* ☎ *805/773-7924.* **Pismo Beach Visitors Information Center** ⊠ *Dolliver St./ Hwy. 1, at Hinds Ave.* ☎ *800/443-7778, 805/773-4382* ⊕ *classiccalifornia.com* ⊗ *Weekdays 9–5, Sat. 11–4, Sun. 10–2.*

BEACHES

Fodor's Choice ★ **Oceano Dunes State Vehicular Recreation Area.** Part of ⇨ *Guadalupe-Nipomo Dunes,* the largest and most ecologically diverse dunes complex in California, this popular state park offers a huge array of activities in a 3,600-acre coastal playground. This is one of the only places in California where you can drive or ride off-highway vehicles on the beach and sand dunes (1,500 acres are open to OHVs.) Hike, ride horses, kiteboard, join a Hummer tour, or rent an ATV or a dune buggy and cruise up the white-sand peaks for spectacular views. At **Oso Flaco Lake Nature Area**—3 miles west of Highway 1 on Oso Flaco Road—a 1½-mile boardwalk over the lake leads to a platform with views up and down the coast. Leashed dogs are allowed in much of the park except Oso Flaco and Pismo Dunes Natural Reserve. **Amenities:** food and drink; lifeguards (seasonal); parking (fee); showers; toilets; water sports. **Best for:** sunset; surfing; swimming; walking. ⊠ *West end of Pier Ave., off Hwy. 1, Oceano* ☎ *805/473-7220* ⊕ *www.parks.ca.gov* ⊠ *$5 per vehicle* ⊗ *Daily 6 am–11 pm; Oso Flaco Lake sunrise–sunset.*

Pismo State Beach. One of the busiest state beaches in the county, Pismo offers a slew of activities along the 17-mile western edges of Oceano, Grover Beach, and Pismo Beach. Hike, surf, golf, ride horses, swim, fish in a lagoon or off the pier, and dig for Pismo clams. From November through late February, one of the nation's largest colonies of monarch

butterflies rests in a grove of eucalyptus and Monterey pine trees
(Hwy. 1, 3 miles north of Pier Ave.).
Entrances to day-use parking areas
are off Hwy. 1 (milepost 8) and at
Pier Ave. in the south. **Facilities:**
food and drink; lifeguards (seasonal); parking (fee); showers; toilets; water sports. **Best for:** sunset;
surfing; swimming; walking. ✉ *555
Pier Ave., Oceano* ☎ *805/489–1869*
⊕ *www.parks.ca.gov* 🖃 *Day use $5
per vehicle if parking at the beach* ⊗ *Day use 6 am–11 pm.*

> **VOLCANOES?**
>
> Those funny looking, sawed-off
> peaks along the drive from Pismo
> Beach to Morro Bay are the Seven
> Sisters—a series of ancient volcanic
> plugs. Morro Rock, the northern-
> most sibling and a state historic
> monument, is the most famous
> and photographed of the clan.

WHERE TO EAT

$$$
SEAFOOD

✕ **Cracked Crab.** This traditional New England–style crab shack imports
fresh seafood daily from Australia, Alaska, and the East Coast. Fish is
line-caught, much of the produce is organic, and everything is made
from scratch. For a real treat, don a bib and sample a bucket of steamed
shellfish with Cajun sausage, potatoes, and corn on the cob, all dumped
right onto your table. ⑤ *Average main: $24* ✉ *751 Price St., near Main St.*
☎ *805/773–2722* ⊕ *www.crackedcrab.com* ⚠ *Reservations not accepted.*

$$
ITALIAN

✕ **Giuseppe's Cucina Italiana.** The classic flavors of southern Italy are
highlighted at this lively downtown spot. Most recipes originate from
Bari, a seaport on the Adriatic; the menu includes breads and pizzas
baked in the wood-burning oven, hearty dishes such as osso buco and
lamb, and homemade pastas. The wait for a table can be long at peak
dinner hours, but sometimes an accordion player gets the crowd singing.
⑤ *Average main: $22* ✉ *891 Price St., at Pismo Ave.* ☎ *805/773–2870*
⊕ *www.giuseppesrestaurant.com* ⚠ *Reservations not accepted* ⊗ *No
lunch weekends.*

$
SEAFOOD

✕ **Splash Café.** Folks stand in line down the block for clam chowder
served in a sourdough bread bowl at this wildly popular seafood stand.
You can also order beach food such as fresh steamed clams, burgers, and fried calamari at the counter (no table service). The grimy,
cramped, but cheery hole-in-the-wall is open daily for lunch and dinner (plus a rock-bottom basic breakfast), but closes early on weekday
evenings during low season. ■**TIP**→ Splash also has two locations in
San Luis Obispo. ⑤ *Average main: $8* ✉ *197 Pomeroy St., at Cypress
St.* ☎ *805/773–4653* ⊕ *www.splashcafe.com.*

WHERE TO STAY

$$$
RESORT

🏨 **The Cliffs Resort.** Perched dramatically on an oceanfront cliff, this full-
service resort is surrounded by lawns and palm trees; the pool, with a
cascading fountain, overlooks the sea. **Pros:** beach access via short down-
hill path; oceanfront restaurant and lounge; bluff-top walking trail. **Cons:**
not close to downtown; rooms near service areas and elevator can be
noisy. ⑤ *Rooms from: $189* ✉ *2757 Shell Beach Rd.* ☎ *805/773–5000,
800/826–7827* ⊕ *www.cliffsresort.com* ⤳ *160 rooms* ⦿**|**❍ *No meals.*

$$$
HOTEL

🏨 **SeaVenture Beachfront Hotel & Restaurant.** The bright, homey rooms
at this hotel all have fireplaces and featherbeds; most have balconies with private hot tubs, and some have beautiful ocean views.

Pros: on the beach; excellent food; romantic rooms. **Cons:** touristy area; some rooms and facilities dated; dark hallways. ⑤ *Rooms from: $179* ✉ *100 Ocean View Ave.* ☎ *805/773–4994* ⊕ *www.seaventure. com* ↝ *50 rooms* ⑩ *No meals.*

$
HOTEL
🛏 **Shell Beach Inn.** Just 2½ blocks from the beach, this basic but cozy motor court is a great bargain for the area. **Pros:** walking distance from the beach; clean rooms; friendly and dependable service. **Cons:** sits on a busy road; small rooms; tiny pool. ⑤ *Rooms from: $100* ✉ *653 Shell Beach Rd.* ☎ *805/773–4373, 800/549–4727* ⊕ *www.shellbeachinn.com* ↝ *10 rooms* ⑩ *No meals.*

AVILA BEACH

4 miles north of Pismo Beach.

FAMILY
Because the village of Avila Beach and the sandy, cove-front shoreline for which it's named face south into the Pacific Ocean, they get more sun and less fog than any other stretch of coast in the area. With its fortuitous climate and protected waters, Avila's public beach draws sunbathers and families; weekends are very busy. Downtown Avila Beach has a lively seaside promenade and some shops and hotels, but for real local color, head to the far end of the cove and watch the commercial fishers offload their catch on the old Port San Luis wharf. A few seafood shacks and fish markets do business on the pier while sea lions congregate below. On Friday from mid-April through mid-September, a fish and farmers' market livens up the beach area with music, fresh local produce and seafood, and children's activities.

GETTING HERE AND AROUND

Exit U.S. 101 at Avila Beach Drive and head 3 miles west to reach the beach. The free Avila Trolley operates weekends year-round, plus Friday afternoon and evening from April to September. The minibuses connect Avila Beach and Port San Luis to Shell Beach, with multiple stops along the way. Service extends to Pismo Beach in summer.

ESSENTIALS

Visitor Information Avila Beach Tourism Alliance ⊕ *visitavilabeach.com.*

EXPLORING

Central Coast Aquarium. You'll learn all about local marine plants and animals from the hands-on exhibits at this science center next to the main beach. ✉ *50 San Juan St., at 1st St., off Avila Beach Dr.* ☎ *805/595–7280* ⊕ *www.centralcoastaquarium.com* 🎫 *$5* ⊙ *June–Aug., Tues.– Sun. 10–5; Sept.–May, weekends 10–4 and holiday breaks.*

FAMILY
Avila Valley Barn. An old-fashioned, family-friendly country store jam-packed with local fruits and veggies, prepared foods and gift items, Avila Valley Barn also gives visitors a chance to experience rural American traditions. You can pet farm animals and savor homemade ice cream and pies daily; on weekends, ride a hay wagon out to the fields to pick your own farm-fresh produce. ✉ *560 Avila Beach Dr., San Luis Obispo* ☎ *805/595–2816* ⊕ *avilavalleybarn.com* ⊙ *Daily 9–5* ⊙ *Closed Tues. and Wed. Jan.–Mar.*

FAMILY **Point San Luis Lighthouse.** Docents lead hikes along scenic Pecho Coast Trail (3½ miles round-trip) to see the historic 1890 lighthouse and its rare Fresnel lens. ■**TIP➜ If you'd prefer a lift out to the lighthouse, join a trolley tour. Hikes and tours require reservations.** ✉ *Point San Luis, 1¾ miles west of Harford Pier, Port San Luis* ☎ *855/533–7843* ⊕ *www.sanluislighthouse.org* ✉ *Trolley tours $20; hikes free ($5 to enter lighthouse)* ☉ *Trolley tours Wed. at noon, Sat. at noon, 1, and 2; hikes Wed. and Sat. at 9.*

BEACHES

FAMILY **Avila State Beach.** At the edge of a sunny cove next to downtown shops and restaurants, Avila's ½-mile stretch of white sand lures scores of beachgoers on weekends year-round and daily in summer. It's especially family-friendly, with a playground, barbecue and picnic tables, volleyball and basketball courts, and lifeguards on watch in summer and on many holiday weekends. Limited free beachfront parking is available but fills up fast; otherwise park in a nearby pay lot ($5 for the day, $1 after 4 pm). Dogs are not allowed on the beach from 10 to 5. **Facilities:** food and drink; lifeguards (seasonal); parking; showers; toilets; water sports. **Best for:** sunset; surfing; swimming; walking. ✉ *Avila Beach Dr., at 1st St.* ⊕ *www.visitavilabeach.com* ✉ *Free* ☉ *Daily 6 am–10 pm.*

WHERE TO STAY

$$$$ 🎏 **Avila Lighthouse Suites.** Families, honeymooners, and business travel-
HOTEL ers all find respite at this two-story, all-suite luxury hotel. **Pros:** directly across from sand; easy walk to restaurants and shops; free underground parking. **Cons:** noise from passersby can be heard in room; some ocean-view rooms have limited vistas. ⑤ *Rooms from: $319* ✉ *550 Front St.* ☎ *805/627–1900, 800/372–8452* 🖶 *805/627–1909* ⊕ *www. avilalighthousesuites.com* ⤳ *54 suites* ⑩ *Breakfast.*

$$ 🎏 **Sycamore Mineral Springs Resort.** This wellness resort's hot mineral
RESORT springs bubble up into private outdoor tubs on an oak-and-sycamore-forest hillside. **Pros:** great place to rejuvenate; nice hiking; incredible spa services. **Cons:** rooms vary in quality; 2½ miles from the beach. ⑤ *Rooms from: $169* ✉ *1215 Avila Beach Dr., San Luis Obispo* ☎ *805/595–7302, 800/234–5831* ⊕ *www.sycamoresprings.com* ⤳ *26 rooms, 50 suites* ⑩ *No meals.*

SAN LUIS OBISPO

8 miles north of Avila Beach.

About halfway between San Francisco and Los Angeles, San Luis Obispo—nicknamed SLO—spreads out below gentle hills and rocky extinct volcanoes. Its main appeal lies in its architecturally diverse, pedestrian-friendly downtown, which bustles with shoppers, restaurant goers, and students from California Polytechnic State University, known as Cal Poly. On Thursday evening from 6 to 9 a farmers' market fills Higuera Street with local produce, entertainment, and food stalls. A Saturday-morning market in the Cost Plus World Market parking lot includes organic meats and wine tasting.

The wineries of the Edna Valley and Arroyo Grande Valley wine regions lie just south of the city off Highway 227, the parallel (to the east) Orcutt Road, and connecting roads. Wine-touring maps are available around town.

GETTING HERE AND AROUND

U.S. 101/Highway 1 traverses the city for several miles. From the north, Highway 1 merges with U.S. 101 when it reaches the city limits. SLO City Transit buses operate daily; Regional Transit Authority (SLORTA) buses connect with north county towns. The Downtown Trolley provides evening service to the city's hub every Thursday, on Friday from June to early September, and on Saturday from April through October.

ESSENTIALS

Visitor Information San Luis Obispo Chamber of Commerce ✉ *895 Monterey St.* ☎ *805/781-2777* ⊕ *www.visitslo.com.* **San Luis Obispo City Visitor Information** ⊕ *www.sanluisobispovacations.com.* **SLO Wine Country** ☎ *805/541-5868* ⊕ *www.slowine.com.*

EXPLORING
TOP ATTRACTIONS

FAMILY **History Center of San Luis Obispo County.** Across the street from the old Spanish mission, the center presents exhibits that explore topics such as Native American life in the county, the California ranchos, and the impact of railroads. On the center's website are links to free downloadable video-podcast walking tours of historic San Luis Obispo. ✉ *696 Monterey St., at Broad St.* ☎ *805/543-0638* ⊕ *historycenterslo.org* ✉ *Free* ☉ *Daily 10–4.*

Mission San Luis Obispo de Tolosa. Sun-dappled Mission Plaza fronts the fifth mission established in 1772 by Franciscan friars. A small museum exhibits artifacts of the Chumash Indians and early Spanish settlers. ✉ *751 Palm St., at Chorro St.* ☎ *805/543-6850* ⊕ *www. missionsanluisobispo.org* ✉ *$3* ☉ *Early Mar.–early Nov. daily 9–5, early Nov.–early Mar. daily 9–4.*

San Luis Obispo Museum of Art. The permanent collection here focuses on the artistic legacy of the Central Coast. Temporary exhibits include traditional and cutting-edge arts and crafts by Central Coast, national, and international artists. ✉ *Mission Plaza, 1010 Broad St., at Monterey St.* ☎ *805/543-8562* ⊕ *www.sloma.org* ☉ *Early Sept.–early July, Wed.– Mon. 11–5; early July–early Sept., daily 11–5.*

Fodor'sChoice **Talley Vineyards.** Acres of Chardonnay and Pinot Noir, plus smaller lots
★   of Sauvignon Blanc, Syrah, and other varietals blanket Talley's mountain-ringed dell in the Arroyo Grande Valley. The estate tour ($35), worth a splurge, includes wine and cheese, a visit to an 1860s adobe, and barrel-room tastings of upcoming releases. ✉ *3031 Lopez Dr., off Orcutt Rd., Arroyo Grande* ☎ *805/489-0446* ⊕ *www.talleyvineyards. com* ✉ *Tastings $8–$15; tours $15–$35* ☉ *Daily 10:30–4:30; tours by appointment.*

WORTH NOTING

Claiborne & Churchill. An eco-friendly winery built from straw bales, C&C makes small lots of Alsatian-style wines such as dry Riesling and Gewürztraminer, plus Pinot Noir and Chardonnay. ✉ *2649 Carpenter Canyon Rd., at Price Canyon Rd.* ☎ *805/544–4066* ⊕ *www.claibornechurchill.com* 🥂 *Tasting $10* ⊙ *Daily 11–5.*

> **DEEP ROOTS**
>
> Way back in the 1700s, the Spanish padres who accompanied Father Junípero Serra planted grapevines from Mexico along California's Central Coast, and began using European wine-making techniques to turn the grapes into delectable vintages.

Edna Valley Vineyard. For sweeping valley views and crisp Sauvignon Blancs and Chardonnays, head to the modern tasting bar here. ■TIP→ **The reserve tasting ($15) is the best option here.** ✉ *2585 Biddle Ranch Rd., off Edna Rd.* ☎ *805/544–5855* ⊕ *www.ednavalleyvineyard.com* 🥂 *Tastings $10–$15* ⊙ *Daily 10–5.*

Niven Family Wine Estates. A refurbished 1909 schoolhouse serves as tasting room for six Niven Family wineries: Baileyana, Cadre, Tangent, Trenza, True Myth, and Zocker. The winemaker for all these labels is Christian Roguenant, whose Cadre Pinot Noirs are worth checking out. ✉ *5828 Orcutt Rd., at Righetti Rd.* ☎ *805/269–8200* ⊕ *www.nivenfamilywines.com* 🥂 *Tasting $8–$12* ⊙ *Daily 10–5.*

Old Edna. This peaceful, 2-acre site once *was* the town of Edna. Nowadays you can peek at the vintage 1897 and 1908 farmhouse cottages, taste wines, pick up sandwiches at the gourmet deli, and stroll along Old Edna Lane. ✉ *1655 Old Price Canyon Rd., at Hwy. 227* ☎ *805/544–8062* ⊕ *www.oldedna.com.*

FAMILY **San Luis Obispo Children's Museum.** Activities at this delightful facility geared to kids under age eight include an "imagination-powered" elevator that transports visitors to a series of underground caverns. Elsewhere, simulated lava and steam sputter from an active volcano. Kids can pick rubber fruit at a farmers' market and race in a fire engine to fight a fire. ✉ *1010 Nipomo St., at Monterey St.* ☎ *805/544–5437* ⊕ *www.slocm.org* 🥂 *$8* ⊙ *May–Aug., Mon.–Wed. 10–3, Thurs.–Sat. 10–5, Sun. and some holidays 11–5; Sept.–Apr., Tues. and Wed. 10–3, Thurs.–Sat. 10–5, Sun. and some holidays 1–5.*

WHERE TO EAT

$$ ╳**Big Sky Café.** Family-friendly Big Sky turns local and organically
ECLECTIC grown ingredients into global dishes, starting with breakfast. Just pick your continent: Brazilian churrasco chicken breast, Thai catfish, North African vegetable stew, Maryland crab cakes. Vegetarians have ample choices. ⑤ *Average main: $17* ✉ *1121 Broad St., at Higuera St.* ☎ *805/545–5401* ⊕ *www.bigskycafe.com* 🍽 *Reservations not accepted.*

$$ ╳**Café Roma.** Authentic northern Italian cuisine is the specialty at this
NORTHERN Railroad Square restaurant. Beneath a mural of Tuscany or out on the
ITALIAN covered patio, you can dine on squash-filled tortelli with a sage-and-butter sauce or beef tenderloin glistening with porcini butter and a Pinot Noir reduction. ⑤ *Average main: $19* ✉ *1020 Railroad Ave., at Osos St.* ☎ *805/541–6800* ⊕ *www.caferomaslo.com* ⊙ *No lunch weekends.*

$$$
INTERNATIONAL

✕ **Luna Red.** A spacious, contemporary space with a festive outdoor patio, this restaurant near Mission Plaza serves creative tapas and cocktails. The small plates include pork-belly buns, avocado-tuna ceviche, and piquillo peppers stuffed with goat cheese. Roast chicken adobo and Kurobuta pork short ribs are two large plates of note. ⑤ *Average main: $25* ⊠ *1023 Chorro St., at Monterey St.* ☎ *805/540–5243* ⊕ *www.lunaredslo.com.*

$$
ECLECTIC

✕ **Novo Restaurant & Lounge.** In the colorful dining room or on the large creek-side deck, this animated downtown eatery will take you on a culinary world tour. The salads, small plates, and entrées come from nearly every continent. The wine and beer list also covers the globe and includes local favorites. ⑤ *Average main: $19* ⊠ *726 Higuera St., at Broad St.* ☎ *805/543–3986* ⊕ *www.novorestaurant.com.*

$$
MODERN
AMERICAN

✕ **Sidecar.** Hip Sidecar serves farm-fresh meals and small plates along with classic cocktails and 16 mostly local beers on tap. Burger patties made from grass-fed beef, free-range chicken, or housemade veggies are served on a brioche bun with inventive sauces such as bacon-maple ketchup. The menu includes many vegetarian and vegan options, among them the raw "green zebra" lasagna, made of basil-pistachio pesto, tomato sauce, and pine-nut "ricotta." Happy hour (daily from 4 to 6) and Sunday brunch (live jazz, five types of eggs Benedict) are very popular here. ⑤ *Average main: $18* ⊠ *1127 Broad St., at Marsh St.* ☎ *805/540–5340* ⊕ *sidecarslo.com.*

WHERE TO STAY

$$$
HOTEL

▥ **Apple Farm.** Decorated to the hilt with floral bedspreads and watercolors by local artists, this Wine Country–theme hotel is highly popular. **Pros:** flowers everywhere; convenient to Cal Poly and U.S. 101; creek-side setting. **Cons:** hordes of tourists during the day; too floral for some people's tastes. ⑤ *Rooms from: $219* ⊠ *2015 Monterey St.* ☎ *800/255–2040, 805/544-2040* ⊕ *www.applefarm.com* ⇱ *104 rooms* ⦿I *No meals.*

$$$
HOTEL

▥ **Granada Hotel & Bistro.** Built in 1922 and sparkling again after renovations completed in 2012, the Granada is the only full-service hotel in the heart of downtown. **Pros:** free parking; easy walk to downtown; luxurious rooms and amenities. **Cons:** some rooms are tiny; sometimes noisy near restaurant kitchen. ⑤ *Rooms from: $229* ⊠ *1126 Morro St.* ☎ *805/544-9100* ⊕ *granadahotelandbistro.com* ⇱ *17 rooms* ⦿I *No meals.*

$$$
HOTEL

▥ **Madonna Inn.** From its rococo bathrooms to its pink-on-pink froufrou steak house, the Madonna Inn is fabulous or tacky, depending on your taste. **Pros:** fun, one-of-a-kind experience. **Cons:** rooms vary widely; must appreciate kitsch. ⑤ *Rooms from: $189* ⊠ *100 Madonna Rd.* ☎ *805/543–3000, 800/543–9666* ⊕ *www.madonnainn.com* ⇱ *106 rooms, 4 suites* ⦿I *No meals.*

$
HOTEL

▥ **Peach Tree Inn.** Extra touches such as rose gardens, a porch with rockers, and flower-filled vases turn this modest, family-run motel into a relaxing creek-side haven. **Pros:** bargain rates; cozy rooms; decent breakfast. **Cons:** near a busy intersection; basic amenities. ⑤ *Rooms from: $99* ⊠ *2001 Monterey St.* ☎ *805/543–3170, 800/227–6396* ⊕ *www.peachtreeinn.com* ⇱ *37 rooms* ⦿I *Breakfast.*

$$
B&B/INN 📺 **Petit Soleil.** A cobblestone courtyard, country-French custom furnishings, and Gallic music piped through the halls evoke a Provençal mood at this cheery inn on upper Monterey Street's motel row. **Pros:** French details throughout; scrumptious breakfasts; cozy rooms. **Cons:** sits on a busy avenue; cramped parking. ⑤ *Rooms from: $169* ✉ *1473 Monterey St.* 📞 *805/549–0321, 800/676–1588* ⊕ *www.psslo.com* ⟿ *15 rooms, 1 suite* ❂ *Breakfast.*

NIGHTLIFE AND THE ARTS
NIGHTLIFE
SLO's club scene is centered on Higuera Street, off Monterey Street.

Koberl at Blue. A trendy crowd hangs out at this upscale restaurant's slick bar to sip on exotic martinis and the many local and imported beers and wines. ✉ *998 Monterey St., at Osos St.* 📞 *805/783–1135* ⊕ *www. epkoberl.com.*

SLO Brew. Handcrafted microbrews and live music most nights make for a winning combination at this downtown watering hole and restaurant that should be relocated to 736 Higuera St. by 2015. ✉ *1119 Garden St.* 📞 *805/543–1843* ⊕ *www.slobrewingco.com.*

THE ARTS
Performing Arts Center, San Luis Obispo. The center hosts live theater, dance, and music performances. ✉ *Cal Poly, 1 Grand Ave., off U.S. 101* 📞 *805/756–7222, 805/756–2787 box office, 888/233–2787 toll-free* ⊕ *www.pacslo.org.*

OFF THE BEATEN PATH
Montaña de Oro State Park. West of San Luis Obispo, Los Osos Valley Road winds past farms and ranches to this state park whose miles of nature trails traverse rocky shoreline, wild beaches, and hills overlooking dramatic scenery. Check out the tide pools, watch the waves roll into the bluffs, and picnic in the eucalyptus groves. From Montaña de Oro you can reach Morro Bay by following the coastline along South Bay Boulevard 8 miles through the quaint residential villages of Los Osos and Baywood Park. ✉ *West about 13 miles from downtown San Luis Obispo on Madonna Rd., to Los Osos Valley Rd., to Pecho Valley Rd.; to continue on to Morro Bay, backtrack east to Los Osos Valley Rd., then head north on S. Bay Blvd., and west on State Park Rd.* 📞 *805/528–0513, 805/772–7434* ⊕ *www.parks.ca.gov.*

MORRO BAY

14 miles north of San Luis Obispo.

Commercial fishermen slog around Morro Bay in galoshes, and beat-up fishing boats bob in the bay's protected waters. Nature-oriented activities take center stage here: kayaking, hiking, biking, fishing, and wildlife-watching around the bay and national marine estuary and along the state beach.

GETTING HERE AND AROUND
From U.S. 101 south or north, exit at Highway 1 in San Luis Obispo and head west. Scenic Highway 1 passes through the eastern edge of town. From Atascadero, two-lane Highway 41 West treks over the mountains to Morro Bay. San Luis Obispo RTA Route 12 buses travel

year-round between Morro Bay, San Luis Obispo, Cayucos, Cambria, San Simeon, and Hearst Castle. The Morro Bay Shuttle picks up riders throughout the town from Friday through Monday in summer ($1.25 one-way, $3 day pass).

ESSENTIALS

Visitor Information Morro Bay Visitors Center ⊠ *255 Morro Bay Blvd., at Morro Ave.* ☎ *805/225–1633, 800/231–0592* ⊕ *www.morrobay.org* ⊙ *Daily 9–5.*

EXPLORING

Embarcadero. The center of the action on land is the Embarcadero, where vacationers pour in and out of souvenir shops and seafood restaurants and stroll or bike along the scenic half-mile Harborwalk to Morro Rock. From here, you can get out on the bay in a kayak or tour boat. ⊠ *On waterfront from Beach St. to Tidelands Park.*

FAMILY **Morro Bay State Park Museum of Natural History.** Entertaining interactive exhibits at this spiffy museum explain the natural environment and how to preserve it—in the bay and estuary and on the rest of the planet. ■**TIP→ Children age 16 and under are admitted free here.** ⊠ *State Park Rd., south of downtown* ☎ *805/772–2694* ⊕ *www.ccnha.org/morrobay* 🎟 *$3* ⊙ *Daily 10–5.*

Morro Rock. At the mouth of Morro Bay stands 576-foot-high Morro Rock, one of nine small volcanic peaks, or morros, in the area. A short walk leads to a breakwater, with the harbor on one side and crashing ocean waves on the other. You may not climb the rock, where endangered falcons and other birds nest. Sea lions and otters often play in the water below the rock. ⊠ *Northern end of Embarcadero.*

WHERE TO EAT

$$ ✕ **Dorn's Original Breakers Cafe.** This restaurant overlooking the harbor
SEAFOOD has satisfied local appetites since 1948. In addition to straight-ahead dishes such as cod or shrimp fish-and-chips or calamari tubes sautéed in butter and wine, Dorn's serves breakfast. ⑤ *Average main: $22* ⊠ *801 Market Ave., at Morro Bay Blvd.* ☎ *805/772–4415* ⊕ *www. dornscafe.com.*

$ ✕ **Taco Temple.** This family-run diner serves some of the freshest food
SOUTHWESTERN around. The seafood-heavy menu includes salmon burritos, superb fish tacos with mango salsa, and other dishes hailing from somewhere between California and Mexico. ■**TIP→ Taco Temple**is in a supermarket parking lot on the frontage road parallel to Highway 1, just north of the Highway 41 junction. ⑤ *Average main: $15* ⊠ *2680 Main St., at Elena St.* ☎ *805/772–4965* ⌓ *Reservations not accepted* ▭ *No credit cards* ⊙ *Closed Tues.*

$$$ ✕ **Windows on the Water.** Diners at this second-floor restaurant view the
SEAFOOD sunset through giant picture windows. Meanwhile, fresh fish and other dishes based on local ingredients emerge from the wood-fired oven in the open kitchen, and oysters on the half shell beckon from the raw bar. The California-centric wine list includes about 20 selections poured by the glass. ⑤ *Average main: $30* ⊠ *699 Embarcadero, at Pacific St.* ☎ *805/772–0677* ⊕ *www.windowsmb.com* ⊙ *No lunch.*

WHERE TO STAY

$$$
B&B/INN
Fodor's Choice
★

⚏ Anderson Inn. Friendly, personalized service and an oceanfront setting keep loyal patrons returning to this Embarcadero inn. **Pros:** walk to restaurants and sights; nice rooms; attentive service. **Cons:** not low-budget; waterfront area can get crowded. ⑤ *Rooms from: $239* ⊠ *897 Embarcadero* ☎ *805/772–3434, 866/950–3434 toll-free reservations* ⊕ *www.andersoninnmorrobay.com* ➳ *8 rooms* ⦶ *No meals.*

$$$
B&B/INN
Fodor's Choice
★

⚏ Cass House. In tiny Cayucos, 4 miles north of Morro Bay, a shipping pioneer's 1867 home is now a luxurious B&B surrounded by rose and other gardens. **Pros:** historic property; some ocean views; excellent meals. **Cons:** away from nightlife and attractions; not good for families. ⑤ *Rooms from: $200* ⊠ *222 N. Ocean Ave., Cayucos* ☎ *805/995–3669* ⊕ *casshouseinn.com* ➳ *5 rooms* ⦶ *Breakfast.*

$$
RESORT

⚏ The Inn at Morro Bay. Surrounded by eucalyptus trees, this inn abuts a heron rookery and Morro Bay State Park. **Pros:** great for wildlife enthusiasts; stellar views from restaurant and some rooms. **Cons:** some rooms on the small side; birds and seals can wake you early. ⑤ *Rooms from: $169* ⊠ *60 State Park Rd.* ☎ *805/772–5651, 800/321–9566* ⊕ *innatmorrobay.com* ➳ *97 rooms, 1 cottage* ⦶ *No meals.*

SPORTS AND THE OUTDOORS

Kayak Horizons. This outfit rents kayaks and paddleboards and gives lessons and guided tours. ⊠ *551 Embarcadero, near Marina St.* ☎ *805/772–6444* ⊕ *www.kayakhorizons.com.*

Sub-Sea Tours & Kayaks. You can view sea life aboard this outfit's glass-bottom boat, watch whales from its catamaran, or rent a kayak or canoe. ⊠ *699 Embarcadero* ☎ *805/772–9463* ⊕ *subseatours.com.*

Virg's Landing. Virg's conducts deep-sea-fishing and whale-watching trips. ⊠ *1169 Market Ave.* ☎ *805/772–1222* ⊕ *virgslanding.com.*

PASO ROBLES

30 miles north of San Luis Obispo; 25 miles northwest of Morro Bay.

In the 1860s tourists began flocking to this dusty ranching outpost to "take the cure" in a luxurious bathhouse fed by underground mineral hot springs. An Old West town, complete with opera house, emerged, and grand Victorian homes went up, followed in the 20th century by Craftsman bungalows. A 2003 earthquake demolished or weakened several beloved downtown buildings, but historically faithful reconstruction has helped the district retain its character.

More than 200 wineries pepper the wooded hills of Paso Robles west of U.S. 101 and blanket the flatter, more open land on the east side. The region's hot summer days and cool nights yield grapes that produce robust Cabernet Sauvignon, Merlot, Syrah, and Zinfandel. Pinot Noir does well in some of the cooler, more fog-heavy western sections. Chardonnay, Sauvignon Blanc, and Viognier are among the white-wine grapes that do well here.

Small-town friendliness prevails at most wineries, especially smaller ones. Pick up a regional wine-touring map at lodgings, wineries, and attractions around town. Many lodgings pass out coupons good for discount tastings. Most tasting rooms close at 5 pm; many charge a small fee.

More attracts people to the Paso Robles area than fine wine and fancy tasting rooms, however. Golfers play the four local courses and spandex-clad bicyclists race along the winding back roads. Down-home and upmarket restaurants, bars, antiques stores, and little shops fill the streets around oak-shaded City Park, where special events of all kinds—custom car shows, an olive festival, Friday-night summer concerts—take place on many weekends. Despite its increasing sophistication, Paso (as the locals call it) more or less remains cowboy country. Each year in late July and early August, the city throws the two-week California Mid-State Fair, complete with livestock auctions, carnival rides, and corn dogs.

GETTING HERE AND AROUND

U.S. 101 runs through the city of Paso Robles. Highway 46 West links Paso Robles to Highway 1 and Cambria on the coast. Highway 46 East connects Paso Robles with Interstate 5 and the San Joaquin Valley. Public transit is not convenient for wine touring and sightseeing.

ESSENTIALS

Visitor Information Paso Robles Wine Country Alliance ☎ 805/239–8463 ⊕ www.pasowine.com. **Travel Paso Robles Alliance** ⊠ 1225 Park St., near 12th St. ☎ 805/238–0506 ⊕ www.travelpaso.com.

EXPLORING

TOP ATTRACTIONS

Fodor'sChoice ★ **Calcareous Vineyard.** Elegant wines, a stylish tasting room, and knockout hilltop views make for a winning experience at this winery along winding Peachy Canyon Road. Cabernet Sauvignon, Syrah, and Zinfandel grapes thrive in the summer heat and limestone soils of the two vineyards near the tasting room, and a third vineyard on cooler York Mountain produces Pinot Noir, Chardonnay, and a Cabernet with a completely different character from the Peachy Canyon edition. ■ TIP→ The picnic area's expansive eastward views invite lingering. ⊠ 3430 Peachy Canyon Rd. ☎ 805/239–0289 ⊕ www.calcareous.com ☜ Tasting $10; tour and tasting (reservations required) $25 ۞ Daily 11–5.

FAMILY **Estrella Warbirds Museum.** An entertaining homage to fighter planes, flyboys, and flygirls, this museum maintains indoor exhibits about wartime aviation and displays retired specimens (of planes) outdoors and in repair shops. Bonus attraction: a huge building with spruced-up autos, drag racers, and "funny cars." ⊠ 4251 Dry Creek Rd., off Airport Rd., north off Hwy. 46E ☎ 805/227–0440 ⊕ www.ewarbirds.org ☜ $10 ۞ Thurs.–Sun. 10–4 and Mon. legal holidays.

Firestone Walker Brewing Company. At this working craft brewery you can sample medal winners such as the Double Barrel Ale and learn about the beer-making process on 30-minute guided tours of the brew house and cellar. ⊠ 1400 Ramada Dr., east side of U.S. 101; exit at Hwy. 46 W/Cambria, but head east ☎ 805/225–5911 ⊕ www.firestonebeer. com ☜ Tasting $1.50–$3 per sample, tour free ۞ Daily 10–5; tours on the half hour Fri.–Sun. 10:30–3:30 and Mon.–Thurs. by appointment.

Fodor's Choice
★

Justin Vineyards & Winery. Suave Justin built its reputation—and, claim some, the Paso Robles wine region's as well—on Isosceles, a hearty Bordeaux blend, usually of Cabernet Sauvignon, Cabernet Franc, and Merlot. Justin's Cabernet Sauvignon is also well regarded, as is the Right Angle blend of Cab and three other varietals. Tastings here take place in an expansive room whose equally expansive windows provide views of Justin's hillside vineyards. ⊠ *11680 Chimney Rock Rd., 15 miles west of U.S. 101's Hwy. 46 E exit; take 24th St. west and follow road (name changes along the way) to Chimney Rock Rd.* ☎ *805/238–6932, 800/726–0049* ⊕ *www.justinwine.com* 🎫 *Tasting $10, tour $10, tour and tasting $15* ☾ *Daily 10–4:30* ☾ *Tours 10:30 and 2:30.*

LAID-BACK WINE COUNTRY

Hundreds of vineyards and wineries dot the hillsides from Paso Robles to San Luis Obispo, through the scenic Edna Valley and south to northern Santa Barbara County. The wineries offer much of the variety of northern California's Napa and Sonoma valleys—without the glitz and crowds. Since the early 1980s the region has developed an international reputation for high-quality wines, most notably Pinot Noir, Chardonnay, and Zinfandel. Wineries here tend to be small, but most have tasting rooms (some have tours), and you'll often meet the winemakers themselves.

Fodor's Choice
★

Pasolivo. While touring the idyllic west side of Paso Robles, take a break from wine tasting by stopping at Pasolivo. Find out how the artisans here make their Tuscan-style olive oils on a high-tech Italian press, and test the acclaimed results. ⊠ *8530 Vineyard Dr., west off U.S. 101 (Exit 224) or Hwy. 46 W (Exit 228)* ☎ *805/227–0186* ⊕ *www.pasolivo.com* 🎫 *Free* ☾ *Daily 11–5.*

River Oaks Hot Springs & Spa. The lakeside spa, on 240 hilly acres near the intersection of U.S. 101 and Highway 46 East, is a great place to relax after wine tasting or festival-going. Soak in a private indoor or outdoor hot tub fed by natural mineral springs, or indulge in a massage or facial. ⊠ *800 Clubhouse Dr., off River Oaks Dr.* ☎ *805/238–4600* ⊕ *www.riveroakshotsprings.com* 🎫 *$20–$24 per hr* ☾ *Tues.–Sun. 9–9.*

Tablas Creek Vineyard. Tucked in the western hills of Paso Robles, Tablas Creek is known for its blends of organically grown, hand-harvested Rhône varietals. Roussanne and Viognier are the two standout whites; the Mourvèdre-heavy blend called Panoplie (it also includes Grenache and Syrah) has received high praise in recent years. ■TIP→ There's a fine picnic area here. ⊠ *9339 Adelaida Rd., west of Vineyard Dr.* ☎ *805/237–1231* ⊕ *www.tablascreek.com* 🎫 *Tasting $10, tour free* ☾ *Daily 10–5; tour 10:30 and 2 by appointment.*

WORTH NOTING

Carnegie Historic Library. Philanthropist and steel magnate Andrew Carnegie funded this sturdy and splendid structure, erected in 1908. The jewel of City Park, it hosts thoughtful exhibits on local history, many of which include quirky products and advertisements from days gone by. ⊠ *800 12th St., at Park St.* ☎ *805/238–4996* ⊕ *www.*

pasorobleshistoricalsociety.org ⊙ *Tues. and Thurs.–Sat. 10–4, Sun. 11–4* ⊙ *Closed Mon., Wed., and holidays.*

Eberle Winery. Even if you don't drink wine, stop here for a fascinating tour of the huge wine caves beneath the vineyards. Eberle produces wines from Bordeaux, Rhône, and Italian varietals and makes intriguing blends including Grenache Blanc–Viognier and Cabernet Sauvignon–Syrah. ⊠ *3810 Hwy. 46 E, 3½ miles east of U.S. 101* ☎ *805/238–9607* ⊕ *www.eberlewinery.com* ⊡ *Basic tasting and tour free; weekend reserve tasting $10* ⊙ *Apr.–Sept. daily 10–6, Oct.–Mar. daily 10–5.*

Paso Robles Pioneer Museum. The museum's one-room schoolhouse and its displays of ranching paraphernalia, horse-drawn vehicles, hot-springs artifacts, and photos evoke Paso's rural heritage. ⊠ *2010 Riverside Ave., at 21st St.* ☎ *805/239–4556* ⊕ *www.pasoroblespioneermuseum. org* ⊡ *Free* ⊙ *Sep.–May Thurs.–Sun. 1–4; Jun.–Aug. Thurs., Fri. and Sun. 1–4, Sat. 10–4.*

WHERE TO EAT

$$$
AMERICAN

✕ **Artisan.** Innovative variations on traditional American comfort foods, well-chosen regional wines, and a sophisticated urban vibe have made this family-run American bistro such a hit with winemakers, locals, and tourists that it recently relocated to larger quarters. Chef Chris Kobayashi, a James Beard Award nominee, uses local, organic, wild-caught ingredients to put a fresh spin on dishes such as rabbit Stroganoff and scallops with cedar-planked spaghetti squash, sherry brown butter, and pork fried wild rice. Save room for chef's home-style desserts: sundaes, puddings, cakes, cookies, and other sweet delights. $ *Average main: $28* ⊠ *843 12th St., at Pine St.* ☎ *805/237–8084* ⊕ *www. artisanpasorobles.com.*

$$$
FRENCH

✕ **Bistro Laurent.** Owner-chef Laurent Grangien's handsome, welcoming French bistro occupies an 1890s brick building across from City Park. He focuses on traditional dishes such as duck confit, rack of lamb, and onion soup, but always prepares a few au courant daily specials as well. The wines, sourced from the adjacent wine shop, come from around the world. $ *Average main: $28* ⊠ *1202 Pine St., at 12th St.* ☎ *805/226–8191* ⊕ *www.bistrolaurent.com* ⊙ *Closed Sun. and Mon.*

$$$
AMERICAN

✕ **McPhee's Grill.** Just south of Paso Robles in tiny Templeton, this casual chophouse in an 1860s wood-frame storefront serves sophisticated, contemporary versions of traditional Western fare such as oak-grilled filet mignon and cedar-planked salmon. The house-label wines, made especially for the restaurant, are quite good. $ *Average main: $25* ⊠ *416 S. Main St., at 5th St., Templeton* ☎ *805/434–3204* ⊕ *mcphees-grill.com* ⊙ *No lunch Sun.*

$
FRENCH

✕ **Panolivo Family Bistro.** Scrumptious, affordable French fare draws patrons to this cheery café just north of the town square. For breakfast, try a fresh pastry or quiche, or build your own omelet. Lunch and dinner choices include sandwiches, salads, and fresh pastas—including cannelloni stuffed with vegetables or house-made beef—along with traditional dishes like snails baked in garlic-butter sauce or beef bourguignon. $ *Average main: $15* ⊠ *1344 Park St., at 14th St.* ☎ *805/239–3366* ⊕ *www.panolivo.com.*

2

$$ ✕**Thomas Hill Organics Market Bistro & Wine Bar.** In casual quarters a
MODERN   block north of City Park, Joe and Debbie Thomas serve inventive loca-
AMERICAN   vore cuisine. Much of the produce comes from their nearby 10-acre
organic farm, and the meats and fish—even the olive oil and cheeses,
not to mention the wines—come mostly from local providers as well.
■TIP➔ When the weather's fine, ask for a table in the outdoor court-
yard. ⑤ *Average main: $17* ✉ *1313 Park St., at 13th St.* ☎ *805/226–
5888* ⊕ *thomashillorganics.com.*

$$$ ✕**Villa Creek.** With a firm nod to the Rancho and Mission cuisine of Cali-
SOUTHWESTERN   fornia's early settlers, chef Tom Fundero conjures distinctly modern magic
with local, organic ingredients. The seasonal menu has included grilled
fish with quinoa pilaf, braised pork belly with sweet-potato hash, mussels
steamed in coconut milk, and seared chicken with whipped potatoes and
preserved-lemon sauce. Central Coast selections dominate the wine list.
All brick and bare wood, the dining room can get loud, but the atmosphere is always festive. For lighter appetites or wallets, the bar serves
smaller plates—and potent margaritas. ⑤ *Average main. $26* ✉ *1114
Pine St., at 12th St.* ☎ *805/238–3000* ⊕ *www.villacreek.com* ☾ *No lunch.*

WHERE TO STAY

$ ⊡**Adelaide Inn.** Family-owned and -managed, this clean, friendly oasis
HOTEL   with meticulous landscaping offers spacious rooms and everything you
need: coffeemaker, iron, hair dryer, and peace and quiet. **Pros:** great
bargain; attractive pool area; ideal for families. **Cons:** not a romantic
retreat; near a busy intersection. ⑤ *Rooms from: $104* ✉ *1215 Ysabel
Ave.* ☎ *805/238–2770, 800/549–7276* ⊕ *www.adelaideinn.com* ⇗ *108
rooms* ⫶○⫶ *Breakfast.*

$$$$ ⊡**Hotel Cheval.** Equestrian themes surface throughout this intimate,
HOTEL   European-style inn a half-block from the main square and near some of
Paso's best restaurants. **Pros:** near downtown restaurants; sophisticated;
personal service. **Cons:** views aren't great; no pool or hot tub. ⑤ *Rooms
from: $330* ✉ *1021 Pine St.* ☎ *805/226–9995, 866/522–6999* ⊕ *www.
hotelcheval.com* ⇗ *16 rooms* ⫶○⫶ *Breakfast.*

$$$$ ⊡**JUST Inn.** Fine wines, a destination restaurant, and a vineyard's-edge
B&B/INN   setting make a stay at Justin winery's on-site inn an exercise in sophisticated seclusion. **Pros:** sophisticated; secluded; vineyard views; destination
restaurant. **Cons:** half-hour drive to town; location may be *too* secluded
for some. ⑤ *Rooms from: $400* ✉ *11680 Chimney Rock Rd.* ☎ *805/238–
6932, 800/726–0049* ⊕ *www.justinwine.com* ⇗ *4 suites* ⫶○⫶ *Breakfast.*

$$ ⊡**La Bellasera Hotel & Suites.** The swankest full-service hotel for miles
HOTEL   around, La Bellasera caters to those looking for high-tech amenities
and easy access to major Central Coast roadways. **Pros:** new property;
tons of amenities. **Cons:** far from downtown; at a major intersection.
⑤ *Rooms from: $169* ✉ *206 Alexa Court* ☎ *805/238–2834, 866/782–
9669* ⊕ *www.labellasera.com* ⇗ *35 rooms, 25 suites* ⫶○⫶ *No meals.*

$$$ ⊡**Paso Robles Inn.** On the site of an old spa hotel of the same name,
HOTEL   the inn is built around a lush, shaded garden with a pool. **Pros:** private
spring-fed hot tubs; historic property; across from town square. **Cons:**
fronts a busy street; rooms vary in size and amenities. ⑤ *Rooms from:
$183* ✉ *1103 Spring St.* ☎ *805/238–2660, 800/676–1713* ⊕ *www.
pasoroblesinn.com* ⇗ *92 rooms, 6 suites* ⫶○⫶ *No meals.*

THE ARTS

Vina Robles Ampitheatre. At this 3,300-seat, mission-style venue that opened in summer 2013, you can wine, dine, and listen to acclaimed musicians in concert. ⊠ *Vina Robles winery, 3800 Mill Rd., off Hwy. 46* ☎ *805/286–3680* ⊕ *www.vinarobles.com* �
 May–Nov.

CAMBRIA

28 miles west of Paso Robles; 20 miles north of Morro Bay.

Cambria, set on piney hills above the sea, was settled by Welsh miners in the 1890s. In the 1970s, the gorgeous, isolated setting attracted artists and other independent types; the town now caters to tourists, but it still bears the imprint of its bohemian past. Both of Cambria's downtowns, the original East Village and the newer West Village, are packed with art and crafts galleries, antiques shops, cafés, restaurants, and B&Bs. Late-Victorian homes stand alongside streets, and the hills are filled with redwood-and-glass residences.

Two diverting detours lie between Morro Bay and Cambria. In the laid-back beach town of Cayucos, 4 miles north of Morro Bay, you can stroll the long pier, feast on chowder (at Duckie's), and sample the namesake delicacies of the Brown Butter Cookie Co. Over in Harmony, a cute former dairy town 7 miles south of Cambria, you can take in the glassworks, pottery, and other artsy enterprises.

GETTING HERE AND AROUND

Highway 1 leads to Cambria from the north and south. Highway 246 West curves from U.S. 101 through the mountains to Cambria. San Luis Obispo RTA Route 12 buses stop in Cambria (and Hearst Castle).

ESSENTIALS

Visitor Information Cambria Chamber of Commerce ☎ *805/927–3624* ⊕ *www.cambriachamber.org.*

EXPLORING

Fiscalini Ranch Preserve. Walk along a mile-long coastal bluff trail to spot migrating whales, otters, and shore birds at this 450-acre public open space. Miles of additional scenic trails crisscross the protected habitats of rare and endangered species of flora and fauna, including a Monterey pine forest, western pond turtles, monarch butterflies, and burrowing owls. Dogs are permitted on-leash everywhere and off-leash on all trails except the bluff. ⊠ *Hwy. 1, between Cambria Rd. and Main St. to the north, and Burton Dr. and Warren Rd. to the south; access either end of bluff trail off Windsor Blvd.* ☎ *805/927–2856* ⊕ *www.ffrpcambria.org.*

Leffingwell's Landing. A state picnic ground, the landing is a good place for examining tidal pools and watching otters as they frolic in the surf. ⊠ *North end of Moonstone Beach Dr.* ☎ *805/927–2070.*

Moonstone Beach Drive. The drive runs along a bluff above the ocean, paralleled by a 3-mile boardwalk that winds along the beach. On this fine walk—a great photo op—you might glimpse sea lions and sea otters, and perhaps a gray whale during winter and spring. Year-round, birds aplenty fly about, and tiny creatures scurry amid the tidepools. ⊠ *Off Hwy. 1.*

Nit Wit Ridge. Arthur Beal (aka Captain Nit Wit, Der Tinkerpaw) spent 51 years building a home above Cambria's West Village out of collected junk: beer cans, rocks, abalone shells, car parts, TV antennas—you name it. The site, sometimes signed as Nitt Witt Ridge, is a state landmark. ■TIP➔ You can drive by and peek in—from the 700 block of Main Street, head southeast on Cornwall Street and east on Hillcrest Drive. Better yet, schedule a guided tour. ⊠ *881 Hillcrest Dr.* ☎ *805/927–2690* ⌑ *$10* ⊙ *Tour daily by appointment.*

WHERE TO EAT

$$$

AMERICAN

✕ **Black Cat Bistro.** Jazz wafts through the several small rooms of this intimate East Village bistro where stylish cushions line the banquettes. Start with an order of the fried olives stuffed with Gorgonzola, accompanied by a glass of local or imported wine. Mains on offer might include asiago pappardelle (vegetarian or with shrimp) or duck breast with mushroom risotto and cherry duck jus. ⑤ *Average main: $25* ⊠ *1602 Main St.* ☎ *805/927–1600* ⊕ *www.blackcatbistro.com* ⌑ *Reservations essential* ⊙ *Closed Tues. and Wed. No lunch.*

$$

AMERICAN

FAMILY

✕ **Linn's Restaurant.** Homemade olallieberry pies, soups, potpies, and other farmhouse comfort foods share the menu with fancier dishes such as free-range chicken cordon bleu at this spacious East Village restaurant. Also on-site are a bakery, a café serving more casual fare (take-out available), and a gift shop that sells gourmet foods. ⑤ *Average main: $18* ⊠ *2277 Main St.* ☎ *805/927–0371* ⊕ *www.linnsfruitbin.com.*

$$

ECLECTIC

✕ **Robin's.** A multiethnic, vegetarian-friendly dining experience awaits you at this cozy East Village cottage. At dinner, choose from lobster enchiladas, Moroccan duck breast, tandoori chicken, and more. Lunchtime's extensive salad and sandwich menu embraces burgers and tofu alike. ■TIP➔ Unless it's raining, ask for a table on the secluded (heated) garden patio. ⑤ *Average main: $22* ⊠ *4095 Burton Dr., at Center St.* ☎ *805/927–5007* ⊕ *www.robinsrestaurant.com.*

$$$

SEAFOOD

✕ **Sea Chest Oyster Bar and Restaurant.** Cambria's best place for seafood fills up soon after it opens at 5:30. Those in the know grab seats at the oyster bar and take in spectacular sunsets while watching the chefs broil fresh halibut, steam garlicky clams, and fry crispy calamari steaks. If you arrive to a wait, play cribbage or checkers in the game room. ⑤ *Average main: $26* ⊠ *6216 Moonstone Beach Dr., near Weymouth St.* ☎ *805/927–4514* ⊕ *www.seachestrestaurant.com* ⌑ *Reservations not accepted* ▭ *No credit cards* ⊙ *Closed Tues. mid-Sept.–May. No lunch.*

WHERE TO STAY

$

HOTEL

▦ **Bluebird Inn.** This sweet motel in Cambria's East Village sits amid beautiful gardens along Santa Rosa Creek. **Pros:** excellent value; well-kept gardens; friendly staff. **Cons:** few frills; basic rooms; on Cambria's main drag; not on beach. ⑤ *Rooms from: $78* ⊠ *1880 Main St.* ☎ *805/927–4634, 800/552–5434* ⊕ *bluebirdmotel.com* ⤴ *37 rooms* ⊙| *No meals.*

$$

RESORT

▦ **Cambria Pines Lodge.** This 25-acre retreat up the hill from the East Village is a good choice for families. **Pros:** short walk from downtown; many recreational facilities; verdant gardens; spacious grounds. **Cons:** service and housekeeping not always top-quality; some units need updating. ⑤ *Rooms from: $169* ⊠ *2905 Burton Dr.* ☎ *805/927–4200, 800/966–6490* ⊕ *www.cambriapineslodge.com* ⤴ *77 rooms, 75 suites* ⊙| *Breakfast.*

$$ ⚑ **J. Patrick House.** Monterey pines and flower gardens surround this
B&B/INN Irish-theme inn, which sits on a hilltop above Cambria's East Village.
Pros: fantastic breakfasts; friendly innkeepers; quiet neighborhood.
Cons: few rooms; fills up quickly. ⑤ *Rooms from: $175* ✉ *2990 Burton Dr.* ☎ *805/927–3812, 800/341–5258* ⊕ *www.jpatrickhouse.com* ⊋ *8 rooms* ⦿ *Breakfast.*

$$ ⚑ **Moonstone Landing.** Friendly staff, lots of amenities, and reasonable
HOTEL rates make this up-to-date motel a top pick of readers who like to stay
right on Moonstone Beach. **Pros:** sleek furnishings; across from the
beach; cheery lounge. **Cons:** narrow property; some rooms overlook
a parking lot. ⑤ *Rooms from: $125* ✉ *6240 Moonstone Beach Dr.* ☎ *805/927–0012, 800/830–4540* ⊕ *www.moonstonelanding.com* ⊋ *29 rooms* ⦿ *Breakfast.*

SAN SIMEON

9 miles north of Cambria; 65 miles south of Big Sur.

Whalers founded San Simeon in the 1850s but had virtually abandoned
it by 1865, when Senator George Hearst began purchasing most of the
surrounding ranch land. Hearst turned San Simeon into a bustling port,
and his son, William Randolph Hearst, further developed the area while
erecting Hearst Castle. Today, San Simeon is basically a strip of unremarkable gift shops and so-so motels that straddle Highway 1 about 4
miles south of the castle's entrance, but Old San Simeon, right across
from the entrance, is worth a peek.

GETTING HERE AND AROUND

Highway 1 is the only way to reach San Simeon. Connect with the
highway off U.S. 101 directly or via rural routes such as Highway 41
West (Atascadero to Morro Bay) and Highway 46 West (Paso Robles
to Cambria).

EXPLORING
TOP ATTRACTIONS

Fodor'sChoice **Hearst Castle.** Officially known as "Hearst San Simeon State Historical
★ Monument," Hearst Castle sits in solitary splendor atop La Cuesta
Encantada (the Enchanted Hill). Its buildings and gardens spread over
127 acres that were the heart of newspaper magnate William Randolph Hearst's 250,000-acre ranch. Hearst devoted nearly 30 years and
about $10 million to building this elaborate estate. He commissioned
renowned California architect Julia Morgan, but he was very much
involved with the final product, a blend of Italian, Spanish, and Moorish styles. The 115-room main building and three huge "cottages" are
connected by terraces and staircases and surrounded by pools, gardens,
and statuary. In its heyday the castle was a playground for Hearst and
his guests—Hollywood celebrities, political leaders, scientists, and other
well-known figures. Construction began in 1919 and was never officially completed. Work was halted in 1947 when Hearst had to leave
San Simeon because of failing health. The Hearst family donated the
property to the State of California in 1958.

Access to the castle is through the visitor center at the foot of the hill, which contains a collection of Hearst memorabilia and a giant-screen theater that shows a 40-minute film giving an overview of Hearst's life and of the castle's construction. Buses from the visitor center zig-zag up to the neoclassical extravaganza, where guides conduct three different daytime tours of parts of the estate: grand rooms, upstairs suites, and cottages and kitchen. Daytime tours take about two hours and include the movie and time at the end to explore the castle exteriors. In spring and fall, docents in period costume portray Hearst's guests and staff for the slightly longer evening tour, which begins at sunset. Reservations are recommended for all the tours, which include a ½-mile walk and between 150 and 400 stairs. ⊠ *San Simeon State Park, 750 Hearst Castle Rd.* ☎ *800/444–4445* ⊕ *www.hearstcastle. com* 🖃 *Daytime tours $25, evening tours $36* ⊘ *Tours daily 9–3:20, later in summer; additional tours take place most Fri. and Sat. evenings Mar.–May and Sept.–Dec.*

FAMILY **Piedras Blancas Elephant Seal Rookery.** A large colony of elephant seals (at last count 15,000 members) gathers every year at Piedras Blancas Elephant Seal Rookery, on the beaches near Piedras Blancas Light-house. The huge males with their pendulous, trunklike noses typically start appearing on shore in late November, and the females begin to arrive in December to give birth—most babies are born in the last two weeks of January. The newborn pups spend about four weeks nursing before their mothers head out to sea, leaving them on their own; the "weaners" leave the rookery when they are about 3½ months old. The seals return in the spring and summer months to molt or rest, but not en masse as in winter. You can watch them from a boardwalk along the bluffs just a few feet above the beach; do not attempt to approach them, as they are wild animals. The nonprofit Friends of the Elephant Seal runs a small visitor center and gift shop at 250 San Simeon Avenue in San Simeon. ⊠ *Off Hwy. 1, 4½ miles north of Hearst Castle, just south of Piedras Blancas Lighthouse* ☎ *805/924–1628* ⊕ *www. elephantseal.org.*

Piedras Blancas Light Station. If you think traversing craggy, twisting Highway 1 is tough, imagine trying to navigate a boat up the rocky coastline (piedras blancas means "white rocks" in Spanish) near San Simeon before lighthouses were built. Captains must have cheered wildly when the beam began to shine here in 1875. Try to time a visit to include a morning tour (reservations not required). ■**TIP**➔ **Do not meet at the gate to the lighthouse—you'll miss the tour. Meet your guide instead at the former Piedras Blancas Motel, a mile and a half north of the light station.** ☎ *805/927–7361* ⊕ *piedrasblancas.org* 🖃 *$10* ⊘ *Tours at 9:45, mid-June–Aug. Mon.–Sat.; Sept.–mid-June Tues., Thurs., and Sat.; no tours on national holidays* ☞ *No pets allowed.*

WORTH NOTING
Old San Simeon. Founded in the 1850s as a whaling village, Old San Simeon morphed into an outpost for employees of Hearst Ranch about two decades later. **Sebastian's General Store,** built in 1852 as a whaling store, was moved by oxen to its present location in 1878. Julia Morgan, William Randolph Hearst's architect, designed some of the village's

mission revival–style buildings. ■TIP➔ Sebastian's houses a deli that serves an excellent French dip sandwich (made from Hearst Ranch beef) and the laid-back tasting room of Hearst Ranch Winery, another delight. ⊠ *West of Hwy. 1, across from Hearst Castle entrance.*

BEACHES

William Randolph Hearst Memorial Beach. This wide, sandy beach edges a protected cove on both sides of San Simeon Pier. Fish from the pier or from a charter boat, picnic and barbecue on the bluffs, or boogie board or bodysurf on relatively gentle waves. In summer, you can rent a kayak and paddle out into the bay for close encounters with marine life and sea caves. **Facilities:** food and drink; parking; toilets; water sports. **Best for:** sunset; swimming; walking. ⊠ *750 Hearst Castle Rd., off Hwy. 1, west of Hearst Castle entrance* ☎ *805/927–2020* ⊕ *www. slostateparks.com* ⊠ *Free* ☉ *Daily sunrise–sunset.*

WHERE TO STAY

$$$
HOTEL
🏨 **Best Western Cavalier Oceanfront Resort.** Reasonable rates, an ocean-front location, evening bonfires, and well-equipped rooms—some with wood-burning fireplaces and private patios—make this motel a great choice. **Pros:** on the bluffs; fantastic views; close to Hearst Castle. **Cons:** room amenities and sizes vary; pools are small and sometimes crowded. ⑤ *Rooms from: $179* ⊠ *9415 Hearst Dr.* ☎ *805/927–4688, 800/826–8168* ⊕ *www.cavalierresort.com* ↝ *90 rooms* ◯| *No meals.*

$$
HOTEL
🏨 **The Morgan San Simeon.** On Highway 1's ocean side, the Morgan offers motel-style rooming options in two Asian-inspired buildings. **Pros:** fascinating artwork; easy access to Hearst Castle; some ocean views. **Cons:** not right on beach; no fitness room or laundry facilities. ⑤ *Rooms from: $149* ⊠ *9135 Hearst Dr.* ☎ *805/927–3878, 800/451–9900* ⊕ *www.hotel-morgan.com* ↝ *54 rooms, 1 suite* ◯| *Breakfast.*

BIG SUR COASTLINE

Long a retreat of artists and writers, Big Sur is a place of ancient forests and rugged shoreline, stretching 90 miles from San Simeon to Carmel. Residents have protected it from overdevelopment, and much of the region lies within several state parks and the more than 165,000-acre Ventana Wilderness, itself part of the Los Padres National Forest.

ESSENTIALS

Visitor Information Big Sur Chamber of Commerce ☎ *831/667–2100* ⊕ *www.bigsurcalifornia.org.*

SOUTHERN BIG SUR

Hwy. 1 from San Simeon to Julia Pfeiffer Burns State Park.

This especially rugged stretch of oceanfront is a rocky world of mountains, cliffs, and beaches.

GETTING HERE AND AROUND

Highway 1 is the only major access route from north or south. From the south, access Highway 1 from U.S. 101 in San Luis Obispo. From the north, take rural route Highway 46 West (Paso Robles to Cambria) or Highway 41 West (Atascadero to Morro Bay). Nacimiento-Fergusson Road snakes through mountains and forest from U.S. 101 at Jolon about 25 miles to Highway 1 at Kirk Creek, about 4 miles south of Lucia; this curving, at times precipitous road is a motorcyclist favorite, not recommended for the faint of heart or during inclement weather.

EXPLORING

Fodor's Choice
★

Highway 1. One of California's most spectacular drives, Highway 1 snakes up the coast north of San Simeon. Numerous pullouts along the way offer tremendous views and photo ops. On some of the beaches, huge elephant seals lounge nonchalantly, seemingly oblivious to the attention of rubberneckers. Heavy rain sometimes causes mudslides that block the highway north and south of Big Sur. ⊕ *www. dot.ca.gov.*

Jade Cove. In Los Padres National Forest just north of the town of Gorda is Jade Cove, a well-known jade-hunting spot. Rock hunting is allowed on the beach, but you may not remove anything from the walls of the cliffs. ✉ *Hwy. 1, 34 miles north of San Simeon.*

Julia Pfeiffer Burns State Park. The park provides fine hiking, from an easy ½-mile stroll with marvelous coastal views to a strenuous 6-mile trek through redwoods. The big draw here, an 80-foot waterfall that drops into the ocean, gets crowded in summer; still, it's an astounding place to contemplate nature. Migrating whales, harbor seals, and sea lions can sometimes be spotted just offshore. ✉ *Hwy. 1, 15 miles north of Lucia* ☎ *831/667–2315* ⊕ *www.parks.ca.gov* ✆ *$10* ☉ *Daily sunrise–sunset.*

WHERE TO STAY

$$
HOTEL

Ragged Point Inn. At this cliff-top resort—the only inn and restaurant for miles around—glass walls in most rooms open to awesome ocean views. **Pros:** on the cliffs; great food; idyllic views. **Cons:** busy road stop during the day; often booked for weekend weddings. ⑤ *Rooms from: $169* ✉ *19019 Hwy. 1, 20 miles north of San Simeon, Ragged Point* ☎ *805/927–4502, 805/927–5708 restaurant* ⊕ *raggedpointinn. com* ✆ *39 rooms* ⦶ *No meals.*

$$$
RESORT

Treebones Resort. Perched on a hilltop, surrounded by national forest and stunning, unobstructed ocean views, this yurt resort provides a stellar back-to-nature experience along with creature comforts. **Pros:** 360-degree views; spacious pool area; comfortable beds. **Cons:** steep paths; no private bathrooms; not good for families with young children. ⑤ *Rooms from: $225* ✉ *71895 Hwy. 1, Willow Creek Rd., 32 miles north of San Simeon, 1 mile north of Gorda* ☎ *805/927–2390, 877/424–4787* ⊕ *www.treebonesresort.com* ✆ *16 yurts, 5 campsites, 1 human nest w/campsite* ⦶ *Breakfast* ☞ *Two-night minimum on weekends and Apr.–Oct.*

CENTRAL BIG SUR

Hwy. 1, from Partington Cove to Bixby Bridge.

The countercultural spirit of Big Sur—which instead of a conventional town is a loose string of coast-hugging properties along Highway 1— is alive and well today. Its few residents include the very wealthy, the enthusiastically outdoorsy, and the thoroughly evolved: since the 1960s the Esalen Institute, a center for alternative education and East–West philosophical study, has attracted seekers of higher consciousness and devotees of the property's hot springs. Today, posh and rustic resorts hidden among the redwoods cater to visitors drawn from near and far by the extraordinary scenery and serene isolation.

GETTING HERE AND AROUND

From the north, follow Highway 1 south from Carmel. From the south, continue the drive north from Julia Pfeiffer Burns State Park *(above)* on Highway 1. Monterey-Salinas Transit operates the Line 22 Big Sur bus from Monterey and Carmel to Central Big Sur (the last top is Nepenthe), daily from late May to early September and weekends only the rest of the year.

Bus Contact Monterey-Salinas Transit ☎ *888/678–2871* ⊕ *www.mst.org.*

EXPLORING

Bixby Creek Bridge. The graceful arc of Bixby Creek Bridge is a photographer's dream. Built in 1932, the bridge spans a deep canyon, more than 100 feet wide at the bottom. From the north-side parking area you can admire the view or walk the 550-foot structure. ⊠ *Hwy. 1, 6 miles north of Point Sur State Historic Park, 13 miles south of Carmel.*

Pfeiffer Big Sur State Park. Among the many hiking trails at Pfeiffer Big Sur, a short route through a redwood-filled valley leads to a waterfall. You can double back or continue on the more difficult trail along the valley wall for views over miles of treetops to the sea. ⊠ *47225 Hwy. 1* ☎ *831/667– 2315* ⊕ *www.parks.ca.gov* ⌨ *$10 per vehicle* ⊙ *Daily sunrise–sunset.*

Point Sur State Historic Park. An 1889 lighthouse still stands watch from atop a large volcanic rock at this state park. Four lighthouse keepers lived here with their families until 1974, when the light station became automated. Their homes and working spaces are open to the public only on 2½- to 3-hour ranger-led tours. Considerable walking, including up two stairways, is involved. Strollers are not allowed. ⊠ *Hwy. 1, 7 miles north of Pfeiffer Big Sur State Park* ☎ *831/625–4419* ⊕ *www.pointsur. org* ⌨ *$12* ⊙ *Tours generally Nov.–Mar., weekends at 10, Wed. at 1; Apr.–Oct., Sat. and Wed. at 10 and 2, Sun. at 10; call to confirm.*

BEACHES

Pfeiffer Beach. Through a hole in one of the gigantic boulders at secluded Pfeiffer Beach, you can watch the waves break first on the sea side and then on the beach side. Keep a sharp eye out for the unsigned, ungated road to the beach: it branches west of Highway 1 between the post office and Pfeiffer Big Sur State Park. The 2-mile, one-lane road descends sharply. **Amenities:** parking (fee); toilets. **Best for:** solitude; sunset. ⊠ *Off Hwy. 1, 1 mile south of Pfeiffer Big Sur State Park* ⌨ *$5 per vehicle* ⊙ *Daily 9–8.*

WHERE TO EAT

$$$ ✗ **Big Sur Roadhouse.** The chef at this colorful bistro perks up California
ECLECTIC favorites with a pinch of Cajun spice. Zesty mains include stewed leg
of lamb with toasted farro, root vegetables, and long-cooked greens,
and seafood gumbo with Dungeness crab and andouille sausage. The
roadhouse, which serves breakfast, lunch, and dinner, is a good stop
for small bites such as oysters, buttermilk biscuits, and fried-chicken
"lollipops." The salted caramel panna cotta with chocolate shortbread
and blood orange caramel is a popular dessert. $ *Average main: $25*
⊠ *Hwy. 1, 1 mile north of Pfeiffer Big Sur State Park* ☎ *831/667–2370*
⊕ *www.glenoaksbigsur.com/roadhouse.html.*

$$$ ✗ **Deetjen's Big Sur Inn.** The candle-lighted, creaky-floor restaurant in the
AMERICAN main house at the historic inn of the same name is a Big Sur institution.
It serves spicy seafood paella, steak, and rack of lamb for dinner and
flavorful eggs Benedict for breakfast. The chef sources most ingredients
from purveyors known for sustainable practices. $ *Average main: $30*
⊠ *Hwy. 1, 3½ mile south of Pfeiffer Big Sur State Park* ☎ *831/667–2378*
⊕ *www.deetjens.com* ☽ *No lunch.*

$$$ ✗ **Nepenthe.** It may be that no other restaurant between San Francisco
AMERICAN and Los Angeles has a better coastal view than Nepenthe. The food
and drink are overpriced but good; there are burgers, sandwiches, and
salads for lunch, and fresh fish and hormone-free steaks for dinner. For
the real show, settle on the terraced deck in the late afternoon, order
a glass from the extensive wine list, and watch the sun slip into the
Pacific Ocean. The less expensive, outdoor Café Kevah serves brunch
and lunch. $ *Average main: $30* ⊠ *48510 Hwy. 1, 2½ miles south of*
Big Sur Station ☎ *831/667–2345* ⊕ *www.nepenthebigsur.com.*

$$$$ ✗ **The Restaurant at Ventana.** The redwood, copper, and cedar elements
AMERICAN at the Ventana Inn's restaurant pay tribute to the historic natural
setting, while gleaming fixtures and dining accoutrements place the
facility firmly in the 21st century. Chef Truman Jones's seasonal menu
showcases meat, fish, and produce—such as organic chicken breast,
wild king salmon, artichokes, and abalone—grown or caught in Cali-
fornia. A full slate of regional and international wines complements
his dishes. The restaurant is also open for lunch. ■ TIP➜ **If the day**
is sunny, ask for a table on the outdoor terrace and take in the ocean
views. $ *Average main: $36* ⊠ *48123 Hwy. 1, 1½ miles south of*
Pfeiffer Big Sur State Park ☎ *831/667–4242* ⊕ *www.ventanainn.com*
⌲ *Reservations essential.*

$$$$ ✗ **Sierra Mar.** Ocean-view dining doesn't get much better than this. At
AMERICAN cliff's edge 1,200 feet above the Pacific at the ultra-chic Post Ranch
Inn, Sierra Mar serves cutting-edge American food made from mostly
organic, seasonal ingredients, some from the on-site chef's garden. The
four-course prix-fixe option always shines. The nine-course Taste of Big
Sur menu centers around ingredients grown and foraged on the property
or sourced locally. The restaurant's wine list is among the nation's most
extensive. $ *Average main: $120* ⊠ *Hwy. 1, 1½ miles south of Pfeiffer*
Big Sur State Park ☎ *831/667–2800* ⊕ *www.postranchinn.com/dining*
⌲ *Reservations essential.*

WHERE TO STAY

$$$
HOTEL

🏨 **Big Sur Lodge.** Modern motel-style cottages with mission-style furnishings and vaulted ceilings sit in a meadow, surrounded by trees and flowering shrubbery. **Pros:** near trailheads; good camping alternative. **Cons:** basic rooms; walk to main lodge. ⑤ *Rooms from: $204* ✉ *Pfeiffer Big Sur State Park, 47225 Hwy. 1* ☎ *831/667–3100, 800/424–4787* ⊕ *www.bigsurlodge.com* ⌁ *61 rooms* ⦿ *No meals.*

$$
B&B/INN

🏨 **Deetjen's Big Sur Inn.** This historic 1930s Norwegian-style property is endearingly rustic, especially if you're willing to go with a camplike flow. **Pros:** tons of character; wooded grounds. **Cons:** thin walls; some rooms don't have private baths. ⑤ *Rooms from: $160* ✉ *Hwy. 1, 3½ miles south of Pfeiffer Big Sur State Park* ☎ *831/667–2377* ⊕ *www. deetjens.com* ⌁ *20 rooms, 15 with bath* ⦿ *No meals.*

$$$$
HOTEL

🏨 **Glen Oaks Big Sur.** At this rustic-modern cluster of adobe-and-redwood buildings, you can choose between motel-style rooms, cabins, and cottages in the woods. **Pros:** in the heart of town; walking distance of restaurants. **Cons:** near busy road and parking lot; no TVs. ⑤ *Rooms from: $275* ✉ *Hwy. 1, 1 mile north of Pfeiffer Big Sur State Park* ☎ *831/667–2105* ⊕ *www.glenoaksbigsur.com* ⌁ *16 rooms, 2 cottages, 7 cabins* ⦿ *No meals.*

$$$$
RESORT
Fodor's Choice
★

🏨 **Post Ranch Inn.** This luxurious retreat, designed exclusively for adult getaways, has remarkable environmentally conscious architecture. **Pros:** world-class resort; spectacular views; gorgeous property with hiking trails. **Cons:** expensive; austere design; not a good choice if heights scare you. ⑤ *Rooms from: $775* ✉ *Hwy. 1, 1½ miles south of Pfeiffer Big Sur State Park* ☎ *831/667–2200, 888/524–4787* ⊕ *www.postranchinn.com* ⌁ *39 units* ⦿ *Breakfast.*

$$$$
HOTEL
Fodor's Choice
★

🏨 **Ventana.** Hundreds of celebrities, from Oprah Winfrey to Sir Anthony Hopkins, have escaped to Ventana, a romantic resort on 243 tranquil acres 1,200 feet above the Pacific. **Pros:** nature trails everywhere; great food; secluded. **Cons:** simple breakfast; some rooms have no ocean view. ⑤ *Rooms from: $650* ✉ *Hwy. 1, almost 1 mile south of Pfeiffer Big Sur State Park* ☎ *831/667–2331, 800/628–6500* ⊕ *www.ventanainn.com* ⌁ *25 rooms, 31 suites* ⦿ *Breakfast.*

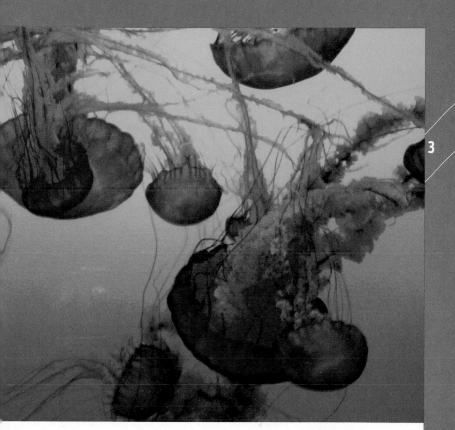

THE MONTEREY BAY AREA

From Carmel to Santa Cruz

WELCOME TO THE MONTEREY BAY AREA

TOP REASONS TO GO

★ **Marine life:** Monterey Bay is the location of the world's third-largest marine sanctuary, home to whales, otters, and other underwater creatures.

★ **Getaway central:** For more than a century, urbanites have come to the Monterey Bay area to unwind, relax, and have fun. It's a great place to browse unique shops and galleries, ride a giant roller coaster, or play a round of golf on a world-class course.

★ **Nature preserves:** More than the sea is protected here: the region boasts nearly 30 state parks, beaches, and preserves—fantastic places for walking, jogging, hiking, and biking.

★ **Wine and dine:** The area's rich agricultural bounty translates into abundant fresh produce, great wines, and fabulous dining. It's no wonder more than 300 culinary events take place here every year.

★ **Small-town vibes:** Even the cities here are friendly, walkable places where you'll feel like a local.

1 Carmel and Pacific Grove. Exclusive Carmel-by-the-Sea and Carmel Valley Village burst with historic charm, fine dining, and unusual boutiques that cater to celebrity residents and well-heeled visitors. Nearby 17-Mile Drive—quite possibly the prettiest stretch of road you'll ever travel—runs between Carmel-by-the-Sea and Victorian-studded Pacific Grove, home to thousands of migrating monarch butterflies between October and February.

2 Monterey. A former Spanish military outpost, Monterey's well-preserved historic district is a hands-on history lesson. Cannery Row, the center of Monterey's once-thriving sardine industry, has been reborn as a tourist attraction with shops, restaurants, hotels, and the Monterey Bay Aquarium.

3 Around Monterey Bay. Much of California's lettuce, berries, artichokes, and brussels sprouts is grown in Salinas and Watsonville. Salinas is also home to the National Steinbeck Center, and Moss Landing and Watsonville encompass pristine wildlife wetlands. Aptos, Capitola, and Soquel are former lumber towns that became popular seaside resorts more than a century ago. Today they're filled with antiques shops, restaurants, and wine-tasting rooms; you'll also find some of the bay's best beaches along the shore here.

4 Santa Cruz. Santa Cruz shows its colors along an old-time beach boardwalk and municipal wharf. A University of California campus imbues the town with arts and culture and a liberal mind-set.

0   5 mi

0   5 km

Santa Cruz

9

1

4

GETTING ORIENTED

3

North of Big Sur the coastline softens into lower bluffs, windswept dunes, pristine estuaries, and long, sandy beaches, bordering one of the world's most amazing marine environments—the Monterey Bay. On the Monterey Peninsula, at the southern end of the bay, are Carmel-by-the-Sea, Pacific Grove, and Monterey; Santa Cruz sits at the northern tip of the crescent. In between, Highway 1 cruises along the coastline, passing windswept beaches piled high with sand dunes. Along the route are wetlands, artichoke and strawberry fields, and workaday towns such as Castroville and Watsonville.

Updated
by Cheryl
Crabtree

Natural beauty is at the heart of the Monterey Bay area's enormous appeal—it's everywhere, from the redwood-studded hillsides to the pristine shoreline with miles of walking paths and bluff-top vistas. Nature even takes center stage indoors at the world-famous Monterey Bay Aquarium, but history also draws visitors, most notably to Monterey's well-preserved waterfront district. Quaint, walkable towns and villages such as Carmel-by-the-Sea and Carmel Valley Village lure with smart restaurants and galleries, while sunny Aptos, Capitola, Soquel, and Santa Cruz, with miles of sand and surf, attract surfers and beach lovers.

Monterey Bay life centers around the ocean. The bay itself is protected by the Monterey Bay National Marine Sanctuary, the nation's largest undersea canyon—bigger and deeper than the Grand Canyon. On-the-water activities abound, from whale-watching and kayaking to sailing and surfing. Bay cruises from Monterey and Moss Landing almost always encounter other enchanting sea creatures, among them sea otters, sea lions, and porpoises.

Land-based activities include hiking, zip-lining in the redwood canopy, and wine tasting along urban and rural trails. Golf has been an integral part of the Monterey Peninsula's social and recreational scene since the Del Monte Golf Course opened in 1897. Pebble Beach's championship courses host prestigious tournaments, and though the greens fees at these courses can run up to $500, elsewhere on the peninsula you'll find less expensive options. And, of course, whatever activity you pursue, natural splendor appears at every turn.

°LANNING

WHEN TO GO

Summer is peak season; mild weather brings in big crowds. In this coastal region, a cool breeze generally blows and fog often rolls in from offshore; you will frequently need a sweater or windbreaker. Off-season, from November through April, fewer people visit and the mood is mellower. Rainfall is heaviest in January and February. Fall and spring days are often clearer than those in summer.

GETTING HERE AND AROUND

AIR TRAVEL

Monterey Regional Airport, 3 miles east of downtown Monterey off Highway 68, is served by Alaska, Allegiant, American, United, and US Airways. Taxi service costs $16 to $18 to downtown, and $24 to $33 to Carmel. Monterey Airbus service between the region and the San Jose and San Francisco airports starts at $40; the Early Bird Airport Shuttle costs $80 to $190 ($195 from Oakland).

Airport Contacts Monterey Regional Airport (MRY). ⊠ 200 Fred Kane Dr., at Olmsted Rd., off Hwy. 68, Monterey ☏ 831/648–7000 ⊕ www.montereyairport.com.

Ground Transportation Central Coast Cab Company ☏ 831/626–3333.
Early Bird Airport Shuttle ☏ 831/462–3933 ⊕ www.earlybirdairportshuttle.com.
Monterey Airbus ☏ 831/373–7777 ⊕ www.montereyairbus.com.
Yellow Cab ☏ 831/333–1234.

BUS TRAVEL

Greyhound serves Santa Cruz and Salinas from San Francisco and San Jose. The trips take about 3 and 4½ hours, respectively. Monterey-Salinas Transit (MST) provides frequent service in Monterey County (from $1.50 to $3.50; day pass $10), and Santa Cruz METRO ($2; day pass from $6 to $10) buses operate throughout Santa Cruz County. You can switch between the lines in Watsonville.

Bus Contacts Greyhound ☏ 800/231–2222 ⊕ www.greyhound.com.
Monterey-Salinas Transit ☏ 888/678–2871 ⊕ www.mst.org.
Santa Cruz METRO ☏ 831/425–8600 ⊕ www.scmtd.com.

CAR TRAVEL

Highway 1 runs south–north along the coast, linking the towns of Carmel-by-the-Sea, Monterey, and Santa Cruz; some sections have only two lanes. The freeway, U.S. 101, lies to the east, roughly parallel to Highway 1. The two roads are connected by Highway 68 from Pacific Grove to Salinas; Highway 156 from Castroville to Prunedale; Highway 152 from Watsonville to Gilroy; and Highway 17 from Santa Cruz to San Jose. ⚠ Traffic near Santa Cruz can crawl to a standstill during commuter hours. In the morning, avoid traveling between 7 and 9; in the afternoon avoid traveling between 4 and 7.

The drive south from San Francisco to Monterey can be made comfortably in three hours or less. The most scenic way is to follow Highway 1 down the coast. An often faster route is Interstate 280 south from San Francisco to Highway 17, north of San Jose, to Highway 1 south.

The drive from the Los Angeles area takes five or six hours. Take U.S. 101 to Salinas and head west on Highway 68. You can also follow Highway 1 up the coast.

TRAIN TRAVEL

Amtrak's *Coast Starlight* runs between Los Angeles, Oakland, and Seattle. From the train station in Salinas, you can connect with buses serving Carmel, Monterey, and Santa Cruz.

Train Contacts Amtrak ☎ *800/872–7245* ⊕ *www.amtrak.com.*

RESTAURANTS

The Monterey Bay area is a culinary paradise. The surrounding waters are full of fish, wild game roams the foothills, and the inland valleys are some of the most fertile in the country—local chefs draw on this bounty for their fresh, truly Californian cuisine. Except at beachside stands and inexpensive eateries, where anything goes, casual but neat dress is the norm.

HOTELS

Accommodations in the Monterey area range from no-frills motels to luxurious hotels. Pacific Grove, amply endowed with ornate Victorian houses, is the region's bed-and-breakfast capital; Carmel also has charming inns. Lavish resorts cluster in exclusive Pebble Beach and pastoral Carmel Valley.

High season runs from May through October. Rates in winter, especially at the larger hotels, may drop by 50% or more, and B&Bs often offer midweek specials. Whatever the month, some properties require a two-night stay on weekends. *Hotel reviews have been shortened. For full information, visit Fodors.com.* △ **Many of the fancier accommodations aren't suitable for children; if you're traveling with kids, ask before you book.**

WHAT IT COSTS				
	$	**$$**	**$$$**	**$$$$**
Restaurants	under $16	$16–$22	$23–$30	over $30
Hotels	under $121	$121–$175	$176–$250	over $250

Restaurant prices are the average cost of a main course at dinner or, if dinner is not served, at lunch, excluding sales tax of 8.25%–9.5% (depending on location). Hotel prices are the lowest cost of a standard double room in high season, excluding service charges and 10%–10.5% tax.

TOUR OPTIONS

Ag Venture Tours & Consulting. Crowd-pleasing half- and full-day wine-tasting, sightseeing, and agricultural tours are Ag Venture's specialty. Tastings are at Monterey and Santa Cruz Mountains wineries; sightseeing opportunities include the Monterey Peninsula, Big Sur, and Santa Cruz; and the agricultural forays take in the Salinas Valley. Customized itineraries can be arranged. ☎ *831/761–8463* ⊕ *www.agventuretours. com* ✉ *From $75.*

California Parlor Car Tours. This outfit operates motor-coach tours from San Francisco that include one or two days in Monterey and Carmel. The company's three-day San Francisco–Los Angeles tours include stops in Monterey and Carmel. ☎ *415/474–7500, 800/227–4250* ⊕ *www. calpartours.com* ✉ *From $80 (day) and $267 (overnight).*

VISITOR INFORMATION

Contacts Monterey County Convention & Visitors Bureau ☎ *877/666–8373* ⊕ *www.seemonterey.com.* **Monterey County Vintners and Growers Association** ☎ *831/375–9400* ⊕ *www.montereywines.org.* **Santa Cruz County Conference and Visitors Council** ✉ *303 Water St., #100, Santa Cruz* ☎ *831/425–1234, 800/833–3494* ⊕ *www.santacruz.org.* **Santa Cruz Mountain Winegrowers Association** ✉ *725 Front St., #112, Santa Cruz* ☎ *831/685–8463* ⊕ *www.scmwa.com.*

CARMEL AND PACIFIC GROVE

As Highway 1 swings inland about 30 miles north of Big Sur, historic Carmel-by-the-Sea anchors the southern entry to the Monterey Peninsula—a gorgeous promontory at the southern tip of Monterey Bay. Just north of Carmel along the coast, the legendary 17-Mile Drive wends its way through private Pebble Beach and the town of Pacific Grove. Highway 1 skirts the peninsula to the east with more direct access to Pebble Beach and Pacific Grove.

CARMEL-BY-THE-SEA

26 miles north of Big Sur.

Even when its population quadruples with tourists on weekends and in summer, Carmel-by-the-Sea, commonly referred to as Carmel, retains its identity as a quaint village. Self-consciously charming, the town is populated by many celebrities, major and minor, and has its share of quirky ordinances. For instance, women wearing high heels do not have the right to pursue legal action if they trip and fall on the cobblestone streets, and drivers who hit a tree and leave the scene are charged with hit-and-run.

Buildings have no street numbers—street names are written on discreet white posts—and consequently no mail delivery. One way to commune with the locals: head to the post office. Artists started this community, and their legacy is evident in the numerous galleries.

GETTING HERE AND AROUND

From north or south follow Highway 1 to Carmel. Head west at Ocean Avenue to reach the main village hub. In summer the MST Carmel-by-the-Sea Trolley loops around town to the beach and mission every 30 minutes or so.

TOURS

Carmel Walks. For insight into Carmel's history and culture, join one of these guided two-hour ambles through hidden courtyards, gardens, and pathways. Tours depart from the Pine Inn courtyard, on Lincoln Street. Call to reserve a spot. ✉ *Lincoln St. at 6th Ave.* ☎ *831/642–2700* ⊕ *www.carmelwalks.com* ✉ *$25* ⊘ *Tues.–Fri. at 10, Sat. at 10 and 2.*

Monterey Bay Area

Santa Cruz — Soquel — Aptos — Gilroy
Capitola

The Forest of Nisene Marks State Park

Natural Bridges State Beach
Twin Lakes State Beach
New Brighton State Beach
Seacliff State Beach
Soquel Cove
Rio del Mar
La Selva Beach
Corralitos
Freedom
Watsonville
Pajaro
Las Lomas
San Juan Bautista

Elkhorn Slough National Estuarine Research Reserve
Moss Landing
Dolan Rd.
Prunedale
Castroville

Asilomar State Beach
Point Pinos
Pacific Grove
Marina
Salinas
Seaside
Sand City
Spreckels

Spanish Bay
17-Mile Drive
Cypress Point
Carmel Beach
Pebble Beach
Del Rey Oaks

Carmel River State Beach
Carmel-by-the-Sea
Carmel Bay
Refuge
Earthbound Farm
Carmel Valley Village
Point Lobos State Natural Reserve
Carmel Highlands
Yankee Point
Garland Ranch Regional Park

TO PINNACLES NATIONAL PARK

0   5 mi
0   5 km

ESSENTIALS

Visitor Information Carmel Chamber of Commerce ⊠ *Visitor Center, San Carlos, between 5th and 6th* ☎ *831/624–2522, 800/550–4333* ⊕ *www.carmelcalifornia.org* ⊗ *Daily 10–5.*

EXPLORING
TOP ATTRACTIONS

Carmel Mission. Long before it became a shopping and browsing destination, Carmel was an important religious center during the establishment of Spanish California. That heritage is preserved in the Mission San Carlos Borroméo del Rio Carmelo, more commonly known as the Carmel Mission. Founded in 1771, it served as headquarters for the mission system in California under Father Junípero Serra. Adjoining the stone church is a tranquil garden planted with California poppies. Museum rooms at the mission include an early kitchen, Serra's spartan sleeping quarters, and the first college library in California. ⊠ *3080 Rio Rd., at Lasuen Dr.* ☎ *831/624–1271* ⊕ *www.carmelmission.org* 🖾 *$6.50* ⊗ *Daily 9:30–4:45.*

Fodor's Choice ★ **Point Lobos State Natural Reserve.** A 350-acre headland harboring a wealth of marine life, the reserve lies a few miles south of Carmel. The best way to explore here is to walk along one of the many trails. The Cypress Grove Trail leads through a forest of Monterey cypress (one of only two natural groves remaining), which clings to the rocks above an emerald-green cove. Sea Lion Point Trail is a good place to view sea lions. From those and other trails you might also spot otters, harbor seals, and (in winter and spring) migrating whales. An additional 750 acres of the reserve is an undersea marine park open to qualified scuba divers. No pets are allowed. ■TIP➔ Arrive early (or in late afternoon) to avoid crowds; the parking lots fill up.

✉ *Hwy. 1* ☏ *831/624–4909, 831/624–8413 for scuba-diving reservations* ⊕ *www.pointlobos.org* 🖃 *$10 per vehicle* ☉ *Daily 8 am–½ hr after sunset in winter, 8 am–7 pm spring–fall.*

WORTH NOTING

Carmel Wine Walk By-the-Sea. Park the car and sample local wines at tasting rooms and shops in downtown Carmel, all within a few blocks of each other. To do so, purchase a Wine Walk Passport, good for flights in nine tasting rooms and free corkage at local restaurants. There's no expiration date—participating venues will stamp it each time you visit. ✉ *Carmel Chamber of Commerce Visitor Center, San Carlos St., between 5th and 6th Aves.* ☏ *831/624–2522, 800/550–4333* ⊕ *www. carmelcalifornia.org* 🖃 *$65.*

Dawson Cole Fine Art. Amazing images of dancers, athletes, and other humans in motion come to life in this gallery that is devoted to the artworks of Monterey Bay resident Richard MacDonald, one of the most famed figurative sculptors of our time. ✉ *Lincoln St., at 6th Ave.* ☏ *800/972–5528* ⊕ *www.dawsoncolefineart.com* 🖃 *Free* ☉ *Mon.–Sat. 10–6, Sun. 10–5:30.*

Ocean Avenue. Downtown Carmel's chief lure is shopping, especially along its main street, Ocean Avenue, between Junipero Avenue and Camino Real. The architecture here is a mishmash of ersatz Tudor, Mediterranean, and other styles.

Tor House. Scattered throughout the pines of Carmel-by-the-Sea are houses and cottages originally built for the writers, artists, and photographers who discovered the area decades ago. Among the most impressive dwellings is Tor House, a stone cottage built in 1919 by poet Robinson Jeffers on a craggy knoll overlooking the sea. Portraits, books, and unusual art objects fill the low-ceilinged rooms. The highlight of the small estate is Hawk Tower, a detached edifice set with stones from the Carmel coastline—as well as one from the Great Wall of China. The docents who lead tours (six people maximum) are well informed about the poet's work and life. ■TIP➔ To reserve a tour, which is recommended, email thf@torhouse.org. ✉ *26304 Ocean View Ave.* ☏ *831/624–1813, 831/624–1840 direct docent office line, Fri. and Sat. only* ⊕ *www.torhouse.org* 🖃 *$10* ☉ *Hourly tours Fri. and Sat. 10–3* ☞ *No children under 12.*

BEACHES

Carmel Beach. Carmel-by-the-Sea's greatest attraction is its rugged coastline, with pine and cypress forests and countless inlets. Carmel Beach, an easy walk from downtown shops, has sparkling white sands and magnificent sunsets. ■TIP→ Dogs are allowed to romp off-leash here. **Amenities:** parking (no fee); toilets. **Best for:** sunset; surfing; walking. ⊠ *End of Ocean Ave.*

Carmel River State Beach. This sugar-white beach, stretching 106 acres along Carmel Bay, is adjacent to a bird sanctuary, where you might spot pelicans, kingfishers, hawks, and sandpipers. **Amenities:** none. **Best for:** sunrise; sunset; walking. ⊠ *Off Scenic Rd., south of Carmel Beach* ☎ *831/624–4909, 831/649–2836* ⊕ *www.parks.ca.gov* ⊡ *Free* ⊙ *Daily 8 am–½ hr after sunset in winter; 8 am–7 pm spring–fall.*

WHERE TO EAT

$$$

FRENCH

✕ **Andre's Bouchée.** The food here represents an innovative bistro-style take on local ingredients. A Monterey Bay sea scallop reduction adorns pan-seared veal tenderloin; grilled rib-eye steaks are topped with a shallot–Cabernet Sauvignon sauce. With its copper wine bar, the dining room feels more urban than most of Carmel. The owners operate the adjacent wineshop, which explains the dizzyingly comprehensive, 52-page wine list. ⑤ *Average main: $28* ⊠ *Mission St., between Ocean and 7th Aves.* ☎ *831/626–7880* ⊕ *www.andresbouchee.com* ⚱ *Reservations essential* ⊙ *No lunch Mon. and Tues.*

$$$

EUROPEAN

✕ **Anton and Michel.** Carefully prepared European cuisine is the draw at this airy restaurant. The rack of lamb is carved at the table, the grilled halloumi cheese and tomatoes are meticulously stacked and served with basil and Kalamata olive tapenade, and the desserts are set aflame before your eyes. ■TIP→ For lighter fare with a worldwide flair, head to the bar, where small plates such as Dungeness crab ravioli and brochette of filet mignon with chimichurri sauce are served. ⑤ *Average main: $30* ⊠ *Mission St. and 7th Ave.* ☎ *831/624–2406* ⊕ *antonandmichel.com* ⚱ *Reservations essential.*

$$$

MEDITERRANEAN

✕ **Casanova.** This cozy restaurant inspires European-style celebration and romance—accordions hang from the walls, and tiny party lights dance along the low ceilings. The food consists of delectable seasonal dishes from southern France and northern Italy. Private dining and a special menu are offered at Van Gogh's Table, a special table imported from France's Auberge Ravoux, the artist's final residence. ⑤ *Average main: $30* ⊠ *5th Ave., between San Carlos and Mission Sts.* ☎ *831/625–0501* ⊕ *www.casanovarestaurant.com* ⚱ *Reservations essential.*

$

AMERICAN

✕ **The Cottage Restaurant.** This family-friendly spot serves sandwiches, pizzas, and homemade soups at lunch, but the best meal is breakfast (good thing it's served all day). The menu offers six variations on eggs Benedict, and all kinds of sweet and savory crepes. ⑤ *Average main: $14* ⊠ *Lincoln St., between Ocean and 7th Aves.* ☎ *831/625–6260* ⊕ *www.cottagerestaurant.com* ⊙ *No dinner.*

$$$

SEAFOOD

✕ **Flying Fish Grill.** Simple in appearance yet bold with its flavors, this Japanese–California seafood restaurant is one of Carmel's most inventive eateries. Among the best entrées is the almond-crusted sea bass served with Chinese cabbage and rock shrimp stir-fry. The warm,

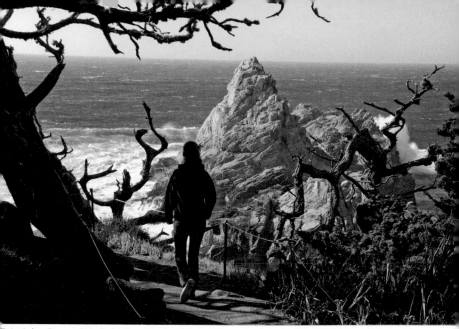

Point Lobos Reserve State Park is home to one of the only two natural stands of Monterey cypress in the world.

wood-lined dining room is broken up into very private booths. ⑤ *Average main: $26* ✉ *Carmel Plaza, Mission St., between Ocean and 7th Aves.* ☎ *831/625–1962* ⊕ *flyingfishgrill.com* ☽ *No lunch.*

$$$ ✕ **Grasing's Coastal Cuisine.** Chef Kurt Grasing draws from fresh Carmel
AMERICAN Coast and Central Valley ingredients to whip up contemporary adaptations of European-provincial and American cooking. Longtime menu favorites include artichoke lasagna in a roasted tomato sauce, duck with fresh cherries and green peppercorns in a red wine sauce, a savory paella, and grilled steaks and chops. ⑤ *Average main: $30* ✉ *6th Ave. and Mission St.* ☎ *831/624–6562* ⊕ *www.grasings.com* ☽ *Reservations essential.*

$$$ ✕ **L'Escargot.** Chef-owner Kericos Loutas personally sees to each plate
FRENCH of food served at this romantic, unpretentious French restaurant. Order the pan-roasted duck breast or the cassoulet de Toulouse; or, if you can't decide, choose the three-course prix-fixe dinner. ⑤ *Average main: $30* ✉ *Mission and 4th Ave.* ☎ *831/620–1942* ⊕ *www.escargot-carmel.com* ☽ *Reservations essential* ☽ *No lunch.*

$$ ✕ **Mundaka.** The traditional Spanish-style tapas, made with fresh local
TAPAS ingredients, and the full bar attract legions of locals to this cozy downtown spot. The menu changes weekly, but longtime favorites include the lamb slider with truffle fries, the authentic Valencian paella, and a platter of housemade charcuterie. At the adjacent Mundaka Cafe, the breakfast menu includes Spanish tortillas, plus Belgian waffles and homemade baked goods; among the lunchtime choices are sandwiches, soups, and salads. Leashed dogs are welcome at the patio tables. After 4 pm, music livens up the scene at High Tide, the restaurant's separate bar in the same cluster of buildings. ⑤ *Average main: $21* ✉ *San Carlos St., between Ocean and 7th Aves.* ☎ *831/624–7400* ⊕ *www.mundakacarmel.com.*

$
AMERICAN
✕ **Tuck Box.** This bright little restaurant is in a cottage right out of a fairy tale, complete with stone fireplace. Handmade scones, good for breakfast or afternoon tea, are the specialty. ⑤ *Average main: $12* ✉ *Dolores St., between Ocean and 7th Aves.* ☎ *831/624–6365* ⊕ *www.tuckbox. com* ⌨ *Reservations not accepted* ▭ *No credit cards* ⊘ *No dinner.*

$$$
ITALIAN
✕ **Vesuvio.** Chef and restaurateur Rich Pèpe heats up the night with his latest venture, a lively trattoria downstairs and a swinging rooftop terrace, Starlight Lounge 65°. Pèpe's elegant take on traditional Italian cuisine yields dishes such as wild-boar Bolognese pappardelle, lobster ravioli, and velvety limoncello mousse cake. Pizzas and small plates are served in the restaurant and two bars. Upstairs, relax in comfy chairs by fire pits and enjoy bird's-eye views of the village. On most nights in summer there's live music. ⑤ *Average main: $24* ✉ *6th and Junipero Aves.* ☎ *831/625–1766* ⊕ *www.vesuviocarmel. com* ⊘ *No lunch.*

WHERE TO STAY

$$$
B&B/INN
☷ **Cypress Inn.** A top-to-bottom redecorating project in 2013 gave this luxurious inn a fresh Mediterranean ambience with Moroccan touches. **Pros:** luxury without snobbery; popular lounge; British-style afternoon tea on weekends. **Cons:** not for the pet-phobic. ⑤ *Rooms from: $235* ✉ *Lincoln St. and 7th Ave.* ☎ *831/624–3871, 800/443–7443* ⊕ *www. cypress-inn.com* ⇥ *39 rooms, 5 suites* ⧉ *Breakfast.*

$$$$
HOTEL
☷ **Hyatt Carmel Highlands.** High on a hill overlooking the Pacific, this place has superb views; accommodations include king rooms with fireplaces, suites with personal Jacuzzis, and full town houses with all the perks. **Pros:** killer views; romantic getaway; great food. **Cons:** thin walls; must drive to Carmel. ⑤ *Rooms from: $369* ✉ *120 Highlands Dr.* ☎ *831/620–1234, 800/233–1234* ⊕ *carmelhighlands.hyatt.com* ⇥ *46 rooms, 2 suites.*

$$$$
B&B/INN
Fodor'sChoice
★
☷ **L'Auberge Carmel.** Stepping through the doors of this elegant inn is like being transported to a little European village. **Pros:** in town but off the main drag; four blocks from the beach; full-service luxury. **Cons:** touristy area; not a good choice for families. ⑤ *Rooms from: $435* ✉ *Monte Verde at 7th Ave.* ☎ *831/624–8578* ⊕ *www.laubergecarmel. com* ⇥ *20 rooms* ⧉ *Breakfast.*

$$$$
HOTEL
☷ **La Playa Hotel.** A historic complex of lush gardens and Mediterranean-style buildings, La Playa reopened in 2012 after a $3.5 million renovation. **Pros:** residential neighborhood; manicured gardens; two blocks from the beach. **Cons:** four stories (no elevator); busy lobby; some rooms are on the small side. ⑤ *Rooms from: $279* ✉ *Camino Real, at 8th Ave.* ☎ *831/293–6100, 800/582–8900* ⊕ *www.laplayahotel.com* ⇥ *75 rooms* ⧉ *Breakfast.*

$$
HOTEL
☷ **Lobos Lodge.** The white-stucco motel units here are set amid cypress, oaks, and pines on the edge of the business district. **Pros:** walking distance from beach and village attractions; inviting lobby; Continental breakfast delivered to your room. **Cons:** no outdoor facilities; sits on a busy avenue. ⑤ *Rooms from: $145* ✉ *Monte Verde St. and Ocean Ave.* ☎ *831/624–3874* ⊕ *www.loboslodge.com* ⇥ *28 rooms, 2 suites* ⧉ *Breakfast.*

$$ **Mission Ranch.** Movie star Clint Eastwood owns this sprawling prop-
HOTEL   erty whose accommodations include rooms in a converted barn, and
several cottages, some with fireplaces. **Pros:** farm setting; pastoral views;
great for tennis buffs. **Cons:** busy parking lot; must drive to the heart
of town. $ *Rooms from: $140* ✉ *26270 Dolores St.* ☎ *831/624–6436,
800/538–8221, 831/625–9040 restaurant* ⊕ *www.missionranchcarmel.
com* ⤳ *31 rooms* ❖ *Breakfast.*

$$$ **Sea View Inn.** In a residential area a few hundred feet from the beach,
B&B/INN   this restored 1905 home has a double parlor with two fireplaces, orien-
tal rugs, canopy beds, and a spacious front porch. **Pros:** quiet; private;
close to the beach. **Cons:** small building; uphill trek to the heart of
town. $ *Rooms from: $200* ✉ *Camino Real, between 11th and 12th
Aves.* ☎ *831/624–8778* ⊕ *www.seaviewinncarmel.com* ⤳ *8 rooms, 6
with private bath* ❖ *Breakfast.*

$$$$ **Tickle Pink Inn.** Atop a towering cliff, this inn has views of the Big
B&B/INN   Sur coastline, which you can contemplate from your private balcony.
Pros: close to great hiking; intimate; dramatic views. **Cons:** close to a
big hotel; lots of traffic during the day. $ *Rooms from: $299* ✉ *155
Highland Dr.* ☎ *831/624–1244, 800/635–4774* ⊕ *www.ticklepink.com*
⤳ *23 rooms, 10 suites, 1 cottage* ❖ *Breakfast.*

$$$ **Tradewinds Carmel.** This converted motel with sleek decor inspired
B&B/INN   by the South Seas encircles a courtyard with waterfalls, a meditation
garden, and a fire pit. **Pros:** serene; within walking distance of restau-
rants; friendly service. **Cons:** no pool; long walk to the beach. $ *Rooms
from: $250* ✉ *Mission St., at 3rd Ave.* ☎ *831/624–2776* ⊕ *www.
tradewindscarmel.com* ⤳ *26 rooms, 2 suites* ❖ *Breakfast.*

NIGHTLIFE

BARS AND PUBS

High Tide. Al Capone and other Prohibition-era legends once sidled up
to this hip nightspot's carved wooden bar. Rock to DJ music and sit
indoors, or head out to the pet-friendly patio. Some menu items pay
homage to California's early days, and you can order Spanish tapas and
wines from the adjacent Mundaka restaurant, which is under the same
ownership. ■**TIP**➜ High Tide only takes cash. ✉ *San Carlos St., between
Ocean and 7th Aves.* ☎ *831/624–7400* ⊕ *www.mundakacarmel.com*
▭ *No credit cards.*

Jack London's. Among the few Carmel restaurants that serve food late,
this publike hangout is a good stop for a beer or cocktail or to watch
sports on TV. On most weekends Jack London's hosts live music. The
weekday happy hour (from 4 to 6) is a bargain. ✉ *Su Vecino Court,
Dolores St., between 5th and 6th Aves.* ☎ *831/624–2336.*

SHOPPING

ART GALLERIES

Carmel Art Association. The association exhibits the original paintings
and sculptures of local artists. ✉ *Dolores St., between 5th and 6th Aves.*
☎ *831/624–6176* ⊕ *www.carmelart.org.*

Galerie Plein Aire. The gallery showcases the oil paintings of a group of
local artists. ✉ *Dolores St., between 5th and 6th Aves.* ☎ *831/625–5686*
⊕ *www.galeriepleinaire.com.*

Gallery Sur. Fine art photography of the Big Sur Coast and the Monterey Peninsula, including scenic shots and golf images, is the focus here. ⊠ *6th Ave., between Dolores and Lincoln Sts.* ☏ *831/626–2615* ⊕ *www.gallerysur.com.*

Weston Gallery. Run by the family of the late Edward Weston, this is hands down the best photography gallery around, with contemporary color photography complemented by classic black-and-whites. ⊠ *6th Ave., between Dolores and Lincoln Sts.* ☏ *831/624–4453* ⊕ *www.westongallery.com.*

MALL

Carmel Plaza. Tiffany & Co. and J. Crew are among the name brands doing business at this mall on Carmel's east side, but what makes it worth a stop are homegrown enterprises such as Homescapes, for marvelous and visually stimulating home and garden objects; Madrigal and Sylvie Unique Boutique, for women's fashion; and J. Lawrence Khaki's for debonair menswear. Flying Fish Grill *(⇨ Where to Eat)* and several other restaurants are here, along with the Wrath Wines tasting room (heavenly Chardonnays and Pinot Noirs). ⊠ *Ocean Ave. and Mission St.* ☏ *831/624–0137* ⊕ *www.carmelplaza.com.*

SPECIALTY SHOPS

Bittner. The shop carries collectible and vintage pens from around the world. ⊠ *Ocean Ave., between Mission and San Carlos Sts.* ☏ *831/626–8828* ⊕ *bittner.com.*

Intima. The European lingerie that ranges from lacy to racy. ⊠ *San Carlos St., between Ocean and 6th Aves.* ☏ *831/625–0599* ⊕ *www.intimacarmel.com.*

Jan de Luz. This shops monograms and embroiders fine linens (including bathrobes) while you wait. ⊠ *Dolores St., between Ocean and 7th Aves.* ☏ *831/622–7621* ⊕ *www.jandeluz.com.*

CARMEL VALLEY

10 miles east of Carmel.

Carmel Valley Road, which heads inland from Highway 1 south of Carmel, is the main thoroughfare through this valley, a secluded enclave of horse ranchers and other well-heeled residents who prefer the area's sunny climate to coastal fog and wind. Once thick with dairy farms, the valley has evolved into an esteemed wine appellation. Carmel Valley Village has crafts shops, art galleries, and the tasting rooms of numerous local wineries.

GETTING HERE AND AROUND

From U.S. 101 north or south, exit at Highway 68 and head west toward the coast. Scenic, two-lane Laureles Grade winds west over the mountains to Carmel Valley Road north of the village.

TOURS

The Carmel Valley Grapevine Express, aka MST's Line 24 bus, travels between downtown Monterey and Carmel Valley Village, with stops near wineries, restaurants, and shopping centers. At $10 for a ride-all-day pass, it's an incredible bargain.

3

Bus Contact **Carmel Valley Grapevine Express** ☎ *888/678–2871* ⊕ *www.mst.org.*

EXPLORING

TOP ATTRACTIONS

Bernardus Tasting Room. At the tasting room of Bernardus, known for its Bordeaux-style red blend, called Marinus, and Chardonnays, you can sample current releases and library and reserve wines. ⊠ *5 W. Carmel Valley Rd., at El Caminito Rd.* ☎ *831/298–8021, 800/223–2533* ⊕ *www.bernardus.com* ☐ *Tastings $12–$20* ⊙ *Daily 11–5.*

Château Julien. The expansive winery, recognized internationally for its Chardonnays and Merlots, offers tours by appointment only, but the tasting room is open daily. ⊠ *8940 Carmel Valley Rd., at Schetter Rd., Carmel* ☎ *831/624–2600* ⊕ *www.chateaujulien.com* ☐ *Tasting $15 (includes tour), private tours $20–$100* ⊙ *Winery: weekdays 8–5, weekends 11–5. Tours: Tues.–Fri. at 10:30 and 2:30, Sat. at 12:30 and 2:30, Sun. at 2:30, and by appointment.*

Cowgirl Winery. Cowgirl chic prevails in the main tasting building here, and it's just plain rustic at the outdoor tables, set amid chickens, a tractor, and a flatbed truck. The wines include Chardonnay, Cabernet Sauvignon, Rosé, and some blends. You can order wood fired pizzas from sister business Corkscrew Café down the block for delivery to your tasting table. ⊠ *25 Pilot Rd.* ☎ *831/298–7030* ⊕ *cowgirlwinery.com* ☐ *Tasting $13* ⊙ *Mon.–Thurs. 11:30–4:30, Fri.–Sun. 11:30–5 (until 6 on Sat. Apr.–Oct.).*

WORTH NOTING

Earthbound Farm. Pick up fresh veggies, ready-to-eat meals, gourmet groceries, flowers, and gifts at Earthbound Farm, the world's largest grower of organic produce. You can also take a romp in the kid's garden, cut your own herbs, and stroll through the chamomile aromatherapy labyrinth. Special events, on Saturday from April through December, include bug walks and garlic-braiding workshops. ⊠ *7250 Carmel Valley Rd., Carmel* ☎ *831/625–6219* ⊕ *www.ebfarm.com* ☐ *Free* ⊙ *Mon.–Sat. 8–6:30, Sun. 9–6.*

Garland Ranch Regional Park. Hiking trails stretch across much of this park's 4,500 acres of meadows, forested hillsides, and creeks. ⊠ *Carmel Valley Rd., 9 miles east of Carmel-by-the-Sea* ☎ *831/659–4488* ⊕ *www.mprpd.org.*

WHERE TO EAT

$$
EUROPEAN
✕ **Café Rustica.** European country cooking is the focus at this lively roadhouse. Specialties include roasted meats, seafood, pastas, and thin-crust pizzas from the wood-fired oven. It can get noisy inside; for a quieter meal, request a table outside. ⑤ *Average main: $20* ⊠ *10 Delfino Pl., at Pilot Rd., off Carmel Valley Rd.* ☎ *831/659–4444* ⊕ *www.caferusticavillage.com* ⚑ *Reservations essential* ⊙ *Closed Mon.*

$$
MODERN
AMERICAN
✕ **Corkscrew Café.** Farm-fresh Wine Country food is the specialty of this casual, Old Monterey–style bistro. Herbs and seasonal produce come from the Corkscrew's own organic gardens, the catch of the day comes from local waters, and the meats are hormone-free. Popular

dishes include the fish tacos, chicken salad, and wood-fired pizzas, which come with classic toppings and unusual ones such as Meyer lemon and prosciutto. You can dine indoors near the open kitchen, or outside in the garden patio. ■TIP→ Don't miss the collection of corkscrews from the 17th century to the present. $ *Average main: $22* ⊠ *55 W. Carmel Valley Rd., at Pilot Rd.* ☎ *831/659–8888* ⊕ *www. corkscrewcafe.com.*

$ ✕**Wagon Wheel Coffee Shop.** This local hangout decorated with wagon
AMERICAN wheels, cowboy hats, and lassos serves terrific hearty breakfasts, including oatmeal and banana pancakes, eggs Benedict, and biscuits and gravy. The lunch menu includes a dozen different burgers and other sandwiches. $ *Average main: $11* ⊠ *Valley Hill Center, 7156 Carmel Valley Rd., next to Quail Lodge, Carmel* ☎ *831/624–8878* ▭ *No credit cards* ⊗ *No dinner.*

WHERE TO STAY

$$$$ 🏨 **Bernardus Lodge.** The spacious guest rooms at this luxury spa resort
RESORT have vaulted ceilings, featherbeds, fireplaces, patios, and bathtubs for
Fodor's Choice two. **Pros:** exceptional personal service; outstanding food and wine.
★ **Cons:** pricey; some guests can seem snooty. $ *Rooms from: $475* ⊠ *415 W. Carmel Valley Rd.* ☎ *831/658–3400, 888/648–9463* ⊕ *www. bernardus.com* ⟿ *56 rooms, 1 suite.*

$$$ 🏨 **Carmel Valley Lodge.** This small inn has rooms surrounding a garden
HOTEL patio as well as separate one- and two-bedroom cottages with fireplaces and full kitchens. **Pros:** peaceful property; good value; friendly staff; close to village. **Cons:** rooms may be too rustic—as in out of date—for some. $ *Rooms from: $179* ⊠ *8 Ford Rd., at Carmel Valley Rd.* ☎ *831/659–2261, 800/641–4646* ⊕ *www.valleylodge.com* ⟿ *19 rooms, 4 suites, 8 cottages* ❑ *Breakfast.*

$$$$ 🏨 **Carmel Valley Ranch.** The activity options at this luxury ranch are so
RESORT varied that the resort provides a program director to guide you through them. **Pros:** stunning natural setting; tons of activities; state-of-the-art amenities. **Cons:** must drive several miles to shops and nightlife; pricey. $ *Rooms from: $400* ⊠ *1 Old Ranch Rd., Carmel* ☎ *831/625–9500* ⊕ *www.carmelvalleyranch.com* ⟿ *139 suites* ❑ *No meals.*

$$$ 🏨 **Quail Lodge & Golf Club.** A sprawling collection of ranch-style build-
HOTEL ings on 850 acres of meadows, fairways, and lakes, Quail Lodge offers
FAMILY luxury rooms and outdoor activities at surprisingly affordable rates. **Pros:** on the golf course; on-site restaurant. **Cons:** extra fees for athletic passes and some services; 5 miles from the beach and Carmel Valley Village. $ *Rooms from: $195* ⊠ *8205 Valley Greens Dr., Carmel* ☎ *831/624–2888* ☎ *866/675–1101 reservations* ⊕ *www.quaillodge. com* ⟿ *77 rooms, 16 suites* ❑ *Breakfast.*

$$$$ 🏨 **Stonepine Estate Resort.** Set on 330 pastoral acres, the former estate of
RESORT the Crocker banking family has been converted to a luxurious inn. **Pros:**
Fodor's Choice supremely exclusive. **Cons:** difficult to get a reservation; far from the
★ coast. $ *Rooms from: $300* ⊠ *150 E. Carmel Valley Rd.* ☎ *831/659– 2245* ⊕ *www.stonepineestate.com* ⟿ *10 rooms, 2 suites, 3 cottages.*

SPORTS AND THE OUTDOORS

GOLF

Quail Lodge & Golf Club. Robert Muir Graves designed this championship semiprivate 18-hole course next to Quail Lodge that provides challenging play for golfers of all skill levels. The course, which incorporates 10 lakes, edges the Carmel River. For the most part flat, the walkable course is well maintained, with stunning views, lush fairways, and ultrasmooth greens. ⊠ *8000 Valley Greens Dr., Carmel* ☎ *831/620–8808 golf shop, 831/620–8866 club concierge* ⊕ *www.quaillodge.com* ☜ *$150 Apr.–Oct., $125 Nov.–Mar.* ⚑ *18 holes, 6500 yards, par 71.*

Rancho Cañada Golf Club. With two 18-hole courses at reasonable rates, this public course is a local favorite. The gently rolling fairways crisscross the Carmel River, and views of the tree-studded Santa Lucia Mountains appear from nearly every vantage point. ⊠ *4860 Carmel Valley Rd., 1 mile east of Hwy. 1, Carmel* ☎ *831/624–0111, 800/536–9459* ⊕ *www.ranchocanada.com* ☜ *$70* ⚑ *East Course: 18 holes, 6125 yards, par 71; West Course: 18 holes, 6357 yards, par 71.*

SHOPPING

Avant Garden & Home. An eclectic array of garden accents, art, jewelry, home furnishings, and handmade gift items from around the world are on display at this family-run shop. ⊠ *14 Delfino Pl.* ☎ *831/659–9899* ⊕ *www.avantgardenandhome.com.*

SPAS

Fodor'sChoice **Refuge.** At this co-ed, European-style center on 2 serene acres you can
★ recharge without breaking the bank. Heat up in the eucalyptus steam room or cedar sauna, plunge into cold pools, and relax indoors in zero-gravity chairs or outdoors in Adirondack chairs around fire pits. Repeat the cycle a few times, then lounge around the thermal waterfall pools. Talk is not allowed, and bathing suits are required. ⊠ *27300 Rancho San Carlos Rd., south off Carmel Valley Rd., Carmel* ☎ *831/620–7360* ⊕ *www.refuge.com* ☜ *$39* ⊙ *Daily 10–10* ☞ *$60 50-min massage, $12 robe rental, hot tubs (outdoor), sauna, steam room. Services: Aromatherapy, hydrotherapy, massage.*

PEBBLE BEACH

Off North San Antonio Road in Carmel-by-the-Sea or off Sunset Drive in Pacific Grove.

Fodor'sChoice In 1919 the Pacific Improvement Company acquired 18,000 acres of
★ prime land on the Monterey Peninsula, including the entire Pebble Beach coastal region and much of Pacific Grove. Pebble Beach Golf Links and the Lodge at Pebble Beach opened the same year, and the private enclave evolved into a world-class golf destination with three posh lodges, five golf courses, and some of the West Coast's ritziest homes.

GETTING HERE AND AROUND

If you drive south from Monterey on Highway 1, exit at 17-Mile-Drive/ Sunset Drive in Pacific Grove to find the northern entrance gate. Coming from Carmel, exit at Ocean Avenue and follow the road almost to the beach; turn right on North San Antonio Road to the Carmel Gate. You can also enter through the Highway 1 Gate at Scenic Drive/Sunridge Road. Monterey–Salinas Transit buses provide regular service in and around Pebble Beach.

EXPLORING

Fodor'sChoice
★

17-Mile Drive. Primordial nature resides in quiet harmony with palatial estates along 17-Mile Drive, which winds through an 8,400-acre microcosm of the Pebble Beach coastal landscape. Dotting the drive are rare Monterey cypress, trees so gnarled and twisted that Robert Louis Stevenson described them as "ghosts fleeing before the wind." Some visitors balk at the $10 per car collected at the gates to drive on the private roads, but most find the drive well worth the price. An alternative is to grab a bike; cyclists tour for free. There are three entrances: the Highway 1 Gate, at Highway 68; the Pacific Grove gate, off Sunset Drive; and the Carmel gate, at San Antonio Road near Carmel Beach. ■ TIP→ If you spend at least $30 on dining or shopping in Pebble Beach and show a receipt at the exit gate, you'll receive a fee refund. ⊠ *West of Hwy. 1 and Hwy. 68 intersection.*

Bird Rock. The largest of several islands at the southern end of the Monterey Peninsula Country Club's golf course, Bird Rock teems with harbor seals, sea lions, cormorants, and pelicans.

Crocker Marble Palace. Many of the stately homes along 17-Mile Drive reflect the classic Monterey or Spanish-mission style typical of the region. A standout is the Crocker Marble Palace, about a mile south of the Lone Cypress (⇨ *below*). The private waterfront estate, inspired by a Byzantine castle, is easily identifiable by its dozens of marble arches.

The Lone Cypress. The most-photographed tree along 17-Mile Drive is the weather-sculpted Lone Cypress, which grows out of a precipitous outcropping above the waves about 1½ miles up the road from Pebble Beach Golf Links. You can't walk out to the tree, but you can stop for a view of it at a small parking area off the road.

Seal Rock. Sea creatures and birds—as well as some very friendly ground squirrels—make use of Seal Rock, the largest of a group of islands about 2 miles north of the Lone Cypress.

WHERE TO STAY

$$$$
RESORT
Fodor'sChoice
★

🖫 **Casa Palmero.** This exclusive boutique hotel evokes a stately Mediterranean villa. **Pros:** ultimate in pampering; sumptuous decor; more private than sister resorts; right on the golf course. **Cons:** pricey; may be *too* posh for some. $ *Rooms from: $885* ⊠ *1518 Cypress Dr.* ☎ *831/622–6650, 800/654–9300* ⊕ *www.pebblebeach.com* ⇱ *20 rooms, 4 suites* ⦿❘ *Breakfast.*

$$$$
RESORT

🖫 **The Inn at Spanish Bay.** This resort sprawls across a breathtaking stretch of shoreline, and has lush, 600-square-foot rooms. **Pros:** attentive service; tons of amenities; spectacular views. **Cons:** huge hotel; 4 miles from other Pebble Beach Resorts facilities. $ *Rooms from: $635* ⊠ *2700 17-Mile Dr.* ☎ *831/647–7500, 800/654–9300* ⊕ *www. pebblebeach.com* ⇱ *252 rooms, 17 suites.*

$$$$
RESORT

🖫 **Lodge at Pebble Beach.** All rooms have fireplaces and many have wonderful ocean views at this circa-1919 resort. **Pros:** world-class golf; borders the ocean and fairways; fabulous facilities. **Cons:** some rooms are on the small side; very pricey. $ *Rooms from: $745* ✉ *1700 17-Mile Dr.* ☎ *831/624–3811, 800/654–9300* ⊕ *www.pebblebeach.com* ⌇ *142 rooms, 19 suites* ⍩ *No meals.*

SPORTS AND THE OUTDOORS

GOLF

Links at Spanish Bay. This course, which hugs a choice stretch of shoreline, was designed by Robert Trent Jones Jr., Tom Watson, and Sandy Tatum in the rugged manner of traditional Scottish links, with sand dunes and coastal marshes interspersed among the greens. There are also chipping and putting greens, and a bagpiper signals the course's closing each day. ■TIP➡ **Nonguests of the Pebble Beach Resorts can reserve tee times up to two months in advance.** ✉ *17-Mile Dr., north end* ☎ *800/654–9300* ⊕ *www.pebblebeach.com* ✑ *$265* ⚐ *18 holes, 6821 yards, par 72.*

Fodor's Choice ★ **Pebble Beach Golf Links.** Pebble Beach Golf Links attracts golfers from around the world. The ocean plays a major role in the 18th hole of the famed links. Each February the course is the main site of the AT&T Pebble Beach National Pro-Am, where show-business celebrities and golf pros team up for one of the nation's most glamorous tournaments. Tee times are available to guests who book a minimum two-night stay. Nonguests can reserve a tee time only one day in advance on a space-available basis (up to a year for groups); resort guests can reserve up to 18 months in advance. ✉ *17-Mile Dr., near Lodge at Pebble Beach* ☎ *800/654–9300* ⊕ *www.pebblebeach.com* ✑ *$495* ⚐ *18 holes, 6828 yards, par 72.*

Peter Hay. A 9-hole, par-3 course, Peter Hay has attracted golfers of all skill levels since 1957. It's an ideal place for warm-ups, practicing short games, and for those who don't have time for a full 18 holes. ✉ *17-Mile Dr.* ☎ *831/622–8723* ⊕ *www.pebblebeach.com* ✑ *$30* ⚐ *9 holes, 725 yards, par 27.*

Poppy Hills. A splendid 18-hole course designed in 1986 by Robert Trent Jones Jr., Poppy Hills reopened in 2014 after an extensive, yearlong renovation Jones also supervised. The reworked course has eco-friendly fairways—the irrigation required is substantially less than before—that meander through the Del Monte Forest. Each hole has been restored to its natural elevation along the forest floor, and all 18 greens have been rebuilt with bentgrass. Individuals may reserve up to one month in advance, groups up to a year. ✉ *3200 Lopez Rd., at 17-Mile Dr.* ☎ *831/622–8239* ⊕ *poppyhillsgolf.com* ✑ *$210* ⚐ *18 holes, 7002 yards, par 73.5.*

Spyglass Hill. Among Pebble Beach's most challenging courses—three of the holes are rated among the toughest on the PGA tour—Spyglass Hill rewards golfers with varied terrain and glorious views. The first five holes border the Pacific, and the other 13 reach deep into the Del Monte Forest. Reservations are essential and may be made up to one month in advance (18 months for resort guests). ✉ *Stevenson Dr. and Spyglass Hill Rd.* ☎ *800/654–9300* ⊕ *www.pebblebeach.com* ✑ *$370* ⚐ *18 holes, 6960 yards, par 72.*

PACIFIC GROVE

3 miles north of Carmel-by-the-Sea.

This picturesque town, which began as a summer retreat for church groups more than a century ago, recalls its prim and proper Victorian heritage in its host of tiny board-and-batten cottages and stately mansions. However, long before the church groups flocked here the area received thousands of annual pilgrims—in the form of bright orange-and-black monarch butterflies. They still come, migrating south from Canada and the Pacific Northwest to take residence in pine and eucalyptus groves from October through March. In Butterfly Town USA, as Pacific Grove is known, the sight of a mass of butterflies hanging from the branches like a long, fluttering veil is unforgettable.

A prime way to enjoy Pacific Grove is to walk or bicycle the 3 miles of city-owned shoreline along Ocean View Boulevard, a cliff-top area landscaped with native plants and dotted with benches meant for sitting and gazing at the sea. You can spot many types of birds here, including the web-footed cormorants that crowd the massive rocks rising out of the surf. Two Victorians of note along Ocean View are the Queen Anne–style Green Gables, at No. 301—erected in 1888, it's now a B&B—and the 1909 Pryor House, at No. 429, a massive, shingled, private residence with a leaded- and beveled-glass doorway.

GETTING HERE AND AROUND

Reach Pacific Grove via Highway 68 off Highway 1, just south of Monterey. From Cannery Row in Monterey, head north until the road merges with Ocean Boulevard and follow it along the coast. MST buses travel within Pacific Grove and surrounding towns.

EXPLORING

FAMILY **Lovers Point Park.** The coastal views are gorgeous from this waterfront park whose sheltered beach has a children's pool and a picnic area. The main lawn has a volleyball court and a snack bar. ⊠ *Ocean View Blvd. northwest of Forest Ave.* ☎ *831/648–5730.*

FAMILY **Monarch Grove Sanctuary.** The sanctuary is a fairly reliable spot for viewing monarch butterflies between October and February. ⊠ *1073 Lighthouse Ave., at Ridge Rd.* ⊕ *www.pgmuseum.org.*

Pacific Grove Museum of Natural History. The museum is a good source for the latest information about the monarch butterflies and has a well-crafted butterfly tree exhibit. ⊠ *165 Forest Ave., at Central Ave.* ☎ *831/648–5716* ⊕ *www.pgmuseum.org* ⌨ *$3, $5 per family* ☉ *Tues.– Sun. 10–5.*

FAMILY **Point Pinos Lighthouse.** At this 1855 structure, the West Coast's oldest continuously operating lighthouse, you can learn about the lighting and foghorn operations and wander through a small museum containing U.S. Coast Guard memorabilia. ⊠ *Asilomar Ave., between Lighthouse Ave. and Del Monte Blvd.* ☎ *831/648–3176* ⊕ *www.pointpinos.org* ⌨ *$2* ☉ *Thurs.–Mon. 1–4.*

BEACHES

Asilomar State Beach. A beautiful coastal area, Asilomar State Beach stretches between Point Pinos and the Del Monte Forest. The 100 acres of dunes, tidal pools, and pocket-size beaches form one of the region's richest areas for marine life—including surfers, who migrate here most winter mornings. Leashed dogs are allowed on the beach. **Amenities:** none. **Best for:** sunrise; sunset; surfing; walking. ⊠ *Sunset Dr. and Asilomar Ave.* ☎ *831/646–6440* ⊕ *www.parks.ca.gov.*

WHERE TO EAT

$$
MODERN
AMERICAN

✕ Beach House. Patrons of this blufftop perch sip classic cocktails, sample California fare, and watch the otters frolic on Lovers Point Beach below. Standouts among the appetizers include the crispy shrimp—tossed in a creamy, spicy sauce—and oysters roasted in garlic-dill butter. Among the entrées worth a try are pan-seared sea scallops in a lobster-cognac bisque, bacon-wrapped meat loaf, and thyme-infused sole almandine with wild-rice pilaf. The sunset discounts between 4 and 6 (reservations recommended) are a great value. ■TIP→ For the best views of the beach and bay, sit on the heated outdoor patio. [$] *Average main: $21* ⊠ *620 Ocean View Blvd.* ☎ *831/375–2345* ⊕ *www.beachhousepg.com* ☉ *No lunch.*

$$$
MEDITERRANEAN

✕ Fandango. The menu here is mostly Mediterranean and southern French, with such dishes as osso bucco and paella served in a skillet. The decor follows suit: stone walls and country furniture lend the restaurant the earthy feel of a European farmhouse. This is where locals come when they want to have a big dinner with friends, drink wine, have fun, and generally feel at home. [$] *Average main: $26* ⊠ *223 17th St., south of Lighthouse Ave.* ☎ *831/372–3456* ⊕ *www.fandangorestaurant.com.*

$$
SEAFOOD

✕ Fishwife. Fresh fish with a Latin accent makes this a favorite of locals for lunch or a casual dinner. Standards are the sea garden salads topped with your choice of fish and the fried seafood plates with fresh veggies. Diners with large appetites appreciate the fisherman's bowls—fresh fish served with rice, black beans, spicy cabbage, salsa, vegetables, and crispy tortilla strips. [$] *Average main: $22* ⊠ *1996½ Sunset Dr., at Asilomar Blvd.* ☎ *831/375–7107* ⊕ *www.fishwife.com.*

$$$
ITALIAN

✕ Joe Rombi's La Mia Cucina. Pasta, fish, steaks, and chops are the specialties at this modern trattoria, which is the best in town for Italian food. The look is spare and clean, with colorful antique wine posters decorating the white walls. Next door, the affiliated La Piccola Casa serves breakfast (baked goods) and lunch daily, plus early dinner from Wednesday through Sunday. [$] *Average main: $23* ⊠ *208 17th St., at Lighthouse Ave.* ☎ *831/373–2416* ⊕ *www.joerombi.com* ☉ *Closed Mon. and Tues. No lunch.*

$$$
MODERN
AMERICAN

✕ Passionfish. South American artwork and artifacts decorate Passionfish, and Latin and Asian flavors infuse the dishes. Chef Ted Walter shops at local farmers' markets several times a week to find the best produce, fish, and meat available, then pairs it with creative sauces. The menu might include sea scallops with tomato-truffle butter and savory rice pudding. [$] *Average main: $23* ⊠ *701 Lighthouse Ave., at Congress Ave.* ☎ *831/655–3311* ⊕ *www.passionfish.net* ☉ *No lunch.*

$ ✕**Peppers Mexicali Cafe.** This cheerful white-walled storefront serves
MEXICAN   traditional dishes from Mexico and Latin America, with an emphasis
on fresh seafood. Excellent red and green salsas are made throughout
the day, and there's a large selection of beers, along with fresh lime margaritas. ⑤ *Average main: $15 ✉ 170 Forest Ave., between Lighthouse
and Central Aves.* ☎ *831/373–6892* ⊕ *www.peppersmexicalicafe.com*
♥ *Closed Tues. No lunch Sun.*

$$ ✕**Red House Café.** When it's nice out, sun pours through the big windows
AMERICAN   of this cozy restaurant and across tables on the porch; when fog rolls
in, the fireplace is lit. The American menu changes with the seasons but
typically includes grilled lamb fillets atop mashed potatoes for dinner
and Dungeness crab cakes over salad for lunch. Breakfast on weekends
is a local favorite. ⑤ *Average main: $20 ✉ 662 Lighthouse Ave., at
19th St.* ☎ *831/643–1060* ⊕ *www.redhousecafe.com* ♥ *No dinner Mon.*

$$ ✕**Taste Café and Bistro.** Grilled marinated rabbit, roasted half chicken,
AMERICAN   filet mignon, and other meats are the focus at Taste, which serves hearty
European-inspired food in a casual, open-kitchen setting. ⑤ *Average
main: $20 ✉ 1199 Forest Ave.* ☎ *831/655–0324* ⊕ *www.tastecafebistro.
com* ♥ *Closed Sun.–Mon.*

WHERE TO STAY

$$ 🏨 **Green Gables Inn.** Stained-glass windows and ornate interior details
B&B/INN   compete with spectacular ocean views at this Queen Anne–style mansion, built by a businessman for his mistress in 1888. **Pros:** exceptional views; impeccable attention to historic detail. **Cons:** some rooms
are small; thin walls. ⑤ *Rooms from: $145 ✉ 301 Ocean View Blvd.*
☎ *831/375–2095, 800/722–1774* ⊕ *www.greengablesinnpg.com* ⪭ *10
rooms, 7 with bath; 1 suite* ⦿Ⅼ *Breakfast.*

$$$ 🏨 **Martine Inn.** The glassed-in parlor and many guest rooms at this 1899
B&B/INN   Mediterranean-style villa have stunning ocean views, and thoughtful
details such as robes and rocking chairs create an ambience of luxury and comfort. **Pros:** romantic; fancy breakfast; ocean views. **Cons:**
not child-friendly; sits on a busy thoroughfare. ⑤ *Rooms from: $209
✉ 255 Ocean View Blvd.* ☎ *831/373–3388, 800/852–5588* ⊕ *www.
martineinn.com* ⪭ *25 rooms* ⦿Ⅼ *Breakfast.*

MONTEREY

2 miles southeast of Pacific Grove; 2 miles north of Carmel.

Early in the 20th century Carmel Martin, the first mayor of the city of
Monterey, saw a bright future for his town: "Monterey Bay is the one
place where people can live without being disturbed by manufacturing
and big factories. I am certain that the day is coming when this will be
the most desirable place in the whole state of California." His Honor
was not far off the mark. Monterey is a scenic city filled with early
California history: adobe buildings from the 1700s, Colton Hall, where
California's first constitution was drafted in 1849, and Cannery Row,
made famous by author John Steinbeck. Thousands of visitors come
each year to mingle with otters and other sea creatures at the world-
famous Monterey Bay Aquarium and in the protected waters of the
national marine sanctuary that hugs the shoreline.

GETTING HERE AND AROUND

From San Jose or San Francisco, take U.S. 101 south to Highway 156 West at Prunedale. Head west about 8 miles to Highway 1 and follow it about 15 miles south. From San Luis Obispo, take U.S. 101 north to Salinas and drive west on Highway 68 about 20 miles.

Many MST bus lines connect at the Monterey Transit Center, at Pearl Street and Munras Avenue. In summer (daily from 10 until at least 7), the free MST Monterey Trolley travels from downtown Monterey along Cannery Row to the Aquarium and back.

TOURS

Monterey Movie Tours. Board a customized motorcoach and relax while a film-savvy local takes you on a scenic tour of the Monterey Peninsula enhanced by film clips shown on overhead monitors. More than 200 movies have been shot in the area, and scenes with Marilyn Monroe, Clint Eastwood, Tom Hanks, and other stars play when the tour passes through the exact film locations. The three-hour adventure travels a 32-mile loop through Monterey, Pacific Grove, and Carmel. ⊠ *Departs from Monterey Conference Center, 1 Portola Plaza* ☎ *831/372–6278, 800/343–6437* ⊕ *www.montereymovietours.com* ⊠ *$55* ⊗ *Daily at 1.*

Old Monterey Walking Tour. Learn all about Monterey's storied past by joining a guided walking tour through the historic district. Tours begin at Custom House Plaza, across from Fisherman's Wharf. ⊠ *$5, includes admission to Custom House and Pacific House* ⊗ *Fri.–Sun. 10:30, 12:30, and 2.*

ESSENTIALS

Visitor Information Monterey County Convention & Visitors Bureau ☎ *877/666–8373* ⊕ *www.seemonterey.com.*

EXPLORING

TOP ATTRACTIONS

Cannery Row. When John Steinbeck published the novel *Cannery Row* in 1945, he immortalized a place of rough-edged working people. The waterfront street, edging a mile of gorgeous coastline, once was crowded with sardine canneries processing, at their peak, nearly 200,000 tons of the smelly silver fish a year. During the mid-1940s, however, the sardines disappeared from the bay, causing the canneries to close. Through the years the old tin-roof canneries have been converted into restaurants, art galleries, and malls with shops selling T-shirts, fudge, and plastic sea otters. Recent tourist development along the row has been more tasteful, however, and includes several stylish inns and hotels, wine tasting rooms, and upscale specialty shops. ⊠ *Cannery Row, between Reeside and David Aves.* ⊕ *www.canneryrow.com.*

Colton Hall. A convention of delegates met here in 1849 to draft the first state constitution. The stone building, which has served as a school, a courthouse, and the county seat, is a city-run museum furnished as it was during the constitutional convention. The extensive grounds outside the hall surround the Old Monterey Jail. ⊠ *570 Pacific St., between*

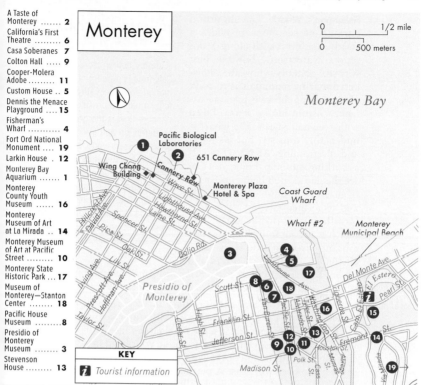

Madison and Jefferson Sts. ☏ *831/646–5640* ⊕ *www.monterey.org/ museums* ✉ *Free* ☉ *Daily 10–4 (Sun. and Tues. noon–3 in winter).*

Cooper-Molera Adobe. The restored 2-acre complex includes a house dating from the 1820s, a gift shop, and a large garden enclosed by a high adobe wall. The mostly Victorian-era antiques and memorabilia that fill the house provide a glimpse into the life of a prosperous sea merchant's family. If the house is closed, you can still stop by the Cooper Store and pick up walking-tour maps and stroll the grounds. ⊠ *Monterey State Historic Park, Polk and Munras Sts.* ☏ *831/649–7111* ⊕ *www.parks.ca.gov/mshp* ✉ *$5 tour* ☉ *Store, daily 10–4; gardens, daily 10–4; tours, Apr.–Aug., Fri.–Sun. and holiday Mon. morning and afternoon (call for hrs).*

Custom House. Built by the Mexican government in 1827 and now California's oldest standing public building, the Custom House was the first stop for sea traders whose goods were subject to duties. In 1846, Commodore John Sloat raised the American flag over this adobe structure and claimed California for the United States. The lower floor displays cargo from a 19th-century trading ship. If the house is closed, you can visit the cactus gardens and stroll the plaza. ⊠ *Monterey State Historic Park, 1 Custom House Plaza, across from Fisherman's Wharf* ☏ *831/649–7118* ⊕ *www.parks.ca.gov/mshp* ✉ *$3 (also includes admission to Pacific House)* ☉ *Fri.–Sun. and Mon. holidays 10–4.*

FAMILY **Fisherman's Wharf.** The mournful barking of sea lions provides a steady soundtrack all along Monterey's waterfront, but the best way to actually view the whiskered marine mammals is to walk along one of the two piers across from Custom House Plaza. Lined with souvenir shops, the wharf is undeniably touristy, but it's lively and entertaining. At Wharf No. 2, a working municipal pier, you can see the day's catch being unloaded from fishing boats on one side and fishermen casting their lines into the water on the other. The pier has a couple of low-key restaurants, from whose seats lucky customers might spot otters and harbor seals. ✉ *At end of Calle Principal* ⊕ *www.montereywharf.com.*

> ### JOHN STEINBECK'S CANNERY ROW
>
> "Cannery Row in Monterey in California is a poem, a stink, a grating noise, a quality of light, a tone, a habit, a nostalgia, a dream. Cannery Row is the gathered and scattered, tin and iron and rust and splintered wood, chipped pavement and weedy lots and junk heaps, sardine canneries of corrugated iron, honky tonks, restaurants and whore houses, and little crowded groceries, and laboratories and flophouses."
>
> —John Steinbeck, *Cannery Row*

FAMILY
Fodor's Choice
★
Monterey Bay Aquarium. Sea creatures surround you the minute you hand over your ticket at this extraordinary facility: right at the entrance dozens of them swim in a three-story-tall, sunlit kelp-forest tank. All the exhibits here provide a sense of what it's like to be in the water with the animals—sardines swim around your head in a circular tank, and jellyfish drift in and out of view in dramatically lighted spaces that suggest the ocean depths. A petting pool puts you literally in touch with bat rays, and the million-gallon Open Seas tank illustrates the variety of creatures, from sharks to placid-looking turtles, that live in the eastern Pacific. At the Splash Zone, which has 45 interactive bilingual exhibits, kids can commune with African black-footed penguins, potbellied seahorses, and other creatures. The only drawback to the aquarium experience is that it must be shared with the throngs that congregate daily, but most visitors think it's worth it. ■TIP→ Through at least fall 2016, don't miss Tentacles: The Astounding Lives of Octopuses, Squid, and Cuttlefishes, a huge and fascinating exhibit of marine mollusks. ✉ *886 Cannery Row, at David Ave.* ☎ *831/648–4800 info, 866/963–9645 for advance tickets* ⊕ *www.montereybayaquarium.org* 🎫 *$40* ⏰ *Mar.–June daily 10–6; July–Aug./holidays weekends 9:30–6, weekends 9:30–8; Nov.–Feb. daily 10–5.*

Monterey State Historic Park. You can glimpse Monterey's early history in the well-preserved adobe buildings scattered along several city blocks. Far from being a hermetic period museum, the park facilities are an integral part of the town's day-to-day business life—within some of the buildings are a store, a theater, and government offices. The gardens at some historic structures are themselves worthy sights, and visitable even if the buildings, among them Casa Soberanes, the Cooper-Molera Adobe, and the Larkin House, are closed. ■TIP→ Because of state budget cuts, some buildings may be closed when you visit, but cell phone tours (☎ 831/998–9498) are available 24/7. The

…rained "seals" that perform in circuses are actually California sea lions—intelligent, social animals that live and sleep) close together in groups.

park's website has up-to-date information. ✉ *20 Custom House Plaza* ☎ *831/649–7118* ⊕ *www.parks.ca.gov/mshp* ✉ *Free* ☽ *Call for hrs.*

Museum of Monterey—Stanton Center. The museum displays maritime artifacts, art, photography, and costumes from Monterey's earliest days to the present. The collection's jewel is the enormous Fresnel lens from the Point Sur Light Station. ✉ *Stanton Center, 5 Custom House Plaza* ☎ *831/372–2608* ⊕ *www.museumofmonterey.org* ✉ *$8, free 1st Wed. of month 1–5* ☽ *May–Aug., Tues.–Sat. 10–7, Sun. noon–5; Sept.–Apr., Wed.–Sat. 11–5, Sun. noon–5.*

WORTH NOTING

A Taste of Monterey. Without driving the back roads, you can taste the wines of nearly 100 area vintners (craft beers, too) while taking in fantastic bay views. Bottles are available for purchase, and food is served from noon until closing. ✉ *700 Cannery Row, Suite KK* ☎ *831/646–5446, 888/646–5446* ⊕ *www.atasteofmonterey.com* ✉ *Tastings $10–$20* ☽ *Sun.–Wed. 11–7, Thurs.–Sat. 11–8.*

California's First Theatre. This adobe began its life in 1846 as a saloon and lodging house for sailors. Four years later stage curtains were fashioned from army blankets, and some U.S. officers staged plays to the light of whale oil lamps. As of this writing, the building is open only for private tours (call for times and fees), but you can stroll in the garden. ✉ *Monterey State Historic Park, Scott and Pacific Sts.* ☎ *831/649–7118* ⊕ *www.parks.ca.gov/mshp* ✉ *Free* ☽ *Call for hrs.*

Casa Soberanes. A classic low-ceiling adobe structure built in 1842, this was once a Custom House guard's residence. Exhibits at the house survey life in Monterey from the era of Mexican rule to the present. The building is open only for private tour requests (call for times and fees), but you can visit the peaceful rear garden and its rose-covered arbor. ⊠ *Monterey State Historic Park, 336 Pacific St., at Del Monte Ave.* ☎ *831/649–7118* ⊕ *www.parks.ca.gov/mshp* 🖾 *Free.*

FAMILY **Dennis the Menace Playground.** The late cartoonist Hank Ketcham designed this play area. Its equipment is on a grand scale and made for Dennis-like daredevils: kid favorites include the roller slide, rock-climbing area, and clanking suspension bridge. You can rent a rowboat or a paddleboat for cruising around U-shaped Lake El Estero, populated with an assortment of ducks, mud hens, and geese. ⊠ *El Estero Park, Pearl St. and Camino El Estero* ☎ *831/646–3866* ⊕ *www.monterey.org/parks* ⊘ *Daily 10–dusk* ⊘ *Closed Tues., Sept.–May.*

Fort Ord National Monument. Scenic beauty, biodiversity, and miles of trails make this former U.S. Army training grounds a haven for nature lovers and outdoor enthusiasts. The 7,200-acre park, which stretches east over the hills between Monterey and Salinas, is also protected habitat for 35 species of rare and endangered plants and animals. There are 86 miles of single-track, dirt, and paved trails for hiking, biking, and horseback riding. The main trailheads are the Creekside, off Creekside Terrace near Portola Road, and Badger Hills. Maps are available at the various trail-access points and on the park's website. ■TIP➔ **Dogs are permitted on trails, but should be leashed when other people are nearby.** ⊠ *Bordered by Hwy. 68 and Gen. Jim Moore and Reservation Rds.* ☎ *831/394–8314* ⊕ *www.blm.gov/pgdata/content/ca/en/fo/hollister/fort_ord/index.html* 🖾 *Free* ⊘ *Daily ½ hr before sunrise–½ hr after sunset.*

Larkin House. A veranda encircles the second floor of this 1835 adobe, whose design bears witness to the Mexican and New England influences on the Monterey style. The building's namesake, Thomas O. Larkin, an early California statesman, brought many of the antiques inside from New Hampshire. From September through March the building is open only for special tour requests (call for times and fees), but you can peek in the windows and stroll the gardens. ⊠ *Monterey State Historic Park, 464 Calle Principal, between Jefferson and Pacific Sts.* ☎ *831/649–7118* ⊕ *www.parks.ca.gov/mshp* 🖾 *Tours $5* ⊘ *Gardens daily 10–4; tours Apr.–Aug. Fri.–Sun and Mon. holidays (call for hrs).*

FAMILY **Monterey County Youth Museum (MY Museum).** Monterey Bay comes to life from a child's perspective in this fun-filled, interactive indoor exploration center. The seven exhibit galleries showcase the science and nature of the Big Sur coast, theater arts, Pebble Beach golf, and beaches. Also here are a live performance theater, a creation station, a hospital emergency room, and an agriculture corner where kids follow artichokes, strawberries, and other fruits and veggies on their evolution from sprout to harvest to farmers' markets. ⊠ *425 Washington St., between E. Franklin St. and Bonifacio Pl.* ☎ *831/649–6444* ⊕ *www.mymuseum. org* 🖾 *$8* ⊘ *Tues.–Sat. 10–5, Sun. noon–5.*

Monterey Museum of Art at La Mirada. Asian and European antiques fill this 19th-century adobe house. A newer 10,000-square-foot gallery space, designed by Charles Moore, houses Asian and California regional art. Outside are magnificent rose and rhododendron gardens. ⊠ *720 Via Mirada, at Fremont St.* ☎ *831/372–3689* ⊕ *www. montereyart.org* ⊠ *$10, also good for admission to museum's Pacific Street facility* ⊙ *Wed.–Sun. 11–5 (Thurs. until 8).*

> ### FORMER CAPITAL OF CALIFORNIA
>
> In 1602 Spanish explorer Sebastián Vizcaíno stepped ashore on a remote California peninsula. He named it after the viceroy of New Spain—Count de Monte Rey. Soon the Spanish built a military outpost, and the site was the capital of California until the state came under American rule.

Monterey Museum of Art at Pacific Street. Photographs by Ansel Adams and Edward Weston, as well as works by other artists who have spent time on the peninsula, are on display here, along with international folk art, from Kentucky hearth brooms to Tibetan prayer wheels. ⊠ *559 Pacific St., across from Colton Hall* ☎ *831/372–5477* ⊕ *www.montereyart. org* ⊠ *$10, also good for admission to museum's La Mirada facility* ⊙ *Wed.–Sun. 11–5.*

Pacific House Museum. Once a hotel and saloon, this facility, also a visitor center, commemorates life in pioneer-era California with gold-rush relics and photographs of old Monterey. On the upper floor are Native American artifacts, including gorgeous baskets and pottery. ⊠ *Monterey State Historic Park, 10 Custom House Plaza* ☎ *831/649–7118* ⊕ *www. parks.ca.gov/mshp* ⊠ *$3 (includes admission to Custom House)* ⊙ *Fri.– Sun. and Mon. holidays 10–4.*

Presidio of Monterey Museum. This spot has been significant for centuries. Its first incarnation was as a Native American village for the Rumsien tribe. The Spanish explorer Sebastián Vizcaíno landed here in 1602, and Father Junípero Serra arrived in 1770. Notable battles fought here include the 1818 skirmish in which the corsair Hipólito Bruchard conquered the Spanish garrison that stood on this site and claimed part of California for Argentina. The indoor museum tells the stories; plaques mark the outdoor sites. ⊠ *Presidio of Monterey, Corporal Ewing Rd., off Lighthouse Ave.* ☎ *831/646–3456* ⊕ *www.monterey.org/museums* ⊠ *Free* ⊙ *Mon. 10–1, Thurs.–Sat. 10–4, Sun. 1–4.*

Stevenson House. This house was named in honor of author Robert Louis Stevenson, who boarded here briefly in a tiny upstairs room. Items from his family's estate furnish Stevenson's room; period-decorated chambers elsewhere in the house include a gallery of memorabilia and a children's nursery stocked with Victorian toys and games. Except on Saturday from April through August, the building is open only for special tour requests (call for times and fees), but you can stroll around the gardens. ⊠ *Monterey State Historic Park, 530 Houston St., near Pearl St.* ☎ *831/649–7118* ⊕ *www.parks.ca.gov/mshp* ⊙ *Gardens daily 9–5; house Apr.–Aug. Sat. 1–4.*

CLOSE UP

The Underwater Kingdom

Although Monterey's coastal landscapes are stunning, their beauty is more than equaled by the wonders that lie offshore. The Monterey Bay National Marine Sanctuary—which stretches 276 miles, from north of San Francisco almost down to Santa Barbara—teems with abundant life, and has topography as diverse as that aboveground.

The preserve's 5,322 square miles include vast submarine canyons, which reach down 10,663 feet at their deepest point. They also encompass dense forests of giant kelp—a kind of seaweed that can grow more than a hundred feet from its roots on the ocean floor. These kelp forests are especially robust off Monterey.

The sanctuary was established in 1992 to protect the habitat of the many species that thrive in the bay. Some animals can be seen quite easily from land. In summer and winter you might glimpse the offshore spray of gray whales as they migrate between their summer feeding grounds in Alaska and their breeding grounds in Baja. Clouds of marine birds—including white-faced ibis, three types of albatross, and more than 15 types of gull—skim the waves, or roost in the rock islands along 17-Mile Drive. Sea otters dart and gambol in the calmer waters of the bay; and of course, you can watch the sea lions—and hear their round-the-clock barking—on the wharves in Santa Cruz and Monterey.

The sanctuary supports many other creatures, however, that remain unseen by most on-land visitors. Some of these are enormous, such as the giant blue whales that arrive to feed on plankton in summer; others, like the more than 22 species of red algae in these waters, are microscopic. So whether you choose to visit the Monterey Bay Aquarium, take a whale-watch trip, or look out to sea with your binoculars, remember you're seeing just a small part of a vibrant underwater kingdom.

WHERE TO EAT

$$
MODERN
AMERICAN
✕ **Bay of Pines.** Local artists painted floor-to-ceiling murals of Monterey's natural habitats—from redwoods and sand dunes to the bay itself—and other homegrown art graces this whimsical organic restaurant. Chicken wontons on Asian slaw are among the appetizers, and the entrées might include seafood pasta puttanesca or seared ahi tuna with lemongrass rice, drizzled with apricot teriyaki sauce. The popular grass-fed beef burger comes with hummus, sautéed wild mushrooms, applewood-smoked bacon strips, and Gruyère. Musicians perform on most nights from 9 to 11:30; the bar here is a popular happy-hour hangout. ⑤ *Average main: $19* ⊠ *150 Del Monte Ave.* ☎ *831/920–3563* ⊕ *www.bayofpinesrestaurant.com.*

$$
SEAFOOD
✕ **Monterey Fish House.** Casual yet stylish and always packed, this seafood restaurant is removed from the hubbub of the wharf. If the dining room is full, you can wait at the bar and savor deliciously plump oysters on the half shell. The bartenders and waitstaff will gladly advise you on the perfect wine to go with your poached, blackened, or oak-grilled seafood. ⑤ *Average main: $21* ⊠ *2114 Del Monte Ave., at Dela Vina Ave.* ☎ *831/373–4647* ⬧ *Reservations essential* ⊘ *No lunch weekends.*

$$$

AMERICAN

Fodor'sChoice

★

✕ **Montrio Bistro.** This quirky, converted firehouse, with its rawhide walls and iron indoor trellises, has a wonderfully sophisticated menu. Chef Tony Baker uses organic produce and meats and sustainably sourced seafood to create imaginative dishes that reflect the area's agriculture—fire-roasted artichokes with Mediterranean relish, for instance, and pesto-rubbed sirloin prepared with brussels sprouts, dates, smoked bacon, and red wine. Monterey wineries are well represented on the California-centric wine list, and the signature cocktails are infused with local fruits, herbs, and veggies. ⑤ *Average main: $24* ✉ *414 Calle Principal, at W. Franklin St.* ☎ *831/648–8880* ⊕ *www.montrio.com* ☖ *Reservations essential* ☽ *No lunch.*

$$$

SEAFOOD

✕ **Old Fisherman's Grotto.** Otters and seals frolic in the water just below this family-run restaurant midway down Fisherman's Wharf that serves seafood, steak, and pasta. The founder's son and current owner, Chris Shake, has updated the decor while retaining the classic nautical style that prevailed when the Grotto opened in 1950. Famed for its creamy clam chowder, the restaurant serves a huge range of dishes, from seafood paella and sand dabs to filet mignon and teriyaki chicken. ■TIP➜ Reserve a windowside table for the best views. ⑤ *Average main: $25* ✉ *39 Fisherman's Wharf* ☎ *831/375–4604* ⊕ *www.oldfishermansgrotto.com.*

$

AMERICAN

✕ **Old Monterey Café.** Breakfast here gets constant local raves. The café's fame rests on familiar favorites: a dozen kinds of omelets, and pancakes from blueberry to cinnamon-raisin-pecan. For lunch are good soups, salads, and sandwiches. This is a fine place to relax with an afternoon cappuccino. ⑤ *Average main: $12* ✉ *489 Alvarado St., at Munras Ave.* ☎ *831/646–1021* ☖ *Reservations not accepted* ☽ *No dinner.*

$$$$

MODERN

AMERICAN

Fodor'sChoice

★

✕ **Restaurant 1833.** Housed in the historic Stokes Adobe, built in 1833, this popular restaurant and bar showcases the region's colorful history and local bounty in one of the most unusual settings anywhere. The two-story structure, a national heritage site, was once the home of the mayor of Monterey. Today it includes seven distinct dining rooms; each honors an era and characters from the adobe's storied past. Sit in a leather booth on the Founder's Balcony for a bird's-eye view of the rocking bar scene below, or outdoors by the courtyard fire pits near giant oak, redwood, palm, and magnolia trees. The casual menu changes daily and centers around seasonal local ingredients. Regular stars include bacon-cheddar biscuits with maple-chili butter and whole roasted truffle chicken, pan-roasted mahimahi, and bacon-wrapped pork loin. The cocktail menu pays tribute to the adobe's 1840s-era apothecary business with four categories: Pain Killers, Stress Relievers, Elixirs, and Aphrodisiacs, which, along with the extensive wine list, fuel a lively atmosphere indoors and out, especially on weekend nights. ⑤ *Average main: $32* ✉ *500 Hartnell St.* ☎ *831/643–1833* ⊕ *www.restaurant1833.com* ☽ *No lunch.*

$$

AMERICAN

✕ **Tarpy's Roadhouse.** Fun, dressed-up American favorites—a little something for everyone—are served in this renovated early-1900s stone farmhouse several miles east of town. The kitchen cranks out everything from Cajun-spiced prawns to meat loaf with marsala-mushroom gravy to grilled ribs and steaks. Eat indoors by a fireplace or outdoors in the courtyard. ⑤ *Average main: $22* ✉ *2999 Monterey–Salinas Hwy., Hwy. 68* ☎ *831/647–1444* ⊕ *www.tarpys.com.*

3

WHERE TO STAY

$$$
RESORT
⊞ Best Western Beach Resort Monterey. One of the area's best values, this hotel has a great waterfront location—2 miles north of Monterey, with views of the bay and the city skyline—and offers a surprising array of amenities. **Pros:** on the beach; great value; family-friendly. **Cons:** several miles from major attractions; big-box mall neighborhood. $ *Rooms from: $189* ⊠ *2600 Sand Dunes Dr.* ☎ *831/394–3321, 800/242–8627* ⊕ *www.montereybeachresort.com* ⤷ *196 rooms* ⦿ *No meals.*

$$
HOTEL
⊞ Hotel Abrego. A half block from Monterey's transit center and a 15-minute walk to Fisherman's Wharf, this full-service hotel has Craftsman-style rooms in four mission-style buildings. **Pros:** central-Monterey location; free parking; near public transit and highways; range of room options. **Cons:** not on waterfront; smallish pool and exercise room; some rooms near busy street. $ *Rooms from: $159* ⊠ *755 Abrego St., at Fremont St.* ☎ *831/372–7551, 800/982–1986 reservations* ▤ *831/324–4625* ⊕ *www.hotelabrego.com* ⤷ *93 rooms* ⦿ *No meals.*

$$$
HOTEL
⊞ InterContinental The Clement Monterey. Spectacular bay views, upscale amenities, assiduous service, and a superb location next to the aquarium propelled this luxury hotel to immediate stardom. **Pros:** a block from the aquarium; fantastic waterfront views from some rooms; great for families. **Cons:** a tad formal; pricey. $ *Rooms from: $199* ⊠ *750 Cannery Row* ☎ *831/375–4500, 866/781–2406 toll free* ⊕ *www.ictheclementmonterey.com* ⤷ *192 rooms, 16 suites* ⦿ *No meals.*

$$
HOTEL
⊞ Monterey Bay Lodge. Its superior amenities and location bordering El Estero Park give this cheerful facility the edge over other area motels. **Pros:** within walking distance of the beach and a playground; quiet at night; good family choice. **Cons:** near a busy boulevard. $ *Rooms from: $130* ⊠ *55 Camino Aguajito* ☎ *831/372–8057, 800/558–1900* ⊕ *www.montereybaylodge.com* ⤷ *43 rooms, 3 suites* ⦿ *No meals.*

$$$$
HOTEL
⊞ Monterey Plaza Hotel & Spa. This hotel commands a waterfront location on Cannery Row, where you can see frolicking sea otters from the wide outdoor patio and many room balconies. **Pros:** on the ocean; many amenities; attentive service. **Cons:** touristy area; heavy traffic. $ *Rooms from: $269* ⊠ *400 Cannery Row* ☎ *831/646–1700, 800/334–3999* ⊕ *www.montereyplazahotel.com* ⤷ *280 rooms, 10 suites.*

$$$$
B&B/INN
Fodor'sChoice
★
⊞ Old Monterey Inn. This three-story manor house was the home of Monterey's first mayor, and today it remains a private enclave within walking distance of downtown, set off by lush gardens shaded by huge old trees and bordered by a creek. **Pros:** gorgeous gardens; refined luxury; serene. **Cons:** must drive to attractions and sights; fills quickly. $ *Rooms from: $289* ⊠ *500 Martin St.* ☎ *831/375–8284, 800/350–2344* ⊕ *www.oldmontereyinn.com* ⤷ *6 rooms, 3 suites, 1 cottage* ⦿ *Breakfast.*

$$$
HOTEL
⊞ Spindrift Inn. This boutique hotel on Cannery Row has beach access and a rooftop garden that overlooks the water. **Pros:** close to aquarium; steps from the beach; friendly staff. **Cons:** throngs of visitors outside; can be noisy; not good for families. $ *Rooms from: $209* ⊠ *652 Cannery Row* ☎ *831/646–8900, 800/841–1879* ⊕ *www.spindriftinn.com* ⤷ *45 rooms* ⦿ *Breakfast.*

NIGHTLIFE

MUSIC CLUBS

Cibo. An Italian restaurant with a big bar area, Cibo brings live jazz and other music to downtown from Tuesday through Sunday. ✉ *301 Alvarado St., at Del Monte Ave.* ☎ *831/649–8151* ⊕ *www.cibo.com.*

MUSIC FESTIVALS

Jazz Bash by the Bay. Traditional jazz bands play early jazz, big band, swing, ragtime, blues, zydeco, and gypsy jazz at waterfront venues during this festival, held on the first full weekend of March. ☎ *831/675–0298, 888/349–6879* ⊕ *www.jazzbashbythebay.com.*

Monterey Jazz Festival. The world's oldest jazz festival attracts top-name performers to the Monterey Fairgrounds on the third full weekend of September. ☎ *888/248–6499 ticket office, 831/373–3366* ⊕ *www. montereyjazzfestival.org.*

THEATER

Bruce Ariss Wharf Theater (*The New Wharf Theatre*). American musicals past and present are the focus here, with dramas and comedies also in the mix. ✉ *One Fisherman's Wharf* ☎ *831/649–2332.*

SPORTS AND THE OUTDOORS

Monterey Bay waters never warm to the temperatures of their Southern California counterparts—the warmest they get is the low 60s. That's one reason why the marine life here is so diverse, which in turn brings out the fishers, kayakers, and whale-watchers. During the rainy winter, the waves grow larger, and surfers flock to the water. On land pretty much year-round, bikers find opportunities to ride, and walkers have plenty of waterfront to stroll.

BIKING

Adventures by the Sea, Inc. You can rent surreys plus tandem, standard, and electric bicycles from this outfit that also conducts bike and kayak tours and rents kayaks. ✉ *299 Cannery Row* ☎ *831/372–1807* ⊕ *www. adventuresbythesea.com* ✉ *210 Alvarado Mall* ✉ *Stillwater Cove, 17-Mile Drive, Pebble Beach* ✉ *Beach at Lovers Point, Pacific Grove.*

Bay Bikes. For bicycle and surrey rentals, visit Bay Bikes at one of its two Monterey shops. ■TIP➔ You can rent a bike on Cannery Row and drop it off at this outfit's Carmel location. ✉ *585 Cannery Row* ☎ *831/655–2453* ⊕ *www.baybikes.com* ✉ *486 Washington St.* ✉ *3600 The Barnyard, Carmel.*

FISHING

Randy's Fishing and Whale Watching Trips. In business since 1949, Randy's takes beginning and experienced fishers out to sea. ✉ *66 Fisherman's Wharf* ☎ *831/372–7440, 800/251–7440* ⊕ *www.randysfishingtrips.com.*

KAYAKING

Fodor's Choice ★ **Monterey Bay Kayaks.** For many visitors the best way to see the bay is by kayak. This company rents equipment and conducts classes and natural-history tours. ⊠ *693 Del Monte Ave.* ☎ *831/373–5357, 800/649–5357* ⊕ *www.monterey baykayaks.com.*

WALKING

Monterey Bay Coastal Trail. From Custom House Plaza, you can walk along the coast in either direction on this 29-mile-long trail for spectacular views of the sea. The trail runs from north of Monterey to Pacific Grove, with sections continuing around Pebble Beach. ☎ *831/372–3196* ⊕ *www.mtycounty.com/ pgs-parks/bike-path.html.*

WHALE-WATCHING

Thousands of gray whales pass close by the Monterey Coast on their annual migration between the Bering Sea and Baja California, and a whale-watching cruise is the best way to see these magnificent mammals close up. The migration south takes place from December through March; January is prime viewing time. The whales migrate north from March through June. Blue whales and humpbacks also pass the coast; they're most easily spotted in late summer and early fall.

Fast Raft Ocean Safaris. Naturalists lead whale-watching and sightseeing tours of Monterey Bay aboard the 33-foot *Ranger,* a six-passenger, rigid-hull inflatable boat. The speedy craft slips into coves inaccessible to larger vessels; its quiet engines enable intimate marine experiences without disturbing wildlife. Children ages 12 and older are welcome to participate. ⊠ *32 Cannery Row, Suite F2* ☎ *831/324–4883 private or custom charter, 800/979-3370 reservations* ⊕ *www.fastraft.com* ⌑ *$140.*

Monterey Bay Whale Watch. The marine biologists here lead three- to five-hour whale-watching tours. ⊠ *84 Fisherman's Wharf* ☎ *831/375–4658* ⊕ *www.montereybaywhalewatch.com.*

Princess Monterey Whale Watching. Tours are offered daily on a 150-passenger high-speed cruiser and a large 75-foot boat. ⊠ *96 Fisherman's Wharf #1* ☎ *831/372–2203, 831/205–2370 reservations, 888/223-9153 international reservations* ⊕ *www.montereywhalewatching.com.*

AROUND MONTEREY BAY

As Highway 1 follows the curve of the bay between Monterey and Santa Cruz, it passes through a rich agricultural zone. Opening right onto the bay, where the Salinas and Pajaro rivers drain into the Pacific, a broad valley brings together fertile soil, an ideal climate, and a good water supply to create optimum growing conditions for crops such as strawberries, artichokes, brussels sprouts, and broccoli. Several beautiful beaches line this part of the coast. Salinas and Moss Landing are in Monterey County; the other cities and towns covered here are in Santa Cruz County.

3

GETTING HERE AND AROUND

All the towns in this area are on or just off Highway 1. MST buses serve Monterey County destinations, connecting in Watsonville with Santa Cruz METRO buses, which operate throughout Santa Cruz County.

SALINAS

17 miles east of Monterey on Hwy. 68.

Salinas, a hard-working city surrounded by vineyards and fruit and vegetable fields, honors the memory and literary legacy of John Steinbeck, its most famous native, with the National Steinbeck Center. The facility spurred the revival of Old Town Salinas, where renovated turn-of-the-20th-century stone buildings house shops and restaurants.

ESSENTIALS

Transportation Information Salinas Amtrak Station ⊠ *11 Station Pl., at W. Market St., Salinas* ☎ *800/872–7245.*

Visitor Information California Welcome Center ⊠ *1213 N. Davis Rd., west of U.S. 101, exit 330, Salinas* ☎ *831/757–8687, 831/759–8687* ⊕ *www.visitcwc.com/salinas* �---- *Open daily 9–5.*

EXPLORING

FAMILY **Monterey Zoo.** More than a hundred exotic animals—many of them retired from film, television, and live production work, or rescued from less-than-ideal environments—find sanctuary at the Monterey Zoo at Vision Quest Ranch. Visit tigers, lions, bears, elephants, and primates on guided hour-long walking tours with professional trainers and handlers. For an in-depth experience, stay in a safari bungalow at Vision Quest Safari B&B where, in the morning, breakfast from a basket is delivered by a resident elephant. ⊠ *400 River Rd., off Hwy. 68, Salinas* ☎ *831/455–1901, 800/228–7382* ⊕ *www.montereyzoo.com* ☐ *Tours $10; optional post-tour elephant feeding $5* ☐ *Tours daily at 1, Jun.–Aug. also at 3.*

National Steinbeck Center. The center's exhibits document the life of Pulitzer- and Nobel-prize winner John Steinbeck and the history of the nearby communities that inspired novels such as *East of Eden*. Highlights include reproductions of the green pickup-camper from *Travels with Charley* and of the bunkroom from *Of Mice and Men*. **Steinbeck House,** the author's Victorian birthplace, at 132 Central Avenue, is two blocks from the center in a so-so neighborhood. Now a decent lunch spot, it displays memorabilia. ⊠ *1 Main St., at Central Ave., Salinas* ☎ *831/775–4721* ⊕ *www.steinbeck.org* ☐ *$15* ☐ *Daily 10–5.*

PINNACLES NATIONAL PARK

38 miles southeast of Salinas

Pinnacles may be the nation's newest national park, but Teddy Roosevelt recognized the uniqueness of this ancient volcano—its jagged spires and monoliths thrusting upward from chaparral-covered mountains—when he made it a national monument in 1908. Though only about two hours from the bustling Bay Area, the outside world seems to recede even before you reach the park's gates.

GETTING HERE AND AROUND

One of the first things you need to decide when visiting Pinnacles is which entrance—east or west—you'll use, because there's no road connecting the two, thanks to the rugged peaks separating them. Entering from Highway 25 on the east is straightforward. The gate is only a mile or so from the turnoff. From the west, once you head east out of Soledad on Highway 146, the road quickly becomes narrow and hilly, with many blind curves. Drive slowly and cautiously along the 11 miles or so before you reach the west entrance.

ESSENTIALS

Pinnacles Visitor Center. This is the main visitor center for the park, located at the east entrance. Here you can purchase your admission passes, get maps, browse books, and buy gifts. Because it's adjacent to the campground store, it's a good place to stock up on last-minute snacks and drinks if you're headed out to hike the trails. ⊠ *Hwy. 146, 2 miles west of Hwy. 25, Paicines* ☎ *831/389–4485* ⊕ *www.nps.gov/ pinn/planyourvisit/hours.htm.*

West Pinnacles Visitor Contact Station. This station is just past the west entrance to the park, about 14 miles east of Soledad. Here you can get maps and information, watch a 13-minute film about the park, view some displays, and browse a small gift shop. Be advised that there isn't any food or drink available at this entrance, so come prepared. ⊠ *Hwy. 146, about 14 miles east of Soledad, Soledad* ☎ *831/537–7220* ⊕ *www. nps.gov/pinn/planyourvisit/hours.htm* ⊙ *Daily 9–4:30.*

EXPLORING

FAMILY **Pinnacles National Park.** This park has many unusual attractions, including talus caves, 30 miles of hiking trails, and hundreds of rock climbing routes. A mosaic of diverse habitats supports an amazing number of wildlife species: 149 birds, 49 mammals, 69 butterflies, and nearly 400 bees. The park is also home to 32 of the world's remaining few hundred condors in captivity and release areas. Fourteen of California's 34 bat species live in caves in the park. President Theodore Roosevelt declared this remarkable 26,000-acre geologic and wildlife preserve a national monument in 1908. President Barack Obama officially designated it a national park in 2013.

The pinnacles are believed to have been created when two major tectonic plates heaved and lurched at their meeting points, spawning extensive volcanic activity in what's now called the Gabilan Mountains, southeast of Salinas and Monterey. The volcano eventually dried up and began to erode, leaving a rugged landscape with rocky spires and crags, or pinnacles, at the plates' intersection. Boulders fell into canyons and valleys, creating talus caves and a paradise for modern-day rock climbers. Spring is the most popular time to visit, when colorful wildflowers blanket the meadows; summer heat can be brutal. The park has two entrances—east and west—but they are not connected (there's no way to build a road over the spires). The Pinnacles Visitor Center, Bear Gulch Nature Center, Park Headquarters, the Pinnacles Campground, and the Bear Gulch Cave and Reservoir are on the east side. The Chaparral Ranger Station is on the west side, where you can feast on fantastic views of the Pinnacles High Peaks from the parking area. Dogs are not allowed on hiking trails. ■ TIP→ **The east entrance is 32 miles southeast of Hollister via Highway 25. The west entrance is about 12 miles east of Soledad via Highway 146.** ⊠ *5000 Hwy. 146, Paicines* ☎ *831/389–4485, 831/389–4427 Westside* ⊕ *www.nps.gov/ pinn* ☒ *$5 per vehicle, $3 per visitor if biking or walking, all valid 7 days* ⊙ *West entrance, daily 7:30 am–8 pm; West Pinnacles Visitor Center, daily 9 5. East entrance, daily 24 hrs; Pinnacles Visitor Center, daily 9:30–5.*

SPORTS AND THE OUTDOORS
HIKING

Hiking is the most popular activity at Pinnacles, with more than 30 miles of trails for every interest and level of fitness. Because there isn't a road through the park, hiking is also the only way to experience the interior of the park, including the High Peaks, the talus caves, and the reservoir.

Balconies Cliffs-Cave Loop. Grab your flashlight before heading out from the Chaparral Trailhead parking lot for this 2.4-mile loop that takes you through the Balconies Caves. This trail is especially beautiful in spring when an abundance of wildflowers carpets the canyon floor. About 0.6 miles from the start of the trail, turn left to begin ascending the Balconies Cliffs Trail, where you'll be rewarded with close-up views of Machete Peak and other steep, vertical formations; you'll probably run across a few rock climbers testing their skills. *Easy.* ⊠ *Pinnacles National Park* ✥ *From West Pinnacles Visitor Contact Station, drive about 2 miles to Chaparral Trailhead parking lot. Trail picks up on west side of lot.*

FAMILY **Moses Spring-Rim Trail Loop.** This is perhaps the most popular hike at Pinnacles, as it's relatively short (2.2 miles in typically 1.5 hours) and fun for both kids and adults alike. It takes you to the Bear Gulch cave system and if your timing is right, you'll pass by several seasonal waterfalls inside the caves (if it's been raining, check with a ranger as the caves could be flooded). The caves are usually closed in spring and early summer to protect the Townsend's big-ear bats and their pups. *Easy.* ⊠ *Trail can be accessed from overflow parking just past Bear Gulch Nature Center, on south side of lot.*

MOSS LANDING

17 miles north of Monterey; 12 miles north of Salinas.

Moss Landing is not much more than a couple of blocks of cafés and restaurants, art galleries, and studios, plus a busy fishing port, but therein lies its charm. It's a fine place to overnight or stop for a meal and get a dose of nature.

GETTING HERE AND AROUND
From Highway 1 north or south, exit at Moss Landing Road on the ocean side. MST buses serve Moss Landing via Watsonville.

TOURS
Elkhorn Slough Safari Nature Boat Tours. This outfit's naturalists lead two-hour tours of Elkhorn Slough aboard a 27-foot pontoon boat. Reservations are required. ⊠ *Moss Landing Harbor* ☎ *831/633–5555* ⊕ *www.elkhornslough.com* ⊠ *$35.*

ESSENTIALS
Visitor Information Moss Landing Chamber of Commerce ☎ *831/633–4501* ⊕ *www.mosslandingchamber.com.*

EXPLORING
Elkhorn Slough National Estuarine Research Reserve. The reserve's 1,400 acres of tidal flats and salt marshes form a complex environment that supports some 300 species of birds. A walk along the meandering waterways and wetlands can reveal hawks, white-tailed kites, owls, herons, and egrets. Also living or visiting here are sea otters, sharks, rays, and many other animals. ■ TIP→ **On weekends, guided walks from the visitor center to the heron rookery begin at 10 and 1.** ⊠ *1700 Elkhorn Rd., Watsonville* ☎ *831/728–2822* ⊕ *www.elkhornslough.org* ⊠ *$4 day use fee* ⊙ *Wed.–Sun. 9–5.*

WHERE TO EAT AND STAY
$$
SEAFOOD
✕ **Phil's Fish Market & Eatery.** Exquisitely fresh, simply prepared seafood (try the cioppino) is on the menu at this warehouselike restaurant on the harbor; all kinds of glistening fish are for sale at the market in the front. ■ TIP→ **Phil's Snack Shack, a tiny sandwich-and-smoothie joint, serves quicker meals at the north end of town.** $ *Average main: $17* ⊠ *7600 Sandholdt Rd.* ☎ *831/633–2152* ⊕ *www.philsfishmarket.com.*

$$
B&B/INN
⌇ **Captain's Inn.** Commune with nature and pamper yourself with upscale creature comforts at this green-certified getaway in the heart of town. **Pros:** walk to restaurants and shops; tranquil natural setting; homey atmosphere. **Cons:** rooms in historic building don't have water views; far from urban amenities; not appropriate for young children. $ *Rooms from: $155* ⊠ *8122 Moss Landing Rd.* ☎ *831/633–5550* ⊕ *www.captainsinn.com* ⊅ *10 rooms* ⏐⊘⏐ *Breakfast.*

SPORTS AND THE OUTDOORS
KAYAKING
Monterey Bay Kayaks. Rent a kayak to paddle out into Elkhorn Slough for up-close wildlife encounters. ⊠ *2390 Hwy. 1, at North Harbor* ☎ *831/373–5357, 800/649–5357 toll free* ⊕ *www.montereybaykayaks.com.*

WATSONVILLE

7 miles north of Moss Landing.

If ever a city was built on berries, Watsonville is it. Produce has long driven the economy here, and this is where the Santa Cruz County Fair takes place each September.

GETTING HERE AND AROUND

From Santa Cruz or Monterey, follow Highway 1 to Watsonville. From U.S. 101, take Highway 152 West from Gilroy (a curving but scenic road over the mountains) or Highway 129 West from just north of San Juan Bautista. MST and Santa Cruz METRO buses connect at the Watsonville Transit Center, at Rodriguez Street and West Lake Avenue.

EXPLORING

FAMILY **Agricultural History Project.** One feature of the Santa Cruz County Fairgrounds is the Agricultural History Project, which preserves the history of farming in the Pajaro Valley. In the Codiga Center and Museum you can examine antique tractors and milking machines, peruse an exhibit on the era when Watsonville was the "frozen food capital of the West," and watch experts restore farm implements and vehicles. ⊠ *2601 E. Lake Ave., Hwy. 152, at Carlton Rd.* ☎ *831/724–5898* ⊕ *www.aghistoryproject.org* ⊠ *$2* ☉ *Thurs.–Sun. noon–4.*

APTOS

7 miles north of Watsonville.

Backed by a redwood forest and facing the sea, downtown Aptos—known as Aptos Village—is a place of wooden walkways and false-fronted shops. Antiques dealers cluster along Trout Gulch Road, off Soquel Drive east of Highway 1.

GETTING HERE AND AROUND

Use Highway 1 to reach Aptos from Santa Cruz or Monterey. Exit at State Park Drive to reach the main shopping hub and Aptos Village. You can also exit at Freedom Boulevard or Rio del Mar. Soquel Drive is the main artery through town.

ESSENTIALS

Visitor Information Aptos Chamber of Commerce ⊠ *7605-A Old Dominion Ct.* ☎ *831/688–1467* ⊕ *www.aptoschamber.com.*

BEACHES

Seacliff State Beach. Sandstone bluffs tower above popular Seacliff State Beach. You can fish off the pier, which leads out to a sunken World War I tanker ship built of concrete. Leashed dogs are allowed on the beach. **Amenities:** food and drink; lifeguards; parking (fee); showers; toilets. **Best for:** sunset; swimming; walking. ⊠ *201 State Park Dr., off Hwy. 1* ☎ *831/685–6442* ⊕ *www.parks.ca.gov* ⊠ *$10 per vehicle* ☉ *Daily 8 am–sunset.*

SAN JUAN BAUTISTA

About as close to early-19th-century California as you can get, San Juan Bautista (15 miles east of Watsonville on Highway 156) has been protected from development since 1933, when much of it became a state park. Small antiques shops and restaurants occupy the Old West and art deco buildings that line 3rd Street.

The wide green plaza of San Juan Bautista State Historic Park is ringed by 18th- and 19th-century buildings, many of them open to the public.

The cemetery of the long, low, colon-naded mission church contains the unmarked graves of more than 4,300 Native American converts. Nearby is an adobe home furnished with Spanish-colonial antiques, a hotel frozen in the 1860s, a blacksmith shop, a stable, a pioneer cabin, and a jailhouse.

The first Saturday of each month, costumed volunteers engage in quilting bees, tortilla making, and other frontier activities. ⊕ *www.san-juan-bautista.ca.us.*

WHERE TO EAT AND STAY

$$$
MEDITERRANEAN
✕ **Bittersweet Bistro.** A large old tavern with cathedral ceilings houses this popular bistro, where chef-owner Thomas Vinolus draws culinary inspiration from the Mediterranean. The menu changes seasonally, but regular highlights include paella, seafood puttanesca, and pepper-crusted skirt steak. The decadent chocolate desserts are not to be missed. Breakfast and lunch are available in the casual Bittersweet Café. Leashed dogs are welcome on the outdoor patio, where they can order from a special menu for pooches. $ *Average main: $25* ⊠ *787 Rio Del Mar Blvd., off Hwy. 1* ☎ *831/662–9799* ⊕ *www.bittersweetbistro.com.*

$$$
HOTEL
FAMILY
Best Western Seacliff Inn. Families and business travelers like this 6-acre property near Seacliff State Beach that's more resort than hotel. **Pros:** walking distance to the beach; family-friendly; hot breakfast buffet. **Cons:** close to freeway; occasional nighttime bar noise. $ *Rooms from: $180* ⊠ *7500 Old Dominion Ct.* ☎ *831/688–7300, 800/367–2003* ⊕ *www.seacliffinn.com* ⇌ *139 rooms, 10 suites* ⦿ *Breakfast.*

$$$
B&B/INN
Flora Vista. Multicolor fields of flowers, strawberries, and veggies unfold in every direction at this luxury neo-Georgian inn set on 2 acres just south of Aptos. **Pros:** private; near Sand Dollar Beach; flowers everywhere. **Cons:** no restaurants or nightlife within walking distance; not a good place for kids. $ *Rooms from: $195* ⊠ *1258 San Andreas Rd., La Selva Beach* ☎ *831/724–8663, 877/753–5672* ⊕ *www.floravistainn.com* ⇌ *5 rooms* ⦿ *Breakfast.*

$$$$
RESORT
FAMILY
Seascape Beach Resort. It's easy to unwind at this full-fledged resort on a bluff overlooking Monterey Bay. **Pros:** time share–style apartments; access to miles of beachfront; superb views. **Cons:** far from city life; most bathrooms are small. $ *Rooms from: $300* ⊠ *1 Seascape Resort Dr.* ☎ *831/688–6800, 800/929–7727* ⊕ *www.seascaperesort.com* ⇌ *285 suites* ⦿ *No meals.*

CAPITOLA AND SOQUEL

4 miles northwest of Aptos.

On the National Register of Historic places as California's first seaside resort town, the village of Capitola has been in a holiday mood since the late 1800s. Casual eateries, surf shops, and ice-cream parlors pack its walkable downtown. Inland, across Highway 1, antiques shops line Soquel Drive in the town of Soquel. Wineries dot the Santa Cruz Mountains beyond.

GETTING HERE AND AROUND

From Santa Cruz or Monterey, follow Highway 1 to the Capitola/Soquel (Bay Avenue) exit about 7 miles south of Santa Cruz and head west to reach Capitola and east to access Soquel Village. On summer weekends, park for free in the lot behind the Crossroads Center, a block west of the freeway, and hop aboard the free Capitola Shuttle to the village.

ESSENTIALS

Visitor Information Capitola-Soquel Chamber of Commerce ⊠ *716-G Capitola Ave., Capitola* ☎ *831/475–6522* ⊕ *www.capitolachamber.com.*

BEACHES

New Brighton State Beach. Once the site of a Chinese fishing village, New Brighton is now a popular surfing and camping spot. Its Pacific Migrations Visitor Center traces the history of the Chinese and other peoples who settled around Monterey Bay and documents the migratory patterns of the area's wildlife, such as monarch butterflies and gray whales. Leashed dogs are allowed in the park. New Brighton connects with Seacliff Beach, and at low tide you can walk or run along this scenic stretch of sand for nearly 16 miles south (though you might have to wade through a few creeks). ■TIP➔ The 1½-mile stroll from New Brighton to Seacliff's concrete ship is a local favorite. **Amenities:** parking (fee); showers; toilets. **Best for:** sunset; swimming; walking. ⊠ *1500 State Park Dr., off Hwy. 1, Capitola* ☎ *831/464–6330* ⊕ *www.parks. ca.gov* ⊠ *$10 per vehicle* ⊗ *Day use daily 8 am–sunset.*

WHERE TO EAT

$
SEAFOOD
FAMILY
✕ **Carpo's.** Locals love this casual counter where seafood predominates but you can also order burgers, salads, and steaks. Baskets of fresh battered snapper are among the favorites, along with calamari, prawns, seafood kebabs, fish and chips, and homemade olallieberry pie. Many items cost less than $10. ■TIP➔ Come early for lunch or dinner to beat the crowds. $ *Average main: $10* ⊠ *2400 Porter St., at Hwy. 1, Capitola* ☎ *831/476–6260* ⊕ *www.carposrestaurant.com/default1.html.*

$
CAFÉ
FAMILY
✕ **Gayle's Bakery & Rosticceria.** Whether you're in the mood for an orange-olallieberry muffin, a wild rice and chicken salad, or tri-tip on garlic toast, this bakery-deli's varied menu is likely to satisfy. Munch your flourless chocolate macaroon on the shady patio, or dig into the daily blue-plate dinner—Yankee pot roast, perhaps, or white-wine coq au vin—amid the whirl of activity inside. $ *Average main: $12* ⊠ *504 Bay Ave., at Capitola Ave., Capitola* ☎ *831/462–1200* ⊕ *www. gaylesbakery.com.*

$$ ✕ **Michael's on Main.** Creative variations on classic comfort food draw lively crowds to this upscale but casual creekside eatery. Chef Michael Clark's menu changes seasonally, but might include pork osso bucco in red-wine tomato-citrus sauce or pistachio-crusted salmon with mint vinaigrette. For a quiet conversation spot, ask for a table on the romantic patio overlooking the creek. The busy bar area hosts live music Tuesday through Saturday. $ *Average main: $22* ⊠ *2591 Main St., at Porter St., Capitola* ☎ *831/479–9777* ⊕ *www.michaels onmain.net* ⊘ *Closed Mon.*

AMERICAN

$$$$ ✕ **Shadowbrook.** To get to this romantic spot overlooking Soquel Creek, you can take a cable car or walk the stairs down a steep, fern-lined bank beside a running waterfall. Dining room options include the rooftop Redwood Room, the wood-paneled Wine Cellar, the creekside, glass-enclosed Greenhouse, the Fireplace Room, and the airy Garden Room with a cypress tree. Prime rib and grilled seafood are the stars of the simple menu. Less expensive light entrées are available in the lounge. $ *Average main: $32* ⊠ *1750 Wharf Rd., at Lincoln Ave., Capitola* ☎ *831/475–1511* ⊕ *www.shadowbrook-capitola.com* ⊘ *No lunch.*

EUROPEAN

CALIFORNIA'S OLDEST RESORT TOWN

As far as anyone knows for certain, Capitola is the oldest seaside resort town on the Pacific Coast. In 1856 a pioneer acquired Soquel Landing, the picturesque lagoon and beach where Soquel Creek empties into the bay, and built a wharf. Another man opened a campground along the shore, and his daughter named it Capitola after a heroine in a novel series. After the train came to town in the 1870s, thousands of vacationers began arriving to bask in the sun on the glorious beach.

WHERE TO STAY

$$$$ ⛿ **Inn at Depot Hill.** This inventively designed B&B in a former rail depot views itself as a link to the era of luxury train travel. **Pros:** short walk to beach and village; historic charm; excellent service. **Cons:** fills quickly; hot tub conversation on the patio may irk second-floor guests. $ *Rooms from: $299* ⊠ *250 Monterey Ave., Capitola* ☎ *831/462–3376, 800/572–2632* ⊕ *www.innatdepothill.com* ⇄ *12 rooms* ⎮◯⎮ *Breakfast.*

B&B/INN

SANTA CRUZ

5 miles west of Capitola; 48 miles north of Monterey.

The big city on this stretch of the California coast, Santa Cruz (pop. 57,500) is less manicured than Carmel or Monterey. Long known for its surfing and its amusement-filled beach boardwalk, the town is a mix of grand Victorian-era homes and rinky-dink motels. The opening of the University of California campus in the 1960s swung the town sharply to the left politically, and the counterculture more or less lives on here. At the same time, the revitalized downtown and an insane real-estate market reflect the city's proximity to Silicon Valley and to a growing wine country in the surrounding mountains.

GETTING HERE AND AROUND

From the San Francisco Bay Area, take Highway 17 south over the mountains to Santa Cruz, where it merges with Highway 1. Use Highway 1 to get around the area. The Santa Cruz Transit Center is at 920 Pacific Avenue, at Front Street, a short walk from the Wharf and Boardwalk, with connections to public transit throughout the Monterey Bay and San Francisco Bay areas. You can purchase day passes for Santa Cruz METRO buses (⇨ *Bus Travel, in Planner*) here.

ESSENTIALS

Visitor Information Santa Cruz County Conference and Visitors Council ⊠ *303 Water St., #100* ☎ *831/425–1234, 800/833–3494* ⊕ *www.santacruz.org.*

EXPLORING

TOP ATTRACTIONS

Pacific Avenue. When you've had your fill of the city's beaches and waters, take a stroll in downtown Santa Cruz, especially on Pacific Avenue between Laurel and Water streets. Vintage boutiques and mountain sports stores, sushi bars and Mexican restaurants, day spas, and nightclubs keep the main drag and the surrounding streets hopping from midmorning until late evening.

FAMILY **Santa Cruz Beach Boardwalk.** Santa Cruz has been a seaside resort since the mid-19th century. Along one end of the broad, south-facing beach, the Boardwalk has entertained holidaymakers for more than a century. Its Looff carousel and classic wooden Giant Dipper roller coaster, both dating from the early 1900s, are surrounded by high-tech thrill rides and easygoing kiddie rides with ocean views. Video and arcade games, a mini-golf course, and a laser-tag arena pack one gigantic building, which is open daily even if the rides aren't running. You have to pay to play, but you can wander the entire boardwalk for free while sampling delicacies such as corn dogs and garlic fries. ⊠ *Along Beach St.* ☎ *831/423–5590 info line* ⊕ *www.beachboardwalk.com* 🎟 *$32 day pass for unlimited rides, or pay per ride* ⊗ *Apr.–early Sept., daily; early Sept.–Mar., weekends and holidays, weather permitting; call for hrs* ⊗ *Some rides may be closed Sept.–May.*

FAMILY **Santa Cruz Municipal Wharf.** Jutting half a mile into the ocean near one end of the boardwalk, the century-old Municipal Wharf is lined with seafood restaurants, a wine bar, souvenir shops, and outfitters offering bay cruises, fishing trips, and boat rentals. A salty soundtrack drifts up from under the wharf, where barking sea lions lounge in heaps on the crossbeams. ■TIP➜ **Docents from the Seymour Marine Discovery Center lead free 30-minute tours on weekeds at 1 and 3; meet at the stage on the west side of the wharf between Olitas Cantina and Marini's Candies.** ⊠ *Beach St., at Pacific Ave.* ☎ *831/459–3800 tour information* ⊕ *www.santacruzwharf.com.*

Santa Cruz Surfing Museum. This museum inside the Mark Abbott Memorial Lighthouse chronicles local surfing history. Photographs show old-time surfers, and a display of boards includes rarities such as a heavy redwood plank predating the fiberglass era and the remains of a modern board chomped by a great white shark. Surfer docents reminisce about the good old days. ⊠ *Lighthouse Point Park, 701 W. Cliff Dr., near Pelton Ave.* ☎ *831/420–6289* ⊕ *www.santacruzsurfingmuseum.org* ⊠ *$2* ☉ *Sept.–June, Thurs.–Mon. noon–4; July–Aug., Wed.–Mon. 10–5.*

West Cliff Drive. The road that winds along an oceanfront bluff from the municipal wharf to Natural Bridges State Beach makes for a spectacular drive, but it's even more fun to walk, blade, or bike the paved path that parallels the road. Surfers bob and swoosh in Monterey Bay at several points near the foot of the bluff, especially at a break known as Steamer Lane. Named for a surfer who died here in 1965, the nearby Mark Abbott Memorial Lighthouse stands at Point Santa Cruz, the cliff's major promontory. From here you can watch pinnipeds hang out, sunbathe, and frolic on Seal Rock.

WORTH NOTING

FAMILY **Monterey Bay National Marine Sanctuary Exploration Center.** The interactive and multimedia exhibits at this fascinating interpretive center reveal and explain the treasures of the nation's largest marine sanctuary. The two-story building, across from the main beach and municipal wharf, has films and exhibits about migratory species, watersheds, underwater canyons, kelp forests, and intertidal zones. The second-floor deck has stellar ocean views and an interactive station that provides real-time weather, surf, and buoy reports. ⊠ *35 Pacific Ave.* ☎ *831/421–9993* ⊕ *montereybay.noaa.gov/vc/sec* ⊠ *Free* ☉ *Wed.–Sun. 10–5.*

Mystery Spot. Hokey tourist trap or genuine scientific enigma? Since 1940, curious throngs baffled by the Mystery Spot have made it one of the most visited attractions in Santa Cruz. The laws of gravity and physics don't appear to apply in this tiny patch of redwood forest, where balls roll uphill and people stand on a slant. ■TIP→ Purchasing online tickets ($6) is advised for weekend and holiday visits. ⊠ *465 Mystery Spot Rd., off Branciforte Dr. (north off Hwy. 1)* ☎ *831/423–8897* ⊕ *www.mysteryspot.com* ⊠ *$5 on-site, $6 in advance, parking $5* ☉ *Late May–early Sept., daily 10–7; early Sept.–late May, weekdays 10–4, weekends 10–5.*

■ OFF THE BEATEN PATH

Santa Cruz Mountains wineries. Highway 9 heads northeast from Santa Cruz into hills densely timbered with massive coastal redwoods. The road winds through the lush San Lorenzo Valley, past hamlets consisting of a few cafés, antiques shops, and old-style tourist cabins. Residents of the hunting-and-fishing persuasion coexist with hardcore flower-power survivors, and a new generation has joined the pioneers who opened wineries decades ago. Mountain grapes produce some superb Chardonnays, Pinot Noirs, and Cabernet Sauvignons, among other wines. To sample some, you can start a **winery tour** in downtown Santa Cruz at Storrs Winery, at 303 Potrero Street—a block off River Street, which, heading north from here becomes Highway 9. Drive north to Felton to visit Hallcrest Vineyards and Organic Wine Works, just west of Highway 9 on Felton Empire Road downtown. Continue north on Highway 9 and east on Bear Creek Road to the classy Byington and David Bruce wineries, both in Los Gatos. ■TIP→ The Santa Cruz Mountains Winegrowers Association (⊕ www.

scmwa.com) distributes a wine-touring map at member wineries and many lodgings and attractions around Santa Cruz.

Surf City Vintners. A dozen tasting rooms of limited-production wineries occupy renovated warehouse spaces west of the beach. MJA, Storrs, and Equinox are good places to start. Also here are the Santa Cruz Mountain Brewing Company and El Salchicheroa, popular for its home-made sausages, jams, and pickled and candied vegetables. ⊠ *Swift Street Courtyard, 334 Ingalls St., at Swift St., off Hwy. 1 (Mission St.)* ⊕ *www. surfcityvintners.com.*

UC Santa Cruz. The 2,000-acre University of California Santa Cruz campus nestles in the forested hills above town. Its sylvan setting, ocean vistas, and redwood architecture make the university worth a visit, as does its **arboretum** ($5, open daily from 9 to 5), whose walking path leads through areas dedicated to the plants of California, Australia, New Zealand, and South Africa. ■TIP→ **Free shuttles help students and visitors get around campus, and you can join a guided tour (online reservation required).** ⊠ *Main entrance at Bay and High Sts. (turn left on High for arboretum)* ☎ *831/459–0111* ⊕ *www.ucsc.edu/visit*

Vinocruz. A slick, contemporary tasting space near the Santa Cruz Museum of Art & History, Vinocruz pours samples from more than five-dozen regional wineries, including small operations without tasting rooms of their own. ⊠ *Abbott Square, 725 Front St., off Cooper St.* ☎ *831/426–8466* ⊕ *www.vinocruz.com* ☉ *Tues.–Thurs. noon–7, Fri. and Sat. noon–8, Sun. 1–6.*

BEACHES

FAMILY **Natural Bridges State Beach.** At the end of West Cliff Drive lies this stretch of soft sand edged with tide pools and sea-sculpted rock bridges. ■TIP→ **From October to early March a colony of monarch butterflies roosts in a eucalyptus grove. Amenities:** lifeguards; parking (fee); toilets. **Best for:** sunrise; sunset; surfing; swimming. ⊠ *2531 W. Cliff Dr.* ☎ *831/423–4609* ⊕ *www.parks.ca.gov* ☒ *Beach free, parking $10* ☉ *Beach: daily 8 am–sunset. Visitor center: Oct.–Feb., daily 10–4; Mar.–Sept., weekends 10–4.*

Twin Lakes State Beach. Stretching a half mile along the coast on both sides of the small-craft jetties, Twin Lakes is one of Monterey Bay's sunniest beaches. It encompasses Seabright State Beach (with access in a residential neighborhood on the upcoast side) and Black's Beach on the downcoast side. Families often come here to sunbathe, picnic, and hike the nature trail around adjacent Schwann Lake. Parking is tricky on summer weekends from April through September, but you can park all day in the harbor pay lot and walk here. Leashed dogs are allowed. **Amenities:** food and drink; lifeguards (seasonal); parking; showers; toilets; water sports (seasonal). **Best for:** sunset; surfing; swimming; walking. ⊠ *7th Ave., at East Cliff Dr.* ☎ *831/427–4868* ⊕ *www.parks.ca.gov/?page_id=547.*

WHERE TO EAT

$$
SEAFOOD
✕ **Crow's Nest.** A classic California beachside restaurant, the Crow's Nest sits right on the water in Santa Cruz Harbor. Vintage surfboards and local surf photography line the walls in the main dining room, and nearly every table overlooks sand and surf. Breakfast favorites include crab-cake eggs Benedict and olallieberry pancakes. Seafood and steaks, served with local veggies, dominate the lunch and dinner menus; favorite appetizers include fried calamari and the chilled shrimp-stuffed artichoke. For sweeping ocean views and fish tacos, burgers, and other casual fare, head upstairs to the Breakwater Bar & Grill. ⑤ *Average main: $20* ✉ *2218 E. Cliff Dr., west of 7th Ave.* ☎ *831/476–4560* ⊕ *www.crowsnest-santacruz.com.*

$$
MEDITERRANEAN
✕ **Laili Restaurant.** Exotic Mediterranean flavors with an Afghan twist take center stage at this artsy, stylish space with soaring ceilings. Traditional dishes range from Moroccan beet salad and apricot chicken flatbread to pomegranate eggplant and *maush-awa*, a soup with lentils, split peas, and lamb, topped with yogurt. The menus also include house-made pastas and numerous vegetarian options; fresh *naan* and delectable chutneys and dips accompany every meal. Evenings are especially lively, when locals come to relax over wine and soft jazz at the blue-concrete bar, the heated patio with twinkly lights, or at a communal table near the open kitchen. ⑤ *Average main: $18* ✉ *101–B Cooper St., near Pacific Ave.* ☎ *831/423–4545* ⊕ *lailirestaurant.com* ⊙ *Closed Mon.*

$$
ITALIAN
✕ **La Posta.** Authentic Italian fare made with fresh local produce lures diners into cozy, modern-rustic La Posta. Nearly everything is housemade, from the pizzas and breads baked in the brick oven to the pasta and the vanilla-bean gelato. The seasonal menu includes flavorful dishes such as fried artichokes, ravioli filled with crab, and sautéed fish from local waters. ⑤ *Average main: $22* ✉ *538 Seabright Ave., at Logan St.* ☎ *831/457–2782* ⊕ *www.lapostarestaurant.com* ⊙ *Closed Mon. No lunch.*

$$$
EUROPEAN
✕ **Oswald.** Sophisticated yet unpretentious European-inspired California cooking is the order of the day at this intimate and stylish bistro. The menu changes seasonally but might include such items as sautéed abalone or roasted rack of lamb. The creative concoctions poured at the slick marble bar include whiskey mixed with apple and lemon juice, and tequila with celery juice and lime. ⑤ *Average main: $25* ✉ *121 Soquel Ave., at Front St.* ☎ *831/423–7427* ⊕ *www.oswaldrestaurant.com* ⊙ *Closed Mon. Lunch Fri. only.*

$
AMERICAN
✕ **Seabright Brewery.** Great burgers, big salads, and stellar microbrews make this a favorite hangout in the youthful Seabright neighborhood east of downtown. Sit outside on the patio or inside at a comfortable, spacious booth; both are popular with families. ⑤ *Average main: $13* ✉ *519 Seabright Ave., at Murray St.* ☎ *831/426–2739* ⊕ *www.seabrightbrewery.com.*

$$
MEDITERRANEAN
✕ **Soif.** Wine reigns at this sleek bistro and wineshop that takes its name from the French word for thirst. The selections come from near and far, and you can order many of them by the taste or glass. Mediterranean-inspired small plates and entrées are served at the copper-top bar, the big communal table, and private tables. A jazz combo or solo pianist plays on some evenings. ⑤ *Average main: $22* ✉ *105 Walnut Ave., at Pacific Ave.* ☎ *831/423–2020* ⊕ *www.soifwine.com* ⊙ *No lunch.*

$ ✕ **Zachary's.** This noisy café filled with students and families defines
AMERICAN the funky essence of Santa Cruz. It also dishes up great breakfasts: stay
simple with sourdough pancakes, or go for Mike's Mess—eggs scrambled with bacon, mushrooms, and home fries, then topped with sour
cream, melted cheese, and fresh tomatoes. ■ TIP→ If you arrive after 9
am, expect a long wait for a table; lunch is a shade calmer (closing time
is 2:30 pm). $ *Average main: $12* ⊠ *819 Pacific Ave.* ☏ *831/427–0646*
🕭 *Reservations not accepted* ⊘ *Closed Mon. No dinner.*

WHERE TO STAY

$$$ ⛴ **Babbling Brook Inn.** Though it's in the middle of Santa Cruz, this B&B
B&B/INN has lush gardens, a running stream, and tall trees that make you feel like
you're in a secluded wood. **Pros:** close to UCSC; within walking distance of downtown shops; woodsy feel. **Cons:** near a high school; some
rooms close to a busy street. $ *Rooms from: $185* ⊠ *1025 Laurel St.*
☏ *831/427–2437, 800/866–1131* ⊕ *www.babblingbrookinn.com* ⇔ *13
rooms* ⎮⊙⎮ *Breakfast.*

$$$$ ⛴ **Chaminade Resort & Spa.** Secluded on 300 hilltop acres of redwood
RESORT and eucalyptus forest with hiking trails, this mission-style complex commands expansive views of Monterey Bay. **Pros:** far from city life; spectacular property; ideal spot for romance and rejuvenation. **Cons:** must
drive to attractions and sights; near a major hospital. $ *Rooms from:*
$269 ⊠ *1 Chaminade La.* ☏ *800/283–6569 reservations, 831/475–5600*
⊕ *www.chaminade.com* ⇔ *112 rooms, 44 suites* ⎮⊙⎮ *No meals.*

$ ⛴ **Harbor Inn.** Family-run, friendly, and funky, this basic but sparkling-
B&B/INN clean lodge offers exceptional value just a few blocks from Santa Cruz
Harbor and Twin Lakes Beach. **Pros:** affordable; free Wi-Fi; park
your car and walk to the beach. **Cons:** not fancy; not near downtown. $ *Rooms from: $99* ⊠ *645 7th Ave.* ☏ *831/479–9731* ⊕ *www.*
harborinnsantacruz.com ⇔ *17 rooms, 2 suites.*

$$$ ⛴ **Hotel Paradox.** Less than 2 miles from the wharf and boardwalk and
HOTEL a short walk to Pacific Avenue, this stylish, forest-theme complex is
among the few full-service hotels in town. **Pros:** close to downtown and
main beach; alternative to beach-oriented lodgings; contemporary feel.
Cons: pool area can get crowded on warm-weather days; some rooms
on the small side. $ *Rooms from: $200* ⊠ *611 Ocean St.* ☏ *831/425–*
7100, 855/425–7200 ⊕ *www.thehotelparadox.com* ⇔ *164 rooms, 6*
suites ⎮⊙⎮ *No meals.*

$$$ ⛴ **Pacific Blue Inn.** Green themes predominate in this three-story, eco-friendly
B&B/INN B&B, built from scratch in 2009 on a sliver of prime property downtown.
Pros: free parking; free bicycles; right in downtown. **Cons:** tiny property; not
suitable for children. $ *Rooms from: $189* ⊠ *636 Pacific Ave.* ☏ *831/600–*
8880 ⊕ *www.pacificblueinn.com* ⇔ *9 rooms* ⎮⊙⎮ *No meals.*

$$$$ ⛴ **Santa Cruz Dream Inn.** A short stroll from the boardwalk and wharf, this
HOTEL full-service luxury hotel is the only lodging in Santa Cruz directly on the
beach. **Pros:** directly on the beach; easy parking; walk to boardwalk and
downtown. **Cons:** expensive; area gets congested on summer weekends.
$ *Rooms from: $309* ⊠ *175 W. Cliff Dr.* ☏ *831/426–4330, 866/774–*
7735 reservations 🖷 *831/427–2025* ⊕ *www.dreaminnsantacruz.com*
⇔ *149 rooms, 16 suites* ⎮⊙⎮ *No meals.*

$$$
B&B/INN
🛏 **West Cliff Inn.** A posh nautical-theme inn with views of the boardwalk and Monterey Bay, the West Cliff perches on the bluffs across from Cowell Beach. **Pros:** killer views; walking distance of the beach; close to downtown. **Cons:** boardwalk noise; street traffic. $ *Rooms from: $185* ✉ *174 West Cliff Dr.* ☎ *800/979–0910 toll free, 831/457–2200* ⊕ *www.westcliffinn.com* ⇆ *7 rooms, 2 suites, 1 cottage* ⏹ *Breakfast.*

NIGHTLIFE AND THE ARTS

NIGHTLIFE

Catalyst. Dance with the crowds at this huge, grimy, and fun club that books rock, indie rock, punk, death-metal, reggae, and other acts. ✉ *1011 Pacific Ave.* ☎ *831/423–1338* ⊕ *www.catalystclub.com.*

Kuumbwa Jazz Center. The renowned center draws top performers such as the Brubeck Brothers Quartet, Ladysmith Black Mambazo, and Chick Corea; the café serves meals an hour before most shows. ✉ *320–2 Cedar St.* ☎ *831/427–2227* ⊕ *kuumbwajazz.org.*

Moe's Alley. Blues, salsa, reggae, funk: delightfully casual Moe's presents it all (and more), six nights a week. ✉ *1535 Commercial Way* ☎ *831/479–1854* ⊕ *www.moesalley.com.*

THE ARTS

Santa Cruz Baroque Festival. From February through May the festival presents classical music at various venues and holds pre- and post-season events. The focus is on 17th- and 18th-century composers such as Bach and Handel. ☎ *831/457–9693* ⊕ *www.scbaroque.org.*

SPORTS AND THE OUTDOORS

ADVENTURE TOURS

Mount Hermon Adventures. Zip-line through the redwoods, climb a giant live oak tree, and hunt for edibles or learn about sand hill habitat restoration at this adventure center in the Santa Cruz Mountains. On some summer weekends, there's an aerial adventure course with obstacles and challenges in the redwoods. ■**TIP→ To join a tour (reservations essential) you must be at least 10 years old and weigh between 75 and 250 pounds.** ✉ *17 Conference Dr., 9 miles north of downtown Santa Cruz near Felton, Mount Hermon* ☎ *831/430–4357* ⊕ *www. mounthermonadventures.com* ▣ *From $50.*

BICYCLING

Another Bike Shop. Mountain bikers should head here for tips on the best area trails and to browse cutting-edge gear made and tested locally. ✉ *2361 Mission St., at King St.* ☎ *831/427–2232* ⊕ *www.anotherbikeshop.com.*

BOATS AND CHARTERS

Chardonnay II **Sailing Charters.** The 70-foot *Chardonnay II* departs year-round from Santa Cruz yacht harbor on whale-watching, sunset, and other cruises around Monterey Bay. Most regularly scheduled excursions cost $64; food and drink are served on many of them. Reservations are essential. ✉ *Santa Cruz West Harbor, 790 Mariner Park Way* ☎ *831/423–1213* ⊕ *www.chardonnay.com.*

O'Neill: A Santa Cruz Icon

O'Neill wet suits and beachwear weren't exactly born in Santa Cruz, but as far as most of the world is concerned, the O'Neill brand is synonymous with Santa Cruz and surfing legend.

The O'Neill wet-suit story began in 1952, when Jack O'Neill and his brother Robert opened their first Surf Shop in a garage across from San Francisco's Ocean Beach. While shaping balsa surfboards and selling accessories, the O'Neills experimented with solutions to a common surfer problem: frigid waters. Tired of being forced back to shore, blue-lipped and shivering, after just 20 or 30 minutes riding the waves, they played with various materials and eventually designed a neoprene vest.

In 1959 Jack moved his Surf Shop 90 miles south to Cowell's Beach in Santa Cruz. It quickly became a popular surf hangout, and O'Neill's new wet suits began to sell like hotcakes. In the early 1960s, the company opened a warehouse for manufacturing on a larger scale. Santa Cruz soon became a major surf city, attracting wave riders to prime breaks at Steamer Lane, Pleasure Point, and the Hook. In 1965 O'Neill pioneered the first wet-suit boots, and in 1971 Jack's son invented the surf leash. By 1980, O'Neill stood at the top of the world wet-suit market.

Stagnaro Sport Fishing, Charters, & Whale Watching Cruises. Stagnaro operates salmon, albacore, and rock-cod fishing expeditions; the fees (from $50 to $85) include bait. The company also runs whale-watching, dolphin, and sea-life cruises ($46) year-round. ⊠ *Santa Cruz West Harbor* ☎ *831/427–2334, 800/979–3370 tickets, 212/209–3370 international tickets* ⊕ *www.stagnaros.com.*

GOLF

Pasatiempo Golf Club. Designed by famed golf architect Dr. Alister MacKenzie in 1929 this semiprivate course, set amid undulating hills just above the city, is among the nation's top championship courses. Golfers rave about the spectacular views and challenging terrain. According to the club, MacKenzie, who also designed the exclusive Cypress Point course, in Pebble Beach, and Augusta National, home of the Masters Golf Tournament, declared this his favorite layout. ⊠ *20 Clubhouse Rd.* ☎ *831/459–9155* ⊕ *www.pasatiempo.com* ⚑ *From $230* ⛳ *18 holes, 6125 yards, par 72.*

KAYAKING

Kayak Connection. From March through May, participants in this outfit's tours mingle with gray whales and their calves on their northward journey to Alaska. Throughout the year, the company rents kayaks and paddleboards and conducts tours of Natural Bridges State Beach, Capitola, and Elkhorn Slough. Most regularly scheduled tours cost $55. ⊠ *Santa Cruz Harbor, 413 Lake Ave. #3* ☎ *831/479–1121* ⊕ *www. kayakconnection.com.*

Venture Quest Kayaking. Explore hidden coves and kelp forests on guided nature tours that depart from Santa Cruz Wharf. An introductory lesson and two-hour kayak tour costs $58. A three-hour kayak rental runs $30, including wet suit and gear. Venture Quest also arranges tours at other Monterey Bay destinations, including Capitola and Elkhorn Slough. ✉ *No. 2 Santa Cruz Wharf* ☎ *831/427–2267 kayak hotline, 831/425–8445 rental office* ⊕ *www.kayaksantacruz.com.*

SURFING

Pleasure Point. Surfers gather for the spectacular waves and sunsets here. ✉ *E. Cliff and Pleasure Point Drs.*

Steamer Lane. This area near the lighthouse on West Cliff Drive has a decent break. Steamer Lane hosts several competitions in summer.

EQUIPMENT AND LESSONS

Club-Ed Surf School and Camps. Find out what all the fun is about at Club-Ed. Your first private or group lesson ($85 and up) includes all equipment. ✉ *Cowell's Beach, at Santa Cruz Dream Inn* ☎ *831/464–0177* ⊕ *www.club-ed.com.*

Cowell's Beach Surf Shop. This shop sells gear, clothing, and swimwear; rents surfboards, standup paddleboards, and wet suits; and offers lessons. ✉ *30 Front St.* ☎ *831/427–2355* ⊕ *www.cowellssurfshop.com.*

SHOPPING

Annieglass. The works of famed Santa Cruz glass artist Annie Morhauser are on display at the Smithsonian and New York's MOMA—but at the gallery in Cooper Square you can collect your own luxury Annieglass tableware, decorative accessories, and jewelry, all designed and handmade in Santa Cruz County. The store also sells discounted studio seconds with barely perceptible flaws and gift items made by other artists. ✉ *110 Cooper St.* ☎ *831/427–4260* ⊕ *www.annieglass.com.*

Bookshop Santa Cruz. The town's best and most beloved independent bookstore has been sating readers' thirst for new, used, and discount books since 1966. The children's section is especially comprehensive, and the shop's special events calendar is packed with readings, social mixers, book signings, and discussions. ✉ *1520 Pacific Ave.* ☎ *831/423–0900* ⊕ *www.bookshopsantacruz.com.*

O'Neill Surf Shop. Local surfers get their wetties (wet suits) and other gear at this O'Neill store or the one in Capitola, at 1115 41st Ave. There's also a satellite shop on the Santa Cruz Boardwalk. ✉ *110 Cooper St.* ☎ *831/469–4377* ⊕ *www.oneill.com.*

The True Olive Connection. Taste your way through boutique extra-virgin olive oils and balsamic vinegars from around the world at this family-run shop just off Pacific Avenue. You can also pick up gourmet food products and olive-oil-based gift items. ✉ *106 Lincoln St.* ☎ *831/458–6457* ⊕ *www.trueoliveconnection.com.*

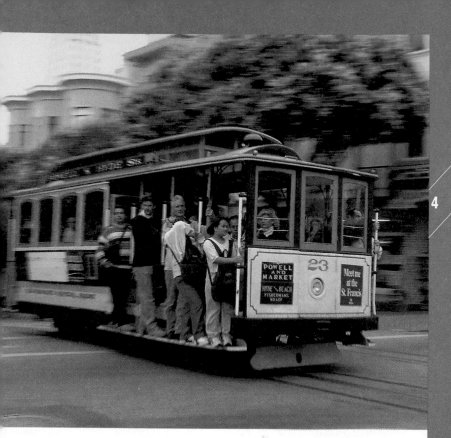

SAN FRANCISCO

WELCOME TO SAN FRANCISCO

TOP REASONS TO GO

★ **The bay:** It's hard not to gasp as you catch sight of sunlight dancing on the water when you crest a hill, or watch the Golden Gate Bridge vanish and reemerge in the summer fog.

★ **The food:** San Franciscans are serious about what they eat, and with good reason. Home to some of the nation's best chefs, top restaurants, and finest local produce, it's hard not to eat well here.

★ **The shopping:** Shopaholics visiting the city will not be disappointed: San Francisco is packed with browsing destinations, everything from quirky boutiques to massive malls.

★ **The good life:** A laid-back atmosphere, beautiful surroundings, and oodles of cultural, culinary, and aesthetic pleasures . . . if you spend too much time here, you might not leave!

★ **The great outdoors:** From Golden Gate Park to sidewalk cafés in North Beach, San Franciscans relish their outdoor spaces.

1 Union Square and Chinatown. Union Square has hotels, public transportation, and shopping; walking through Chinatown is like visiting a bustling street in Beijing.

2 SoMa and Civic Center. SoMa is anchored by SFMOMA and Yerba Buena Gardens; the city's performing arts venues are in Civic Center.

3 Nob Hill and Russian Hill. Nob Hill is old-money San Francisco; Russian Hill's steep streets have excellent eateries and shopping.

4 North Beach. This small Italian neighborhood is a great place to enjoy an espresso.

5 On the Waterfront. Head here to visit the exquisitely restored Ferry Building, Fisherman's Wharf, Pier 39, the Exploratorium and Ghirardelli Square.

6 The Marina and the Presidio. The Marina has trendy boutiques, restaurants, and cafés; the wooded Presidio offers great views of the Golden Gate Bridge.

5 WATERFRONT
Fisherman's Wharf
♦ Pier 39
4
Marina Green
Ghirardelli Square
Bay St.
NORTH BEACH
6 MARINA
Palace of Fine Arts
RUSSIAN HILL
Lombard St.
Columbus Ave.
♦ Coit Tower
TELEGRAPH HILL
101
Broadway
Hyde St.
Larkin St.
(tunnel)
3 CHINATOWN
Ferry Building
The Embarcadero
San Francisco–Oakland Bay Bridge
PACIFIC HEIGHTS
NOB HILL
Washington St.
Sacramento St.
California St.
1
FINANCIAL DISTRICT
Grant Ave.
Pewell St.
80
San Francisco Bay
Presidio Ave.
Pine St.
Bush St.
Polk St.
Van Ness Ave.
Franklin St.
Gough St.
Laguna St.
Post St.
Geary St.
UNION SQUARE
1st St.
2nd St.
Geary Blvd.
JAPANTOWN
Turk St.
Mission St.
4th St.
5th St.
Turk St.
Golden Gate Ave.
Fulton St.
Steiner St.
Divisadero St.
CIVIC CENTER
Hayes St.
Market St.
2 SOMA
8th St.
9th St.
10th St.
Folsom St.
Harrison St.
Bryant St.
Brannan St.
Townsend St.
Berry St.
7th St.
3rd St.
Fell St.
HAIGHT
Haight St.
Duboce
280
Buena Vista Park
Clayton St.
Stanyan St.
8 CASTRO
Castro Theater
Market St.
9
17th St.
Harrison St.
Potrero Ave.
Mariposa St.
Central Basin
Indiana St.
3rd St.
Castro St.
MISSION
Dolores St.
Guerrero St.
Mission St.
Van Ness Ave.
20th St.
Pennsylvania Ave.
Clarendon Ave.
Twin Peaks
24th St.
25th St.
101
Cesar Chavez St.
Islais Cr. Channel

San Francisco Bay

7 **Golden Gate Park and the Western Shoreline.** San Francisco's 1,000-acre backyard has sports fields, windmills, museums, and gardens; the windswept Western Shoreline stretches for miles.

8 **The Haight, the Castro, and Noe Valley.** After you've seen the blockbuster sights, come to these neighborhoods to see where the city's heart beats.

9 **The Mission.** This hip neighborhood has destination restaurants, bargain ethnic eateries, and a lively bar scene.

10 **Pacific Heights and Japantown.** Pacific Heights has some of the city's most opulent real estate; Japantown is packed with authentic Japanese shops and restaurants.

GETTING ORIENTED

San Francisco is a compact city; just 46.7 square miles. Essentially a tightly packed cluster of extremely diverse neighborhoods, the city dearly rewards walking. The areas that most visitors cover are easy (and safe) to reach on foot, but many have steep— make that *steep*—hills.

Updated by
Michele Bigley

On a 46½-square-mile strip of land between San Francisco
Bay and the Pacific Ocean, San Francisco has charms great
and small. Residents cherish their city for the same reasons
visitors do: the proximity to the bay, rows of Victorian homes
clinging precariously to the hillsides, the sun setting behind
the Golden Gate Bridge, the world-class cuisine. Locals and
visitors alike spend hours exploring downtown, Chinatown,
North Beach, the northern and western waterfronts, and
Golden Gate Park, along with colorful neighborhoods like
the Haight, the Mission murals, and the Castro.

The city's attraction, though, goes much deeper than its alluring physical space, from the diversity of its neighborhoods to its free-spirited tolerance. Take all these things together and you'll understand why many San Franciscans—despite the dizzying cost of living and the chilly summers—can't imagine calling anyplace else home.

You won't want to miss the City by the Bay's highlights, whether it's a cable car ride over Nob Hill, a walk down the Filbert Street Steps; or gazing at the thundering Pacific from the cliffs of Lincoln Park; or cheering the San Francisco Giants to *beat L.A.* in the lively AT&T Park; or eating freshly shucked oysters at the Ferry Building. San Francisco is a beautiful metropolis packed with diverse wonders that inspire at every turn.

PLANNING

WHEN TO GO

You can visit San Francisco comfortably any time of year. Probably the best months are September and October, when the city's summer-like weather brings outdoor concerts and festivals. The climate here always feels Mediterranean and moderate—with a foggy, sometimes chilly bite. The temperature rarely drops below 40°F, and anything warmer than

80°F is considered a heat wave. Be prepared for rain in winter, especially December and January. Winds off the ocean can add to the chill factor. That old joke about summer in San Francisco feeling like winter is true at heart, but once you move inland, it gets warmer. (And some locals swear that the thermostat has inched up in recent years.)

GETTING HERE AND AROUND
AIR TRAVEL

The major gateway to San Francisco is San Francisco International Airport (SFO), 15 miles south of the city. It's off U.S. 101 near Millbrae and San Bruno. Oakland International Airport (OAK) is across the bay, not much farther away from downtown San Francisco (via I–80 east and I–880 south), but rush-hour traffic on the Bay Bridge may lengthen travel times considerably. San Jose International Airport (SJC) is about 40 miles south of San Francisco; travel time depends largely on traffic flow, but plan on an hour and a half with moderate traffic.

Airports San Francisco International Airport (SFO). ✉ McDonnell and Link Rds. ☎ 800/435–9736, 650/821–8211 ⊕ www.flysfo.com. **Oakland International Airport** (OAK). ✉ 1 Airport Dr., Oakland ☎ 510/563–3300 ⊕ www.flyoakland.com. **San Jose International Airport** (SJC). ✉ 1701 Airport Blvd., San Jose ☎ 408/392–3600 ⊕ www.flysanjose.com.

Airport Transfers American Airporter ☎ 415/202–0733 ⊕ www.americanairporter.com. **BayPorter Express** ☎ 415/467–1800 ⊕ www.bayporter.com. **Caltrain** ☎ 800/660–4287 ⊕ www.caltrain.com. **East Bay Express Airporter** ☎ 877/526–0304 ⊕ www.eastbaytransportation.com. **GO Lorrie's Airport Shuttle** ☎ 415/334–9000 ⊕ www.gosfovan.com. **Marin Airporter** ☎ 415/461–4222 ⊕ www.marinairporter.com. **Marin Door to Door** ☎ 415/457–2717 ⊕ www.marindoortodoor.com. **SamTrans** ☎ 800/660–4287 ⊕ www.samtrans.com. **South and East Bay Airport Shuttle** ☎ 800/548–4664 ⊕ www.southandeastbayairportshuttle.com. **SuperShuttle** ☎ 800/258–3826 ⊕ www.supershuttle.com.

BART TRAVEL

BART (Bay Area Rapid Transit) trains, which run until midnight, travel under the bay via tunnel to connect San Francisco with Oakland, Berkeley, and other cities and towns beyond. Within San Francisco, stations are limited to downtown, the Mission, and a couple of outlying neighborhoods.

Trains travel frequently from early morning until evening on weekdays. After 8 pm weekdays and on weekends there's often a 20-minute wait between trains on the same line. Trains also travel south from San Francisco as far as Millbrae. BART trains connect downtown San Francisco to San Francisco International Airport; the ride costs $8.65.

Intracity San Francisco fares are $1.85; intercity fares are $3.15 to $11.65. BART bases its ticket prices on miles traveled and does not offer price breaks by zone. The easy-to-read maps posted in BART stations list fares based on destination, radiating out from your starting point of the current station.

Contact Bay Area Rapid Transit (BART). ☎ 415/989-2278 ⊕ www.bart.gov.

BOAT AND FERRY TRAVEL

Several ferry lines run out of San Francisco. Blue & Gold Fleet operates a number of routes, including service to Sausalito ($11 one-way) and Tiburon ($11 one-way). Tickets are sold at Pier 41 (between Fisherman's Wharf and Pier 39), where the boats depart. Alcatraz Cruises, owned by Hornblower Yachts, operates the ferries to Alcatraz Island ($30 including audio tour and National Park Service ranger-led programs) from Pier 33, about a half-mile east of Fisherman's Wharf ($3 shuttle buses serve several area hotels and other locations). Boats leave 10 times a day (14 times a day in summer), and the journey itself takes 30 minutes. Allow roughly 2½ hours for a round-trip jaunt. Golden Gate Ferry runs daily to and from Sausalito and Larkspur ($10.25 one-way), leaving from Pier 1, behind the San Francisco Ferry Building. The Alameda/Oakland Ferry operates daily between Alameda's Main Street Ferry Building, Oakland's Jack London Square, and San Francisco's Pier 41 and the Ferry Building ($6.25 one-way); some ferries go only to Pier 41 or the Ferry Building, so ask when you board. Purchase tickets on board.

Ferry Lines Alameda/Oakland Ferry ☎ 510/522–3300 ⊕ www.eastbayferry. com. **Alcatraz Cruises** ☎ 415/981–7625 ⊕ www.alcatrazcruises.com. **Blue & Gold Fleet** ☎ 415/705–8200 ⊕ www.blueandgoldfleet.com. **Golden Gate Ferry** ☎ 415/455–2000 ⊕ www.goldengateferry.org. **San Francisco Ferry Building** ⊠ 1 Ferry Bldg., at foot of Market St. on Embarcadero ☎ 415/983–8030 ⊕ www.ferrybuildingmarketplace.com.

CABLE CAR TRAVEL

The fare (for one direction) is $6 (Muni Passport holders only pay a $1 supplement). You can buy tickets on board (exact change isn't necessary) or at the kiosks at the cable-car turnarounds at Hyde and Beach streets and at Powell and Market streets.

The heavily traveled Powell–Mason and Powell–Hyde lines begin at Powell and Market streets near Union Square and terminate at Fisherman's Wharf; lines for these routes can be long, especially in summer. The California Street line runs east and west from Market and California streets to Van Ness Avenue; there is often no wait to board this route.

CAR TRAVEL

Driving in San Francisco can be a challenge because of the one-way streets, snarly traffic, and steep hills. The first two elements can be frustrating enough, but those hills are tough for unfamiliar drivers. ■TIP→ Remember to curb your wheels when parking on hills—turn wheels away from the curb when facing uphill, toward the curb when facing downhill. You can get a ticket if you don't do this.

MUNI TRAVEL

The San Francisco Municipal Railway, or Muni, operates light-rail vehicles, the historic F-line streetcars along Fisherman's Wharf and Market Street, trolley buses, and the world-famous cable cars. Light rail travels along Market Street to the Mission District and Noe Valley (J-line), the Ingleside District (K-line), and the Sunset District (L-, M-, and N-lines); during peak hours (weekdays from 6 am to 9 am and 3 pm to 7 pm) the J-ine continues around the Embarcadero to the Caltrain station at 4th and King streets. The T-line light rail runs from the Castro, down Market Street, around the Embarcadero, and south past Hunters Point and Monster Park to Sunnydale Avenue and Bayshore Boulevard. Muni provides 24-hour service on select lines to all areas of the city.

On buses and streetcars the fare is $2. Exact change is required (coins or bills). For all Muni vehicles other than cable cars, 90-minute transfers are issued free upon request when the fare is paid. These are valid for two transfers in any direction. Cable cars cost $6 and include no transfers (⇨ *Cable-Car Travel, above*).

One-day ($15), three-day ($23), and seven-day ($29) Passports valid on the entire Muni system can be purchased at several outlets, including the cable-car ticket booth at Powell and Market streets and the visitor information center downstairs in Hallidie Plaza. A monthly ticket, called a Fast Pass, is available for $76, and can be used on all Muni lines (including cable cars) and on BART within city limits. The San Francisco CityPass, a discount ticket booklet to several major city attractions, also covers all Muni travel for seven consecutive days.

The San Francisco Municipal Transit and Street Map ($3) is a useful guide to the extensive transportation system. You can buy the map at most bookstores and at the San Francisco Visitor Information Center, on the lower level of Hallidie Plaza at Powell and Market streets. The Muni+ app provides updates and other info.

Muni Info San Francisco Municipal Railway System (*Muni*). ☎ *311, 415/701–3000* ⊕ *www.sfmta.com.*

TAXI TRAVEL

Hailing a cab can be frustratingly difficult in some parts of the city, especially on weekends. Popular nightspots such as the Mission, SoMa, North Beach, the Haight, and the Castro have a lot of cabs but a lot of people looking for taxis, too. Midweek, and during the day, you shouldn't have much of a problem—unless it's raining. In a pinch, hotel taxi stands are an option, as is calling for a pick-up. But be forewarned: taxi companies frequently don't answer the phone in peak periods. The absolute worst times to find a taxi are Friday afternoon and evening; plan well ahead, and if you're going to the airport, make a reservation or book a shuttle instead. Most taxi companies take reservations for airport and out-of-town runs but not in-town rides.

Alternatively, you can download the Uber or Lyft apps to participate in the city's user-generated car services. You basically join the group and pay via a credit card on your app, then order a car to pick you up from your destination and deliver you anywhere in the city. Rates vary by company, but are generally comparable to taxi rates.

Taxis in San Francisco charge $3.50 for the first 1/5 mile (one of the highest base rates in the United States), 55¢ for each additional 1/5 mile, and 55¢ per minute in stalled traffic; a $2 surcharge is added for trips to the airport. There is no charge for additional passengers; there is no surcharge for luggage. For trips outside city limits, multiply the metered rate by 1.5; tolls and tip are extra.

Taxi Companies DeSoto Cab ☎ *415/970–1300* ⊕ *www.desotosf.com.*
Luxor Cab ☎ *415/282–4141* ⊕ *www.luxorcab.com.* Veteran's Taxicab
☎ *415/648–1313.* Yellow Cab ☎ *415/626–2345* ⊕ *yellowcabsf.com.*

Complaints San Francisco Police Department Taxi Complaints
☎ *415/553–1447.*

TRAIN TRAVEL

Amtrak trains serve the Bay Area from major population centers in California and the United States. Amtrak doesn't have a train station in San Francisco, instead shuttling its passengers by bus from its Emeryville station, just across the Bay Bridge, to the Ferry Building and other points in downtown San Francisco. A California Rail Pass gives you 7 days of travel in a 21-day period for $159.

Caltrain connects San Francisco to San Jose and many smaller cities en route. The main depot in San Francisco is at 4th and Townsend streets. One-way fares cost from $3 to $13, depending on the number of zones through which you travel. A ticket from San Francisco to Palo Alto costs $7, to San Jose at least $9. A day pass (from $6 to $26) buys you unlimited travel for a 24-hour period. There are no onboard ticket sales. You must buy tickets before boarding the train or risk paying a $250 fine for fare evasion.

Train Contacts Amtrak ☎ *800/872–7245* ⊕ *www.amtrak.com.*
Caltrain ☎ *800/660–4287* ⊕ *www.caltrain.com.* San Francisco Caltrain
station ✉ *700 4th St., at King St.* ☎ *800/660–4287.*

VISITOR INFORMATION

The San Francisco Convention and Visitors Bureau can mail you brochures, maps, and events listings. Once in town, you can stop by the bureau's info center near Union Square.

Contacts San Francisco Visitor Information Center ✉ *Hallidie Plaza, lower level, 900 Market St., at Powell St., Union Sq.* ☎ *415/391–2000 TDD*
⊕ *www.onlyinsanfrancisco.com.*

EXPLORING SAN FRANCISCO

UNION SQUARE AND CHINATOWN

The Union Square area bristles with big-city bravado, while just a stone's throw away is a place that feels like a city unto itself, Chinatown. The two areas share a strong commercial streak, although manifested very differently. In Union Square the crowds zigzag among international brands, trailing glossy shopping bags. A few blocks north, people dash between small neighborhood stores, their arms draped with plastic totes filled with groceries or souvenirs.

UNION SQUARE

TOP ATTRACTIONS

Union Square. Ground zero for big-name shopping in the city and within walking distance of many hotels, Union Square is home base for many visitors. The Westin St. Francis Hotel and Macy's line two of the square's sides, and Saks, Neiman-Marcus, and Tiffany & Co. edge the other two. Four globular lamp sculptures by the artist R. M. Fischer preside over the landscaped, 2½-acre park, which has a café with outdoor seating, an open-air stage, and a visitor-information booth—along with a familiar kaleidoscope of characters: office workers sunning and brown-bagging, street musicians, shoppers taking a rest, kids chasing pigeons, and a fair number of homeless people. The constant clang of cable cars traveling up and down Powell Street helps maintain a festive mood.

The heart of San Francisco's downtown since 1850, the square takes its name from the violent pro-Union demonstrations staged here before the Civil War. At center stage, Robert Ingersoll Aitken's *Victory Monument* commemorates Commodore George Dewey's victory over the Spanish fleet at Manila in 1898. The 97-foot Corinthian column, topped by a bronze figure symbolizing naval conquest, was dedicated by Theodore Roosevelt in 1903 and withstood the 1906 earthquake. After the earthquake and fire of 1906, the square was dubbed "Little St. Francis" because of the temporary shelter erected for residents of the St. Francis Hotel. Actor John Barrymore (grandfather of actress Drew Barrymore and a notorious carouser) was among the guests pressed into volunteering to stack bricks in the square. His uncle, thespian John Drew, remarked, "It took an act of God to get John out of bed and the United States Army to get him to work."

The square sits atop a handy four-level garage, allegedly the world's first underground parking structure. Aboveground the convenient **TIX Bay Area** (☎ 415/433–7827 ⊕ *www.tixbayarea.com*) provides half-price, day-of-performance tickets to performing-arts events, as well as regular full-price box-office services. ■TIP→ Tired of shopping? Grab a coffee and pastry right in the square at Emporio Rulli, sit at a small outdoor table, and take in the action. ⊠ *Bordered by Powell, Stockton, Post, and Geary Sts., Union Sq.*

WORTH NOTING

Maiden Lane. Known as Morton Street in the raffish Barbary Coast era, this former red-light district reported at least one murder a week during the late 19th century. Things cooled down after the 1906 fire destroyed the brothels, and these days Maiden Lane is a chic, boutique-lined pedestrian mall (favored by brides to be) stretching two blocks, between Stockton and Kearny streets. Wrought-iron gates close the street to traffic most days between 11 and 5, when the lane becomes a patchwork of umbrella-shaded tables.

At **140 Maiden Lane** you can see the only Frank Lloyd Wright building in San Francisco. Walking through the brick archway and recessed entry feels a bit like entering a glowing cave. The interior's graceful, curving ramp and skylights are said to have been his model for the Guggenheim Museum in New York. Xanadu Gallery, which showcases expensive Baltic, Latin American, and African folk art, occupies the space and welcomes Frank Lloyd Wright fans. ⊠ *Between Stockton and Kearny Sts., Union Sq.*

4

The epicenter of high-end shopping, Union Square is lined with department stores.

San Francisco Visitor Information Center. Head downstairs from the cable-car terminus to the visitor center, where multilingual staffers answer questions and provide maps and pamphlets. Muni Passports are sold here, and you can pick up discount coupons—the savings can be significant, especially for families. If you're planning to hit the big-ticket stops like the California Academy of Sciences and the Exploratorium and ride the cable cars, consider purchasing a CityPass (⊕ *www.citypass.com/san-francisco*) here. ■TIP→ **The CityPass ($86, $64 ages 5–11), good for nine days, including seven days of transit, will save you more than 40%.** The pass is also available at the attractions it covers, though if you choose the pass that includes Alcatraz—an excellent deal—you'll have to buy it directly from Alcatraz Cruises (⇨ *On the Waterfront, below*). ⊠ *Hallidie Plaza, lower level, 900 Market St., at Market and Powell Sts., Union Sq.* ☎ *415/391–2000* ⊕ *www.sanfrancisco.travel* ☉ *Weekdays 9–5, Sat. 9–3; also Sun. 9–3 May–Oct.*

Westin St. Francis Hotel. Architects Walter Danforth Bliss and William Baker Faville visited the great hotels of Europe seeking inspiration for the St. Francis, established in 1904 and renowned from the start for its sumptuous surroundings. After San Francisco's 1906 fire ravaged the hotel, a larger, more luxurious Italian Renaissance–style residence was opened in 1907 to attract loyal clients from among the world's rich and powerful. The hotel's checkered past includes the ill-fated 1921 bash in the suite of the silent-film superstar Fatty Arbuckle, at which a woman became ill and later died. Arbuckle endured three sensational trials for rape and murder before being acquitted, by which time his career was kaput. In 1975 Sara Jane Moore, standing among a crowd outside the hotel, attempted to shoot then-president Gerald Ford. As might be imagined, the grand lobby contains no plaques commemorating these events, though every November the hotel's pastry chef adds a new touch to his spectacular, rotating 12-foot-high gingerbread castle on display here—a fun holiday treat for families. ■TIP➔ Some visitors make the St. Francis a stop whenever they're in town, soaking up the lobby ambience or enjoying a cocktail in Clock Bar or a meal at Michael Mina's Bourbon Steak. ⊠ *335 Powell St., at Geary St., Union Sq.* ☎ *415/397–7000* ⊕ *www.westinstfrancis.com.*

CABLE CAR TERMINUS

Two of the three cable-car lines begin and end their runs at Powell and Market streets, a couple of blocks south of Union Square. These two lines are the most scenic, and both pass near Fisherman's Wharf, so they're usually clogged with first-time sightseers. The wait to board a cable car at this terminus is longer than at any other stop in the system. To avoid the mob, board the less-touristy California line at the bottom of Market Street, at Drumm Street.

4

CHINATOWN
TOP ATTRACTIONS

Chinatown Gate. This is the official entrance to Chinatown. Stone lions flank the base of the pagoda-topped gate; the lions, dragons, and fish up top symbolize wealth, prosperity, and other good things. The four Chinese characters immediately beneath the pagoda represent the philosophy of Sun Yat-sen (1866–1925), the leader who unified China in the early 20th century. Sun Yat-sen, who lived in exile in San Francisco for a few years, promoted the notion of friendship and peace among all nations based on equality, justice, and goodwill. The vertical characters under the left pagoda read "peace" and "trust," the ones under the right pagoda "respect" and "love." The whole shebang telegraphs the internationally understood message of "photo op." Immediately beyond the gate, dive into souvenir shopping on Grant Avenue, Chinatown's tourist strip. ⊠ *Grant Ave. at Bush St., Chinatown.*

Kong Chow Temple. This ornate temple sets a somber, spiritual tone right away with a sign warning visitors not to touch *anything*. The god to whom the members of this temple pray represents honesty and trust. Chinese stores and restaurants often display his image because he's thought to bring good luck in business. Chinese immigrants established the temple in 1851; its congregation moved to this building in 1977. Take the elevator up to the fourth floor, where incense fills the air. You can show respect by placing a dollar or two in the donation box and by leaving your camera in its case. Amid the statuary, flowers, and richly colored altars (red wards off evil spirits and signifies virility, green symbolizes longevity, and gold connotes majesty), a couple of plaques announce that "Mrs. Harry S. Truman came to this temple in June 1948 for a prediction on the outcome of the election . . . this fortune came true." ■TIP➔ The temple's balcony has a good view of Chinatown. ⊠ *855 Stockton St., Chinatown* 🎫 *Free* ☺ *Mon.–Sat. 9–4.*

Fodor's Choice
★

Tin How Temple. Duck into the inconspicuous doorway, climb three flights of stairs, and be assaulted by the aroma of incense in this tiny, altar-filled room. In 1852, Day Ju, one of the first three Chinese to arrive in San Francisco, dedicated this temple to the Queen of the Heavens and the Goddess of the Seven Seas, and the temple looks largely the same today as it did more than a century ago. In the entryway, elderly ladies can often be seen preparing "money" to be burned as offerings to various Buddhist gods or as funds for ancestors to use in the afterlife. Hundreds of red-and-gold lanterns cover the ceiling; the larger the lamp, the larger its donor's contribution to the temple. Gifts of oranges, dim sum, and money left by the faithful, who kneel mumbling prayers, rest on altars to different gods. Tin How presides over the middle back of the temple, flanked by one red and one green lesser god. Take a good look around, since taking photographs is not allowed. ⊠ *125 Waverly Pl., between Clay and Washington Sts., Chinatown* ☎ *Free, donations accepted* ⊗ *Daily 9–4.*

WORTH NOTING

Chinese Historical Society of America Museum and Learning Center. The displays at this light-filled gallery document the Chinese-American experience—from 19th-century agriculture to 21st-century food and fashion trends—and include a thought-provoking collection of racist games and toys. The facility also exhibits works by contemporary Chinese-American artists. ⊠ *965 Clay St., between Stockton and Powell Sts., Chinatown* ☎ *415/391–1188* ⊕ *www.chsa.org* ☎ *$5, free 1st Thurs. of month* ⊗ *Tues.–Fri. noon–5, Sat. 11–4.*

FAMILY **Golden Gate Fortune Cookie Factory.** Follow your nose down Ross Alley to this tiny but fragrant cookie factory. Workers sit at circular motorized griddles and wait for dollops of batter to drop onto a tiny metal plate, which rotates into an oven. A few moments later out comes a cookie that's pliable and ready for folding. It's easy to peek in for a moment, and hard to leave without a few free samples. A bagful of cookies—with mildly racy "adult" fortunes or more benign ones—costs under $5. You can also purchase the cookies "fortuneless" in their waferlike unfolded state, which makes snacking that much more efficient. ■**TIP**➔ **Photographing the cookie makers at work will set you back 50¢.** ⊠ *56 Ross Alley, off Washington or Jackson St. west of Grant Ave., Chinatown* ☎ *415/781–3956* ☎ *Free* ⊗ *Daily 9–8.*

Old Chinese Telephone Exchange. After the 1906 earthquake, many Chinatown buildings were rebuilt in Western style with pagoda roof and fancy balconies slapped on. This building—today EastWest Bank—is the exception, an example of top-to-bottom Chinese architecture. The intricate three-tier pagoda was built in 1909. To the Chinese, it's considered rude to refer to a person as a number, so the operators were required to memorize each subscriber's name. As the San Francisco Chamber of Commerce boasted in 1914: "These girls respond all day with hardly a mistake to calls that are given (in English or one of five Chinese dialects) by the name of the subscriber instead of by his number—a mental feat that would be practically impossible for most high-schooled American misses." ⊠ *EastWest Bank, 743 Washington St., Chinatown.*

Union Square and Chinatown

Jackson Square Historic District

CHINATOWN

♦ Chinese Culture Center

Fresno St.
Dunne's Al.

Columbus Ave.

Kearny St.

Pacific Ave.

Churchill St.

Stark St.

J. Kerouac Al.

Cordelia St.

Reynolds Pl.

Pelton Pl.

Jason Ct.

Jackson St.

St. Louis Pl.

Beckett St.

Balance Al.

Hotaling St.

Custom House Pl.

Gibb St.

Washington St.

Merchant St.

M. Twain Pl.

Clay St.

Montgomery St.

Sansome St.

Battery St.

Bedford Pl.

James Al.

Stone St.

Stockton St.

Spofford St.

Waverly Pl.

Clay St.

Commercial St.

Sacramento St.

Spring St.

Leidesdorff St.

Hallcck St.

Parkhurst Al.

Old St. Mary's Cathedral

California St.

NOB HILL

Powell St.

Joice St.

Pratt Pl.

Tunnel

Quincy St.

St. Mary's Sq.

Pine St.

Vinton Ct.

Grant Ave.

Kearny St.

St. George Al.

Belden St.

Pine St.

Trinity St.

Pine St.

Emma St.

Bush St.

Harlan Pl.

Mark La.

Claude La.

Hardie Pl.

Hallidie Building

Anson Pl.

Sutter St.

Campton Pl.

Tillman Pl.

Market St.

b MONTGOMERY ST.

Maiden La.

Lotta's Fountain

Geary St.

Annie St.

A. Bierce St.

New Montgomery St.

UNION SQUARE

Geary St.

Security Pacific Pl.

3rd St.

Pacific Telephone Bldg.

O'Farrell St.

Minna St.

Market St.

Howard St.

4th St.

Jessie St.

Mission St.

3rd St.

b POWELL ST.

Pioneer Pl.

Yerba Buena Gardens

Moscone Convention Center

Eddy St.

Folsom St.

5th St.

Mission St.

Old U.S. Mint

0 _____ 350 M
0 _____ 1,000 ft.

Portsmouth Square. Chinatown's living room buzzes with activity. The square, with its pagoda-shape structures, is a favorite spot for morning tai chi; by noon dozens of men huddle around Chinese chess tables, engaged in not-always-legal competition. Kids scamper about the square's two grungy playgrounds (warning: the bathrooms are sketchy). Back in the late 19th century this land was near the waterfront. The square is named for the USS *Portsmouth*, the ship helmed by Captain John Montgomery, who in 1846 raised the American flag here and claimed the then-Mexican land for the United States. A couple of years later, Sam Brannan kicked off the gold rush at the square when he waved his loot and proclaimed, "Gold from the American River!" Robert Louis Stevenson, the author of *Treasure Island*, often dropped by, chatting up the sailors who hung out here. Some of the information he gleaned about life at sea found its way into his fiction. A bronze galleon sculpture, a tribute to Stevenson, anchors the square's northwest corner. A plaque marks the site of California's first public school, built in 1847. ⊠ *Bordered by Walter Lum Pl. and Kearny, Washington, and Clay Sts., Chinatown.*

SOMA, CIVIC CENTER, AND HAYES VALLEY

To a newcomer, SoMa (short for "south of Market") and the Civic Center may look like cheek-by-jowl neighbors—they're divided by Market Street. To locals, though, these areas are separate entities. Both neighborhoods have a core of cultural sights but more than their share of sketchy blocks. Locals love Hayes Valley, due west of Civic Center, for its terrific eateries and cool watering holes, the SFJAZZ Center, and the great browsing in funky clothing, home-decor, and design boutiques. Swing down the main drag, Hayes Street, between Franklin and Laguna streets and you can hit the neighborhood's highlights.

SOMA
TOP ATTRACTIONS
California Historical Society. If you're not a history buff, the CHS might seem like an obvious skip—who wants to look at fading old photographs and musty artifacts?—but these airy galleries are worth a stop. The shows here draw from the society's vast repository of Californiana—hundreds of thousands of photographs, publications, paintings, and gold-rush paraphernalia. Special exhibits have included *A Wild Flight of the Imagination: The Story of the Golden Gate Bridge* and *Hobos to Street People: Artists' Responses to Homelessness from the New Deal to the Present.* ■TIP➡ From out front, take a look across the street: this is the best view of the Museum of the African Diaspora's three-story photo mosaic. ⊠ *678 Mission St., SoMa* ☎ *415/357–1848* ⊕ *www.californiahistoricalsociety.org* 🔊 *$5* ☉ *Tues.–Sun. noon–5; galleries close between exhibitions.*

Contemporary Jewish Museum. Daniel Liebeskind designed the postmodern CJM, whose impossible-to-ignore diagonal blue cube juts out of a painstakingly restored power substation. A physical manifestation of the Hebrew phrase *l'chaim* (to life), the cube may have obscure philosophical origins, but Liebeskind created a unique, light-filled space

Continued on page 171

CHINATOWN

Chinatown's streets flood the senses. Incense and cigarette smoke mingle with the scents of briny fish and sweet vanilla. Rooflines flare outward, pagoda-style. Loud Cantonese bargaining and honking car horns rise above the sharp clack of mah-jongg tiles and the eternally humming cables beneath the street.

Most Chinatown visitors march down Grant Avenue, buy a few trinkets, and call it a day. Do yourself a favor and dig deeper. This is one of the largest Chinese communities outside Asia, and there is far more to it than buying a back-scratcher near Chinatown Gate. To get a real feel for the neighborhood, wander off the main drag. Step into a temple or an herb shop and wander down a flag-draped alley. And don't be shy: residents welcome guests warmly, though rarely in English.

Whatever you do, don't leave without eating something. Noodle houses, bakeries, tea houses, and dim sum shops seem to occupy every other storefront. There's a feast for your eyes as well: in the market windows on Stockton and Grant, you'll see hanging whole roast ducks, fish, and shellfish swimming in tanks, and strips of shiny, pink-glazed Chinese-style barbecued pork. (For the scoop on dim sum, *see* the Union Square and Chinatown spotlight in the Where to Eat chapter.)

CHINATOWN'S HISTORY

Sam Brannan's 1848 cry of "Gold!" didn't take long to reach across the world to China. Struggling with famine, drought, and political upheaval at home, thousands of Chinese jumped at the chance to try their luck in California. Most came from the Pearl River Delta region, in the Guangdong province, and spoke Cantonese dialects. From the start, Chinese businesses circled around Portsmouth Square, which was conveniently central. Bachelor rooming houses sprang up, since the vast majority of new arrivals were men. By 1853, the area was called Chinatown.

The Street of Gamblers (Ross Alley), 1898 (top). The first Chinese telephone operator in Chinatown (bottom).

COLD WELCOME

The Chinese faced discrimination from the get-go. Harrassment became outright hostility as first the gold rush, then the work on the Transcontinental Railroad petered out. Special taxes were imposed to shoulder aside competing "coolie labor." Laws forbidding the Chinese from moving outside Chinatown kept the residents packed in like sardines, with nowhere to go but up and down—thus the many basement establishments in the neighborhood. State and federal laws passed in the 1870s deterred Chinese women from immigrating, deeming them prostitutes. In the late 1870s, looting and arson attacks on Chinatown businesses soared.

The coup de grace, though, was the Chinese Exclusion Act, passed by the U.S.

Chinatown's Grant Avenue.

Women and children flooded into the neighborhood after the Great Quake.

Congress in 1882, which slammed the doors to America for "Asiatics." This was the country's first significant restriction on immigration. The law also prevented the existing Chinese residents, including American-born children, from becoming naturalized citizens. With a society of mostly men (forbidden, of course, from marrying white women), San Francisco hoped that Chinatown would simply die out.

OUT OF THE ASHES

When the devastating 1906 earthquake and fire hit, city fathers thought they'd seize the opportunity to kick the Chinese out of Chinatown and get their hands on that desirable piece of downtown real estate. Then Chinatown businessman Look Tin Eli had a brainstorm of Disneyesque proportions.

He proposed that Chinatown be rebuilt, but in a tourist-friendly, stylized, "Oriental" way. Anglo-American architects would design new buildings with pagoda roofs and dragon-covered columns. Chinatown would attract more tourists—the curious had been visiting on the sly

for decades—and add more tax money to the city's coffers. Ka-ching: the sales pitch worked.

PAPER SONS

For the Chinese, the 1906 earthquake turned the virtual "no entry" sign into a flashing neon "welcome!" All the city's immigration records went up in smoke, and the Chinese quickly began to apply for passports as U.S. citizens, claiming their old ones were lost in the fire. Not only did thousands of Chinese become legal overnight, but so did their sons in China, or "sons," if they weren't really related. Whole families in Chinatown had passports in names that weren't their own; these "paper sons" were not only a windfall but also an uncomfortable neighborhood conspiracy. The city caught on eventually and set up an immigration center on Angel Island in 1910. Immigrants spent weeks or months being inspected and interrogated while their papers were checked. Roughly 250,000 people made it through. With this influx, including women and children, Chinatown finally became a more complete community.

A GREAT WALK THROUGH CHINATOWN

■ Start at the Chinatown Gate and walk ahead on Grant Avenue, entering the souvenir gauntlet. (You'll also pass Old St. Mary's Cathedral.)

■ Make a right on Clay Street and walk to Portsmouth Square. Sometimes it feels like the whole neighborhood's here, playing chess and exercising.

■ Head up Washington Street to the Old Chinese Telephone Exchange building, now the EastWest Bank. Across Grant, look left for Waverly Place. Here Free Republic of China (Taiwanese) flags flap over some of the neighborhood's most striking buildings, including Tin How Temple.

■ At the Sacramento Street end of Waverly Place stands the First Chinese Baptist Church of 1908. Just across the way, the Clarion Music Center is full of unusual instruments, as well as exquisite lion-dance sets.

■ Head back to Washington Street and check out the herb shops, like the Superior Trading Company (No. 839) and the Great China Herb Co. (No. 857).

■ Follow the scent of vanilla down Ross Alley (entrance across from Superior Trading Company) to the Golden Gate Fortune Cookie Factory. Then

head across the alley to Sam Bo Trading Co., where religious items are stacked in the narrow space. Tell the owners your troubles and they'll prepare a package of joss papers, joss sticks, and candles, and tell you how and when to offer them up.

■ Turn left on Jackson Street; ahead is the real Chinatown's

main artery, Stockton Street, where most residents do their grocery shopping. Vegetarians will want to avoid Luen Fat Market (No. 1135), with tanks of live frogs, turtles, and lobster as well as chickens and ducks. Look toward the back of stores for Buddhist altars with offerings of oranges and grapefruit. From here you can loop one block east back to Grant.

ALL THE TEA IN CHINATOWN

Preparing a perfect brew at Red Blossom Tea.

San Francisco's close ties to Asia have always made it more tea-conscious than other American burgs, but these days the city is in the throes of a tea renaissance, with new tasting rooms popping up in every neighborhood. Below are our favorite spots for every tea under the sun.

Blest Tea. Chinatown's smallest tea shop is a calm, modern space with a thoughtful selection of teas by the pound. The Taiwanc owners sell teas from many Asian countries, but their offerings emphasize Taiwan. Regulars rave about the service. ✉ *752 Grant Ave.* ☎ *415/951–8516.*

Red Blossom Tea. A light and modern shop—the staff really know their stuff. It's a favorite among younger tea enthusiasts, who swear by its excellent bang-for-the-buck value. While Red Blossom doesn't do formal tastings or sell tea by the cup, they'll gladly brew up perfect samples of the teas you're interested in. ✉ *831 Grant Ave.* ☎ *415/395–0868.*

Vital Tea Leaf. Tastings here work like those for wine—one of the gregarious, knowledgeable servers chooses the teas and describes them as you sample. It's a great spot for tea newbies to get their feet wet without a hard sell, but local connoisseurs grumble about the high prices and the self-promotion. ✉ *1044 Grant Ave.* ☎ *415/981–2388.*

Imperial Tea Court. If you want to visit the most respected of traditional tea purveyors, you'll need to venture outside of Chinatown. Imperial Tea Court may have left Chinatown, but you'll find the same great selection and expertise at their fancy digs in the Ferry Building. ☎ *415/544–9830.*

WAITING FOR CUSTARD

As you're strolling down Grant Avenue, past the plastic Buddhas and yin/yang balls, be sure to stop at the Golden Gate Bakery (No. 1029) for some delicious eggy *dan tat* (custard tarts). These flaky-crusted treats are heaven for just a buck. There's often a line, but it's worth the wait.

DON'T-MISS SHOPS

Locals snap up flowers from an outdoor vendor.

If you're in the market for a pair of chirping metal crickets (oh you'll hear them, trust us), you can duck into any of the obvious souvenir-stuffed storefronts. But if you're looking for something special, head for these tempting sources. ■TIP→ Fierce neighborhood competition keeps prices within reason, but for popular wares like jade, it pays to shop around before making a serious investment. Many stores accept cash only.

Chinatown Kite Shop. Family-run shop selling bright, fun-shaped kites—dragons, butterflies, sharks—since the 1960s. ☒ 717 Grant Ave. ☎ 415/989–5182.

Dragon House. A veritable museum: the store sells authentic, centuries-old antiques like ivory carvings. ☒ 455 Grant Ave. ☎ 415/421–3693.

Old Shanghai. One of the largest selections of hand-painted robes, formal dresses, and jackets in Chinatown, plus chic Asian-inspired pieces. ☒ 645 Grant Ave. ☎ 415/986–1222.

CHINATOWN WITH KIDS

It can be tough for the little ones to keep their hands to themselves, especially when all sorts of curios spill out onto the sidewalk at just the right height. To burn off some steam (in them) and relieve some stress (in you), take them to the small but spruce playground in the park in St. Mary's Square, across California from Old St. Mary's. If that setting's too tranquil, head to the more boisterous Willie Wong Playground, on Sacramento Street at Waverly Place.

that merits a stroll through the lobby even if current exhibits don't entice you into the galleries. Be sure to check out the seam where old building meets new, and check the website for fun children's activities linked to exhibits. San Francisco's best Jewish deli, Wise Sons, recently opened a counter in the museum, giving you a chance to sample the company's wildly popular smoked trout. ■TIP➔ At the StoryCorps StoryBooth, a project of the NPR oral-history series, you can listen to past interviews—or slip into the recording studio and preserve a loved one's memories right on the spot. ✉ *736 Mission St., between 3rd and 4th Sts., SoMa* ☎ *415/655–7800* ⊕ *www.thecjm.org* ✉ *$12; $5 Thurs. after 5 pm, free 1st Tues. of month* ⊘ *Thurs. 1–8, Fri.–Tues. 11–5.*

Museum of the African Diaspora (MoAD). Dedicated to the influence that people of African descent have had all over the world, MoAD provokes discussion from the get-go with the question, "When did you discover you are African?" painted on the wall at the entrance. With no permanent collection, the museum is light on displays and heavy on interactive exhibits. For instance, you can sit in a darkened theater and listen to the moving life stories of slaves; hear snippets of music that helped create genres from gospel to hip-hop; and see videos about the civil rights movement or the Haitian Revolution. Some grumble that the presentations favor sweeping generalities over specifics, but almost everyone can appreciate the museum's most striking exhibit in the front window. The three-story mosaic, made from thousands of photographs, forms the image of a young girl's face. ■TIP➔ Walk up the stairs inside the museum to view the photographs up close—Malcolm X is there, Muhammad Ali, too, along with everyday folks—but the best view is from across the street. ✉ *685 Mission St., SoMa* ☎ *415/358–7200* ⊕ *www.moadsf.org* ✉ *$10* ⊘ *Wed.–Sat. 11–6, Sun. noon–5.*

FAMILY
Fodor'sChoice
★
Yerba Buena Gardens. There's not much south of Market Street that encourages lingering outdoors—or indeed walking at all—with this notable exception. These two blocks encompass the Center for the Arts, the Metreon, Moscone Convention Center, and the convention center's rooftop Children's Creativity Museum, but the gardens themselves are the everyday draw. Office workers escape to the green swath of the East Garden, the focal point of which is the memorial to Martin Luther King Jr. Powerful streams of water surge over large, jagged stone columns, mirroring the enduring force of King's words that are carved on the stone walls and on glass blocks behind the waterfall. Moscone North is behind the memorial, and an overhead walkway leads to Moscone South and its rooftop attractions. ■TIP➔ The gardens are liveliest during the week and especially during the Yerba Buena Gardens Festival from May through October (⊕ www.ybgf.org), with free performances of everything from Latin music to Balinese dance.

LOOK UP!

When wandering around Chinatown, don't forget to look up! Above the chintziest souvenir shop might loom an ornate balcony or a curly pagoda roof. The best examples are on the 900 block of Grant Avenue (at Washington Street) and at Waverly Place.

4

Atop the Moscone Convention Center perch a few lures for kids. The historic Looff carousel (🎫 *$3 for two rides*) twirls daily 11 to 6. South of the carousel is the Children's Creativity Museum (☎ *415/820–3320* 🌐 *creativity.org*), a high-tech, interactive arts-and-technology center (🎫 *$11*) geared to children from age 3 to 12. Kids can make Claymation videos, work in a computer lab, check out new games and apps, and perform and record music videos. The museum is open year-round between 10 and 4 from Wednesday through Sunday, and on Tuesday during the summer. Just outside, kids adore the excellent slides, including a 25-foot tube slide, at the play circle. Also part of the rooftop complex are gardens, an ice-skating rink, and a bowling alley. ✉ *Bordered by 3rd, 4th, Mission, and Folsom Sts., SoMa* 🌐 *www. yerbabuenagardens.com* 🎫 *Free* 🕐 *Daily sunrise–10 pm.*

WORTH NOTING

Cartoon Art Museum. Krazy Kat, Zippy the Pinhead, Batman, and other colorful cartoon icons greet you at the Cartoon Art Museum, established with an endowment from cartoonist-icon Charles M. Schulz. The museum's strength is its changing exhibits, which explore such topics as America from the perspective of international political cartoons, and the output of women and African American cartoonists. Serious fans of cartoons—especially those on the quirky underground side—will likely enjoy the exhibits; those with a casual interest may be bored. The store here carries cool titles to add to your collection. ✉ *655 Mission St., SoMa* ☎ *415/227–8666* 🌐 *www.cartoonart.org* 🎫 *$8, pay what you wish 1st Tues. of month* 🕐 *Tues.–Sun. 11–5.*

San Francisco Museum of Modern Art. SFMOMA closed for a massive expansion project in 2013 and is scheduled to reopen in 2016. Until then, the museum will draw from its collection to create joint exhibitions with the Asian Art Museum, the Yerba Buena Center for the Arts, and other institutions. SFMOMA's store—known for its fun gadgets, artsy doodads, and superb art and kids' books—is relocating temporarily to 51 Yerba Buena Lane, off Mission and Market Streets near 4th Street. ✉ *151 3rd St., SoMa* ☎ *415/357–4000* 🌐 *www.sfmoma.org.*

Yerba Buena Center for the Arts. You never know what's going to be on display at this facility in Yerba Buena Gardens, but whether it's an exhibit of Mexican street art (graffiti to laypeople), innovative modern dance, or a baffling video installation, it's likely to be memorable. The productions here, which lean toward the cutting edge, tend to draw a young, energetic crowd. ■ **TIP→ Present any library card to receive a $2 discount.** ✉ *701 Mission St., SoMa* ☎ *415/978–2787* 🌐 *www.ybca. org* 🎫 *Galleries $10, free 1st Tues. of month* 🕐 *Thurs.–Sat. noon–8, Sun. noon–6, 1st Tues. of the month noon–8.*

CIVIC CENTER
TOP ATTRACTIONS

Fodor's Choice
★

Asian Art Museum. You don't have to be a connoisseur of Asian art to appreciate a visit to this museum whose monumental exterior conceals a light, open, and welcoming space. The fraction of the Asian's collection on display (about 2,500 pieces out of 15,000-plus total) is laid out thematically and by region, making it easy to follow historical developments.

SoMa and Civic Center

KEY

b̄ Bart Stop

Asian Art Museum **8**
California Historical
Society **7**
Cartoon Art Museum **6**
City Hall **9**

Contemporary Jewish
Museum **1**
Museum of the
African Diaspora **4**
San Francisco
Museum of Modern Art **5**

Yerba Buena Center
for the Arts **3**
Yerba Buena Gardens **2**

Begin on the third floor, where highlights of Buddhist art in Southeast Asia and early China include a large, jewel-encrusted, exquisitely painted 19th-century Burmese Buddha and clothed rod puppets from Java. On the second floor you can find later Chinese works, as well as pieces from Korea and Japan. The joy here is all in the details: on a whimsical Korean jar, look for a cobalt tiger jauntily smoking a pipe, or admire the delicacy of the Japanese tea implements. The ground floor is devoted to temporary exhibits, often traveling shows such as recent ones about Balinese art, and the transformation of yoga. ■TIP→ For much of the year the museum stays open late on Thursday and hosts Matcha, an evening of cocktails, music, and activities related to current exhibitions. ⊠ 200 Larkin St., between McAllister and Fulton Sts., Civic Center ☎ 415/581–3500 ⊕ www.asianart.org ⊠ $12, free 1st Sun. of month; $10 Thurs. 5–9; tea ceremony $27, includes museum admission ☉ Tues.–Sun. 10–5; Feb.–Oct., Thurs. until 9.

City Hall. This imposing 1915 structure with its massive gold-leaf dome— higher than the U.S. Capitol's—is about as close to a palace as you're going to get in San Francisco. (Alas, the metal detectors detract from the grandeur.) The classic granite-and-marble behemoth was modeled after St. Peter's Basilica in Rome. Architect Arthur Brown Jr., who also designed Coit Tower and the War Memorial Opera House, designed an interior with grand columns and a sweeping central staircase. San Franciscans were thrilled, and probably a bit surprised, when his firm built City Hall in just a few years. The 1899 structure it replaced had taken 27 years to erect, as corrupt builders and politicians lined their pockets with funds earmarked for it. That building collapsed in about 27 seconds during the 1906 earthquake, revealing trash and newspapers mixed into the construction materials.

City Hall was spruced up and seismically retrofitted in the late 1990s, but the sense of history remains palpable. Some noteworthy events that have taken place here include the marriage of Marilyn Monroe and Joe DiMaggio (1954); the hosing—down the central staircase— of civil-rights and freedom-of-speech protesters (1960); the murders of Mayor George Moscone and openly gay supervisor Harvey Milk (1978); the torching of the lobby by angry members of the gay community in response to the light sentence given to the former supervisor who killed both men (1979); and the registrations of scores of gay couples in celebration of the passage of San Francisco's Domestic Partners Act (1991). February 2004 has come to be known as the Winter of Love: thousands of gay and lesbian couples responded to Mayor Gavin Newsom's decision to issue marriage licenses to same-sex partners, turning City Hall into the site of raucous celebration and joyful nuptials for a month before the state Supreme Court ordered the practice stopped. That celebratory scene replayed during 2008, when scores of couples were wed between the court's June ruling that everyone enjoys the civil right to marry and the November passage of California's ballot proposition banning same-sex marriage. In 2013, the U.S. Supreme Court resolved the issue, ruling against the proposition.

On display in the South Light Court are artifacts from the collection of the **Museum of the City of San Francisco** (⊕ www.sfmuseum.org), including maps, documents, and photographs. That enormous, 700-pound iron head once crowned the *Goddess of Progress* statue, which topped the old City Hall building until it crumbled during the 1906 earthquake. City Hall's centennial in 2013 kicked off three years of exhibits—the same amount of time it took to raise the building.

Across Polk Street from City Hall is **Civic Center Plaza,** with lawns, walkways, seasonal flower beds, a playground, and an underground parking garage. This sprawling space is generally clean but somewhat grim. A large part of the city's homeless population hangs out here, so the plaza can feel dodgy. ⊠ *Bordered by Van Ness Ave. and Polk, Grove, and McAllister Sts., Civic Center* ☎ *415/554–6023 recorded tour info* ⊕ *sfgsa.org/index.aspx?page=1172* ⌖ *Free* ☼ *Weekdays 8–8 except holidays; free tours weekdays at 10, noon, and 2.*

4

NOB HILL AND RUSSIAN HILL

In place of the quirky charm and cultural diversity that mark other San Francisco neighborhoods, Nob Hill exudes history and good breeding. Topped with some of the city's most elegant hotels, Gothic Grace Cathedral, and private blue-blood clubs, it's the pinnacle of privilege. One hill over, across Pacific Avenue, is another old-family bastion, Russian Hill. It may not be quite as wealthy as Nob Hill, but it's no slouch—and it's got jaw-dropping views.

NOB HILL

TOP ATTRACTIONS

FAMILY **Cable Car Museum.** One of the city's best free offerings, this museum is an absolute must for kids. You can even ride a cable car here—all three lines stop between Russian Hill and Nob Hill. The facility, which is inside the city's last cable-car barn, takes the top off the system to let you see how it all works. Eternally humming and squealing, the massive powerhouse cable wheels steal the show. You can also climb aboard a vintage car and take the grip, let the kids ring a cable-car bell (briefly), and check out vintage gear dating from 1873.

The gift shop sells cable-car paraphernalia, including an authentic gripman's bell for $600 (it'll sound like Powell Street in your house every day). For significantly less, you can pick up a key chain made from a piece of worn-out cable. ⊠ *1201 Mason St., at Washington St., Nob Hill* ☎ *415/474–1887* ⊕ *www.cablecarmuseum.org* ⌖ *Free* ☼ *Oct.–Mar., daily 10–5; Apr.–Sept., daily 10–6.*

Grace Cathedral. Not many churches can boast an altarpiece by Keith Haring and not one, but two labyrinths. The seat of the Episcopal Church in San Francisco, this soaring Gothic-style structure, erected on the site of the 19th-century railroad baron Charles Crocker's mansion, took 53 years to build, wrapping up in 1964. The gilded bronze doors at the east entrance were taken from casts of Lorenzo Ghiberti's incredible Gates of Paradise, which are on the Baptistery in Florence, Italy. A black-and-bronze stone sculpture of St. Francis by Beniamino Bufano greets you as you enter.

The 35-foot-wide limestone labyrinth is a replica of the 13th-century stone maze on the floor of Chartres Cathedral. All are encouraged to walk the ¼-mile-long labyrinth, a ritual based on the tradition of meditative walking. There's also a terrazzo outdoor labyrinth on the church's north side. The AIDS Interfaith Chapel, to the right as you enter Grace, contains a metal triptych by the late artist Keith Haring and panels from the AIDS Memorial Quilt. ■ **TIP→ Especially dramatic times to view the cathedral are during Thursday-night evensong (5:15 pm) and during special holiday programs.** ⊠ *1100 California St., at Taylor St., Nob Hill* ☎ *415/749–6300* ⊕ *www.gracecathedral.org* ⊡ *Free* ⊙ *Weekdays 7–6, Sat. 8–6, Sun. 8–7; tours weekdays at 1, Sat. at 11:30, and Sun. at 12:40.*

RUSSIAN HILL
TOP ATTRACTIONS

Fodor's Choice
★

Ina Coolbrith Park. If you make it all the way up here, you may have the place all to yourself, or at least feel that you do. The park's terraces are carved from a hill so steep that it's difficult to see if anyone else is there or not. Locals love this park because it feels like a secret no one else knows about—one of the city's magic hidden gardens, with a meditative setting and spectacular views of the bay peeking out from among the trees. A poet, Oakland librarian, and niece of Mormon prophet Joseph Smith, Ina Coolbrith (1842–1928) introduced Jack London and Isadora Duncan to the world of books. For years she entertained literary greats in her Macondray Lane home near the park. In 1915 she was named poet laureate of California. ⊠ *Vallejo St. between Mason and Taylor Sts., Russian Hill.*

Lombard Street. The block-long "Crookedest Street in the World" makes eight switchbacks down the east face of Russian Hill between Hyde and Leavenworth streets. Residents bemoan the traffic jam outside their front doors, but the throngs continue. Join the line of cars waiting to drive down the steep hill, or avoid the whole mess and walk down the steps on either side of Lombard. You take in super views of North Beach and Coit Tower whether you walk or drive—though if you're the one behind the wheel, you'd better keep your eye on the road lest you become yet another of the many folks who ram the garden barriers. ■ **TIP→ Can't stand the traffic? Thrill seekers of a different stripe may want to head two blocks south of Lombard to Filbert Street. At a gradient of 31.5%, the hair-raising descent between Hyde and Leavenworth streets is the city's steepest. Go slowly!** ⊠ *Lombard St. between Hyde and Leavenworth Sts., Russian Hill.*

Fodor's Choice
★

Macondray Lane. San Francisco has no shortage of impressive, grand homes, but it's the tiny fairy-tale lanes that make most folks want to move here, and Macondray Lane is the quintessential hidden garden. Enter under a lovely wooden trellis and proceed down a quiet, cobbled pedestrian lane lined with Edwardian cottages and flowering plants and trees. Watch your step—the cobblestones are quite uneven in spots. A flight of steep wooden stairs at the end of the lane leads to Taylor Street—on the way down you can't miss the bay views. If you've read any of Armistead Maupin's *Tales of the City* books, you may find the lane vaguely familiar. It's the thinly disguised setting for part of the series' action. ⊠ *Between Jones and Taylor Sts., and Union and Green Sts., Russian Hill.*

WORTH NOTING

San Francisco Art Institute. A Moorish-tile fountain in a tree-shaded court-yard draws the eye as soon as you enter the institute. The number-one reason for a visit is Mexican master Diego Rivera's *The Making of a Fresco Showing the Building of a City* (1931), in the student gallery to your immediate left inside the entrance. Rivera himself is in the fresco—his broad behind is to the viewer—and he's surrounded by his assistants. They in turn are surrounded by a construction scene, laborers, and city notables such as sculptor Robert Stackpole and architect Timothy Pfleuger. *Making* is one of three San Francisco murals painted by Rivera. The number-two reason to come here is the café, or more precisely the eye-popping, panoramic view from the café, which serves surprisingly decent food for a song.

The older portions of the Art Institute, including the lovely mission-style bell tower, were erected in 1926. To this day, otherwise pragmatic people claim that ghostly footsteps can be heard in the tower at night. Ansel Adams created the school's fine-arts photography department in 1946, and school directors established the country's first fine-arts film program. Notable faculty and alumni have included painter Richard Diebenkorn and photographers Dorothea Lange, Edward Weston, and Annie Leibovitz.

The **Walter & McBean Galleries** (☎ 415/749–4563 ⊙ *Open Tues. 11–7, Wed.–Sat. 11–6*) exhibit the often provocative works of established artists. ✉ *800 Chestnut St., North Beach* ☎ *415/771–7020* ⊕ *www.sfai.edu* ☑ *Galleries free* ⊙ *Hrs vary but building generally open Mon.–Sat. 9–7.*

NORTH BEACH

Italian bakeries appear frozen in time, homages to Jack Kerouac and Allen Ginsberg pop up everywhere, and strip joints, the modern equivalent of the Barbary Coast's "houses of ill repute," do business on Broadway. With its outdoor café tables, throngs of tourists, and holiday vibe, this is probably the part of town Europeans are thinking of when they say San Francisco is the most European city in America.

TOP ATTRACTIONS

Fodor's Choice
★

City Lights Bookstore. Take a look at the exterior of the store: the replica of a revolutionary mural destroyed in Chiapas, Mexico, by military forces; the art banners hanging above the windows; and the sign that says "Turn your sell [sic] phone off. Be here now." This place isn't just doling out best sellers. Designated a city landmark, the hangout of Beat-era writers—Allen Ginsberg and store founder Lawrence Ferlinghetti among them—and independent publisher remains a vital part of San Francisco's literary scene. Browse the three levels of sometimes haphazardly arranged poetry, philosophy, politics, fiction, history, and local zines, to the tune of creaking wood floors. ■ TIP➔ Be sure to check the calendar of literary events.

Back in the day, the basement was a kind of literary living room, where writers like Ginsberg and Jack Kerouac would read and even receive mail. Ferlinghetti cemented City Lights' place in history by publishing Ginsberg's *Howl and Other Poems* in 1956. The small volume was ignored in the mainstream . . . until Ferlinghetti and the bookstore manager were arrested for obscenity and corruption of youth. In the landmark First Amendment trial that followed, the judge exonerated both men, declaring that a work that has "redeeming social significance" can't be obscene. *Howl* went on to become a classic.

Stroll Kerouac Alley, branching off Columbus Avenue next to City Lights, to read the quotes from Ferlinghetti, Maya Angelou, Confucius, John Steinbeck, and the street's namesake embedded in the pavement. ✉ *261 Columbus Ave., North Beach* ☎ *415/362–8193* ⊕ *www. citylights.com* ⊙ *Daily 10 am–midnight.*

Coit Tower. Whether or not you agree that it resembles a fire-hose nozzle, this 210-foot tower is among San Francisco's most distinctive skyline sights. Although the monument wasn't intended as a tribute to firemen, it's often considered as such because of the donor's special attachment to the local fire company. As the story goes, a young gold rush–era girl, Lillie Hitchcock Coit (known as Miss Lil), was a fervent admirer of her local fire company—so much so that she once deserted a wedding party and chased down the street after her favorite engine, Knickerbocker No. 5, while clad in her bridesmaid finery.

Continued on page 183

CABLE CARS

The moment it dawns on you that you severely underestimated the steepness of the San Francisco hills will likely be the same moment you look down and realize those tracks aren't just for show—or just for tourists.

Sure, locals rarely use the cable cars for commuting these days. (That's partially due to the $6 fare—hear that, Muni?) So you'll likely be packed in with plenty of fellow sightseers. You may even be approaching cable-car fatigue after seeing its image on so many souvenirs. But if you fear the magic is gone, simply climb on board, and those jaded thoughts will dissolve. Grab the pole and gawk at the view as the car clanks down an insanely steep grade toward the bay. Listen to the humming cable, the clang of the bell, and the occasional quip from the gripman. It's an experience you shouldn't pass up, whether on your first trip or your fiftieth.

HOW CABLE CARS WORK

The mechanics are pretty simple: cable cars grab a moving subterranean cable with a "grip" to go. To stop, they release the grip and apply one or more types of brakes. Four cables, totaling 9 miles, power the city's three lines. If the gripman doesn't adjust the grip just right when going up a steep hill, the cable will start to slip and the car will have to back down the hill and try again. This is an extremely rare occurrence—imagine the ribbing the gripman gets back at the cable car barn!

Gripman: Stands in front and operates the grip, brakes, and bell. Favorite joke, especially at the peak of a steep hill: "This is my first day on the job folks…"

Conductor: Moves around the car, deals with tickets, alerts the grip about what's coming up, and operates the rear wheel brakes.

❶ Cable: Steel wrapped around flexible sisal core; 2 inches thick; runs at a constant 9½ mph.

❷ Bells: Used for crew communication; alerts other drivers and pedestrians.

❸ Grip: Vice-like lever extends through the center slot in the track to grab or release the cable.

❹ Grip Lever: Left-hand lever; operates grip.

❺ Car: Entire car weighs 8 tons.

❻ Wheel Brake: Steel brake pads on each wheel.

❼ Wheel Brake Lever: Foot pedal; operates wheel brakes.

❽ Rear Wheel Brake Lever: Applied for extra traction on hills.

❾ Track Brake: 2-foot-long sections of Monterey pine push down against the track to help stop the car.

❿ Track Brake Lever: Middle lever; operates track brakes.

⓫ Emergency Brake: 18-inch steel wedge, jams into street slot to bring car to an immediate stop.

⓬ Emergency Brake Lever: Right-hand lever, red; operates emergency brake.

ROUTES

Powell–Hyde line: Most scenic, with classic Bay views. Begins at Powell and Market streets, then crosses Nob Hill and Russian Hill before a white-knuckle descent down Hyde Street, ending near the Hyde Street Pier.

Powell–Mason line: Also begins at Powell and Market streets, but winds through North Beach to Bay and Taylor streets, a few blocks from Fisherman's Wharf.

California line: Runs from the foot of Market Street, at Drumm Street, up Nob Hill and back. Great views (and aromas and sounds) of Chinatown on the way up. Sit in back to catch glimpses of the Bay. ■TIP→ Take the California line if it's just the cable-car experience you're after—the lines are shorter, and the grips and conductors say it's friendlier and has a slower pace.

Cars run at least every 15 minutes, from around 6 AM to about 1 AM.

RULES OF THE RIDE

Tickets. A whopping $6 each way. There are ticket booths at all three turnarounds, or you can pay the conductor after you board (they can make change). Try not to grumble about the price—they're embarrassed enough as it is.

■TIP→ If you're planning to use public transit a few times, or if you'd like to ride back and forth on the cable car without worrying about the price, consider a one-day Muni passport ($14). You can get passports online, at the Powell Street turnaround, the TIX booth on Union Square, or the Fisherman's Wharf cable-car ticket booth at Beach and Hyde streets.

All Aboard. You can board on either side of the cable car. It's legal to stand on the running boards and hang on to the pole, but keep your ears open for the gripman's warnings. ■TIP→ Grab a seat on the outside bench for the best views.

Most people wait (and wait) in line at one of the cable car turnarounds, but you can also hop on along the route. Board wherever you see a white sign showing a figure climbing aboard a brown cable car; wave to the approaching driver, and wait until the car stops.

Riding on the running boards can be part of the thrill.

CABLE CAR HISTORY

HALLIDIE FREES THE HORSES

In the 1850s and '60s, San Francisco's streetcars were drawn by horses. Legend has it that the horrible sight of a car dragging a team of horses downhill to their deaths roused Andrew Smith Hallidie to action. The English immigrant had invented the "Hallidie Ropeway," essentially a cable car for mined ore, and he was convinced that his invention could also move people. In 1873, Hallidie and his intrepid crew prepared to test the first cable car high on Russian Hill. The anxious engineer peered down into the foggy darkness, failed to see the bottom of the hill, and promptly turned the controls over to Hallidie. Needless to say, the thing worked . . . but rides were free for the first two days because people were afraid to get on.

SEE IT FOR YOURSELF

The **Cable Car Museum** is one of the city's best free offerings and an absolute must for kids. (You can even ride a cable car there, since all three lines stop between Russian Hill and Nob Hill.) The museum, which is inside the city's last cable-car barn, takes the top off the system to let you see how it all works.

Eternally humming and squealing, the massive powerhouse cable wheels steal the show. You can also climb aboard a vintage car and take the grip, let the kids ring a cable-car bell (briefly, please!), and check out vintage gear dating from 1873.

✉ *1201 Mason St., at Washington St., Nob Hill* ☎ *415/474–1887* ⊕ *www. cablecarmuseum.com* 🎟 *Free* 🕐 *Oct.– Mar., daily 10–5; Apr.–Sept., daily 10–6*

▣ TIP➔ The gift shop sells cable car paraphernalia, including an authentic gripman's bell for $600 (it'll sound like Powell Street in your house every day). For significantly less, you can pick up a key chain made from a piece of worn-out cable.

CHAMPION OF THE CABLE CAR BELL

Each September the city's best and brightest come together to crown a bell-ringing champion at Union Square. The crowd cheers gripmen and conductors as they stomp, shake, and riff with the rope. But it's not a popularity contest; the ringers are judged by former bell-ringing champions who take each ping and gong very seriously.

The Birds

While on Telegraph Hill, you might be startled by a chorus of piercing squawks and a rushing sound of wings. No, you're not about to have a Hitchcock bird-attack moment. These small, vivid green parrots with cherry red heads number in the hundreds; they're descendants of former pets that escaped or were released by their owners. (The birds dislike cages, and they bite if bothered... must've been some disillusioned owners along the way.)

The parrots like to roost high in the aging cypress trees on the hill, chattering and fluttering, sometimes taking wing en masse. They're not popular with some residents, but they did find a champion in local bohemian Mark Bittner, a former street musician. Bittner began chronicling their habits, publishing a book and battling the homeowners who wanted to cut down the cypresses. A documentary, *The Wild Parrots of Telegraph Hill,* made the issue a cause célèbre. In 2007 City Hall, which recognizes a golden goose when it sees one, stepped in and brokered a solution to keep the celebrity birds in town. The city would cover the homeowners' insurance worries and plant new trees for the next generation of wild parrots.

She became the Knickerbocker Company's mascot and always signed her name "Lillie Coit 5." When Lillie died in 1929 she left the city $125,000 to "expend in an appropriate manner . . . to the beauty of San Francisco."

You can ride the elevator to the top of the tower—the only thing you have to pay for here—to enjoy the view of the Bay Bridge and the Golden Gate Bridge; due north is Alcatraz Island. Most visitors saunter right past the 19 fabulous Depression-era murals inside the tower that depict California's economic and political life, but take the time to appreciate the first New Deal art project supported by taxpayer money. The federal government commissioned the paintings from 25 local artists, and ended up funding a controversy. The radical Mexican painter Diego Rivera inspired the murals' socialist-realist style, with its biting cultural commentary, particularly about the exploitation of workers. At the time the murals were painted, clashes between management and labor along the waterfront and elsewhere in San Francisco were widespread. The elements, the thousands of visitors that pass by them every year, and the lack of climate control in the tower have taken their toll on the murals, but restoration work done on the tower in 2013 should help protect them. ■ TIP→ The views from the tower's base are also expansive—and free. Parking at Coit Tower is limited; in fact, you may have to wait (and wait) for a space. Spare yourself the frustration and hike up, if you're in good shape, or take the 39 bus. ✉ *Telegraph Hill Blvd. at Greenwich St. or Lombard St., North Beach* ☏ *415/362–0808* 🖅 *Free; elevator to top $7* ⊙ *Mar.–Sept., daily 10–5:30; Oct.–Feb., daily 9–4:30.*

Grant Avenue. Originally called Calle de la Fundación, Grant Avenue is the oldest street in the city, but it's got plenty of young blood. Here dusty bars such as the Saloon and perennial favorites like the Savoy

Tivoli mix with hotshot boutiques, odd curio shops like the antique jumble that is Aria, atmospheric cafés such as the boho haven Caffè Trieste, and authentic Italian delis. While the street runs from Union Square through Chinatown, North Beach, and beyond, the fun stuff in this neighborhood is crowded into the four blocks between Columbus Avenue and Filbert Street. ⊠ *North Beach.*

Fodor'sChoice
★

Telegraph Hill. Residents here have some of the city's best views, as well as the most difficult ascents to their aeries. The hill rises from the east end of Lombard Street to a height of 284 feet and is capped by Coit Tower *(see above)*. Imagine lugging your groceries up that! If you brave the slope, though, you can be rewarded with a "secret treasure" San Francisco moment. Filbert Street starts up the hill, then becomes the **Filbert Steps** when the going gets too steep. You can cut between the Filbert Steps and another flight, the **Greenwich Steps,** on up to the hilltop. As you climb, you can pass some of the city's oldest houses and be surrounded by beautiful, flowering private gardens. In some places the trees grow over the stairs so it feels as if you're walking through a green tunnel; elsewhere, you'll have wide-open views of the bay. And the telegraphic name? It comes from the hill's status as the first Morse code signal station back in 1853. ⊠ *Bordered by Lombard, Filbert, Kearny, and Sansome Sts., North Beach.*

Washington Square. Once the daytime social heart of Little Italy, this grassy patch has changed character numerous times over the years. The Beats hung out here in the 1950s, hippies camped out in the 1960s and early '70s, and nowadays you're more likely to see kids of Southeast Asian descent tossing a Frisbee than Italian folks reminiscing about the old country. In the morning, elderly Asians perform the motions of tai chi. Then and later you might see homeless people hanging out on the benches, and by midday young locals sunbathing or running their dogs. Lillie Hitchcock Coit, in yet another show of affection for San Francisco's firefighters, donated the statue of two firemen with a child they rescued. ■TIP➔ The North Beach Festival, the city's oldest street fair, celebrates the area's Italian culture here each June. ⊠ *Bordered by Columbus Ave. and Stockton, Filbert, and Union Sts., North Beach.*

WORTH NOTING

Beat Museum. This two-level museum is likely to see an uptick in visitors in response to the 2012 film version of *On the Road*, whose director donated the 1949 Hudson from the movie. Check out exhibits such as the *Beat Pad*, a mock-up of one of the cheap, tiny North Beach apartments the writers and artists populated in the 1950s, complete with bongos and bottle-as-candleholder. Memorabilia include the shirt Neal Cassady wore while driving Ken Kesey's Merry Prankster bus, "Further." An early photo of the legendary bus is juxtaposed with a more current picture showing it covered with moss and overgrowth, labeled "Nothing lasts." Indeed. There are also manuscripts, letters, and early editions by Jack Kerouac, Allen Ginsberg, and Lawrence Ferlinghetti. The gift store has a good selection of Beat philosophy, though it's nothing you won't find across the street at City Lights. ⊠ *540 Broadway, North Beach* ☏ *415/399–9626* ⊕ *www.thebeatmuseum.org* ☐ *$8* ☉ *Daily 10–7.*

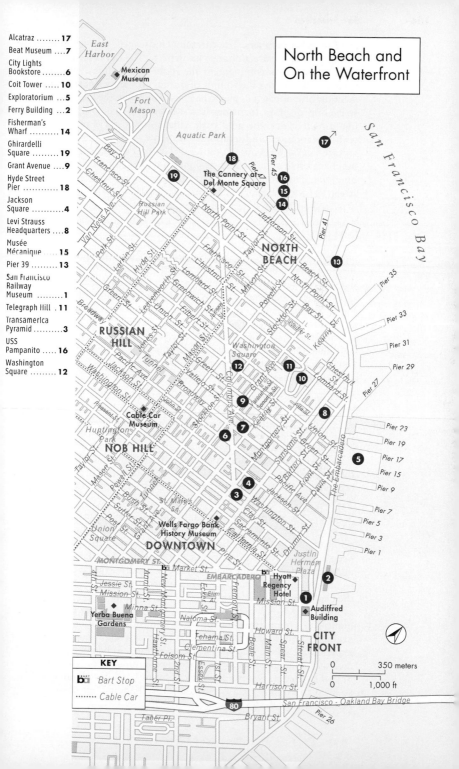

North Beach and
On the Waterfront

San Francisco Bay

East
Harbor

Mexican
Museum

Fort
Mason

Aquatic Park

Pier 45

NORTH
BEACH

The Cannery at
Del Monte Square

RUSSIAN
HILL

Washington
Square

NOB HILL

Cable Car
Museum

Huntington
Park

Wells Fargo Bank
History Museum

DOWNTOWN

Union
Square

MONTGOMERY ST.

Market St.

EMBARCADERO

Jessie St.
Mission St.

Minna St.

Natoma St.

Tehama St.

Clementina St.

Folsom St.

Hyatt
Regency
Hotel

Audiffred
Building

Justin
Herman
Plaza

CITY
FRONT

Yerba Buena
Gardens

Howard St.

Harrison St.

San Francisco - Oakland Bay Bridge

Bryant St.

Taber Pl.

Pier 35
Pier 33
Pier 31
Pier 29
Pier 27
Pier 23
Pier 19
Pier 17
Pier 15
Pier 9
Pier 7
Pier 5
Pier 3
Pier 1

Pier 26

KEY

bart Bart Stop

.... Cable Car

350 meters

1,000 ft

Levi Strauss headquarters. The carefully landscaped complex appears so collegiate that it's affectionately known as LSU—short for Levi Strauss University. Lawns complement the redbrick buildings, and gurgling fountains drown out the sounds of traffic, providing a perfect environment for brown-bag and picnic lunches. The Vault, the lobby exhibition space, has displays focusing on the history of the company, including jeans that saw the gold rush, videos about Levi's marketing and textile restoration, and temporary displays such as decades' worth of vintage Levi's shirts on a rotating dry-cleaner's rack. ■ TIP→ You can purchase Levi's and Dockers straight from the source at the cozy lobby boutique. The wonderful Filbert Steps to Coit Tower are across the street. ⊠ *Levi's Plaza, 1155 Battery St., North Beach* ☎ *415/501–6000* ⊕ *www.levistrauss.com* ☉ *Weekdays 9–6, weekends noon–5.*

ON THE WATERFRONT

San Francisco's waterfront neighborhoods have fabulous views and utterly different personalities. Kitschy, overpriced Fisherman's Wharf struggles to maintain the last shreds of its existence as a working wharf, while Pier 39 is a full-fledged consumer circus. The Ferry Building draws well-heeled locals with its culinary pleasures, firmly reconnecting the Embarcadero to downtown. Between the Ferry Building and Pier 39 a former maritime no-man's-land is filling in with the recently relocated Exploratorium, a $90 million cruise-ship terminal, Alcatraz Landing, fashionable waterfront restaurants, and restored, pedestrian-friendly piers.

TOP ATTRACTIONS

Alcatraz. Thousands of visitors come every day to walk in the footsteps of Alcatraz's notorious criminals. The stories of life and death on "The Rock" may sometimes be exaggerated, but it's almost impossible to resist the chance to wander the cellblock that tamed the country's toughest gangsters and saw daring escape attempts of tremendous desperation. Fewer than 2,000 inmates ever did time on the Rock, and though they weren't the worst criminals, they were definitely the worst prisoners, include Al "Scarface" Capone, Robert "The Birdman" Stroud, and George "Machine Gun" Kelly.

Some tips for escaping to Alcatraz: 1) Buy your ticket in advance. Visit the website for Alcatraz Cruises (⊕ *www.alcatrazcruises.com*) to scout out available departure times for the ferry. Prepay by credit card and keep a receipt record; the ticket price covers the boat ride and the audio tour. Pick up your ticket at the "will call" window at Pier 33 up to an hour before sailing. 2) Dress smart. Bring a jacket to ward off the chill from the boat ride and wear comfortable shoes. 3) Go for the evening tour. You'll get even more out of your Alcatraz experience at night. The evening tour has programs not offered during the day, the bridge-to-bridge view of the city twinkles at night, and your "prison experience" will be amplified as darkness falls. 4) Be mindful of scheduled and limited-capacity talks. Some programs are only given once a day (the schedule is posted in the cell house) and have limited seating, so keep an eye out for a cell-house staffer handing out passes shortly before the start time.

Thousands of visitors take ferries to Alcatraz each day to walk in the footsteps of the notorious criminals who were held on "The Rock."

The boat ride to the island is brief (15 minutes), but affords beautiful views of the city, Marin County, and the East Bay. The audio tour, highly recommended, includes observations by guards and prisoners about life in one of America's most notorious penal colonies. Plan your schedule to allow at least three hours for the visit and boat rides combined. Not inspired by the prison? Wander around the lovely native plant gardens and (if the tide is cooperating) the tide pools on the north side of the island. ⊠ *Pier 33, Embarcadero* ☎ *415/981–7625* ⊕ *www.nps.gov/alca* 🎟 *$30, including audio tour; $37 evening tour, including audio* ☉ *Ferry departs every 30–45 mins Sept.–late May, daily 9:30–2:15, 4:20 for evening tour Thurs.–Mon. only; late May–Aug., daily 9:30–4:15, 6:30 and 7:30 for evening tour.*

The Bay Lights. Adored by romance seekers, local families, and tourists alike, installation artist Leo Villareal's jaw-dropping LED light sculpture on the San Francisco–Oakland Bay Bridge has become an iconic San Francisco experience. As you travel west into the city along the bridge's upper deck you can view the sculpture's 25,000 lights dancing across its western span, but this installation is best seen from the Embarcadero. As of this writing, the Bay Lights was slated to end in March 2015, but locals are rallying for it to become permanent. ⊠ *Embarcadero* ⊕ *thebaylights.org.*

FAMILY
Fodor's Choice
★

Exploratorium. Walking into this fascinating "museum of science, art, and human perception" is like visiting a mad scientist's laboratory. Most of the exhibits are supersize, and you can play with everything. After moving into larger digs on the Embarcadero in 2013, the Exploratorium has even more space for its signature experiential exhibits, including a brand-new Tinkering Studio and a glass Bay Observatory building, where the exhibits inside help visitors better understand what they see outside.

Quintessential exhibits remain: Get an *Alice in Wonderland* feeling in the distortion room, where you seem to shrink and grow as you walk across the slanted, checkered floor. In the shadow room, a powerful flash freezes an image of your shadow on the wall; jumping is a favorite pose. *Pushover* demonstrates cow-tipping, but for people: stand on one foot and try to keep your balance while a friend swings a striped panel in front of you (trust us, you're going to fall).

More than 650 other exhibits focus on sea and insect life, computers, electricity, patterns and light, language, the weather, and more. "Explainers"—usually high-school students on their days off—demonstrate cool scientific tools and procedures, like DNA sample-collection and cow-eye dissection. One surefire hit is the pitch-black, touchy-feely Tactile Dome ($15 extra; reservations required). In this geodesic dome strewn with textured objects, you crawl through a course of ladders, slides, and tunnels, relying solely on your sense of touch. Lovey-dovey couples sometimes linger in the "grope dome," but be forewarned: the staff will turn on the lights if necessary. ■TIP➜ Patrons must be at least seven years old to enter the Tactile Dome, and the space is not for the claustrophobic. ✉ *Piers 15–17, Embarcadero* ☎ *415/561–0360 general information, 415/561–0362 Tactile Dome reservations* ⊕ *www. exploratorium.edu* ✍ *$25* ⊙ *Tues. and Thurs.–Sun. 10–5, Wed. 10–10; Thurs. 6 pm–10 pm ages 18 and over only.*

F-line. The city's system of vintage electric trolleys, the F-line, gives the cable cars a run for their money as a beloved mode of transportation. The beautifully restored streetcars—some dating from the 19th century—run from the Castro District down Market Street to the Embarcadero, then north to Fisherman's Wharf. Each car is unique, restored to the colors of its city of origin, from New Orleans and Philadelphia to Moscow and Milan. ■TIP➜ Purchase tickets on board; exact change is required. ⊕ *www.streetcar.org* ✍ *$2.*

Fodor's Choice
★

Ferry Building. The jewel of the Embarcadero, erected in 1896, is topped by a 230-foot clock tower modeled after the campanile of the cathedral in Seville, Spain. On the morning of April 18, 1906, the tower's four clock faces, powered by the swinging of a 14-foot pendulum, stopped at 5:17—the moment the great earthquake struck—and stayed still for 12 months.

Today San Franciscans flock to the street-level marketplace, stocking up on supplies from local favorites such as Acme Bread, Scharffen Berger Chocolate, Cowgirl Creamery, and Blue Bottle Coffee. Lucky diners claim a coveted table at Slanted Door, the beloved high-end Vietnamese restaurant. The seafood bar at Hog Island Oyster Company has fantastic bay-view panoramas, including the Bay Bridge. On Saturday morning the plazas outside the building buzz with an upscale farmers' market where you can buy exotic sandwiches and other munchables. Extending south from the piers north of the building all the way to the Bay Bridge, the waterfront promenade out front is a favorite among joggers and picnickers, with a front-row view of sailboats plying the bay.

True to its name the Ferry Building still serves actual ferries: from its eastern flank they sail to Sausalito, Larkspur, Tiburon, and the East Bay. ⊠ *Embarcadero at foot of Market St., Embarcadero* ☎ *415/983–8030* ⊕ *www.ferrybuildingmarketplace.com.*

QUICK
BITES

Buena Vista Café. At the end of the Hyde Street cable-car line, the Buena Vista packs 'em in for its famous Irish coffee—which, according to owners, was the first served stateside (in 1952). The place oozes nostalgia, drawing devoted locals as well as out-of-towners relaxing after a day of sightseeing. It's narrow and can get crowded, but this spot provides a fine alternative to the overpriced tourist joints nearby. ⊠ *2765 Hyde St., at Beach St., Fisherman's Wharf* ☎ *415/474–5044* ⊕ *www.thebuenavista.com.*

FAMILY
Fodor'sChoice
★

Hyde Street Pier. Cotton candy and souvenirs are all well and good, but if you want to get to the heart of the Wharf—boats—there's no better place to do it than at this pier, one of the Wharf area's best bargains. Depending on the time of day, you might see boatbuilders at work or children pretending to man an early-1900s ship.

Don't pass up the centerpiece collection of historic vessels, part of the **San Francisco Maritime National Historic Park,** almost all of which can be boarded. The *Balclutha,* an 1886 full-rigged three-masted sailing vessel that's more than 250 feet long, sailed around Cape Horn 17 times. Kids especially love the *Eureka,* a side-wheel passenger and car ferry, for her onboard collection of vintage cars. The *Hercules* is a steam-powered tugboat. The *C.A. Thayer,* a three-masted schooner, recently underwent a painstaking restoration.

Across the street from the pier and almost a museum in itself is the maritime park's **Visitor Center** (⊠ *499 Jefferson St.* ☎ *415/447–5000* ☉ *June–Aug., daily 9:30–5:30; Sept.–May, daily 9:30–5),* whose fun, large-scale exhibits, such as a huge First Order Fresnel lighthouse lens and a shipwrecked boat, make it an engaging quick stop. ⊠ *Hyde and Jefferson Sts., Fisherman's Wharf* ☎ *415/561–7100* ⊕ *www.nps.gov/safr* ⊠ *Ships $5 (ticket good for five days)* ☉ *June–Aug., daily 9:30–5:30; Sept.–May, daily 9:30–5.*

Jackson Square Historic District. This was the heart of the Barbary Coast of the Gay Nineties—the 1890s, that is. Although most of the red-light district was destroyed in the fire that followed the 1906 earthquake, the remaining old redbrick buildings, many of them now occupied by advertising agencies, law offices, and antiques firms, retain hints of the romance and rowdiness of San Francisco's early days.

With its gentrified gold rush–era buildings, the 700 block of **Montgomery Street** just barely evokes the Barbary Coast days, but this was a colorful block in 19th century and on into the 20th. Writers Mark Twain and Bret Harte were among the contributors to the spunky *Golden Era* newspaper, which occupied No. 732 (now part of the building at No. 744). From 1959 to 1996 the late ambulance-chaser extraordinaire, lawyer Melvin Belli, had his headquarters at Nos. 722 and 728–730. There was never a dull moment in Belli's world; he represented clients from the actress Mae West to Gloria Sykes (who in 1964 claimed that a cable-car accident turned her into a nymphomaniac) to the disgraced

4

televangelists Jim and Tammy Faye Bakker. Whenever he won a case, he fired a cannon and raised the Jolly Roger. Belli was also known for receiving a letter from the never-caught Zodiac killer.

Restored 19th-century brick buildings line Hotaling Place, which connects Washington and Jackson streets. The lane is named for the head of the **A.P. Hotaling Company whiskey distillery** (⊠ *451 Jackson St., at Hotaling Pl.*), the largest liquor repository on the West Coast in its day. (Anchor Distillery still makes an occasional Hotaling whiskey in the city, by the way; look for this single malt for a sip of truly local flavor.) ■**TIP**➔ The exceptional City Guides (☎ 415/557–4266 ⊕ www.sfcityguides.org) Gold Rush City walking tour covers this area and brings its history to life. ⊠ *Bordered by Columbus Ave., Broadway and Pacific Ave., Washington St., and Sansome St., Jackson Square.*

FAMILY
Fodor's Choice
★
Musée Mécanique. A time-warped arcade with antique mechanical contrivances, including peep shows and nickelodeons, Musée Mécanique is one of the most worthwhile attractions at the Wharf. Some favorites are the giant and rather creepy Laffing Sal, an arm-wrestling machine, the world's only steam-powered motorcycle, and mechanical fortune-telling figures that speak from their curtained boxes. Note the depictions of race that betray the prejudices of the time: stoned Chinese figures in the Opium-Den and clown-faced African Americans eating watermelon in the Mechanical Farm. ■**TIP**➔ Admission is free, but you'll need quarters to bring the machines to life. ⊠ *Pier 45 Shed A, Fisherman's Wharf* ☎ 415/346–2000 ⊕ *www.museemechanique.org* ⊠ *Free* ☉ *Weekdays 10–7, weekends 10–8.*

FAMILY
Pier 39. The city's most popular waterfront attraction draws millions of visitors each year who come to browse through its shops and concessions hawking every conceivable form of souvenir. The pier can be quite crowded, and the numerous street performers may leave you feeling more harassed than entertained. Arriving early in the morning ensures you a front-row view of the sea lions that bask here, but if you're here to shop—and make no mistake about it, Pier 39 wants your money—be aware that most stores don't open until 9:30 or 10 (later in winter).

Brilliant colors enliven the double-decker **San Francisco Carousel** (⊠ *$3 per ride*), decorated with images of such city landmarks as the Golden Gate Bridge and Lombard Street.

Follow the sound of barking to the northwest side of the pier to view the **sea lions** that flop about the floating docks. During the summer, orange-clad naturalists answer questions and offer fascinating facts about the playful pinnipeds—for example, that all the animals here are males.

At the **Aquarium of the Bay** (☎ 415/623–5300 or 888/732–3483 ⊕ *www.aquariumofthebay.org* ⊠ *$19.95* ☉ *Hours vary but at least 10–6 daily*) moving walkways transport you through a space surrounded on three sides by water filled with indigenous San Francisco Bay marine life, from fish and plankton to sharks. Many find the aquarium overpriced; if you can, take advantage of the family rate (⊠ *$64 for two adults and two kids under 12*).

The **California Welcome Center** (☎ 415/981–1280 ⊕ *www.visitcwc. com* ☉ *Daily 9–7*), on Pier 39's second level, can help you reserve tours and plan your time in the city.

Parking is across the street at the **Pier 39 Garage** (✉ *With validation from a Pier 39 restaurant, one hour free before 6 pm, two hours after 6 pm*), off Powell Street at the Embarcadero. ✉ *Beach St. at Embarcadero, Fisherman's Wharf* ⊕ *www.pier39.com.*

WORTH NOTING

FAMILY **Fisherman's Wharf.** It may be one of the city's best-known attractions, but the Wharf is a no-go zone for most locals, who shy away from the tourist crowds, overpriced food, and cheesy shops. If you can't resist a visit, come early to avoid the crowds and get a sense of the Wharf's functional role—it's not just an amusement park replica. Two delights amid the tackiness, both at Pier 45, are the ⇨ *Museé Mécanique*, a repository of old-fashioned but still working penny-arcade entertainments, and the World War II–era sub the ⇨ *USS Pampanito*. ✉ *Jefferson St. between Leavenworth St. and Pier 39, Fisherman's Wharf* ⊕ *www.fishermanswharf.org*

Ghirardelli Square. Most of the redbrick buildings in this early-20th-century complex were once part of the Ghirardelli factory. Now tourists come here to pick up the famous chocolate, though you can purchase it all over town and save yourself a trip to what is essentially a mall. But this is the only place to watch the cool chocolate manufactory in action. Placards throughout the square describe the factory's history. ✉ *900 North Point St., Fisherman's Wharf* ☎ *415/775–5500* ⊕ *www.ghirardellisq.com.*

USS Pampanito. Get an intriguing, if mildly claustrophobic, glimpse into life on a submarine during World War II on this sub, which sank six Japanese warships and damaged four others. ✉ *Pier 45, Fisherman's Wharf* ☎ *415/775–1943* ⊕ *www.maritime.org/pamphome.htm* ☞ *$12 (family pass $25)* ⊘ *Oct.–late May, Sun.–Thurs. 9–6, Fri. and Sat. 9–8; late May–Sept., Thurs.–Tues. 9–8, Wed. 9–6.*

FAMILY **San Francisco Railway Museum.** A labor of love brought to you by the same vintage-transit enthusiasts responsible for the F-line's revival, this one-room museum and store celebrates the city's streetcars and cable cars with photographs, models, and artifacts. The permanent exhibit includes the replicated end of a streetcar with a working cab—complete with controls and a bell—for kids to explore; the cool, antique Wiley birdcage traffic signal; and models and display cases to view. Right on the F-line track, just across from the Ferry Building, this is a great quick stop. ✉ *77 Steuart St., Embarcadero* ☎ *415/974–1948* ⊕ *www.streetcar. org* ☞ *Free* ⊘ *Tues.–Sun. 10–6.*

Transamerica Pyramid. It's neither owned by Transamerica nor is it a pyramid, but this 853-foot-tall obelisk *is* the most photographed of the city's high-rises. Excoriated in the design stages as "the world's largest architectural folly," the icon was quickly hailed as a masterpiece when it opened in 1972. Today it's probably the city's most recognized structure after the Golden Gate Bridge. Visit the small, street-level visitor center to see the virtual view from the top, watch videos about the building's history, and perhaps pick up a T-shirt. ■**TIP➜** A fragrant redwood grove along the east side of the building, replete with benches and a cheerful fountain, is a placid patch in which to unwind. ✉ *600 Montgomery St., Financial District* ⊕ *www.thepyramidcenter.com.*

THE MARINA, COW HOLLOW, AND THE PRESIDIO

Yachts bob at their moorings, satisfied-looking folks jog along the Marina Green, and multimillion-dollar homes overlook the bay in the picturesque, if somewhat sterile, Marina neighborhood. Does it all seem a bit too perfect? Well, it got this way after the hard knock of Loma Prieta—the current pretty face was put on after hundreds of homes collapsed in the 1989 earthquake. Between the Marina and old-money Pacific Heights lies comfortably upscale Cow Hollow. The neighborhood's name harks back to the 19th-century dairy farms whose owners eked out a living here despite the fact that there was more sand than grass. To get a feel for this accessible bastion of affluence, stroll down Union Street. Just west of Cow Hollow and the Marina stands the Presidio. Once a military base, this sprawling beauty is mostly green space, with hills, woods, and the marshlands of Crissy Field.

THE MARINA
TOP ATTRACTIONS

Fodor's Choice
★
Palace of Fine Arts. At first glance this stunning, rosy rococo palace seems to be from another world, and indeed, it's the sole survivor of the many tinted-plaster structures (a temporary classical city of sorts) built for the 1915 Panama-Pacific International Exposition, the world's fair that celebrated San Francisco's recovery from the 1906 earthquake and fire. The expo buildings originally extended about a mile along the shore. Bernard Maybeck designed this faux–Roman classic beauty, which was reconstructed in concrete and reopened in 1967. A victim of the elements, the Palace required a piece-by-piece renovation that was completed in 2008.

The pseudo-Latin language adorning the Palace's exterior urns continues to stump scholars. The massive columns (each topped with four "weeping maidens"), great rotunda, and swan-filled lagoon have been used in countless fashion layouts, films, and wedding photo shoots. After admiring the lagoon, look across the street to the house at 3460 Baker Street. If the maidens out front look familiar, they should—they're original casts of the "garland ladies" you can see in the Palace's colonnade.

Inside the palace is a performance venue favored by local community groups and international musicians. ⊠ *3301 Lyon St., at Beach St., Marina* ☎ *415/561–0364 Palace history tours* ⊕ *www.palaceoffinearts. org* ☐ *Free* ☉ *Daily 24 hrs.*

COW HOLLOW
WORTH NOTING

Octagon House. This eight-sided home sits across the street from its original site on Gough Street; it's one of two remaining octagonal houses in the city (the other is on Russian Hill), and the only one open to the public. White quoins accent each of the eight corners of the pretty blue-gray exterior, and a colonial-style garden completes the picture. The house is full of antique American furniture, decorative arts (paintings, silver, rugs), and documents from the 18th and 19th centuries. A deck of Revolutionary-era hand-painted playing cards takes an antimonarchist position: in place of kings, queens, and jacks, the American upstarts

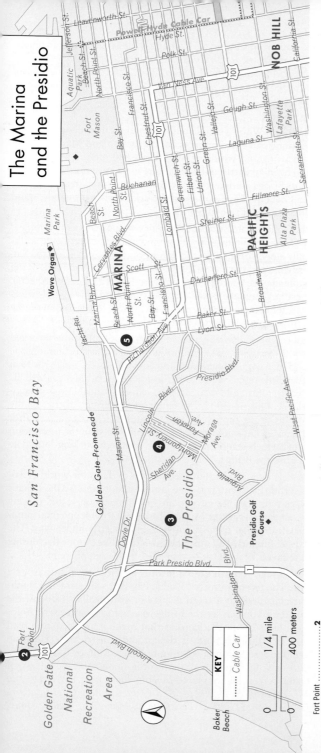

The Marina and the Presidio

San Francisco Bay

Golden Gate National Recreation Area

The Presidio

MARINA

PACIFIC HEIGHTS

NOB HILL

Golden Gate Promenade

Marina Park

Fort Mason

Aquatic Park

Presidio Golf Course

Baker Beach

Fort Point

Wave Organ

Lafayette Park

Alta Plaza Park

Powell-Hyde Cable Car

KEY

.... Cable Car

0 — 1/4 mile

0 — 400 meters

Jefferson St.
Leavenworth St.
Hyde St.
Polk St.
Beach St.
North Point St.
Francisco St.
Van Ness Ave.
Bay St.
Chestnut St.
Gough St.
Vallejo St.
Green St.
Washington St.
Laguna St.
Sacramento St.
California St.
Buchanan
North Point St.
Greenwich St.
Filbert St.
Union St.
Lombard St.
Fillmore St.
Steiner St.
Divisadero St.
Broadway
Baker St.
Lyon St.
Beach St.
North Point St.
Bay St.
Francisco St.
Scott St.
Marina Blvd.
Cervantes Blvd.
Richardson Ave.
Presidio Blvd.
Lincoln Blvd.
Funston Ave.
Moraga Ave.
Montgomery St.
Sheridan Ave.
Arguello Blvd.
West Pacific Ave.
Park Presidio Blvd.
Washington Blvd.
Lincoln Blvd.
Mason St.
Doyle Dr.
Yacht Rd.
101
1

substituted American statesmen, Roman goddesses, and Indian chiefs. ☒ *2645 Gough St., near Union St., Cow Hollow* ☏ *415/441–7512* ⬚ *Free, donations encouraged* ☉ *Feb.–Dec., 2nd Sun. and 2nd and 4th Thurs. of month noon–3; group tours weekdays by appointment.*

THE PRESIDIO

TOP ATTRACTIONS

Fodor's Choice
★

Golden Gate Bridge. With its simple but powerful art deco design, the 1.7-mile suspension span that connects San Francisco and Marin County was built to withstand winds of more than 100 mph. It's also not a bad place to be in an earthquake: designed to sway almost 28 feet, the Golden Gate Bridge (unlike the Bay Bridge) was undamaged by the 1989 Loma Prieta quake. If you're on the bridge when it's windy, stand still and you can feel it swaying a bit.

Crossing the Golden Gate Bridge under your own power is exhilarating—a little scary, and definitely chilly. From the bridge's eastern-side walkway, the only side pedestrians are allowed on, you can take in the San Francisco skyline and the bay islands; look west for the wild hills of the Marin Headlands, the curving coast south to Lands End, and the Pacific Ocean. On sunny days, sailboats dot the water, and brave windsurfers test the often-treacherous tides beneath the bridge. A vista point on the Marin County side provides a spectacular city panorama.

A structural engineer, dreamer, and poet named Joseph Strauss worked tirelessly for 20 years to make the bridge a reality, first promoting the idea of it and then overseeing design and construction. Though the final structure bore little resemblance to his original plan, Strauss guarded his legacy jealously, refusing to recognize the seminal contributions of engineer Charles A. Ellis. In 2007, the Golden Gate Bridge district finally recognized Ellis's role, though Strauss, who died less than a year after opening day in 1937, would doubtless be pleased with the inscription on his statue, which stands sentry in the southern parking lot: "The Man Who Built the Bridge."

You won't see it on a T-shirt, but the bridge is perhaps the world's most publicized suicide platform, with one jumper about every 10 days. Signs on the bridge refer the disconsolate to special telephones, and officers patrol the walkway and watch by security camera to spot potential jumpers. A public campaign to install a suicide barrier is under way. The unobtrusive net supported by most locals—not unlike the one that during construction saved 19 workers—completed the design phase in 2013.

While at the bridge you can grab a healthy snack at the art deco–style Bridge Café. The recently erected Bridge Pavilion sells attractive, high-quality souvenirs and has a small display of historical artifacts. At the outdoor exhibits, you can see the bridge rise before your eyes on hologram panels, learn about the features that make it art deco, and read about the personalities behind its design and construction. Head up to the Round House to join a 45-minute bridge tour, or have a photo taken ($20) of your family walking up the main cable—courtesy of a background screen, of course. ☒ *Lincoln Blvd. near Doyle Dr. and Fort Point, Presidio* ☏ *415/921–5858* ⊕ *www.goldengatebridge.org* ⬚ *Bridge free, tour $12.95* ☉ *Pedestrians: Mar.–Oct., daily 5 am–9* *pm; Nov.–Feb., daily 5 am–6 pm; hrs change with daylight saving time. Bikers: daily 24 hrs. Tour: on the half hour, 10:30–3:30.*

Fodor's Choice
★

Presidio. When San Franciscans want to spend a day in the woods, they head here. The Presidio has 1,400 acres of hills and majestic woods, two small beaches, and stunning views of the bay, the Golden Gate Bridge, and Marin County. Famed environmental artist Andy Goldsworthy's sculpture greets visitors at the Arguello Gate entrance. The 100-plus-foot *Spire*, made of 37 cypress logs reclaimed from the Presidio, looks like a rough, natural version of a church spire. ■TIP→ **The Presidio's best lookout points lie along Washington Boulevard, which meanders through the park.**

Part of the **Golden Gate National Recreation Area**, the Presidio was a military post for more than 200 years. Don Juan Bautista de Anza and a band of Spanish settlers first claimed the area in 1776. It became a Mexican garrison in 1822, when Mexico gained its independence from Spain; U.S. troops forcibly occupied the Presidio in 1846. The U.S. Sixth Army was stationed here until 1994.

Presidio is now a thriving community of residential and nonresidential tenants, who help to fund the Presidio's operations by rehabilitating and leasing its more than 700 buildings. In 2005 Bay Area filmmaker George Lucas opened the **Letterman Digital Arts Center**, his 23-acre digital studio "campus," along the eastern edge of the land. Seventeen of those acres are exquisitely landscaped and open to the public. If you have kids in tow or are a *Star Wars* fan yourself, sidle over to the **Yoda Fountain** (Letterman Drive at Dewitt Road), between two of the arts-center buildings.

The Presidio Trust, created to manage the Presidio and guide its transformation from military post to national park, has now turned its focus to rolling out the welcome mat to the public. The Presidio's visitor-serving tenants, such as the Asian-theme SenSpa, the House of Air Trampoline Park, Planet Granite climbing gym, the Walt Disney museum, a fabulous lodge at the Main Post, the newly reopened Officers' Club and 12 restaurants have helped with this goal. With old military housing now repurposed as apartments and homes with rents up to $10,000 a month the Presidio is a very popular place to live and boasts a much higher rate of families with children than the rest of San Francisco (36% versus16% in the rest of the city). Still, the $6 million that Lucas Film Ltd.—since 2012 a subsidiary of the Walt Disney Company—shells out annually for rent does plant a lot of saplings.

The Presidio also has a golf course, a visitor center, and picnic sites; the views from the many overlooks are sublime.

Especially popular is **Crissy Field**, a stretch of restored marshland along the sand of the bay. Kids on bikes, folks walking dogs, and joggers share the paved path along the shore, often winding up at the Warming Hut, a combination café and fun gift store at the end of the path, for a hot chocolate in the shadow of the Golden Gate Bridge. Midway along the Golden Gate Promenade that winds along the shore is the Gulf of the Farallones National Marine Sanctuary Visitor Center, where kids can get a close-up view of small sea creatures and learn about the rich ecosystem offshore. Temporarily relocated to East Beach, just across from the Palace

4

of Fine Arts, Crissy Field Center offers great children's programs and has cool science displays; grab lunch at the Beach Hut Café next door. West of the Golden Gate Bridge is sandy **Baker Beach,** beloved for its spectacular views and laid-back vibe (read: you'll see naked people here). This is one of those places that inspires local pride. ⊠ *Between Marina and Lincoln Park, Presidio* ⊕ *www.nps.gov/prsf and www.presidio.gov.*

Walt Disney Family Museum. This beautifully refurbished brick barracks house is a tribute to the man behind Mickey Mouse, the Disney Studios, and Disneyland. The smartly organized displays include hundreds of family photos, and well-chosen videos play throughout. Disney's legendary attention to detail becomes particularly evident in the cels and footage of *Fantasia, Sleeping Beauty,* and other animation classics. *The Toughest Period in My Whole Life* exhibit sheds light on lesser-known bits of history: the animators' strike at Disney Studios, the films Walt Disney made for the U.S. military during World War II, and his testimony before the House Un-American Activities Committee during its investigation of Communist influence in Hollywood. The glass-walled gallery showcasing Disney's wildlife films takes full advantage of the museum's location, with a lovely view of Presidio trees and the Golden Gate Bridge in the background. The liveliest exhibit and the largest gallery documents the creation of Disneyland with a fun, detailed model of what Disney imagined the park would be. Teacups spin, the Matterhorn looms, and that world-famous castle leads the way to Fantasyland. You won't be the first to leave humming "It's a Small World." In the final gallery, titled simply *December 16, 1966,* a series of sweet cartoons chronicles the world's reaction to Disney's sudden death. The one-way flow of the galleries deposits you near the attractive gift shop, which carries cool Disney-related stuff, and a café serving sandwiches, salads, and drinks. The downstairs theater shows Disney films (free with admission, $7 without) twice daily. ⊠ *Main Post, 104 Montgomery St., off Lincoln Blvd., Presidio* ☎ *415/345–6800* ⊕ *www.waltdisney.org* ⊠ *$20* ☉ *Wed.–Mon. 10–6.*

WORTH NOTING

FAMILY **Fort Point.** Dwarfed today by the Golden Gate Bridge, this brick fortress constructed between 1853 and 1861 was designed to protect San Francisco from a Civil War sea attack that never materialized. It was also used as a coastal-defense fortification post during World War II, when soldiers stood watch here. This National Historic Site is now a sprawling museum of military memorabilia. The building, which surrounds a lonely, windswept courtyard, has a gloomy air and is suitably atmospheric. It's usually chilly, too, so bring a jacket. The top floor affords a unique angle on the bay. ■ TIP➔ Take care when walking along the front side of the building, as it's slippery, and the waves have a dizzying effect.

On the days when Fort Point is staffed (on Friday and weekends), guided group tours and cannon drills take place. The popular, guided candlelight tours, available only in winter, sell out in advance, so book ahead. Living-history days take place throughout the year, when Union soldiers perform drills, a drum-and-fife band plays, and a Civil War–era doctor shows his instruments and describes his surgical technique (gulp). ⊠ *Marine Dr. off Lincoln Blvd., Presidio* ☎ *415/556–1693* ⊕ *www.nps.gov/fopo* ⊠ *Free* ☉ *Fri.–Sun. 10–5.*

Armed with only helmets, safety harnesses, and painting equipment, a full-time crew of 38 painters keeps the Golden Gate Bridge clad in International Orange.

GOLDEN GATE PARK AND THE WESTERN SHORELINE

More than 1,000 acres, stretching from the Haight all the way to the windy Pacific coast, Golden Gate Park is a vast patchwork of woods, trails, lakes, lush gardens, sports facilities, museums—even a herd of buffalo. There's more natural beauty beyond the park's borders, along San Francisco's wild Western Shoreline.

GOLDEN GATE PARK

TOP ATTRACTIONS

FAMILY
Fodor's Choice
★

California Academy of Sciences. With its native plant–covered living roof, retractable ceiling, three-story rain forest, gigantic planetarium, living coral reef, and frolicking penguins, the California Academy of Sciences is one of the city's most spectacular treasures. Dramatically designed by Renzo Piano, it's an eco-friendly, energy-efficient adventure in bio-diversity and green architecture. The roof's large mounds and hills mirror the local topography, and Piano's audacious design completes the dramatic transformation of the park's Music Concourse. Moving away from a restrictive role as a museum that catalogued natural history, the academy these days is all about sustainability and the future. The locally beloved dioramas in African Hall have survived the transition, however.

By the time you arrive, hopefully you've decided which shows and programs to attend, looked at the academy's floor plan, and designed a plan to cover it all in the time you have. And if not, here's the quick version: Head left from the entrance to the wooden walkway over otherworldly rays in the Philippine Coral Reef, then continue to the

Swamp to see Claude, the famous albino alligator. Swing through African Hall and gander at the penguins, take the elevator up to the living roof, then return to the main floor and get in line to explore the Rainforests of the World, ducking free-flying butterflies and watching for other live surprises. You'll end up below ground in the Amazonian Flooded Rainforest, where you can explore the academy's other aquarium exhibits. Phew.

■TIP➔ During peak periods the museum adds a $5 surcharge to tickets purchased at the door, so buy yours online ahead of time. ⊠ *55 Music Concourse Dr., Golden Gate Park* ☎ *415/379–8000* ⊕ *www. calacademy.org* ⊠ *$29.95, free 1 Sun. per quarter* ☉ *Mon.–Sat. 9:30–5, Sun. 11–5.*

Conservatory of Flowers. Whatever you do, be sure to at least drive by the Conservatory of Flowers—it's too darn pretty to miss. The gorgeous, white-framed 1878 glass structure is topped with a 14-ton glass dome. Stepping inside the giant greenhouse is like taking a quick trip to the rain forest, with its earthy smell and humid warmth. The undeniable highlight is the Aquatic Plants section, where lily pads float and carnivorous plants dine on bugs to the sounds of rushing water. On the east side of the conservatory (to the right as you face the building), cypress, pine, and redwood trees surround the Dahlia Garden, which blooms in summer and fall. Adding to the allure are temporary exhibits such as a past one devoted to prehistoric plants; an annual model-train display punctuated with mini buildings, found objects, and dwarf plants; and a butterfly garden that returns periodically. To the west is the **Rhododendron Dell,** which contains 850 varieties, more than any other garden in the country. It's a favorite local Mother's Day picnic spot. ⊠ *John F. Kennedy Dr. at Conservatory Dr., Golden Gate Park* ☎ *415/666–7001* ⊕ *www.conservatoryofflowers.org* ⊠ *$8, free 1st Tues. of month* ☉ *Tues.–Sun. 10–4:30* ☞ *No strollers allowed inside.*

de Young Museum. It seems that everyone in town has a strong opinion about the de Young Museum: Some adore its striking copper facade, while others just hope that the green patina of age will mellow the effect. Most maligned is the 144-foot tower, but the view from its ninth-story observation room, ringed by floor-to-ceiling windows and free to the public, is worth a trip here by itself. The building almost overshadows the de Young's respected collection of American, African, and Oceanic art. The museum also plays host to major international exhibits, such as postimpressionist works on loan from the Musée d'Orsay and 100 works from Paris's Musée National Picasso. The annual Bouquet des Art is a fanciful tribute to the museum's collection by notable Bay Area floral designers. ■TIP➔ On many Friday evenings, the museum hosts fun, free, family-centered events, with live music, art projects for children, and a wine and beer bar (the café stays open late, too). ⊠ *50 Hagiwara Tea Garden Dr., Golden Gate Park* ☎ *415/750–3600* ⊕ *deyoung.famsf.org* ⊠ *$10, good for same-day admittance to the Legion of Honor; free 1st Tues. of month* ☉ *Tues.–Sun. 9:30–5:15; mid-Jan.– Nov., Fri. until 8:45.*

Golden Gate Park and the Western Shoreline

California Academy of Sciences **2**
Cliff House **8**
Conservatory of Flowers **1**
de Young Museum **3**
Legion of Honor **7**
Lincoln Park **6**
Ocean Beach **9**
San Francisco Botanical Garden at Strybing Arboretum **5**
San Francisco Japanese Tea Garden **4**
San Francisco Zoo **10**

San Francisco Japanese Tea Garden. As you amble through the manicured landscape, past Japanese sculptures and perfect miniature pagodas, and over ponds of carp, you may feel transported to a more peaceful plane. Or maybe the shrieks of kids clambering over the almost vertical "humpback" bridges will keep you firmly in the here and now. Either way, this garden is one of those tourist spots that's truly worth a stop (a half hour will do). And at 5 acres, it's large enough that you'll always be able to find a bit of serenity, even when the tour buses drop by. The garden is especially lovely in March and April, when the cherry blossoms are in bloom. ⊠ *Hagiwara Tea Garden Dr., off John F. Kennedy Dr., Golden Gate Park* ☎ *415/752–4227* ⊕ *www.japaneseteagardensf. com* ✉ *$7, free Mon., Wed., and Fri. if you enter by 10 am* ⊙ *Mar.– Oct., daily 9–6; Nov.–Feb., daily 9–4:45.*

San Francisco Botanical Garden at Strybing Arboretum. One of the best picnic spots in a very picnic-friendly park, the 55-acre arboretum specializes in plants from areas with climates similar to that of the Bay Area. Walk the Eastern Australian garden to see tough, pokey shrubs and plants with cartoon-like names, such as the hilly-pilly tree. Kids gravitate toward the large shallow fountain and the pond with ducks, turtles, and egrets. ⊠ *Lincoln Way and 9th Ave. entrance, Golden Gate Park* ☎ *415/661–1316* ⊕ *www.sfbotanicalgarden.org* ✉ *$7, free 2nd Tues. of month* ⊙ *Apr.–Oct., daily 9–6; Nov.–Mar., daily 9–5.*

THE WESTERN SHORELINE

TOP ATTRACTIONS

Cliff House. A meal at the Cliff House isn't just about the food—the spectacular ocean view is what brings folks here—but the cuisine won't leave you wanting. The vistas, which include offshore Seal Rock (the barking marine mammals who reside there are actually sea lions), can be 30 miles or more on a clear day—or less than a mile on foggy days. ∎TIP➔ Come for drinks just before sunset; then head back into town for dinner.

Three buildings have occupied this site since 1863. The current building dates from 1909; a 2004 renovation has left a strikingly attractive restaurant and a squat concrete viewing platform out back. The complex, owned by the National Park Service, includes a gift shop.

Sitting on the observation deck is the **Giant Camera,** a camera obscura with its lens pointing skyward housed in a cute yellow-painted wooden shack. Built in the 1940s and threatened many times with demolition, it's now on the National Register of Historic Places. Step into the dark, tiny room inside (for a $3 fee); a fascinating 360-degree image of the surrounding area—which rotates as the "lens" on the roof rotates—is projected on a large, circular table. ∎TIP➔ In winter and spring you may also glimpse migrating gray whales from the observation deck.

To the north of the Cliff House lie the ruins of the once grand glass-roof **Sutro Baths,** which you can explore on your own (they look a bit like water-storage receptacles). Adolf Sutro, eccentric onetime San Francisco mayor and Cliff House owner, built the bath complex, including a train out to the site, in 1896, so that everyday folks could enjoy the benefits of swimming. Six enormous baths (some freshwater and some seawater), more than 500 dressing rooms, and several restaurants covered 3 acres north of the Cliff House and accommodated 25,000 bathers. Likened to Roman baths in a European glass palace, the baths were for decades the favorite destination of San Franciscans in search of entertainment. The complex fell into disuse after World War II, was closed in 1952, and burned down (under questionable circumstances) during demolition in 1966. ✉ *1090 Point Lobos Ave., Richmond* ☎ *415/386–3330* ⊕ *www.cliffhouse.com* ✉ *Free* ☼ *Weekdays 9 am–9:30 pm, weekends 9 am–10 pm.*

Fodor's Choice
★

Legion of Honor. The old adage of real estate—location, location, location—is at full force here. You can't beat the site of this museum of European art atop cliffs overlooking the ocean, the Golden Gate Bridge, and the Marin Headlands. A pyramidal glass skylight in the entrance court illuminates the lower-level galleries, which exhibit prints and drawings, English and European porcelain, and ancient Assyrian, Greek, Roman, and Egyptian art. The 20-plus galleries on the upper level display the permanent collection of European art (paintings, sculpture, decorative arts, and tapestries) from the 14th century to the present day.

The noteworthy Auguste Rodin collection includes two galleries devoted to the master and a third with works by Rodin and other 19th-century sculptors. An original cast of Rodin's *The Thinker* welcomes you as you walk through the courtyard. As fine as the museum is, the setting and view outshine the collection and also make a trip here worthwhile.

The **Legion Café,** on the lower level, serves tasty light meals (soup, sandwiches, grilled chicken) inside and on a garden terrace. (Unfortunately, there's no view.) Just north of the museum's parking lot is George Segal's *The Holocaust,* a stark white installation that evokes life in concentration camps during World War II. It's haunting at night, when backlighted by lights in the Legion's parking lot. ■TIP→ **Admission to the Legion is also good for same-day admission to the de Young Museum in Golden Gate Park.** ✉ *34th Ave. at Clement St., Richmond* ☎ *415/750–3600* ⊕ *legionofhonor.famsf.org* ✉ *$10, $2 off with Muni transfer, free 1st Tues. of month* ☼ *Tues.–Sun. 9:30–5:15.*

Fodor's Choice
★

Lincoln Park. Although many of the city's green spaces are gentle and welcoming, Lincoln Park is a wild, 275-acre park in the Outer Richmond with windswept cliffs and panoramic views. The newly renovated Coastal Trail, the park's most dramatic one, leads out to **Lands End;** pick it up west of the Legion of Honor (at the end of El Camino del Mar) or from the parking lot at Point Lobos and El Camino del Mar. Time your hike to hit Mile Rock at low tide, and you might catch a glimpse of two wrecked ships peeking up from their watery graves. ⚠ **Be careful if you hike here; landslides are frequent, and people have fallen into the sea by standing too close to the edge of a crumbling bluff top.**

On the tamer side, large Monterey cypresses line the fairways at Lincoln Park's 18-hole golf course, near the Legion of Honor. At one time this land was the Golden Gate Cemetery, where the dead were segregated by nationality; most were indigent and interred without ceremony in the potter's field. In 1900 the Board of Supervisors voted to ban burials

4

within city limits, and all but two city cemeteries (at Mission Dolores and the Presidio) were moved to Colma, a small town just south of San Francisco. When digging has to be done in the park, bones occasionally surface again. ⊠ *Entrance at, 34th Ave. at Clement St, Richmond.*

WORTH NOTING

Ocean Beach. Stretching 3 miles along the western side of the city from the Richmond to the Sunset, this sandy swath of the Pacific coast is good for jogging or walking the dog—but not for swimming. The water is so cold that surfers wear wet suits year-round, and riptides are strong, so only brave the waves if you are a strong swimmer or surfer. As for sunbathing, it's rarely warm enough here; think meditative walking instead of sun worshipping.

Paths on both sides of the Great Highway lead from Lincoln Way to Sloat Boulevard (near the zoo); the beachside path winds through landscaped sand dunes, and the paved path across the highway is good for biking and in-line skating. (Though you have to rent bikes elsewhere.) The **Beach Chalet** restaurant and brewpub is across the Great Highway from Ocean Beach, about five blocks south of the Cliff House. ⊠ *Along Great Hwy. from Cliff House to Sloat Blvd. and beyond.*

FAMILY **San Francisco Zoo.** Occupying prime oceanfront property, the zoo is touting its metamorphosis into the "New Zoo," a wildlife-focused recreation center that inspires visitors to become conservationists. Integrated exhibits group different species of animals from the same geographic areas together in enclosures that don't look like cages. More than 250 species reside here, including endangered species such as the snow leopard, Sumatran tiger, grizzly bear, and a Siberian tiger.

The zoo's superstar exhibit is **Grizzly Gulch,** where orphaned grizzly bear sisters Kachina and Kiona enchant visitors with their frolicking and swimming. When the bears are in the water, the only thing between you and them is (thankfully thick) glass. Grizzly feedings are at 11:30 am daily.

The **Lemur Forest** has five varieties of the bug-eyed, long-tailed primates from Madagascar. You can help hoist food into the lemurs' feeding towers and watch the fuzzy creatures climb up to chow down. African Kikuyu grass carpets the circular outer area of **Gorilla Preserve,** one of the largest and most natural gorilla habitats of any zoo in the world. Trees and shrubs create communal play areas.

Ten species of rare primates—including black howler monkeys, black-and-white ruffed lemurs, and macaques—live and play at the two-tier **Primate Discovery Center,** which contains 23 interactive learning exhibits on the ground level.

Magellanic penguins waddle about the rather sad concrete **Penguin Island,** splashing and frolicking in its 200-foot pool. Feeding times are 10:30 and 3:30. Koalas peer out from among the trees in **Koala Crossing,** and kangaroos and wallabies headline the **Australian Walkabout** exhibit. The 7-acre **Puente al Sur** (Bridge to the South) re-creates habitats in South America, replete with giant anteaters and capybaras.

An **African Savanna** exhibit mixes giraffes, zebras, kudus, ostriches, and many other species, all living together in a 3-acre section with a central viewing spot accessed by a covered passageway.

The 6-acre **Children's Zoo** has about 300 mammals, birds, and reptiles, plus an insect zoo, a meerkat and prairie-dog exhibit, a nature trail, a nature theater, a huge playground, a restored 1921 Dentzel carousel, and a mini–steam train. A ride on the train costs $4, and you can hop astride one of the carousel's 52 hand-carved menagerie animals for $2. ⊠ *Sloat Blvd. and 47th Ave., Sunset* ☎ *415/753–7080* ⊕ *www.sfzoo.org* 🎟 *$17, $1 off with Muni transfer (take Muni L–Taraval streetcar from downtown)* ⊘ *Mid-Mar.–Oct., daily 10–5; Nov.–mid-Mar., daily 10–4.*

THE HAIGHT, THE CASTRO, AND NOE VALLEY

4

These distinct neighborhoods are where the city's soul resides. They wear their personalities large and proud, and all are perfect for just strolling around. Like a slide show of San Franciscan history, you can move from the Haight's residue of 1960s counterculture to the Castro's connection to 1970s and '80s gay life to 1990s gentrification in Noe Valley. Although historic events thrust the Haight and the Castro onto the international stage, both are anything but stagnant—they're still dynamic areas well worth exploring.

THE HAIGHT
TOP ATTRACTION

Haight-Ashbury Intersection. On October 6, 1967, hippies took over the intersection of Haight and Ashbury streets to proclaim the "Death of Hip." If they thought hip was dead then, they'd find absolute confirmation of it today, what with the only tie-dye in sight on the famed corner being Ben & Jerry's storefront.

Everyone knows the Summer of Love had something to do with free love and LSD, but the drugs and other excesses of that period have tended to obscure the residents' serious attempts to create an America that was more spiritually oriented, more environmentally aware, and less caught up in commercialism. The Diggers, a radical group of actors and populist agitators, for example, operated a free shop a few blocks off Haight Street. Everything really was free at the free shop; people brought in things they didn't need and took things they did.

Among the folks who hung out in or near the Haight during the late 1960s were writers Richard Brautigan, Allen Ginsberg, Ken Kesey, and Gary Snyder; anarchist Abbie Hoffman; rock performers Marty Balin, Jerry Garcia, Janis Joplin, and Grace Slick; LSD champion Timothy Leary; and filmmaker Kenneth Anger. If you're keen to feel something resembling the hippie spirit these days, there's always Hippie Hill, just inside the Haight Street entrance of Golden Gate Park. Think drum circles, guitar players, and whiffs of pot smoke. ⊠ *Haight.*

THE CASTRO
TOP ATTRACTION

Fodor'sChoice
★

Castro Theatre. Here's a classic way to join in the Castro community: grab some popcorn and catch a flick at this 1,500-seat art deco theater; opened in 1922, it's the grandest of San Francisco's few remaining movie palaces. The neon marquee, which stands at the top of the Castro strip, is the neighborhood's great landmark. The Castro was the fitting host of 2008's red-carpet preview of Gus Van Sant's film *Milk*, starring Sean Penn as openly gay San Francisco supervisor Harvey Milk. The theater's elaborate Spanish baroque interior is fairly well preserved. Before many shows the theater's pipe organ rises from the orchestra pit and an organist plays pop and movie tunes, usually ending with the Jeanette McDonald standard "San Francisco" (go ahead, sing along). The crowd can be enthusiastic and vocal, talking back to the screen as loudly as it talks to them. Classics such as *Who's Afraid of Virginia Woolf?* take on a whole new life, with the assembled beating the actors to the punch and fashioning even snappier comebacks for Elizabeth Taylor. Head here to catch sing-along classics like *Mary Poppins*, a Fellini film retrospective, or the latest take on same-sex love. ⊠ *429 Castro St., Castro* ☎ *415/621–6120* ⊕ *www.castrotheatre.com.*

WORTH NOTING

QUICK
BITES

✕ **Cafe Flore.** Sometimes referred to as Cafe Floorshow because it's such a see-and-be-seen place, Cafe Flore serves coffee drinks, beer, and tasty café fare. It's a good place to catch the latest Castro gossip. ⊠ *2298 Market St., at Noe St., Castro* ☎ *415/621–8579* ⊕ *cafeflore.com.*

GLBT Historical Society Museum. The one-room Gay, Lesbian, Bisexual, and Transgender (GLBT) Historical Society Museum presents multimedia exhibits from its vast holdings covering San Francisco's queer history. You might hear the audiotape Harvey Milk made for the community in the event of his assassination, view an exhibit of prominent African Americans, gays, and lesbians in the city, or flip through a memory book with pictures and thoughts on some of the more than 20,000 San Franciscans lost to AIDS. Though perhaps not for the faint of heart (those offended by sex toys and photos of lustily frolicking naked people may, well, be offended), the museum offers an inside look at these communities so integral to the fabric of San Francisco life. ⊠ *4127 18th St., near Castro St., Castro* ☎ *415/621–1107* ⊕ *www.glbthistory.org* ▭ *$5, free 1st Wed. of the month* ☉ *Mon. and Wed.–Sat. 11–7, Sun. noon–5.*

Harvey Milk Plaza. An 18-foot-long rainbow flag, the symbol of gay pride, flies above this plaza named for the man who electrified the city in 1977 by being elected to its board of supervisors as an openly gay candidate. In the early 1970s Milk had opened a camera store on the block of Castro Street between 18th and 19th streets. The store became the center for his campaign to open San Francisco's social and political life to gays and lesbians.

The Haight, the Castro, Noe Valley, and the Mission District

The liberal Milk hadn't served a full year of his term before he and Mayor George Moscone, also a liberal, were shot in November 1978 at City Hall. The murderer was a conservative ex-supervisor named Dan White, who had recently resigned his post and then became enraged when Moscone wouldn't reinstate him. Milk and White had often been at odds on the board, and White thought Milk had been part of a cabal to keep him from returning to his post. Milk's assassination shocked the gay community, which became infuriated when the infamous "Twinkie defense"—that junk food had led to diminished mental capacity—resulted in a manslaughter verdict for White. During the so-called White Night Riot of May 21, 1979, gays and their allies stormed City Hall, torching its lobby and several police cars.

Milk, who had feared assassination, left behind a tape recording in which he urged the community to continue the work he had begun. His legacy is the high visibility of gay people throughout city government; a bust of him was unveiled at City Hall on his birthday in 2008, and the 2008 film *Milk* gives insight into his life. A plaque at the base of the flagpole lists the names of past and present openly gay and lesbian state and local officials. ⊠ *Southwest corner of Castro and Market Sts., Castro.*

NOE VALLEY
WORTH NOTING
Golden fire hydrant. When all the other fire hydrants went dry during the fire that followed the 1906 earthquake, this one kept pumping. Noe Valley and the Mission District were thus spared the devastation wrought elsewhere in the city, which explains the large number of pre-quake homes here. Every year on April 18th (the anniversary of the quake) folks gather here to share stories about the earthquake, and the famous hydrant gets a fresh coat of gold paint. ⊠ *Church and 20th Sts., southeastern corner, across from Dolores Park, Noe Valley.*

CASTRO
AND NOE
WALK

The Castro and Noe Valley neighborhoods beg to be walked—or ambled through, really, without time pressure or an absolute destination. Fortify yourself with a coffee, or get one to go, at the amusing **Cafe Flore**, then head west up **Market Street** to check out the shops and boutiques in the block before **Castro Street**. You've at Castro arrived when you're standing under the gigantic rainbow flag at **Harvey Milk Plaza**. Enjoy the plaza's perspective on the art deco **Castro Theatre**, then head south past the theater, popping into the shops along the way (Cliff's Variety, at 479 Castro Street, is a must). To tour Noe Valley, go east down **18th Street** to Church (at Dolores Park), and then head south over the hill—or hop on the J–Church light-rail car—to **24th Street**, this rambling neighborhood's center.

A colorful mosaic mural in the Castro

MISSION DISTRICT

The Mission has a number of distinct personalities: it's the Latino neighborhood, where working-class folks raise their families and where gangs occasionally clash; it's the hipster hood, where tattooed and pierced twenty- and thirtysomethings hold court in too-cool cafés and bars; it's a culinary epicenter, with destination restaurants and affordable ethnic cuisine; and it's the artists' quarter, where murals adorn literally blocks of walls. It's also the city's equivalent of the Sunshine State—this neighborhood's always the last to succumb to fog.

TOP ATTRACTIONS

Balmy Alley murals. Mission District artists have transformed the walls of their neighborhood with paintings, and Balmy Alley is one of the best-executed examples. Many murals adorn the one-block alley, with newer ones continually filling in the blank spaces. In 1971, artists began teaming with local children to create a space to promote peace in Central America, community spirit, and (later) AIDS awareness; since then dozens of artists have added their vibrant works. ■TIP➜ Be alert here: the 25th Street end of the alley adjoins a somewhat dangerous area. ✉ *24th St. between and parallel to Harrison and Treat Sts., alley runs south to 25th St., Mission.*

Fodor's Choice ★ **Dolores Park.** A two-square-block microcosm of life in the Mission, Dolores Park is one of San Francisco's liveliest green spaces: dog lovers and their pampered pups congregate, kids play at the extravagant, recently reconstructed playground, and hipsters hold court, drinking beer on sunny days. During the summer, the park hosts movie nights; performances by Shakespeare in the Park, the San Francisco Mime

Troupe, and the San Francisco Symphony; and any number of pop-up events and impromptu parties. Spend a warm day here—maybe sitting at the top of the park with a view of the city and the Bay Bridge—surrounded by locals and that laid-back San Francisco energy, and you may well find yourself plotting your move to the city. The park continues to be well visited during a major renovation expected to continue through 2015. ⊠ *Between 18th and 20th Sts. and Dolores and Church Sts., Mission.*

Mission Dolores. Two churches stand side by side at this mission, including the small adobe **Mission San Francisco de Asís,** the oldest standing structure in San Francisco. Completed in 1791, it's the sixth of the 21 California missions founded by Franciscan friars in the 18th and early 19th centuries. Its ceiling depicts original Ohlone Indian basket designs, executed in vegetable dyes. The tiny chapel includes frescoes and a hand-painted wooden altar.

There's a hidden treasure here, too. In 2004 an archaeologist and an artist crawling along the ceiling's rafters opened a trap door behind the altar and rediscovered the mission's original mural, painted with natural dyes by Native Americans in 1791. The centuries have taken their toll, so the team photographed the 20-by-22-foot mural and began digitally restoring the photographic version. Among the images is a dagger-pierced Sacred Heart of Jesus.

The small museum here covers the mission's founding and history, and the pretty little cemetery—which appears in Alfred Hitchcock's film *Vertigo*—contains the graves of mid-19th-century European immigrants. (The remains of an estimated 5,000 Native Americans lie in unmarked graves.) Services are held in both the old mission and next door in the handsome multidome basilica. ⊠ *Dolores and 16th Sts., Mission* ☎ *415/621–8203* ⊕ *www.missiondolores.org* ✉ *$5, audio tour $7* ☉ *Nov.–Apr., daily 9–4; May–Oct., daily 9–4:30.*

WORTH NOTING

Clarion Alley murals. A new generation of muralists is creating a fresh alley-cum-gallery here. The works by the loosely connected artists of the Clarion Alley Mural Project (CAMP) represent a broad range of styles and imagery. Carpet-draped Indonesian elephants plod calmly down the block; kung fu movie–style headlines shout slogans. The alley's murals offer a quick but dense glimpse into the Mission's contemporary art scene. ⊠ *Between Valencia and Mission Sts. and 17th and 18th Sts., Mission.*

Galería de la Raza. San Francisco's premier showcase for contemporary Latino art, the gallery exhibits the works of mostly local artists. Events include readings and spoken word by local poets and writers, screenings of Latin American and Spanish films, and theater works by local minority theater troupes. Just across the street, murals and mosaics festoon the 24th Street/York Street Minipark, a tiny urban playground. A mosaic-covered Quetzalcoatl serpent plunges into the ground and rises, creating hills for little ones to clamber over, and mural-covered walls surround the space. ⊠ *2857 24th St., at Bryant St., Mission* ☎ *415/826–8009* ⊕ *www.galeriadelaraza.org* ☉ *Gallery Wed.–Sat. noon–6.*

Precita Eyes Mural Arts and Visitors Center. The muralists of this nonprofit arts organization design and create murals and lead guided walks of area murals. The Classic Mission Mural Walk ($20) starts with a 45-minute slide presentation before participants head outside to view murals on Balmy Alley and 24th Street. The Mission Trail Mural Walk ($15) includes some of the same murals and impressive ones at Cesar Chavez Elementary School. You can pick up a map of 24th Street's murals at the center and buy art supplies, T-shirts, postcards, and other mural-related items. ✉ *2981 24th St., Mission* ☎ *415/285–2287* ⊕ *www.precitaeyes. org* ⌨ *Center free, tours $15–$20* ⊙ *Center: weekdays 10–5, Sat. 10–4, Sun. noon–4. Walks: weekends at 11 (Mission Trail) and 1:30 (Classic).*

DOGPATCH

East of the Mission District and Potrero Hill and a short T-Third Muni Metro ride from SoMa, the Dogpatch neighborhood has been on the rise for the last decade. Artisans, designers, and craftspeople eager to protect the area's historical industrial legacy have all moved here in recent years, providing a solid customer base for shops, galleries, and boutique restaurants and artisanal food producers. The Museum of Craft and Design moved to Dogpatch in 2013 and instantly became the neighborhood's cultural anchor.

TOP ATTRACTION

Museum of Craft and Design. Right at home in this once-industrial neighborhood now bursting with creative energy, this small, four-room space mounts temporary art and design exhibitions. The focus might be sculpture, metalwork, furniture, or jewelry—or industrial design, architecture, or other topics. The MakeArt Lab gives kids the opportunity to create their own exhibit-inspired work, and the beautifully curated shop sells tempting textiles, housewares, jewelry, and other well-crafted items. ✉ *2569 3rd St. near 22nd St., Dogpatch* ☎ *415/773–0303* ⊕ *sfmcd.org* ⌨ *$8, free first Tues. of month* ⊙ *Tues.–Sat. 11–6 (Thurs. until 7), Sun. noon–5.*

PACIFIC HEIGHTS AND JAPANTOWN

Pacific Heights and Japantown are something of an odd couple: privileged, old-school San Francisco and the workaday commercial center of Japanese American life in the city, stacked virtually on top of each other. The extravagant mansions of Pacific Heights gradually give way to the more modest Victorians and unassuming housing tracts of Japantown. The most interesting spots in Japantown huddle in the Japan Center, the neighborhood's two-block centerpiece, and along Post Street. You can find plenty of authentic Japanese treats in the shops and restaurants. ■TIP→ Japantown is a relatively safe area, but the Western Addition, south of Geary Boulevard, can be dangerous even during the daytime.

PACIFIC HEIGHTS
TOP ATTRACTIONS

Haas-Lilienthal House. A small display of photographs on the bottom floor of this elaborate, gray 1886 Queen Anne house makes clear that despite its lofty stature and striking, round third-story tower, the house was modest compared with some of the giants that fell victim to the 1906 earthquake and fire. The Foundation for San Francisco's Architectural Heritage operates the home, whose carefully kept rooms provide a glimpse into late-19th-century life through period furniture, authentic details (antique dishes in the kitchen built-in), and photos of the family that occupied the house until 1972. ■TIP➡ You can admire hundreds of gorgeous San Francisco Victorians from the outside, but this is the only one that's open to the public, and it's worth a visit. Volunteers conduct one-hour house tours three days a week, and informative two-hour walking tours of Pacific Heights on Sunday afternoon (call or check website for schedule). ⊠ *2007 Franklin St., between Washington and Jackson Sts., Pacific Heights* ☏ *415/441–3004* ⊕ *www.sfheritage.org* 🖙 *Tours $8* ⏱ *1-hr tour Wed. and Sat. noon–3, Sun. 11–4; 2-hr tour Sun. at 12:30.*

Spreckels Mansion. Shrouded behind tall juniper hedges at the corner of winding, redbrick Octavia Street, overlooking Lafayette Park, the estate was built for sugar heir Adolph Spreckels and his wife Alma. Mrs. Spreckels was so pleased with her house that she commissioned George Applegarth to design another building in a similar vein: the Legion of Honor. One of the city's great iconoclasts, Alma Spreckels was the model for the bronze figure atop the Victory Monument in Union Square. These days an iconoclast of another sort owns the mansion: romance novelist Danielle Steel, whose dust-up with local columnists over the size of those hedges entertained aficionados of local gossip in early 2014. ⊠ *2080 Washington St., at Octavia St., Pacific Heights.*

WORTH NOTING

FAMILY **Alta Plaza Park.** Golden Gate Park's longtime superintendent, John McLaren, designed Alta Plaza in 1910, modeling its terracing on that of the Grand Casino in Monte Carlo, Monaco. From the top you can see Marin to the north, downtown to the east, Twin Peaks to the south, and Golden Gate Park to the west. ■TIP➡ Kids love the many play structures at the large, enclosed playground at the top; everywhere else is dog territory. ⊠ *Bordered by Clay, Steiner, Jackson, and Scott Sts., Pacific Heights.*

Franklin Street buildings. The three blocks south of the ⇨ *Haas-Lilienthal House* contain a few curiosities of interest to architecture buffs. What at first looks like a stone facade on the **Golden Gate Church** (⊠ *1901 Franklin St.*) is actually redwood painted white. A handsome Georgian-style residence built in the early 1900s for a coffee merchant sits at 1735 Franklin. On the northeast corner of Franklin and California streets is a **Christian Science church**; built in the Tuscan revival style, it's noteworthy for its terra-cotta detailing. **The Coleman House** (⊠ *1701 Franklin St.*) is an impressive twin-turret Queen Anne mansion that was built for a gold-rush mining and lumber baron. Don't miss the large, brilliant-purple stained-glass window on the house's north side. ⊠ *Franklin St. between Washington and California Sts., Pacific Heights.*

JAPANTOWN
TOP ATTRACTIONS

Japan Center. Cool and curious trinkets, noodle houses and sushi joints, a destination bookstore, and a peek at Japanese culture high and low await at this 5-acre complex designed in 1968 by noted American architect Minoru Yamasaki. The Japan Center includes the shop- and restaurant-filled Kintetsu and Kinokuniya buildings; the excellent Kabuki Springs & Spa; the Hotel Kabuki; and the Sundance Kabuki, Robert Redford's fancy, reserved-seating cinema/restaurant complex.

The Kinokuniya Bookstores, in the Kinokuniya Building, have an extensive selection of Japanese-language books, *manga* (graphic novels), books on design, and English-language translations and books on Japanese topics. Just outside, follow the Japanese teenagers to Pika Pika, where you and your friends can step into a photo booth and then use special effects and stickers to decorate your creation. On the bridge connecting the center's two buildings, check out Shige Antiques for *yukata* (lightweight cotton kimonos) for kids and lovely silk kimonos, and Asakichi and its tiny incense shop for tinkling wind chimes and display-worthy teakettles. Continue into the Kintetsu Building for a selection of Japanese restaurants.

Between the Miyako Mall and Kintetsu Building are the five-tier, 100-foot-tall **Peace Pagoda** and the Peace Plaza, where seasonal festivals are held. The pagoda, which draws on the 1,200-year-old tradition of miniature round pagodas dedicated to eternal peace, was designed in the late 1960s by Yoshiro Taniguchi to convey the "friendship and goodwill" of the Japanese people to the people of the United States. The plaza itself is a shadeless, unwelcoming space with little seating. Continue into the Miyako Mall to Ichiban Kan, a Japanese dollar store where you can pick up fun Japanese kitchenware, tote bags decorated with hedgehogs, and erasers shaped like food. ⊠ *Bordered by Geary Blvd. and Fillmore, Post, and Laguna Sts., Japantown.*

Fodor's Choice ★ **Kabuki Springs & Spa.** This serene spa is one Japantown destination that draws locals from all over town, from hipster to grandma, Japanese-American or not. Balinese urns decorate the communal bath area of this house of tranquillity.

The massage menu has also expanded well beyond traditional shiatsu technique. The experience is no less relaxing, however, and the treatment regimen includes facials, salt scrubs, and mud and seaweed wraps. You can take your massage in a private room with a bath or in a curtained-off area.

The communal baths ($25) contain hot and cold tubs, a large Japanese-style bath, a sauna, a steam room, and showers. Bang the gong for quiet if your fellow bathers are speaking too loudly. The clothing-optional baths are open for men only on Monday, Thursday, and Saturday; women bathe on Wednesday, Friday, and Sunday. Bathing suits are required on Tuesday, when the baths are coed.

Pacific Heights and Japantown

Men and women can reserve private rooms daily. An 80-minute massage-and-private-bath package costs $140 weekdays, $152 weekends; a package that includes a 50-minute massage and the use of the communal baths costs $105 weekdays, $114 weekends. ✉ *1750 Geary Blvd., Japantown* ☎ *415/922–6000* ⊕ *www.kabukisprings.com* ☉ *Daily 10–10.*

New People. The kids' counterpart to the Japan Center, this fresh shopping center combines a cinema, a café, shops, and a gallery with a successful synergy. The basement cinema shows classic and cutting-edge Asian (largely Japanese) films and is home to the San Francisco Film Society. Grab some *onigiri* (rice balls) and a cup of Blue Bottle coffee at the café, then head upstairs and peruse Japanese pop-culture items and anime-inspired fashion. The cuteness radiating from the Rilakkuma store may overwhelm you. The tiny Superfrog Gallery upstairs exhibits cutting-edge contemporary art. ✉ *1746 Post St., Japantown* ☎ *415/525–8630 store, 415/525–8600 cinema* ⊕ *www. newpeopleworld.com* ☉ *Mon.–Sat. noon–7, Sun. noon–6.*

WHERE TO EAT

Make no mistake, San Francisco is one of America's top food cities. Some of the biggest landmarks are restaurants; and Gary Danko is probably just as big a draw as Alcatraz. On a Saturday, the Ferry Building might attract more visitors than the Golden Gate Bridge. This temple to local eating sells cheeses, breads, "salty pig parts," homemade delicacies, and sensory-perfect vegetables and fruits that attract a rabidly dedicated group. You see, San Franciscans are a little loco about their edibles. If you ask them what their favorite season is, don't be surprised if they respond, "tomato season."

Some renowned restaurants are booked weeks or even months in advance. But you can get lucky at the last minute if you're flexible—and friendly. Most restaurants keep a few tables open for walk-ins and VIPs. Show up for dinner early (5:30 pm) or late (after 9 pm) and politely inquire about any last-minute vacancies or cancellations. *Use the coordinate (✛ A1) at the end of each listing to locate a site on the corresponding map.*

WHAT IT COSTS				
	$	$$	$$$	$$$$
Restaurants	under $16	$16–$22	$23–$30	over $30

Restaurant prices are the average cost of a main course at dinner or, if dinner is not served, at lunch.

UNION SQUARE AND CHINATOWN

$
JAPANESE

✗ **Katana-Ya.** From the moment it opens, there's a line in front of this hole-in-the-wall ramen house across from the American Conservatory Theater. Hand-drawn pictures of specials punctuate a colorful interior with too-close tables and a couple of stools around the bar. There's nothing fancy, but the ramen is among the most authentic in town. Add a couple of sushi rolls and gyozas to your order and be on your way. ⑤ *Average main: $8* ⊠ *430 Geary St., Union Square* ☎ *415/771–1280* ⊕ *www.katanayausa.com* ⌲ *Reservations not accepted* ✛ *E4.*

$$
CHINESE
FAMILY

✗ **R&G Lounge.** The name conjures up an image of a dark, smoky bar with a piano player, but this Cantonese restaurant is actually as bright as a new penny. On the lower level (entrance on Kearny Street) is a no-tablecloth dining room that's packed at lunch and dinner. The classy upstairs space (entrance on Commercial Street) is a favorite stop for special-occasion banquets and Chinese businessmen on expense accounts. The street-level room on Kearny is a comfortable spot to wait for an open table. A menu with photographs helps you pick from the many wonderful, sometimes pricey, always authentic dishes, such as the famous salt-and-pepper Dungeness crab, Peking duck, and shrimp-stuffed tofu. Much of the seafood is fresh from the tank. ⑤ *Average main: $16* ⊠ *631 Kearny St., Chinatown* ☎ *415/982–7877* ⊕ *www.rnglounge.com* ✛ *F3.*

BEST BETS FOR SAN FRANCISCO DINING

With thousands of restaurants to choose from, how will you decide where to eat? Fodor's writers and editors have selected their favorite restaurants by price, cuisine, and experience in the Best Bets lists below. In the first column, Fodor's Choice designations represent the "best of the best" in every price category. You can also search by neighborhood for excellent eats—just peruse the following pages.

Fodor's Choice★

Acquerello, $$$$, p. 224
Benu, $$$$, p. 218
Boulevard, $$$$, p. 226
Central Kitchen, $$$, p. 230
Coi, $$$$, p. 224
Coqueta, $$$, p. 226
Delfina, $$$, p. 230
Dosa on Fillmore, $$, p. 233
Dosa on Valencia, $$, p. 230
Gary Danko, $$$$, p. 226
Nopalito, $, p. 234
Rich Table, $$$, p. 219
State Bird Provisions, $$$, p. 234
Swan Oyster Depot, $$, p. 224
Zuni Café, $$$, p. 219

By Price

$

Burma Superstar, p. 235
Katana-Ya, p. 214
Nopalito, p. 234
Park Chow, p. 235
SanJalisco, p. 232
Tony's Pizza Napoletana, p. 225

$$

Bar Tartine, p. 229
Citizen's Band, p. 218
Dosa on Fillmore, p. 233
Nojo, p. 219
Zarzuela, p. 223

$$$

Cavalier, p. 218
Central Kitchen, p. 230
Coqueta, p. 226
Delfina, p. 230
Flour + Water, p. 231
Local's Corner, p. 231
Locanda, p. 231

Rich Table, p. 219
St. Vincent, p. 232
Wexler's, p. 222

$$$$

Acquerello, p. 224
Benu, $$$$, p. 218
Boulevard, p. 226
Coi, p. 224
Gary Danko, p. 226

By Cuisine

AMERICAN

Central Kitchen, $$$, p. 230
Citizen's Band, $$, p. 218
Greens, $$, p. 228
Nopa, $$$, p. 234
Park Chow, $, p. 235
Rich Table, $$$, p. 219
Verbena, $$, p. 223
Wexler's, $$$, p. 222

CHINESE

Yank Sing, $$, p. 223

ITALIAN

A16, $$$, p. 228
Delfina, $$$, p. 230
Locanda, $$$, p. 231

JAPANESE

Katana-Ya, $, p. 214
Nojo, $$, p. 219

MEDITERRANEAN

Coqueta, $$$, p. 226
Zarzuela, $$, p. 223
Zuni Café, $$$, p. 219

MEXICAN

Nopalito, $, p. 234
SanJalisco, $, p. 232

SEAFOOD

Hog Island Oyster Company, $$, p. 227
Local's Corner, $$$, p. 231
Swan Oyster Depot, $$, p. 224

By Experience

BAY VIEWS

Coqueta, $$$, p. 226
Greens, $$, p. 228
Slanted Door, $$$, p. 227

BRUNCH

Bar Tartine, $$, p. 229
Greens, $$, p. 228
Local's Corner, $$$, p. 231
Rose's Café, $$$, p. 228

4

NORCAL'S LOCAVORE FOOD MOVEMENT

Organic, local, and *sustainable* are buzzwords in Northern California, home to hundreds of small family farmers, sustainable ranchers, and artisan producers leading the country's back-to-the-earth food movement.

When Alice Waters opened Chez Panisse in Berkeley in 1971, she sparked a culinary revolution that continues today. Initially called California cuisine, the cooking style showcased local, seasonal ingredients in fresh preparations. It also marked a new willingness by American chefs to experiment with international influences. As the movement spread, it became known as New American cooking. This "eat local, think global" ethos has led to a resurgence of artisanal producers across the country.

The *locavore* (focused on sustainable, local foods) movement's epicenter is still Northern California. At the Ferry Plaza Farmers' Market in San Francisco alone, farmers bring more than 1,200 varieties of fruits and vegetables to market every year. Chefs proudly call out their purveyors on menus and websites, elevating humble vegetable growers to starring culinary roles.

FARMERS' MARKETS

One of the best ways to taste Northern California's bounty is by stopping by the Ferry Plaza Farmers' Market, held outside the Ferry Building on the Embarcadero, at Market Street on Tuesday, Thursday, and Saturday morning. The market offers produce, meats, fish, and flowers from small regional farmers and ranchers, many of whom are certified organic producers.

It is also a great place to pick up items for a picnic. Prepared foods such as tamales and pasta are available, as are jams, breads, and cheeses from local artisan producers.

Check ⊕ *www.cuesa.org* for hours.

FRUIT

Northern California's diverse climate makes it an ideal place to grow all types of fruit, from berries to stone fruit. Farmers' markets and restaurants abound with a staggering selection of produce: Blossom Bluff Orchards, south of San Francisco, offers more than 150 varieties of stone fruits, like apricots, nectarines, and peaches. North of the city, the Apple Farm grows 80 varieties of apples, pears, persimmons, quince, and French plums. The Bay Area is also one of the best places in the country to find rare fruit varieties such as aprium, cherimoya, cactus pear, jujube, and loquat; California's famous Meyer lemons—sweeter and less acidic than common lemons—are celebrated in restaurant desserts.

VEGETABLES

Some chefs give top billing to their produce purveyors, as in a recently observed menu touting a salad of Star Route Farm field greens with Picholine olives, sweet herbs, and goat cheese. Along with these tantalizing items, be on the lookout for locally grown artichokes, Asian vegetables, multihued beets and carrots, and heirloom varieties of tomatoes, squash, and beans.

MEAT

Family-owned ranches and farms are prominent in the region, with many raising organic or "humane certified"

beef, pork, lamb, and poultry. Upscale Bay Area restaurants are fervent about recognizing their high-quality protein producers. From recent menus at two well-known San Francisco restaurants: Wolfe Ranch quail with Murcott mandarins, smoked bacon and bok choy, and vanilla gastrique; and Prather Ranch lamb with fava greens, cranberry beans, crispy artichokes, and salsa verde.

FISH

Diners and shoppers will find myriad seafood from local waters, from farm-raised scallops to line-caught California salmon. On menus, look for Hog Island Oysters, a local producer that raises more than 3 million oysters a year in Tomales Bay. Sardines netted in Monterey Bay are popular in preparations like mesquite-grilled sardines with fava beans, French radish and fennel salad, and preserved Meyer lemon.

CHEESE

Restaurant cheese plates, often served before—or in lieu of—dessert, are a great way to experience the region's excellent local cheeses. Look for selections from Cypress Grove Chevre, popular for its artisan goat cheeses, and Cowgirl Creamery, a renowned local producer of fresh and aged cow's milk cheeses. Additionally, some shops and bakeries offer fresh local butter and cheeses.

4

SOMA

$$$$
MODERN
AMERICAN
Fodor's Choice
★

✕ **Benu.** One of the city's most high-profile establishments, chef-owner Corey Lee's contemporary American restaurant delights food-obsessed locals and travelers alike. Lee's pedigree spans 15 years in fine dining, including a position as chef de cuisine at Thomas Keller's the French Laundry, but Benu is decidedly more relaxed—no jacket required. The dining room is very minimalist, with bare-wood tables and high-backed banquettes along the walls. The pricy tasting menu ($195 per person) of 14 to 18 courses is mandatory. Each dish is a marvel, from the meticulous presentation (Lee has had pieces specifically designed for the restaurant and each course) to the sophisticated flavors and textures. Fans of Asian cuisine will be particularly thrilled to see his elegant handling of ingredients like a thousand-year-old quail egg, *xiao long bao* dumplings, and sea cucumber. He utilizes many modern techniques, but never in an alienating way. You may find dishes like Hokkaido sea cucumber stuffed with lobster, pork belly, eggplant, fermented pepper or eel, *feuille de brik* (flaky pastry), crème fraiche, lime. An extremely professional staff is behind the quick pacing and on-point wine pairings. Couples expecting an ultraromantic environment may be a bit disappointed by the stark atmosphere, but culinary adventurers will be thrilled. ⑤ *Average main: $195* ✉ *22 Hawthorne St., SoMa* ☎ *415/685–4860* ⊕ *www.benusf.com* ⌂ *Reservations essential* ⊘ *Closed Sun. and Mon. No lunch* ✛ *G5.*

$$$
MODERN BRITISH

✕ **Cavalier.** Occupying a hefty slice of Hotel Zetta's ground floor, Cavalier is a British pub with a Nor Cal sensibility. The celebratory space, the brainchild of restaurateur Anna Weinberg and chef Jennifer Puccio, has high ceilings, red walls, stuffed animal heads, large arched windows, and clusters of paintings imparting a decidedly British temperament. The gin-based cocktails pair well with starters such as deviled crab, rock shrimp, and duck-egg confit, and hearty mains include the Sunday chicken—bathed in a bacon-mustard *jus*—and rib-eye steak atop a bed of horseradish mashed potatoes. The service here is top-notch. ⑤ *Average main: $23* ✉ *Hotel Zetta, 360 Jessie St., SoMa* ☎ *415/321–6000* ⊕ *thecavaliersf.com* ⌂ *Reservations essential* ✛ *E5.*

$$
DINER

✕ **Citizen's Band.** A fresh take on the classic American diner, this busy corner spot seems to always pack in its coveted 40 seats. The draw: one of the city's tastiest versions of mac and cheese (topped with onion rings), fried chicken with red-eye gravy, and an excellent burger sandwiched inside a bun from the next-door neighbor, Pinkie's Bakery. Other "fine diner" dishes—among them seasonal salads and pan-roasted rock cod—further reveal chef-owner Chris Beerman's experience in upscale restaurants. Brunch brings eggs Benedict, while lunch has more sandwich options (try the fried chicken). The vibe is very SoMa, with an edgy and eclectic crowd that can match the rock-and-roll playing (sometimes loudly) on the stereo or at the club next door, but the well-chosen wine list keeps things elevated. Solo diners can try for a seat at the counter. The restaurant shares restrooms with the rock club next door. ⑤ *Average main: $22* ✉ *1198 Folsom St., at 8th St., SoMa* ☎ *415/556–4901* ⊕ *www.citizensbandsf.com* ✛ *E6.*

HAYES VALLEY

$$ ✕ **Nojo.** For a little bonhomie before the symphony, this buzzy yakitori
JAPANESE and izakaya spot serves stellar Japanese pub food, made from Bay
Area ingredients, and it encourages sharing. The menu is divided into
items "on a stick" and "not on a stick." For the stick items, much of
it is *yakitori* (grilled chicken), like chicken skin with matcha sea salt,
neck with *tare* (a thick grilled sauce), or *tsukune* (a chicken meatball)
with egg yolk sauce—all the different notes in the varied sauces are
part of the taste adventure. The savory, rich custard, *chawan mushi*,
has chunks of Dungeness crabmeat and shiitake mushrooms. Seating
is at bamboo tables in a mod-Japanese-slash-San Franciscan setting
with large windows overlooking Hayes Valley's main thoroughfare of
Franklin. There are 20 sakes by the glass. ■TIP➜ Nojo requires a credit
card number to hold a reservation. ⑤ *Average main: $20* ✉ *231 Frank-
lin St., Hayes Valley* ☏ *415/896–4587* ⊕ *www.nojosf.com* ☾ *Closed
Tues. No lunch Mon.* ✛ *C6.*

$$$ ✕ **Rich Table.** This Hayes Valley restaurant is a brilliant example of fine
MODERN dining without preciousness or formality. Beginning with the bar bites
AMERICAN co-chefs Evan and Sarah Rich, alumni of Manhattan's Bouley restau-
Fodor's Choice rant and Mas (farmhouse) and San Francisco's Quince, Michael Mina,
★ and Coi, magically transform simple ingredients such as Castelvetrano
olives by marinating them in wasabi, seaweed, and lime juice. Casual
doughnuts become exquisite delicacies—the dried-porcini ones are
served with a raclette béchamel sauce for dipping. To this point, it's
all finger food, but forks and knives are put to use for the half-dozen
pastas and an equal number of appetizer and mains. Vased branches
decorate the dining room, which has weathered-wood wallboards
repurposed from a Northern California sawmill. There's a nice selection of wines by the glass and artisanal cocktails. There are even some
original dessert cocktails, including the 1 Up (for Mario Bros. fans),
with porcini-infused gin, sherry, egg, and cream. ■TIP➜ Ten bar seats
are available for walk-ins. ⑤ *Average main: $30* ✉ *199 Gough St., at
Oak, Hayes Valley* ☏ *415/355–9085* ⊕ *www.richtablesf.com* ⟋ *Reservations essential* ☾ *Closed Tues. No lunch* ✛ *C6.*

$$$ ✕ **Zuni Café.** After one bite of Zuni's succulent brick-oven-roasted
MEDITERRANEAN whole chicken with Tuscan bread salad, you'll understand why the
Fodor's Choice café is a perennial star. Food is served on two floors; the rabbit war-
★ ren of rooms on the second level includes a balcony overlooking the
main dining room. At the long copper bar a disparate mix of patrons
reflecting the city's diversity—casual and dressy, young and old, hip
and staid—communes over fresh oysters on the half shell and cocktails
and wine. The southern French–Italian menu changes daily, though
the signature chicken, prepared for two, is a fixture.
The simple dishes, made with excellent ingredients, include house-
cured anchovies with Parmigiano-Reggiano, deep-fried squid and lem-
ons, ricotta gnocchi with seasonal vegetables, and brick-oven squab
with polenta. Nearly as famous as the chicken is the chocolatey flour-
less *gâteau Victoire*, served since the '80s. The most cheerful spot to sit
is at the tip of the "pyramid window" near the bar, easier to score if
you plan a late lunch. Zuni's world famous chef-owner, Judy Rodgers,

passed away in 2013, but thanks to her strong guidance, the food remains outstanding. $ *Average main: $28* ⊠ *1658 Market St., Hayes Valley* ☏ *415/552–2522* ⊕ *www.zunicafe.com* ⊘ *Closed Mon.* ✛ *C6.*

FINANCIAL DISTRICT

$$
SPANISH
✕ **Bocadillos.** The name means "sandwiches," but that's only half the story here. You'll find a baker's dozen of bocadillos at lunchtime: plump rolls (pick two for $12) filled with everything from Serrano ham to Catalan sausage with arugula to a memorable lamb burger. At night chef-owner Gerald Hirigoyen, who also owns the high-profile Piperade, focuses on tapas, offering two-dozen choices, including roasted Monterey Bay squid, pig's trotters with chopped egg salad, and *patatas bravas* (potatoes) with *romesco* sauce (a thick combination of red pepper, tomato, almonds, and garlic). His wine list is well matched to the dishes. A youngish crowd typically piles into the redbrick dining space, whose aesthetic includes wire chairs and small, square light fixtures. Be prepared to wait for a seat. The large communal table is a good perch for singles. ■ TIP→ Breakfast is served here, too. The choices include house-made chorizo and eggs and a scrambled-eggs-and-cheese bocadillo. $ *Average main: $18* ⊠ *710 Montgomery St., Financial District* ☏ *415/982–2622* ⊕ *www.bocasf.com* ⊘ *Reservations not accepted* ⊘ *Closed Sun. No lunch Sat.* ✛ *F3.*

$$$$
ECLECTIC
✕ **Michael Mina.** Chef Michael Mina moved his eponymous restaurant and reopened in the former AQUA location on California Street, where he got his start (and worked for 13 years). In another flashback, Mina hired chef Ron Siegel, a former AQUA cook, to collaborate with him in the kitchen. The Euro-Japanese menu remains a treat, with luxurious renditions of shabu shabu, as well as classics like the lemon-poached fluke with black truffles. The most popular item, a lobster pot pie with Meyer lemons and smoked potatoes, blew up the blogosphere with raves. The space is chic and airy, highlighting natural elements like dark walnut tables and custom porcelain. The lounge area is the center of activity, drawing a busy Financial District scene after work (the cocktails and hors d'oeuvres sampler are recommended). Lunch is the time to sample the mastery of Mina at half the price, like his ahi tuna tartare with habanero-infused sesame oil, Asian pear, pine nuts, and quail egg yolk. $ *Average main: $38* ⊠ *252 California St., Financial District* ☏ *415/397–9222* ⊕ *www.michaelmina.net* ⊘ *No lunch Sat. and Sun.* ✛ *G3.*

$$$
BARBECUE
✕ **Wexler's.** Four words: bourbon banana cream pie. Of course, there's a slew of tempting barbecue items that threaten whether you'll have room at the end of the meal. This upscale comfort-food joint neighbors Wayfare Tavern, but for our food money Wexler's is first choice. The interior is chic, almost minimalist, with one mighty interesting ceiling sculpture and a couple of red chandeliers to liven up the place. Barbecue traditionalists should come with an open mind. The crispy Scotch eggs, fork-tender short ribs, and smoked wings (with Point Reyes blue cheese dressing) take their cues from barbecue but wander into more creative territory—chef Charlie Kleinman earned accolades while at the Hotel Palomar's late Fifth Floor restaurant. Purists might do better with Wexler's food truck parked out back on weekdays, serving pulled

pork, chicken, and brisket with traditional sides such as hush puppies. ■TIP→ The cocktails are fantastic here. ⑤ *Average main: $24* ⊠ *568 Sacramento St., Financial District* ☎ *415/983–0102* ⊕ *www.wexlerssf. com* ⊘ *Closed Sun. No dinner Mon. No lunch weekends* ✦ *F3.*

$$
CHINESE
FAMILY

✕ **Yank Sing.** The granddaddy of local dim sum teahouses opened in a plain-Jane storefront in Chinatown in 1959 but left its Cantonese neighbors behind for the high-rises of downtown in the 1970s. This brightly decorated location on quiet Stevenson Street—there's also a big, brassy branch in the Rincon Center—serves some of San Francisco's best dim sum to office workers on weekdays and boisterous families on weekends. The several dozen varieties of dim sum prepared daily include both the classic (steamed pork buns, shrimp dumplings, egg custard tartlets) and the creative (scallion-skewered prawns tied with bacon, lobster and *tobiko* roe dumplings, basil seafood dumplings). The Shanghai soup dumplings are perfection. Staffers pushing food carts whiz by tables constantly, and the tab can rise quickly, so pace yourself. The take-out counter makes a meal on the run a satisfying and penny-wise compromise when office duties—or touring—won't wait. ⑤ *Average main: $16* ⊠ *49 Stevenson St., Financial District* ☎ *415/541–4949* ⊕ *www.yanksing.com* ⊘ *No dinner* ✦ *F4.*

RUSSIAN HILL

$$
MODERN
AMERICAN

✕ **Verbena.** Attention to detail and artistic presentations are the hallmarks of this recent venture from the creators of Berkeley's Gather restaurant. The dining room's brick walls, soft lighting, and dark-wood accents hint at chef Sean Baker's meticulous approach, and jars of pickled onions, peppers, and other vegetables—backlit and stacked high on wooden shelves—make clear the important role plant life plays in his menu. Each element seems carefully thought out, from the artisanal bread and butter to the carrots swimming in a smoky, barbecue-like sauce whose ingredients include cashews, lemon verbena, and mulberry-date molasses. The menu changes often but might include sardines with cauliflower, horseradish, trout roe, and chickweed; Koji quail served on Sonoma grains with slices of hedgehog mushroom awash in pumpkin juice; or duck meatballs in mole sauce. ⑤ *Average main: $22* ⊠ *2323 Polk St, Russian Hill* ☎ *415/441–2323* ⊕ *www.verbenarestaurant.com* ⌲ *Reservations essential* ⊘ *No lunch weekdays* ✦ *C1.*

$$
TAPAS

✕ **Zarzuela.** Full-blooded Spaniards swear by the paella at this tiny old world–style bistro, complete with matador art on the wall, not far from the crookedest street in the world (Lombard). Also not to be missed is the homemade sangria—or the goat cheese baked in tomato sauce or poached octopus prepared by chef Lucas Gasco, who grew up in Madrid. Opened in 1994, Zarzuela was among the Bay Area's first wave of modern tapas restaurants and today offers about 30 small plates, as well as heartier dishes such as Catalan seafood stew. Arched windows overlook Hyde Street and the cable cars rolling by. Riding the Powell–Hyde line to and from dinner adds to the romance of the evening and saves you the nightmare of parking in this neighborhood where spaces are scarce. ⑤ *Average main: $21* ⊠ *2000 Hyde St., Russian Hill* ☎ *415/346–0800* ⌲ *Reservations not accepted* ⊘ *Closed Sun. and Mon. No lunch* ✦ *D2.*

VAN NESS/POLK

$$$$
ITALIAN
Fodor'sChoice
★

✕**Acquerello.** Devotees of chef-owner Suzette Gresham-Tognetti's high-end but soulful Italian cooking have swooned for years over her incomparable Parmesan *budino* (pudding) as well as the ridged pasta with foie gras and truffles. The latter dish, even with the California ban on foie gras, is still a favorite—Tognetti's chef de cuisine Mark Pensa has created a faux foie that is a dead ringer for the real item. Classics pepper the menu but there are also some cutting-edge touches, techniques, and flavors. Dinners are prix-fixe, with three ($82), four ($96), or five ($110) courses and at least six choices within each course. Tognetti also tempts with a seasonal eight-course tasting menu ($145). The cheese course is not to be missed, with rare cheeses from Piemonte, and other regions, rolled tableside. Co-owner Giancarlo Paterlini oversees the service and his son Gianpaolo presides over the roughly 1,900-bottle list of Italian wines. The room, in a former chapel, with wooden vaulted ceiling and terra-cotta and pale-ocher palette, is refined but never stuffy—and neither is the service. Every member of the dining staff is honest and welcoming, knowing that many people here are celebrating special occasions. They will make it a night to be remembered. This true San Francisco dining gem is worth every penny. ⑤ *Average main: $82* ✉ *1722 Sacramento St., Van Ness/Polk* ☎ *415/567–5432* ⊕ *www.acquerello.com* ⌖ *Reservations essential* ⊗ *Closed Sun. and Mon. No lunch* ✛ *C3.*

$$
SEAFOOD
Fodor'sChoice
★

✕**Swan Oyster Depot.** Half fish market and half diner, this small, slim, family-run seafood operation, open since 1912, has no tables, just a narrow marble counter with about a dozen-and-a-half stools. Most people come in to buy perfectly fresh salmon, halibut, crabs, and other seafood to take home. Everyone else hops onto one of the rickety stools to enjoy a bowl of clam chowder—the only hot food served—a dozen oysters, half a cracked crab, a slice of crusty sourdough, a big shrimp salad, or a smaller shrimp cocktail. It's all served up with a side of big personality from the jovial folks behind the counter who make you feel like a regular. ■**TIP➜** Come before 11 am or after 2 pm to avoid a long wait, and bring a full wallet: old-school Swan only takes cash. ⑤ *Average main: $18* ✉ *1517 Polk St., Nob Hill* ☎ *415/673–1101* ⌖ *Reservations not accepted* ▬ *No credit cards* ⊗ *Closed Sun. No dinner* ✛ *D3.*

NORTH BEACH

$$$$
MODERN
AMERICAN
Fodor'sChoice
★

✕**Coi.** Daniel Patterson, who has made a name for himself internationally both as a chef and as a pundit on contemporary restaurant trends, has created a destination restaurant, an enchanting spot on the gritty end of Broadway. There are two dining rooms: the front room, casual with chocolate-color leather chairs and rustic wood tables, and the 30-seat formal dining room, with soft lighting, natural linens, and hand-crafted pottery. The 11-course meal ($195) chef Patterson prepares fully expresses the bounty of Bay Area produce and other ingredients. The highly seasonal and obsessively sourced food—some of it foraged by Patterson himself—matches the space in sophistication. The inspired

Eating with Kids

Kids can be fussy eaters, and parents can be, too. Fortunately, there are plenty of excellent options in the city that will satisfy both.

✕ **City View Restaurant.** Over in Chinatown, City View serves a varied selection of dim sum, with tasty pork buns for kids and more exotic fare such as chicken feet and turnip cakes for adults. Though less expensive than nearby Yank Sing, this bustling restaurant is no less busy, so be prepared for epic weekend waits. ⑤ *Average main: $1* ⊠ *662 Commercial St., near Kearny St.* ☎ *415/398–2838.*

The Ferry Building on the Embarcadero has plenty of kid-friendly options, from **Mijita Cocina Mexicana,** which has its own kids' menu, to **Gott's Roadside,** for burgers, shakes, and more. (And the outdoor access can help keep the little ones entertained.)

✕ **La Corneta.** The Mission has dozens of no-frills taco-and-burrito parlors; especially worthy is La Corneta, known for its baby burrito (which is basically just a smaller-sized

version) and the huge quesadillas. Vegetarians will be satisfied by the bean selection. ⑤ *Average main: $1* ⊠ *2731 Mission St., between 23rd and 24th Sts.* ☎ *415/643–7001.*

Rosamunde Sausage Grill. In Lower Haight, the small Rosamunde serves a slew of different sausages, from Polish to duck to *Weisswurst* (Bavarian veal). Toppings (choose two) include grilled onions, sauerkraut, chili, and sweet and hot peppers. There are only six stools, so plan on take-out. ■ **TIP➜ Nearby Duboce Park has a cute playground.** ⊠ *545 Haight St., between Steiner and Fillmore Sts.* ☎ *415/437–6851.*

Park Chalet. Finally, both kids and adults love to be by the ocean, and the Park Chalet, hidden behind the two-story Beach Chalet, offers pizza, mac and cheese, sticky ribs, and a big banana split. On sunny days, you'll be hard-pressed to find a plot of grass to claim as families gather on blankets and folding chairs to sip the house-brewed beers and listen to live music. ⊠ *1000 Great Hwy., at Fulton St.* ☎ *415/386–8439.*

dishes include Dungeness crab raviolo with sheep sorrel and butter crab broth, and aged duck breast with stuffed cabbage, roasted beets, horseradish, and dill. Patterson is always tinkering and innovating, brining and curing, so the culinary experience always feels new and exciting. ⑤ *Average main: $195* ⊠ *373 Broadway, North Beach* ☎ *415/393–9000* ⊕ *www.coirestaurant.com* ⋈ *Reservations essential* ⊘ *Closed Sun. and Mon. No lunch* ✛ *F2.*

$ ✕ **Tony's Pizza Napoletana.** Locals hotly debate who makes the city's
PIZZA best pizza, and for many Tony Gemignani takes the prize. His reputa-
FAMILY tion extends well beyond the city: at the World Pizza Cup in Naples he eclipsed the Italians for the title of World Champion Pizza Maker. The dough at his restaurant is flavorful and fired just right, with multiple wood-burning ovens in his casual, modern pizzeria turning out many different pies—the famed Neapolitan-style Margherita, but also Sicilian, Romana, and Detroit styles, and even coal-fired. Salads, antipasti, homemade pastas, and calzone, round out the menu. At the counter

next door you can grab a slice quickly. ■TIP→ If you're dining with kids, ask for some pizza dough to keep them entertained. $ *Average main: $15 ⊠ 1570 Stockton St., North Beach* ☎ *415/835–9888* ⊕ *www. tonyspizzanapoletana.com* ⩙ *Reservations not accepted* ☼ *Closed Mon. and Tues.* ✛ *E2.*

FISHERMAN'S WHARF

$$$$
MODERN
AMERICAN
Fodor's Choice
★

✕ **Gary Danko.** In high season plan on reserving two months ahead at Chef Danko's namesake restaurant—his legion of fans typically keep the reservation book full. The cost of a meal ($73–$107) is pegged to the number of courses, from three to five, and the menu spans a classic yet Californian style that changes seasonally. Dishes might include risotto with lobster and rock shrimp, lemon pepper duck breast with duck hash, and herb-crusted lamb loin. A diet-destroying chocolate soufflé with two sauces is usually among the desserts. The wine list is the size of a small-town phone book, and the banquette-lined rooms, with beautiful wood floors and stunning (but restrained) floral arrangements, are as memorable as the food and impeccable service. $ *Average main: $73 ⊠ 800 N. Point St., Fisherman's Wharf* ☎ *415/749–2060* ⊕ *www.garydanko.com* ⩙ *Reservations essential* 🎩 *Jacket required* ☼ *No lunch* ✛ *D1.*

EMBARCADERO

$$$$
AMERICAN
Fodor's Choice
★

✕ **Boulevard.** Two local restaurant celebrities—chef Nancy Oakes and designer Pat Kuleto—are behind this high-profile, high-priced eatery in the 1889 Audiffred Building, a Parisian look-alike that survived the 1906 quake. Kuleto's Belle-Époque interior and Oakes's sophisticated American food with a French accent attract well-dressed locals and flush out-of-towners. The menu changes seasonally, but count on generous portions of dishes such as Maine lobster ravioli, grilled king salmon with wild rice and vegetables that include chanterelle mushrooms, and a wood-grilled pork prime rib chop with Kabocha squash gnocchi (all the entrées come with delicious side dishes). Save room for one of the dynamite desserts, among them the dark-chocolate brioche custard. There's counter seating for folks too hungry to wait for a table, and an American Wagyu beef burger with Cowgirl Creamery cheese at lunchtime for those who want to dine here without raiding the piggy bank. The wine list and excellent service are two additional Boulevard hallmarks. $ *Average main: $36 ⊠ 1 Mission St., Embarcadero* ☎ *415/543–6084* ⊕ *www.boulevardrestaurant.com* ⩙ *Reservations essential* ☼ *No lunch weekends* ✛ *H4.*

$$$
SPANISH
Fodor's Choice
★

✕ **Coqueta.** With its Embarcadero perch, Bay Bridge views, and stellar Spanish tapas, celebrity chef Michael Chiarello's San Francisco debut was an instant hit. Equal parts rustic and chic, his dining room's bold decor—stained wooden beams, cowhide rugs, marble bar—sends out the visual message that Chiarello is at the top of his game, and it's fun to see him mingling with diners as they enjoy toothpicked *pintxos* (small snacks) such as quail egg with Serrano ham. The real draws, though, are the inventive cocktails, luscious paella, and dazzling variation on the cut of pork *secreto Ibérico* (Iberian secret). The desserts are also small bites, so you'll likely have room to end your experience on a sweet note. ■TIP→ Book well in advance for dinner. $ *Average main: $30* ⊠ *Pier 5, on the Embarcadero, near Broadway, Embarcadero* ☎ *415/704–8866* ⊕ *coquetasf.com* ⚲ *Reservations essential* ✛ *G3.*

$$ ✕ **Hog Island Oyster Company.** A thriving oyster farm north of San Francisco in Tomales Bay, Hog Island serves up its harvest at its newly expanded raw bar and restaurant in the busy Ferry Building. Devotees come here for impeccably fresh oysters (from Hog Island and elsewhere) and clams (from Hog Island) on the half shell. Other mollusk-centered options include a first-rate oyster stew, baked oysters, clam chowder, and "steamer" dishes atop a bed of local greens. The bar also turns out one of the city's best grilled-cheese sandwiches, made with three artisanal cheeses on artisanal bread. $ *Average main: $20* ⊠ *Ferry Bldg., Embarcadero at Market St., Embarcadero* ☎ *415/391–7117* ⊕ *www. hogislandoysters.com* ⚲ *Reservations not accepted* ✛ *H3.*

SEAFOOD

$$$ ✕ **La Mar Cebicheria Peruana.** Right on the water's edge, the casually chic La Mar is divided into three areas: a lounge with a long ceviche bar where diners watch the chefs put plates together; the Pisco Bar facing the Embarcadero, where bartenders mix cocktails based on Peru's famed Pisco brandy; and a bright blue and whitewashed dining room overlooking an outdoor patio and the bay. Your waiter will start you out with a pile of potato and plantain chips with three dipping sauces, but after that you're on your own, choosing from a long list of ceviches, can't-miss *causas* (whipped potatoes topped with a choice of fish, shellfish, or vegetable salads), and everything from crisp, lightly deep-fried fish and shellfish to soups and stews and rice dishes, many spiked with Peruvian chilis. The original La Mar is in Lima, Peru. San Francisco was the first stop in its campaign to open a string of *cebicherías* across the United States and Latin America. The view of the water is especially enjoyable during lunch or a warm evening. $ *Average main: $25* ⊠ *Pier 1½ between Washington and Jackson Sts., Embarcadero* ☎ *415/397–8880* ⊕ *www.lamarcebicheria.com* ✛ *G3.*

PERUVIAN

$$$ ✕ **Slanted Door.** If you're looking for homey Vietnamese food served in a down-to-earth dining room at a decent price, *don't* stop here. Celebrated chef-owner Charles Phan has mastered the upmarket, Western-accented Vietnamese menu. To showcase his cuisine, he built a big space with sleek wooden tables and chairs, white marble floors, a cocktail lounge, a bar, and an enviable bay view. Among his popular cult dishes are green-papaya salad, daikon rice cakes, cellophane crab noodles, chicken clay pot, and shaking beef (tender beef cubes with garlic and onion). They don't come cheap, but they're made with quality ingredients. The restaurant has also become a regular stop for those who appreciate finely made cocktails, many of them created by star bartender Erik Adkins. ■TIP→ To avoid the midday and evening crowds (and to save some bucks), dine at the bar, drop by for afternoon tea (2:30–4:30), or visit Out the Door, Phan's take-out counter around the corner. $ *Average main: $29* ⊠ *Ferry Bldg., Embarcadero at Market St., Embarcadero* ☎ *415/861–8032* ⊕ *www.slanteddoor.com* ⚲ *Reservations essential* ✛ *H3.*

VIETNAMESE

4

MARINA

$$$
ITALIAN
✗**A16.** Marina residents—and, judging from the crowds, everybody else—gravitate to this trattoria named for the autostrada that traverses Italy's sunny south. The kitchen serves the food of Naples and surrounding Campania, with the added twist of seasonal California ingredients. Cult classics include the creamy burrata with olive oil and crostini and crisp-crust pizzas, including a classic Neapolitan Margherita (mozzarella, tomato, and basil). Rustic pasta favorites such as *maccaronara* with *ragu napoletana* and house-made salted ricotta might show up on the menu, and for an entrée perhaps petrale sole with crispy black trumpet mushrooms. The selection of primarily southern Italian wines, augmented by some well-chosen California vintages, supports the food perfectly, and there's a substantial beer list. ■**TIP➜ The animated bar scene near the door sets the tone at A16; for a quieter time request a table in the alcove at the far end or try for the patio.** ⑤ *Average main: $25* ✉ *2355 Chestnut St., Marina* ☎ *415/771–2216* ⊕ *www.a16sf.com* ⌕ *Reservations essential* ⊘ *No lunch Sat.–Tues.* ✛ *A1.*

$$
VEGETARIAN
✗**Greens.** Owned and operated by the San Francisco Zen Center, this nonprofit vegetarian restaurant gets some of its fresh produce from the center's organic Green Gulch Farm. Floor-to-ceiling windows give diners a sweeping view of the Marina and the Golden Gate Bridge. Despite the lack of meat, hearty dishes from chef Annie Somerville—shepherd's pie with wild mushrooms, for example, or the vegetable brochette plate—really satisfy. Other standouts include thin-crust pizza with local cheese, potato, and grilled onions, and the salads are something special, especially the wilted spinach salad with croutons, feta, and olives. An à la carte menu is offered on Sunday and weeknights, but on Saturday a $56 four-course prix-fixe dinner is served. Weekend brunch is a good time to watch boaters on the bay. A small counter just inside the front door stocks sandwiches, soups, and sweets for easy takeout, and it's open in the morning. ⑤ *Average main: $19* ✉ *Bldg. A, Fort Mason, enter across Marina Blvd. from Safeway, Marina* ☎ *415/771–6222* ⊕ *www.greensrestaurant.com* ⌕ *Reservations essential* ⊘ *No lunch Mon.* ✛ *B1.*

COW HOLLOW

$$$
ITALIAN
FAMILY
✗**Rose's Café.** Sleepy-headed locals turn up at Rose's for the breakfast pizza of smoked ham, eggs, and fontina; house-baked pastries and breads; poached eggs with Yukon Gold potato and mushroom hash; and soft polenta with mascarpone and jam. Midday is time for pizza with wild nettles, or linguine with clams. Evening hours find customers eating their way through more pizza and pasta if on a budget, and skirt steak and a glorious roasted chicken if not. The ingredients are top-notch, the service is friendly, and the seating is in comfortable booths and at tables and a counter. Heaters above the outdoor tables keep things toasty when the temperature dips. ■**TIP➜ Expect long lines for Sunday brunch.** ⑤ *Average main: $27* ✉ *2298 Union St., Cow Hollow* ☎ *415/775–2200* ⊕ *www.rosescafesf.com* ✛ *A2.*

THE HAIGHT

$ ✕ **Indian Oven.** This white-tablecloth northern Indian restaurant draws
INDIAN diners from all over the city who come for the tandoori specialties—chicken, lamb, breads. Classics like *saag paneer* (spinach with Indian cheese), *aloo gobhi* (potato, cauliflower, and spices), and *bengan bartha* (roasted eggplant with onions and spices) are also excellent. The chef wants to keep his clientele around for the long haul, too, and puts a little "heart healthy" icon on the menu next to items that warrant it. On Friday and Saturday night, famished patrons overflow onto the sidewalk to wait for open tables; some retreat next door to the affiliated Clay Oven. If you linger too long over a mango *lassi* or the excellent *kheer* (rice pudding) on one of these nights, you'll likely be hurried along by a waiter. For better service, come on a weeknight or for lunch. ⑤ *Average main: $13* ⊠ *233 Fillmore St., Lower Haight* ☎ *415/626–1628* ✛ *A6.*

THE CASTRO

$$$ ✕ **Frances.** Still one of the hottest tickets in town, Frances is located,
FRENCH ironically, on one of the Castro's quieter streets. Chef-owner Melissa Percello's California and French cuisine is well executed and, for the quality, notably affordable. Bacon beignets, tender gnocchi, and a savory bavette steak are longtime favorites on the seasonally driven menu, with newer entries such as baked clams with bacon cream and a duck confit and baby kale salad angling to become standbys as well. The apple galette for dessert hits all the right notes. The small space is simply designed, with a limited number of tables (hence the difficulty in landing a reservation) and a small bar area with counter seating for walk-ins desperate to dine here. Service is professional and warm. ⑤ *Average main: $27* ⊠ *3870 17th St., Castro* ☎ *415/621–3870* ⊕ *www.frances-sf.com* ⌂ *Reservations essential* ◷ *No lunch* ✛ *A6.*

THE MISSION

$$ ✕ **Bar Tartine.** An offshoot of the cultlike Tartine Bakery, this neigh-
MODERN borhood restaurant in an artsy space provides a way to taste the bak-
AMERICAN ery's famed (and nearly always sold-out) country loaf. Chef Nicolaus Balla's flavor-packed cuisine combines an Eastern European sensibility with California seasonality and some Japanese influences. The menu includes many house-pickled items, tempting *langos* (fried potato bread), and seasonal salads such as one with persimmons, pressed cheese, chicories, walnuts, and orange honey. Chicken *paprikas* and fisherman's stew are among the larger, homey dishes Balla prepares. The extensive wine-and-beer list makes this a fun place to swing by for a glass—if you can find a seat. Weekend brunch is one of the city's more distinct offerings in that category, with an array of *smørrebrød* (toppings like trumpet mushrooms, mizuna, and cultured butter on sprouted rye) and buckwheat blintzes, and a beef-brisket hash with celery root, parsnip, Yukon Gold potatoes, and fried eggs. On Wednesday, Thursday, and Friday afternoon, the restaurant operates

a shop that serves sandwiches, smørrebrød, and light snacks. $ *Average main: $16* ✉ *561 Valencia St., Mission* ☎ *415/487–1600* ⊕ *www. bartartine.com* ⊘ *Closed Mon. No lunch Tues.* ✛ *B6.*

$$$
MODERN
AMERICAN
Fodor'sChoice
★

✕ **Central Kitchen.** It's nearly impossible to score seats at chef Thomas McNaughton's highly lauded Flour + Water. That's why many had plum visions of sampling his cuisine again when the Gary Danko alumnus opened this spot in a former sausage factory. Central Kitchen is the centerpiece of a modern open space, with tea lights strung along the ceiling; also in the building are Salumeria (a deli and larder, which sells Flour + Water pastas) and Trick Dog, an energetic cocktail bar. The menu is original, with playful combos and surprising flavors: Parker House rolls baked with coffee and caraway; raw Hamachi topped with fennel (from the rooftop garden) roasted until it's ash, for a strong smokiness that combines with citruses into a vinaigrette; an inky cioppino, with burnt peppers as its base that make the broth luscious. In addition to the starters, there are about four main-dish items nightly. The seven-course tasting menu ($95) provides the ultimate food journey. $ *Average main: $30* ✉ *3000 20th St., Mission* ☎ *415/826–7004* ⊕ *www. centralkitchensf.com* ⊘ *No lunch Mon.–Sat.* ✛ *D6.*

$$$
ITALIAN
Fodor'sChoice
★

✕ **Delfina.** "Irresistible." That's how countless die-hard fans describe Craig and Anne Stoll's Delfina. Such wild enthusiasm has made patience the critical virtue for anyone wanting a reservation here (although walk-ins can find some success at a counter and in the bar area). The urban interior is comfortable, with hardwood floors, aluminum-top tables, and a tile bar. Although the menu changes daily, among the usual offerings are grilled squid with warm white-bean salad and excellent tripe. As boring as spaghetti with tomato sauce may sound, it's been dialed to perfection here, and there would be a neighborhood revolt if it ever disappeared. If Piemontese fresh white truffles have made their way to San Francisco, you are likely to find hand-cut tagliarini dressed with butter, cream, and the pricey aromatic fungus on the menu alongside dishes built on more prosaic ingredients. The panna cotta is the best in its class. The storefront next door is home to pint-size Pizzeria Delfina. And for folks who can't get to the Mission, the Stolls have opened a second pizzeria on California Street in Lower Pacific Heights. $ *Average main: $25* ✉ *3621 18th St., Mission* ☎ *415/552–4055* ⊕ *www.delfinasf. com* ⌕ *Reservations essential* ⊘ *No lunch* ✛ *B6.*

$$
INDIAN
Fodor'sChoice
★

✕ **Dosa on Valencia.** If you like Indian food but crave more than chicken tikka masala and naan, Dosa is for you. This temple of South Indian cuisine, done in cheerful tones of tangerine and turmeric, serves not only the large, thin savory pancake for which it is named, but also curries, *uttapam* (open-face pancakes), and various starters, breads, rice dishes, and chutneys. You can select from about 10 different dosa fillings, ranging from traditional potatoes, onions, and cashews to spinach and fennel stems. Each comes with tomato and fresh coconut chutneys and *sambar* (lentil curry) for dipping. Tamil lamb curry with fennel and tomatoes and poppy seed prawns are popular, as are starters such as *Chennai* chicken (chicken marinated in yogurt and spices and lightly fried), and the new Indian street-food additions, among them *vada pav* (a vegetarian slider). The wine and beer lists are top drawer, and both include some Indian brands; the cocktail list is also very food-friendly. Weekend brunch offers a nice change from the usual menu suspects (the flavorful *pani puri* are a must). Queues for this spot inspired the owners to open a second, splashier and much bigger, branch at the corner of Fillmore and Post streets in Japantown. ⑤ *Average main: $18* ✉ *995 Valencia St., at 21st St., Mission* ☎ *415/642–3672* ⊕ *www.dosasf.com* ☽ *No lunch weekdays* ✛ *B6.*

$$$ **ITALIAN** ✕ **Flour + Water.** Diners used to flood into this hot spot for the blistery thin-crust Neapolitan pizza, but these days it's the pasta that holds attention, merging beautifully with chef Thomas McNaughton's whole-animal sensibilities. The grand experience here is the seven-course pasta-tasting menu at $65 per person (plus $45 for wine pairings). The homemade mustard tagliatelle with smoked lamb's tongue is surprisingly zippy, with lemon zest lifting and extracting flavors. The perfectly chewy rigatoni comes with a braised pork–laced tomato sauce. Pizzas are still being pulled from the 900-degree wood-burning oven, but they aren't what they used to be. Paxton Gate designed the dining room, and the local firm's whimsical touches are in evidence throughout: tabletop beakers as candleholders, for instance, a moth-wing wall mural, and a cabinet of taxidermy in the bathroom. Expect a noisy, boisterous scene. Trying to get a reservation at Flour + Water is one of the longest-running jokes in town. Walk-ins are ecstatic to nab a seat at the reclaimed wood bar, made from wine-barrel staves. Your best bet is to come when the doors open. ⑤ *Average main: $26* ✉ *2401 Harrison St., Mission* ☎ *415/826–7000* ⊕ *www. flourandwater.com* ☽ *No lunch* ✛ *D6.*

$$$ **SEAFOOD** ✕ **Local's Corner.** Hang on, because chef Jake Des Voignes is about to take you on a seafood joyride. With no industrial ovens or high-powered burners, this 30-seat place is really about the delicate, natural flavors of California's seasonal bounty, from the fish to the fennel, Japanese yams, and sunchokes. In typical San Francisco style, the menu reads like a jumble of ingredients, making it difficult to imagine how they might taste together, but each dish works beautifully, like creamy uni with crunchy English peas and preserved Meyer lemon, or cured halibut with diced, sweet pluots. To immerse yourself in Des Voignes's genius, make a reservation for the seven-course tasting ($65) at the chef's counter. The three-course brunches are as well-crafted as dinner, with dishes that include waffles with chicory syrup, and chicken sausage and polenta. Although the food is solid, the service is too casual. ⑤ *Average main: $25* ✉ *2500 Bryant St., Mission* ☎ *415/800–7945* ⊕ *www. localscornersf.com* ☽ *Closed Mon.* ✛ *C6.*

$$$ **ITALIAN** ✕ **Locanda.** Annie and Craig Stoll, the owners of Delfina, have bestowed another culinary gift on the city. This time her name is Locanda, and the menu is Roman inspired. A dangerously addictive starter is *pizza bianca*: chewy, hot bread that holds mini puddles of olive oil and is sprinkled with sea salt. It's hard to decide on a pasta with so many represented. A signature one, *tonnarelli cacio e pepe*, is a creamy, peppery smack of flavor. A good strategy here is to double down on pastas and antipasti, then share a main, like the lamb *scottadito*, seasoned with anchovies and coriander. Finely made cocktails (Negroni flights even) arrive at dark-wood tables on a candlelit tray, and white Heath wall tiles pump up the sophisticated interior. This is a busy place with the bar stools constantly occupied, and the communal table filling quickly each night. [$] *Average main: $28* ✉ *557 Valencia St., Mission* ☎ *415/863–6800* ⊕ *www.locandasf.com* ⊙ *No lunch* ✛ *B6.*

$ ✕ **SanJalisco.** This old-time, sun-filled, colorful, family-run restaurant is
MEXICAN   a neighborhood gem—and not only because it serves breakfast all day.
FAMILY   Try the hearty *chilaquiles,* made from day-old tortillas cut into strips and cooked with cheese, eggs, chilies, and sauce. Or order eggs scrambled with cactus or with *chicharrones* (crisp pork skins) and served with freshly made tortillas. Soup offerings change daily, with Tuesday's *albondigas* (meatballs) comfort food at its best. On weekends, adventurous eaters may opt for *birria,* a spicy goat stew, or *menudo,* a tongue-searing soup made from tripe, calf's foot, and hominy. The latter is a time-honored hangover cure—but don't come expecting margaritas here (though you will find beer and sangria). Bring plenty of change for the jukebox loaded with Latin hits. [$] *Average main: $11* ✉ *901 S. Van Ness Ave., Mission* ☎ *415/648–8383* ⊕ *www.sanjalisco.com* ✛ *C6.*

$$$ ✕ **St. Vincent.** Sommelier David Lynch is behind this modern-day Ameri-
MODERN   can tavern with a Bay Area spin. Previously at Babbo in New York
AMERICAN   and Quince in San Francisco, Lynch has put together a list of mostly European wines, with an innovative half-bottle program, and chef Bill Niles, formerly of Bar Tartine, creates rustic upscale food to accompany them. On the snacky side of things, we challenge you to eat just *one* curried, pickled egg. These starters are outrageously good, as is the hand-rolled pretzel, and the dry-aged sirloin for two comes with some of the best gratin potatoes known to man. This is lick-your-plate-clean food served in a welcoming, somewhat noisy place (wood surfaces, soaring ceilings) where Lynch himself will suggest a wine, or cicerone Sayre Piotrkowski will pair a beer with dinner or dessert. Winning seats are at the zinc-topped bar, where you can bend the ear of both men. They also run a retail wine business. [$] *Average main: $27* ✉ *1270 Valencia St., Mission* ☎ *415/285–1200* ⊕ *www.stvincentsf.com* ⊙ *Closed Sun. No lunch* ✛ *B6.*

POTRERO HILL

$$ ✕ **Chez Papa Bistrot.** France arrived on Potrero Hill with this restaurant,
FRENCH   which delivers food, waiters, and charm that would be right at home in Provence. The modest corner spot, with a Mediterranean blue awning, big windows overlooking the street, and a small heated patio, caters to a lively crowd that can make conversation difficult. Small plates include bistro classics such as beef tartare, mussels in pastis, and a leek and tomato tart. Duck confit, grilled flat-iron steak and frites, and homey lamb daube are among the big plates. The lavender crème brûlée and chocolate fondant provide sweet endings. The $36.95 prix-fixe menu is an excellent deal. To accommodate the overflow of Hill residents, who have packed this place since day one, the owners opened the tiny, more casual Chez Maman (crepes, burgers, salads) a few doors away. [$] *Average main: $24* ✉ *1401 18th St., Potrero Hill* ☎ *415/824–8205* ⊕ *www.chezpapasf.com* ⊙ *No lunch Sun.* ✛ *H6.*

PACIFIC HEIGHTS

$$$
MODERN
AMERICAN

✕ **Spruce.** A hot reservation from the day it opened, Spruce caters to the social set, with the older crowd sliding into oversized faux ostrich leather chairs for an early dinner and the younger set appearing after 8. There's also quite the lunch club during the week. The large space, an auto barn from the 1930s, contains a high-style dining room and a more casual bar and library lounge. Charcuterie, bavette steak with bordelaise sauce and duck-fat potatoes, and sweetbreads reflect the modern American menu's French leanings. The wine list, a star here, provides special delights for Riesling fans. If you can't wrangle a table, stop by the take-out café next door, which in addition to sandwiches, salads, and pastries (like the exquisite palmiers) will supply anything from the dining room menu. If you're watching your pocketbook, you can graze off the bar menu—which includes an excellent burger and *boudin blanc* (white sausage)—and over a well-crafted cocktail watch the swells come and go. $ *Average main: $34* ✉ *3640 Sacramento St., Pacific Heights* ☎ *415/931–5100* ⊕ *www.sprucesf.com* ☌ *Reservations essential* ⊗ *No lunch weekends* ✛ *A3.*

JAPANTOWN

$$
INDIAN
Fodor's Choice
★

✕ **Dosa on Fillmore.** As soon as the large door swings open to this happening two-level space, diners are greeted with a sexy atmosphere with bright colors, vivid artwork, upbeat music, a lively bar, and the smell of spices in the air. This is the second location of the popular Dosa on Valencia, but it's definitely the glamorous younger sister, with a full bar, an expanded menu, and much more room. The menu entices with savory fish dishes, fall-off-the-bone pepper chicken, and papery dosas stuffed with various fillings. The restaurant handles group dining often, and has a special menu you can customize. Return for lunch and indulge in the Indian street-food selections, and the famed *pani puri* (little crisp puffs you fill with mint and tamarind water and pop all at once into your mouth). $ *Average main: $17* ✉ *1700 Fillmore St., Japantown* ☎ *415/441–3672* ⊕ *www.dosasf.com* ⊗ *No lunch Mon. and Tues.* ✛ *A4.*

$
JAPANESE
FAMILY

✕ **Mifune.** Thin brown soba and thick white udon are the stars at this long-popular North American outpost of an Osaka-based noodle empire. A line regularly snakes out the door, but the house-made noodles, served both hot and cold and with a score of toppings, are worth the wait (and the line moves quickly). Seating is at wooden tables, where diners of every age can be heard slurping down big bowls of such traditional Japanese combinations as *nabeyaki udon,* wheat noodles topped with tempura, chicken, and fish cake; and *tenzaru,* cold noodles and hot tempura with gingery dipping sauce served on lacquered trays. The noodle-phobic can choose from a few rice dishes and sushi. $ *Average main: $12* ✉ *Japan Center, Kintetsu Bldg., 1737 Post St., Japantown* ☎ *415/922–0337* ⊕ *www.mifune.com* ✛ *B4.*

WESTERN ADDITION

$$$
AMERICAN

✕ **Nopa.** In the mid-2000s North of the Panhandle became the city's newest talked-about neighborhood in part because of big, bustling Nopa, which was cleverly named after it. The casual space, with its high ceilings, concrete floor, long bar, and sea of tables, suits the high-energy crowd of young professionals and stylish neighborhood residents. Because the kitchen doesn't close until 1 am, restaurant-industry types pack the bar late into the night. The rustic fare includes an always winning flatbread topped with fennel sausage and caramelized onions; Moroccan-style vegetable *tagine* (stew) with lemon yogurt; smoky, crisp-skin rotisserie chicken; a juicy grass-fed hamburger with thick-cut fries; one of the city's best pork chops; and, for dessert, the doughnut-like sopapillas. This place is so lively that raised voices are sometimes the only way to communicate with fellow diners. A big communal table and the friendly bar ease the way for those dining solo. The wine list is excellent, and weekend brunch is among the city's best—and most popular, so arrive a few minutes before the 11 am opening to score a table. ⑤ *Average main: $24* ✉ *560 Divisadero St., Western Addition* ☎ *415/864–8643* ⊕ *www.nopasf. com* ⊘ *No lunch weekdays* ✛ *A6.*

$
MEXICAN
FAMILY
Fodor's Choice
★

✕ **Nopalito.** The two chefs at this unusual Mexican restaurant formerly worked in the kitchen at nearby Nopa; they made such delicious staff/family meals there that Nopa's owners developed this restaurant around their cuisine. The authentic, skillfully prepared dishes range from seasonal salads and a spicy beef empanada to succulent pork carnitas and a fulfilling posole. All the tortillas are made from organic house-ground *masa* (dough), also used in the tortilla chips layering the *chilaquiles* at weekend brunch. Mexico's flavorful peppers, among them the *guajillo, chile de arbol,* and *pasilla,* find their way into many of the offerings. Casual Nopalito is popular with families yet equally pleasing to adult groups lured by the well-selected tequilas. Expect a substantial wait in the evening. You must leave your name on a list, but you can call ahead to be put on it. (There's a take-out window if you're feeling truly impatient.) To avoid waiting, try weekday lunch, after 2, when the place clears out. A second location in the inner Sunset is less crowded. ⑤ *Average main: $15* ✉ *306 Broderick St., Western Addition* ☎ *415/437–0303* ⊕ *www.nopalitosf.com* ✛ *A6.*

$$$
MODERN
AMERICAN
Fodor's Choice
★

✕ **State Bird Provisions.** Eating at this 14-table spot can be described as a festive parade of hors d'oeuvre, with bite-sized "provisions" rolled around on carts and diners picking what they want. Prices for provisions, ranging from $3 to $8, are displayed on placards and tallied up as the dinner unfolds. Those who eat with their eyes, and not their stomachs, should be cautious. This is dim-sum format, only rather than dumplings, the choices include half dollar–sized thick savory pancakes stuffed with sauerkraut; giant nori chips topped with Hamachi, radishes, and avocados; and kimchi yuba noodles with house-made egg bottarga. Each night roughly a dozen provisions are offered, along with commandables (larger dishes, including the state bird, quail, batter-dipped), and desserts. The colorful, airy dining room with pegboard walls has a high school art-room vibe, decorated as it is with string art and folksy wooden cutouts shaped like food. The staff is superfriendly. Because a reservation here is among the most sought-after in the city the wait can be onerous, but the host will take your number, recommend a nearby wine bar, and call when a table is ready. $ *Average main: $30* ⊠ *1529 Fillmore St., Western Addition* ☎ *415/795–1272* ⊕ *www.statebirdsf.com* ⌂ *Reservations essential* ⊗ *Closed Sun. No lunch* ✛ *A4.*

RICHMOND

$
ASIAN

✗ **Burma Superstar.** Locals make the trek to the "Avenues" for the extraordinary tea-leaf salad, a combo of spicy, salty, crunchy, and sour that is mixed table-side, with fermented tea leaves from Burma, fried garlic, and peanuts. Another hit is the hearty vegetarian *samusa* soup. Forget having to decide between Thai, Indian, or Chinese. Burmese fuses flavors and techniques from all these (mostly) bordering countries. The modestly decorated, no-reservations restaurant is small, so lines can be long during peak times. Leave your number and wait for the call, or walk a couple of blocks east to B-Star, owned by the same people but lesser known and often less crowded. $ *Average main: $14* ⊠ *309 Clement St., Richmond* ☎ *415/387–2147* ⊕ *www. burmasuperstar.com* ⌂ *Reservations not accepted* ✛ *A4.*

$
AMERICAN
FAMILY

✗ **Park Chow.** What do spaghetti and meatballs, Thai noodles with chicken and shrimp, salads in three sizes, and big burgers have in common? They're all on the eclectic comfort-food menu at Park Chow, and all are made with sustainable ingredients yet offered at unbeatable prices. This neighborhood standby is also known for its desserts: the fresh-baked pies and ginger cake with pumpkin ice cream are among the standouts. Kids get their own menu, with items such as burgers, grilled-cheese sandwiches, chicken fingers (made with organic chicken), fish, and mini pizzas. In cool weather fires roar in the dining-room fireplaces; in warm weather, the outdoor tables are the place to be—but arrive early for lunch or dinner. For either meal, call ahead to put your name on the waiting list. Breakfast is served on weekdays, brunch on weekends. There's another Chow in the Castro neighborhood at 215 Church St. $ *Average main: $13* ⊠ *1240 9th Ave., Inner Sunset* ☎ *415/665–9912* ⊕ *www.chowfoodbar.com* ✛ *A6.*

WHERE TO STAY

Hotels here are more than hotels: they are a part of the cityscape, some as old as the city itself, beloved by visitors and locals alike. Like its neighborhoods, San Francisco's accommodations are diverse, from cozy inns and kitschy motels, to chic boutiques and true grande dames. *Hotel reviews have been shortened. For full information, visit Fodors. com. Use the coordinate (⊕ A1) at the end of each listing to locate a site on the corresponding map.*

WHAT IT COSTS				
	$	$$	$$$	$$$$
Hotels	under $151	$151–$199	$200–$250	over $250

Hotel prices are the lowest cost of a standard double room in high season.

UNION SQUARE

$
B&B/INN
FAMILY
Fodor's Choice
★

⊞ Golden Gate Hotel. Budget seekers looking for accommodations in the Union Square area will enjoy this homey, family-run B&B. **Pros:** friendly staff; free Wi-Fi; spotless rooms; comfortable bedding; good location if you're a walker. **Cons:** some rooms without private bath. ⑤ *Rooms from: $135* ⊠ *775 Bush St., Union Sq.* ☎ *415/392–3702, 800/835–1118* ⊕ *www.goldengatehotel.com* ⤴ *25 rooms, 14 with bath* ⭐ *Breakfast* ⊕ *E4.*

$$$
HOTEL
FAMILY
Fodor's Choice
★

⊞ Hotel Diva. Entering this hotel requires stepping over footprints, handprints, and autographs embedded in the sidewalk by visiting stars; with two major theaters, the Curran and the American Conservatory, across the street, this hotel is a magnet for actors, musicians, writers, and artists. **Pros:** punchy design; in the heart of the theater district; accommodating service. **Cons:** few frills; tiny bathrooms. ⑤ *Rooms from: $201* ⊠ *440 Geary St., Union Sq.* ☎ *415/885–0200, 800/553–1900* ⊕ *www. hoteldiva.com* ⤴ *115 rooms, 3 suites* ⭐ *No meals* ⊕ *E4.*

$$$
HOTEL
FAMILY
Fodor's Choice
★

⊞ Hotel Nikko, San Francisco. The vast surfaces of gray-flecked white marble that dominate the Nikko's neoclassical lobby have the starkness of an airport, but the crisply designed rooms, in muted tones and with Bluetooth-enabled headboards, flat-screen TVs, and modern bathrooms with sinks atop granite bases, please the business-traveler clientele. **Pros:** friendly multilingual staff; tastefully designed rooms; large indoor pool; very clean. **Cons:** lobby lacks color; atmosphere feels cold to some patrons; expensive parking. ⑤ *Rooms from: $239* ⊠ *222 Mason St., Union Sq.* ☎ *415/394–1111, 800/248–3308* ⊕ *www.hotelnikkosf.com* ⤴ *510 rooms, 22 suites* ⭐ *No meals* ⊕ *E4.*

$$
HOTEL
Fodor's Choice
★

⊞ Hotel Triton. A spirit of fun has taken up full-time residence in this Kimpton property, which has a youngish, superfriendly staff, pink- and blue-neon elevators, and a colorful psychedelic lobby mural depicting the San Francisco art and music scene—think flower power mixed with Andy Warhol. **Pros:** attentive service; refreshingly funky atmosphere; hip arty environs; good location. **Cons:** rooms and baths are on the small side. ⑤ *Rooms from: $189* ⊠ *342 Grant Ave., Union*

Sq. ☎ 415/394–0500, 800/800–1299 ⊕ *www.hoteltriton.com* ⟿ 133 *rooms, 7 suites* ⊙ *No meals* ⊹ *F4.*

$$$$ ⚏ **Westin St. Francis.** The survivor of two major earthquakes, some
HOTEL   headline-grabbing scandals, and even an attempted presidential assassination, this grande dame that dates to 1904 remains ever above the fray—richly appointed, serenely elegant, and superbly located. **Pros:** fantastic beds; prime Union Square location; spacious rooms, some with great views. **Cons:** some guests comment on the long wait at check-in; rooms in original building can be small; glass elevators are not for the faint of heart. ⑤ *Rooms from: $325* ✉ *335 Powell St., Union Sq.* ☎ 415/397–7000, 800/917–7458 ⊕ *www.westinstfrancis.com* ⟿ *1,157 rooms, 38 suites* ⊙ *No meals* ⊹ *E4.*

SOMA

$$$$ ⚏ **Four Seasons Hotel San Francisco.** Occupying floors 5 through 17 of a
HOTEL   skyscraper, this exclusive, award-winning hotel is sandwiched between
Fodor's Choice multimillion-dollar condos, elite shops, and a premier sports-and-fit-
★   ness complex. **Pros:** near museums, galleries, restaurants, shopping, and clubs; terrific fitness facilities; luxurious rooms and amenities; MKT restaurant is worth the splurge. **Cons:** priccy; staff can be uppity. ⑤ *Rooms from: $425* ✉ *757 Market St., SoMa* ☎ 415/633–3000, 800/332–3442, 800/819–5053 ⊕ *www.fourseasons.com/sanfrancisco* ⟿ *231 rooms, 46 suites* ⊙ *No meals* ⊹ *F4.*

$$$$ ⚏ **InterContinental San Francisco.** The arctic-blue glass exterior and sub-
HOTEL   dued, Zen-like lobby of this sparkling hotel may be as bland as an airport concourse, but they're merely a prelude to the spectacularly light, expansive, thoughtfully laid-out guest rooms, which have all the ultramodern conveniences. **Pros:** a stone's throw from Moscone Center; well-equipped gym; near hip clubs and restaurants. **Cons:** decor is short on character; borders a rough neighborhood; a few blocks off the major tourist path. ⑤ *Rooms from: $329* ✉ *888 Howard St., SoMa* ☎ 415/616–6500, 866/781–2364 ⊕ *www.intercontinentalsanfrancisco. com* ⟿ *536 rooms, 14 suites* ⊙ *No meals* ⊹ *E5.*

$$$$ ⚏ **The St. Regis San Francisco.** Though this may be the most luxurious hotel
HOTEL   in the city, guests often remark that it's hipper and more modern than
Fodor's Choice other hotels in the St. Regis chain. **Pros:** tasteful, yet current; lap pool;
★   good location; luxe spa; views. **Cons:** expensive; some guests report inconsistent service; hallway noise; long waits for room service and valet parking. ⑤ *Rooms from: $575* ✉ *125 3rd St., SoMa* ☎ 415/284–4000 ⊕ *www. stregis.com/sanfrancisco* ⟿ *214 rooms, 46 suites* ⊙ *No meals* ⊹ *F4.*

THE TENDERLOIN

$$$$ ⚏ **Phoenix Hotel.** A magnet for the hip at heart and ultracool—Little
HOTEL   Richard, Elijah Wood, Sean Lennon, and members of R.E.M. and Pearl Jam have stayed here—the Phoenix isn't the best choice for those seeking peace and quiet (or anyone put off by the hotel's location, on the fringes of the sketchy Tenderloin District). **Pros:** boho atmosphere; cheeky design; popular with musicians; hip new restaurant/ bar; free parking. **Cons:** somewhat seedy location; no elevators; can be

loud in the evenings. $ *Rooms from: $409 ✉ 601 Eddy St., Tenderloin ☎ 415/776–1380, 800/248–9466 ⊕ www.thephoenixhotel.com ↘ 41 rooms, 3 suites* ¡O¡ *Breakfast ✛ D5.*

FINANCIAL DISTRICT

$$$$ 🖳 **Mandarin Oriental, San Francisco.** Two towers connected by glass-
HOTEL   enclosed sky bridges compose the top 11 floors of one of San Francisco's tallest buildings, offering spectacular panoramas from every room; the windows open so you can hear that trademark San Francisco sound: the "ding ding" of the cable cars some 40 floors below (and rooms even include binoculars). **Pros:** spectacular "bridge-to-bridge" views; attentive service; in the running for the most comfy beds in the city. **Cons:** in a business area that's quiet on weekends; extremely pricey. $ *Rooms from: $695 ✉ 222 Sansome St., Financial District ☎ 415/276–9600, 800/622–0404 ⊕ www.mandarinoriental.com/sanfrancisco ↘ 151 rooms, 7 suites* ¡O¡ *No meals ✛ F3.*

NOB HILL

$$$$ 🖳 **The Huntington Hotel.** Stars from Bogart and Bacall to Picasso and
HOTEL   Pavarotti have stayed in this ivy-covered hotel famed for its gracious
Fodor'sChoice   personal service and spacious rooms and suites, most of which have
★   great views of Grace Cathedral, the bay, or the city skyline. **Pros:** city icon; personalized service; spacious rooms; the aura of old San Francisco; first-rate spa with city views; cable cars pass by right out front. **Cons:** up a steep hill from downtown. $ *Rooms from: $459 ✉ 1075 California St., Nob Hill ☎ 415/474–5400, 800/227–4683 ⊕ www. huntingtonhotel.com ↘ 96 rooms, 40 suites* ¡O¡ *No meals ✛ E3.*

$$$$ 🖳 **Ritz-Carlton, San Francisco.** A preferred destination for travel-industry
HOTEL   honchos, movie stars, and visitors alike, this hotel—a stunning tribute
Fodor'sChoice   to beauty and attentive, professional service—completed a $12.5-mil-
★   lion renovation in 2012 to offer a modern twist to that classic Ritz style. **Pros:** terrific service; all-day food available on Club Level; beautiful surroundings; fantastic new restaurant and Lobby Lounge; renovated fitness center. **Cons:** expensive; hilly location; no pool. $ *Rooms from: $495 ✉ 600 Stockton St., at California St., Nob Hill ☎ 415/296–7465 ⊕ www.ritzcarlton.com ↘ 276 rooms, 60 suites* ¡O¡ *No meals ✛ E3.*

NORTH BEACH

$ 🖳 **San Remo Hotel.** A few blocks from Fisherman's Wharf, this three-
HOTEL   story 1906 Italianate Victorian—once home to longshoremen and Beat
Fodor'sChoice   poets—has a narrow stairway from the street leading to the front desk
★   and labyrinthine hallways; rooms are small but charming, with lace curtains, forest-green-painted wood floors, and brass beds and other antique furnishings. **Pros:** inexpensive; historic; cozy. **Cons:** some rooms are dark; only the penthouse suite has a private bath; spartan amenities. $ *Rooms from: $89 ✉ 2237 Mason St., North Beach ☎ 415/776–8688, 800/352–7366 ⊕ www.sanremohotel.com ↘ 64 rooms with shared baths, 1 suite* ¡O¡ *No meals ✛ E1.*

FISHERMAN'S WHARF

$$$$
HOTEL
FAMILY
Fodor's Choice
★

Argonaut Hotel. When the four-story Haslett Warehouse was a fruit-and-vegetable canning complex, boats docked right up against the 1909 structure; a century later it contains a hotel with a nautical decor—think anchors, ropes, compasses, and a row of cruise-ship deck chairs in the lobby. **Pros:** bay views; near Hyde Street cable car; sofa beds; toys for the kids. **Cons:** nautical theme isn't for everyone; cramped public areas; service can be hit or miss; location requires a bit of a trek to many SF attractions. $ *Rooms from: $309* ⊠ *495 Jefferson St., at Hyde St., Fisherman's Wharf* ☎ *415/563–0800, 866/415–0704* ⊕ *www.argonauthotel.com* ⇆ *239 rooms, 13 suites* ⦿ *No meals* ✛ *D1.*

$$$$
HOTEL

Best Western Plus–The Tuscan. The redbrick facade of this hotel some Fodors.com users describe as a "hidden treasure" barely hints at the Tuscan country villa that lies within. **Pros:** wine and beer hour; cozy feeling; great location near Fisherman's Wharf. **Cons:** congested touristy area; small rooms. $ *Rooms from: $259* ⊠ *425 North Point St., at Mason St., Fisherman's Wharf* ☎ *415/561–1100, 800/648–4626* ⊕ *www.tuscaninn.com* ⇆ *212 rooms, 12 suites* ⦿ *No meals* ✛ *E1.*

$$$$
RENTAL
FAMILY
Fodor's Choice
★

Fairmont Heritage Place, Ghirardelli Square. Housed in the former Ghirardelli chocolate factory, these one-to-three-bedroom serviced apartments just might be the most luxurious accommodations in San Francisco. **Pros:** luxury at its finest; gigantic apartments; many amenities; bay views from most accommodations; free car service within a 2-mile radius. **Cons:** a bit of a trek from downtown; expensive. $ *Rooms from: $699* ⊠ *950 North Point St., Fisherman's Wharf* ☎ *415/268–9900* ⊕ *www.fairmont.com/ghirardelli* ⇆ *53 rooms* ⦿ *Breakfast* ✛ *C1.*

EMBARCADERO

$$$$
HOTEL
FAMILY
Fodor's Choice
★

Hotel Vitale. "Luxury, naturally," the theme of this eight-story, terraced bay-front hotel, is apparent in every thoughtful detail: little vases of lavender mounted outside each room; the penthouse-level day spa with soaking tubs set in a rooftop bamboo forest; and the restaurant Americano, whose outdoor terrace is packed with hip jet-setters. **Pros:** family-friendly studios; great views; fanciful spa; luxurious amenities throughout. **Cons:** some rooms can feel cramped or be noisy; some guests report inconsistent service; rates are expensive. $ *Rooms from: $479* ⊠ *8 Mission St., Embarcadero* ☎ *415/278–3700, 888/890–8688* ⊕ *www.hotelvitale.com* ⇆ *190 rooms, 9 suites* ⦿ *No meals* ✛ *H3.*

THE MARINA, COW HOLLOW, AND THE PRESIDIO

$$
HOTEL
Fodor's Choice
★

Cow Hollow Motor Inn and Suites. The suites at this large, family-owned, modern motel are more spacious than average, featuring one or two bedrooms, hardwood floors, sitting and dining areas, marble wood-burning fireplaces, big living rooms, and fully equipped kitchens. **Pros:** suites are the size of apartments; good for families; free covered parking in building for one vehicle. **Cons:** congested neighborhood has a

4

BEST BETS FOR SAN FRANCISCO LODGING

Fodor's offers a selective listing of quality lodging experiences at every price range, from the city's best budget motel to its most sophisticated luxury hotel. Here we've compiled our top recommendations by price and experience. The very best properties—in other words, those that provide a particularly remarkable experience in their price range—are designated in the listings with the Fodor's Choice logo.

Fodor'sChoice★

By Price

$

$$

$$$

$$$$

By Experience

BUSINESS TRAVELERS

GREAT CONCIERGE

HISTORICAL FLAVOR

MOST KID-FRIENDLY

MOST ROMANTIC

TOP B&BS

TOP SPAS

college-rush-week feel; standard rooms are on a loud street. ⑤ *Rooms from: $155* ✉ *2190 Lombard St., Marina* ☎ *415/921–5800* ⊕ *www. cowhollowmotorinn.com* ⌁ *117 rooms, 12 suites* ⦿⦿ *No meals* ✛ *A1.*

$$$$
HOTEL
FAMILY

🏨 **Hotel Del Sol.** The proximity of this beach-themed, three-story 1950s motor lodge to Funston Playground, Fort Mason, the Walt Disney Family Museum, the Presidio, Crissy Field, and Chestnut Street's munchkin-favored shops already qualify this place as kid-friendly, but the toys, games, DVDs, outdoor saltwater heated pool with plenty of inflatable playthings, snow cones on summer weekends, and afternoon cookies and milk make it a virtual haven for little ones. **Pros:** kid-friendly; plenty of nearby places to eat and shop; recently renovated; $10 parking. **Cons:** far from downtown and the landmark attractions around Fisherman's Wharf; faces a busy thoroughfare. ⑤ *Rooms from: $329* ✉ *3100 Webster St., Marina* ☎ *415/921–5520, 877/433–5765* ⊕ *www. thehoteldelsol.com* ⌁ *47 rooms, 10 suites* ⦿⦿ *Breakfast* ✛ *B2.*

$$$
B&B/INN
Fodor's Choice
★

🏨 **The Inn at the Presidio.** A brick facade, porches with rocking chairs, and an outdoor fire pit set the backdrop for this idyllic hotel at the base of numerous hiking and biking trails in the Presidio, a National Land Trust. **Pros:** playful design; outdoor fire pit; only hotel in the Presidio; spacious rooms; views of Golden Gate Bridge. **Cons:** no on-site restaurant; no elevator; challenging to get a taxi; very far from downtown attractions. ⑤ *Rooms from: $215* ✉ *42 Moraga Ave., Presidio* ☎ *415/800–7356* ⊕ *www.innatthepresidio.com* ⌁ *8 rooms, 18 suites* ⦿⦿ *Breakfast* ✛ *A2.*

$$$
B&B/INN
Fodor's Choice
★

🏨 **Union Street Inn.** Precious family antiques and unique artwork helped British innkeepers Jane Bertorelli and David Coyle (former chef for the Duke and Duchess of Bedford) transform this green-and-cream 1902 Edwardian into a delightful B&B. **Pros:** personal service; Jane's excellent full breakfast; romantic setting. **Cons:** parking is difficult; no air-conditioning; no elevator. ⑤ *Rooms from: $249* ✉ *2229 Union St., Cow Hollow* ☎ *415/346–0424* ⊕ *www.unionstreetinn.com* ⌁ *6 rooms* ⦿⦿ *Breakfast* ✛ *A2.*

PACIFIC HEIGHTS AND JAPANTOWN

$$$$
HOTEL
Fodor's Choice
★

🏨 **Hotel Drisco.** Pretend you're a resident of one of the wealthiest residential neighborhoods in San Francisco at this understated, elegant 1903 Edwardian hotel. **Pros:** great service; comfortable rooms; quiet residential retreat; 24-hour room service. **Cons:** far from downtown. ⑤ *Rooms from: $475* ✉ *2901 Pacific Ave., Pacific Heights* ☎ *415/346–2880, 800/634–7277* ⊕ *www.hoteldrisco.com* ⌁ *29 rooms, 19 suites* ⦿⦿ *Breakfast* ✛ *A3.*

$$
HOTEL
FAMILY
Fodor's Choice
★

🏨 **Hotel Tomo.** Inspired by the comic phenomena manga and anime, the Tomo draws hipsters and Japanophiles eager to surround themselves with Japanese pop culture, or J-Pop as it is known across the pond. **Pros:** cool J-Pop style; anime playing on the lobby TV and manga in your room; great price in a fun neighborhood. **Cons:** tight quarters; away from downtown. ⑤ *Rooms from: $169* ✉ *1800 Sutter St., Japantown* ☎ *415/921–4000* ⊕ *www.hoteltomo.com* ⌁ *125 rooms, 1 suite* ⦿⦿ *No meals* ✛ *B1.*

NIGHTLIFE

After hours, business folk and the working class give way to costume-clad partygoers, hippies and hipsters, downtown divas, frat boys, and those who prefer something a little more clothing-optional.

Entertainment information is printed in the pink Sunday "Datebook" section and the more calendar-based Thursday "96 Hours" section (⊕ *www.sfgate.com/96hours*) in the *San Francisco Chronicle*. Also consult any of the free alternative weeklies, notably the *SF Weekly* (⊕ *www.sfweekly.com*), which blurbs nightclubs and music, and the *San Francisco Bay Guardian* (⊕ *www.sfbg.com*), which lists neighborhood, avant-garde, and budget events. SF Station (⊕ *www.sfstation.com*; online only) has an up-to-date calendar of entertainment goings-on.

UNION SQUARE

BARS

Cantina. Let the skull and crossbones over the entryway of this intimate Latin bar provide fair warning, because the magic the bartenders perform here is pure voodoo. The drinks are handcrafted with fresh ingredients, homemade bitters, and even homegrown citrus fruits. Because of this, the service can be slow during busy times; fortunately, many cocktails are served in pitchers. ■TIP→ The most popular cocktail is the vibrant Laughing Buddha—lime, ginger, and Serrano chilis. ⊠ *580 Sutter St., at Mason St., Union Sq.* ☎ *415/398–0195* ⊕ *www.cantinasf.com.*

Redwood Room. Opened in 1933 and updated by designer Philippe Starck in 2001, the Redwood Room at the Clift Hotel is a San Francisco icon. The entire room, floor to ceiling, is paneled with the wood from a single redwood tree, giving the place a rich, monochromatic look. The gorgeous original art deco sconces and chandeliers still hang, but bizarre video installations on plasma screens also adorn the walls. It's packed on weekend evenings after 10, when young scenesters swarm in; for maximum glamour, visit on a weeknight. ⊠ *Clift Hotel, 495 Geary St., at Taylor St., Union Sq.* ☎ *415/929–2372 for table reservations, 415/775–4700 for hotel* ⊕ *www.clifthotel.com.*

SOMA

BARS

City Beer Store. Called CBS by locals, this friendly tasting room cum liquor mart has a wine bar's sensibility. Perfect for connoisseurs and the merely beer curious, CBS stocks more than 300 different bottled beers, and more than a dozen are on tap. The indecisive can mix and match six-packs to go. ■TIP→ Come early: The small space, which fills up quickly on event nights, closes at 10 pm except Sunday, when it closes at 6. ⊠ *1168 Folsom St., at 8th St., SoMa* ☎ *415/503–1033* ⊕ *www.citybeerstore.com.*

GAY NIGHTLIFE

The Stud. Glam trannies, gay bears, tight-teed pretty boys, ladies and their ladies, and a handful of straight onlookers congregate here to dance to live DJ sounds and watch world-class drag performers on the small stage. The entertainment is often campy, pee-your-pants funny, and downright fantastic. Each night's music is different—from funk, soul, and hip-hop to '80s tunes and disco favorites. ■TIP➜ At Frolic, the Stud's most outrageous party (second Saturday of the month), club goers dance the night away dressed as bunnies, kittens, and even stranger creatures. ✉ *1284 Harrison St., at 9th St., SoMa* ☎ *415/863–6623* ⊕ *www.studsf.com* ◷ *Closed Mon.*

THE TENDERLOIN

4

BARS

Fodor'sChoice ★ **Bourbon & Branch.** The address and phone are unlisted, the black outer door unmarked, and when you make your reservation (required), you get a password for entry. In short, Bourbon & Branch reeks of Prohibition-era speakeasy cool. It's not exclusive, though: everyone is granted a password. The place has sex appeal, with tin ceilings, bordello-red silk wallpaper, intimate booths, and low lighting; loud conversations and cell phones are not allowed. The menu of expertly mixed cocktails and quality bourbon and whiskey is substantial, though the servers aren't always authorities. ■TIP➜ Your reservation dictates your exit time, which is strictly enforced. There's also a speakeasy within the speakeasy, called Wilson & Wilson, that is more exclusive but just as funky. ✉ *501 Jones St., at O'Farrell St., Tenderloin* ⊕ *www.bourbonandbranch.com.*

ROCK, POP, HIP-HOP, FOLK, AND BLUES CLUBS

Fodor'sChoice ★ **Great American Music Hall.** You can find top-drawer entertainment at this eclectic nightclub. Acts range from the best in blues, folk, and jazz to up-and-coming college-radio and American-roots artists to indie rockers such as OK Go, Mates of State, and the Cowboy Junkies. The colorful marble-pillared emporium (built in 1907 as a bordello) also accommodates dancing at some shows. Pub grub is available on most nights. ✉ *859 O'Farrell St., between Polk and Larkin Sts., Tenderloin* ☎ *415/885–0750* ⊕ *www.slimspresents.com.*

HAYES VALLEY

BARS

Hôtel Biron Wine Bar and Art Gallery. Sharing an alleylike block with the backs of Market Street restaurants, this tiny, cave-like (in a good way) spot displays artworks of the Mission School aesthetic on its brick walls. The well-behaved twenty- to thirtysomething clientele enjoys the off-the-beaten-path quarters, the wines from around the world, the soft lighting, and the hip music. ✉ *45 Rose St., off Market St. near Gough St., Hayes Valley* ☎ *415/703–0403* ⊕ *www.hotelbiron.com.*

Smuggler's Cove. With the decor of a pirate ship and a slew of rum-based cocktails, you half expect Captain Jack Sparrow to sidle up next to you at this offbeat, Disney-esque hangout. But don't let the kitschy

Built as a bordello in 1907, the Great American Music Hall now pulls in top-tier performers.

ambience fool you. The folks at Smuggler's Cove take rum so seriously they even make their own, which you can sample along with more than 200 other offerings, some of them vintage and very hard to find. A punchcard is provided so you can try all 70 cocktails and remember where you left off without getting shipwrecked. The small space fills up quickly, so arrive early. ⊠ *650 Gough St., at McAllister St., Hayes Valley* 🕿 *415/869–1900* ⊕ *www.smugglerscovesf.com.*

EMBARCADERO

BARS

Hard Water. A waterfront restaurant and bar with stunning bay views, Hard Water pays homage to America's most iconic spirit—bourbon—with a wall of whiskeys and a lineup of specialty cocktails. The menu, crafted by Charles Phan of Slanted Door fame, includes spicy pork-belly cracklings, cornbread-crusted alligator, and other fun snacks. ⊠ *Pier 3, Suite 3–102, at Embarcadero, Embarcadero* 🕿 *415/392–3021* ⊕ *www.hardwaterbar.com.*

NORTH BEACH

BARS

Vesuvio Cafe. If you're only hitting one bar in North Beach, it should be this one. The low-ceiling second floor of this raucous boho hangout, little altered since its 1960s heyday (when Jack Kerouac frequented the place), is a fine vantage point for watching the colorful Broadway and Columbus Avenue intersection. Another part of Vesuvio's appeal is its diverse clientele, from older neighborhood regulars and young couples to Bacchanalian posses. ⊠ *255 Columbus Ave., at Broadway, North Beach* ☎ *415/362–3370* ⊕ *www.vesuvio.com.*

ROCK, POP, HIP-HOP, FOLK, AND BLUES CLUBS

Bimbo's 365 Club. The plush main room and adjacent lounge of this club, here since 1951, retain a retro vibe perfect for the "Cocktail Nation" programming that keeps the crowds entertained. For a taste of the old-school San Francisco nightclub scene, you can't beat Bimbo's. Indie low-fi and pop bands such as Stephen Malkmus and the Jicks and Camera Obscura play here. ⊠ *1025 Columbus Ave., at Chestnut St., North Beach* ☎ *415/474–0365* ⊕ *www.bimbos365club.com.*

THE WESTERN SHORELINE

BARS

Cliff House. Classier than the nearby Beach Chalet, with a more impressive view of Ocean Beach, the Cliff House is our pick if you must choose just one oceanfront restaurant/bar. Sure, it's the site of many high school prom dates, and you could argue that the food and drinks are overpriced, and some say the sleek facade seems more suitable for a mausoleum—but the views are terrific. The best window seats are reserved for diners, but there's a small upstairs lounge where you can watch gulls sail high above the vast blue Pacific. ■TIP→ Come before sunset. ⊠ *1090 Point Lobos, at Great Hwy., Lincoln Park* ☎ *415/386–3330* ⊕ *www.cliffhouse.com.*

THE MISSION

GAY NIGHTLIFE

Lexington Club. According to its slogan, "every night is ladies' night" at this all-girl club geared to urban alterna-dykes in their 20s and 30s—expect piercings and tattoos, not lipstick. ■TIP→ The women's room has awesome graffiti. ⊠ *3464 19th St., at Valencia, Mission* ☎ *415/863–2052* ⊕ *www.lexingtonclub.com.*

Martuni's. A mixed crowd enjoys cocktails in the semirefined environment of this bar where the Castro, the Mission, and Hayes Valley intersect; variations on the martini are a specialty. In the intimate back room a pianist plays nightly, and patrons take turns boisterously singing show tunes. Martuni's often gets busy after symphony and opera performances—Davies Hall and the Opera House are both within walking distance. ■TIP→ The Godiva Chocolate Martini is a crowd favorite. ⊠ *4 Valencia St., at Market St., Mission* ☎ *415/241–0205.*

POTRERO HILL

ROCK, POP, HIP-HOP, FOLK, AND BLUES CLUBS

Bottom of the Hill. This is a great live-music dive—in the best sense of the word—and truly the epicenter for Bay Area indie rock. The club has hosted some great acts over the years, including the Strokes and the Throwing Muses. Rap and hip-hop acts occasionally make it to the stage. ⊠ *1233 17th St., at Texas St., Potrero Hill* ☎ *415/621–4455* ⊕ *www.bottomofthehill.com.*

WESTERN ADDITION

JAZZ CLUBS

Fodor's Choice
★

Yoshi's. The legendary Oakland jazz venue's San Francisco location has terrific acoustics, a 9-foot Steinway grand piano (broken in by Chick Corea), and seating for 411; it's been hailed as "simply the best jazz club in the city." Yoshi's serves Japanese food in an adjoining restaurant set in a soaring two-story space, decorated with blond wood and hanging paper lanterns (you can also order food at café tables in the club). And yes, the coupling of sushi and jazz *is* as elegant as it sounds. Sightlines are good from just about anywhere, including the back balcony. Yoshi's is in the old Fillmore District, which was known as the "Harlem of the West" in its 1940s and '50s heyday. ■TIP➔ **The club is on a tough block in the even tougher Western Addition neighborhood, so take advantage of the valet parking.** ✉ *1330 Fillmore St., at Eddy St., Western Addition* ☎ *415/655–5600* ⊕ *www.yoshis.com.*

ROCK, POP, HIP-HOP, FOLK, AND BLUES CLUBS

The Fillmore. This is *the* club that all the big names, from Coldplay to Clapton, want to play. San Francisco's most famous rock-music hall presents national and local acts: rock, reggae, grunge, jazz, folk, acid house, and more. Most tickets cost between $20 and $30, and some shows are open to all ages. Go upstairs to view the amazing collection of rock posters lining the walls. At the end of each show, free apples are set near the door, and staffers hand out collectible posters. ■TIP➔ **Avoid steep service charges by purchasing tickets at the club's box office on Sunday from 10 to 4.** ✉ *1805 Geary Blvd., at Fillmore St., Western Addition* ☎ *415/346–6000* ⊕ *www.thefillmore.com.*

THE ARTS

Sophisticated, offbeat, and often ahead of the curve, San Francisco's performing arts scene supports world-class opera, ballet, and theater productions, along with alternative-dance events, avant-garde plays, groundbreaking documentaries, and a slew of spoken-word and other literary happenings.

The best guide to the arts is the Sunday "Datebook" section of the *San Francisco Chronicle.* The four-day entertainment supplement "96 Hours" (⊕ *www.sfgate.com/96hours*) is in the Thursday *Chronicle.* Also check out the city's free alternative weeklies, including *SF Weekly* (⊕ *www.sfweekly.com*) and the *San Francisco Bay Guardian* (⊕ *www. sfbg.com*).

Online, SF Station (⊕ *www.sfstation.com*) has a frequently updated arts and nightlife calendar. San Francisco Arts Monthly (⊕ *www.sfarts. org*), which is published at the end of the month, has arts features and events listings, plus a helpful "Visiting San Francisco?" section. For offbeat, emerging-artist performances, consult CounterPULSE (⊕ *www. counterpulse.org*).

TICKETS

City Box Office. This charge-by-phone service, sells tickets for many performances and lectures. You can also buy tickets online, or in person on weekdays from 9:30 to 5:30. ✉ *180 Redwood St., Ste. 100, off Van Ness Ave., between Golden Gate Ave. and McAllister St., Civic Center* ☎ *415/392–4400* ⊕ *www.cityboxoffice.com.*

San Francisco Performances. SFP brings an eclectic array of top-flight global music and dance talents to various venues—mostly the Yerba Buena Center for the Arts, Davies Symphony Hall, and Herbst Theatre. Artists have included Yo-Yo Ma, Edgar Meyer, the Paul Taylor Dance Company, and Midori. Tickets can be purchased in person, online, or by phone. ✉ *500 Sutter St., Ste. 710* ☎ *415/392–2545* ⊕ *www.performances.org.*

TIX Bay Area. Half-price, same-day tickets for many local and touring shows go on sale (cash only) at the TIX booth in Union Square, which is open daily from 10 to 6. Discount purchases can also be made online. ✉ *Powell St. between Geary and Post Sts., Union Sq.* ☎ *415/433–7827* ⊕ *www.tixbayarea.com.*

DANCE

Fodor's Choice ★ **San Francisco Ballet.** For ballet lovers the nation's oldest professional company is reason alone to visit the Bay Area. SFB's performances, for the past three decades under direction of Helgi Tomasson, have won critical raves. The primary season runs from February through May. The repertoire includes full-length ballets such as *Don Quixote* and *Sleeping Beauty*; the December presentation of *The Nutcracker* is truly spectacular. The company also performs bold new dances from star choreographers such as William Forsythe and Mark Morris, alongside modern classics by George Balanchine and Jerome Robbins. Tickets are available at the **War Memorial Opera House.** ✉ *War Memorial Opera House, 301 Van Ness Ave., at Grove St., Civic Center* ☎ *415/865–2000* ⊕ *www.sfballet.org* ☉ *Weekdays 10–4.*

FILM

Fodor's Choice ★ **Castro Theatre.** A large neon sign marks the exterior of this 1,400-plus seat art deco movie palace whose exotic interior transports you back to 1922, when the theater first opened. High-profile festivals present films here, and classic revivals and foreign flicks also unfold. ■ **TIP→** Lines for the Castro's popular sing-along movie musicals often trail down the block. ✉ *429 Castro St., near Market St., Castro* ☎ *415/621–6120* ⊕ *www.castrotheatre.com.*

MUSIC

Fodor's Choice ★ **San Francisco Symphony.** One of America's top orchestras, the symphony performs from September through May, with additional summer performances of light classical music and show tunes. The orchestra and its charismatic music director, Michael Tilson Thomas, known for his daring programming of 20th-century American works, often perform with soloists of the caliber of Andre Watts, Gil Shaham, and Renée Fleming. The symphony's adventurous projects include its collaboration with the heavy metal band Metallica. ■**TIP**➜ Tickets cost between $15 and $100; deep discounts are often available through Travelzoo, Groupon, and other vendors. ☒ *Davies Symphony Hall, 201 Van Ness Ave., at Grove St., Civic Center* ☏ *415/864–6000* ⊕ *www.sfsymphony.org.*

SFJAZZ Center. Jazz legends Branford Marsalis and Herbie Hancock have performed at the snazzy center, as have Rosanne Cash and world-music favorite Esperanza Spaulding. The sightlines and acoustics here impress. Shows often sell out quickly. ☒ *201 Franklin St., Hayes Valley* ☏ *866/920–5299* ⊕ *www.sfjazz.org.*

MUSIC FESTIVALS

Fodor's Choice
★ **Stern Grove Festival.** The nation's oldest continual free summer music festival hosts Sunday-afternoon performances of symphony, opera, jazz, pop music, and dance. The amphitheater is in a beautiful eucalyptus grove, perfect for picnicking before the show. World-music favorites such as Ojos de Brujas, Seu Jorge, and Shuggie Otis get the massive crowds dancing. ■**TIP**➜ Shows generally start at 2 pm, but arrive hours earlier if you want to see the performances up close—and dress for cool weather, as the fog often rolls in. ☒ *Sloat Blvd. at 19th Ave., Sunset* ☏ *415/252–6252* ⊕ *www.sterngrove.org.*

OPERA

Fodor's Choice
★ **San Francisco Opera.** Founded in 1923, this internationally recognized organization has occupied the War Memorial Opera House since the building's completion in 1932. From September through January and June through July, the company presents a dozen or so operas. SF opera frequently collaborates with European companies and presents unconventional, sometimes edgy projects designed to attract younger audiences. Translations are projected above the stage during most non-English productions. Ticket prices range from $25 to $195. ☒ *War Memorial Opera House, 301 Van Ness Ave., at Grove St., Civic Center* ☏ *415/864–3330 tickets* ⊕ *www.sfopera.com* ☞ *Box office: 199 Grove St., at Van Ness Ave.; open Mon. 10–5, Tues.–Fri. 10–6.*

THEATER

American Conservatory Theater. Among the nation's leading regional theater companies, ACT presents about eight plays a year, from classics to contemporary works, often in repertory. The season runs from early fall to late spring. In December ACT stages a beloved version of Charles Dickens's *A Christmas Carol.* ☒ *415 Geary St., Union Sq.* ☏ *415/749–2228* ⊕ *www.act-sf.org.*

Fodor's Choice
★ **Teatro ZinZanni.** In a fabulous antique Belgian dance-hall tent, contortionists, chanteuses, jugglers, illusionists, and circus performers entertain audiences who dine on a surprisingly good five-course dinner. The show, which ran for 11 years on a waterfront pier, is scheduled to debut in its new permanent home in 2015. Tickets cost between $125 and $150; during summer and on most weekends, reservations are essential. ☒ *Broadway and the Embarcadero, Northern Waterfront* ☏ *415/438–2668* ⊕ *www.zinzanni.org.*

SPORTS AND THE OUTDOORS

BASEBALL

FAMILY **San Francisco Giants.** Two World Series titles (2010 and 2012) and the
Fodor'sChoice classic design of AT&T Park lead to sellouts for nearly every home
★ game the National League team plays. ☒ *AT&T Park, 24 Willie Mays Plaza, between 2nd and 3rd Sts., SoMa* ☎ *415/972–2000, 800/734–4268* ⊕ *sanfrancisco.giants.mlb.com.*

BIKING

San Francisco Bicycle Coalition. The San Francisco Bicycle Coalition has
extensive information about the policies and politics of riding and lists
local events for cyclists on its website. You can download (but not print)
a PDF version of the *San Francisco Bike Map and Walking Guide.*
☎ *415/431–2453* ⊕ *www.sfbike.org.*

WHERE TO RENT

Bike and Roll. You can rent bikes at this national outfit's locations for
$8 per hour or $32 per day; discounted weekly rates are available, and
complimentary maps are provided. ☒ *899 Columbus Ave., at Lombard St., North Beach* ☎ *415/229–2000* ⊕ *www.bikethegoldengate.com* ☒ *353 Jefferson St., between Jones and Leavenworth Sts., Fisherman's Wharf* ☒ *2800 Leavenworth St., at Beach St., Fisherman's Wharf* ☒ *Pier 43½, Embarcadero at Taylor St., North Beach* ☒ *Hyatt Regency, 5 Embarcadero Center, outside, ground level, North Beach.*

Blazing Saddles. This outfitter rents bikes for $8 to $9 an hour ($32 to
$105 a day), depending on the type of bike, and shares tips on sights to
see along the paths. ☒ *2715 Hyde St., at Beach St., Fisherman's Wharf* ☎ *415/202–8888* ⊕ *www.blazingsaddles.com* ☒ *433 Mason St., at Post St., Union Sq.* ☒ *Pier 41, Fisherman's Wharf* ☒ *465 Jefferson St., at Hyde St., Fisherman's Wharf* ☒ *2555 Powell St., at the Embarcadero, Fisherman's Wharf* ☒ *1095 Columbus, at Francisco St., North Beach* ☒ *721 Beach St., at Hyde St., North Beach.*

FOOTBALL

San Francisco 49ers. The city's NFL team is set to debut its new Levi's
Stadium for the 2014 season. The state-of-the-art facility, 44 miles south
of San Francisco, will have complete Wi-Fi capability, IPTV, and more
than 13,000 square feet of HD video boards. The 49ers may have left
town, but the team hasn't forgotten SF cuisine: at time of writing restaurateur and season-ticket holder Michael Mina was planning to open
Tailgate, based on his Bourbon and Steak restaurants. Home games usually sell out far in advance. **Ticketmaster** (⊕ *www.ticketmaster.com*) and
StubHub! (⊕ *www.stubhub.com*) are sources for single-game tickets.
☒ *Levi's Stadium, 4949 Marie P. DeBartolo Way, from San Francisco, take U.S. 101 south to the Lawrence Expressway and follow signs, Santa Clara* ☎ *800/745–3000 Ticketmaster, 866/788–2482 StubHub!, 408/579–4400 Santa Clara stadium* ⊕ *www.49ers.com*

4

RUNNING

The *San Francisco Bike Map and Walking Guide* (⊕ *www.sfbike.org/ maps*), which indicates hill grades on city streets by color, is a great resource. The **San Francisco Road Runners Club** (⊕ *www.sfrrc.org*) recommends routes on its website and has links to the websites of other clubs.

SHOPPING

UNION SQUARE

ART GALLERIES

Fodor'sChoice
★
Hang Art. A spirit of fun imbues this inviting gallery that showcases emerging artists. Prices range from a few hundred dollars to several thousand, making it an ideal place for novice collectors to get their feet wet. ⊠ *567 Sutter St., 2nd fl., near Mason St., Union Sq.* ☏ *415/434–4264* ⊕ *www.hangart.com.*

CLOTHING: MEN AND WOMEN

Fodor'sChoice
★
Margaret O'Leary. If you can only buy one piece of clothing in San Francisco, make it a hand-loomed, cashmere sweater by this Irish-born local legend. The perfect antidote to the city's wind and fog, the sweaters are so beloved by San Franciscans that some of them never wear anything else. Pick up an airplane wrap for your trip home, or a media cozy to keep your iPod toasty. Another store is in Pacific Heights, at 2400 Fillmore St. ⊠ *1 Claude La., at Sutter St., just west of Kearny St., Union Sq.* ☏ *415/391–1010* ⊕ *www.margaretoleary.com.*

DEPARTMENT STORES

Gump's. It's a San Francisco institution, dating to the 19th century, and it's a strikingly luxurious one. The airy store exudes a museumlike vibe, with its large decorative vases, sumptuous housewares, and Tahitian-pearl display. It's a great place to pick up gifts, such as the Golden Gate Bridge note cards or silver-plated butter spreaders in a signature Gump's box. ⊠ *135 Post St., near Kearny St., Union Sq.* ☏ *415/982–1616* ⊕ *www.gumps.com.*

Nordstrom. Somehow Nordstrom manages to be all things to all people, and this location, with spiral escalators circling a four-story atrium, is no exception. Whether you're an elegant lady of a certain age shopping for a new mink coat or a teen on the hunt for a Roxy hoodie, the salespeople are known for being happy to help. Nordstrom carries the best selections in town of designers such as Tory Burch, but its own brands have loyal followings, too. ■TIP➔ The café upstairs is a superb choice for a ladies-who-lunch shopping break. ⊠ *San Francisco Shopping Centre, 865 Market St., at 5th St., Union Sq.* ☏ *415/243–8500* ⊕ *shop.nordstrom.com.*

FURNITURE, HOUSEWARES, AND GIFTS

Fodor'sChoice
★
Diptyque. The original Diptyque boutique in Paris has attracted a long line of celebrities. You can find the full array of scented candles and fragrances in this chic shop that would be at home on the boulevard

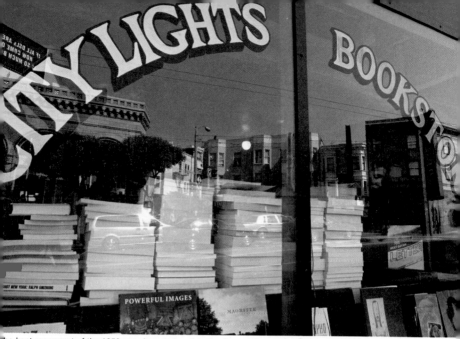

The beat movement of the 1950s was born in San Francisco's most famous bookstore, City Lights.

St-Germain. Trademark black-and-white labels adorn the popular L'eau toilet water, scented with geranium and sandalwood. Candles come in traditional and esoteric scents, including lavender, basil, leather, and fig tree. Also available are French Mariage Frères teas. ✉ *171 Maiden La., near Stockton St., Union Sq.* ☎ *415/402–0600* ⊕ *www.diptyqueparis.com.*

CHINATOWN

TOYS AND GADGETS

Chinatown Kite Shop. The kites sold here range from basic diamond shapes to box- and animal-shaped configurations. ■**TIP→** Colorful dragon kites make great souvenirs. ✉ *717 Grant Ave., near Sacramento St., Chinatown* ☎ *415/989–5182* ⊕ *www.chinatownkite.com.*

SOMA

BOOKS

Chronicle Books. This local beacon of publishing produces inventively designed fiction, cookbooks, art books, and other titles, as well as diaries, planners, and address books—all of which you can purchase at three airy and attractive spaces. The other stores are at 680 2nd Street, near AT&T Park, and 1846 Union Street, in Cow Hollow. ✉ *Metreon Westfield Shopping Center, 165 4th St., near Howard St., SoMa* ☎ *415/369–6271* ⊕ *www.chroniclebooks.com.*

FOOD AND DRINK

K&L Wine Merchants. More than any other wine store, this one has an ardent cult following around town. The friendly staffers promise not to sell what they don't taste themselves, and weekly events—on Thursday from 5 pm to 6:30 pm and Saturday from noon to 3 pm—open the tastings to customers. The best-seller list for varietals and regions for both the under- and over-$30 categories appeals to the wine lover in everyone. ⊠ *638 4th St., between Brannan and Townsend Sts., SoMa* 🕾 *415/896–1734* ⊕ *www.klwines.com.*

HAYES VALLEY

FOOD AND DRINK

Miette Confiserie. There is truly nothing sweeter than a cellophane bag tied with blue-and-white twine and filled with malt balls or chocolate sardines from this European-style apothecary. Grab a gingerbread cupcake or a tantalizing macaron or some shortbread. The pastel-color cake stands make even window-shopping a treat. ⊠ *449 Octavia Blvd., between Hayes and Fell Sts., Hayes Valley* 🕾 *415/626–6221* ⊕ *www.miette.com.*

NORTH BEACH

BOOKS

Fodor's Choice ★ **City Lights Bookstore.** The city's most famous bookstore is where the Beat movement of the 1950s was born. Neal Cassady and Jack Kerouac hung out in the basement, and now regulars and tourists while hours away in this well-worn space. The upstairs room holds impressive poetry and Beat literature collections. Poet Lawrence Ferlinghetti, the owner, remains involved in the workings of this three-story shop. City Lights Publishers, which issued the poet Allen Ginsberg's *Howl* in 1956, publishes a dozen new titles each year. ⊠ *261 Columbus Ave., at Broadway, North Beach* 🕾 *415/362–8193* ⊕ *www.citylights.com.*

FOOD AND DRINK

Fodor's Choice ★ **Molinari Delicatessen.** This store has been making its own salami, sausages, and cold cuts since 1896. Other homemade specialties include meat and cheese ravioli, tomato sauces, and fresh pastas. ■ TIP→ Do like the locals: grab a made-to-order sandwich for lunch and eat it at one of the sidewalk tables or over at Washington Square Park. ⊠ *373 Columbus Ave., at Vallejo St., North Beach* 🕾 *415/421–2337.*

EMBARCADERO

FARMERS' MARKETS

Fodor's Choice ★ **Ferry Plaza Farmers' Market.** The partylike Saturday edition of the city's most upscale and expensive farmers' market places baked goods, gourmet cheeses, smoked fish, and fancy pots of jam alongside organic basil, specialty mushrooms, heirloom tomatoes, handcrafted jams, and juicy-ripe locally grown fruit. On Saturday about 100 vendors pack along three sides of the building, and sandwiches and other prepared foods are for sale in addition to fruit, vegetable, and other samples free for the nibbling. Smaller markets take place on Tuesday and Thursday (the Thursday one doesn't operate from about late December through March.) ⊠ *Ferry Plaza at Market St., Embarcadero* ☎ *415/291–3276* ⊕ *www.ferrybuildingmarketplace.com* ✆ *Tues. and Thurs. 10–2, Sat. 8–2.*

THE HAIGHT

MUSIC

Fodor's Choice ★ **Amoeba Music.** With more than 2.5 million new and used CDs, DVDs, and records, this warehouselike offshoot of the Berkeley original carries titles you can't find on Amazon at bargain prices. No niche is ignored—from electronica and hip-hop to jazz and classical—and the stock changes daily. ■**TIP➔** Weekly in-store performances attract large crowds. ⊠ *1855 Haight St., between Stanyan and Shrader Sts., Haight* ☎ *415/831–1200* ⊕ *www.amoeba.com.*

THE MISSION

CERAMICS

Heath Ceramics. A darling of restaurateurs and local party hosts, Heath opened a 60,000-square-foot Mission District warehouse, complete with a Blue Bottle Coffee kiosk, to showcase its simple yet beautifully crafted ceramic bowls, plates, and vases. ⊠ *2900 18th St., at Alabama St., Mission* ☎ *415/361–5552* ⊕ *www.heathceramics.com.*

FURNITURE, HOUSEWARES, AND GIFTS

Fodor's Choice ★ **Paxton Gate.** Elevating gardening to an art, this serene shop offers beautiful earthenware pots, amaryllis and narcissus bulbs, decorative garden items, and coffee-table books such as *An Inordinate Fondness for Beetles.* The collection of taxidermy and preserved bugs provides more unusual gift ideas. A couple of storefronts away is too-cute Paxton Gate Curiosities for Kids, jam-packed with retro toys, books, and other stellar finds. ⊠ *824 Valencia St., between 19th and 20th Sts., Mission* ☎ *415/824–1872* ⊕ *www.paxtongate.com.*

PACIFIC HEIGHTS

BEAUTY

BeneFit Cosmetics. You can find this locally based line of cosmetics and skin-care products at Macy's and Sephora, but it's much more fun to come to one of the eponymous boutiques. No-pressure salespeople dab you with whimsical makeup such as Ooh La Lift concealer and Tinted Love, a stain for lips and cheeks. ⊠ *2117 Fillmore St., between California and Sacramento Sts., Pacific Heights* ☎ *415/567–0242* ⊕ *www.benefitcosmetics.com.*

JAPANTOWN

BOOKS

Kinokuniya Bookstore. The selection of English-language books about Japanese culture—everything from medieval history to origami instructions—is one of the finest in the country. Kinokuniya is the city's biggest seller of Japanese-language books. Dozens of glossy Asian fashion magazines attract the young and trendy; the manga and anime books and magazines are wildly popular, too. ⊠ *Kinokuniya Bldg., 1581 Webster St., at Geary Blvd., Japantown* ☎ *415/567–7625.*

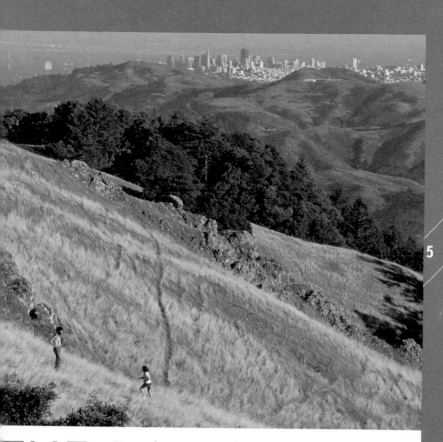

THE BAY AREA

WELCOME TO THE BAY AREA

TOP REASONS TO GO

★ **Bite into the "Gourmet Ghetto":** Eat your way through this area of North Berkeley, starting with a slice of perfect pizza from the Cheese Board (just look for the line).

★ **Find solitude at Point Reyes National Seashore:** Hike beautifully rugged—and often deserted—beaches at one of the most beautiful places on earth, period.

★ **Sit on a dock by the bay:** Admire the beauty of the Bay Area from the rocky, picturesque shores of Sausalito or Tiburon.

★ **Go barhopping in Oakland's hippest hood:** Spend an evening swinging through the watering holes of Uptown, Oakland's artsy-hip and fast-rising corner of downtown.

★ **Walk among giants:** Walking into Muir Woods, a mere 12 miles north of the Golden Gate Bridge, is like entering a cathedral built by God.

1 Berkeley. This college town has long been known for its liberal ethos, stimulating university community (and perhaps even more stimulating coffee shops), and activist streak. But these days, the lively restaurant and arts scenes are luring even those who wouldn't be caught dead in Birkenstocks.

2 Oakland. Life in this harbor-front city is strongly defined by a turbulent history. But the up-and-coming downtown scene and rejuvenated waterfront are signals of good things ahead.

3 **Marin County.** Marin is considered the prettiest of the Bay Area counties, primarily because of its wealth of open space. Anchored by water on three sides, the county is mostly parkland, including long stretches of undeveloped coastline. The picturesque small towns here—Sausalito, Tiburon, Mill Valley, and Bolinas among them—may sometimes look rustic, but they're mostly in a dizzyingly high tax bracket. There's a reason why people call BMWs "basic Marin wheels."

GETTING ORIENTED

East of the city, across the San Francisco Bay, lie Berkeley and Oakland, which most Bay Area residents refer to as the East Bay. These two towns have distinct personalities, but life here feels more relaxed than in the city—though every bit as vibrant. Cross the Golden Gate Bridge and head north to reach Marin County's rolling hills and green expanses, where residents enjoy a haute-suburban lifestyle. Farther afield, the wild landscapes of the Muir Woods, Mt. Tamalpais, Stinson Beach, and Point Reyes National Seashore await.

Updated by
Denise M. Leto

It's rare for a metropolis to compete with its suburbs for visitors, but the view from any of San Francisco's hilltops shows that the Bay Area's temptations extend far beyond the city limits. East of town are two energetic urban centers, Berkeley and Oakland. Famously radical Berkeley is also comfortably sophisticated, while Oakland has an art and restaurant scene so hip that it pulls San Franciscans to this side of the bay. To the north is Marin County, the beauty queen, with dramatic coastal scenery of breathtaking beauty and chic, affluent villages like Tiburon and Mill Valley.

PLANNING

WHEN TO GO

As with San Francisco, you can visit the rest of the Bay Area comfortably at any time of year, and it's especially nice in late spring and fall. Unlike in San Francisco, though, the surrounding areas are reliably sunny in summer—it gets hotter as you head inland. Even the rainy season has its charms, as hills that are golden the rest of the year turn a rich green and wildflowers become plentiful. Precipitation is usually the heaviest between November and March. Berkeley is a university town, so the rhythm of the school year might affect your visit. It's easier to navigate the streets and find parking near the university between semesters, but there's also less buzz around town.

GETTING HERE AND AROUND
BART TRAVEL

Using public transportation to reach Berkeley or Oakland is ideal. The under- and aboveground BART (Bay Area Rapid Transit) trains make stops in both towns. Trips to either take about a half hour one-way from the center of San Francisco. BART does not serve Marin County.

Contacts BART ☎ 510/465–2278 ⊕ www.bart.gov.

BOAT AND FERRY TRAVEL

For sheer romance, nothing beats the ferry; there's service from San Francisco to Sausalito, Tiburon, and Larkspur in Marin County, and to Alameda and Oakland in the East Bay.

The Golden Gate Ferry crosses the bay to Sausalito from San Francisco's Ferry Building (⊠ *Market Street and the Embarcadero*). Blue & Gold Fleet ferries depart daily for Sausalito and Tiburon from Pier 41 at Fisherman's Wharf; weekday commuter ferries leave from the Ferry Building for Tiburon. The trip to Sausalito takes 25 minutes to an hour; to Tiburon, it takes 25 to 55 minutes.

The Angel Island–Tiburon Ferry sails to the island daily April through October and weekends the rest of the year.

The San Francisco Bay Ferry runs several times daily between San Francisco's Ferry Building or Pier 41 and Alameda and Jack London Square in Oakland; one-way tickets are $6.25. The trip lasts 20 to 45 minutes, depending on your departure point, and leads to Oakland's waterfront shopping and restaurant district. Purchase tickets on board.

Boat and Ferry Lines Angel Island–Tiburon Ferry ☎ 415/435–2131 ⊕ www.angelislandferry.com. **Blue & Gold Fleet** ☎ 415/705–8200 ⊕ www.blueandgoldfleet.com. **Golden Gate Ferry** ☎ 511 ⊕ www.goldengateferry.org. **San Francisco Bay Ferry** ☎ 510/522–3300 ⊕ sanfranciscobayferry.com.

BUS TRAVEL

Golden Gate Transit buses travel to Sausalito, Tiburon, and Mill Valley from Folsom and 8th streets and from other points in San Francisco. For Mt. Tamalpais State Park and West Marin (e.g., Stinson Beach, Bolinas, and Point Reyes Station), take one of the many routes to Marin City and transfer there to the West Marin Stagecoach (schedules vary). San Francisco Muni bus 76X runs hourly from Sutter and Sansome streets to the Marin Headlands Visitor Center on weekends and major holidays only. The trip takes about 45 minutes.

Though much less convenient than BART, AC Transit buses run between San Francisco's Transbay Temporary Terminal (on the block bordered by Main, Folsom, Beale and Howard streets) and the East Bay. AC Transit's F and FS lines stop near the university and 4th Street shopping, respectively, in Berkeley. Lines C and P travel to Piedmont in Oakland. The O bus stops at the edge of Chinatown near downtown Oakland.

Bus Lines AC Transit ☎ 511 ⊕ www.actransit.org. **Golden Gate Transit** ☎ 511 ⊕ www.goldengate.org. **San Francisco Muni** ☎ 311 ⊕ www.sfmta.com. **West Marin Stagecoach** ☎ 415/526–3239 ⊕ www.marintransit.org/stage.html.

CAR TRAVEL

To reach the East Bay from San Francisco, take Interstate 80 East across the San Francisco–Oakland Bay Bridge. Take the University Avenue exit through downtown Berkeley to reach U.C. Berkeley, or take the Ashby Avenue exit and turn left on Telegraph Avenue; there's a parking garage on Channing Way near the campus. For Oakland, take Interstate 580 off the Bay Bridge. To reach downtown and the waterfront, take Interstate 980 from Interstate 580 and exit at 12th Street. Both trips take about 30 minutes unless it's rush hour or a weekend afternoon, when you should count on an hour.

Head north on U.S.101 and cross the Golden Gate Bridge to reach all points in Marin by car, which is essential to visit the outer portions unless you want to spend all day on the bus. From San Francisco, the towns of Sausalito and Tiburon and the Marin Headlands and Point Reyes National Seashore are accessed off U.S. 101. The coastal route, Highway 1, also known as Shoreline Highway, can be accessed off U.S. 101 as well. Follow this road to Mill Valley, Muir Woods, Mt. Tamalpais State Park, Muir Beach, Stinson Beach, and Bolinas. From Bolinas, you can continue north on Highway 1 to Point Reyes. Depending on traffic, it takes from 20 to 45 minutes to get to the Marin Headlands, Sausalito, and Tiburon; driving directly to Point Reyes from San Francisco takes about 90 minutes in moderate traffic if you drive north on U.S. 101 and west on Sir Francis Drake Boulevard. Trips to Muir Woods take from 35 minutes to an hour from San Francisco. Add another 30 minutes for the drive to Stinson Beach (the curving roads make the going slower), 10 more if you continue on to Bolinas. The drive from Bolinas to Point Reyes takes an additional half hour.

RESTAURANTS

The Bay Area is home to some of the most popular and innovative restaurants in the country, including Chez Panisse in Berkeley and Commis in Oakland—for which reservations must be made well in advance. Expect an emphasis on locally grown produce, hormone-free meats, and California wine. Keep in mind that many Marin cafés don't serve dinner, and that dinner service ends on the early side.

HOTELS

Hotels in Berkeley and Oakland tend to be standard-issue, but many Marin hotels package themselves as cozy retreats. Summer is often booked well in advance, despite weather that can be downright chilly. Check for special packages during this season. *Hotel reviews have been shortened. For full information, visit Fodors.com.*

WHAT IT COSTS

	$	$$	$$$	$$$$
Restaurants	under $16	$16–$22	$23–$30	over $30
Hotels	under $151	$151–$199	$200–$250	over $250

Restaurant prices are the average price of a main course at dinner or, if dinner is not served, at lunch. Hotel prices are the lowest cost of a standard double room in high season.

TOURS

Dylan's Tours. Spend three hours exploring San Francisco with some of the friendliest local guides around, then head to Muir Woods for an hour among giant redwoods, with a stop in Sausalito on the way back. Groups are limited to 14 people; past patrons rave about the tour's in-the-know feel. ⊠ *782 Columbus Ave., North Beach, San Francisco* ☎ *415/932–6993* ⊕ *www.dylanstours.com* ⊠ *From $65.*

Extranomical Tours. Take a combination Muir Woods–Sausalito tour with Extranomical, and you can choose to ferry back to San Francisco from Sausalito. Another tour combines a Muir Woods visit with a Wine Country excursion. ☎ *866/231–3752* ⊕ *www.extranomical.com* ⊠ *From $49.*

Great Pacific Tour Co. Morning and afternoon tours to Muir Woods and Sausalito run 3½ hours, with hotel pickup, in 14-passenger vans. ☎ *415/626–4499* ⊕ *www.greatpacifictour.com* ⊠ *From $55.*

THE EAST BAY

When San Franciscans refer to it, the East Bay often means nothing more than what you can see across the bay from the city—mainly Oakland and Berkeley. There's far more here—industrial-chic Emeryville, the wooded ranchland of Walnut Creek, and sprawling, urban Richmond, to name a few other communities—but Berkeley, anchored by its world-class university, and Oakland, which struggles with violence but has booming arts, nightlife, and restaurant scenes, are the magnets that draw folks across the bay.

BERKELEY

2 miles northeast of Bay Bridge.

The birthplace of the Free Speech Movement, the radical hub of the 1960s, the home of arguably the nation's top public university, and the city whose government condemned the bombing of Afghanistan—Berkeley is all of those things. The city of 100,000 facing San Francisco across the bay is also culturally diverse, a breeding ground for social trends, a bastion of the counterculture, and an important center for writers, artists, and musicians. Berkeley residents, students, and faculty spend hours nursing various coffee concoctions while they read, discuss, and debate at any of the dozens of cafés that surround the campus. It's the quintessential university town, and many who graduated years ago still bask in daily intellectual conversation, great weather, and good food. Residents will walk out of their way to go to the perfect bread shop or consult with their favorite wine merchant.

Oakland may have Berkeley beat when it comes to cutting-edge arts, and the city may have forfeited some of its renegade 1960s spirit over the years, but unless a guy in a hot-pink satin body suit, skullcap, and cape rides a unicycle around *your* town, you'll likely find Berkeley offbeat indeed.

The epicenter of Berkeley's energy and activism: the University of California.

GETTING HERE AND AROUND

BART is the easiest way to get to Berkeley from San Francisco. Alight at the Downtown Berkeley (not North Berkeley) station, and walk a block up Center Street to get to the western edge of campus. AC Transit buses F and FS stop near the university and 4th Street shopping. By car, take Interstate 80 east across the Bay Bridge then take the University Avenue exit through downtown Berkeley to the campus or take the Ashby Avenue exit and turn left on Telegraph Avenue. Once you arrive, explore on foot. Berkeley is very pedestrian-friendly.

ESSENTIALS

Visitor Information Visit Berkeley ⊠ *2030 Addison St., Ste. 102* ☎ *510/549–7040* ⊕ *www.visitberkeley.com.*

EXPLORING
TOP ATTRACTIONS

4th Street. Several blocks centering on 4th Street north of University Avenue have evolved from light industrial uses into an upscale shopping and dining district. The compact area is busiest on bright weekend afternoons. Stained Glass Garden, Builders Booksource, and the Apple Store are among shoppers' favorites, along with a minislew of boutiques and wonderful paper stores. ■TIP➜ **A walk through the East Bay Vivarium, at 1827 5th St., where turtles swim, Amazonian snakes slither, and baby mice (dinner) cower, is better than a walk through the reptile house at the zoo—and it's free.** ⊠ *4th St., between University Ave. and Delaware Sts.* ⊕ *www.fourthstreet.com.*

QUICK
BITES

✕ **Cheese Board Pizza.** With a jazz combo playing in the storefront and a long line snaking down the block, Cheese Board Pizza taps into the pulse of the Gourmet Ghetto. The cooperatively owned take-out spot and restaurant draws devoted customers with the smell of just-baked garlic, fresh vegetables, and perfect sauces: one pizza a day, always vegetarian. For just a nibble, the Cheese Board bakery–cheese shop next door sells cookies, muffins, scones, bialys, and the best sourdough baguettes in town. ✉ *1504–1512 Shattuck Ave., at Vine St.* ☎ *510/549-3055* ⊕ *cheeseboardcollective.coop/pizza* ⊙ *Tues.–Sat. 11:30–3 and 4:30–8.*

A TASTING TOUR

For an unforgettable foodie experience, take Lisa Rogovin's **Culinary Walking Tour** (☎ 415/806–5970 ⊕ www.edible-excursions.net). You'll taste your way through the Gourmet Ghetto, learn some culinary history, and meet the chefs behind the food. Tours ($88) run on Thursday from 11 to 2:15 and on Saturday from 10 to 1.

5

Fodor'sChoice
★

Gourmet Ghetto. The success of Chez Panisse restaurant attracted other food-related enterprises to its stretch of Shattuck Avenue, and the area surrounding the intersection of Shattuck and Vine Street became known as the Gourmet Ghetto. Foodies will do well to spend a couple of hours here, poking around the food shops, grabbing a quick bite, or indulging in a full meal at one of the neighborhood's many excellent eateries.

The line stretches down the block in front of **Cheese Board Pizza,** at 1512 Shattuck, where live jazz bands sometimes serenade the diners that spill out onto the sidewalk and median. Next door is the **Cheese Board Collective**—worker owned since 1971—and its fabulous bakery and extensive cheese counter. Next door to Chez Panisse, César (No. 1515) wine bar and tapas house is a good place for an afternoon quaff or late-night drink.

The small food stands of **Epicurious Garden,** at 1509–1513 Shattuck, sell everything from sushi to gelato. Out back, you can find a small terraced garden—the best place to sit—that winds up four levels and ends at the **Imperial Tea Court.** Around the corner just off Vine Street is **Love at First Bite,** a cupcakery that sells scrumptious confections. Across Vine, the **Vintage Berkeley** wine shop occupies the historic former pump house at No. 2113; the offerings here are shrewdly selected and reasonably priced. Coffee lovers of the **Peet's** persuasion may want to pay respects at No. 2124, where the famed roaster got its start; the small café includes a display chronicling Peet's history.

South of Cedar Street in the next block of Shattuck is the art-filled **Guerilla Cafe** (No. 1620), a breakfast and lunch spot beloved for its waffles (the Blue Bottle Coffee doesn't hurt). Also look for the **Local Butcher Shop** (No. 1600), with locally sourced meat and hearty made-to-order sandwiches. A former Ritz-Carlton chef brings white-linen quality to his to-go counter, **Grégoire,** around the corner on Cedar Street (No. 2109). In the block north of Vine Street on Shattuck are popular **Saul's** deli and restaurant and beautiful **Masse's Pastries**. On Thursday, an organic farmers' market thrives here. We could go on, but you get the idea. ⊠ *Shattuck Ave. between Cedar and Rose Sts., North Berkeley* ⊕ *www.gourmetghetto.org.*

FAMILY **Tilden Regional Park.** The **Regional Parks Botanic Garden** is the star of this beautiful 2,000-acre park in the hills east of the U.C. Berkeley campus. Botanically speaking, a stroll through the garden, which focuses on native plants of California, provides a whirlwind tour of the entire state. At the garden's visitor center, you can pick up information about Tilden's other attractions, including its picnic spots, Lake Anza swimming site, golf course, and hiking trails (the paved **Nimitz Way**, at Inspiration Point, is a popular hike with wonderful views, especially at sunset). ■TIP➜ Children love Tilden Park's miniature steam trains; Little Farm, where kids can feed the animals; and the vintage carousel with wooden animals. ⊠ *Regional Parks Botanic Garden, Wildcat Canyon Rd. and South Park Dr., Tilden Park* ☎ *510/544–2747* ⊕ *www. ebparks.org/parks/tilden* ⊡ *Free to park and botanic garden* ⊙ *Daily 8 am–10 pm.*

University of California. Known simply as "Cal," the founding campus of California's university system is one of the leading intellectual centers in the United States and a major site for scientific research. Chartered in 1868, the university sits on 178 oak-covered acres split by Strawberry Creek. Bounded by Bancroft Way to the south, Hearst Avenue to the north, Oxford Street to the west, and Gayley Road to the east, Cal has more than 30,000 students and a full-time faculty of 1,500.

Below are a few places of note on campus:

Berkeley Art Museum & Pacific Film Archive. The museum's collection spans five centuries and is strong on mid-20th-century art, particularly abstract expressionist works; admission to the downstairs galleries is free. The Pacific Film Archive, at 2575 Bancroft Way, is a major venue for foreign, independent, and avant-garde film. ⊠ *2626 Bancroft Way, at Bowditch St.* ☎ *510/642–0808, film info 510/642–1124* ⊕ *www. bampfa.berkeley.edu* ⊡ *$10, free 1st Thurs. of month* ⊙ *Wed.–Sun. 11–5, some Fridays 11–9.*

Berkeley Visitor Information Center. You can get your bearings here and find out about campus events. Free 90-minute tours leave from here on weekdays. ⊠ *101 Sproul Hall, Bancroft Way and Telegraph Ave.* ☎ *510/642–5215* ⊕ *visitors.berkeley.edu* ⊙ *Weekdays 8:30–4:30, tours at 10 am.*

Sather Tower. Weekend campus tours leave from this landmark, popularly known as the Campanile, at 10 am on Saturdays and 1 pm on Sundays. The 307-foot structure, modeled on St. Mark's Tower in Venice, can be seen for miles. For a view of the campus and beyond, take the elevator up 175 feet, then walk another 38 steps to the observation deck. ⊡ *Elevator $3,* ⊙ *Weekdays 10–4, Sat. 10–5, Sun. 10–1:30 and 3–5.*

Sproul Plaza. The site of free-speech and civil-rights protests in the 1960s, the plaza remains a platform for political and social activists, musicians, and students. Preachers orate atop milk crates, amateur entertainers bang on makeshift drum sets, and protesters distribute leaflets about everything from marijuana to the Middle East. Walk through at noon for the liveliest show of student spirit. ⊠ *Telegraph Ave. and Bancroft Way.*

University of California Botanical Garden. Thanks to Berkeley's temperate climate, about 13,500 species of plants from all over the world flourish in this 34-acre garden. Free tours are given on Thursdays and weekends at 1:30; the views are breathtaking. ⊠ *200 Centennial Dr.* ☎ *510/643–2755* ⊕ *botanicalgarden.berkeley.edu* ☑ *$10, free 1st Thurs. of month* ⊙ *Daily 9–5, closed 1st Tues. of month.* ⊕ *www. berkeley.edu.*

WORTH NOTING

Elmwood. Shops and cafés pack this pleasant neighborhood centered on College Avenue, just south of the U.C. campus. You'll know you're here when you see the logo for the beloved art-house cinema and performance space, the **Elmwood theater,** near College and Ashby avenues, though you're just as apt to see a line snaking outside nearby **Ici Ice Cream,** at 2948 College. All the treats here are made on the premises. While you're waiting, check out the architectural details of the nearby pre-World War II storefronts. Century-old shingled houses line the tree-shaded streets nearby. ⊠ *College Ave. between Dwight Way and Alcatraz Ave., Elmwood.*

OFF THE
BEATEN
PATH

Indian Rock. An outcropping of nature in a sea of North Berkeley homes, this is an unbeatable spot for a sunset picnic. You know you've reached the rock when you see amateur rock climbers clinging precariously to its side. After-work walkers and cuddling couples, all watching the sun sinking beneath the Golden Gate Bridge, join you at the top. Come early to grab a spot on the rock while it's still light. ✉ *Head east on Indian Rock Path at Solano Ave. and the Alameda.*

FAMILY **Lawrence Hall of Science.** At this dazzling hands-on science museum, kids can look at insects under microscopes, solve crimes using chemical forensics, and explore the physics of baseball. Out front they'll climb on Pheena, a life-size blue-whale model, and clamber over a giant strand of DNA. Out back, it's all about how earthquakes and water have shaped the bay, and from all vantage points sweeping views of the bay and beyond can be had. On weekends come special lectures, demonstrations, and planetarium shows. ✉ *1 Centennial Dr.* ☎ *510/642–5132* ⊕ *www.lawrencehallofscience.org* 🎫 *$12, planetarium $4 extra* ⊙ *Daily 10–5.*

San Pablo Avenue. Berkeley's diversity is front and center along this evolving north–south artery in West Berkeley, where the old and new stand side by side: sari shops and a Mexican grocery do business near a hipster dive bar, a bait-and-tackle store, a typewriter store, and a dozen cool boutiques, all cheek by jowl in a six-block microhood that doesn't have a name . . . yet.

Start at University Avenue, where you can duck into **Mi Tierra Foods** (No. 2082) for piñatas and chorizo—notice the Mission District–like mural—and **Middle East Market** (No. 2054) for rose water and rockin' baklava. **Café V** (No. 2056) has fresh, reliably good, and reasonably priced Vietnamese food, and pretty much everyone loves the thin-crust pies at **Lanesplitter Pizza & Pub** (No. 2033). The coffee at **Local 123** (No. 2049) is strong, delicious, and beautiful, and the back patio is a lovely surprise.

Old-fashioned, family-run **Country Cheese** (No. 2101) has hundreds of cheeses, of course, but it also carries great bulk foods and makes a heck of a sandwich to order. Or grab a table at industrial-cute **Gaumenkitzel** (No. 2121) and tuck in to schnitzel and other traditional German fare. The pierced-and-tattooed set loves **Acme Bar & Company** (No. 2115) for its Bloody Marys and whiskey selection.

As you move south, you'll pass lots of home-decor shops. Witness the reupholstering genius on display at **Mignonne Décor** (No. 2447). One of the Bay Area's oldest salvage shops, **Ohmega Salvage** (Nos. 2400–2407) makes for fun browsing, though its claw-foot tubs and Victorian window frames are pricey.

At the corner of Dwight Way, stop for more caffeine at **Caffè Trieste** (No. 2500), Berkeley's homey branch of North Beach's bohemian coffee bar. Arousing browsing can be had at sex-positive, woman-friendly **Good Vibrations** (No. 2504). Find wonderful gifts at **Juniper Tree Supplies** (No. 2520), with everything for the soap and candle maker, and **Kiss My Ring** (No. 2522), which stocks jewelry designed by the owner. ✉ *San Pablo Ave., between University Ave. and Parker St.*

Telegraph Avenue. Berkeley's student-oriented thoroughfare, Telegraph Avenue is the best place to get a dose of the city's famed counterculture. On any given day, you might encounter a troop of chanting Hare Krishnas or a drumming band of Rastafarians. First and foremost, however, Telegraph is a place for socializing and shopping, the only uniquely Berkeley shopping experience in town and a definite don't-miss (though locals complain that Telegraph is heading downhill fast, with too many panhandlers, and businesses closing up shop). ■**TIP➔ Take care at night, when things get edgier. The nearby People's Park, mostly harmless by day, is best avoided after sunset.** Cafés, bookstores, poster shops, and street vendors line the avenue. T-shirt vendors and tarot-card readers come and go on a whim, but a few establishments—**Rasputin Music** (No. 2401), **Amoeba Music** (No. 2455), and **Moe's Books** (No. 2476)—are neighborhood landmarks. Allen Ginsberg wrote his acclaimed poem "Howl" at **Caffe Mediterraneum** (No. 2475), a relic of 1960s-era café culture that also lays claim to inventing the café latte.

WHERE TO EAT

Dining in Berkeley is a low-key affair; even in the finest restaurants, most folks dress casually. Late diners be forewarned: Berkeley is an "early to bed" kind of town.

$
SOUTHERN

✕**Angeline's Louisiana Kitchen.** There's always a line winding out the door for the delicious food at Angeline's. The brick walls, maps of Louisiana, ceiling fans, and New Orleans music create a festive atmosphere that is both welcoming and exciting. Specialties include Voo Doo shrimp with blue lake beans, crawfish étouffée, and buttermilk fried chicken. The Creole pecan pie is so good you'll be coming back for more. $ *Average main: $14* ✉ *2261 Shattuck Ave., near Kittredge St.* ☎ *510/548–6900* ⊕ *www.angelineskitchen.com* ☾ *No lunch Mon.*

$
AMERICAN

✕**Bette's Oceanview Diner.** Buttermilk pancakes are just one of the specialties at this 1930s-inspired diner complete with checkered floors and burgundy booths. Huevos rancheros and lox and eggs are other breakfast options; kosher franks, generous slices of pizza, and a slew of sandwiches are available for lunch. The wait for a seat can be quite long; thankfully, 4th Street was made for strolling. ■**TIP➔ If you're starving, head to Bette's to Go, next door, for takeout.** $ *Average main: $10* ✉ *1807 4th St., near Delaware St., 4th Street* ☎ *510/644–3230* ⊕ *www.bettesdiner.com* 🍴 *Reservations not accepted* ☾ *No dinner.*

$
SPANISH

✕**César.** In true Spanish style, dinners are served late at César, whose kitchen closes at 11:30 pm on Friday and Saturday and at 11 pm the rest of the week. Couples spill out from its street-level windows on warm nights, or rub shoulders at the polished bar or center communal table. Founded by a trio of former Chez Panisse chefs, César is like a first cousin to that stalwart eatery right next door, each restaurant recommending the other if there's a long wait ahead. For tapas and perfectly grilled *bocadillos* (small sandwiches), there's no better choice. The bar also makes a mean martini and has an impressive wine list. ■**TIP➔ Come early to get seated quickly and to hear your tablemates; the room gets loud when the bar is in full swing.** $ *Average main: $15* ✉ *1515 Shattuck Ave., at Vine St., North Berkeley* ☎ *510/883–0222* ⊕ *cesarberkeley.com* 🍴 *Reservations not accepted.*

5

$$$$　✕**Chez Panisse Café & Restaurant.** At Chez Panisse even humble pizza is
AMERICAN　reincarnated, with innovative toppings of the freshest local ingredients.
Fodor's Choice　The downstairs portion of Alice Waters's legendary eatery is noted
★　for its formality and personal service. The daily-changing multicourse
dinners are prix-fixe ($$$$), with the cost slightly lower on weekdays.
Upstairs, in the informal café, the crowd is livelier, the prices are lower
($$–$$$), and the ever-changing menu is à la carte. The food is sim-
pler, too: penne with new potatoes, arugula, and sheep's-milk cheese;
fresh figs with Parmigiano-Reggiano cheese and arugula; and grilled
tuna with savoy cabbage, for example. Legions of loyal fans insist that
Chez Panisse lives up to its reputation and delivers a dining experience
well worth the price. ■**TIP➔** It's wise to make your reservation a few
weeks ahead of your visit. ⑤ *Average main: $95* ✉ *1517 Shattuck Ave.,
at Vine St., North Berkeley* ☎ *510/548–5525 restaurant, 510/548–5049
café* ⊕ *www.chezpanisse.com* ⌑ *Reservations essential* ☉ *Closed Sun.
No lunch in the restaurant.*

$$　✕**Corso Trattoria.** On the edge of Berkeley's Gourmet Ghetto, this lively
TUSCAN　spot serves up excellent Florentine cuisine in a spare but snazzy space.
The open kitchen at the back dominates the room (which can get smoky
at times), and the closely spaced tables add to the festivity of dining
here. The seasonal menu might include pan-roasted sturgeon with brus-
sels sprouts or butter-roasted chicken breast. Side dishes are ordered
separately; the baked polenta with mascarpone and Parmesan is a
definite crowd pleaser. An extensive Italian wine list complements the
menu; save room for the memorable panna cotta. ⑤ *Average main: $18*
✉ *1788 Shattuck Ave., at Delaware St., North Berkeley* ☎ *510/704–
8004* ⊕ *www.trattoriacorso.com* ☉ *No lunch.*

$$　✕**Gather.** Here organic, sustainable, and all things Berkeley reside har-
AMERICAN　moniously beneath one tasty roof. This vibrant, well-lit eatery boasts
funky lighting fixtures, a variety of shiny wood furnishings, and banquettes made of recycled leather belts. Everything feels contemporary
and local, especially the food. The vegan "charcuterie," made of root
vegetables, put the restaurant on the national map; the stinging nettles
pizza is refreshing, and the grilled chicken is oh so juicy. This is a
haven for vegetarian, vegan, and gluten-free eaters, but there's plenty
for meat eaters to choose from, too. Desserts don't get much better
than the chocolate semifreddo with Zinfandel-braised Mission figs and
pine nuts. ⑤ *Average main: $20* ✉ *2200 Oxford St., at Allston Way*
☎ *510/809–0400* ⊕ *www.gatherrestaurant.com.*

$$　✕**Ippuku.** More Tokyo street chic than standard sushi house, this
JAPANESE　*izakaya*—the Japanese equivalent of a bar with appetizers—with
bamboo-screen booths serves up surprising fare, from chicken tartare
to wonderful *yakitori*, skewers such as bacon-wrapped enoki, bacon-
wrapped mushrooms, and pork belly. (Anything skewered here is sure
to please.) Dinner beats lunch at Ippuku, and savvy diners make reserva-
tions and arrive early for the best selection. The bar, which opens onto
the street, pours an impressive array of sakes and *shōchū* (liquor dis-
tilled from sweet potatoes, rice, or barley). ⑤ *Average main: $19* ✉ *2130
Center St., Downtown* ☎ *510/665–1969* ⊕ *www.ippukuberkeley.com*
☉ *No lunch Sun.–Thurs.*

The pioneering restaurant Chez Panisse focuses on seasonal local ingredients.

$$$ ✕ **Lalime's.** Inside a charming, flower-covered house, this restaurant
MEDITERRANEAN serves dishes that reflect the entire Mediterranean region. The menu,
Fodor's Choice constantly changing and unfailingly great, depends on the availability
★ of fresh seasonal ingredients. Choices might include grilled ahi tuna or
creamy Italian risotto. Light colors used in the dining room, which has
two levels, help to create a cheerful mood. Excellent and long-lived but
not flashy, the restaurant has a legion of dedicated fans, many middle-
aged and up. ■ TIP➔ Lalime's is a good second choice if Chez Panisse
is booked up. ⑤ *Average main: $27* ✉ *1329 Gilman St., at Tevlin St.,
North Berkeley* ☎ *510/527–9838* ⊕ *www.lalimes.com* ✍ *Reservations
essential* ⊗ *Closed Mon. and Tues. No lunch.*

$ ✕ **Picante.** A barnlike space full of cheerful Mexican tiles and folk-art
MEXICAN masks, Picante is a find for anyone seeking good, Cal-Mex food for a
FAMILY song. The masa is freshly ground for the tortillas and tamales (it's fun to
watch the tamale maker in action), the salsas are complex, and the flavor
combinations are inventive. Try tamales filled with butternut squash and
chilis or a simple taco of roasted poblanos and sautéed onions; we chal-
lenge you to finish a plate of supernachos. Picante is beloved of Berkeley
families with raucous children, as they fit right in to the festival-like
atmosphere and are happily distracted by the fountain on the back patio.
⑤ *Average main: $12* ✉ *1328 6th St., near Camelia St.* ☎ *510/525–3121*
⊕ *www.picanteberkeley.com* ✍ *Reservations not accepted.*

$ ✕ **Saul's.** Well known for its homemade sodas and enormous sand-
AMERICAN wiches, the Saul's of today uses sustainably sourced seafood, grass-fed
FAMILY beef, and organic eggs. The restaurant is a Berkeley institution, and its
loyal clientele swears by the pastrami sandwiches, stuffed-cabbage rolls,
and tuna melts. For breakfast, the challah French toast is so thick it's

almost too big to bite, and the deli omelets are served pancake style. The high ceilings and red-leather booths add to the friendly, retro atmosphere. ■**TIP**➔ **Don't overlook the glass deli case, where you can order food to go.** ⑤ *Average main: $14* ✉ *1475 Shattuck Ave., near Vine St., North Berkeley* ☎ *510/848–3354* ⊕ *www.saulsdeli.com* ⌕ *Reservations not accepted* ⊘ *Closed Thanksgiving and Yom Kippur.*

WHERE TO STAY

For inexpensive lodging, investigate University Avenue, west of campus. The area can be noisy, congested, and somewhat dilapidated, but it does include a few decent motels and chain properties. All Berkeley lodgings, except for the swanky Claremont, are strictly mid-range.

$
HOTEL
⛼ The Bancroft Hotel. Lovingly remodeled in 2012, this green boutique hotel—across from the U.C. campus—is fresh, stylish, and completely eco-friendly. **Pros:** heating under the floorboards; great rooftop deck; closest hotel in Berkeley to campus. **Cons:** some rooms are small; bathrooms could be freshened up; no elevator. ⑤ *Rooms from: $149* ✉ *2680 Bancroft Way* ☎ *510/549–1000* ⊕ *bancrofthotel.com* ☞ *22* ⦿*Breakfast.*

$$$$
HOTEL
Fodor'sChoice
★
⛼ Claremont Resort and Spa. Straddling the Oakland–Berkeley border, this amenities-rich resort—which celebrates its centennial in 2015—beckons like a gleaming white castle in the hills. **Pros:** amazing spa; supervised child care; solid business amenities; great bay views from some rooms. **Cons:** parking is pricey; resort charge for use of spa, tennis courts, pool, gym, etc.; additional fee for breakfast. ⑤ *Rooms from: $260* ✉ *41 Tunnel Rd., at Ashby and Domingo Aves., Claremont* ☎ *510/843–3000, 800/551–7266* ⊕ *www.claremontresort.com* ☞ *249 rooms, 30 suites* ⦿*No meals.*

$$
HOTEL
⛼ Holiday Inn Express. Convenient to the freeway and 4th Street shopping, this peach-and-beige hotel provides good bang for the buck. **Pros:** good breakfast; short walk to restaurant options on San Pablo and University; free Internet in rooms. **Cons:** area can be noisy and congested with traffic during commute hours; neighborhood can feel sketchy after dark. ⑤ *Rooms from: $189* ✉ *1175 University Ave., at Curtis St.* ☎ *510/548–1700, 866/548–1700* ⊕ *www.hiexberkeley.com* ☞ *69 rooms, 3 suites* ⦿*Breakfast.*

$$
HOTEL
⛼ Hotel Durant. A mainstay of parents visiting their children at U.C. Berkeley, this boutique hotel is also a good option for those who want to be a short walk from Telegraph Avenue. **Pros:** convenient location to Cal and public transit; blackout shades; organic bathrobes. **Cons:** downstairs bar can get noisy during Cal games; parking can be pricey. ⑤ *Rooms from: $180* ✉ *2600 Durant Ave., at Bowditch St.* ☎ *510/845–8981* ⊕ *www.hoteldurant.com* ☞ *143 rooms* ⦿*No meals.*

$$
HOTEL
Fodor'sChoice
★
⛼ Hotel Shattuck Plaza. This historic boutique hotel sits amid Berkeley's downtown arts district, just steps from the U.C. campus and a short walk from the Gourmet Ghetto. **Pros:** central location; near public transit; modern facilities; good views; great restaurant. **Cons:** pricey parking; limited fitness center. ⑤ *Rooms from: $195* ✉ *2086 Allston Way, at Shattuck Ave., Downtown* ☎ *510/845–7300* ⊕ *www. hotelshattuckplaza.com* ☞ *199 rooms, 17 suites* ⦿*No meals.*

NIGHTLIFE AND THE ARTS

NIGHTLIFE

Fodor's Choice
★

Freight & Salvage Coffeehouse. Some of the most talented practitioners of folk, blues, Cajun, and bluegrass perform in this alcohol-free space, one of the country's finest folk houses. Most tickets cost less than $25. ✉ *2020 Addison St., between Shattuck Ave. and Milvia St.* ☎ *510/644–2020* ⊕ *www.thefreight.org.*

THE ARTS

Berkeley Repertory Theatre. One of the region's highly respected resident professional companies, Berkeley Rep performs classic and contemporary plays. Well-known pieces such as *Crime and Punishment* and *The Arabian Nights* mix with edgier fare like Green Day's *American Idiot* and Lemony Snicket's *The Composer Is Dead.* The theater's complex is in the heart of downtown Berkeley's arts district, near BART's Downtown Berkeley station. ✉ *2025 Addison St., near Shattuck Ave.* ☎ *510/647–2949* ⊕ *www.berkeleyrep.org.*

Berkeley Symphony Orchestra. The works of 20th-century composers are a focus of this prominent orchestra, but traditional pieces are also performed. BSO plays a handful of concerts each year, in Zellerbach Hall and other locations. ✉ *1942 University Ave., Ste. 207* ☎ *510/841–2800* ⊕ *www.berkeleysymphony.org.*

Cal Performances. The series, running from September through May at Zellerbach Hall and various other U.C. Berkeley venues, offers the Bay Area's most varied bill of internationally acclaimed artists in all disciplines, from classical soloists to the latest jazz, world-music, theater, and dance ensembles. Look for frequent campus colloquiums or preshow talks featuring Berkeley's professors. ✉ *Zellerbach Hall, Telegraph Ave. and Bancroft Way* ☎ *510/642–9988* ⊕ *calperformances.org.*

SHOPPING

Fodor's Choice
★

Amoeba Music. Heaven for audiophiles, this legendary Berkeley favorite is *the* place to head for new and used CDs, records, cassettes, and DVDs. The dazzling stock includes thousands of titles for all music tastes. The store even has its own record label. There are branches in San Francisco and Hollywood, but this is the original. ✉ *2455 Telegraph Ave., at Haste St.* ☎ *510/549–1125* ⊕ *www.amoeba.com.*

Body Time. Founded in Berkeley in 1970, this local chain uses premium-quality ingredients to create its natural perfumes and skin-care and aromatherapy products. Sustainably harvested essential oils that you can combine and dilute to create your own personal fragrances are the specialty. The Citrus, Lavender-Mint, and China Rain scents are all popular. ✉ *1950 Shattuck Ave., at Berkeley Way* ☎ *510/841–5818* ⊕ *www.bodytime.com.*

Kermit Lynch Wine Merchant. Lynch's newsletters describing his finds are legendary, as is his friendship with Alice Waters of Chez Panisse. Credited with taking American appreciation of French wine to another level, this shop is a great place to peruse as you educate your palate. The friendly salespeople can direct you to the latest French bargains. ✉ *1605 San Pablo Ave., at Dwight Way* ☎ *510/524–1524* ⊕ *kermitlynch.com.*

Moe's Books. The spirit of Moe—the cantankerous, cigar-smoking late proprietor—lives on in this four-story house of books. Students and professors come here to browse the large selection of used books, including literary and cultural criticism, art titles, and literature in foreign languages. ⊠ *2476 Telegraph Ave., near Haste St.* ☎ *510/849–2087* ⊕ *moesbooks.com.*

Rasputin Music. A huge selection of new music for every taste draws crowds. In any other town, Rasputin's stock of used CDs and vinyl would likely be unsurpassed. ⊠ *2403 Telegraph Ave., at Channing Way* ☎ *510/848–9004* ⊕ *www.rasputinmusic.com.*

OAKLAND

Directly east of Bay Bridge.

Often overshadowed by San Francisco's beauty and Berkeley's storied counterculture, Oakland's allure lies in its amazing diversity. Here you can find a Nigerian clothing store, a beautifully renovated Victorian home, a Buddhist meditation center, and a lively salsa club, all within the same block.

Oakland's multifaceted nature reflects its colorful and often tumultuous history. Once a cluster of Mediterranean-style homes and gardens that served as a bedroom community for San Francisco, the city became a hub of shipbuilding and industry almost overnight when the United States entered World War II. New jobs in the city's shipyards and factories attracted thousands of workers, including some of the first female welders, and the city's neighborhoods were imbued with a proud but gritty spirit. In the 1960s and '70s this intense community pride gave rise to such militant groups as the Black Panther Party and the Symbionese Liberation Army, but they were little match for the economic hardships and racial tensions that plagued Oakland. In many neighborhoods the reality was widespread poverty and gang violence—subjects that dominated the songs of such Oakland-bred rappers as the late Tupac Shakur. The highly publicized protests of the Occupy Oakland movement in 2011 and 2012 illustrated just how much Oakland remains a mosaic of its past.

The affluent reside in the city's hillside homes, wooded enclaves like Claremont and Montclair, which provide a warmer, more spacious, and more affordable alternative to San Francisco, while a constant flow of newcomers—many from Central America and Asia—ensures continued diversity, vitality, and growing pains. Many neighborhoods to the west and south of the city center remain run-down and unsafe, but a renovated downtown area—sparking a vibrant arts scene—and the waterfront around Jack London Square on the edge of finding its footing have injected new energy into the city. Even San Franciscans, often loathe to cross the Bay Bridge—why should they?—come to Uptown and Temescal for the crackling arts and restaurant scenes there.

Everyday life here revolves around the neighborhood, with a main business strip attracting both shoppers and strollers. In some areas, such as high-end Piedmont and Rockridge, you'd swear you were in Berkeley

5

or San Francisco's Noe Valley or Cow Hollow. Along Telegraph Avenue just south of 51st Street, Temescal is pulsing with creative culinary and design energy. These are perfect places for browsing, eating, or just relaxing between sightseeing trips to Oakland's architectural gems, rejuvenated waterfront, and numerous green spaces.

GETTING HERE AND AROUND

Driving from San Francisco, take Interstate 80 East across the Bay Bridge, then take Interstate 580 to the Grand Avenue exit for Lake Merritt. To reach downtown and the waterfront, take Interstate 980 from Interstate 580 and exit at 12th Street; exit at 18th Street for Uptown. For Temescal, take Interstate 580 to Highway 24 and exit at 51st Street.

By BART, use the Lake Merritt Station for the Oakland Museum and southern Lake Merritt; the Oakland City Center–12th Street Station for downtown, Chinatown, and Old Oakland; and the 19th Street Station for Uptown, the Paramount Theatre, and the north side of Lake Merritt.

By bus, take the AC Transit's C and P lines to get to Piedmont in Oakland. The O bus stops at the edge of Chinatown near downtown Oakland.

Oakland's Jack London Square is an easy hop on the ferry from San Francisco. Those without cars can take advantage of the free Broadway Shuttle, which runs from the square down Broadway through Chinatown/Old Oakland, downtown, Uptown, and Lake Merritt, all the way to 27th Street. The shuttle runs late on Friday and Saturday nights; its website has full schedule information.

Once you arrive, be aware of how quickly neighborhoods can change. Walking is safe downtown and in the Piedmont and Rockridge areas, but avoid walking west and south of downtown.

ESSENTIALS

Shuttle Contact Broadway Shuttle ⊕ *www.meetdowntownoak.com.*

Visitor Information Visit Oakland ⊠ *481 Water St.* ☎ *510/839–9000* ⊕ *www.visitoakland.org.*

EXPLORING
TOP ATTRACTIONS

FAMILY

Fodor'sChoice

★

Oakland Museum of California. One of Oakland's top attractions, the museum surveys the state's art, history, and natural wonders in three galleries of absorbing, detailed exhibits. You can travel through myriad ecosystems in the Gallery of California Natural Sciences, from the sand dunes of the Pacific to the coyotes and brush of the Nevada border. Kids love the lifelike wild-animal exhibits, especially the snarling wolverine, big-eyed harbor seal, and trove of hidden creatures. The rambling Gallery of California History includes everything from Spanish-era armor to a small but impressive collection of vintage vehicles, including a candy-apple-red "Mystery" car from the 1960s and a gleaming red, gold, and silver fire engine that battled the flames in San Francisco following the 1906 earthquake. The Gallery of California Art holds an eclectic collection of modern works and early landscapes. Of particular interest are paintings by Richard Diebenkorn, Joan Brown, Elmer Bischoff, and David Park, all members of the Bay Area figurative school, which flourished here after World War II. Fans of Dorothea Lange won't want to miss the gallery's comprehensive collection of her work. The museum also has a sculpture garden with a view of the Oakland and Berkeley hills in the distance. ⊠ *1000 Oak St., at 10th St., Downtown* ☎ *510/238–2200* ⊕ *www.museumca.org* ⊠ *$15, free 1st Sun. of month* ☉ *Wed.–Sun. 11–5, Fri. until 9.*

Fodor'sChoice

★

Paramount Theatre. Perhaps the most glorious art deco specimen in the city, if not the entire Bay Area, the Paramount operates as a venue for concerts and performances of all kinds, from the Oakland East Bay Symphony to Tom Waits and Elvis Costello. The popular monthly movie nights start off with a 30-minute Wurlitzer concert preceding classic films such as *Casablanca.* ■ **TIP➜ At 10 am on the first and third Saturday of each month, you can take a marvelous two-hour tour of the building.** ⊠ *2025 Broadway, at 20th St., Uptown* ☎ *510/465–6400* ⊕ *www.paramounttheatre.com* ⊠ *Tour $5.*

Rockridge. This upscale neighborhood is one of Oakland's most desirable places to live. Explore the tree-lined streets that radiate out from **College Avenue** just north and south of the Rockridge BART station for a look at California bungalow architecture at its finest. By day

College Avenue between Broadway and Alcatraz Avenue is crowded with shoppers buying fresh flowers, used books, and clothing; by night the same folks are back for dinner and locally brewed ales in the numerous restaurants and pubs. With its pricey specialty-food shops, **Market Hall,** an airy European-style marketplace at Shafter Avenue, is a hub of culinary activity. ⊕ *www.rockridgedistrict.com.*

Fodor's Choice
★
Temescal. Centering on Telegraph Avenue between Piedmont and South Berkeley, up-and-coming Temescal ("sweat house" in the language of the Aztec) is a low-pretension, moneyed-hipster hood with a lot of young families and—gasp—middle-aged folks thrown into the mix. A critical mass of excellent eateries, from veteran Doña Tomás and favorites Pizzaiola and Aunt Mary's to **Bakesale Betty** (⊠ *5098 Telegraph Ave.*), where folks line up for the fried-chicken sandwich on the one-item menu, and **Doughnut Dolly** (⊠ *482B 49th St.*), who fills her fried treats to order, draws folks from around the Bay Area. Old-time dive bars and check-cashing places share space with newer arrivals like crafty, local children's clothing shop **Ruby's Garden** (⊠ *5026 Telegraph Ave.*); **Article Pract** (⊠ *5010 Telegraph Ave.*), purveyor of gorgeous yarn; and the **East Bay Depot for Creative Reuse** (⊠ *4695 Telegraph Ave.*), where you might find a bucket of buttons or 1,000 muffin wrappers for $1 among bird cages, furniture, lunch boxes, and ribbon.

Around the corner, **Temescal Alley** (⊠ *49th St.*), a tucked-away lane of tiny storefronts, crackles with the creative energy of the craftspeople who have set up shop there, among them fashion designer Ali Golden and jewelry designer Marisa Haskell. You can make some surprising finds at Crimson Horticultural Rarities and the fresh home-decor shop Bounty and Feast.

This neighborhood is *the* place to go to put your finger on the pulse of Oakland right now. ⊠ *Telegraph Ave., between 45th and 51st Sts.* ⊕ *www.temescaldistrict.org.*

Uptown. This is where nightlife and cutting-edge art happens in Oakland, along the formerly gritty, currently crazy-cool Telegraph Avenue/Broadway corridor north of downtown. Dozens of galleries cluster around Telegraph, showing everything from photography and video installations to glasswork and textile arts. On the first Friday of the month, thousands descend for the neighborhood's biggest happening, the gallery walk **Art Murmur** (⊕ *oaklandartmurmur.org*). In addition to galleries open late, Art Murmur has expanded into **First Friday,** a veritable festival featuring food trucks, street vendors, and live music along Telegraph Avenue. Less raucous and more intimate is the **Saturday Stroll,** with 17 galleries and eight mixed-use venues open on Saturday from 1 to 5, often with special events.

Lively restaurants with a distinctly urban vibe make the neighborhood a dining destination; favorites include friendly **Luka's Taproom and Lounge** (⊠ *2221 Broadway*); beautiful art deco **Flora** (⊠ *1900 Telegraph Ave.*), one of the best brunch places in town; trendy, graffiti-walled **Hawker Fare** (⊠ *2300 Webster St.*), serving Asian street food; elegant **Picán** (⊠ *2295 Broadway*), for upscale Southern comfort food; and the sophisticated **Plum** (⊠ *2214 Broadway*) and its attached bar, just to name a few.

5

Toss in the bevy of bars, and there's plenty within walking distance to keep you busy for an entire evening: **Cafe Van Kleef** (✉ *1621 Telegraph Ave.*), the friendly jumble that started it all Uptown; **Bar Three Fifty-Five** (✉ *355 19th St.*), a house of great cocktails; strikingly beautiful but low-key **Dogwood** (✉ *1644 Telegraph Ave.*), which has tasty nibbles; and **Somar** (✉ *1727 Telegraph Ave.*), a bar, music lounge, and gallery in one. Uptown's shopping element hasn't yet gelled, making this more of an evening destination. The Paramount Theatre, the Fox Theater, and other late-art deco architectural gems distinguish this neighborhood. ✉ *Telegraph Ave. and Broadway from 16th to 26th Sts.*

WORTH NOTING

Chinatown. Across Broadway from Old Oakland but worlds apart, Chinatown is a densely packed, bustling neighborhood. Unlike its San Francisco counterpart, Oakland's Chinatown makes no concessions to tourists; you won't find baskets of trinkets lining the sidewalk and souvenir displays in the shop windows. But supermarkets such as **Yuen Hop Noodle Company** and **Asian Food Products** (✉ *824 Webster St.*), open since 1931, overflow with goodies. And the line for sweets, breads, and towering cakes snakes out the door of **Napoleon Super Bakery** (✉ *810 Franklin St.*). ✉ *Between Broadway and Lakeside Dr. and between 6th and 12th Sts.*

Fox Theater. An art deco movie palace built in 1928, the Fox sat decaying and mostly unused for decades until the last of several redevelopment schemes culminated in a stunning renovation. The Mediterranean Moorish–style theater and its attached buildings contain the main theater, these days used for music concerts; the Oakland School for the Arts; and the Den, a gorgeous lounge. The theater's restoration helped revive what's now known as the Uptown neighborhood. ✉ *1807 Telegraph Ave., at 18th St., Uptown* ☎ *510/302–2250* ⊕ *www.thefoxoakland.com.*

Jack London Square. A few shops, some minor historic sites, and a growing number of noteworthy restaurants (along with the well-established Yoshi's Jazz Club) line Jack London Square, which is named after the author of *The Call of the Wild, The Sea Wolf,* and other books. London, who was born in San Francisco, also lived in Oakland, where he spent many a day boozing and brawling in the waterfront area, most notably at the tiny, wonderful **Heinold's First and Last Chance Saloon** (✉ *48 Webster St., at Embarcadero W.*). The saloon has been serving since 1883, although it's a little worse for the wear since the 1906 earthquake. Next door is the Klondike cabin in which London spent a summer in the late 1890s. The cabin was moved from Alaska and reassembled here in 1970.

During the week, the square can feel desolate, albeit with great views. Weekends are much livelier, with diners filling the many outdoor patios, and shoppers perusing Sunday's farmers' market, which takes place from 9 am to 2 pm. ■**TIP➔** The square is an obvious spot for tourists to visit, and it's worth a peek if you've arrived on the ferry that docks here; but to get a real feel for Oakland, you'll do better to check out downtown, Temescal, or at least Rockridge. ✉ *Embarcadero W. at Broadway* ☎ *510/645–9292* ⊕ *www.jacklondonsquare.com.*

A fun place to wet your whistle, Heinold's First and Last Chance Saloon

Lake Merritt. Joggers and power walkers charge along the 3-mile path that encircles this 155-acre natural saltwater lake in downtown Oakland. Crew teams often glide across the water, and boatmen guide snuggling couples in authentic Venetian gondolas (✉ *Fares start at $40 per couple for 30 minutes* ☎ *510/663–6603* ⊕ *gondolaservizio.com*). **Lakeside Park,** which surrounds the north side of Lake Merritt, has several outdoor attractions, including a small children's park and a waterfowl refuge. The lake is less an attraction than a pleasant backdrop to Oaklanders' everyday life. ✉ *Lakeside Park, Bellevue and Grand Aves.* ⊕ *www.lakemerritt.org.*

Old Oakland. In the shadow of the convention center and towering downtown hotels, Old Oakland was once a booming business district. Today the restored Victorian storefronts lining four historic blocks house restaurants, cafés, shops, galleries, and a lively three-block farmers' market, which takes place on Friday morning. Architectural consistency distinguishes the area from surrounding streets and lends it a distinct neighborhood feel. The Italian grocery **Ratto's International Market** (✉ *827 Washington St.*) has been in business for more than a century. Stop in for a deli sandwich, or head over to the genial **Pacific Coast Brewing Company** (✉ *902 Washington St.*) for a microbrew on the patio. One of the best beer bars in California, the **Trappist** (✉ *460 8th St.*) wins loyalty for its exhaustive selection of Belgian ales. Various pop-up boutiques throughout the neighborhood are reinvigorating the storefront scene. ✉ *Bordered by 7th, 10th, Clay, and Washington Sts.* ⊕ *old-oakland.com.*

WHERE TO EAT

$$
MEDITERRANEAN

✗**À Côté.** This place for Mediterranean food is all about small plates, cozy tables, family-style eating—and truly excellent food. The butternut-squash ravioli, wild-boar chestnut sausage, and duck confit flatbread with apples and cantelet cheese are all fine choices, and you won't find a better plate of *pommes frites* (french fries) anywhere. The restaurant pours more than 40 wines by the glass. Among the tempting desserts here are the lemon pudding cake with lemon cream, huckleberries, and candied pistachios, and the tangy pomegranate sorbet. Heavy wooden tables, cool tiles, and natural light make this a destination for students, families, couples, and the after-work crowd; the heated back patio is warm and welcoming in any weather. $ *Average main: $20* ✉ *5478 College Ave., at Taft Ave., Rockridge* ☎ *510/655–6469* ⊕ *www. acoterestaurant.com* ⊗ *No lunch.*

$
AMERICAN
Fodor'sChoice
★

✗**Brown Sugar Kitchen.** Chef and owner Tanya Holland, named chef of 2012 by the California Travel Association, has turned an isolated corner in West Oakland into a breakfast and lunch destination. Influenced by her African American heritage and her culinary education in France—and using local, organic, and seasonal products—she blends sweet and savory flavors like no one else and pairs her dishes with well-chosen wines. The dining room is fresh and bright, with a long, sleek counter, red-leather stools, and spacious booths and tables. ■**TIP➔ This is the place to come for chicken and waffles.** $ *Average main: $13* ✉ *2534 Mandela Pkwy., at 26th St., West Oakland* ☎ *510/839–7685* ⊕ *www. brownsugarkitchen.com* ⊗ *Closed Mon. No dinner.*

$$$
AMERICAN

✗**Camino.** Chef-owner Russell Moore cooked at Chez Panisse for two decades before opening this restaurant with co-owner Allison Hopelain that focuses on simple, seasonal, straightforward dishes cooked in an enormous, crackling *camino* (Italian for "fireplace"). Everything is made with top-notch ingredients, including local sardines and smelts, grilled lamb and sausage, and Dungeness crab (cooked in the fireplace with rutabagas). The menu changes nightly and includes vegetarian options such as eggplant gratin. Camino is decorated in a Craftsman-meets-refectory style, with brick walls and two long redwood communal tables. ■**TIP➔ The small bar here turns out delicious, seasonally inspired cocktails, among them a gin-based one with house-made cherry and hibiscus bitters.** $ *Average main: $26* ✉ *3917 Grand Ave., at Boulevard Way, Grand Lake* ☎ *510/547–5035* ⊕ *www.caminorestaurant. com* ⊗ *Closed Tues. No lunch (weekend brunch 10–2).*

$$
MODERN
AMERICAN

✗**Chop Bar.** The walls and tables are made of reclaimed wood at this small, stylish space whose knowing, tattooed bartenders serve potent cocktails to a crowd of hipsters and area residents and workers. A great neighborhood joint for every meal of the day (and brunch on weekends), Chop Bar serves upmarket gastro-pub grub, including favorites such as oxtail poutine, pork confit with polenta and kale, and burgers that rank among the Bay Area's best. On sunny days when the glass garage door is raised, extending the outdoor seating area out front, you'll feel like an insider who's stumbled upon an industrial neighborhood's cool secret. $ *Average main: $18* ✉ *247 4th St., at Alice St., Jack London Square* ☎ *510/834–2467* ⊕ *www.oaklandchopbar.com.*

$$$$ ✕**Commis.** Blink and you'll miss the only East Bay restaurant with a
MODERN   Michelin star. No sign announces Commis, a slender, unassuming store-
AMERICAN front in Oakland's Piedmont neighborhood, and the room is simple and
polished: nothing distracts from the artistry of the food served here.
Chef James Syhabout creates a fixed, multicourse menu ($95, wine
pairing $55 additional) based on the season and his distinctive vision.
Dishes might include poached egg yolk with smoked dates and alliums
(members of the onion/garlic family) in malt vinegar, or duck roasted on
the bone over charcoal with renderings, walnut, and persimmon. Diners
don't see the menu until after the meal, the chef's way of ensuring that
everyone comes to the table with an open mind. This isn't a place to
grab a quick bite: meals last about three hours. The service is excellent.
⑤ *Average main: $95* ✉ *3859 Piedmont Ave., at Rio Vista Ave., Pied-
mont* ☎ *510/653–3902* ⊕ *www.commisrestaurant.com* ⌂ *Reservations
essential* ◷ *Closed Mon.–Tues. No lunch.*

$$ ✕**Doña Tomás.** A neighborhood favorite, this spot in Oakland's hot
MEXICAN Temescal District serves seasonal Mexican fare to a hip but low-key
crowd. Mexican textiles and art adorn walls in two long rooms; there's
also a vine-covered patio. Banish all images of taqueria grub and tuck
into starters such as quesadillas filled with butternut squash and goat
cheese and entrées such as *albondigas en sopa zanahoria* (pork-and-
beef meatballs in carrot purée). Some mighty fine tequilas comple-
ment the offerings. Brunch is served on weekends. ⑤ *Average main:
$19* ✉ *5004 Telegraph Ave., near 51st St., Temescal* ☎ *510/450–0522*
⊕ *www.donatomas.com* ◷ *Closed Mon. No lunch weekdays. No din-
ner Sun.*

$$$ ✕**Haven.** Daniel Patterson of San Francisco's revered Coi opened this
MODERN   waterfront space in 2011, focusing on vegetables, whole-animal prepa-
AMERICAN rations, dishes to share, and great cocktails. Floor-to-ceiling windows
overlook the yachts of Jack London Square, and warm lighting casts a
glow over the wood-and-brick dining room. Look for anything smoked
or with marrow on executive chef Kim Alter's menu and you can't miss;
smoked black rice with citrus and uni is striking and flavorful, and
the shepherd's pie—pig belly, rutabaga, and potato purée—is earthy
and delicious. The family menu ($35 per person), three courses served
family-style and based on what's fresh at the market, is a fun way to
experience this restaurant's inventive approach. Sunday brunch is served
from 10:30 am to 1:30 pm. ⑤ *Average main: $26* ✉ *44 Webster St.,
at 1st St. and Embarcadero W, Jack London Square* ☎ *510/663–4440*
⊕ *www.havenoakland.com* ◷ *No lunch Mon.–Sat.*

$ ✕**Le Cheval Restaurant.** This cavernous restaurant, a lunchtime favorite,
VIETNAMESE is a good place to sample *pho*, Hanoi-style beef noodle soup fragrant
with star anise. Other entrées include lemon chicken, cubed beefsteak,
and clay-pot snapper. It's hard to spend more than $20 for an entire
meal unless you order the seven courses of beef ($28). The complimen-
tary minibowls of soup that are placed on the table as soon as you sit
down are a great balm to hungry diners, though the service is lightning-
quick anyway. ⑤ *Average main: $12* ✉ *1019 Clay St., at 11th St., Old
Oakland* ☎ *510/763–8495* ⊕ *www.lecheval.com* ◷ *No lunch Sun.*

5

$$ ✕ **Luka's Taproom & Lounge.** Hip and urban, with an unpretentious vibe,
BELGIAN Luka's is a real taste of Uptown. Diners nibble on *frites* (fries) any Belgian
would embrace and entrées such as crispy-skin salmon or gratinéed mac
and cheese. The brews draw them in, too—a nice selection of Trappist
ales complements plentiful beers on tap and international bottles—and
the DJs in the adjacent lounge keep the scene going late. ■TIP→ Hungry
night owls appreciate the late-night menu, served daily until midnight.
ⓢ *Average main: $17* ✉ *2221 Broadway, at West Grand Ave., Uptown*
☎ *510/451–4677* ⊕ *www.lukasoakland.com* ⊘ *No lunch Sat.*

$$ ✕ **Pizzaiolo.** Apparently no length of a wait can discourage locals who
PIZZA persevere to enjoy the legendary thin-crust, wood-fired pizza served up
by Chez Panisse alum Charlie Hallowell in this rustic-chic dining room.
Diners—mostly neighborhood hipsters but also young families and foodies of all ages—perch in wooden chairs with red-leather backs; weathered
wood floors and brick walls peeking through the plaster create an always-
been-here feel. Seasonal pizza options might include wild nettles and
pecorino, or rapini and house-made sausage; don't overlook non-pizza
dishes such as wild steelhead salmon with fava greens, English peas, and
Meyer-lemon butter. Except on Sunday, early risers get to skip the crowds
and enjoy Blue Bottle Coffee and pastries from 8 until noon. ⓢ *Average
main: $17* ✉ *5008 Telegraph Ave., at 51st St., Temescal* ☎ *510/652–4888*
⊕ *www.pizzaiolooakland.com* ⊘ *Closed Sun. No lunch.*

WHERE TO STAY

$$ ⊞ **Best Western Plus Bayside Hotel.** Sandwiched between the serene and
HOTEL scenic Oakland Estuary on one side and train tracks and an eight-lane
freeway on the other, this all-suites property has handsome accommo-
dations with balconies or patios, many overlooking the water. **Pros:**
attractive, budget-conscious choice; free parking; recently renovated;
water views make city bustle seem far away. **Cons:** not near anything
of interest; city-side rooms can be loud. ⓢ *Rooms from: $179* ✉ *1717
Embarcadero, off I–880, at 16th St. exit* ☎ *510/356–2450* ⊕ *www.
baysidehoteloakland.com* ⤳ *81 suites* ⛾ *Breakfast.*

$$ ⊞ **Waterfront Hotel.** The only bayfront hotel in town, this thoroughly
HOTEL modern, pleasantly appointed Joie de Vivre property sits among the
appealing restaurants (including the hotel's own) of Jack London
Square. **Pros:** great location; lovely views; dog-friendly. **Cons:** passing
trains can be noisy; parking is pricey; hotel is beginning to show its
age. ⓢ *Rooms from: $159* ✉ *10 Washington St., Jack London Square*
☎ *510/836–3800, 800/729–3638* ⊕ *www.waterfrontplaza.com* ⤳ *143
rooms* ⛾ *No meals.*

NIGHTLIFE AND THE ARTS

Artists have found cheap rent and loft spaces in Oakland, giving rise to
an underground cultural scene—visual arts, indie music, spoken word,
film—that's definitely buzzing, especially in Uptown (which is pretty
much downtown). Trendy bars and clubs seem to pop up by the week—
everything from artisan breweries to all-out retro dives. The nightlife
scene here is less crowded and more intimate than what you'll find in
San Francisco. Music is just about everywhere, though the most popular
venues are downtown.

NIGHTLIFE

Fodor's Choice ★ **Café Van Kleef.** Dutch artist Peter Van Kleef's candle-strewn, funky café-bar crackles with creative energy. Van Kleef has a lot to do with the convivial atmosphere; the garrulous owner loves sharing tales about his quirky, floor-to-ceiling collection of mementos, including what he claims are Cassius Clay's boxing gloves and Dorothy's ruby slippers from *The Wizard of Oz*. The café also has a consistently solid calendar of live music, heavy on the jazz side. The drinks are among the stiffest in town. ⊠ *1621 Telegraph Ave., between 16th and 17th Sts., Uptown* ☎ *510/763–7711* ⊕ *www.cafevankleef.com* ☽ *No lunch Sat.–Mon.*

Fox Theater. Willie Nelson, Counting Crows, Rebelution, and B.B. King have all played at this renovated art deco stunner that has good sight lines, a state-of-the-art sound system and acoustics, and bars and other amenities. ⊠ *1807 Telegraph Ave., at 18th St., Uptown* ☎ *510/548–3010* ⊕ *www.thefoxoakland.com.*

The Layover Music Bar and Lounge. Bright, bold, and very hip, this hangout filled with recycled furniture is constantly evolving because everything is for sale, from the artwork to the pillows, rugs, and lamps. The busy bar serves up organic cocktails, and depending on the night, the entertainment might include comedy or live or DJ music. ⊠ *1517 Franklin St., near 15th St., Uptown* ☎ *510/834–1517* ⊕ *www.oaklandlayover.com.*

Mua. Cuisine, cocktails, and culture—Mua puts it all together in a bright and airy former garage. The chefs serve up beautifully crafted meals like softshell crab and duck confit; the bartenders shake up elegant cocktails; and the rich cultural offerings include poetry readings, art shows, DJ music, and more. ⊠ *2442a Webster St., between 16th and 17th Sts., Uptown* ☎ *510/238–1100* ⊕ *www.muaoakland.com.*

The Trappist. Grand pillars, brick walls, soft lighting, and the buzz of conversation set a warm and mellow tone inside this Victorian space that's been renovated to resemble a traditional Belgian pub. The setting is definitely a draw, but the real stars are the artisan beers: more than a hundred Belgian, Dutch, and North American ones. The light fare includes panini made with organic ingredients. ⊠ *460 8th St., at Broadway, Old Oakland* ☎ *510/238–8900* ⊕ *www.thetrappist.com.*

THE ARTS

Paramount Theatre. The art deco movie palace is home to the Oakland East Bay Symphony and also presents ballet, comedy (Cedric, Sinbad, Bill Cosby), well-known rock and other musical acts, and monthly classic films. ⊠ *2025 Broadway, at 20th St., Uptown* ☎ *510/465–6400* ⊕ *www.paramounttheatre.com.*

Fodor's Choice ★ **Yoshi's.** Omar Sosa and Charlie Hunter are among the musicians who play at Yoshi's, one of the area's best jazz venues. Shows start at 8 pm and 10 pm except on Sunday, when they're usually at 6 and 8. The cover runs from $16 to $50. ⊠ *510 Embarcadero St., between Washington and Clay Sts., Jack London Square* ☎ *510/238–9200* ⊕ *www.yoshis.com.*

SPORTS AND THE OUTDOORS

BASEBALL

Oakland A's. Billy Beane of *Moneyball* fame is the general manager of the American League baseball team. Same-day tickets can usually be purchased at the **O.co Coliseum** box office (Gate D). To get to the game, take a BART train to the Coliseum/Oakland Airport Station. ✉ *O.co Coliseum, 7000 Coliseum Way, off I–880, north of Hegenberger Rd.* ☎ *510/638–4900* ⊕ *oakland.athletics.mlb.com.*

BASKETBALL

Golden State Warriors. The NBA team plays basketball at **Oracle Arena** from late October into April. BART trains serve the arena; get off at the Coliseum/Oakland Airport Station. Purchase single tickets through Ticketmaster (☎ *800/653–8000* ⊕ *www.ticketmaster.com*). ✉ *Oracle Arena, 7000 Coliseum Way, off I–880, north of Hegenberger Rd.* ☎ *888/479–4667 tickets* ⊕ *www.nba.com/warriors.*

FOOTBALL

Oakland Raiders. The National Football League's brawling Oakland Raiders play at **O.co Coliseum.** Tickets are available through Ticketmaster. ✉ *O.co Coliseum, 7000 Coliseum Way, off I–880, north of Hegenberger Rd.* ☎ *510/864–5000* ⊕ *www.raiders.com*

SHOPPING

College Avenue and Piedmont Avenue are great for upscale strolling, shopping, and people-watching. Temescal—especially Temescal Alley—is another shopping hot spot, with bespoke clothing and artisan jewelry in tiny storefronts. The more casual streets around Lake Merritt and Grand Lake have smaller, less fancy boutiques.

Diesel. Wandering bibliophiles collect armfuls of the latest fiction and nonfiction here. The loftlike space, with its high ceilings and spare design, encourages contemplation, and on chilly days a fire burns in the hearth. Past participants in the excellent authors' events have included Ian Rankin, Annie Leibovitz, Kareem Abdul-Jabbar, and Michael Moore. ✉ *5433 College Ave., at Kales Ave., Rockridge* ☎ *510/653–9965* ⊕ *www.dieselbookstore.com.*

Maison d'Etre. Close to the Rockridge BART station, this store epitomizes the Rockridge neighborhood's funky-chic shopping scene. Look for impulse buys like whimsical watches, imported fruit-tea blends, and funky slippers. ✉ *5640 College Ave., at Keith Ave., Rockridge* ☎ *510/658–2801* ⊕ *maisondetre.com.*

MARIN COUNTY

Marin is quite simply a knockout—some go so far as to call it spectacular and wild. This isn't an extravagant claim, since more than 40% of the county (180,000 acres), including the majority of the coastline, is parkland. The territory ranges from chaparral, grassland, and coastal scrub to broadleaf and evergreen forest, redwood, salt marsh, and rocky shoreline. It's well worth the drive over the Golden Gate Bridge to explore the Headlands and the stunning beauty of sprawling Point Reyes National Seashore, with more than 80 miles of shoreline.

Regardless of its natural beauty, what gave the county its reputation was Cyra McFadden's 1977 book *The Serial,* a literary soap opera that depicted the county as a bastion of hot-tubbing and "open" marriages. Indeed old-time bohemian, but also increasingly jet-set, Marinites still spend a lot of time outdoors, and surfing, cycling, and hiking are common after-work and weekend activities. Adrenaline junkies mountain bike down Mt. Tamalpais, and those who want solitude take a walk on one of Point Reyes's many empty beaches. The hot tub remains a popular destination, but things have changed since the boho days. Artists and musicians who arrived in the 1960s have set the tone for mellow country towns, but Marin is now undeniably chic, with BMWs supplanting VW buses as the cars of choice.

After exploring Marin's natural beauty, consider a stop in one of its lovely villages. Most cosmopolitan is Sausalito, the town just over the Golden Gate Bridge from San Francisco. Across the inlet from Sausalito, Tiburon and Belvedere are lined with grand homes that regularly appear on fund-raising circuits, and to the north, landlocked Mill Valley is a hub of wining and dining and tony boutiques.

In general, the farther west of U.S. 101 you go the more country things become, and West Marin is about as far as you can get from the big city, both physically and ideologically. Separated from the inland county by the slopes and ridges of giant Mt. Tamalpais, this territory beckons to mavericks, artists, ocean lovers, and other free spirits. Stinson Beach has tempered its isolationist attitude to accommodate out-of-towners, as have Inverness and Point Reyes Station. Bolinas, on the other hand, would prefer you not know its location.

VISITOR INFORMATION
Contact Marin Convention & Visitors Bureau ✉ *1 Mitchell Blvd., Suite B, San Rafael* ☎ *415/925–2060* ⊕ *www.visitmarin.org.*

THE MARIN HEADLANDS

Due west of the Golden Gate Bridge's northern end.

The term *Golden Gate* may now be synonymous with the world-famous bridge, but it originally referred to the grassy, poppy-strewn hills flanking the passageway into San Francisco Bay. To the north of the gate lie the Marin Headlands, part of the Golden Gate National Recreation Area (GGNRA) and among the most dramatic scenery in these parts. Windswept hills plunge down to the ocean, and creek-fed thickets shelter swaying wildflowers.

GETTING HERE AND AROUND
Driving from San Francisco, head north on U.S. 101. Just after you cross the Golden Gate Bridge, take the Alexander Avenue exit. From there take the first left (signs read "San Francisco/U.S. 101 South"), go through the tunnel under the freeway, and turn right up the hill where the sign reads "Forts Barry and Cronkhite." Muni bus 76X runs hourly from Sutter and Sansome streets to the Marin Headlands Visitor Center on weekends and major holidays only. Once here, you can explore this beautiful countryside on foot.

EXPLORING
TOP ATTRACTIONS

FAMILY

Fodor'sChoice

★

Marin Headlands. The headlands stretch from the Golden Gate Bridge to Muir Beach. Photographers perch on the southern headlands for shots of the city, with the bridge in the foreground and the skyline on the horizon. Equally remarkable are the views north along the coast and out to sea, where the Farallon Islands are visible on clear days. ■TIP➔ Nearly all the roads, all of them windy and winding, offer great coastal views.

The headlands' strategic position at the mouth of San Francisco Bay made them a logical site for World War II military installations. Today you can explore the crumbling concrete batteries where naval guns protected the approaches from the sea. The headlands' main attractions are centered on Forts Barry and Cronkhite, which lie just across Rodeo Lagoon from each other. Fronting the lagoon is Rodeo Beach, a dark stretch of sand that attracts sand-castle builders and dog owners. The beaches at the Marin Headlands are not safe for swimming. The giant cliffs are steep and unstable, so hiking down them can be dangerous. Stay on trails.

The visitor center is a worthwhile stop for its exhibits on the area's history and ecology, and kids enjoy the "please touch" educational sites and small play area inside. You can pick up guides to historic sites and wildlife at the center, as well as the park's newspaper, which has a schedule of guided walks. ⊠ *Visitor Center, Fort Barry Chapel, Fort Barry, Bldg. 948, Field and Bunker Rds., Sausalito* ☎ *415/331–1540* ⊕ *www.nps.gov/goga/marin-headlands.htm* ⊙ *Park: sunrise–sunset. Visitor center: daily 9:30–4.*

FAMILY

Point Bonita Lighthouse. At the end of Conzelman Road, in the southern headlands, is the Point Bonita Lighthouse, a restored beauty that still guides ships to safety with its original 1855 refractory lens. Half the fun of a visit is the steep ½-mile walk from the parking area down to the lighthouse, which takes you through a rock tunnel and across a suspension bridge. Signposts along the way detail the bravado of surfmen, as the early lifeguards were called, and the tenacity of the "wickies," the first keepers of the light. ⊠ *End of Conzelman Rd.* ⊕ *www.nps.gov/ goga/pobo.htm* 🖾 *Free* ⊙ *Sat.–Mon. 12:30–3:30.*

WORTH NOTING

Hawk Hill. Craggy Hawk Hill is the best place on the West Coast to watch the migration of eagles, hawks, and falcons as they fly south for winter. The main migration period is from September through November. As many as 1,000 birds have been sighted in a single day. The viewing area is about 2 miles up Conzelman Road from U.S. 101; look for a Hawk Hill sign and parking, right before the road becomes one way. In September and October, on rain- and fog-free weekends at noon, enthusiastic docents from the Golden Gate Raptor Observatory give free lectures on Hawk Hill, and a raptor-banding demonstration follows at 1 pm. ⊠ *Sausalito* ⊕ *www.ggro.org.*

Headlands Center for the Arts. The center's main building, formerly the army barracks, exhibits contemporary art in a rustic natural setting; the downstairs "archive room" contains objects found and created by residents, such as natural rocks, interesting glass bottles filled with collected items, and unusual masks. Stop by the industrial gallery space, two flights up, to see what the resident visual artists are up to—most of the work is quite contemporary. ⊠ *Fort Barry, 944 Simmonds Rd., Sausalito* ☎ *415/331–2787* ⊕ *www.headlands.org* ⊙ *Sun.–Thurs. noon–5.*

FAMILY **Marine Mammal Center.** If you're curious about the rehabilitation of sea mammals from the Pacific—and the human practices that endanger them—stop by this amazing facility for rescued seals, sea lions, dolphins, and otters. An observation area overlooks the pools where the animals convalesce, and nearby plaques describe what you're seeing. ■TIP→ You'll learn even more—and get closer to the animals—on a worthwhile, docent-led tour. ⊠ *Fort Cronkhite, 2000 Bunker Rd., off U.S. 101's Alexander Ave. exit, Sausalito* ☎ *415/289–7325* ⊕ *www. marinemammalcenter.org* ✉ *Center free, tour $9* ⊙ *Daily 10–5.*

Nike Missile Site SF-88-L. For a look at a relatively recent episode in the area's military history, head to the now defunct Nike missile site, above Fort Barry, which is the only accessible site of its kind in the United States. It gives you a firsthand view of menacing Hercules missiles and missile-tracking radar. Free, guided tours take place at 12:45, 1:45, and 2:30 pm. ■TIP→ On the first Saturday of the month the site holds an open house at which some of the docents leading walking tours are Nike veterans who describe their experiences. The site is closed to the public during inclement weather, so call ahead to confirm open hours. ⊠ *Field Rd., off Bunker Hill Rd.* ☎ *415/331–1453* ⊕ *www.nps.gov/ goga/nike-missile-site.htm* ⛟ *Free* ⊙ *Thurs.–Sat. 12:30–3:30.*

SAUSALITO

2 miles north of Golden Gate Bridge.

Bougainvillea-covered hillsides and an expansive yacht harbor give Sausalito the feel of an Adriatic resort. The town sits on the northwestern edge of San Francisco Bay, where it's sheltered from the ocean by the Marin Headlands; the mostly mild weather here is perfect for strolling and outdoor dining. Nevertheless, morning fog and afternoon winds can roll over the hills without warning, funneling through the central part of Sausalito once known as Hurricane Gulch.

South on Bridgeway (toward San Francisco), which snakes between the bay and the hills, a waterside esplanade is lined with restaurants on piers that lure diners with good seafood and even better views. Stairs along the west side of Bridgeway climb the hill to wooded neighborhoods filled with both rustic and opulent homes. As you amble along Bridgeway past shops and galleries, you'll notice the absence of basic services. If you need an aspirin or some groceries (or if you want to see the locals), you'll have to head to Caledonia Street, which runs parallel to Bridgeway, north of the ferry terminus and inland a couple of blocks. The streets closest to the ferry landing flaunt their fair share of shops selling T-shirts and kitschy souvenirs. Venture into some of the side streets or narrow alleyways to catch a bit more of the town's taste for eccentric jewelry and handmade crafts.

■ **TIP→** The ferry is the best way to get to Sausalito from San Francisco; you get more romance (and less traffic) and disembark in the heart of downtown.

Sausalito developed its bohemian flair in the 1950s and '60s, when creative types, led by a charismatic Greek portraitist named Varda, established an artists' colony and a houseboat community here. Today more than 450 houseboats are docked in Sausalito, which has since also become a major yachting center. Some of these floating homes are ragged, others deluxe, but all are quirky (one, a miniature replica of a Persian castle, even has an elevator inside). For a close-up view of the community, head north on Bridgeway—Sausalito's main thoroughfare—from downtown, turn right on Gate Six Road, park where it dead-ends at the public shore, and enter through the unlocked gates. Keep a respectful distance; these are homes, after all, and the residents become a bit prickly from too much ogling.

GETTING HERE AND AROUND

From San Francisco by car or bike, follow U.S. 101 north across the Golden Gate Bridge and take the first exit, Alexander Avenue, just past Vista Point; continue down the winding hill to the water to where the road becomes Bridgeway. Golden Gate Transit buses 10 and 2 will drop you off in downtown Sausalito, and the ferries dock downtown as well.

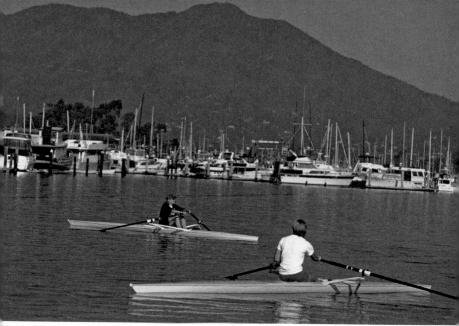
...he crowded piers and rolling hillside of the Sausalito waterfront

The center of town is flat, with plenty of sidewalks and bay views. It's a pleasure and a must to explore on foot.

ESSENTIALS

Visitor Information Sausalito Chamber of Commerce ⊠ *780 Bridgeway* ☎ *415/332–0505* ⊕ *www.sausalito.org.*

EXPLORING

FAMILY **Bay Area Discovery Museum.** Sitting at the base of the Golden Gate Bridge, this indoor-outdoor museum offers entertaining and enlightening hands-on exhibits for children under eight. Kids can fish from a boat at the indoor wharf, imagine themselves as marine biologists in the Wave Workshop, and play outdoors at Lookout Cove (made up of scaled-down sea caves, tidal pools, and even a re-created shipwreck). At Tot Spot, toddlers and preschoolers dress up in animal costumes and crawl through miniature tunnels. ■TIP➔ From San Francisco, take U.S. 101's Alexander Avenue exit and follow signs to East Fort Baker. ⊠ *557 McReynolds Rd., at East Rd. off Alexander Ave.* ☎ *415/339–3900* ⊕ *www.baykidsmuseum. org* ☞ *$11, free 1st Wed. of the month* ☉ *Tues.–Sun. 9–5.*

FAMILY **Bay Model.** An anonymous-looking World War II shipyard building holds a great treasure: the sprawling (more than 1½ acres) Bay Model of the entire San Francisco Bay and the San Joaquin–Sacramento River delta, complete with flowing water. The U.S. Army Corps of Engineers uses the model to reproduce the rise and fall of tides, the flow of currents, and the other physical forces at work on the bay. ⊠ *2100 Bridgeway, at Marinship Way* ☎ *415/332–3870 recorded information, 415/332–3871 operator assistance* ⊕ *www.spn.usace.army.mil* ☞ *Free* ☉ *Late May–early Sept., Tues.–Fri. 9–4, weekends 10–5; early Sept.–late May, Tues.–Sat. 9–4.*

Drinking Fountain. On the waterfront between the Hotel Sausalito and the Sausalito Yacht Club is an unusual historic landmark—a drinking fountain. It's inscribed with "Have a drink on Sally" in remembrance of Sally Stanford, the former San Francisco madam who became the town's mayor in the 1970s. Sassy Sally, as they called her, would have appreciated the fountain's eccentric custom attachment: a knee-level basin that reads "Have a drink on Leland," in memory of her beloved dog.

QUICK BITES

✕ Hamburgers. Patrons queue up daily for a sandwich made from the juicy, hand-formed beef patties sizzling on the grill here. Brave the line (it moves fast), get your food to go, and head to the esplanade to enjoy the sweeping views. ⑤ *Average main: $25* ⊠ *737 Bridgeway, at Humboldt Ave.* ☎ *415/332-9471* ⊘ *Daily 11-5.*

Plaza Viña del Mar. The landmark Plaza Viña del Mar, named for Sausalito's sister city in Chile, marks the center of town. Flanked by two 14-foot-tall elephant statues (created in 1915 for the Panama-Pacific International Exposition), the fountain is a great setting for snapshots and people-watching. ⊠ *Bridgeway and Park St.*

Sausalito Visitors Center and Historical Exhibit. The local historical society operates the center, where you can get your bearings, learn some history, and find out what's happening in town. ⊠ *780 Bridgeway, at Bay St.* ☎ *415/332-0505* ⊕ *www.sausalitohistoricalsociety.com* ⊘ *Closed Mon.*

WHERE TO EAT

$$
SEAFOOD
FAMILY
Fodor's Choice
★

✕ Fish. When locals want fresh seafood, they head to this gleaming dockside fish house a mile north of downtown. Order at the counter and then grab a seat by the floor-to-ceiling windows or at a picnic table on the pier, overlooking the yachts and fishing boats. Most of the sustainably caught fish is hauled in from the owner's boats, docked right outside. Try the ceviche, crab Louis, cioppino, barbecue oysters, or anything fresh that's being grilled over the oak-wood fire. Outside, kids can doodle with sidewalk chalk on the pier. ⑤ *Average main: $20* ⊠ *350 Harbor Dr., off Bridgeway* ☎ *415/331-3474* ⊕ *www.331fish. com* ⚆ *Reservations not accepted* ▭ *No credit cards.*

$$$
FRENCH

✕ Le Garage. Brittany-born Olivier Souvestre serves traditional French bistro fare in a relaxed, sidewalk café–style bayside setting. The menu is small, but the dishes are substantial in flavor and presentation. Standouts include frisée salad with poached egg, bacon, croutons, and pancetta vinaigrette; steak frites with a shallot confit and crispy fries; and a chef's selection of cheese or charcuterie with soup and mixed greens. The restaurant only seats 35 inside and 15 outside, so to avoid a long wait for lunch, arrive before 11:30 or after 1:30. ⑤ *Average main: $23* ⊠ *85 Liberty Ship Way, off Marinship Way* ☎ *415/332-5625* ⊕ *www.legaragebistrosausalito.com* ⚆ *Reservations essential* ⊘ *No dinner Sun.*

$$
ITALIAN

✕ Poggio. One of the few restaurants in Sausalito to attract both food-savvy locals and tourists, Poggio serves modern Tuscan cuisine in a handsome, open-wall space that spills onto the street. Expect dishes such as grilled chicken with roasted beets and sunchokes, braised artichokes with polenta, featherlight gnocchi, and pizzas from the open kitchen's wood-fired oven. $ *Average main: $22* ✉ *777 Bridgeway, at Bay St.* ☎ *415/332–7771* ⊕ *www.poggiotrattoria.com* ⌂ *Reservations essential.*

$$
JAPANESE
Fodor's Choice
★

✕ **Sushi Ran.** Sushi aficionados swear that this is the Bay Area's best option for raw fish, but don't overlook the excellent Pacific Rim fusions, a melding of Japanese ingredients and French cooking techniques, served up in unusual presentations. Because Sushi Ran is so highly ranked among area foodies, book two to seven days in advance for dinner. Otherwise, expect a long wait, which you can soften by sipping one of the 45 by-the-glass sakes from the outstanding wine-and-sake bar. ■**TIP→** If you arrive without a reservation and can't get a table, you can sometimes dine in the noisy bar. $ *Average main: $18* ✉ *107 Caledonia St., at Pine St.* ☎ *415/332–3620* ⊕ *www.sushiran.com* ⌂ *Reservations essential* ⊘ *No lunch weekends.*

$
WINE BAR

✕ **Wellingtons Wine Bar.** British memorabilia decorates the walls of this establishment that celebrates English and Californian liquid culture. The space is bright, warm, and welcoming, and when the weather is nice, you can sit on the boat dock and drink your pint of lager or sip a glass of wine while scooping up hummus with garlic pita chips. The menu is as big as a book. ■**TIP→** Wellingtons opens at 3 pm on Fridays and weekends, and at 4 the rest of the week. $ *Average main: $12* ✉ *300 Turney St., at Bridgeway* ☎ *415/331–9463* ⊕ *www.wellingtonswinebar. com* ⌂ *Reservations not accepted* ⊘ *No lunch.*

WHERE TO STAY

$$$$
HOTEL

🏨 **Cavallo Point.** Set in the Golden Gate National Recreation Area, this luxury hotel and resort's location is truly one of a kind, featuring turn-of-the-20th-century buildings converted into well-appointed yet eco-friendly rooms. **Pros:** stunning views and numerous activities: a cooking school, yoga classes, and nature walks; spa with a tea bar; art gallery. **Cons:** landscaping feels incomplete; isolated from urban amenities. $ *Rooms from: $375* ✉ *601 Murray Circle, Fort Baker* ☎ *415/339–4700* ⊕ *www.cavallopoint.com* ⟿ *68 historic and 74 contemporary guest rooms* ⏐❍⏐ *No meals.*

$$
B&B/INN

🏨 **Hotel Sausalito.** Handmade furniture and tasteful original art and reproductions give this well-run inn the feel of a small European hotel. **Pros:** great staff; excellent central location; feels like home away from home. **Cons:** no room service; some rooms feel cramped. $ *Rooms from: $180* ✉ *16 El Portal* ☎ *415/332–0700, 888/442–0700* ⊕ *www. hotelsausalito.com* ⟿ *14 rooms, 2 suites* ⏐❍⏐ *No meals.*

$$$$
B&B/INN

🏨 **The Inn Above Tide.** This is the only hotel in the Bay Area with balconies literally hanging over the water, and each of its rooms has a perfect-10 view that takes in wild Angel Island as well as the city lights across the bay. **Pros:** great complimentary breakfast; minutes from restaurants/attractions; in-room binoculars let you indulge in the incredible views. **Cons:** costly parking; some rooms are on the small side. $ *Rooms from: $360* ✉ *30 El Portal* ☎ *415/332–9535, 800/893–8433* ⊕ *www.innabovetide.com* ⟿ *29 rooms, 3 suites* ⏐❍⏐ *Breakfast.*

5

THE ARTS

Sausalito Art Festival. The annual event, held over Labor Day weekend, attracts more than 30,000 people to the northern waterfront; Blue & Gold Fleet ferries from San Francisco dock at the pier adjacent to the festival. ☎ *415/332–3555* ⊕ *www.sausalitoartfestival.org* ⊠ *$25.*

SPORTS AND THE OUTDOORS

Sea Trek Ocean Kayaking and SUP Center. The center (SUP stands for stand-up paddleboarding) offers guided half-day sea-kayaking trips underneath the Golden Gate Bridge and full- and half-day trips to Angel Island, both for beginners. Trips for experienced kayakers, classes, and rentals are also available. ■ TIP→ Starlight and full-moon paddles are particularly popular. ⊠ *Schoonmaker Point Marina, off Libertyship Way* ☎ *415/332–8494* ⊕ *www.seatrek.com* ⊠ *From $20 per hr for rentals, $65 for 3-hr guided trip.*

SF Bay Adventures. This outfit's expert skippers conduct sunset and full-moon sails around the bay, as well as fascinating eco and whale-watching tours with the possibility of viewing great white sharks. If you're interested, they can arrange for you to barbecue on Angel Island or even spend the night in a lighthouse. ⊠ *60 Liberty Ship Way, Ste. 4* ☎ *415/331–0444* ⊕ *www.sfbayadventures.com.*

SHOPPING

FAMILY **Sausalito Ferry Co.** Eccentric and fun, this shop is a great place to buy trendy T-shirts, wallets, and clocks—not to mention solar-powered bobbleheads, outrageous cocktail napkins, and one-of-a-kind key chains. ⊠ *688 Bridgeway, near Princess St.* ☎ *415/332–9590* ⊕ *www.sausalitoferry.com.*

Something/Anything Gallery. Where Bridgeway ends and curves toward the dock, this gallery with a friendly staff carries jewelry and gifts, from unique watches to humorous pendants. ■ TIP→ This a good spot to pick up your Sausalito memento. ⊠ *20 Princess St., at Broadway* ☎ *415/339–8831* ⊕ *www.somethinganythinggallery.com.*

TIBURON

2 miles north of Sausalito, 7 miles north of Golden Gate Bridge.

On a peninsula that was called Punta de Tiburon (Shark Point) by the Spanish explorers, this beautiful Marin County community retains the feel of a village—it's more low-key than Sausalito—despite the encroachment of commercial establishments from the downtown area. The harbor faces Angel Island across Raccoon Strait, and San Francisco is directly south across the bay—which makes the views from the decks of harbor restaurants a major attraction. Since its incarnation, in 1884, when ferries from San Francisco connected the point with a railroad to San Rafael, the town has centered on the waterfront. ■ TIP→ The ferry is the most relaxing (and fastest) way to get here, particularly in summer, allowing you to skip traffic and parking problems. If visiting midweek, keep in mind that many shops close either Tuesday or Wednesday, or both.

ESSENTIALS

Visitor Information Tiburon ⊠ *Town Hall, 1505 Tiburon Blvd.* ☎ *415/435–7373* ⊕ *www.townoftiburon.org.*

GETTING HERE AND AROUND

Blue & Gold Fleet ferries travel between San Francisco and Tiburon daily. By car, head north from San Francisco on U.S. 101 and get off at CA 131/Tiburon Boulevard/East Blithedale Avenue (Exit 447). Turn right onto Tiburon Boulevard and drive just over 4 miles to downtown. Golden Gate Transit bus 8 serves downtown Tiburon from San Francisco on weekdays. Tiburon's Main Street is made for wandering, as are the footpaths that frame the water's edge.

EXPLORING

Ark Row. Past the pink-brick bank building, Main Street is known as Ark Row, and has a tree-shaded walk lined with antiques and specialty stores. Some of the buildings are actually old houseboats that floated in Belvedere Cove before being beached and transformed into stores. ■ **TIP→** If you're curious about architectural history, the Tiburon Heritage & Arts Commission has a self-guided walking-tour map, available online and at local businesses. ⊠ *Ark Row, parallel to Main St.* ⊕ *tiburonheritageandarts.org.*

Old St. Hilary's Landmark and Wildflower Preserve. The architectural centerpiece of the Old St. Hilary's Landmark and Wildflower Preserve is a stark-white 1886 Carpenter Gothic church that overlooks the town and the bay from its hillside perch. Surrounding the church, which was barged over from Strawberry Point in 1957, is a wildflower preserve that's spectacular in May and June, when the rare black jewelflower blooms. Expect a steep walk uphill to reach the preserve. ■ **TIP→** The hiking trails behind the landmark wind up to a peak that has 360-degree views of the entire Bay Area (great photo op). ⊠ *201 Esperanza St., off Mar West St. or Beach Rd.* ☎ *415/435–1853* ⊕ *landmarkssociety.com* ☞ *$3 suggested donation* ☉ *Apr.–Oct., Sun. 1–4 and by appointment.*

WHERE TO EAT

$$$$
AMERICAN
✕ **The Caprice.** For more than 50 years this Tiburon landmark that overlooks the bay has been the place to come to mark special occasions. The views are spectacular, and soft-yellow walls and starched white tablecloths help to make the space bright and light. Elegant comfort food is the premise, with choices like seared day-boat scallops or pan-roasted filet mignon. Polishing off the warm chocolate cake with almond ice cream while gazing out at the sunset and porpoises bobbing in the waves below is a near perfect end to the evening. ⑤ *Average main: $31* ⊠ *2000 Paradise Dr.* ☎ *415/435–3400* ⊕ *www.thecaprice.com* ☉ *No lunch.*

$
AMERICAN
✕ **New Morning Cafe.** Omelets and scrambles are served all day long at this homey café. If you're past morning treats, choose from the many soups, salads, and sandwiches. The café is open from 6:30 until 2:30 on weekdays, until 4 on weekends. ⑤ *Average main: $13* ⊠ *1696 Tiburon Blvd., near Main St.* ☎ *415/435–4315* ☉ *No dinner.*

$$$
AMERICAN
✕ **Sam's Anchor Cafe.** Open since 1921, this casual dockside restaurant with mahogany wainscoting is the town's most famous eatery. Today most people flock here for the deck, where out-of-towners and old

salts sit shoulder to shoulder for bay views, beer, seafood, and Ramos fizzes. The lunch menu has the usual suspects—burgers, sandwiches, salads, fried fish with tartar sauce—and you'll sit on plastic chairs at tables covered with blue-and-white-checked oilcloths. At night you can find standard seafood dishes with vegetarian and meat options. Mind the seagulls; they know no restraint. ■TIP→ Expect a wait for outside tables on sunny summer days or weekends; there are no reservations for deck seating or weekend lunch. $ *Average main: $23* ✉ *27 Main St.* ☎ *415/435–4527* ⊕ *www.samscafe.com.*

WHERE TO STAY

$$$
B&B/INN
🏨 **Waters Edge Hotel.** Checking into this elegant hotel feels like tucking away into an inviting retreat by the water—the views are stunning and the lighting is perfect. **Pros:** complimentary wine and cheese for guests every evening; restaurants/sights are minutes away; free bike rentals for guests. **Cons:** downstairs rooms lack privacy and views; except for breakfast delivery, no room service; fitness center is off-site; not a great place to bring small children. $ *Rooms from: $250* ✉ *25 Main St., off Tiburon Blvd.* ☎ *415/789–5999, 877/789–5999* ⊕ *www.marinhotels. com* ⇋ *23 rooms* ⦿ *Breakfast.*

MILL VALLEY

2 miles north of Sausalito, 4 miles north of Golden Gate Bridge.

Chic and woodsy Mill Valley has a dual personality. Here, as elsewhere in the county, the foundation is a superb natural setting. Virtually surrounded by parkland, the town lies at the base of Mt. Tamalpais and contains dense redwood groves traversed by countless creeks. But this is no lumber camp. Smart restaurants and chichi boutiques line the streets, and more rock stars than one might suspect live here.

The rustic village flavor isn't a modern conceit but a holdover from the town's early days as a logging camp. In 1896 the Mill Valley and Mt. Tamalpais Scenic Railroad—called "the crookedest railroad in the world" because of its curvy tracks—began transporting visitors from Mill Valley to the top of Mt. Tam and down to Muir Woods, and the town soon became a vacation retreat for city slickers. The trains stopped running in the 1940s, but the old railway depot still serves as the center of town: the 1924 building has been transformed into the popular Depot Bookstore & Cafe, at 87 Throckmorton Avenue.

The small downtown area has the constant bustle of a leisure community; even at noon on a Tuesday, people are out shopping for fancy cookware and lacy pajamas.

ESSENTIALS

Visitor Information Mill Valley Chamber of Commerce ✉ *85 Throckmorton Ave.* ☎ *415/388–9700* ⊕ *www.millvalley.org.*

GETTING HERE AND AROUND

By car from San Francisco, head north on U.S. 101 and get off at CA 131/Tiburon Boulevard/East Blithedale Avenue (Exit 447). Turn left onto East Blithedale and continue west to Throckmorton Avenue; turn left to reach Lytton Square, then park. Golden Gate Transit bus

4 leaves for Mill Valley from San Francisco every 30 minutes during afternoon commute hours. Once here, explore the town on foot; it's great for strolling.

EXPLORING

FAMILY **Lytton Square.** Mill Valley locals congregate on weekends to socialize in the many coffeehouses near the town's central square (which is unmarked), but it bustles most any time of day. Shops, restaurants, and cultural venues line the nearby streets. ⊠ *Miller and Throckmorton Aves.*

OFF THE BEATEN PATH

Marin County Civic Center. A wonder of arches, circles, and skylights about 8 miles north of Mill Valley, the civic center was Frank Lloyd Wright's last major architectural undertaking. Docent-led tours ($5) leave from the gift shop, on the second floor, on Wednesday mornings at 10:30. You can also wander about on your own; pick up a self-guided tour map at the gift shop (50¢) or access one on the center's website. ■ TIP→ Don't miss the photographs on the first floor, which show Marin County homes designed by Wright. ⊠ *3501 Civic Center Dr., off N. San Pedro Rd., San Rafael* ☎ *415/473–3762 for docent tour* ⊕ *www. marincounty.org/depts/cu/visitor-services* ☞ *Free* ☉ *Weekdays 8–5.*

WHERE TO EAT

$$$

AMERICAN

✕ **Buckeye Roadhouse.** This is Mill Valley's secret den of decadence, where house-smoked meats and fish, grilled steaks, and old-fashioned dishes such as brisket bring the locals coming back for more. The restaurant also serves beautiful organic salads and desserts so heavenly—like the s'more pie—you'll just about melt into the floor. The look of the 1937 roadhouse is decidedly hunting-lodge chic, with a river-rock fireplace, topped by a trophy fish, dominating one wall. The busy but cozy bar with elegant mahogany paneling and soft lighting is a good place to quench your thirst for a Marin martini or Napa Valley Merlot. ⑤ *Average main: $23* ⊠ *15 Shoreline Hwy., off U.S. 101* ☎ *415/331–2600* ⊕ *buckeyeroadhouse.com* ⚇ *Reservations essential.*

$$$

CONTEMPORARY

Fodor's Choice

★

✕ **El Paseo House of Chops.** Chef Tyler Florence and rocker Sammy Hagar teamed up to restore El Paseo, which was established in 1947 and remains *the* place for a romantic and culinary night out. You'll feel as if you're on one of Spain's tiny cobbled lanes as you enter the secluded brick walkway that wraps around a candlelit dining room. If you reserve well in advance you can sit in the bougainvillea-framed courtyard, but the dining room casts its own atmospheric charms, with soft leather chairs, white tablecloths, and dark wooden walls. And then there's Tyler Florence's famous seasonal Californian cuisine. Favorites include pan-roasted duck breast and the traditional steak frites. Don't overlook the decadent desserts. ⑤ *Average main: $27* ⊠ *17 Throckmorton Ave., at E. Blithedale Ave.* ☎ *415/388–0741* ⊕ *www.elpaseomillvalley.com* ⚇ *Reservations essential* ☉ *No lunch.*

$

BURGER

FAMILY

✕ **Pearl's Phat Burgers.** Families, couples, and teenagers flock to Pearl's for juicy, grass-fed organic burgers stacked high with tomatoes, lettuce, bacon, and cheese; sweet-potato fries that are not too crispy and not too soft; and thick, creamy milk shakes. The food here is among the freshest, biggest, and fastest in town. No wonder there's always a line out the door. ⑤ *Average main: $14* ⊠ *8 E. Blithedale Ave., at Sunnyside Ave.* ☎ *415/381–6010.*

5

WHERE TO STAY

$$$
B&B/INN

🏨 **Mill Valley Inn.** The only hotel in downtown Mill Valley has smart-looking rooms done up in Tuscan colors of ocher and olive, with hand-crafted beds, armoires, and lamps by local artisans. **Pros:** minutes from local shops and restaurants; great complimentary Continental breakfast; free parking; free mountain bikes. **Cons:** some rooms are noisy; dark in winter because of surrounding trees; some rooms are not accessible via elevator; no in-room coffeemakers. $ *Rooms from: $239* ✉ *165 Throckmorton Ave., near Miller Ave.* ☎ *415/389–6608, 800/595–2100* ⊕ *www.marinhotels.com* ⇌ *22 rooms, 1 suite, 2 cottages* ⦿ *Breakfast.*

$$$$
B&B/INN
Fodor's Choice
★

🏨 **Mountain Home Inn.** Abutting 40,000 acres of state and national parks, the inn sits on the skirt of Mt. Tamalpais, where you can follow hiking trails all the way to Stinson Beach. **Pros:** amazing deck and views; peaceful, remote setting. **Cons:** nearest town is a 20-minute drive away; restaurant can get crowded on sunny weekend days; too rustic for some. $ *Rooms from: $279* ✉ *810 Panoramic Hwy., at Edgewood Ave.* ☎ *415/381–9000* ⊕ *www.mtnhomeinn.com* ⇌ *10 rooms* ⦿ *Breakfast.*

NIGHTLIFE AND THE ARTS

NIGHTLIFE

Mill Valley Beerworks. A place to rest your feet after shopping or hiking, Beerworks serves more than 100 local, national, and international beers, from ale to port to lager. For food, you'll find cheese plates, olives, homemade pretzels, and sandwiches. ✉ *173 Throckmorton Ave., at Madrona St.* ☎ *415/888–8218* ⊕ *millvalleybeerworks.com.*

THE ARTS

Sweetwater Music Hall. With the help of part-owner Bob Weir of the Grateful Dead, this renowned club reopened in an old Masonic Hall. The location may be new, but the Sweetwater's reputation as the best music club and bar in Marin remains. In its former life, it hosted the likes of John Lee Hooker and Jerry Garcia. Today, famous as well as up-and-coming bands play nightly, and local stars such as Bonnie Raitt and Huey Lewis have been known to stop in for a pickup session. ✉ *19 Corte Madera Ave., between Throckmorton and Lovell Aves.* ☎ *415/388–3850* ⊕ *www.sweetwatermusichall.com.*

MUIR WOODS NATIONAL MONUMENT

12 miles northwest of the Golden Gate Bridge.

Climbing hundreds of feet into the sky, *Sequoia sempervirens* are the tallest living things on Earth. One of the last remaining old-growth stands of these redwood behemoths, Muir Woods is nature's cathedral: imposing, awe-inspiring, reverence-inducing, and not to be missed.

GETTING HERE AND AROUND

Driving to Muir Woods, especially in summer and early fall, causes epic traffic jams around the tiny parking areas and miles-long walks to reach the entrance. Do yourself (and everyone else) a favor and take a shuttle instead, if you can. On weekends and holidays, from Memorial Day through Labor Day, Marin Transit's Route 66 shuttle (✉ *$5 round-trip* ⊕ *www.marintransit.org*) is timed to meet boats at Sausalito's ferry

landing four times daily en route to Muir Woods. The shuttle also runs every half hour from the Manzanita Park-and-Ride three miles north of the ferry. To get there, take the Highway 1 exit off U.S. 101 (look for the lot under the elevated freeway), or take connecting bus service from San Francisco with Golden Gate Transit. To drive directly from San Francisco by car, take U.S. 101 north across the Golden Gate Bridge to the Mill Valley/Stinson Beach exit, then follow signs to Highway 1 north. Once here, you can wander by foot through this pristine patch of nature.

EXPLORING

Fodor'sChoice   **Muir Woods National Monument.** Walking among some of the last old-
★   growth redwoods on the planet, trees hundreds of feet tall and a millennium or more old, is magical, an experience like few others to clearly illustrate our tiny place in a bigger world. Ancestors of redwood and sequoia trees grew throughout what is now the United States 150,000,000 years ago. Today the *Sequoia sempervirens* can be found only in a narrow, cool coastal belt from Monterey to Oregon. The 550 acres of Muir Woods National Monument contain some of the most majestic redwoods in the world—some more than 250 feet tall. (To see the real giants, though, you'll have to head north to Humboldt County, where the tallest redwood, in Redwood National Park, has been measured at 380 feet.) The Marin stand was saved from destruction in 1905, when it was purchased by a couple who donated it to the federal government. Three years later it was named after naturalist John Muir, whose environmental campaigns helped to establish the national park system. His response: "Saving these woods from the ax and saw is in many ways the most notable service to God and man I have heard of since my forest wandering began."

Muir Woods, part of the Golden Gate National Recreation Area, is a pedestrian's park. Old paved trails have been replaced by wooden walkways, and the trails vary in difficulty and length. Beginning from the park headquarters, an easy 2-mile, wheelchair-accessible **loop trail** crosses streams and passes ferns and azaleas, as well as magnificent redwood groves. Among the most famous are **Bohemian Grove** and the circular formation called **Cathedral Grove.** On summer weekends visitors oohing and aahing in a dozen languages line the trail. If you prefer a little serenity, consider the challenging **Dipsea Trail,** which climbs west from the forest floor to soothing views of the ocean and the Golden Gate Bridge. For a complete list of trails, check with rangers, who can also help you pick the best one for your ability level.

■**TIP**→ The weather in Muir Woods is usually cool and often wet, so wear warm clothes and shoes appropriate for damp trails. Picnicking and camping aren't allowed, and pets aren't permitted. Crowds can be large, especially from May through October, so try to come early in the morning or late in the afternoon. The **Muir Woods Visitor Center** has books and exhibits about redwood trees and the woods' history; the café here serves locally sourced, organic food, and the gift shop has plenty of souvenirs. ⊠ *1 Muir Woods Trail, off Panoramic Hwy., Mill Valley* ☎ *415/388–2595 park information, 415/526–3239 shuttle information* ⊕ *www.nps.gov/muwo* ☒ *$7* ☉ *Daily 8 am–sunset.*

MT. TAMALPAIS STATE PARK

16 miles northwest of Golden Gate Bridge.

The view of Mt. Tamalpais from all around the bay can be a beauty, but that's nothing compared to the views *from* the mountain, which range from jaw-dropping to spectacular and take in San Francisco, the East Bay, the coast, and beyond—on a clear day, all the way to the Farallon Islands, 26 miles away.

GETTING HERE AND AROUND

By car, take the Highway 1–Stinson Beach exit off U.S. 101 and follow the road west and then north. From San Francisco, the trip can take from 30 minutes up to an hour, depending on traffic. By bus, take the 10, 70 or 80 (on weekdays also the 92) to Marin City; in Marin City transfer to the West Marin Stagecoach (☎ *415/226–0855* ⊕ *www.marintransit. org/stage.html*). Once here, the only way to explore is on foot or by bike.

EXPLORING

Mt. Tamalpais State Park. Although the summit of Mt. Tamalpais is only 2,571 feet high, the mountain rises practically from sea level, dominating the topography of Marin County. Adjacent to Muir Woods National Monument, Mt. Tamalpais State Park affords views of the entire Bay Area and the Pacific Ocean to the west. The mountain was sacred to Native Americans, who saw in its profile—as you can see today—the silhouette of a sleeping Indian maiden. Locals fondly refer to it as the "Sleeping Lady." For years the 6,300-acre park has been a favorite destination for hikers. There are more than 200 miles of trails, some rugged but many developed for easy walking through meadows, grasslands, and forests and along creeks. Mt. Tam, as it's called by locals, is also the birthplace (in the 1970s) of mountain biking, and today many spandex-clad bikers whiz down the park's winding roads.

The park's major thoroughfare, Panoramic Highway, snakes its way up from U.S. 101 to the **Pantoll Ranger Station.** The office is staffed sporadically, depending on funding. From the ranger station, Panoramic Highway drops down to the town of Stinson Beach. Pantoll Road branches off the highway at the station, connecting up with Ridgecrest Boulevard. Along these roads are numerous parking areas, picnic spots, scenic overlooks, and trailheads. Parking is free along the roadside, but there's a fee at the ranger station and at some of the other parking lots ($8).

The **Mountain Theater,** also known as the Cushing Memorial Amphitheatre, is a natural amphitheater with terraced stone seats (for nearly 4,000 people) constructed in its current form by the Civilian Conservation Corps in the 1930s. The theater celebrated its 100th year of performances in 2013.

The **Rock Spring Trail** starts at the Mountain Theater and gently climbs about 1¾ miles to the **West Point Inn,** once a stop on the Mt. Tam railroad route. Relax at a picnic table and stock up on water before forging ahead, via Old Railroad Grade Fire Road and the Miller Trail, to Mt. Tam's Middle Peak, about 2 miles uphill.

Starting from the Pantoll Ranger Station, the precipitous **Steep Ravine Trail** brings you past stands of coastal redwoods and, in the springtime, numerous small waterfalls. Take the connecting **Dipsea Trail** to reach the town of Stinson Beach and its swath of golden sand. ■ **TIP→ If you're too weary to make the 3½-mile trek back up, Marin Transit Bus 61 takes you from Stinson Beach back to the ranger station.** ⊠ *Pantoll Ranger Station, 3801 Panoramic Hwy., at Pantoll Rd.* ☎ *415/388–2070* ⊕ *www.parks.ca.gov.*

NIGHTLIFE AND THE ARTS

FAMILY **Mountain Play.** Every May and June, locals tote overstuffed picnic baskets to the Mountain Theater to see the Mountain Play, popular musicals such as *The Music Man* and *My Fair Lady*. Depending on the play, this can be a great family activity. Summer 2013 marked the 100th anniversary of this Bay Area tradition. ⊠ *Mt. Tamalpais, Richardson Blvd. off Panoramic Hwy.* ☎ *415/383–1100* ⊕ *www.mountainplay.org* ☜ *$40.*

BEACH TOWNS

The winds whip wildly around Marin County's miles of coastline. If you've never heard sand "sing" as the wind rustles through it you're in for a treat— though when it lands in your sandwich you might not rejoice. But when the weather's calm and sunny as you stroll Stinson Beach—or you're communing with nature at rocky Muir Beach—you'll realize this landscape is ever so choice.

GETTING HERE AND AROUND

If you're driving, take the Highway 1–Stinson Beach exit off U.S. 101 and follow Highway 1, also signed as Shoreline Highway, west and then north. Public transit serves Stinson Beach and Bolinas but not Muir Beach.

MUIR BEACH

12 miles northwest of Golden Gate Bridge; 6 miles southwest of Mill Valley.

Except on the sunniest of weekends Muir Beach is relatively quiet. But this craggy cove has seen its share of history. Sir Francis Drake disembarked here five centuries ago, rock star Janis Joplin's ashes were scattered here among the sands, and this is where author Ken Kesey hosted the second of his famed Acid Tests.

GETTING HERE AND AROUND

A car is the best way to reach Muir Beach. From Highway 1, follow Pacific Way southwest ¼ mile.

EXPLORING

Green Gulch Farm Zen Center. Giant eucalyptus trees frame the long and winding road that leads to this tranquil retreat. Meditation programs, workshops, and various events take place here, and there's an extensive organic garden. Visitors are welcome to roam the acres of gardens that reach down toward Muir Beach. ■ **TIP→ Follow the main dirt road to a peaceful path (birds, trees, ocean breezes) that meanders to the beach.** ⊠ *1601 Shoreline Hwy., at Green Gulch Rd.* ☎ *415/383–3134* ⊕ *www.sfzc.org* ☜ *Free* ☉ *Tues.–Sat. 9–noon and 2–4, Sun. 9–10 am.*

Shutterbugs rejoice in catching a scenic Muir Beach sunset.

BEACHES

FAMILY **Muir Beach.** Small but scenic, this beach—a rocky patch of shoreline off Highway 1 in the northern Marin Headlands—is a good place to stretch your legs and gaze out at the Pacific. Locals often walk their dogs here; families and cuddling couples come for picnicking and sunbathing. At one end of the sand are waterfront homes (and where nude sunbathers lay their towels), and at the other are the bluffs of Golden Gate National Recreation Area. **Amenities:** parking (free); toilets. **Best for:** solitude; nudists; walking. ⊠ *190 Pacific Way, off Shoreline Highway* ⊕ *www. nps.gov/goga/planyourvisit/muirbeach.htm.*

WHERE TO STAY

$$$ ▦ **Pelican Inn.** From its slate roof to its whitewashed plaster walls, this
B&B/INN inn looks so Tudor that it's hard to believe it was built in the 1970s, but the Pelican is English to the core, with its smallish guest rooms upstairs (no elevator), high half-tester beds draped in heavy fabrics, and bangers and grilled tomatoes for breakfast. **Pros:** five-minute walk to beach; great bar and restaurant; peaceful setting. **Cons:** 20-minute drive to nearby attractions; some rooms are quite small. Ⓢ *Rooms from: $220* ⊠ *10 Pacific Way, off Hwy. 1* ☎ *415/383–6000* ⊕ *www.pelicaninn.com* ⤴ *7 rooms* Ⓞ *Breakfast.*

STINSON BEACH

20 miles northwest of Golden Gate Bridge; 5½ miles north of Muir Beach.

This laid-back hamlet is all about the beach, and folks come from all over the Bay Area to walk its sandy, often windswept shore. Ideal day trip: a morning Mt. Tam hike followed by lunch at one of Stinson's unassuming eateries and leisurely beach stroll.

GETTING HERE AND AROUND

By car from U.S. 101, take the Highway 1–Stinson Beach exit off U.S. 101 and head west on Highway 1, also signed as Shoreline Highway. Follow signs to 12½ miles to Stinson Beach. Or take Golden Gate Transit bus 10, 70, or 80 to Marin City; in Marin City transfer to the West Marin Stagecoach. Intimate Stinson is perfect for casual walking.

BEACHES

FAMILY **Stinson Beach.** When the fog hasn't rolled in, this expansive stretch of sand is about as close as you can get in Marin to the stereotypical feel of a Southern California beach. There are several clothing-optional areas, among them a section called Red Rock Beach. ⚠ Swimming at Stinson Beach is recommended only from early May through September, when lifeguards are on duty, because the undertow can be strong and shark sightings, although infrequent, aren't unheard of. On any hot summer weekend, every road to Stinson is jam-packed, so factor this into your plans. The down-to-earth town itself—population 600, give or take—has a surfer vibe, with a few good eating options and pleasant hippie-craftsy browsing. **Amenities:** food and drink; lifeguards; parking (free); showers; toilets. **Best for:** nudists; sunset; surfing; swimming; walking. ⊠ *Hwy. 1* ⊕ *www.stinsonbeachonline.com.*

WHERE TO EAT AND STAY

$$ ✕ **Parkside Cafe.** The Parkside is popular for its beachfront snack bar
AMERICAN (cash only), but inside is tiny Stinson's best restaurant, with classic Cal-
FAMILY cuisine offerings such as the day-boat-scallop and ceviche appetizers, and mains like the lamb with goat-cheese-stuffed red peppers. Breakfast is served until 2 pm. Creeping vines on the sunny patio shelter diners from the wind; for a cozier ambience eat by the fire in the dining room. ⑤ *Average main: $20* ⊠ *43 Arenal Ave., off Shoreline Hwy. 1* ☎ *415/868–1272* ⊕ *www.parksidecafe.com.*

$$ ✕ **Sand Dollar.** The town's oldest restaurant still attracts all the old salts
AMERICAN from Muir Beach to Bolinas, but these days they sip whiskey over an up-to-date bar or beneath market umbrellas on the spiffy deck. The food is good—try the panfried sand dabs (small flatfish) and pear salad with blue cheese—but the big draw is the lively atmosphere. Musicians play on Sundays in summer, and on sunny afternoons the deck gets so packed that people sit on the fence rails sipping beer. From Monday through Thursday the restaurant opens at 3. ⑤ *Average main: $20* ⊠ *3458 Shoreline Hwy.* ☎ *415/868–0434* ⊕ *www.stinsonbeachrestaurant.com* ☉ *No lunch Mon.–Thurs.*

$$ ⬛ **Sandpiper Lodging.** Recharge, rest, and enjoy the local scenery at this
B&B/INN ultra-popular lodging that books up months, even years, in advance.
FAMILY **Pros:** bright rooms; lush gardens; minutes from the beach. **Cons:** walls

are thin; some guests say motel rooms are overpriced. ⑤ *Rooms from: $145* ✉ *1 Marine Way, at Arenal Ave.* ☎ *415/868–1632* ⊕ *www. sandpiperstinsonbeach.com* ⇄ *6 rooms, 4 cabins* ❍*| No meals.*

$$
B&B/INN

🏠 **Stinson Beach Motel.** Built in the 1930s, this motel surrounds three courtyards that burst with flowering greenery, and rooms are clean, simple, and summery; the two cottages have kitchenettes. **Pros:** minutes from the beach; cozy, unpretentious rooms. **Cons:** smaller rooms are cramped; some linens need replacing. ⑤ *Rooms from: $130* ✉ *3416 Shoreline Hwy.* ☎ *415/868–1712* ⊕ *www.stinsonbeachmotel.com* ⇄ *6 rooms, 2 cottages* ❍*| No meals.*

EN ROUTE

Martin Griffin Preserve. A 1,000-acre wildlife sanctuary along the Bolinas Lagoon, this Audubon Canyon Ranch preserve gets the most traffic during late spring, when great blue herons and egrets nest in the evergreens covering the hillside. It's spectacular to see these large birds in white and gray, dotting the tops of the trees. Quiet trails through the rest of the preserve offer tremendous vistas of the Bolinas Lagoon and Stinson Beach—and fabulous birding. On weekends, "Ranch Guides" are posted throughout to point out nests—scopes are provided—and answer questions. During the week, check in at the small bookstore and take a self-guided tour. ✉ *4900 Shoreline Hwy. 1, between Stinson Beach and Bolinas* ☎ *415/868–9244* ⊕ *www.egret.org* 🎟 *Free* ⊘ *Mid-Dec.–mid-Mar.*

5

BOLINAS

7 miles north of Stinson Beach.

The tiny town of Bolinas wears its 1960s idealism on its sleeve, attracting potters, poets, and peace lovers to its quiet streets. With a funky gallery, a general store selling organic produce, a café, and an offbeat saloon, the main thoroughfare, Wharf Road, looks like a hippie-fied version of Main Street, USA.

GETTING HERE AND AROUND

Bolinas isn't difficult to find, though locals notoriously remove the street sign for their town from the highway: heading north from Stinson Beach, follow Highway 1 west and then north. Make a left at the first road just past the Bolinas Lagoon (✉ *Olema–Bolinas Road*), and then turn left at the stop sign. The road dead-ends smack-dab in the middle of town. By bus, take the 10, 70, or 80 to Marin City; in Marin City, transfer to the West Marin Stagecoach. Walking is the only way to see this small town.

WHERE TO EAT

$$
AMERICAN

✕ **Coast Cafe.** Decked out in a nautical theme with surfboards and buoys, the dining room at the Coast serves dependably good American fare, including specials such as shepherd's pie, pot roast, local fresh fish, grass-fed steaks, and gorgeous salads. Live music accompanies dinner on Thursday and Sunday. On weekends, the café is open for brunch. ⑤ *Average main: $19* ✉ *46 Wharf Rd., off Olema–Bolinas Rd.* ☎ *415/868–2298.*

POINT REYES NATIONAL SEASHORE

Bear Valley Visitor Center is 12 miles north of Bolinas.

With sandy beaches stretching for miles, a dramatic rocky coastline, a gem of a lighthouse, and idyllic, century-old dairy farms, Point Reyes National Seashore is one of the most varied and strikingly beautiful corners of the Bay Area.

GETTING HERE AND AROUND

From San Francisco, take U.S. 101 north, head west at Sir Francis Drake Boulevard (Exit 450B), and follow the road just under 20 miles to Bear Valley Road. From Stinson Beach or Bolinas, drive north on Highway 1 and turn left on Bear Valley Road. If you're going by bus, take Golden Gate Transit bus 70 to the San Rafael Transit Center and transfer to the West Marin Stagecoach, which stops at the Bear Valley Visitor Center. Allow two and a half hours for the trip.

EXPLORING

FAMILY **Bear Valley Visitor Center.** A life-size orca model hovers over the center's engaging exhibits about the wildlife and history of the Point Reyes National Seashore. The rangers at the barnlike facility are fonts of information about beaches, whale-watching, hiking trails, and camping. Winter hours may be shorter; call or check the website for details. ⊠ *Bear Valley Visitor Center Access Rd., west of Hwy. 1* ☎ *415/464–5100* ⊕ *www.nps.gov/pore/planyourvisit* ☉ *Weekdays 9–5; weekends 8–5.*

FAMILY **Duxbury Reef.** Excellent tide pooling can be had along mile-long Duxbury Reef, the largest shale intertidal reef in North America. Look for sea stars, barnacles, sea anemones, purple urchins, limpets, sea mussels, and the occasional abalone. But check a tide table (⊕ *www.wrh. noaa.gov/mtr/marine.php*) or the local papers if you plan to explore the reef—it's accessible only at low tide. The reef is a 30-minute drive from the Bear Valley Visitor Center. Take Highway 1 south from the center, turn right at Olema-Bolinas Road (keep an eye peeled; the road is easy to miss), left on Horsehoe Hill Road, right on Mesa Road, left on Overlook Drive, and then right on Elm Road, which dead-ends at the Agate Beach County Park parking lot.

FAMILY **Point Blue Conservation Science.** Birders adore Point Blue (formerly the Point Reyes Bird Observatory), which lies in the southernmost part of Point Reyes National Seashore and is accessed through Bolinas. (Those not interested in birds might find it ho-hum.) The unstaffed Palomarin Field Station, open daily from sunrise to sunset, has excellent interpretive exhibits, including a comparative display of real birds' talons. The surrounding woods harbor more than 200 bird species. As you hike the quiet trails through forest and along ocean cliffs, you're likely to see biologists banding birds to aid in the study of their life cycles. ■ TIP→ Visit Point Blue's website to find out when banding will occur; it's a fun time to come here. ⊠ *Mesa Rd., Bolinas* ☎ *415/868–0655* ⊕ *www.pointblue.org* ⊠ *Free* ☉ *Daily sunrise–sunset.*

FAMILY

Fodor's Choice

★

Point Reyes Lighthouse. In operation since December 1, 1870, this light-house is one of the premier attractions of the Point Reyes National Seashore. It occupies the tip of Point Reyes, 22 miles from the Bear Valley Visitor Center, a scenic 45-minute drive over hills scattered with longtime dairy farms. The lighthouse originally cast a rotating beam lighted by four wicks that burned lard oil. Keeping the wicks lighted and the 6,000-pound Fresnel lens soot-free in Point Reyes's perpetually foggy climate was a constant struggle that reputedly drove the early attendants to alcoholism and insanity. ■ TIP→ The lighthouse is one of the best spots on the coast for watching gray whales: on both legs of their annual migration, the magnificent animals pass close enough to see with the naked eye. Southern migration peaks in mid-January, and the whales head back north in March; see the slower mothers and calves in late April and early May.

On busy whale-watching weekends (from late December through mid-April), buses shuttle visitors from the Drakes Beach parking lot to the top of the stairs leading down to the lighthouse (🚌 Bus $5, admission free) and the road is closed to private vehicles. However you've arrived, consider whether you have it in you to walk down—and up—the 308 steps to the lighthouse. The view from the bottom is worth the effort, but the whales are visible from the cliffs above the lighthouse. ⊠ Visitor Center, Western end of Sir Francis Drake Blvd., Inverness ☎ 415/669–1534 ☉ Fri.–Mon. 10–4:30; weather lens room 2:30–4, except during very windy weather.

Fodor's Choice

★

Point Reyes National Seashore. One of the Bay Area's most spectacular treasures and the only national seashore on the West Coast, the 66,500-acre Point Reyes National Seashore encompasses hiking trails, secluded beaches, and rugged grasslands as well as Point Reyes itself, a triangular peninsula that juts into the Pacific. The town of **Point Reyes Station** is a quaint, one-main-drag affair, with a charming bakery, some good gift shops with locally made and imported goods, and a few places to eat. It's nothing fancy, but that's part of its relaxed charm.

When explorer Sir Francis Drake sailed along the California coast in 1579, he missed the Golden Gate and San Francisco Bay, but he did land at what he described as a convenient harbor. In 2012 the federal government finally officially recognized Drake's Bay, which flanks the point on the east, as that harbor, designating the spot a National Historic Landmark and silencing competing claims in the 433-year-old controversy. Today Point Reyes's hills and dramatic cliffs attract other kinds of explorers: hikers, whale-watchers, and solitude seekers.

The infamous San Andreas Fault runs along the eastern edge of the park and up the center of Tomales Bay; take the short **Earthquake Trail** from the visitor center to see the impact near the epicenter of the 1906 earthquake that devastated San Francisco. A ½-mile path from the visitor center leads to **Kule Loklo**, a brilliantly reconstructed Miwok village that sheds light on the daily lives of the region's first inhabitants. From here, trails also lead to the park's free, hike-in campgrounds (camping permits are required).

■**TIP➔** In late winter and spring, take the short walk at Chimney Rock, just before the lighthouse, to the Elephant Seal Overlook. Even from the cliff, the male seals look enormous as they spar, growling and bloodied, for resident females.

You can experience the diversity of Point Reyes's ecosystems on the scenic **Coast Trail**, which starts at the Palomarin Trailhead, just outside Bolinas. From here, it's a 3-mile trek through eucalyptus groves and pine forests and along seaside cliffs to beautiful and tiny Bass Lake. To reach the Palomarin Trailhead, take Olema–Bolinas Road toward Bolinas, follow signs to Point Blue Conservation Science, and then continue until the road dead-ends.

The 4.7-mile-long (one-way) **Tomales Point Trail** follows the spine of the park's northernmost finger of land through a Tule Elk Preserve, providing spectacular ocean views from the high bluffs. Expect to see elk, but keep your distance from the animals. To reach the fairly easy hiking trail, look for the Pierce Point Road turnoff on the right, just north of the town of Inverness; park at the end of the road by the old ranch buildings. ⊠ *Bear Valley Visitor Center, Bear Valley Visitor Center Access Rd., off Hwy. 1, Point Reyes Station* ☎ *415/464–5100* ⊕ *www.nps.gov/pore.*

WHERE TO EAT

$$ ✕ **Osteria Stellina.** The vaguely industrial-chic overtones of this West
ITALIAN Marin star's otherwise rustic-contemporary decor hint at the panache
Fodor's Choice that enlivens chef-owner Christian Caiazzo's "Point Reyes Italian" cui-
★ sine. The emphasis on locally sourced ingredients makes for ingenious combinations—oysters harvested just a few miles away, for instance, anchor a pizza with leeks braised in cream from Marin and Sonoma cows and garnished with parsley and lemon thyme. Pastas and pizzas dominate the menu, which might contain as few as two entrées for lunch and a handful for dinner. The hit at lunch, tomato minestra, is a lightly spiced seafood concoction reminiscent of gumbo; dinner might include osso buco that pairs Niman Ranch veal with Marin-grown kale, or braised goat with greens from Stellina's own farm. ⑤ *Average main: $19* ⊠ *11285 Hwy. 1, at 3rd St., Point Reyes Station* ☎ *415/663–9988* ⊕ *www.osteriastellina.com* ⊗ *Closed Thurs.*

$$$ ✕ **Station House Cafe.** In good weather, hikers fresh from the park fill
AMERICAN the Station House's garden to enjoy alfresco dining, and on weekends there's not a spare seat on the banquettes in the dining room, so prepare for a wait. The focus is on local, seasonal, and sustainable food: oyster shooters, Niman Ranch braised lamb, Californian white sea bass, and sweet bread pudding are the standbys. The place is also open for breakfast, and there's a full bar. ⑤ *Average main: $30* ⊠ *11180 Hwy. 1, Point Reyes Station* ☎ *415/663–1515* ⊕ *www.stationhousecafe.com* ⊗ *Closed Wed.*

$$$ ✕ **Tomales Bay Foods.** A renovated hay barn off the main drag houses this
AMERICAN collection of food shops, a favorite stopover among Bay Area foodies.
FAMILY Watch workers making Cowgirl Creamery cheese; then buy some at a counter that sells exquisite artisanal cheeses from around the world. Tomales Bay Foods showcases local organic fruits and vegetables and

premium packaged foods, and the kitchen turns the best ingredients into creative sandwiches, salads, and soups. You can eat at a small café table or the picnic areas outside. ⑤ *Average main: $23* ⊠ *80 4th St., at B St., Point Reyes Station* ☎ *415/663–9335 cheese shop* ⊕ *No dinner* ⊘ *Closed Mon. and Tues.*

WHERE TO STAY

$$
B&B/INN
FAMILY

🏠 **Cottages at Point Reyes Seashore.** Amid a 15-acre valley on the north end of town, this secluded getaway offers spacious one- and two-bedroom cabins with fireplaces and patios perfect for sunset barbecues and leisurely breakfasts. **Pros:** spacious accommodations; great place to bring kids. **Cons:** 3-plus miles from downtown Inverness; small pool. ⑤ *Rooms from: $160* ⊠ *13275 Sir Francis Drake Blvd., Inverness* ☎ *415/669–7250, 800/406–0405* ⊕ *www.cottagespointreyes.com* ⟿ *20 cabins* ❙⊚❙ *No meals.*

$$$$
B&B/INN

🏠 **Manka's Inverness Lodge.** Chef-owner Margaret Grade takes rustic fantasy to extravagant heights in her 1917 hunting lodge and cabins, where mica-shaded lamps cast an amber glow, and bearskin rugs warm wide-planked floors. **Pros:** extremely romantic, remote and quiet. **Cons:** no on-site restaurant; sounds from neighboring rooms are easily heard; some question the value for the price. ⑤ *Rooms from: $365* ⊠ *30 Callendar Way, at Argyle Way, Inverness* ☎ *415/669–1034* ⊕ *www.mankas. com* ⟿ *5 rooms, 2 suites, 1 boathouse, 2 cabins.*

$$
B&B/INN

🏠 **Ten Inverness Way.** This is the kind of down-to-earth place where you sit around after breakfast and share tips for hiking Point Reyes or linger around the living room and its stone fireplace and library. **Pros:** great base for exploring the nearby wilderness; peaceful garden and friendly staff. **Cons:** overly folksy decor; some rooms are on the small side; poor cell-phone reception. ⑤ *Rooms from: $170* ⊠ *10 Inverness Way, Inverness* ☎ *415/669–1648* ⊕ *www.teninvernessway.com* ⟿ *5 rooms* ❙⊚❙ *Breakfast.*

SPORTS AND THE OUTDOORS

Blue Waters Kayaking. This outfit rents kayaks ($50 for two hours), stand-up paddleboards ($25 for one hour), and electric bikes ($30 for one hour, $10 for each additional hour) and offers tours and lessons. ⊠ *12944 Sir Francis Drake Blvd., Inverness* ☎ *415/669–2600* ⊕ *www. bwkayak.com.*

Five Brooks Stable. Tour guides here lead private and group horse rides lasting from one to six hours; trails from the stable wind through Point Reyes National Seashore and along the beaches. ⊠ *8001 Hwy. 1, north of town, Olema* ☎ *415/663–1570* ⊕ *www.fivebrooks.com* ⊠ *From $40.*

THE WINE
COUNTRY

WELCOME TO WINE COUNTRY

TOP REASONS TO GO

★ **Biking:** Cycling is one of the best ways to see the Wine Country—the Russian River and Dry Creek valleys, in Sonoma County, are particularly beautiful.

★ **Browsing the farmers' markets:** Many towns in Napa and Sonoma have seasonal farmers' markets, each rounding up an amazing variety of local produce.

★ **Wandering di Rosa:** Though this art and nature preserve is just off the busy Carneros Highway, it's a relatively unknown treasure. The galleries and gardens are filled with hundreds of artworks.

★ **Canoeing on the Russian River:** Trade in your car keys for a paddle and glide down the Russian River in Sonoma County. From May through October is the best time to be on the water.

★ **Touring Wineries:** Let's face it: this is the reason you're here, and the range of excellent sips to sample would make any oeno-phile (or novice drinker, for that matter) giddy.

1 Napa Valley.
You'll find big names all around, from high-profile wineries to world-renowned chefs. Napa, the valley's oldest town, sweet-life St. Helena, and down-to-earth Calistoga all make good home bases here. Calistoga has the extra draw of local thermal springs. Yountville has become a culinary boomtown, while the tiny communities of Oakville and Rutherford are home to major wineries such as Robert Mondavi and Beaulieu. Rutherford in particular is the source for outstanding Cabernet Sauvignon.

2 Sonoma Valley.
Historic attractions and an unpretentious attitude prevail here. The town of Sonoma, with its picture-perfect central plaza, is rich with 19th-century buildings. Glen Ellen, meanwhile, has a special connection with author Jack London.

GETTING ORIENTED

The Napa and Sonoma valleys run roughly parallel, northwest to southeast, and are separated by the Mayacamas Mountains. Northwest of the Sonoma Valley are several more important viticultural areas in Sonoma County, including the Dry Creek, Alexander, and Russian River valleys. The Carneros region, which spans southern Sonoma and Napa counties, is just north of San Pablo Bay.

6

3 Elsewhere in Sonoma.
The winding, rural roads here feel a world away from Napa's main drag. The Russian River, Dry Creek, and Alexander valleys are all excellent places to seek out Pinot Noir, Zinfandel, and Sauvignon Blanc. The small town of Healdsburg gets lots of attention, thanks to its terrific restaurants, bed-and-breakfasts, and chic boutiques.

Updated by
Daniel Mangin

Life is lived well in California's premiere wine-making region, where eating and drinking are cultivated as high arts. Prestigious wineries can be found in the Napa Valley and in Sonoma County's Russian River, Dry Creek, and Sonoma valleys, and boutique operations flourish throughout. Marquee chefs preside over restaurants everywhere, though the largest concentrations are in the Napa Valley's Yountville and St. Helena and the Sonoma County towns of Sonoma and Healdsburg. The food fest continues at shops and farmers' markets selling artisanal produce, olive oils, cheeses, charcuterie, and baked goods.

The Wine Country is also rich in history. In Sonoma you can explore California's Spanish and Mexican pasts at the Sonoma Mission, and the origins of modern California wine making at Buena Vista Winery. Well before the mission or the wineries existed, Native Americans bathed in the hot mineral waters on the site now occupied by the Fairmont Sonoma Mission Inn & Spa. Some wineries, among them St. Helena's Beringer and Rutherford's Inglenook, have cellars or tasting rooms dating to the late 1800s. Calistoga is a flurry of late-19th-century Steamboat Gothic architecture, though the town's oldest-looking building, the medieval-style Castello di Amorosa, is a 21st-century creation.

Tours at the Napa Valley's Beringer, Mondavi, and Inglenook—and at Buena Vista in the Sonoma Valley—provide an entertaining overview of Wine Country history. The tour at the splashy visitor center at St. Helena's Hall winery will introduce you to 21st-century wine-making technology, and over in Glen Ellen's Benziger Family Winery you can see how its vineyard managers apply biodynamic farming principles to grape growing. At numerous facilities you can play winemaker for a day at seminars in the fine art of blending wines.

If blending strikes you as too much work, fear not. Sit-down tastings that pair food and wine—all the rage these days—provide an elegant way to experience the lifestyle that attracted so many vintners and chefs here in the first place. If even that sounds too much effort, you can always pamper yourself at a luxury spa. To delve further into the fine art of Wine Country living, grab a copy of *Fodor's InFocus Napa & Sonoma.*

PLANNING

WHEN TO GO

"Crush," the term used to indicate the time when grapes are picked and crushed, usually takes place in September or October, depending on the weather. From September until November the Wine Country celebrates its bounty with street fairs and festivals. The Sonoma County Harvest Fair, with its famous grape stomp, is held on the first weekend in October. Wine auctions and art and food fairs occur from spring through fall.

The Wine Country is usually hot and dry all summer and into autumn, so dress appropriately if you visit during these seasons. From May through November the Napa Valley draws crowds of tourists, and traffic along Highway 29 from St. Helena to Calistoga often backs up on weekends. The Sonoma Valley and northern Sonoma County are less crowded, though even that's changing. To avoid crowds, visit during the week. Because many wineries close as early as 4 or 4:30—and few are open past 5—you'll need to get a reasonably early start if you want to fit in more than one or two, especially if you're going to enjoy the leisurely lunch customary in these parts. Keep in mind that many wineries require appointments for tastings and most do so for tours.

GETTING HERE AND AROUND
AIR TRAVEL

Wine Country regulars often bypass San Francisco and Oakland and fly into Santa Rosa's Charles M. Schulz Sonoma County Airport (STS) on Alaska Airlines, which has nonstop flights from San Diego, Los Angeles, Portland, and Seattle. Avis, Budget, Enterprise, Hertz, and National rent cars here. ■ TIP→ Alaska allows passengers flying out of STS to check up to one case of wine for free.

BUS TRAVEL

Bus travel is an inconvenient way to explore the Wine Country. Greyhound and Golden Gate Transit travel from San Francisco to Petaluma and Santa Rosa, where you can transfer to Sonoma County Transit buses, but connections aren't always smooth. VINE provides service in the Napa Valley; the San Francisco Bay Ferry *(see Ferry Travel, below)* is the easiest way to connect with the VINE network from San Francisco.

Bus Lines Golden Gate Transit ☎ *415/455–2000* ⊕ *www.goldengatetransit.org.* **Greyhound** ☎ *800/231–2222* ⊕ *www.greyhound.com.* **Sonoma County Transit** ☎ *707/576–7433, 800/345–7433* ⊕ *www.sctransit.com.* **VINE** ☎ *707/251–2800, 800/696–6443* ⊕ *www.ridethevine.com.*

CAR TRAVEL

Driving your own car is by far the most convenient way to explore the Wine Country. Distances between towns are fairly short, and in normal traffic you can drive from one end of the Napa or Sonoma valley to the other in less than an hour. Although this is a mostly rural area, the usual rush hours still apply, and high-season weekend traffic can often be slow.

Five major roads serve the region. U.S. 101 and Highways 12 and 121 travel through Sonoma County. Highway 29 and the parallel, more scenic, and often less crowded Silverado Trail travel north–south between Napa and Calistoga.

The easiest way to travel from Napa Valley to Sonoma County is along Highway 12/121 to the south, or Highway 128 to the north. Travel between the middle sections of either area requires taking the slow, winding drive over the Mayacamas Mountains on the Oakville Grade, which links Oakville, in Napa, and Glen Ellen, in Sonoma.

■TIP➜ If you're wine tasting, either select a designated driver or be careful of your wine intake—the police keep an eye out for tipsy drivers.

From San Francisco to Napa: Cross the Golden Gate Bridge, then go north on U.S. 101. Head east on Highway 37 toward Vallejo, then north on Highway 121, aka the Carneros Highway. Turn left (north) when Highway 121 runs into Highway 29. This should take about an hour in light traffic.

From San Francisco to Sonoma: Cross the Golden Gate Bridge, then go north on U.S. 101, east on Highway 37 toward Vallejo, and north on Highway 121. When you reach Highway 12, take it north to the town of Sonoma. This trip takes about an hour in light traffic. For Sonoma County destinations north of Sonoma Valley stay on U.S. 101, which passes through Santa Rosa and Healdsburg.

From Berkeley and Oakland: Take Interstate 80 north to Highway 37 west, then on to Highway 29 north. For the Napa Valley, continue on Highway 29; to reach Sonoma County, head west on Highway 121. The trip from Berkeley or Oakland to Napa takes about 50 minutes in normal traffic, to Sonoma about an hour.

FERRY TRAVEL

The San Francisco Bay Ferry sails from the Ferry Building and Pier 41 in San Francisco to Vallejo, where you can board a VINE bus to Napa. Buses sometimes fill in for the ferries.

Contact San Francisco Bay Ferry ☎ *510/522–3300* ⊕ *sanfranciscobayferry.com.*

RESTAURANTS

Excellent meals can be found in all the major Wine Country towns, but tiny Yountville has become a culinary crossroads under the influence of chef Thomas Keller. In St. Helena the elegant Restaurant at Meadowood has achieved almost as much critical acclaim as Keller's French Laundry, yet is easier to get into. And the buzzed-about restaurants in Sonoma County, including Glen Ellen Star and the Farmhouse Inn, offer plenty of mouthwatering options.

If you're on a budget, many high-end delis prepare superb picnic fare. Stopping for lunch or brunch can be a cost-effective strategy at pricey restaurants, as can sitting at the bar and ordering appetizers instead of having a full meal.

Except as noted in individual restaurant listings, dress is informal. Where reservations are indicated as essential, book a week or more ahead in summer and early fall.

HOTELS

Wine Country inns and hotels range from low-key to sumptuous, and generally maintain high standards. Many inns are in historic Victorian buildings, and when rates include breakfast the preparations often involve fresh local produce. The newer hotels tend to have a more modern, streamlined aesthetic and elaborate, spa-like bathrooms, and many have excellent restaurants on-site.

Accommodations generally have lower rates on weeknights, and prices are about 20% lower in winter. The towns of Napa and Santa Rosa have the widest selection of moderately priced rooms. On weekends, two- or even three-night minimum stays are commonly required at smaller lodgings. Book well ahead for stays at such places during the busy summer or fall season. If your party will include travelers under age 16, inquire about policies regarding younger guests; some smaller lodgings discourage (or discreetly forbid) children.

The Napa Valley Hotels & Resorts page on the Visit Napa Valley website lists hotels, inns, and other accommodations throughout Napa County. The members of the Sonoma Valley Bed & Breakfast Association operate noteworthy small inns and vacation-rental properties throughout the valley; Wine Country Inns represents small lodgings throughout Sonoma County. *Hotel reviews have been shortened. For full information, visit Fodors.com.*

Contacts Napa Valley Hotels & Resorts ☎ 707/251-9188, 855/333-6272 ⊕ www.visitnapavalley.com/napa_valley_hotels.htm. **Wine Country Inns** ✉ Cloverdale ☎ 800/946-3268 ⊕ www.winecountryinns.com.

WHAT IT COSTS				
	$	$$	$$$	$$$$
Restaurants	under $16	$16–$22	$23–$30	over $30
Hotels	under $121	$121–$300	$301–$400	over $400

Restaurant prices are the average cost of a main course at dinner or, if dinner is not served, at lunch. Hotel prices are for the lowest cost of a standard double room in high season.

TOURS

Whether you want to tour wineries in a van or bus along with other passengers or spring for a private limo, there are plenty of operators who can accommodate you. Tours generally last from five to seven hours and stop at four or five wineries. Rates vary—from $80 to $100 per person to $250 or more, depending on the vehicle and whether the tour includes other guests. Some include lunch and tasting and other fees, but not all do, so ask. On most tours, at least one of the day's stops includes a behind-the-scenes look at wine-production facilities and the chance to meet winemakers or others involved in the wine-making process. Most tour operators will pick you up at Wine Country hotels or a specified meeting place.

Fodor's Choice
★
Perata Luxury Tours & Car Services. Perata's customized private tours, led by well-trained, knowledgeable drivers, are tailored to its patrons' interests—you can create your own itinerary or have your guide craft one for you. Tours, in luxury SUVs, cover Napa and Sonoma. The options include exclusive, appointment-only boutique wineries. ☎ 707/227–8271 ⊕ *www.perataluxurycarservices.com* ✉ *From $325 per day, plus fuel surcharge ($25–$35), tasting fees, and 18% gratuity charge.*

Fodor's Choice
★
Platypus Wine Tours. The emphasis at Platypus is on "fun" experiences at off-the-beaten-path wineries. Expect intimate winery experiences with jolly, well-informed guides. You can join an existing tour with other guests or book a private one. ☎ 707/253–2723 ⊕ *www.platypustours. com* ✉ *From $99, excluding tasting fees.*

Valley Wine Tours. Historic, family-owned wineries are the specialty of this Sonoma-based company that provides a gourmet picnic lunch—on china with cloth napkins, no less. The Valley Wine tour rate includes tasting fees. ☎ 707/975–6462 ⊕ *www.valleywinetours.com* ✉ *From $135.*

Woody's Wine Tours. The amiable, well-informed Woody Guderian favors small wineries but will customize a tour to suit your taste and budget. In addition to winery tours in both Napa and Sonoma, Woody also conducts tours of local craft breweries. ☎ 707/396–8235 ⊕ *www. woodyswinetours.com* ✉ *From $80 per hr, excluding tasting fees.*

VISITOR INFORMATION

Pre-Trip Planning Visit Napa Valley ☎ *707/251–5895* ⊕ *www.visitnapavalley. com.* **Visit Sonoma** ☎ *707/522–5800, 800/576–6662* ⊕ *www.sonomacounty.com.*

Visitor Centers California Welcome Center ✉ *9 4th St., at Wilson St., Santa Rosa* ☎ *800/404–7673* ⊕ *www.visitcalifornia.com/california-welcome-centers/ santa-rosa.* **Napa Valley Welcome Center** ✉ *600 Main St., at 5th St., Napa* ☎ *707/251–5895* ⊕ *www.visitnapavalley.com/welcome_centers.htm.* **Sonoma Valley Visitors Center** ✉ *453 1st St. E, east side of Sonoma Plaza, Sonoma* ☎ *707/996–1090, 866/996–1090* ⊕ *www.sonomavalley.com.*

THE NAPA VALLEY

With more than 450 wineries and many of the biggest brands in the business, the Napa Valley is the Wine Country's star. But what's the area like beyond the glossy advertising and boldface names? The small towns strung along Highway 29 are where many wine-industry workers live, and they're where most of the lodging is. Napa—population 78,340 and the valley's largest town—lures with its cultural attractions and (relatively) reasonably priced accommodations. A few miles farther north, compact Yountville is densely packed with top-notch restaurants and hotels, and Rutherford and Oakville are renowned for their Cabernet Sauvignon–friendly soils (Merlot, too). Beyond them, St. Helena teems

Continued on page 324

Napa Valley

Mount Helena

Robert Louis Stevenson State Park

Aetna Springs

THE PALISADES

29
35
3
34
28
29

Calistoga
32
31

Dunaweal Ln.

Howell Mtn Rd.

Larkmead Ln.

Pope Valley

POPE VALLEY

Lake Berryessa

Angwin
Angwin Airport

Lake Berryessa Recreation Area

Bothe Napa State Park
30
29

Petrified Forest Rd.

Diamond Mountain

NOMA OUNTY

Bale Grist Mill State Historic Park

29 128

26
28

Deer Park
Sanitarium Rd.

NAPA COUNTY

Knoxville Rd.

Lake Hennessy

Chiles Pope Valley Rd.

Sage Canyon Rd.

128

Lake Hennessy City Recreation Area

Atlas Peak

FOSS VALLEY

27
Saint Helena

Sugarloaf Ridge State Park

24
23

NAPA

Silverado Trail

128

llood Mountain Regional Park

Adobe Canyon Rd.

Sonoma Hwy.

12

Bald Mountain

Mt St. John

25

21
22
18
17
13
19
20
16

Rutherford

Oakville

Oakville Grade Rd.

14
15

Yountville Hills

10
9

Yountville

12
11

Silverado Trail

Napa River

Oak Knoll

nnadel ate Park

Kenwood

Trinity Rd.

Mt Veeder

VALLEY

Glen Ellen

SONOMA VALLEY

12

Agua Caliente

Boyes Hot Springs

Sonoma Mountain

Jack London State Park

SONOMA MOUNTAINS

Arnold Dr.

VALLEY OF THE MOON

Sonoma

Napa Rd.

RENWOOD CANYON

Dry Creek Rd.

CARNEROS VALLEY

8
Redwood Rd.

Browns Valley Rd.

4
Dealy La.

Carneros Valley Henry Rd.

29

7
St. Clair Brown Winery

Big Ranch Rd.

Trancas St.
Pueblo
6
5
Lincoln

Napa

121

Old Sonoma Rd.

12

Imola Ave.

Adobe Rd.

Lakeville Hwy.

aluma

01

Bonness Rd.

Carneros Hwy.

116

121

12

12 121

Naha Rd.

1
2
3

29

0   4 mi

0   4 km

Napa County Airport

WINE TASTING *in* NAPA *and* SONOMA

VISITING WINERIES

Napa and Sonoma are outstanding destinations for both wine newcomers and serious wine buffs. Tasting rooms range from modest to swanky, offering everything from a casual conversation over a few sips of wine to in-depth tours of wine-making facilities and vineyards. And there's a tremendous variety of wines to taste. The one constant is a deep, shared pleasure in the experience of wine tasting.

Wineries in Napa and Sonoma range from faux châteaus with vast gift shops to rustic converted barns where you might have to step over the vintner's dog in the doorway. Many are regularly open to the public, usually daily from around 10 am to 5 pm. Others require reservations to visit, and still others are closed to the public entirely. When in doubt, call ahead.

There are many, many more wineries in Napa and Sonoma than we could possibly include here. Free maps pinpointing most of them are widely available, though; ask the staff at the tasting rooms you visit or look for the ubiquitous free tourist magazines.

Pick a designated driver before setting out for the day. Although wineries rarely advertise it, many will provide a free nonalcoholic drink for the designated driver; it never hurts to ask.

Fees. In the past few years, tasting fees have skyrocketed. Most Napa wineries charge $20 or $25 to taste four or so wines, though $35, $45 or even $65 fees aren't unheard of. Sonoma wineries are often a bit cheaper, in the $10 to $25 range, and you'll still find the occasional freebie.

Some winery tours are free, in which case you're usually required to pay a separate fee if you want to taste the wine. If you've paid a fee for the tour—often $20 to $40—your wine tasting is usually included in that price.

he tantalizing pop of a cork. oads unspooling through hypotically even rows of vines. Sun linting through a glass of sparling wine or ruby colored caberet. If these are your daydreams, ou won't be disappointed when ou get to Napa and Sonoma. The neyard-blanketed hills, shady wn squares, and ivy-draped winies—not to mention the luxurious staurants, hotels, and spas— ally *are* that captivating.

posite page) Carneros vineyards in autumn, Napa ley. (top) Pinot Gris grapes (bottom) Bottles from Niente winery.

6

IN FOCUS WINE TASTING IN NAPA AND SONOMA

MAKING THE MOST OF YOUR TIME

(top) Sipping and swirling in the De Loach tasting room. (bottom) Learning about barrel aging at Robert Mondavi Winery.

■**Call ahead.** Some wineries require reservations to visit or tour and others are closed to the public entirely. It's wise to check before visiting.

■**Come on weekdays,** especially if you're visiting during high season (May to November), to avoid traffic-clogged roads and crowded tasting rooms. For more info on the best times of year to visit, see this chapter's Planner.

■**Get an early start.** Tasting rooms are often deserted before 11 am or so, when most visitors are still lingering over a second cup of coffee. If you come early, you'll have the staff's undivided attention. You'll usually encounter the largest crowds between 3 and 5 pm.

■**Consider skipping Napa.** If you've got less than two days to spend in the Wine Country, dip into the Carneros area or the Sonoma Valley rather than Napa Valley or northern Sonoma County. Though you might find fewer big-name wineries and critically acclaimed res-

taurants, these regions are only about an hour away from San Francisco . . . if you don't hit traffic.

■**Divide your attention.** If you're lucky enough to have three nights or more here, split your overnights between Napa and Sonoma to easily see the best that both counties have to offer.

Domaine Carneros.

AT THE BAR

In most tasting rooms, you'll be handed a list of the wines available that day. The wines will be listed in a suggested tasting order, starting with the lightest-bodied whites, progressing to the most intense reds, and ending with dessert wines. If you can't decide which wines to choose, tell the server what types of wines you usually like and ask for a recommendation.

The server will pour you an ounce or so of each wine you select. As you taste it, feel free to take notes or ask questions. Don't be shy—the staff are there to educate you about the wine. If you don't like a wine, or you've simply tasted enough, feel free to pour the rest into one of the dump buckets on the bar.

TOURS

Tours tend to be the most exciting (and the most crowded) in September and October, when the harvest and crushing are underway. Tours typically last from 30 minutes to an hour and give you a brief overview of the wine-making process. At some of the older wineries, the tour guide might focus on the history of the property.

■ TIP→ If you plan to take any tours, wear comfortable shoes, since you might be walking on wet floors or dirt or gravel pathways or stepping over hoses or other equipment.

MONEY-SAVING TIPS

■ Many hotels and B&Bs distribute coupons for free or discounted tastings to their guests—don't forget to ask.

■ If you and your travel partner don't mind sharing a glass, servers are happy to let you split a tasting.

■ Some wineries will refund all or part of the tasting fee if you buy a bottle. Usually one fee is waived per bottle purchased, though sometimes you must buy two or more.

■ Most wineries will waive the fee if you join their wine club program. This typically commits you to buying a certain number of bottles on a regular basis, so be sure you really like the wines before signing up.

Preston Vineyards bottles only estate-grown grapes.

TOP 2-DAY ITINERARIES

First-Timer's Napa Tour

Start: Oxbow Public market, Napa. Get underway by browsing the shops selling wines, spices, locally grown produce, and other fine foods, for a taste of what the Wine Country has to offer.

Inglenook, Rutherford. The tour here is a particularly fun way to learn about the history

of Napa winemaking—and you can see the old, atmospheric, ivy-covered château.

Frog's Leap, Rutherford. Its friendly, unpretentious, and knowledgeable staff makes this place great for wine newbies. (Make sure you get that reservation lined up.)

Dinner and Overnight: St. Helena. Splurge at Meadowood Napa Valley and you won't need to leave the property for

Domaine Carneros

di Rosa Preserve

Old Sonoma Rd.

121
12

Oxbow Public Market
Napa
29

NAPA COUNTY

Rob Mond

Far Niente
Yountville
Oakville

KEY
First-Timer's Napa Tour
Wine Buff's Tour

Silverado Trail

Stag's Leap Wine Cellars

Wine Buff's Tour

Start: Stag's Leap Wine Cellars, Yountville. Famed for its Cabernet Sauvignon and Bordeaux blends.

Beaulieu Vineyard, Rutherford. Pony up the extra fee to visit the reserve tasting room to try the flagship Cabernet Sauvignon.

Mumm Napa, Rutherford. Come for the bubbly—which is available in a variety of tastings—stay for the photography exhibits.

Dinner and Overnight: Yountville. Have dinner at one of the Thomas Keller restaurants. Splurge at Bardessono; save at

Maison Fleurie.

Next Day: Robert Mondavi, Oakville. Spring for the reserve room tasting so you can sip the top-of-the-line wines, especially the Cabernet Sauvignon. Head across Highway 29 to the Oakville Grocery to pick up a picnic lunch.

an extravagant dinner at its restaurant. Save at El Bonita Motel with dinner at Gott's.

Next Day: Poke around St. Helena's shops, then drive to Yountville for lunch.

di Rosa, Napa. Call ahead to book a one- or two-hour tour of the acres of gardens and galleries here

showcasing about 2,000 artworks.

Domaine Carneros, Napa. Toast your trip with a glass of outstanding bubbly.

Sonoma Backroads

Start: Iron Horse Vineyards, Russian River Valley. Soak up a view of vine-covered hills and Mount St. Helena while sipping a sparkling wine or Pinot Noir at this beautifully rustic spot.

Hartford Family Winery, Russian River Valley. A terrific source for Pinot Noir and Chardonnay, the stars of this valley.

Dinner and Overnight: Forestville. Go all out with a stay at the Farmhouse Inn, whose award-winning restaurant is one of the best in all of Sonoma.

Next Day: Westside Road, Russian River Valley. This scenic route, which follows the river, is crowded with worthwhile wineries like Gary Farrell and Rochioli—but it's not crowded with visitors. Pinot fans will find a lot to love.

Matanzas Creek Winery, near Santa Rosa. End on an especially relaxed note with a walk through the lavender fields (best in June).

ar Niente, Oakville. ou have to make a eservation and the ee for the tasting and ur is steep, but the

payoff is an especially intimate winery experience. You'll taste excellent Cabernet and Chardonnay, then end your trip on a sweet note with a dessert wine.

WINE TASTING 101

TAKE A GOOD LOOK.
Hold your glass by the stem, raise it to the light, and take a close look at the wine. Check for clarity and color. (This is easiest to do if you can hold the glass in front of a white background.) Any tinge of brown usually means that the wine is over the hill or has gone bad.

BREATHE DEEP.
1. Sniff the wine once or twice to see if you can identify any smells.

2. Swirl the wine gently in the glass. Aerating the wine this way releases more of its aromas. (It's called "volatilizing the esters," if you're trying to impress someone.)

3. Take another long sniff. You might notice that experienced wine tasters spend more time sniffing the wine than drinking it. This is because this step is where the magic happens. The number of scents you might detect is almost endless, from berries, apricots, honey, and wildflowers to leather, cedar, or even tar. Does the wine smell good to you? Do you detect any "off" flavors, like wet dog or sulfur?

AT LAST! TAKE A SIP.
1. Swirl the wine around your mouth so that it makes contact with all your taste buds and releases more of its aromas. Think about the way the wine feels in your mouth. Is it watery or rich? Is it crisp or silky? Does it have a bold flavor, or is it subtle? The weight and intensity of a wine are called its body.

2. Hold the wine in your mouth for a few seconds and see if you can identify any developing flavors. More complex wines will reveal many different flavors as you drink them.

SPIT OR SWALLOW.
The pros typically spit, since they want to preserve their palate (and sobriety!) for the wines to come, but you'll find that swallowers far outnumber the spitters in the winery tasting rooms. Whether you spit or swallow, notice the flavor that remains after the wine is gone (the finish).

Sniff

Sip

DODGE THE CROWDS

To avoid bumping elbows in the tasting rooms, look for wineries off the main drags of Highway 29 in Napa and Highway 12 in Sonoma. The back roads of the Russian River, Dry Creek, and Alexander valleys, all in Sonoma, are excellent places to explore. In Napa, try the northern end. Also look for wineries that are open by appointment only; they tend to schedule visitors carefully to avoid a big crush at any one time.

HOW WINE IS MADE

1. CRUSHING
Harvested grapes go into a stemmer-crusher, which separates stems from fruit and crushes the grapes to release "free-run" juice.

2. PRESSING
Remaining juice is gently extracted from grapes. Usually done by pressing grapes against the walls of a tank with an inflatable bladder.

3. FERMENTING
Extracted juice (and also grape skins and pulp, when making red wine) goes into stainless-steel tanks or oak barrels to ferment. During fermentation, sugars convert to alcohol.

4. AGING
Wine is stored in stainless-steel or oak casks or barrels to develop flavors.

5. RACKING
Wine is transferred to clean barrels; sediment is removed. Wine may be filtered and fined (clarified) to improve its clarity, color, and sometimes flavor.

6. BOTTLING
Wine is bottled either at the winery or at a special facility, then stored again for bottle-aging.

WHAT'S AN APPELLATION?

A specific region with a particular set of grape-growing conditions, such as soil type, climate, and elevation, is called an appellation. What makes things a little confusing is that appellations, which are defined by the Alcohol and Tobacco Tax and Trade Bureau, often overlap. California is an appellation, for example, but so is the Napa Valley. Napa and Sonoma counties are each county appellations, but they, too, are divided into even smaller regions, usually called subappellations or AVAs (American Viticultural Areas). You'll hear a lot about these AVAs from the staff in the tasting rooms; they might explain, for example, why the Russian River Valley AVA is such an excellent place to grow Pinot Noir grapes.

By law, if the label on a bottle of wine lists the name of an appellation, then at least 85% of the grapes in that wine must come from that appellation.

with elegant boutiques and restaurants, and casual Calistoga, known for spas and hot springs, has the feel of an Old West frontier town.

NAPA

46 miles northeast of San Francisco

Visitors who glimpse Napa's malls and big-box stores from Highway 29 often speed past the town on the way to the more seductive Yountville or St. Helena. But Napa is changing. After many years as a blue-collar burg detached from the Wine Country scene, Napa has spent the past decade reshaping its image.

A recently completed walkway that follows the Napa River has made downtown more pedestrian-friendly, and each year high-profile new restaurants pop up. The shopping has become more chic and varied, and the Oxbow Public Market, a klatch of high-end food purveyors, is popular with locals and tourists. If you establish your base in Napa, you'll undoubtedly want to explore the wineries amid the surrounding countryside, but plan on spending at least a half a day strolling the downtown district of the valley's least pretentious town.

GETTING HERE AND AROUND

Downtown Napa lies a mile east of Highway 29—take the 1st Street exit and follow the signs. Ample parking, much of it free for the first three hours and some for the entire day, is available on or near Main Street. Several VINE buses serve downtown and beyond.

EXPLORING
TOP ATTRACTIONS

Fodor'sChoice ★ **Artesa Vineyards & Winery.** From a distance the modern, minimalist architecture of Artesa blends harmoniously with the surrounding Carneros landscape, but up close its pools, fountains, and outdoor sculptures make a vivid impression. So, too, do the wines crafted by Mark Beringer—a great-great-grandson of the 19th-century Napa winemaking pioneer Jacob Beringer—who focuses on Chardonnay and Pinot Noir but also produces Cabernet Sauvignon and other limited-release wines such as Albariño and Tempranillo. You can taste wines by themselves or paired with chocolate ($50), cheese ($60), tapas ($60), and gourmet small bites ($80). ⊠ *1345 Henry Rd., off Old Sonoma Rd. and Dealy La.* ☎ *707/224–1668* ⊕ *www.artesawinery.com* ⊠ *Tastings $15–$80, tours $20–$45* ☉ *Daily 10–5, winery tour daily at 11 and 2.*

Fodor'sChoice ★ **di Rosa.** About 2,000 works from the 1960s to the present by Northern California artists are displayed on this 217-acre art property. They can be found not only in galleries and in the former residence of its late founder, Rene di Rosa, but also on every lawn, in every courtyard, and even on the lake. Some works were commissioned especially for di Rosa, among them Paul Kos's meditative *Chartres Bleu,* a video installation in a chapel-like setting that replicates a stained-glass window from the cathedral in Chartres, France. ■**TIP**→ You can view the current temporary exhibition and a few permanent works at the Gatehouse Gallery, but to experience the breadth of this incomparable collection you'll need to book a tour. ⊠ *5200 Sonoma Hwy./Hwy. 121*

Wine and contemporary art find a home at di Rosa.

☎ 707/226–5991 ⊕ *www.dirosaart.org* ✉ *Gatehouse Gallery $5, tours $12–$15* ⊗ *Wed.–Sun. 10–4.*

Fodor's Choice **Domaine Carneros.** A visit to this majestic château is an opulent way
★ to enjoy the Carneros District—especially in fine weather, when the vineyard views are spectacular. The château was modeled after an 18th-century French mansion owned by the Taittinger family. Carved into the hillside beneath the winery, the cellars produce delicate sparkling wines reminiscent of those made by Taittinger, using only Los Carneros AVA grapes. The winery sells full glasses, flights, and bottles of its wines, which also include Chardonnay, Pinot Noir, and other still wines. Enjoy them all with cheese and charcuterie plates, caviar, or smoked salmon. Seating is in the Louis XV–inspired salon or on the terrace overlooking the vines. The tour here covers traditional methods of making sparkling wines. ✉ *1240 Duhig Rd., at Hwy. 121* ☎ *707/257–0101, 800/716–2788* ⊕ *www.domainecarneros.com* ✉ *Tastings $7–$30, tour $30* ⊗ *Daily 10–5:45; tour daily at 11, 1, and 3.*

Fodor's Choice **The Hess Collection.** About 9 miles northwest of Napa, up a winding road
★ ascending Mt. Veeder, this winery is a delightful discovery. The limestone structure, rustic from the outside but modern and airy within, contains Swiss owner Donald Hess's art collection, including large-scale works by contemporary artists such as Andy Goldsworthy, Anselm Kiefer, and Robert Rauschenberg. Cabernet Sauvignon is a major strength, and the 19 Block Cuvée, Mt. Veeder, a Cabernet blend, shows off the Malbec and other estate varietals. ■TIP→ Food-wine pairings include one with chocolates that go well with the Mount Veeder Cabernet Sauvignon. ✉ *4411 Redwood Rd., west off Hwy. 29 at Trancas St./Redwood Rd.*

exit ☎ 707/255–1144 ⊕ www.hesscollection.com ☜ Art gallery free, tasting $15–$85 ☉ Daily 10–5:30; guided tours daily 10:30–3:30.

Fodor's Choice
★
Oxbow Public Market. The market's two-dozen shops, wine bars, and artisanal food producers provide an introduction to Napa Valley's wealth of foods and wines. Swoon over decadent charcuterie at the Fatted Calf, slurp bivalves at Hog Island Oyster Company, or chow down on tacos with homemade tortillas at C Casa. Afterward, sip wine at Ca' Momi Enoteca or sample the barrel-aged cocktails and handcrafted vodka of the Napa Valley Distillery. The owner of C Casa also runs Cate & Co., a bakeshop that makes going gluten-free an absolute delight. ■ TIP➔ Locals head to Model Bakery around 3 pm for hot-from-the-oven "late bake" bread. ⊠ 610 and 644 1st St., at McKinstry St. ⊕ www. oxbowpublicmarket.com ☜ Free ☉ Weekdays 9–9, weekends 10–9; merchants hrs vary.

WORTH NOTING

Etude Wines. Wine and food seminars are a big draw at Etude, but the most seductive part of a visit here is tasting the suave Pinot Noirs. Though the handsome, modern winery is in Napa County, its flagship Carneros Estate Pinot Noir comes from grapes grown in the Sonoma portion of Los Carneros, as does the rarer Heirloom Carneros Pinot Noir. Both are sophisticated wines whose smooth tannins linger on the palate. These or other Pinots—along with Pinot Gris, Chardonnay, Cabernet Sauvignon, and other wine—are paired with small bites of food at informative tasting seminars ($35). ■ TIP➔ Don't leave without stopping to survey the landscape. You're apt to see (or hear) geese, hawks, egrets, and other wildlife. ⊠ 1250 Cuttings Wharf Rd., 1 mile south of Hwy. 121 ☎ 877/586–9361 ⊕ www.etudewines.com ☜ Tastings $15–$35 ☉ Daily 10–4:30.

Napa Valley Wine Train. Several restored Pullman railroad cars travel a scenic route between Napa and St. Helena. Although the Wine Train is no bargain and can feel hokey, the staffers are pleasant and the meals served are generally good. ■ TIP➔ It's best to make this trip during the day, when you can enjoy the vineyard views. ⊠ 1275 McKinstry St., off 1st St. ☎ 707/253–2111, 800/427–4124 ⊕ www.winetrain.com ☜ Lunch and dinner $119 ☉ Lunch: Jan. and Feb., Fri.–Sun. 11:30; Mar.–Dec. daily 11:30. Dinner: Jan.–Mar., Sat. 6:30; Apr. and Nov.–Dec., Fri. and Sat. 6:30; May, Fri.–Sun. 6:30; June–Oct., Thurs.–Mon. 6:30.

St. Clair Brown Winery. Tastings at this women-run "urban winery" a few blocks north of downtown take place in an intimate, light-filled greenhouse. Winemaker Elaine St. Clair, well regarded for her stints at Domaine Carneros and Black Stallion, produces elegant vintages—crisp yet complex whites and smooth, French-style reds whose star is Syrah from grapes grown in the Coombsville appellation. The wines are paired with addictive appetizers that include almonds roasted with rosemary, cumin, and Meyer lemon juice. ■ TIP➔ You can sip single wines by the glass or half glass, or opt for the four-wine sampler. ⊠ 850 Vallejo St., off Soscol Ave. ☎ 707/255–5591 ⊕ www.stclairbrownwinery.com ☜ Tasting $4–$20 ☉ Daily 11–8.

Where to Eat and Stay in Napa Valley

Climbing ivy and lily pads decorate the Hess Collection's rustic exterior.

WHERE TO EAT

$$
MODERN
AMERICAN
Fodor's Choice
★

✕ **Boon Fly Café.** This small spot melds rural charm with industrial chic. Outside, swings occupy the porch of a modern red barn; inside, things get sleek with high ceilings and galvanized-steel tabletops. The menu of three squares a day updates American classics such as roasted pork chop, served here with sweet potatoes, and chicken and waffles. The flatbread topped with bacon, Point Reyes blue cheese, and portobello mushrooms is a local favorite. There's a good selection of wines by the glass. ■TIP→ One of the rare Wine Country restaurants open all day, Boon Fly makes a convenient midmorning or late-afternoon stop. $ *Average main: $20 ⊠ Carneros Inn, 4048 Sonoma Hwy.* ☎ *707/299–4870* ⊕ *www.theboonflycafe.com.*

$$$
AMERICAN
Fodor's Choice
★

✕ **Bounty Hunter.** A triple threat, Bounty Hunter is a wine store, wine bar, and restaurant in one. You can stop by for just a glass—about 40 choices are available in both 2- and 5-ounce pours—or a bottle, but it's best to come with an appetite. Every dish on the small menu is a standout, including the pulled-pork and beef brisket sandwiches served with three types of barbecue sauce, the signature beer-can chicken, and meltingly tender St. Louis–style ribs. The space is whimsically rustic, with stuffed game trophies mounted on the wall and leather saddles standing in for seats at a couple of tables. $ *Average main: $26 ⊠ 975 1st St., near Main St.* ☎ *707/226–3976* ⊕ *www.bountyhunterwinebar. com* ⟵ *Reservations not accepted.*

$$$$
STEAKHOUSE
Fodor's Choice
★

✕ **Cole's Chop House.** When only a fat slab of steak will do, popular Cole's is the best choice in town. The prime steaks—New York, porterhouse, and filet mignon among them—are dry-aged by Allen Brothers of Chicago, purveyors to America's top steak houses. New Zealand lamb chops are the house's non-beef favorite, and seasonal additions might include pork tenderloin. Inside a handsome 1886 stone building, Chops hews to tradition with the starters and sides. Expect oysters Rockefeller, creamed spinach, grilled asparagus with hollandaise, and other standbys, all prepared with finesse. The wine list is borderline epic, with the best of the Napa Valley amply represented. Ⓢ *Average main: $38* ✉ *1122 Main St., at Pearl St.* ☎ *707/224–6328* ⊕ *www.coleschophouse. com* ⚐ *Reservations essential* ☾ *No lunch.*

$$$$ ✕**Morimoto Napa.** *Iron Chef* star Masuharu Morimoto is the big name
JAPANESE behind this downtown Napa hot spot. Organic materials such as twisting grapevines above the bar and rough-hewn wooden tables seem simultaneously earthy and modern, creating a fitting setting for the gorgeously plated Japanese fare, from sashimi served with grated fresh wasabi to elaborate concoctions that include sea-urchin *carbonara*, made with udon noodles. Everything's delightfully overdone, right down to desserts. ■**TIP➔ For the full experience, leave the choice up to the chef and opt for the omakase menu ($120 $160).** Ⓢ *Average main: $44* ✉ *610 Main St., at 5th St.* ☎ *707/252–1600* ⊕ *www. morimotonapa.com.*

$$ ✕**Tarla Mediterranean Grill.** The menu at Tarla challenges the Napa Val-
MEDITERRANEAN ley's notoriously Italo-centric diners to venture deeper into the Mediterranean. You can build a meal by combining such traditional *mezes* (tapas) as stuffed grape leaves with fresh *tzatziki* (a thick yogurt sauce with cucumber, dill, and mint) and *spanakopita* (phyllo dough stuffed with spinach and feta cheese) with more contemporary, seasonally offered creations—perhaps a crab, spinach, and hearts of palm fondue. The entrées include updates of moussaka and other Mediterranean mainstays, along with fancifully modern items such as beef short ribs braised with a pomegranate-wine sauce and accompanying them with a corn-and-white-truffle risotto. A sister restaurant, Napkins Bar + Grill, at Main and 2nd streets, serves high-style comfort food and stays open late. Ⓢ *Average main: $19* ✉ *Andaz Napa, 1480 1st St., at School St.* ☎ *707/255–5599* ⊕ *www.tarlagrill.com.*

$$$ ✕**Torc.** *Torc* means "wild boar" in an early Celtic dialect, and chef
MODERN Sean O'Toole occasionally incorporates his restaurant's namesake beast
AMERICAN into dishes at his eclectic downtown restaurant. Bolognese sauce, for example, might include ground wild boar, tomato, lime, and cocoa. O'Toole has helmed kitchens at top New York City, San Francisco, and Yountville establishments. Torc is the first restaurant he's owned, and he crafts meals with style and precision that are reflected in the gracious service and classy, contemporary decor. ■**TIP➔ The Bengali sweet potato–pakora appetizer, which comes with a dreamy-creamy yogurt-truffle dip, has been a hit since day one.** Ⓢ *Average main: $25* ✉ *1140 Main St., at Pearl St.* ☎ *707/252–3292* ⊕ *www.torcnapa.com* ☾ *No lunch weekdays.*

$$$ ✕**ZuZu.** A recent seismic retrofitting changed ZuZu's look but not its
SPANISH festive vibe or the sharp focus on Spanish favorites like tapas and paella.
Fodor'sChoice Diners down *Cava* (Spanish sparkling wine) or sangria with such dishes
★ as white anchovies with boiled egg and remoulade on grilled bread. Locals revere the paella, made with Spanish Bomba rice. Latin jazz

6

on the stereo helps make this place a popular spot for get-togethers. ■ TIP→ Reservations aren't accepted, so expect a wait on weekends, when a young crowd floods the zone. $ *Average main: $29* ⊠ *829 Main St., near 3rd St.* ☎ *707/224–8555* ⊕ *www.zuzunapa.com* ⌂ *Reservations not accepted* ⊘ *No lunch weekends.*

WHERE TO STAY

$$$
HOTEL
Fodor's Choice
★
🛏 **Andaz Napa.** By far Napa's hippest place to stay, this boutique hotel has luxurious rooms, many of them suites. **Pros:** proximity to downtown restaurants, theaters, and tasting rooms; access to modern fitness center; complimentary snacks and nonalcoholic beverages. **Cons:** parking can be a challenge on weekends; unremarkable views from some rooms. $ *Rooms from: $309* ⊠ *1450 1st St.* ☎ *707/224–3900* ⊕ *www.napa.andaz.hyatt.com* ⇴ *50 rooms, 91 suites* ⎮◯⎮ *No meals.*

$$$$
RESORT
Fodor's Choice
★
🛏 **Carneros Inn.** Freestanding board-and-batten cottages with rocking chairs on each porch are simultaneously rustic and chic at this luxurious property. **Pros:** cottages have lots of privacy; beautiful views from hilltop pool and hot tub; heaters on private patios; excellent Boon Fly Café is open all day. **Cons:** a long drive from destinations up-valley; smallish rooms with limited seating options. $ *Rooms from: $600* ⊠ *4048 Sonoma Hwy./Hwy. 121* ☎ *707/299–4900, 888/400–9000* ⊕ *www.thecarnerosinn.com* ⇴ *76 cottages, 10 suites.*

$$$
B&B/INN
🛏 **Milliken Creek Inn.** Wine-and-cheese receptions at sunset set a romantic mood in this hotel's intimate lobby, with its terrace overlooking a lush lawn and the Napa River. **Pros:** soft-as-clouds beds; serene spa; breakfast delivered to your room (or elsewhere on the beautiful grounds). **Cons:** expensive; road noise audible in outdoor areas. $ *Rooms from: $379* ⊠ *1815 Silverado Trail* ☎ *707/255–1197* ⊕ *www.millikencreekinn.com* ⇴ *12 rooms.*

$$
B&B/INN
🛏 **Napa River Inn.** Part of a complex of restaurants, shops, a nightclub, and a spa, this waterfront inn is within easy walking distance of downtown hot spots. **Pros:** wide range of room sizes and prices; near downtown action; pet-friendly. **Cons:** river views could be more scenic; some rooms get noise from nearby restaurants. $ *Rooms from: $249* ⊠ *500 Main St.* ☎ *707/251–8500, 877/251–8500* ⊕ *www.napariverinn.com* ⇴ *65 rooms, 1 suite* ⎮◯⎮ *Breakfast.*

$$
HOTEL
🛏 **Westin Verasa Napa.** Near the Napa Valley Wine Train depot and the Oxbow market, this spacious resort is sophisticated and soothing. **Pros:** two heated saline pools; most rooms have well-equipped kitchenettes (some have full kitchens); spacious double-headed showers; good value for the price. **Cons:** "amenities fee" added to room rate. $ *Rooms from: $259* ⊠ *1314 McKinstry St.* ☎ *707/257–1800, 800/937–8461* ⊕ *www.westinnapa.com* ⇴ *160 suites, 20 rooms* ⎮◯⎮ *No meals.*

NIGHTLIFE AND THE ARTS

Fodor's Choice
★
1313 Main. Cool, sexy 1313 Main attracts a youngish crowd for top-drawer spirits and sparkling and still wines. The on-site **LuLu's Kitchen** serves comfort food ranging from the classic (mini lobster rolls) to the intricate (shaved black truffle with ricotta) to the highly whimsical (s'mores *semifreddo*). ⊠ *1313 Main St., at Clinton St.* ☎ *707/258–1313* ⊕ *www.1313main.com.*

City Winery Napa. A recent makeover transformed the 1879 Napa Valley Opera House into a combination wine bar, restaurant, and live-music venue that features top singer-songwriters and small acts. Many of the three-dozen wines on tap are exclusive to the club from prestigious area wineries. ⊠ *1030 Main St., near 1st St.* ☎ *707/260–1600* ⊕ *www.citywinery.com/napa.*

Empire. This groovy nightclub attached to the Andaz Napa hotel draws locals and tourists for cocktails, gourmet bites, and, on some nights, dancing to DJ music. If the beautiful people in motion don't mesmerize you, perhaps the jellyfishes undulating in their tubular tanks will. ⊠ *1400 1st St., at Franklin St.* ☎ *707/254–8888* ⊕ *empirenapa.com.*

Uptown Theatre. This top-notch live-music venue, a former movie house, attracts B.B. King, Ani DiFranco, Napa Valley resident and winery owner Boz Scaggs, and other performers. ⊠ *1350 3rd St., at Franklin St.* ☎ *707/259–0123* ⊕ *www.uptowntheatrenapa.com.*

YOUNTVILLE

9 miles north of the town of Napa.

These days Yountville is something like Disneyland for food lovers. You could stay here for a week and not exhaust all the options—several of them owned by the French Laundry's Thomas Keller—and the tiny town is full of small inns and high-end hotels that cater to those who prefer to walk (not drive) after an extravagant meal. It's also well located for excursions to many big-name Napa wineries, especially those in the Stags Leap District, from which big, bold Cabernet Sauvignons helped make the Napa Valley's wine-making reputation.

GETTING HERE AND AROUND

Downtown Yountville sits just off Highway 29. Approaching from the south take the Yountville exit—from the north take Madison—and proceed to Washington Street, home to the major shops and restaurants. Yountville Cross Road connects downtown to the Silverado Trail, along which many noted wineries do business. The free Yountville Trolley serves the town daily from 10 am to 7 pm (on-call service until 11 except on Sunday).

Contact Yountville Trolley ☎ *707/944–1234 10 am–7 pm, 707/312–1509 7–11 pm.*

EXPLORING
TOP ATTRACTIONS

Domaine Chandon. On a knoll shaded by ancient oak trees, this French-owned maker of sparkling wines claims one of Yountville's prime pieces of real estate. Chandon is best known for bubblies, but the still wines—Cabernet Sauvignon, Chardonnay, Pinot Meunier, and Pinot Noir—are also worth a try. Tours of the production facility, which focus on how the winemakers adapt traditional Champagne-making methods to 21st-century wine science and technology, end with a seated tasting. For the complete experience, order hors d'oeuvres to accompany the wines in the tasting room. ⊠ *1 California Dr., at Solano Ave., west of Hwy. 29* ☎ *707/204–7530, 888/242–6366* ⊕ *www.chandon.com* ⌕ *Tastings $18–$30, tours $40–$45* ☉ *Daily 10–5; tours daily at 10:30, 11:30, and 3.*

Fodor's Choice ★ **Ma(i)sonry Napa Valley.** An art-and-design gallery that also pours the wines of two-dozen limited-production wineries, Ma(i)sonry occupies an atmospheric stone manor house constructed in 1904. Tasting flights can be sampled in fair weather in the beautiful garden, in a private nook, or at the communal redwood table, and in any weather indoors among the contemporary artworks and some well-chosen *objets*—which might include 17th-century furnishings, industrial lamps, or slabs of petrified wood. ■ TIP➔ Walk-ins are welcome space permitting, but during summer, at harvest time, and on weekends and holidays it's best to book in advance. ✉ *6711 Washington St., at Pedroni St.* ☎ *707/944–0889* ⊕ *www.maisonry.com* ⌑ *Tasting $15–$35* ☉ *Sun.–Thurs. daily 10–6, Fri. and Sat. daily 10–7; check for later hrs in summer and early fall.*

Stag's Leap Wine Cellars. A 1973 Stag's Leap Cabernet Sauvignon put this winery and the Napa Valley on the oenological map by placing first in the famous Paris tasting of 1976. The grapes for that wine came from a vineyard visible from a new stone-and-glass tasting room that is scheduled to open in fall 2014. The room will have views of a second fabled Cabernet vineyard and the promontory that gives both the winery and the Stags Leap District AVA their names. ■ TIP➔ A $30 tasting includes the top-of-the-line estate-grown Cabernets, which sell for more than $100; a $15 tasting of more modestly priced wines is also available. ✉ *5766 Silverado Trail, at Wappo Hill Rd., Napa* ☎ *707/944–2020, 866/422–7523* ⊕ *www.cask23.com* ⌑ *Tastings $15–$30, tour $40* ☉ *Daily 10–4:30; tours by appointment.*

WORTH NOTING

Fodor's Choice ★ **Robert Sinskey Vineyards.** Although the winery produces a well-regarded Stags Leap Cabernet Sauvignon, two supple red blends called Marcien and POV, and white wines, Sinskey is best known for its intense, brambly Carneros District Pinot Noirs. All the grapes are grown in organic, certified biodynamic vineyards. The influence of Robert's wife, Maria Helm Sinskey—a chef and cookbook author and the winery's culinary director—is evident during the tastings, which are accompanied by a few bites of food with each wine. ■ TIP➔ The Farm to Table Tour ($75) takes in the winery's gardens and ends with a seated pairing of food and wine. ✉ *6320 Silverado Trail, at Yountville Cross Rd., Napa* ☎ *707/944–9090* ⊕ *www.robertsinskey.com* ⌑ *Tasting $25, tour $75* ☉ *Daily 10–4:30; tours daily at 11 by appointment.*

WHERE TO EAT

$$$$
MODERN
AMERICAN
Fodor's Choice ★

✕ **Ad Hoc.** At this casual spot, superstar chef Thomas Keller offers a single, fixed-price menu ($52) nightly, with a small lineup of decadent brunch items served on Sunday. The dinner selection might include a juicy pork loin and buttery polenta, served family style, or a delicate *panna cotta* with a citrus glaze. The dining room is warmly low-key, with zinc-top tables, wine served in tumblers, and rock and jazz on the stereo. Call a day ahead to find out the next day's menu. ■ TIP➔ From Thursday through Saturday, except in winter, you can pick up a boxed lunch to go—the buttermilk fried chicken one is delicious—at the on-site and aptly named Addendum. ⑤ *Average main: $52* ✉ *6476 Washington St., at Oak Circle* ☎ *707/944–2487* ⊕ *www.adhocrestaurant. com* ☉ *No lunch Mon.–Sat. No dinner Tues. and Wed.*

$$$
FRENCH

✕ Bistro Jeanty. French classics and obscure delicacies tickle patrons' palates at chef Philippe Jeanty's genteel country bistro. Jeanty prepares the greatest hits—escargots, cassoulet, *daube de boeuf* (beef stewed in red wine)—with the utmost precision and turns out pike dumplings and lamb tongue with equal élan. Regulars often start with the extraordinary, rich tomato soup in a flaky puff pastry before proceeding to sole *meunière*, slow-roasted pork shoulder, or coq au vin (always choosing the simple, suggested side: thin egg noodles cooked with just the right amount of butter and salt). Chocolate pot de crème, warm apple tart tartin, and other authentic desserts complete the French sojourn. ⑤ *Average main: $26* ⊠ *6510 Washington St., at Mulberry St.* ☎ *707/944–0103* ⊕ *www.bistrojeanty.com.*

$$$
ITALIAN

✕ Bottega. The food at chef Michael Chiarello's trattoria is simultaneously soulful and inventive, transforming local ingredients into regional Italian dishes with a twist. The antipasti shine: you can order grilled short-rib meatballs, house-made charcuterie, or incredibly fresh fish. Potato gnocchi might be served with pumpkin *fonduta* (Italian-style fondue) and roasted root vegetables, and hearty main courses such as twice-cooked pork chops with peck seasoning might be accompanied by cinnamon stewed plums and crispy black kale. The vibe is festive, with exposed-brick walls and an open kitchen, but service is spot-on, and the wine list includes interesting choices from Italy and California. ⑤ *Average main: $27* ⊠ *V Marketplace, 6525 Washington St., near Mulberry St.* ☎ *707/945–1050* ⊕ *www.botteganapavalley.com* ⊘ *No lunch Mon.*

$$$
FRENCH

✕ Bouchon. The team that created the French Laundry is also behind this place, where everything—the lively and crowded zinc-topped bar, the elbow-to-elbow seating, the traditional French onion soup—could have come straight from a Parisian bistro. Roast chicken with sautéed chicken livers and button mushrooms, and steamed mussels served with crispy, addictive *frites* (french fries) are among the dishes served. ■TIP→ The adjacent Bouchon Bakery sells marvelous macarons (meringue cookies) in many flavors, along with brownies, pastries, and other baked goods. ⑤ *Average main: $27* ⊠ *6534 Washington St., near Humboldt St.* ☎ *707/944–8037* ⊕ *www.bouchonbistro.com.*

$$$$
AMERICAN
Fodor's Choice
★

✕ Étoile. Domaine Chandon's quietly elegant restaurant seems built for romance, with delicate orchids on each table and views of the wooded grounds from the large windows. Chef Perry Hoffman has racked up numerous awards for his sophisticated California cuisine. The menu might include a salad of tender Spanish octopus and heirloom melon or a slow-poached egg and caviar on a blini as preludes to entrées such as roulade of rabbit prepared with applewood bacon and chanterelles. Four- and six-course tasting menus can be ordered with or without wine pairings. The wine list features Domaine Chandon sparklers but is strong in wines from throughout California as well. ⑤ *Average main: $34* ⊠ *1 California Dr., at Solano Ave., west of Hwy. 29* ☎ *888/242–6366* ⊕ *www.chandon.com/etoile-restaurant* ⊘ *Closed Jan. and Tues. and Wed.*

$$$$
AMERICAN
Fodor's Choice
★

✕ French Laundry. An old stone building laced with ivy houses the most acclaimed restaurant in the Napa Valley—and, indeed, one of the most highly regarded in the country. The two nine-course prix-fixe menus (both $270), one of which highlights vegetables, vary, but

6

"oysters and pearls," a silky dish of pearl tapioca with oysters and white sturgeon caviar, is a signature starter. Some courses rely on luxe ingredients like *calotte* (cap of the rib eye), while others take humble foods such as fava beans and elevate them to art. Many courses also offer the option of "supplements"—sea urchin, for instance, or black truffles. ■TIP➔ Reservations are hard-won here; to get one call two months ahead to the day at 10 am, on the dot. $ *Average main: $270* ⊠ *6640 Washington St., at Creek St.* ☎ *707/944–2380* ⊕ *www. frenchlaundry.com* ⌕ *Reservations essential* ⋔ *Jacket required* ☉ *No lunch Mon.–Thurs.*

$$$$
MODERN
AMERICAN

✕ **Lucy Restaurant & Bar.** In a sleek modern space radiating offhand elegance, Lucy seduces with sophisticated flavors and suave service. Chef Victor Scargle builds his menu around produce from an on-site garden. Being one of its farmers he's intimately acquainted with its bounty, which includes the components of the (truly) freshly dug carrot salad. Sunchoke soup and ahi tuna ceviche also make excellent starters, and you can stay small even with the entrées, which come in full and half portions. A modern take on duck à l'orange is a consistent pleaser, but game diners can opt for a chop—in this case antelope—served with wild rice and tangy huckleberry jus. The sommelier, formerly of the French Laundry and New York City's Per Se, graciously guides diners through the well-conceived wine list. $ *Average main: $33* ⊠ *Bardessono, 6526 Yount St., at Finnell St.* ☎ *707/204–6030* ⊕ *www.bardessono.com/restaurant_bar.*

$$$
AMERICAN

✕ **Mustards Grill.** Cindy Pawlcyn's Mustards fills day and night with fans of her hearty cuisine. The menu mixes updated renditions of traditional American dishes (what Pawlcyn dubs "deluxe truck stop classics")—among them barbecued baby back pork ribs and a lemon-lime tart piled high with browned meringue—with more fanciful choices such as sweet corn tamales with tomatillo-avocado salsa and wild mushrooms. A black-and-white marble tile floor and upbeat artworks keep the mood jolly. $ *Average main: $27* ⊠ *7399 St. Helena Hwy./Hwy. 29, 1 mile north of Yountville, Napa* ☎ *707/944–2424* ⊕ *www.mustardsgrill.com.*

$$$
MODERN
AMERICAN
Fodor'sChoice
★

✕ **Redd.** The minimalist dining room here seems a fitting setting for chef Richard Reddington's up-to-date menu. The culinary influences include California, Mexico, Europe, and Asia, but the food always feels modern and never fussy. The glazed pork belly with apple purée, set amid a pool of soy caramel, is a prime example of the East-meets-West style. The seafood preparations—among them petrale sole, clams, and chorizo poached in a saffron-curry broth—are deft variations on the original dishes. For the full experience, consider the five-course tasting menu ($80 per person, $125 with wine pairing). ■TIP➔ For a quick bite, order small plates and a cocktail and sit at the bar. $ *Average main: $30* ⊠ *6480 Washington St., at Oak Circle* ☎ *707/944–2222* ⊕ *www. reddnapavalley.com* ⌕ *Reservations essential.*

$$
ITALIAN

✕ **Redd Wood.** Chef Richard Reddington's casual restaurant specializes in thin-crust wood-fired pizzas and contemporary variations on rustic Italian classics. The cool nonchalance of the industrial decor mirrors the service, which is less officious than elsewhere in town, and the cuisine itself. The glazed beef short ribs, for instance, seem like yet another fancy take on a down-home favorite until you realize how cleverly the sweetness of the glaze plays off the creamy polenta and the piquant splash of salsa verde. Redd Wood does for Italian comfort food what nearby Mustards Grill does for the American version: it spruces it up but retains its innate pleasures. $ *Average main: $22 ⊠ North Block Hotel, 6755 Washington St., at Madison St.* ☎ *707/299–5030* ⊕ *www.redd-wood.com.*

WHERE TO STAY

$$$$
RESORT
Fodor's Choice
★

🏨 **Bardessono.** Although Bardessono bills itself as the "greenest luxury hotel in America," there's nothing spartan about its accommodations; arranged around four landscaped courtyards, the rooms have luxurious organic bedding, gas fireplaces, and huge bathrooms with walnut floors. **Pros:** large rooftop lap pool; exciting restaurant; excellent spa, with in-room treatments available; polished service. **Cons:** expensive; limited view from some rooms. $ *Rooms from: $550 ⊠ 6526 Yount St.* ☎ *707/204–6000* ⊕ *www.bardessono.com* ⇌ *56 rooms, 6 suites* ⦿ *No meals.*

$
B&B/INN

🏨 **Maison Fleurie.** A stay at this comfortable inn places you within easy walking distance of Yountville's fine restaurants. **Pros:** smallest rooms a bargain; outdoor hot tub; pool (open in season); free bike rental. **Cons:** breakfast room can be crowded at peak times. $ *Rooms from: $160 ⊠ 6529 Yount St.* ☎ *707/944–2056, 800/788–0369* ⊕ *www. maisonfleurienapa.com* ⇌ *13 rooms* ⦿ *Breakfast.*

$$$$
HOTEL

🏨 **North Block Hotel.** With a chic Tuscan style, this 20-room hotel has dark-wood furniture and soothing decor in brown and sage. **Pros:** extremely comfortable beds; attentive service; room service by Redd Wood restaurant. **Cons:** outdoor areas get some traffic noise. $ *Rooms from: $420 ⊠ 6757 Washington St.* ☎ *707/944–8080* ⊕ *northblockhotel.com* ⇌ *20 rooms* ⦿ *Breakfast.*

$$$
RESORT

🏨 **Villagio Inn & Spa.** With a layout that resembles a Tuscan village, this relaxing haven has streamlined furnishings, subdued color schemes, and high ceilings that create a sense of spaciousness in the guest rooms, each of which has a wood-burning fireplace and, beyond louvered doors, a balcony or a patio. **Pros:** amazing buffet breakfast; no extra charge for the spa facilities; steps from many dining options. **Cons:** can be bustling with large groups; highway noise audible from many balconies or patios. $ *Rooms from: $375 ⊠ 6481 Washington St.* ☎ *707/944–8877, 800/351–1133* ⊕ *www.villagio.com* ⇌ *86 rooms, 26 suites* ⦿ *Breakfast.*

SPORTS AND THE OUTDOORS
BALLOONING

Napa Valley Aloft. Between 8 and 12 passengers soar over the Napa Valley in balloons that launch from downtown Yountville. The rates include preflight refreshments and a huge breakfast. ⊠ *V Marketplace, 6525 Washington St., near Mulberry St.* ☎ *707/944–4400, 855/944–4408* ⊕ *www.nvaloft.com* 🎫 *From $220 per person.*

Napa Valley Balloons. The valley's oldest balloon company offers trips that are elegant from start to finish. Satisfied customers include Chelsea Clinton and *Today* show host Matt Lauer. ⊠ *Domaine Chandon, 1 California Dr., at Solano Ave., west of Hwy. 29* ☎ *707/944–0228, 800/253–2224* ⊕ *www.napavalleyballoons.com* 🎫 *$215 per person.*

BIKING

Fodor's Choice ★ **Napa Valley Bike Tours.** With dozens of wineries within 5 miles, this shop makes a fine starting point for vineyard and wine-tasting excursions. The outfit also rents bikes. ✉ *6500 Washington St., at Mulberry St.* ☎ *707/944–2953* ⊕ *www.napavalleybiketours.com* ⌗ *From $89.*

SPAS

Spa Villagio. The perks abound at this 13,000-square-foot Mediterranean-style facility equipped with huge spa suites—complete with flat-screen TVs and wet bars—that are perfect for couples and groups. The pièce de résistance among the treatments, the Suite Sensations experience ($575), draws on Asian, Mediterranean, and Middle-Eastern traditions and includes matching wine-and-food pairings. Body peels, facials, manicures, and massages are among the à la carte services. ✉ *6481 Washington St., at Oak Circle* ☎ *707/948–5050, 800/351–1133* ⊕ *www.villagio.com/spavillagio* ⌗ *Treatments $75–$575.*

SHOPPING

V Marketplace. The clothing boutiques, art galleries, and gift stores amid this vine-covered market include NapaStyle, which sells cookbooks, kitchenware, and prepared foods that are perfect for picnics. ✉ *6525 Washington St., near Mulberry St.* ☎ *707/944–2451* ⊕ *www. vmarketplace.com.*

OAKVILLE

2 miles northwest of Yountville.

A large butte that runs east–west just north of Yountville blocks the cooling fogs from the south, facilitating the myriad microclimates of the Oakville AVA, home to several high-profile wineries.

GETTING HERE AND AROUND

Driving along Highway 29, you'll know you've reached Oakville when you see the Oakville Grocery on the east side of the road. You can reach Oakville from the Sonoma County town of Glen Ellen by heading east on Trinity Road from Highway 12. The twisting route, along the mountain range that divides Napa and Sonoma, eventually becomes the Oakville Grade. The views on this drive are breathtaking, though the continual curves make it unsuitable for those who suffer from motion sickness.

EXPLORING
TOP ATTRACTIONS

Fodor's Choice ★ **Far Niente.** Though the fee for the combined tour and tasting is high, guests at Far Niente are welcomed by name and treated to a glimpse of one of the Napa Valley's most beautiful properties. Small groups are escorted through the historic 1885 stone winery, including some of the 40,000 square feet of caves, for a lesson on the labor-intensive method of making Far Niente's two wines: a Cabernet Sauvignon blend and a Chardonnay. The next stop is the Carriage House, which holds a gleaming collection of classic cars. The tour concludes with a seated tasting of wines and cheeses. ✉ *1350 Acacia Dr., off Oakville Grade Rd.* ☎ *707/944–2861* ⊕ *www.farniente.com* ⌗ *Tasting and tour $65* ☉ *Daily 10–3 by appointment.*

Far Niente's wine cellars have a touch of ballroom elegance.

PlumpJack. With its metal chandelier and wall hangings, the tasting room at this casual winery looks like a stage set for a modern Shakespearean production. (The name "PlumpJack" is a nod to Shakespeare's Falstaff.) A youngish crowd assembles here to sample vintages that include the citrusy reserve Chardonnay and a Merlot that's blended like a Cab, providing the wine sufficient tannins to ensure it can age at least another five years. The luscious Syrah, from Atlas Peak and Carneros grapes, is available only through the winery. ■**TIP➜** The Hilltop Tasting and Tour takes in the cellar and grounds and ends with a seated tasting overlooking the vineyards. Limited to six guests, it books up quickly in summer. ⊠ *620 Oakville Cross Rd., off Silverado Trail* ☎ *707/945–1220* ⊕ *www. plumpjack.com* ✉ *Tastings $20–$30; tour $30* ☉ *Daily 10–4; hilltop tour spring and summer Tues.–Fri. at 11 by appointment.*

Oakville Grocery. Built in 1881 as a general store, Oakville Grocery carries unusual and high-end groceries and prepared foods. On busy summer weekends the grocery is often packed with customers stocking up on picnic provisions: meats, cheeses, breads, and hearty sandwiches. ■**TIP➜** This is a fine place to sit on a bench and sip an espresso between winery visits. ⊠ *7856 St. Helena Hwy./Hwy. 29, at Oakville Rd.* ☎ *707/944–8802* ⊕ *www.oakvillegrocery.com.*

WORTH NOTING

Robert Mondavi Winery. The arch at the center of the sprawling mission-style building frames the lawn and the vineyard behind, inviting a stroll under the lovely arcades. You can head for one of the two tasting rooms, but if you've not toured a winery before, the Signature Tour and Tasting ($30) is a good way to learn about oenology, as well as the late Robert Mondavi's role in California wine making. Those new to tasting and mystified by all that swirling and sniffing should consider the 45-minute Wine Tasting Basics experience ($20). Serious wine lovers should opt for the one-hour $55 Exclusive Cellar tasting, during which a server pours and explains limited-production, reserve, and older-vintage wines. ■TIP➜ Concerts, mostly jazz and R&B, take place in summer on the lawn; call ahead for tickets. ✉ 7801 St. Helena Hwy./ Hwy. 29 ☎ 888/766–6328 ⊕ www.robertmondaviwinery.com ⌑ Tastings and tours $15–$55 ⊙ Daily 10–5; tour times vary.

RUTHERFORD

2 miles northwest of Oakville.

With its singular microclimate and soil, Rutherford is an important viticultural center, with more big-name wineries than you can shake a corkscrew at. Cabernet Sauvignon is king here. The well-drained, loamy soil is ideal for those vines, and since this part of the valley gets plenty of sun, the grapes develop exceptionally intense flavors.

GETTING HERE AND AROUND

Wineries around Rutherford are dotted along Highway 29 and the parallel Silverado Trail north and south of Rutherford Road/Conn Creek Road, on which wineries can also be found.

EXPLORING
TOP ATTRACTIONS

FAMILY

Fodor's Choice

★

Frog's Leap. John Williams, owner of Frog's Leap, maintains a goofy sense of humor about wine that translates into an entertaining yet informative experience—if you're a novice, the tour here is a fine way to begin your education. You'll taste wines that might include Zinfandel, Cabernet Sauvignon, Merlot, Chardonnay, Sauvignon Blanc, and Frögenbeerenauslese, a variation on the German dessert wine Trockenbeerenauslese. The winery includes a barn built in 1884, 5 acres of organic gardens, an eco-friendly visitor center, and a frog pond topped with lily pads. ■TIP➜ The tour is highly recommended, but you can also just sample wines either inside or on a porch overlooking the garden. ✉ 8815 Conn Creek Rd. ☎ 707/963–4704, 800/959–4704 ⊕ www.frogsleap.com ⌑ Tasting $20, tour $20 ⊙ Tastings daily 10–4 by appointment only; tours weekdays at 10:30 and 2:30 by appointment.

Inglenook. Filmmaker Francis Ford Coppola began his wine-making career in 1975, when he bought part of the historic Inglenook estate. Over the next few decades he reunited the original property acquired by Inglenook founder Gustave Niebaum, purchased Niebaum's ivy-covered 1880s château, and purchased the rights to the Inglenook name. Various tours cover the estate's history, the local climate and geology, the sensory evaluation of wine, and the evolution of Coppola's signature wine, Rubicon, a Cabernet Sauvignon–based blend. Some tastings are held in an opulent, high-ceilinged room, others in a wine-aging cave. ■TIP➜ You can taste wines by the glass (or the bottle) at The Bistro, an on-site wine bar with a picturesque courtyard. ✉ 1991 St. Helena Hwy./Hwy. 29 ☎ 707/968–1100, 800/782–4266 ⊕ www.inglenook.com ⌑ Tastings $45–$60, tours $50–$85 ⊙ Daily 10–5; call for tour times.

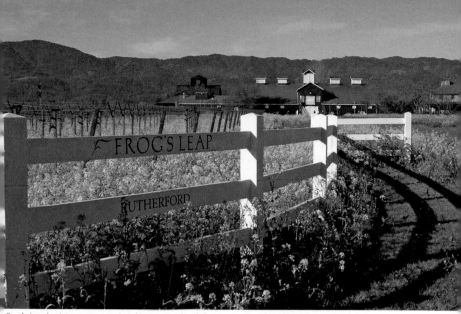

Frog's Leap's picturesque country charm extends all the way to the white picket fence.

Mumm Napa. Although this is one of California's best-known sparkling-wine producers, enjoying the bubbly from the light-filled tasting room—available in either single flutes or by the flight—isn't the only reason to visit Mumm. An excellent gallery displays 30 Ansel Adams prints and presents temporary exhibits by local photographers. You can even take that glass of crisp Brut Rosé with you as you wander. ■ TIP➔ For a leisurely tasting of library wines while seated on the Oak Terrace ($40), reserve in advance. ⊠ *8445 Silverado Trail* ☎ *707/967–7700, 800/686–6272* ⊕ *www.mummnapa.com* ✉ *Tastings $8–$40, tour $25 (includes tasting)* ⊙ *Daily 10–4:45; tours daily at 10, 11, 1, and 3.*

Fodor's Choice
★
Round Pond Estate. Sophisticated wines come from Round Pond, but the estate also produces premium olive oils, most from olives grown and crushed on the property. Informative olive-related seminars begin with a look at some trees and a tour of the high-tech mill, followed by tastings of the aromatic oils, both alone and with house-made red-wine vinegars. You'll also sip wines, but for a full tasting, head across the street to the winery. The basic tasting includes a suave Sauvignon Blanc and Round Pond's supple, well-rounded reds. The flagship Estate Cabernet Sauvignon has the structure and heft of the classic 1970s Rutherford Cabs, but gracefully acknowledges 21st-century palates with smoother, if still sturdy, tannins. The Estate Tasting ($45) pairs small morsels with the wines. ⊠ *875 Rutherford Rd., near Conn Creek Rd.* ☎ *707/302–2575, 888/302–2575* ⊕ *www.roundpond.com* ✉ *Wine tasting $25, tour and tasting $55; olive mill tour and tasting $45* ⊙ *All tastings and tours by appointment 24–48 hrs in advance.*

WORTH NOTING

Beaulieu Vineyard. The influential André Tchelistcheff (1901–1994), who helped define the California style of wine making, worked his magic here for many years. BV, founded in 1900 by Georges de Latour and his wife, Fernande, is known for its widely distributed Chardonnay, Pinot Noir, and Cabernet Sauvignon wines, but many others are produced in small lots and are available only at the winery. The most famous of the small-lot wines is the flagship Georges De Latour Cabernet Sauvignon, first crafted by Tchelistcheff himself in the late 1930s. ■TIP→ The historic tour ($35) includes a peek at Prohibition-era artifacts and tastes of finished wines and ones still aging in their barrels. ⊠ *1960 St. Helena Hwy./Hwy. 29* ☎ *707/967–5233, 800/264–6918 Ext. 5233* ⊕ *www. bvwines.com* ⊠ *Tasting $15–$50, tours $20* ☉ *Daily 10–5.*

Cakebread Cellars. The Cakebreads, at first Jack and Dolores and these days also their children, have been making luscious, complex Chardonnays, Cabernet Sauvignons, and Sauvignon Blancs since the 1970s. With a portfolio that now includes Merlot, Pinot Noir, and other varietals, Cakebread has built its reputation on crafting food-friendly wines. Case in point: winemaker Julianne Laks's Sauvignon Blanc. Blended with Sèmillon and Sauvignon Musqué grapes and aged lightly in neutral French oak, it's both accessible and sophisticated and the ideal accompaniment to seafood and pasta dishes. A basic tasting includes six current releases; the all-reds option is popular with Cab and Merlot fans. ⊠ *8300 St. Helena Hwy./Hwy. 29* ☎ *707/963–5222, 800/588–0298* ⊕ *www.cakebread.com* ⊠ *Tastings $15–$45, tour $25* ☉ *Daily 10–4; tastings and tour by appointment.*

Rutherford Hill Winery. This place is a Merlot lover's paradise in a Cabernet Sauvignon world. When the winery's founders were deciding what grapes to plant, they discovered that the climate and soil conditions resembled those of Pomerol, a region of Bordeaux where Merlot is king. Now owned by the Terlato family, Rutherford Hill has extensive wine caves—nearly a mile of tunnels and passageways. You can glimpse them and the barrels inside on the tours, and you can make your own Merlot at entertaining Saturday blending sessions ($95). The winery's hillside picnic area, amid oak and olive trees, is a magical spot. ■TIP→ The $35 picnic-reservation fee includes a $20 voucher toward the purchase of wine and two glasses. ⊠ *200 Rutherford Hill Rd., east of Silverado Trail* ☎ *707/963–1871* ⊕ *www.rutherfordhill.com* ⊠ *Tastings $20–$75; tour $30 (includes tasting)* ☉ *Daily 10–5; tours daily at 11:30, 1:30, and 3:30.*

WHERE TO EAT

$$$$
MODERN
AMERICAN
Fodor's Choice
★

✕ **Restaurant at Auberge du Soleil.** Possibly the most romantic roost for a dinner in all the Wine Country is a terrace seat at the Auberge du Soleil's illustrious restaurant, and the Mediterranean-inflected cuisine more than matches the dramatic vineyards views. The prix-fixe dinner menu ($105 for three courses, $125 for four; $150 for six-course tasting menu), which relies largely on local produce, might include veal sweetbreads with slow-cooked egg yolk, frisée, fried capers, and salsa verde or prime beef pavé with hand-foraged wild rice and chanterelles. The service is polished, and the wine list is comprehensive. ⑤ *Average* *main: $105 ⊠ Auberge du Soleil, 180 Rutherford Hill Rd., off Silverado Trail ☎ 707/963–1211, 800/348–5406 ⊕ www.aubergedusoleil.com ⚲ Reservations essential.*

$$$
AMERICAN
Fodor'sChoice
★

✕**Rutherford Grill.** Dark-wood walls, subdued lighting, and red-leather banquettes make for a perpetually clubby mood at this trusty Rutherford hangout. Many of the entrées—steaks, burgers, fish, succulent rotisserie chicken, and barbecued pork ribs—emerge from an oak-fired grill operated by master technicians. So, too, do alluring starters such as the grilled jumbo artichokes and the iron-skillet cornbread, a ton of butter being the secret of success with both. The French dip sandwich is a local legend, and the wine list includes rare selections from Caymus and other celebrated producers at (for Napa) reasonable prices. ∎**TIP➔** Between or after wine tastings, the margaritas and other clever cocktails the bartenders shake, stir, and pour are superb palate cleansers. ⑤ *Average main: $25 ⊠ 1180 Rutherford Rd., at Hwy. 29 ☎ 707/963–1792 ⊕ www.rutherfordgrill.com ⚲ Reservations essential.*

WHERE TO STAY

$$$$
RESORT
Fodor'sChoice
★

🏨 **Auberge du Soleil.** Taking a cue from the olive-tree-studded landscape, this hotel with a renowned restaurant and spa cultivates a luxurious Mediterranean look—earth-tone tile floors, heavy wood furniture, and terra-cotta colors. **Pros:** stunning views over the valley; spectacular pool and spa areas; the most expensive suites are fit for a superstar. **Cons:** stratospheric prices; least expensive rooms get some noise from the bar and restaurant. ⑤ *Rooms from: $850 ⊠ 180 Rutherford Hill Rd. ☎ 707/963–1211, 800/348–5406 ⊕ www.aubergedusoleil.com ⤴ 31 rooms, 21 suites* ⑩*Breakfast.*

ST. HELENA

2 miles northwest of Oakville.

Downtown St. Helena is a symbol of how well life can be lived in the Wine Country. Sycamore trees arch over Main Street (Highway 29), a funnel of outstanding restaurants and tempting boutiques. At the north end of town looms the hulking stone building of the Culinary Institute of America. Weathered stone and brick buildings from the late 1800s give off that gratifying whiff of history.

By the time pioneering winemaker Charles Krug planted grapes in St. Helena around 1860, vineyards already existed in the area. Today the town is hemmed in by wineries, and you could easily spend days visiting vintners within a few miles.

GETTING HERE AND AROUND

Downtown St. Helena stretches along Highway 29, which is called Main Street here. Many wineries lie north and south of downtown along Highway 29. More can be found off Silverado Trail, and some of the most scenic spots are on Spring Mountain, which rises southwest of town.

EXPLORING
TOP ATTRACTIONS

Beringer Vineyards. Arguably the Napa Valley's most beautiful winery, the 1876 Beringer Vineyards is also the oldest continuously operating property. In 1884 Frederick and Jacob Beringer built the Rhine House Mansion to serve as Frederick's family home. Today it serves as the reserve tasting room, where you can sample wines surrounded by Belgian art nouveau hand-carved oak and walnut furniture and stained-glass windows. The assortment includes a limited-release Chardonnay, a few big Cabernets, and a luscious white dessert wine named Nightingale. A less expensive tasting takes place in the original stone winery. ■TIP➜ First-time visitors to the valley will learn a lot about the region's wine-making history on the introductory tour. Longer tours, which might pass through a demonstration vineyard or end with a seated tasting in the Rhine House, are also offered. ⊠ *2000 Main St./ Hwy. 29, near Pratt Ave.* ☎ *707/963–8989, 866/708–9463* ⊕ *www. beringer.com* ✉ *Tastings $20–$50, tours $25–$40* ☉ *June–mid-Oct. daily 10–6; mid-Oct.–May daily 10–5; many tours daily, call for times.*

Culinary Institute of America. The West Coast headquarters of the country's leading school for chefs are in the 1889 Greystone Winery, an imposing building that once was the world's largest stone winery. On the ground floor you can check out the quirky Corkscrew Museum and browse a shop stocked with gleaming gadgets and many cookbooks. At the adjacent Flavor Bar you can sample various ingredients (for example, chocolate or olive oil). Plaques upstairs at the Vintners Hall of Fame commemorate winemakers past and present. Beguiling one-hour cooking demonstrations (reservations required) take place on weekends. The student-run Bakery Café by Illy serves soups, salads, sandwiches, and baked goods; the Institute also operates a full restaurant. ⊠ *2555 Main St./ Hwy. 29* ☎ *707/967–1100* ⊕ *www.ciachef.edu* ✉ *Museum and store free, cooking demonstrations $20, tastings $10–$15, tour $10* ☉ *Museum and store: daily 10:30–6 (Mon.–Thurs. 11–5 in winter). Tour: 11:45, 2:45, 5.*

Fodor's Choice
★ **Hall.** The award-winning Cabs, Merlots, and an impeccable Syrah produced here are works of art—and of up-to-the-minute organic-farming science and high technology. A new glass-wall tasting center allows you to see in action some of the technology winemaker Steve Leveque employs to craft wines that also include a Cabernet Franc and late-harvest Sauvignon Blanc dessert wines. The Production Tour and Barrel Tasting provides an even more in-depth look. For an understatedly elegant experience, book an Artisan Tasting at Hall's Rutherford winery, where the hilltop vistas enthrall and even the stainless-steel aging tanks are dazzlingly ornate. Tastings take place deep inside a dramatic brick-lined cave. ⊠ *401 St. Helena Hwy./Hwy. 29, near White La.* ☎ *707/967–2626, 800/688–4255* ⊕ *www.hallwines.com* ✉ *Tastings $35–$60; tours (with tastings) $40–$75* ☉ *St. Helena daily: 10–5:30. Rutherford: by appointment only.*

Fodor's Choice
★ **Joseph Phelps Vineyards.** An appointment is required for tastings at the winery started by the legendary Joseph Phelps—his son Bill now runs the operation—but it's well worth the effort. Phelps makes fine whites, but the blockbuster wines are reds, particularly the Cabernet

Sauvignon and the flagship Bordeaux-style blend called Insignia. The luscious-yet-subtle Insignia sells for more than $200 a bottle. Luckily, all tastings include the current vintage. The 90-minute seminars include one on wine-and-cheese pairing and another focusing on blending. In the latter you mix the various varietals that go into the Insignia blend. ■TIP➔ **Through early 2015, a visit to the winery will take place in a temporary tasting pavilion among the vines while the main guest center undergoes renovation.** ⊠ *200 Taplin Rd., off Silverado Trail* ☎ *707/963–2745, 800/707–5789* ⊕ *www.josephphelps.com* ✉ *Tastings $35–$150, seminars $75* ⊙ *Weekdays 9–5, weekends 10–4; tastings by appointment.*

WORTH NOTING

St. Clement Vineyards. A winery steeped in history, St. Clement is blessed with such splendid views that you might drift into reverie even before tasting the signature Bordeaux-style blend, Oroppas. (That's Sapporo spelled backward—the famous Japanese brewery once owned this place.) The tasting room is inside the 1878 Rosenbaum House, named for the wealthy merchant who built it on land purchased from his neighbor, the winemaker Charles Krug. You can also sip wine at café tables on the front porch while taking in views of nearby vineyards and beyond them Howell Mountain. Wines of note include three single-vineyard Cabernet Sauvignons made from grapes grown on Mt. Veeder and Howell and Diamond mountains. ⊠ *2867 St. Helena Hwy. N/Hwy. 29, near Deer Park Rd.* ☎ *707/967–3030* ⊕ *www.stclement. com* ✉ *Tastings $20–$30* ⊙ *Daily 11–5.*

WHERE TO EAT

$$
MODERN
AMERICAN
Fodor'sChoice
★

✕**Cindy's Backstreet Kitchen.** At her upscale-casual St. Helena outpost, Cindy Pawlcyn serves variations on the comfort food she made popular at Mustards Grill, but spices things up with dishes influenced by Mexican, Central American, and occasionally Asian cuisines. Along with mainstays such as herb-marinated hanger steak, meat loaf with garlic mashed potatoes, and beef and duck burgers served with flawless fries, the menu might include a rabbit tostada or chicken served with avocado salsa and a two-cheese stuffed green chili. Two dessert favorites are the high-style yet homey warm pineapple upside-down cake and the nearly ethereal parfait. ⑤ *Average main: $21* ⊠ *1327 Railroad Ave., at Hunt St., 1 block east of Main St.* ☎ *707/963–1200* ⊕ *www. cindysbackstreetkitchen.com.*

$$$
MODERN
AMERICAN

✕**Farmstead at Long Meadow Ranch.** Housed in a former barn, Farmstead revolves around an open kitchen where chef Stephen Barber cooks with as many local and organic ingredients as possible. Many of them—including grass-fed beef, fruits and vegetables, eggs, extra-virgin olive oil, wine, and honey—come from the property of parent company Long Meadow Ranch. Entrées might include grilled rainbow trout with wild mushrooms, or potato gnocchi with beef *ragù*, herbs, and Parmesan. Tuesday is the popular pan-fried chicken night—$35 for a three-course meal. ■TIP➔ **In warm weather, you can dine on an open-air patio among apple trees.** ⑤ *Average main: $23* ⊠ *738 Main St., at Charter Oak Ave.* ☎ *707/963–4555* ⊕ *www.longmeadowranch. com/Farmstead-Restaurant.*

$$$
MODERN
AMERICAN
Fodor'sChoice
★

✕ **Goose & Gander.** The pairing of food and drink at clubby Goose & Gander is as likely to involve cocktails as it is wine. Main courses such as Scottish salmon with shaved brussels sprouts, chanterelles, and crispy prosciutto work well with starters that include an heirloom chicory salad with smoked trout and cream of mushroom soup made from both wild and cultivated varieties. You might enjoy your meal with a top-notch Chardonnay or Pinot Noir—or a Manhattan made with three kinds of bitters and poured over a hand-carved block of ice. On cold days a fireplace warms the main dining room, and in good weather the outdoor patio is a splendid spot for dining alfresco. ■ **TIP→ Year-round the basement bar is a good stop for a drink.** ⑤ *Average main: $25* ✉ *1245 Spring St., at Oak St.* ☎ *707/967–8779* ⊕ *www.goosegander.com.*

$
AMERICAN

✕ **Gott's Roadside.** A 1950s-style outdoor hamburger stand goes upscale at this spot whose customers brave long lines to order breakfast sandwiches, juicy burgers, root-beer floats, and garlic fries. Choices not available a half century ago include the ahi tuna burger and the chili spice–marinated chicken breast served with Mexican slaw. ■ **TIP→ Arrive early or late for lunch, or all of the shaded picnic tables on the lawn might be filled.** A second branch does business at Napa's Oxbow Public Market. ⑤ *Average main: $12* ✉ *933 Main St./Hwy. 29* ☎ *707/963–3486* ⊕ *www.gotts.com* ⚐ *Reservations not accepted* ⑤ *Average main: $12* ✉ *Oxbow Public Market, 644 1st St., at McKinstry St., Napa* ☎ *707/224–6900* ⚐ *Reservations not accepted.*

$$$$
MODERN
AMERICAN
Fodor'sChoice
★

✕ **Press.** Few taste sensations surpass the combination of a sizzling steak and a Napa Valley red, a union that the chef and sommeliers here celebrate with a reverence bordering on obsession. Beef from carefully selected local and international purveyors is the star—especially the rib eye for two—but chef Stephen Rogers also prepares pork chops and free-range chicken and veal on his cherry-and-almond-wood-fired grill and rotisserie. The cellar holds thousands of wines; if you recall having a great steak with a 1985 Mayacamas Mt. Veeder Cab, you'll be able to recreate, and perhaps exceed, the original event. The kitchen's attention to detail is matched by the efforts at the bar, whose tenders know their way around both rad and trad cocktails. ⑤ *Average main: $36* ✉ *587 St. Helena Hwy./Hwy. 29, at White La.* ☎ *707/967–0550* ⊕ *www.pressthelena. com* ⚐ *Reservations essential* ⊘ *Closed Tues. No lunch.*

$$$$
MODERN
AMERICAN
Fodor'sChoice
★

✕ **The Restaurant at Meadowood.** Chef Christopher Kostow has garnered rave reviews—and three Michelin stars for several years running—for creating a unique dining experience. After you reserve your table, your party will be interviewed about food likes and dislikes, allergies, and desired level of culinary adventure. Inspired by these conversations, Kostow will transform seasonal local ingredients, some grown on or near the property, into an elaborate, multi-course experience. If you choose the Tasting Menu option ($225, $450 with wine pairings), you'll enjoy your meal in the romantic dining room, its beautiful finishes aglow with warm lighting. Choose the Counter Menu ($500, $850 with wine pairings), and you and up to three guests can sit inside the kitchen and watch Kostow's team prepare your meal. ■ **TIP→ The restaurant also offers a limited, three-course menu ($90) at its bar.** ⑤ *Average main: $225* ✉ *900 Meadowood La., off Silverado Trail N*

☎ *707/967–1205, 800/458–8080* ⊕ *www.meadowood.com* ⊙ *Closed Sun. No lunch.*

$$$$
MEDITERRANEAN
Fodor's Choice
★

✕ **Terra.** For old-school romance and service, many diners return year after year to this quiet favorite in an 1884 fieldstone building. Beloved chef Hiro Sone gives an unexpected twist to Italian and southern French cuisine in such dishes as porcini mushroom soup with grilled Berkshire pork jowl. A few standouts, like the signature sake-marinated black cod in a *shiso* broth, draw on Sone's Japanese background. Homey yet elegant desserts, courtesy of Sone's wife, Lissa Doumani, might include a chocolate brownie parfait with vanilla bean ice cream, caramelized bananas, and fudge sauce. Next door, the lively Bar Terra serves cocktails, local wines, and a menu of smaller, lighter dishes, among them succulent fried rock shrimp served with a chive-mustard sauce. ⑤ *Average main: $36* ⊠ *1345 Railroad Ave., off Hunt Ave.* ☎ *707/963–8931* ⊕ *www.terrarestaurant.com* ⊙ *Closed Tues. No lunch.*

$$$
MEDITERRANEAN

✕ **Wine Spectator Greystone Restaurant.** On busy nights at the Culinary Institute's stone-walled restaurant you may find the student chefs toiling in their open stations more entertaining than your dining companions. The dishes prepared are Mediterranean in spirit and emphasize locally grown produce. Typical main courses include seared breast of Sonoma duck with a celery-root purée and house-made pasta with trumpet mushrooms and a sherry cream sauce. ■TIP➔ **The terrace, with broad vineyard views and tables shaded by red umbrellas, is a delightful place to dine in fine weather.** ⑤ *Average main: $26* ⊠ *2555 Main St./Hwy. 29* ☎ *707/967–1010* ⊕ *www.ciachef.edu* ⊙ *Closed Sun. and Mon. late Dec.–Apr.*

WHERE TO STAY

$
HOTEL

🏨 **El Bonita Motel.** For budget-minded travelers the tidy rooms at this roadside motel are pleasant enough, and the landscaped grounds and picnic tables elevate this property over similar places. **Pros:** cheerful rooms; hot tub; microwaves and mini-refrigerators. **Cons:** road noise is a problem in some rooms. ⑤ *Rooms from: $149* ⊠ *195 Main St./Hwy. 29* ☎ *707/963–3216, 800/541–3284* ⊕ *www.elbonita.com* ⇘ *38 rooms, 4 suites* ⑩ *Breakfast.*

$$$$
HOTEL

🏨 **Harvest Inn.** Although this inn sits just off Highway 29, its patrons remain mostly above the fray, strolling 8 acres of landscaped gardens with views of adjoining vineyards, partaking in spa services, and drifting off to sleep in beds adorned with fancy linens and down pillows. **Pros:** garden setting; spacious rooms; professional staff; off-season packages a good value. **Cons:** some lower-priced rooms lack elegance; high weekend rates; ho-hum breakfast. ⑤ *Rooms from: $439* ⊠ *1 Main St.* ☎ *707/963–9463, 800/950–8466* ⊕ *www.harvestinn.com* ⇘ *69 rooms, 5 suites* ⑩ *Breakfast.*

$$$$
RESORT
Fodor's Choice
★

🏨 **Meadowood Napa Valley.** Founded in 1964 as a country club, Meadowood has evolved into a five-star resort, a gathering place for Napa's wine-making community, and a celebrated dining destination. **Pros:** superb restaurant; pleasant hiking trails; gracious service. **Cons:** very expensive; far from downtown St. Helena. ⑤ *Rooms from: $700* ⊠ *900 Meadowood La.* ☎ *707/963–3646, 800/458–8080* ⊕ *www.meadowood.com* ⇘ *85 rooms, suites, and cottages.*

6

CALISTOGA

3 miles northwest of St. Helena.

With false-fronted, Old West–style shops and 19th-century inns and hotels lining its main drag, Lincoln Avenue, Calistoga comes across as more down-to-earth than its more polished neighbors. Don't be fooled, though. On its outskirts lie some of the Wine Country's swankest (and priciest) resorts and its most fanciful piece of architecture, the medieval-style Castello di Amorosa.

Calistoga was developed as a tourist-oriented getaway from the start. In 1859 entrepreneur Sam Brannan snapped up 2,000 acres of prime property, intending to use the area's natural hot springs as the centerpiece of a resort complex. Brannan's gamble didn't pay off as he'd hoped, but some of his era's hotels and bathhouses still operate. You can come for an old-school mud bath or a dip in a spring-fed pool at one of them, or go completely 21st century and experience lavish treatments based on the latest innovations in skin and body care.

GETTING HERE AND AROUND

Highway 29 heads east (turn right) at Calistoga, where in town it is signed as Lincoln Avenue. If arriving via the Silverado Trail, head west at Highway 29/Lincoln Avenue.

EXPLORING
TOP ATTRACTIONS

Castello di Amorosa. An astounding medieval structure complete with drawbridge and moat, chapel, stables, and secret passageways, the Castello commands Diamond Mountain's lower eastern slope. Some of the 107 rooms contain replicas of 13th-century frescoes (cheekily signed [the-artist's-name].com), and the dungeon has an actual iron maiden from Nuremberg, Germany. You must pay for a tour to see most of Dario Sattui's extensive eight-level property, though basic tastings include access to part of the complex. Wines of note include several Italian-style wines, including La Castellana, a robust "super Tuscan" blend of Cabernet Sauvignon, Sangiovese, and Merlot; and Il Barone, a praiseworthy cab made largely from Diamond Mountain grapes. ■TIP➜ The two-hour food-and-wine pairing ($72) by sommelier Mary Davidek is among the Wine Country's best. ✉ 4045 N. St. Helena Hwy./ Hwy. 29 ☎ 707/967–6272 ⊕ www.castellodiamorosa.com ⌑ Tastings $19–$29, tours $34–$44 ☉ Mar.–Oct., daily 9:30–6; Nov.–Feb., daily 9:30–5; tours and food-wine pairing by appointment.

Chateau Montelena. Set amid a bucolic northern Calistoga landscape, this winery helped establish the Napa Valley's reputation for high-quality wine making. At the legendary Paris tasting of 1976, the Chateau Montelena 1973 Chardonnay took first place, beating out four white Burgundies from France and five other California Chardonnays. The 2008 movie *Bottle Shock* immortalized the event, and the winery honors its four decades of classic wine making with a special Beyond Paris & Hollywood tasting of the winery's Napa Valley Chardonnays ($40). You can also opt for a Current Release Tasting ($20) or a Limited Release Tasting ($50) that includes some stellar Cabernet Sauvignons.

oor-to-ceiling stacked bottles are no exaggeration in Schramsberg's cellars.

⊠ *1429 Tubbs La., off Hwy. 29* ☎ *707/942–5105* ⊕ *www.montelena. com* 🎫 *Tastings $20–$50, tours $30–$40; appointment required for some tastings and tours* ☉ *Daily 9:30–4, tour times vary.*

Fodor's Choice
★

Schramsberg. Founded in 1865, Schramsberg produces bubblies made using the traditional *méthode champenoise*. To taste, you first must tour, but what a tour: in addition to glimpsing the winery's historic architecture, you see the underground cellars dug in the late 19th century by Chinese laborers. A mind-boggling 2 million–plus bottles are stacked in gravity-defying configurations. The tour includes generous pours of very different sparkling wines. To learn more about them, consider the three-day **Camp Schramsberg.** Fall participants harvest grapes and explore food-and-wine pairing, riddling (the process of turning the bottles every few days to nudge the sediment into the neck of the bottle), and other topics. In spring the focus is on blending sparklers. ⊠ *1400 Schramsberg Rd., off Hwy. 29* ☎ *707/942–4558, 800/877–3623* ⊕ *www.schramsberg.com* 🎫 *Tasting and tour $50* ☉ *Tours at 10, 11:30, 12:30, 1:30, and 2:30 by appointment.*

WORTH NOTING

Dutch Henry Winery. The casual style and lack of crowds at this pet-friendly winery make it a welcome change of pace from some of its overly serious neighbors. Towering oak barrels hold excellent Cabernet Sauvignon, Pinot Noir, Zinfandel, Syrah, and other single-varietal wines, along with a well-regarded Bordeaux blend called Argos. Dutch Henry also sells a Sauvignon Blanc and a charming Rosé. ⊠ *4310 Silverado Trail, near Dutch Henry Canyon Rd., Calistoga* ☎ *707/942–5771, 888/224–5879* ⊕ *www.dutchhenry.com* 🎫 *Tasting $25* ☉ *Daily 10–4:30.*

Jericho Canyon Vineyard. It takes a Polaris all-terrain vehicle to tour the vineyards at this family-owned winery whose grapes grow on hillsides that slope as much as 45 degrees. The rocky, volcanic soils of this former cattle ranch yield intensely flavored grapes that winemaker Aaron Potts fashions into old world–style Cabernet Sauvignons, some 100%, others blended with Cabernet Franc, Merlot, Petit Verdot, and other estate-grown varietals. Tastings, which might also include a Sauvignon Blanc or a Chardonnay, are held in an underground barrel cave dug into the canyon and redolent of French oak and red wine. Topics covered on the Polaris tour include the nuances of sustainable farming in this challenging environment. ⊠ *3322 Old Lawley Toll Rd., off Hwy. 29* ☎ *707/942–9665* ⊕ *jerichocanyonvineyard.com* ⊠ *Winery tour and tasting $40, Polaris tour and tasting $80* ☉ *Tastings and tours: daily at 10, 11:30, 1, and 2:30 by appointment only.*

Lava Vine Winery. The owners and staff of this jolly spot pride themselves on creating a family- and dog-friendly environment, and you're apt to hear rock, pop, and other tunes as you taste small-lot wines that include Cabernet Sauvignon, Chenin Blanc, Syrah, and Port. The wry Pete might even start playing the banjo. If they're available, be sure to taste the Suisun Valley Petite Sirah and the Knights Valley Reserve Cabernet. ⊠ *965 Silverado Trail N.* ☎ *707/942–9500* ⊕ *www.lavavine. com* ⊠ *Tasting $10* ☉ *Daily 10–5.*

Tamber Bey Vineyards. Endurance riders Barry and Jennifer Waitte share their passion for horses and wine at their glam-rustic winery north of Calistoga. Their 22-acre Sundance Ranch remains a working equestrian facility, but the site has been revamped to include a state-of-the-art winery with separate fermenting tanks for grapes from Tamber Bey's vineyards in Yountville, Oakville, and elsewhere. The winemakers produce two Chardonnays and a Sauvignon Blanc, but the winery's stars are several subtly powerful reds, including a flagship Cabernet Sauvignon, a Merlot, and blends dominated by Cabernet Franc, Cabernet Sauvignon, and Petit Verdot. ■**TIP→** Appointments are required, but even on a few minutes' notice they're generally easy to get. ⊠ *1251 Tubbs La., at Myrtledale Rd.* ☎ *707/942–2100* ⊕ *www.tamberbey. com* ⊠ *Tastings $25–$35, tour and tasting $45* ☉ *Daily 10–5, by appointment only.*

WHERE TO EAT

$$
MODERN
AMERICAN

✕ **1226 Washington.** At this appealing homage to comfort foods worldwide you can take your meal in the boisterous but classy tavern, in a placid outdoor garden, or in the pine-walled, high-ceilinged dining room. Fried pickles, the egg-topped bubble and squeak (a Yankee's take on a Brit version of hash), pulled-chicken sliders with caramelized bacon slaw, and similar starters shake up the palate for less frolicsome mains, which might include the day's fresh fish rubbed in green tea or stuffed breast of pheasant with a parsnip purée. The cuisine here is satisfying and often tantalizing. Ⓢ *Average main: $21* ⊠ *1226 Washington St., near Lincoln Ave.* ☎ *707/942–4268* ⊕ *www.1226washington. com* ☉ *Closed Mon. and Tues.*

$$
AMERICAN

✕ **All Seasons Bistro.** Flowers top the tables at this Calistoga mainstay, a delightful stop for lunch or dinner. The seasonal menu might include braised lamb shank with creamy polenta or seared salmon fillet with chive-scallion mashed potatoes, and year-round the grilled Angus-beef burger comes with super-crispy fries and a smoked-onion aioli. Among the homey desserts are a well-executed vanilla-bean crème brûlée and a warm dark-chocolate torte. ■TIP→ You can order reasonably priced wines from the extensive list, or buy a bottle at the attached shop and have it poured at your table. ⑤ *Average main: $21* ✉ *1400 Lincoln Ave., at Washington St.* ☎ *707/942–9111* ⊕ *www. allseasonsnapavalley.net* ◷ *Closed Mon.*

$$
ITALIAN
✕ **Bosko's Trattoria.** Affable Bosko's provides tasty Italian cuisine at a fair price. The specialties include house-made pastas and thin-crust pizzas cooked in a wood-fired oven. Two of the hefty sandwiches worth trying are the free-range chicken breast sandwich on garlicky focaccia (also made in-house) and the Italian sausage on a sourdough roll. Both come with a salad or a bowl of minestrone or other soup. Nothing super-fancy here, just good value in a pleasant setting. ⑤ *Average main: $17* ✉ *1364 Lincoln Ave., at Washington St.* ☎ *707/942–9088* ⊕ *www.boskos.com* ⌫ *Reservations not accepted.*

$$$
MODERN
AMERICAN
✕ **Jolē.** Local produce plays a starring role at this modern American restaurant, not surprising as chef Matt Spector is one of the area's biggest proponents of farm-to-table dining. Depending on when you visit, you might enjoy roasted cauliflower served with almonds, dates, capers, and balsamic; kale stew with Tasso ham, kabocha squash, and fingerling potatoes; and molasses-glazed quail with farro risotto, roasted pumpkin, and a maple-bourbon demi-glace. The menu is available à la carte, and there are four-, five-, and six-course prix-fixe options. With about four-dozen wines by the glass, it's easy to find something to pair with each course. ⑤ *Average main: $25* ✉ *Mount View Hotel, 1457 Lincoln Ave., near Fair Way* ☎ *707/942–9538* ⊕ *jolerestaurant. com* ◷ *No lunch.*

$$$$
MODERN
AMERICAN
Fodor's Choice
★
✕ **Solbar.** Chef Brandon Sharp is known around the region for his subtle and sophisticated take on Wine Country cooking. As befits a restaurant at a spa resort, the menu here is divided into "healthy, lighter dishes" and "hearty cuisine." On the lighter side, the lemongrass-poached petrale sole comes with jasmine rice and hearts of palm. On the heartier side you might find a New York strip steak served with Yukon gold potatoes, sautéed rapini, oxtail marmalade, and sauce bordelaise. The service at Solbar is uniformly excellent, and in good weather the patio is a festive spot for breakfast, lunch, or dinner. ⑤ *Average main: $31* ✉ *Solage Calistoga, 755 Silverado Trail, at Rosedale Rd.* ☎ *707/226–0850* ⊕ *www.solagecalistoga.com/solbar.*

WHERE TO STAY

$
HOTEL
🛏 **Best Western Plus Stevenson Manor.** Budget travelers get what they pay for—and a little bit more—at this clean, well-run motel a few blocks from Calistoga's downtown. **Pros:** great price for region; friendly staff; nice pool area; complimentary full breakfast. **Cons:** decidedly lacking in glamour. ⑤ *Rooms from: $159* ✉ *1830 Lincoln Ave.* ☎ *707/942–1112, 800/780–7234* ⊕ *www.bestwestern.com* ⇆ *34 rooms* ⎮⊙⎮ *Breakfast.*

$$$$
RESORT
Fodor'sChoice
★
🏨 **Calistoga Ranch.** Spacious cedar-shingle lodges throughout this posh, wooded property have outdoor living areas, and even the restaurant, spa, and reception space have outdoor seating and fireplaces. **Pros:** almost half the lodges have private hot tubs on the deck; lovely hiking trails on the property; guests have reciprocal privileges at Auberge du Soleil and Solage Calistoga. **Cons:** innovative indoor-outdoor organization works better in fair weather than in rain or cold. ⑤ *Rooms from: $750* ⊠ *580 Lommel Rd.* ☎ *707/254–2800, 800/942–4220* ⊕ *www.calistogaranch.com* ↘ *50 rooms* ⦿ *No meals.*

$$$
B&B/INN
🏨 **Cottage Grove Inn.** A long driveway lined with freestanding cottages, each shaded by elm trees and with rocking chairs on the porch, looks a bit like Main Street, USA, but inside the skylighted buildings include all the perks necessary for a romantic weekend getaway. **Pros:** loaner bicycles available; plenty of privacy; huge bathtubs. **Cons:** no pool; some may find the decor too old school. ⑤ *Rooms from: $375* ⊠ *1711 Lincoln Ave.* ☎ *707/942–8400, 800/799–2284* ⊕ *www.cottagegrove.com* ↘ *16 cottages* ⦿ *Breakfast.*

$$
RESORT
🏨 **Indian Springs Resort and Spa.** Stylish Indian Springs—operating as a spa since 1862—ably splits the difference between laid-back style and ultrachic touches. **Pros:** lovely grounds with outdoor seating areas; stylish for the price; enormous mineral pool; free touring bikes. **Cons:** lodge rooms are small; service could be more polished. ⑤ *Rooms from: $262* ⊠ *1712 Lincoln Ave.* ☎ *707/942–4913* ⊕ *www.indianspringscalistoga.com* ↘ *24 rooms, 17 suites* ⦿ *No meals.*

$$
B&B/INN
Fodor'sChoice
★
🏨 **Meadowlark Country House.** Two charming European gents run this laid-back but sophisticated inn on 20 wooded acres just north of downtown. **Pros:** charming innkeepers; tasty sit-down breakfasts; welcoming vibe that attracts diverse guests. **Cons:** clothing-optional pool policy isn't for everyone. ⑤ *Rooms from: $210* ⊠ *601 Petrified Forest Rd.* ☎ *707/942–5651, 800/942–5651* ⊕ *www.meadowlarkinn.com* ↘ *5 rooms, 3 suites, 1 cottage, 1 guesthouse* ⦿ *Breakfast.*

$$$$
RESORT
🏨 **Solage Calistoga.** The aesthetic at this 22-acre property is Napa Valley barn meets San Francisco loft, so the rooms have high ceilings, polished concrete floors, recycled walnut furniture, and all-natural fabrics in soothingly muted colors. **Pros:** great service; complimentary bikes; separate pools for kids and adults. **Cons:** the vibe may not suit everyone. ⑤ *Rooms from: $465* ⊠ *755 Silverado Trail* ☎ *855/942–7442, 707/226–0800* ⊕ *www.solagecalistoga.com* ↘ *83 rooms, 6 suites* ⦿ *No meals.*

SPAS

Fodor'sChoice
★
Spa Solage. This eco-conscious spa has reinvented the traditional Calistoga mud and mineral water therapies. Case in point: the hour-long "Mudslide," a three-part treatment that includes a mud body mask (in a heated lounge), a soak in a thermal bath, and a power nap in a comfy sound/vibration chair. The mud here is a mix of clay, volcanic ash, and essential oils. Traditional spa services—combination Shiatsu-Swedish and other massages, full-body exfoliations, facials, and waxes—are available, as are fitness and yoga classes. ⊠ *755 Silverado Trail, at Rosedale Rd.* ☎ *707/226–0825* ⊕ *www.solagecalistoga.com/spa* 🎫 *Treatments $35–$335* ⊗ *Daily 8–8.*

it needs is a fair maiden: Castello di Amorosa's re-created castle.

SPORTS AND THE OUTDOORS

Calistoga Bikeshop. Options here include regular and fancy bikes that rent for $12 an hour and up, and there's a self-guided wine tour ($90) that includes tastings at three or four small wineries. ✉ *1318 Lincoln Ave., near Washington St.* ☎ *707/942–9687* ⊕ *www.calistogabikeshop.net.*

HE SONOMA VALLEY

Although the Sonoma Valley may not have the cachet of the neighboring Napa Valley, wineries here entice with an unpretentious attitude and, for the most part, smaller crowds. Sonoma's landscape seduces, too, its roads gently climbing and descending on their way to wineries hidden from the road by trees.

The scenic valley, bounded by the Mayacamas Mountains on the east and Sonoma Mountain on the west, extends north from San Pablo Bay nearly 20 miles to the eastern outskirts of Santa Rosa. The varied terrain, soils, and climate (cooler in the south because of the bay influence and hotter toward the north) allow grape growers to raise cool-weather varietals such as Chardonnay and Pinot Noir as well as Merlot, Cabernet Sauvignon, and other heat-seeking vines. The valley is home to dozens of wineries, many of them on or near Highway 12, which runs the length of the valley.

ESSENTIALS

Contact Sonoma Valley Visitors Bureau ☎ *707/996–1090, 866/996–1090* ⊕ *www.sonomavalley.com.*

SONOMA

14 miles west of Napa, 45 miles northeast of San Francisco.

Founded in the early 1800s, Sonoma is the oldest town in the Wine Country. The central Sonoma Plaza dates from the mission era; surrounding it are 19th-century adobes, atmospheric hotels, and the swooping marquee of the 1930s Sebastiani Theatre. On summer days the plaza is a hive of activity, with children blowing off steam in the playground while their folks stock up on picnic supplies and browse the boutiques surrounding the square. On your way into town from the south, you pass through the vineyards of the Carneros District, which straddles the southern sections of Sonoma and Napa counties.

GETTING HERE AND AROUND

Highway 12 (signed as Broadway as it approaches Sonoma Plaza) heads north into Sonoma from Highway 121 and south from Santa Rosa into downtown Sonoma, where (signed as West Spain Street) it travels east to the plaza. Parking is relatively easy to find on or near the plaza, and you can walk to many restaurants, shops, and tasting rooms. You'll likely want to drive to the several wineries a mile or more east of the plaza. Signs on East Spain Street or East Napa Street point the way.

EXPLORING

TOP ATTRACTIONS

Fodor'sChoice
★
Bartholomew Park Winery. Although this winery was founded in 1994, grapes were grown in some of its vineyards as early as the 1830s. The emphasis here is on handcrafted, single-varietal wines—Cabernet Sauvignon, Chardonnay, Sauvignon Blanc, Syrah, and Zinfandel—made from organically farmed grapes. A small museum off the tasting room contains vivid exhibits about the history of the winery and the Sonoma region. Another plus is the beautiful, slightly off-the-beaten-path location amid a 375-acre private park about 2 miles from downtown Sonoma. Gather a lunch to enjoy on the woodsy grounds, one of Sonoma's prettier picnic spots, or hike 3 miles on the property's marked trails. ■ TIP➔ To get here from Sonoma Plaza, head east on East Napa Street and follow the signs. ⊠ *1000 Vineyard La., off Castle Rd.* ☎ *707/935–9511* ⊕ *www.bartpark.com* 🍷 *Tasting $10, tour $20* ☉ *Daily 11–4:30; tours Fri. and Sat. at 11:30 and 2, Sun. at 2, by reservation.*

Fodor'sChoice
★
Gundlach Bundschu. Visitors may mispronounce this winery's name ("gun lock bun shoe" gets you close), but still they flock here to sample polished wines served by some of Sonoma's friendliest pourers. Most of the winery's land has been in the Bundschu family since 1858. Fine Cabernet Franc, Cabernet Sauvignon, Chardonnay, Merlot, and Tempranillo wines all are available in the standard $10 tasting. Add $5 to taste the signature Vintage Reserve red blend. For a more comprehensive experience, tour the cave ($20) or head into the vineyard ($50; available only between May and October). ■ TIP➔ In fine weather you can taste outdoors at tables that have splendid vineyard views. ⊠ *2000 Denmark St., at Bundschu Rd., off 8th St. E.* ☎ *707/938–5277* ⊕ *www. gunbun.com* 🍷 *Tastings $10–$15, tours $20–$50* ☉ *June–mid.-Oct., daily 11–5:30; mid.-Oct.–May, daily 11–4:30.*

Fodor's Choice ★ **Ram's Gate Winery.** Stunning views, ultrachic architecture, and wines made from grapes grown by acclaimed producers make a visit to Ram's Gate an event. The welcoming interior spaces—think Restoration Hardware with a dash of high-style whimsy—open up to the entire western Carneros. During fine weather you'll experience (in comfort) the cooling breezes that sweep through the area while sipping sophisticated wines, mostly Pinot Noirs and Chardonnays, but also Sauvignon Blanc, Cabernet Sauvignon, Syrah, late-harvest Zinfandel, and even a sparkler. With grapes sourced from the Sangiacomo, Lee Hudson, and other illustrious vineyards, winemaker Jeff Gaffner focuses on creating balanced vintages that express what occurred in nature that year. One food-wine pairing ($60) includes tapas, wine tasting, and a winery tour; the other ($125) focuses on food and wine education. ✉ *28700 Arnold Dr./Hwy. 121* ☎ *707/721–8700* ⊕ *www. ramsgatewinery.com* 🍷 *Tasting $7–$125* ⊗ *Thurs.–Mon. 10–6; tours (times vary) by appointment.*

Sonoma Mission. The northernmost of the 21 missions established by Franciscan friars in California, Sonoma Mission was founded in 1823 as Mission San Francisco Solano. It serves as the centerpiece of **Sonoma State Historic Park,** which includes several other sites in Sonoma and nearby Petaluma. Some early structures were destroyed, but all or part of several remaining buildings date to the days of Mexican rule over California. These include the **Sonoma Barracks,** a block west of the mission at 20 East Spain Street, which housed troops under the command of General Mariano Guadalupe Vallejo, who controlled vast tracks of land in the region. The modest museum contains displays about the missions and information about the other historic sites. ✉ *114 E. Spain St., at 1st St. E.* ☎ *707/938–9560* ⊕ *www.parks. ca.gov/?page_id–479* 🍷 *$3, includes same day admission to other historic sites* ⊗ *Daily 10–5.*

Fodor's Choice ★ **Walt Wines.** You could spend a full day sampling wines in the tasting rooms bordering Sonoma Plaza, but one not to miss is Walt, which specializes in Pinot Noir. Fruit-forward yet subtle, these wines win over even the purists who pine for the genre's days of lighter, more perfumey vintages. Walt is a good place to compare the Pinots one winemaker crafts from local grapes with others from grapes grown in Mendocino County (just north of Sonoma County), California's Central Coast, and even Oregon's Willamette Valley. Critics routinely bestow high ratings on all these wines. ✉ *380 1st St. W, at W. Spain St.* ☎ *707/933–4440* ⊕ *www.waltwines.com* 🍷 *Tastings $10–$20.*

WORTH NOTING

Buena Vista Winery. The site where modern California wine making got its start has been transformed into an entertaining homage to the accomplishments of the 19th-century wine pioneer Count Agoston Haraszthy. Tours, sometimes conducted by the count himself—as channeled by actor George Webber and others—pass through the original aging caves dug deep into the hillside by Chinese laborers. Reserve tastings ($50) include library and current wines, plus ones still aging in barrels. The stylish former press house (used for pressing grapes into wine), which dates to 1862, hosts the standard tastings. The barrel tour and

Sonoma County

tasting ($30) includes finished and barrel wines. ■**TIP→** Chardonnays and Pinot Noirs from Los Carneros AVA are this winery's strong suits. ⊠ *18000 Old Winery Rd., off Napa Rd.* ☏ *800/926–1266* ⊕ *www. buenavistawinery.com* ⊠ *Tastings $15–$50; tours $10–$30* ⊙ *Daily 10–5; tours by appointment 1–2 days in advance.*

WHERE TO EAT

$$
AMERICAN
Fodor's Choice
★

✕ **Cafe La Haye.** In a postage-stamp-size open kitchen, the skillful chef turns out main courses that star on a small but worthwhile seasonal menu emphasizing local ingredients. Chicken, beef, pasta, and fish get deluxe treatment without fuss or fanfare. The daily roasted chicken and the risotto specials are always good. Butterscotch pudding is a homey signature dessert. The dining room is compact, but the friendly owner, always there to greet diners, maintains a particularly welcoming vibe. Ⓢ *Average main: $22* ⊠ *140 E. Napa St., at 1st. St. E.* ☏ *707/935–5994* ⊕ *www.cafelahaye.com* ⊙ *Closed Sun. and Mon. No lunch.*

$$$
MODERN
AMERICAN
Fodor's Choice
★

✕ **El Dorado Kitchen.** The visual delights at this winning restaurant include its clean lines and handsome decor, but the eye inevitably drifts westward to the open kitchen, where chef Armando Navarro and his diligent crew craft flavorful dishes full of subtle surprises. Pumpkin seeds and spiced marshmallows top the popular butternut squash soup, for instance, adding a crunchy-sweet piquancy that plays well off the dish's predominantly savory sentiments. Focusing on locally sourced ingredients, the menu might include Petaluma duck breast enlivened by the tangy flavors of parsnip purée, braised endive, roasted turnips, persimmons, and huckleberries. Even a simple dish, like truffle-oil fries liberally sprinkled with Parmesan cheese, charms with its combination of tastes and textures. The noteworthy desserts include an apple tart tatin, banana crisp with lime curd, and molten chocolate cake. Ⓢ *Average main: $26* ⊠ *El Dorado Hotel, 405 1st St. W., at W. Spain St.* ☏ *707/996–3030* ⊕ *www.eldoradosonoma.com/restaurant.*

$$$
FRENCH

✕ **The Girl & the Fig.** Chef Sondra Bernstein transformed the historic bar room of the Sonoma Hotel into a hot spot for inventive French cooking. You can always find a dish with the signature figs on the menu, whether it's a fig-and-arugula salad or an aperitif blending sparkling wine with fig liqueur. Also look for duck confit, a burger with matchstick fries, or wild flounder *meunière.* The wine list is notable for its emphasis on Rhône varietals, and a counter in the bar area sells artisanal cheese platters for eating here as well as cheese by the pound to go. The indulgent Sunday brunch includes potato pancakes with smoked salmon, dill crème fraîche, and caviar. Ⓢ *Average main: $24* ⊠ *Sonoma Hotel, 110 W. Spain St., at 1st St. W.* ☏ *707/938–3634* ⊕ *www.thegirlandthefig.com.*

$$
AMERICAN
Fodor's Choice
★

✕ **Harvest Moon Cafe.** It's easy to feel like one of the family at this little restaurant with an odd, zigzagging layout. Diners seated at one of the two tiny bars chat with the servers like old friends, but the husband-and-wife team in the kitchen is serious about the food, much of which relies on local produce. The ever-changing menu might include homey dishes such as grilled pork loin with crispy polenta and artichokes, Niman Ranch rib-eye steak with a red-wine sauce, or seared ahi tuna au poivre. Everything is so perfectly executed and the vibe is so genuinely warm that a visit here is deeply satisfying. ■TIP➔ A spacious back patio with tables arranged around a fountain more than doubles the seating; a heated tent keeps this area warm in winter. ⑤ *Average main: $22* ✉ *487 1st St. W., at W. Napa St.* ☎ *707/933–8160* ⊕ *www. harvestmooncafesonoma.com* ☯ *Closed Tues. No lunch.*

$$$ ✕ **Hot Box Grill.** Comfort foods aren't often described as *nuanced*, but
MODERN the term aptly describes the locally sourced preparations chef Norm
AMERICAN Owens conjures up at his modest roadside restaurant. Take the fries (but not too many): long and not at all lean, they're cooked in duck fat and served with malt-vinegar aioli, lending them a richness that lingers pleasingly in your memory. There's lots of frying going on—even Cornish game hen gets the treatment. Up against these dishes, the pasta offerings almost seem light, and the appetizers—among them spicy ahi tuna with a ponzu sauce, avocado mousse, and crispy wontons— downright dainty. ⑤ *Average main: $24* ✉ *18350 Sonoma Hwy./Hwy. 12* ☎ *707/939–8383* ⊕ *www.hotboxgrill.com* ☯ *Closed Mon. and Tues. No lunch.*

$$$ ✕ **LaSalette.** Born in the Azores and raised in Sonoma, chef-owner Man-
PORTUGUESE uel Azevedo serves dishes inspired by his native Portugal in this warmly decorated spot. The best seats are on a patio along an alleyway off Sonoma Plaza. Such boldly flavored dishes as pork tenderloin *recheado*, stuffed with olives and almonds and topped with a Port sauce, might be followed by a dish of rice pudding with Madeira-braised figs or a Port from the varied list. The daily seafood specials are also well worth a try. ⑤ *Average main: $24* ✉ *452 1st St. E., near E. Spain St.* ☎ *707/938–1927* ⊕ *www.lasalette-restaurant.com.*

$$$$ ✕ **Santé.** This elegant dining room has evolved into a destination res-
AMERICAN taurant through its focus on seasonal and locally sourced ingredients.
Fodor's Choice The room is understated, with dark walls and soft lighting, but the
★ food is anything but. Dishes such as the Sonoma Liberty duck breast and confit leg, served with wild rice, gray shallots, and quince mustard, are sophisticated without being fussy. Others, like the sampler of Niman Ranch beef that includes a petite filet mignon, a skirt steak, and braised *pavé beef à la bourguignonne*, are pure decadence. The restaurant offers a seasonal tasting menu ($135). ⑤ *Average main: $43* ✉ *Fairmont Sonoma Mission Inn & Spa, 100 Boyes Blvd./Hwy. 12, 2½ miles north of Sonoma Plaza, Boyes Hot Springs* ☎ *707/938–9000* ⊕ *www.santediningroom.com* ☯ *No lunch.*

$ ✕ **Sunflower Caffé.** The food at this casual eatery, mostly salads and
AMERICAN sandwiches, is simple but satisfying. Highlights include the smoked duck breast sandwich, served on a baguette and slathered with caramelized onions. A meal of soup and local cheeses is a good option if you just want to nibble. Both the pretty patio, which is in the back, and the sidewalk seating area facing Sonoma Plaza are equipped with heating lamps and get plenty of shade, so they're comfortable in all but the most inclement weather. Cheerful artwork brightens up the interior, where locals hunker over their computers and take advantage of the free Wi-Fi. Omelets and waffles are the stars at breakfast. ⑤ *Average main: $13* ✉ *421 1st St. W, at W. Spain St.* ☎ *707/996–6645* ⊕ *www. sonomasunflower.com* ☯ *No dinner.*

Where to Eat and Stay in Sonoma County

WHERE TO STAY

$$
B&B/INN

El Dorado Hotel. Rooms in this remodeled 1843 building strike a spare, modern pose with their pristine white bedding, but the Mexican-tile floors hint at Sonoma's mission-era past. **Pros:** stylish for the price; hip on-site restaurant; good café for breakfast; central location. **Cons:** rooms are small; lighting could be better; noisy. $ *Rooms from: $200* ✉ *405 1st St. W.* ☎ *707/996–3030* ⊕ *www.eldoradosonoma.com/hotel* ⬐ *27 rooms* ⦿ *No meals.*

$$$$
RESORT

Fairmont Sonoma Mission Inn & Spa. The real draw at this mission-style resort is the extensive, swank spa with its array of massages and treatments, some designed for couples. **Pros:** enormous spa; excellent restaurant; free shuttle to downtown. **Cons:** standard rooms on the smaller side; lacks intimacy of similarly priced options. $ *Rooms from: $439* ✉ *100 Boyes Blvd./Hwy. 12, 2½ miles north of Sonoma Plaza, Boyes Hot Springs* ☎ *707/938–9000* ⊕ *www.fairmont.com/sonoma* ⬐ *166 rooms, 60 suites* ⦿ *No meals.*

$
B&B/INN
FAMILY

Sonoma Creek Inn. The small but cheerful rooms at this motel-style inn are individually decorated with painted wooden armoires, cozy quilts, and brightly colored contemporary artwork. **Pros:** clean, well-lighted bathrooms; lots of charm for the price; popular with bicyclists. **Cons:** office not staffed 24 hours a day; a 10-minute drive from Sonoma Plaza. $ *Rooms from: $145* ✉ *239 Boyes Blvd., off Hwy. 12* ☎ *707/939–9463, 888/712–1289* ⊕ *www.sonomacreekinn.com* ⬐ *16 rooms.*

SPAS

Willow Stream Spa at Fairmont Sonoma Mission Inn & Spa. With 40,000 square feet and 30 treatment rooms, the Wine Country's largest spa provides every amenity you could possibly want, including pools and hot tubs fed by local thermal springs. Although the place bustles with patrons in summer and on some weekends, the vibe is always soothing. The signature bathing ritual includes an exfoliating shower, dips in two mineral-water soaking pools, an herbal steam, a dry sauna, and cool-down showers. Other popular treatments include the warm ginger-oil float, which involves relaxation in a weightless environment, and the perennially popular caviar facial. The most requested room among couples is outfitted with a two-person copper bathtub. ✉ *100 Boyes Blvd./Hwy. 12, 2½ miles north of Sonoma Plaza, Boyes Hot Springs* ☎ *707/938–9000* ⊕ *www.fairmont.com/sonoma/willow-stream* ⬐ *Treatments $65–$485.*

SHOPPING

Sonoma Plaza is the town's main shopping magnet, with tempting boutiques and specialty food purveyors facing the square or just a block or two away.

Fodor's Choice
★

Chateau Sonoma. The fancy furniture, lighting fixtures, and objets d'art at this upscale shop make it a dangerous place to enter: after just a few minutes you may find yourself reconsidering your entire home's aesthetic. The owner's keen eye for style and sense of whimsy make a visit here a delight. ✉ *153 W. Napa St., near 2nd St. W* ☎ *707/935–8553* ⊕ *www.chateausonoma.com.*

Horseback riding tours loop around Jack London State Historic Park.

The Epicurean Connection. In addition to selling Délice de La Vallée, her award-winning cheese made from triple-cream cow and goat milk, Sheana Davis offers jams, sauces, tapenades, and other toppings from local producers. She also sells sandwiches and sweets, and stages good live music from Thursday through Saturday evening and on Sunday afternoon. ⊠ *122 W. Napa St., at 1st St.* ☏ *707/935-7960* ⊕ *www.the epicureanconnection.com.*

GLEN ELLEN

7 miles north of Sonoma.

Unlike its flashier Napa Valley counterparts, Glen Ellen eschews well-groomed sidewalks lined with upscale boutiques and restaurants, preferring instead its crooked streets, some with no sidewalks at all, shaded with stands of old oak trees. Jack London, who represents Glen Ellen's rugged spirit, lived in the area for many years; the town commemorates him with place names and nostalgic establishments. Hidden among sometimes-ramshackle buildings abutting Sonoma and Calabasas creeks are low-key shops and galleries worth poking through, and several fine dining establishments.

GETTING HERE AND AROUND

Glen Ellen sits just off Highway 12. From the north or south, take Arnold Drive west and follow it south less than a mile. The walkable downtown straddles a half-mile stretch of Arnold Drive.

EXPLORING

Fodor'sChoice ★ **Benziger Family Winery.** One of the best-known Sonoma County wineries sits on a sprawling estate in a bowl with 360-degree sun exposure, the benefits of which are explored on popular tram tours that depart several times daily. Guides explain Benziger's biodynamic farming practices and give you a glimpse of the extensive cave system. The regular tram tour costs $20; another tour costing $40 concludes with a seated tasting. Noted for its Chardonnay, Cabernet Sauvignon, Merlot, Pinot Noir, and Sauvignon Blanc wines, the winery is a beautiful spot for a picnic. ■ TIP→ Reserve a seat on the tram tour through the winery's website or arrive early in the day on summer weekends and during harvest season. ⊠ *1883 London Ranch Rd., off Arnold Dr.* ☎ *707/935–3000, 888/490–2739* ⊕ *www.benziger.com* ☜ *Tastings $10–$20, tours $20–$40* ⊙ *Daily 10–5; tours daily at 11:15, 12:45, 2:15.*

Fodor'sChoice ★ **Jack London State Historic Park.** The pleasures are both pastoral and intellectual at the beloved former ranch of the late Jack London. You could easily spend the afternoon hiking along the edge of vineyards and through stands of oaks. Several manuscripts and a handful of personal effects are on view at the House of Happy Walls Museum, which provides a tantalizing overview of the author's life and literary passions. A short hike away lie the ruins of Wolf House, which mysteriously burned down just before the writer was to move in. Also open to the public are a few restored farm outbuildings and the Cottage, a wood-framed building where he penned many of his later works. London is buried on the property. ⊠ *2400 London Ranch Rd., off Arnold Dr.* ☎ *707/938–5216* ⊕ *www.jacklondonpark.com* ☜ *Parking $10 ($5 walk-in or bike), includes admission to museum; cottage $4* ⊙ *Mar.–Nov. park daily 9:30–5, museum 10–5, cottage noon–4; Dec.–Feb., Thurs.–Mon. park 9:30–5, museum 10–5, cottage noon–4.*

WHERE TO EAT

$$
FRENCH
Fodor'sChoice ★ **✕ The Fig Cafe.** Pale sage walls, a sloping ceiling, and casual but warm service set a sunny mood in this little bistro. The compact menu focuses on California and French comfort food—pot roast and duck confit, for instance, as well as thin-crust pizza. Steamed mussels are served with terrific crispy fries, which also accompany the sirloin burger. Weekend brunch brings out locals and tourists for French toast, pizza with applewood-smoked bacon and poached eggs, corned-beef hash, and other delights. ■ TIP→ The unusual no-corkage-fee policy makes this a great place to drink the wine you discovered down the road. ⑤ *Average main: $18* ⊠ *13690 Arnold Dr., at O'Donnell La.* ☎ *707/938–2130* ⊕ *www.thefigcafe.com* ⚄ *Reservations not accepted* ⊙ *No lunch weekdays.*

$$
ECLECTIC **✕ Glen Ellen Inn Oyster Grill & Martini Bar.** Tucked inside a creekside 1940s cottage, this cozy restaurant exudes romance, especially if you sit in the shady garden or on the patio strung with tiny lights. After taking the edge off your hunger with some oysters on the half shell and an ice-cold martini, order from a menu that plucks elements from California, French, and other cuisines. You might find ginger tempura calamari with grilled pineapple salsa, or hanger steak with chimichurri sauce

and a side of garlic fries. Desserts tend toward the indulgent; witness the warm cinnamon-pecan bread pudding with a chocolate center that sits in a puddle of brandy sauce. $ *Average main: $20* ⊠ *13670 Arnold Dr., at O'Donnell La.* ☎ *707/996–6409* ⊕ *www.glenelleninn. com* ☺ *No lunch Wed.*

$$ ✕ **Glen Ellen Star.** Chef Ari Weiswasser honed his craft at the French
ECLECTIC Laundry, Daniel, and other bastions of culinary finesse, but the goal
Fodor'sChoice at his hot-ticket Wine Country boîte is haute-rustic cuisine, much of
★ which emerges from a wood-fired oven that burns a steady 600°F. Pizzas such as the crisp-crusted, richly sauced Margherita thrive in the torrid heat, as do root and other vegetables roasted in small iron skillets. Ditto for entrées that include juicy, tender roasted whole fish. Weiswasser signs each dish with a sauce, emulsion, or sly blend of spices that jazzes things up without upstaging the primary ingredient. The restaurant's decor is equally restrained, with an open-beam ceiling, exposed hardwood floors, and utilitarian seating. ■TIP➔ Many regulars perch on a stool at the kitchen-view counter to watch the chefs at work. $ *Average main: $21* ⊠ *13648 Arnold Dr., at Warm Springs Rd.* ☎ *707/343–1384* ⊕ *glenellenstar.com* ⌲ *Reservations essential* ☺ *No lunch.*

WHERE TO STAY

$ ⊡ **Beltane Ranch.** On a slope of the Mayacamas range a few miles from
B&B/INN Glen Ellen, this 1892 ranch house, shaded by magnificent oak trees,
Fodor'sChoice contains charmingly old fashioned rooms, each individually deco-
★ rated with antiques and original artwork by noted artists. **Pros:** casual, friendly atmosphere; reasonable prices; beautiful grounds with ancient oak trees. **Cons:** downstairs rooms get some noise from upstairs rooms; ceiling fans instead of air-conditioning. $ *Rooms from: $185* ⊠ *11775 Sonoma Hwy./Hwy. 12* ☎ *707/996–6501* ⊕ *www.beltaneranch.com* ⌲ *3 rooms, 2 suites, 1 cottage* ⌷ *Breakfast.*

$$ ⊡ **Gaige House.** Asian objets d'art and leather club chairs cozied up to
B&B/INN the lobby fireplace are just a few of the graceful touches in this luxuri-
Fodor'sChoice ous but understated bed-and-breakfast. **Pros:** beautiful lounge areas;
★ lots of privacy; excellent service; full breakfasts, afternoon wine and appetizers. **Cons:** sound carries in the main house; the least expensive rooms are on the small side. $ *Rooms from: $275* ⊠ *13540 Arnold Dr.* ☎ *707/935–0237, 800/935–0237* ⊕ *www.gaige.com* ⌲ *10 rooms, 13 suites* ⌷ *Breakfast.*

$$ ⊡ **Olea Hotel.** The husband-and-wife team of Ashish and Sia Patel
B&B/INN gave an extreme makeover to a run-down former B&B, and after
Fodor'sChoice a year's labor unveiled a boutique lodging that's at once sophisti-
★ cated and down-home country casual. **Pros:** beautiful style; welcoming staff; chef-prepared breakfasts; complimentary wine throughout stay. **Cons:** fills up quickly on weekends; minor road noise in some rooms. $ *Rooms from: $257* ⊠ *5131 Warm Springs Rd., west off Arnold Dr.* ☎ *707/996–5131* ⊕ *www.oleahotel.com* ⌲ *10 rooms, 2 cottages* ⌷ *Breakfast.*

6

Hitching a ride on the Benziger Family Winery tram tour

KENWOOD

3 miles north of Glen Ellen.

Tiny Kenwood consists of little more than a few restaurants and shops and a historic train depot. But hidden in this pretty landscape of meadows and woods at the north end of Sonoma Valley are several good wineries, most just off the Sonoma Highway (Highway 12).

GETTING HERE AND AROUND
To get to Kenwood from Glen Ellen, drive north on Highway 12.

EXPLORING
Deerfield Ranch Winery. The focus at Deerfield is on producing "clean wines"—ones low in histamines and sulfites—the better to eliminate the headaches and allergic reactions some red-wine drinkers experience. Winemaker Robert Rex accomplishes this goal with no loss of flavor or complexity. Deerfield wines are bold, fruit-forward wines with a long finish. The lush DRX and Meritage Bordeaux-style red blends invite contemplation about the vineyards, weather, and winemaking skills involved in their creation. To taste these and other wines, including a finely tuned blend of four white grapes, you walk deep into a 23,000-square-foot cave. ■**TIP→** Standard tastings ($15) include five wines; for an additional $5, you can sample more, including at least one older, library wine. ✉ *10200 Sonoma Hwy./Hwy. 12* ☎ *707/833–5215* ⊕ *www.deerfieldranch.com* 🍷 *Tastings $15–$20* 🕙 *Daily 10:30–4:30.*

Kunde Estate Winery & Vineyards. On your way into Kunde you pass a terrace flanked by fountains, virtually coaxing you to stay for a picnic with views over the vineyard. Best known for its toasty Chardonnays, the winery also makes well-regarded Sauvignon Blanc, Cabernet Sauvignon, Merlot, and Zinfandel wines. Among the Destination wines available only through the winery, the Dunfillan Cuvée, an astute blend of Cabernet and Syrah grapes, is worth checking out. The free basic tour of the grounds includes the caves, some of which stretch 175 feet below a vineyard. ■**TIP→** Reserve ahead for the Mountain Top Tasting, a popular tour that ends with a sampling of reserve wines ($40). ✉ *9825 Sonoma Hwy./Hwy. 12* ☎ *707/833–5501* ⊕ *www.kunde.com* ⌑ *Tastings $10–$40, tours free–$50* ◔ *Daily 10:30–5, tours daily at various times.*

St. Francis Winery. Nestled at the foot of Mt. Hood, St. Francis has earned national acclaim for its food-and-wine pairings. With its red-tile roof and dramatic bell tower, the winery's California mission–style visitor center occupies one of Sonoma's most scenic locations. The charm of the surroundings is matched by the wines, most of them red, including rich, earthy Zinfandels from the Dry Creek, Russian River, and Sonoma valleys. Chef David Bush's five-to-seven-course small bites and wine pairings ($50)—bouillabaisse with a mellifluous Cabernet Franc, for example—are offered from Thursday through Monday; pairings with cheeses and charcuterie ($30) are available daily. ✉ *100 Pythian Rd., off Hwy. 12* ☎ *888/675–9463, 707/833–6146* ⊕ *www.stfranciswinery. com* ⌑ *Tastings $10–$50* ◔ *Daily 10–5.*

WHERE TO EAT AND STAY

$ | ✕**Café Citti.** Classical music in the background, a friendly staff, and a
ITALIAN | roaring fire when it's cold outside keep this roadside café from feeling too spartan. Order dishes such as roast chicken and slabs of tiramisu from the counter and they're delivered to your table, indoors or on an outdoor patio. The array of prepared salads and sandwiches means the café does a brisk business in takeout for picnic packers, but you can also choose pasta made to order. $ *Average main: $13* ✉ *9049 Sonoma Hwy./Hwy. 12* ☎ *707/833–2690* ⊕ *www.cafecitti.com* ⌑ *Reservations not accepted.*

$$$$ | ⌂**Kenwood Inn and Spa.** French doors opening onto terraces or balconies,
B&B/INN | fluffy featherbeds, and wood-burning fireplaces give the uncommonly
Fodor'sChoice | spacious guest rooms, many with tile floors, at this inn a particularly
★ | romantic air. **Pros:** large rooms; lavish furnishings; excellent restaurant; romantic. **Cons:** road or lobby noise in some rooms; expensive. $ *Rooms from: $475* ✉ *10400 Sonoma Hwy./Hwy. 12* ☎ *707/833–1293, 800/353–6966* ⊕ *www.kenwoodinn.com* ⌑ *25 rooms, 4 suites* ◉*|Breakfast.*

SPAS

Spa at Kenwood Inn. A pretty setting, expert practitioners, and rejuvenating French therapies make a visit to the Spa at Kenwood Inn a marvelously ethereal experience. The wine-based Vinothérapie treatments and beauty products from the French line Caudalíe combine in the delicious-sounding Honey Wine Wrap, which involves a warming, full-body slathering of wine yeast and honey, the better to rehydrate your parched and neglected skin. The Crushed Cabernet Scrub, designed to stimulate and soften your skin, raises the sweetness ante by adding brown sugar to the honey, along with crushed grape seeds and grape-seed oil. The spa's other services include massages and facials using the products and treatments by iS Clinical and Intraceuticals. ✉ *10400 Sonoma Hwy./Hwy. 12* ☎ *707/833–1293, 800/353–6966* ⊕ *www.kenwoodinn.com/spa.php* ☞ *Treatments $125–$390.*

ELSEWHERE IN SONOMA COUNTY

At nearly 1,598 square miles, there's more to Sonoma County than the day-tripper favorites of Sonoma, Glen Ellen, and Kenwood. To the north is Healdsburg, a small town that receives national media attention for its swank hotels and remarkable restaurants. An ideal base for wine tasting in northern Sonoma County, it's within easy striking distance of the scenic vineyards of the Alexander, Dry Creek, and Russian River valleys, home to some of the country's best Pinot Noir, Cabernet Sauvignon, Zinfandel, and Sauvignon Blanc vineyards. Though hardly unknown regions, the quiet roads that pass by them feel a world away from Highway 29 in Napa. The western stretches of Sonoma County are sparsely populated in comparison to the rest of Sonoma and have fewer wineries.

ESSENTIALS

Sonoma County Tourism Bureau ✉ *3637 Westwind Blvd., Santa Rosa* ☎ *707/522–5800, 800/576–6662* ⊕ *www.sonomacounty.com.*

SANTA ROSA

8 miles northwest of Kenwood; 55 miles north of San Francisco.

With more than 170,000 people, Santa Rosa, the Wine Country's largest city, isn't likely to charm you with its malls, office buildings, and frequent traffic snarls. Its moderately priced lodgings, however, can come in handy, especially since Santa Rosa is roughly equidistant from Sonoma, Healdsburg, and notable Russian River wineries.

GETTING HERE AND AROUND

Santa Rosa straddles U.S. 101, the route to take (north) from San Francisco. From the Sonoma Valley, take Highway 12 north. Factor in extra time when driving around sprawling Santa Rosa, especially during morning and evening commute hours.

EXPLORING

TOP ATTRACTIONS

Fodor'sChoice
★

Matanzas Creek Winery. The visitor center at Matanzas Creek sets itself apart with an understated Japanese aesthetic, extending to a tranquil fountain, a koi pond, and a vast field of lavender. The winery specializes in Sauvignon Blanc, Chardonnay, and Merlot wines, although it also produces Pinot Noirs and a rich Bordeaux blend called Journey. All tours take in the beautiful estate and include tastings. The Signature tour concludes with tastings of limited-production and library wines paired with artisanal cheeses. ■TIP→ The ideal time to visit is in May and June, when lavender perfumes the air. ✉ *6097 Bennett Valley Rd.* ☎ *707/528–6464, 800/590–6464* ⊕ *www.matanzascreek.com* 🍷 *Tastings $10–$20, tours $10–$35* ⊙ *Daily 10–4:30; estate tour ($10) daily at 10:30, others by appointment.*

FAMILY **Safari West.** An unexpected bit of wilderness in the Wine Country, this African wildlife preserve covers 400 acres. A visit begins with a stroll around enclosures housing lemurs, cheetahs, giraffes, and rare birds such as the brightly colored scarlet ibis. Next, climb with your guide onto open-air vehicles that spend about two hours combing the expansive property, where more than 80 species—including gazelles, wildebeests, and zebras—inhabit the hillsides. ✉ *3115 Porter Creek Rd., off Mark West Springs Rd.* ☎ *707/579–2551, 800/616–2695* ⊕ *www. safariwest.com* 🍷 *$78–$80* ⊙ *Safaris: mid-Mar.–early Sept. at 9, 10, 1, 2, and 4; hrs vary rest of year.*

WORTH NOTING

FAMILY **Charles M. Schulz Museum.** Fans of Snoopy and Charlie Brown will love this museum dedicated to the late Charles M. Schulz, who lived his last three decades in Santa Rosa. Permanent installations include a re-creation of the cartoonist's studio, and temporary exhibits often focus on a particular theme in his work. ■TIP→ Children and adults can take a stab at creating cartoons in the Education Room. ✉ *2301 Hardies La., at W. Steele La.* ☎ *707/579–4452* ⊕ *www.schulzmuseum. org* 🍷 *$10* ⊙ *Labor Day–Memorial Day, Mon. and Wed.–Fri. 11–5, weekends 10–5; Memorial Day–Labor Day, weekdays 11–5, weekends 10–5.*

DeLoach Vineyards. Slightly off the beaten track in western Santa Rosa, DeLoach is best known for its Russian River Valley Pinot Noirs, among them the much-lauded Pennacchio Vineyard edition and the Estate Collection Pinot Noir. The winery also produces old-vine Zinfandels, Chardonnays, and a handful of other varietals. Some of the reds are made using open-top wood fermentation vats that are uncommon in Sonoma but have been used in France for centuries to intensify a wine's flavor. The history-rich tour focuses on the estate vineyards outside the tasting-room door, where you can learn about the winery's labor-intensive biodynamic and organic farming methods. ✉ *1791 Olivet Rd., off Guerneville Rd.* ☎ *707/526–9111* ⊕ *www.deloachvineyards.com* 🍷 *Tastings $10–$50, tour and tasting $15* ⊙ *Daily 10–5; tour at 11.*

WHERE TO EAT

$$$ ╳ **Willi's Wine Bar.** Don't let the name fool you: instead of a sedate spot ECLECTIC serving wine and delicate nibbles, you'll find a cozy warren of rooms Fodor'sChoice where boisterous crowds snap up small plates from the globe-trotting ★ menu. Dishes such as the pork-belly pot stickers represent Asia, and Moroccan-style lamb chops and balsamic roasted fig and Serrano-ham flatbread are some of the Mediterranean-inspired foods. The plate of crispy-skin Mt. Lassen trout is among the many using California-sourced ingredients. Wines are available in 2-ounce pours, making it easier to pair each of your little plates with a different glass. ■TIP→ It

6

can get noisy inside on busy nights, so consider a table on the covered patio. $ *Average main: $28* ⊠ *4404 Old Redwood Hwy., at Ursuline Rd.* ☎ *707/526–3096* ⊕ *williswinebar.net* ⊘ *No lunch Sun. and Mon.*

WHERE TO STAY

$$
HOTEL

🖵 **Vintners Inn.** The owners of Ferrari-Carano Vineyards operate this oasis set amid 80 acres of vineyards that's known for its comfortable lodgings. **Pros:** spacious rooms with comfortable beds; jogging path through the vineyards; online deals pop up year-round. **Cons:** occasional noise from adjacent events center; some decor seems dated. $ *Rooms from: $265* ⊠ *4350 Barnes Rd.* ☎ *707/575–7350, 800/421–2584* ⊕ *www.vintnersinn.com* ⇦ *38 rooms, 6 suites* ◎ *No meals.*

RUSSIAN RIVER VALLEY

10 miles northwest of Santa Rosa.

The Russian River flows from Mendocino to the Pacific, but Russian River Valley wine making centers on a triangle with points at Healdsburg, Guerneville, and Sebastopol. Tall redwoods shade the two-lane roads of this scenic area, where, thanks to the cooling marine influence, Pinot Noir and Chardonnay are the king and queen of grapes.

GETTING HERE AND AROUND

Many Russian River Valley visitors base themselves in Healdsburg. You can find noteworthy purveyors of Pinots and Chards by heading west from downtown on Mill Street, which eventually becomes Westside Road. For Forestville and Sebastopol wineries, continue south and west along Westside until it intersects River Road and turn west. Turn south at Mirabel Road and follow it to Highway 116. Turn west for Forestville and east for Sebastopol. Follow Highway 12 west 6 miles from Sebastopol to visit Freestone; Occidental is 4 miles north on the Bohemian Highway.

ESSENTIALS

Contacts Russian River Wine Road ☎ *707/433–4335, 800/723–6336* ⊕ *www.wineroad.com.*

EXPLORING

TOP ATTRACTIONS

Fodor'sChoice
★

Hartford Family Winery. Pinot Noir lovers appreciate the subtle differences in the wines Hartford's Jeff Stewart crafts from grapes grown in Sonoma County's three top AVAs for the varietal—Los Carneros, Russian River Valley, and the Sonoma Coast—along with one from the Anderson Valley, just north in Mendocino County. The Pinot Noirs win praise from major wine critics, and Stewart also makes highly rated Chardonnays and old-vine Zinfandels. A reserve tasting ($15) includes a flight of six wines; a tour of the winery is part of the seated private library tasting ($35). ■**TIP→** If the weather's good and you've made a reservation, your reserve tasting can take place on the patio outside the opulent main winery building. ⊠ *8075 Martinelli Rd., off Hwy. 116 or River Rd., Forestville* ☎ *707/887–8030, 800/588–0234* ⊕ *www.hartfordwines.com* ◳ *Tastings $15–$35* ⊘ *Daily 10–4:30, tours by appointment.*

Fodor's Choice
★
Iron Horse Vineyards. A meandering one-lane road leads to this winery known for its sparkling wines and estate Chardonnays and Pinot Noirs. The sparklers have made history: Ronald Reagan served them at his summit meetings with Mikhail Gorbachev; George Herbert Walker Bush took some along to Moscow for treaty talks; and Barack Obama has included them at official state dinners. Despite Iron Horse's brushes with fame, a casual rusticity prevails at its outdoor tasting area (large heaters keep things comfortable on chilly days), which gazes out on acres of rolling, vine-covered hills. Tours take place on weekdays at 10 am. ■**TIP**➜ Winemaker David Munksgard leads the Friday tour when his schedule permits. ✉ *9786 Ross Station Rd., off Hwy. 116, Sebastopol* ☎ *707/887–1507* ⊕ *www.ironhorsevineyards. com* ⚏ *Tasting $20, tour $25* ☉ *Daily 10–4:30, tour (by appointment) weekdays at 10.*

Fodor's Choice
★
Merry Edwards Winery. Winemaker Merry Edwards describes the Russian River Valley as "the epicenter of great Pinot Noir," and she produces wines that express the unique characteristics of the soils, climates, and Pinot Noir clones from which they derive. (Edwards's research into Pinot Noir clones is so extensive that there's even one named after her.) The valley's advantages, says Edwards, are warmer-than-average daytime temperatures that encourage more intense fruit, and evening fogs mitigate the extra heat's potential negative effects. Group tastings of the well-composed single-vineyard and blended Pinots take place throughout the day, and there are five sit-down appointment slots available except on Sunday. Edwards also makes a fine Sauvignon Blanc that's lightly aged in old oak. Tastings end, rather than begin, with this singular white wine so as not to distract guests' palates from the Pinot Noirs. ✉ *2959 Gravenstein Hwy. N/Hwy. 116, near Oak Grove Ave., Sebastopol* ☎ *707/823–7466, 888/388–9050* ⊕ *www.merryedwards.com* ⚏ *Tasting free* ☉ *Daily 9:30–4:30; call for appointment or drop in and join next available tasting.*

Fodor's Choice
★
Rochioli Vineyards and Winery. Claiming one of the prettiest picnic sites in the area, with tables overlooking the vineyards, this winery has an airy little tasting room with an equally romantic view. Production is small and fans on the winery's mailing list snap up most of the bottles, but the winery is still worth a stop. Because of the cool growing conditions in the Russian River Valley, the flavors of the Chardonnay and Sauvignon Blanc are intense and complex, and the Pinot Noir, which helped cement the Russian River's status as a Pinot powerhouse, is consistently excellent. ✉ *6192 Westside Rd., Healdsburg* ☎ *707/433–2305* ⊕ *www.rochioliwinery.com* ⚏ *Tasting $10* ☉ *Early Jan.–mid-Dec., Thurs.–Mon. 11–4, Tues. and Wed. by appointment.*

WORTH NOTING

The Barlow. On the site of a former apple cannery, this cluster of buildings celebrates Sonoma County's "maker" culture with an inspired combination production space and marketplace. The complex contains breweries and wine-making facilities, along with areas where people create or sell crafts, large-scale artwork, and artisanal food, herbs, and beverages. There's even a studio where artists using traditional methods are creating the world's largest *thangka* (Tibetan painting). Only club

members can visit the anchor wine tenant, Kosta Browne, but La Follette (sublimely aromatic Pinot Noirs and velvety Chardonnays) and other small producers have tasting rooms open to the public. Warped Brewing Company and Woodfour Brewing Company make and sell ales on-site, and you can have a nip of gin at Spirit Works Distillery. ⊠ 6770 McKinley St., at Morris St., north off Hwy. 12, Sebastopol ☎ 707/824–5600 ⊕ www.thebarlow.net ⊠ Free to complex; tasting fees at wineries, breweries, distillery ⊘ Daily, hrs vary.

Gary Farrell Winery. Pass through an impressive metal gate and wind your way up a steep hill to reach Gary Farrell, a spot with knockout views over the rolling hills and vineyards below. Though its Zinfandels and Chardonnays often excel, the winery built its reputation on Pinot Noirs, crafted these days by winemaker Theresa Heredia. ■TIP➜ Worth seeking out are the wines in the Inspiration Series, made from small lots of grapes—perhaps from certain vineyard blocks or a particular clone—that Heredia finds of special merit. ⊠ 10701 Westside Rd., Healdsburg ☎ 707/473–2909 ⊕ www.garyfarrellwines.com ⊠ Tastings $15–$25, tour $35 ⊘ Daily 10:30–4:30, tour by appointment.

WHERE TO EAT

$$$$
FRENCH
Fodor's Choice
★

✕ **The Farmhouse Inn.** From the sommelier who assists you with wine choices to the servers who describe the provenance of the black truffles shaved over the intricate pasta dishes, the staff matches the quality of this restaurant's French-inspired cuisine. The signature dish, "Rabbit Rabbit Rabbit," a trio of confit of leg, rabbit loin wrapped in applewood-smoked bacon, and roasted rack of rabbit with a whole-grain mustard sauce, is typical of preparations that are both rustic and refined. The menu is prix-fixe (three courses $69, four $84). ■TIP➜ The inn is a favorite of wine-industry foodies, so reserve well in advance; if it's full, you might be able to dine in the small lounge. Ⓢ Average main: $69 ⊠ 7871 River Rd., at Wohler Rd., Forestville ☎ 707/887–3300, 800/464–6642 ⊕ www.farmhouseinn.com ⌖ Reservations essential ⊘ Closed Tues. and Wed. No lunch.

$$$
MODERN
AMERICAN

✕ **Zazu Kitchen + Farm.** "Serve food from people you know" is the motto at Zazu, and some of the local ingredients in dishes here come from the owners themselves: executive chef Duskie Estes and her husband, John Stewart, the house *salumist* (specialist in all things pig). Small plates such as *chicharrones* (fried pork rinds), tamarind Petaluma chicken wings, and baby back ribs can add up to a meal, or you can sample a few appetizers before moving on to a bacon burger, duck-leg cassoulet, pasta, or steak and fries. In good weather the industrial-looking space's huge doors lift up to admit the breeze that often graces the open-air patio, which is surrounded by raised garden beds that supply produce and spices for diners' meals. Service can be chaotic. Ⓢ Average main: $26 ⊠ The Barlow, 6770 McKinley St., No. 150, Sebastopol ☎ 707/523–4814 ⊕ www.zazukitchen.com ⊘ Closed Tues. No lunch Mon.

WHERE TO STAY

$$$

B&B/INN

Fodor's Choice

★

The Farmhouse Inn. With a rustic-farmhouse-meets-modern-loft aesthetic, the spacious rooms in this pale yellow farmhouse dating from 1873 are filled with king-size four-poster beds, whirlpool tubs, and terraces overlooking the hillside. **Pros:** fantastic restaurant; luxury bath products; full-service spa. **Cons:** road noise audible in rooms closest to the street. $ *Rooms from: $350* ✉ *7871 River Rd., Forestville* ☎ *707/887–3300, 800/464–6642* ⊕ *www.farmhouseinn.com* ⇆ *12 rooms, 6 suites* ❑ *Breakfast.*

$

HOTEL

FAMILY

Sebastopol Inn. The cheerful rooms clustered around a pleasant courtyard at this reasonably priced inn are steps away from the Barlow, a hip collection of restaurants, wine-tasting rooms, brewpubs, galleries, and other spaces occupied by artisans and entrepreneurs. **Pros:** good rates; friendly staff; across from the Barlow complex; near noteworthy wineries. **Cons:** no frills; bland decor; beds too firm for some guests. $ *Rooms from: $139* ✉ *6751 Sebastopol Ave., Sebastopol* ☎ *707/829–2500* ⊕ *www.sebastopolinn.com* ⇆ *29 rooms, 2 suites* ❑ *No meals.*

SPORTS AND THE OUTDOORS

CANOE TRIPS

Burke's Canoe Trips. You get a real feel for the Russian River's flora and fauna on a leisurely 10-mile paddle from Burke's downstream to Guerneville. A shuttle bus returns you to your car at the end of the journey, which is best taken from late May through mid-October. The cost is $65 per canoe. ✉ *8600 River Rd., at Mirabel Rd., Forestville* ☎ *707/887–1222* ⊕ *www.burkescanoetrips.com.*

6

HEALDSBURG

17 miles north of Santa Rosa.

Just when it seems that the buzz about Healdsburg couldn't get any more intense, another glossy food or wine magazine will publish an article about the chic hotels and restaurants that keep popping up here. Despite all the hype, you needn't be a tycoon to enjoy this town. For every ritzy restaurant or hotel there's a great bakery, modest B&B, or swell motel. The tin-roof bandstand on Healdsburg Plaza hosts free concerts, at which you might hear anything from bluegrass to Sousa marches. Add to that the plaza's fragrant magnolia trees and bright flower beds, and the whole ensemble seems right out of a Norman Rockwell painting.

The setting is no less idyllic in the adjacent countryside, where food stands along relatively untrafficked roads sell just-plucked fruits and vine-ripened tomatoes. Tucked behind groves of eucalyptus or hidden high on fog-shrouded hills, the winery buildings here are barely visible.

GETTING HERE AND AROUND

Healdsburg sits just off U.S. 101. Heading north, take the Central Healdsburg exit to reach Healdsburg Plaza; heading south, take the Westside Road exit and pass east under the freeway. From the plaza you can walk to many of its restaurants, shops, and tasting rooms.

Annual barrel tasting along Russian River's wine road

WHERE TO EAT

$$$$
AMERICAN

✕ **Barndiva.** This hip joint abandons the homey vibe of many Wine Country spots for a more urban feel. Electronic music plays quietly in the background while servers ferry inventive seasonal cocktails. The food is as stylish as the couples cozying up next to each other on the banquette seats. Make a light meal out of starters like "The Artisan," a bountiful plate of cheeses and charcuterie, or settle in for the evening with such dishes as bacon-wrapped pork tenderloin with stone-ground polenta or crispy young chicken served with roasted brussels sprouts, and egg-yolk ravioli. ■ **TIP→ During warm weather the open-air patio is the place to be.** ⑤ *Average main: $31* ⊠ *231 Center St., at Matheson St.* ☎ *707/431–0100* ⊕ *www.barndiva.com* ⊘ *Closed Mon. and Tues.*

$$
MODERN
AMERICAN
Fodor's Choice
★

✕ **Chalkboard.** Unvarnished oak flooring, wrought-iron accents, and a vaulted white ceiling create a polished yet rustic ambience for the playfully ambitious cuisine of chef Shane McAnelly. Starters such as pork-belly biscuits might at first glance seem frivolous, but the silky flavor blend—maple glaze, pickled onions, and chipotle mayo playing off feathery biscuit halves—signals a supremely capable tactician at work. Likewise with vegetable sides such as fried brussels sprouts perched upon a perky kimchi purée, or moist and crispy buttermilk-fried quail. House-made pasta dishes favor rich country flavors—the robust Sonoma lamb *sugo* (sauce) with Pecorino-Romano tickles the entire palate—while desserts named The Candy Bar and Donuts O' the Day aim to please (and do). The canny wine selections ably support McAnelly's cuisine. ⑤ *Average main: $19* ⊠ *Hotel Les Mars, 29 North St., west of Healdsburg Ave.* ☎ *707/473–8030* ⊕ *chalkboard healdsburg.com.*

$
FRENCH

✕**Costeaux.** This French-style bakery and café has won numerous awards for its bread, and the croissants are among Sonoma County's best. Breakfast, served all day, includes homemade quiche, the signature omelet (sun-dried tomatoes, applewood-smoked bacon, and Brie), and French toast made from thick slabs of cinnamon-walnut bread. Among the lunch items are two au courant variations on classic sandwiches: a French dip made from house-roasted rib eye and a Monte Cristo (turkey, ham, and Jarlsberg cheese) on that addictive cinnamon-walnut bread. ■**TIP**➔ Arrive early on weekends to grab a seat on the open-air patio. ⑤ *Average main: $13* ✉ *417 Healdsburg Ave., at North St.* ☏ *707/433–1913* ⊕ *www.costeaux.com* ☾ *No dinner.*

$
BAKERY
Fodor'sChoice
★

✕**Downtown Bakery & Creamery.** To catch the Healdsburg spirit, hit the plaza in the early morning to down a cup of coffee and a fragrant sticky bun or a too-darlin' *canelé,* a French-style pastry with a soft custard center surrounded by a dense caramel crust. Until 2 pm you can also go the full breakfast route: pancakes, granola, poached farm eggs on polenta, or perhaps the dandy bacon-and-egg pizza. For lunch there are sandwiches and focaccia. ⑤ *Average main: $8* ✉ *308A Center St., at North St.* ☏ *707/431–2719* ⊕ *www.downtownbakery.net* ⊿ *Reservations not accepted* ☾ *No dinner.*

$$
ITALIAN
Fodor'sChoice
★

✕**Scopa.** At his tiny, deservedly popular eatery, chef Ari Rosen prepares rustic Italian specialties such as *sugo Calabrese* (tomato-braised beef and pork rib served with smoked mozzarella in a tomato sauce) and house-made ravioli stuffed with braised rabbit, leeks, and black trumpets. Simple thin-crust pizzas make fine meals, too. Locals love the restaurant for its lack of pretension: wine is served in juice glasses, and the friendly hostess makes the rounds to ensure everyone is satisfied. You'll be packed in elbow-to-elbow with your fellow diners, but for a convivial evening over a bottle of Nebbiolo, there's no better choice. ⑤ *Average main: $20* ✉ *109A Plaza St., near Healdsburg Ave.* ☏ *707/433–5282* ⊕ *www.scopahealdsburg.com* ☾ *No lunch.*

$$$
MODERN
AMERICAN
Fodor'sChoice
★

✕**Spoonbar.** Cantina doors that open onto Healdsburg Avenue make this trendy eatery especially appealing in summer, when a warm breeze wafts into the stylish space. Midcentury modern furnishings, concrete walls, and a long communal table fashioned from rough-hewn acacia wood create an urbane setting for chef Louis Maldonado's contemporary American fare. Divided into five sections, the menu lets you mix and match to create a memorable meal. The mains might include Cornish game hen roulade with artichokes or loin of beef in red wine *jus,* served with quinoa and cider-braised root vegetables. The perpetually packed bar, known for inventive seasonal and historic cocktails, is the real draw for many locals. ⑤ *Average main: $23* ✉ *h2hotel, 219 Healdsburg Ave., at Vine St.* ☏ *707/433–7222* ⊕ *www.h2hotel.com/spoonbar* ☾ *No lunch Mon.–Thurs. in winter.*

$$$
SEAFOOD
Fodor'sChoice
★

✕**Willi's Seafood & Raw Bar.** The perpetually packed Willi's draws a festive crowd that likes to enjoy specialty cocktails at the full bar before sitting down to a dinner of small, mostly seafood-oriented plates. The warm Maine lobster roll with garlic butter and fennel conjures up a New England fish shack, while the ceviches and the scallops served with a cilantro-and-pumpkin-seed pesto suggest Latin

6

America. $ *Average main: $25* ✉ *403 Healdsburg Ave., at North St.* ☎ *707/433–9191* ⊕ *www.willisseafood.net* ☞ *Reservations not accepted Fri.–Sun.*

$$$
AMERICAN

✕ **Zin Restaurant and Wine Bar.** Concrete floors and large canvases on the walls lend this restaurant a casual, industrial, and slightly artsy feel. The American cuisine—such as the roasted pork belly with pickled apples or the free-range chicken braised in red wine—is hearty and highly seasoned. Portions are large, so consider sharing if you hope to save room for such desserts as the brownie sundae with house-made ice cream. As you might have guessed from the name, Zinfandel is the drink of choice here, though Sonoma County's other major varietals show up on the 100-bottle wine list. ■**TIP→** From Sunday through Thursday, blue-plate specials featuring homey fare (think pot roast and chicken and dumplings) make this place a bargain. $ *Average main: $25* ✉ *344 Center St., at North St.* ☎ *707/473–0946* ⊕ *zinrestaurant.com* ☉ *No lunch weekends.*

WHERE TO STAY

$$
HOTEL

🛏 **Best Western Plus Dry Creek Inn.** Spotless rooms and easy access both to downtown and outlying hot spots make this Spanish mission–style motel near U.S. 101 Healdsburg's best low-budget option. **Pros:** laundry facilities; frequent Internet discounts. **Cons:** thin walls; highway noise audible in many rooms; bland furnishings in standard rooms. $ *Rooms from: $172* ✉ *198 Dry Creek Rd.* ☎ *707/433–0300, 800/222–5784* ⊕ *www.drycreekinn.com* ⤙ *163 rooms* ⏐⦾⏐ *Breakfast.*

$$
B&B/INN
Fodor's Choice
★

🛏 **h2hotel.** Eco-friendly touches abound at this hotel, from the plant-covered "green" roof to wooden decks made from salvaged lumber. **Pros:** stylish modern design; popular bar; complimentary bikes. **Cons:** least expensive rooms lack bathtubs; no fitness facilities. $ *Rooms from: $275* ✉ *219 Healdsburg Ave.* ☎ *707/922–5251* ⊕ *www.h2hotel. com* ⤙ *34 rooms, 2 suites* ⏐⦾⏐ *Breakfast.*

$$$
B&B/INN
Fodor's Choice
★

🛏 **The Honor Mansion.** An 1883 Italianate Victorian houses this photogenic hotel; rooms in the main house preserve a sense of the building's heritage, whereas the larger suites are comparatively understated. **Pros:** homemade sweets available at all hours; spa pavilions by pool available for massages in fair weather. **Cons:** almost a mile from Healdsburg's plaza; walls can seem thin. $ *Rooms from: $325* ✉ *891 Grove St.* ☎ *707/433–4277, 800/554–4667* ⊕ *www.honormansion. com* ⤙ *5 rooms, 7 suites, 1 cottage* ☉ *Closed 2 wks around Christmas* ⏐⦾⏐ *Breakfast.*

$$$
RESORT

🛏 **Hotel Healdsburg.** Across the street from the tidy town plaza, this spare, sophisticated hotel caters to travelers with an urban sensibility. **Pros:** several rooms overlook the town plaza; comfortable lobby with a small attached bar; extremely comfortable beds. **Cons:** exterior rooms get some street noise; rooms could use better lighting. $ *Rooms from: $375* ✉ *25 Matheson St.* ☎ *707/431–2800, 800/889–7188* ⊕ *www. hotelhealdsburg.com* ⤙ *49 rooms, 6 suites* ⏐⦾⏐ *Breakfast.*

$$$$
HOTEL
Fodor's Choice
★

🛏 **Hôtel Les Mars.** This Relais & Châteaux property takes the prize for opulence with guest rooms spacious and elegant enough for French nobility, 18th- and 19th-century antiques and reproductions, canopy beds dressed in luxe linens, and gas-burning fireplaces. **Pros:** large rooms; just off Healdsburg's plaza; fancy bath products. **Cons:** very expensive. ⑤ *Rooms from: $625* ⊠ *27 North St.* ☎ *707/433–4211* ⊕ *www.hotellesmars.com* ⇨ *16 rooms* ⦿ *Breakfast.*

SPAS

Fodor's Choice **Spa Dolce.** Owner Ines von Majthenyi Scherrer has a good local rep, ★ having run a popular nearby spa before opening this stylish facility just off Healdsburg Plaza. Spa Dolce specializes in skin and body care for men and women, and makeup, waxing, and nail care for women. Curved white walls and fresh-cut floral arrangements set a subdued tone for such treatments as the exfoliating Hauschka body scrub, which combines organic brown sugar with scented oil. There's a romantic room for couples to enjoy massages for two. Many guests come just for the facials, which range from a straightforward cleansing to an anti-aging peel. ⊠ *250 Center St., at Matheson St.* ☎ *707/433–0177* ⊕ *www. spadolce.com* ⊠ *Treatments $20–$210* ⊙ *Tues.–Sun. 10–7.*

SPORTS AND THE OUTDOORS

Wine Country Bikes. This shop in downtown Healdsburg is perfectly located for single or multi-day treks into the Dry Creek and Russian River valleys. Bikes, including tandems, rent for $39 to $145 a day. One-day tours start at $149. ⊠ *61 Front St., at Hudson St.* ☎ *707/473–0610, 866/922–4537* ⊕ *www.winecountrybikes.com.*

SHOPPING

Fodor's Choice **Saint Dizier Home.** With its selection of furniture and contemporary items ★ for the home, this shop reminds mere mortals why the universe provides us with decorators and designers—they really do know best. ⊠ *259 Center St., at Matheson St.* ☎ *707/473–0980* ⊕ *www.saintdhome.com.*

Fodor's Choice **The Shed.** Inside a glass-front, steel-clad variation on a traditional ★ grange hall, this shop-cum-eatery celebrates local agriculture with specialty foods. It also stocks seeds and plants, gardening and farming implements, cookware, and everything a smart pantry should hold. ⊠ *25 North St., west of Healdsburg Ave.* ☎ *707/431–7433* ⊕ *healdsburgshed.com.*

DRY CREEK AND ALEXANDER VALLEYS

With its diverse terrain and microclimates, the Dry Creek Valley supports an impressive range of varietals. Zinfandel grapes flourish on the benchlands, whereas the gravelly, well-drained soil of the valley floor is better known for Chardonnay and, in the north, Sauvignon Blanc. Pinot Noir, Syrah, and other cool-climate grapes thrive on eastern-facing slopes that receive less afternoon sun than elsewhere in the valley.

Dry Creek wineries tend to be smaller, which make them a good bet on summer weekends, when tourists flood more easily accessible locales. The Alexander Valley, which lies northeast of Healdsburg, is similarly rustic. The largely family-owned wineries are known for Zinfandels, Chardonnays, and Cabernet Sauvignons, though Cabernet Franc and other less high-profile wines are also made here.

GETTING HERE AND AROUND

To reach the Dry Creek Valley from Healdsburg, drive north on Healdsburg Avenue and turn left on Dry Creek Road. West of U.S. 101, you'll see signs pointing the way to wineries on that road and West Dry Creek Road, which runs roughly parallel about a mile to the west. To get to the Alexander Valley from the plaza, drive north on Healdsburg Avenue and veer right onto Alexander Valley Road. Follow it to Highway 128, where many of this appellation's best wineries lie.

EXPLORING

TOP ATTRACTIONS

Dry Creek Vineyard. Fumé Blanc is king at Dry Creek, where the refreshing white wine is made in the style of those in Sancerre, France. The winery also makes well-regarded Zinfandels, a zesty dry Chenin Blanc, a Pinot Noir, and a handful of Cabernet Sauvignon blends. Since many wines are priced below $30 a bottle (some less than $20), it's a popular stop for wine lovers looking to stock their cellars for a reasonable price. You can picnic on the lawn next to a flowering magnolia tree. Conveniently, a general store and deli is close by. ✉ *3770 Lambert Bridge Rd., off Dry Creek Rd., Healdsburg* ☎ *707/433–1000, 800/864–9463* ⊕ *www.drycreekvineyard.com* ✉ *Tastings $5–$45, tour $15* ⊘ *Daily 10:30–4:30, tour 11 and 1 by appointment.*

FAMILY **Francis Ford Coppola Winery.** The film director's over-the-top fantasyland is the sort of place the midlevel Mafiosi in his *The Godfather* saga might declare had real class—the "everyday wines" poured here are pretty much beside the point. The fun here is all in the excess, and you may find it hard to resist having your photo snapped standing next to Don Corleone's desk from *The Godfather* or beside memorabilia from other Coppola films, including some directed by his daughter, Sofia. A bandstand reminiscent of one in *The Godfather Part II* is the centerpiece of a large pool area where you can rent a changing room, complete with shower, and spend the afternoon lounging poolside, perhaps ordering food from the adjacent café. A more elaborate restaurant, Rustic, overlooks the vineyards. ✉ *300 Via Archimedes, off U.S. 101, Geyserville* ☎ *707/857–1400* ⊕ *www.franciscoppolawinery.com* ✉ *Tastings free–$15, tours $20–$75, pool pass $30* ⊘ *Tasting room daily 11–6, restaurant daily 11–9; pool hrs vary seasonally.*

Fodor'sChoice **Locals Tasting Room.** Though trending upscale, downtown Geyserville
★ remains little more than a crossroads with a few shops and restaurants. But if you're serious about wine, Carolyn Lewis's tasting room is alone worth a trek. Connoisseurs come to sample the output of a dozen or so small wineries, most without tasting rooms of their own. There's no fee for tasting—a bargain for wines of this quality—and the extremely knowledgeable staff is happy to pour you a flight of several wines so you can compare, say, different Cabernet Sauvignons. ✉ *21023A Geyserville Ave., at Hwy. 128, Geyserville* ☎ *707/857–4900* ⊕ *www.tastelocalwines.com* ✉ *Tasting free* ⊘ *Daily 11–6.*

Quivira Vineyards and Winery. An unassuming winery in a modern wooden barn topped by solar panels, Quivira produces some of Dry Creek's most interesting wines. Hugh Chappelle, the winemaker since

2010, crafts well-balanced reds, among them a lush Syrah, several hearty Zinfandels, and a Petite Sirah that showcases this unheralded varietal's noblest attributes. He also makes a zesty yet refined Sauvignon Blanc. The excellent tour provides information about the winery's biodynamic and organic farming practices and offers a glimpse of the beautiful garden and the property's pigs, chickens, and beehives. ■TIP→ You can take a free self-guided tour through the garden, some of whose bounty—including estate-grown honey and olive oil—is available for sale. ⊠ *4900 W. Dry Creek Rd., near Wine Creek Rd., Healdsburg* ☎ *707/431–8333, 800/292–8339* ⊕ *www.quivirawine.com* ☜ *Tasting $10, tours $20–$30* ⊙ *Daily 11–5; tours by appointment.*

Fodor's Choice **Ridge Vineyards.** Ridge stands tall among California wineries, and not
★ merely because one of its 1971 Cabernet Sauvignons placed first in a 2006 re-creation of the 1976 Judgment of Paris tasting. The winery built its reputation on Cabernet Sauvignons, Zinfandels, and Chardonnays of unusual depth and complexity, but you'll also find blends of Rhône varietals. Ridge makes wines using grapes from several California locales—including the Dry Creek Valley, Sonoma Valley, Napa Valley, and Paso Robles—but the focus is on single-vineyard estate wines such as the exquisitely textured Lytton Springs Zinfandel blend from grapes grown near the tasting room. In good weather you can taste outside, taking in views of rolling vineyard hills while you sip. ■TIP→ The $20 tasting option includes a pour of the top-of-the-line Monte Bello Cabernet Sauvignon blend from grapes grown in the Santa Cruz Mountains. ⊠ *650 Lytton Springs Rd., off U.S. 101, Healdsburg* ☎ *707/433–7721* ⊕ *www.ridgewine.com* ☜ *Tastings $5–$20, tours $30–$40* ⊙ *Daily 11–4.*

WHERE TO EAT AND STAY

$$ ✕ **Diavola Pizzeria & Salumeria.** A cozy dining room with hardwood
ITALIAN floors, a pressed-tin ceiling, and exposed-brick walls provide a fitting
Fodor's Choice setting for the rustic cuisine at this Geyserville charmer. Chef Dino
★ Bugica studied with several artisans in Italy before opening this restaurant that specializes in pizzas pulled from a wood-burning oven and several types of house-cured meats. A few salads and meaty main courses round out the menu. ■TIP→ If you're impressed by the antipasto plate, you can pick up some smoked pork belly, pancetta, or spicy Calabrese sausage to take home. ⑤ *Average main: $19* ⊠ *21021 Geyserville Ave., at Hwy. 128, Geyserville* ☎ *707/814–0111* ⊕ *www.diavolapizzeria.com* ⌨ *Reservations not accepted.*

$$ ▦ **Geyserville Inn.** Clever travelers give the Healdsburg hubbub and
HOTEL prices the heave-ho but still have easy access to outstanding Dry Creek and Alexander Valley wineries from this modest, well-run inn. **Pros:** pool; second-floor rooms in back have vineyard views; picnic area. **Cons:** occasional noise bleed-through from corporate and other events. ⑤ *Rooms from: $155* ⊠ *21714 Geyserville Ave., Geyserville* ☎ *707/857–4343, 877/857–4343* ⊕ *www.geyservilleinn.com* ⇆ *41 rooms* ❏ *No meals.*

6

THE NORTH COAST

From the Sonoma Coast to
Redwood National Park

WELCOME TO THE NORTH COAST

TOP REASONS TO GO

★ **Scenic coastal drives:** There's hardly a road here that *isn't* scenic.

★ **Wild beaches:** This stretch of California is one of nature's masterpieces. Revel in the unbridled, rugged coastline, without a building in sight.

★ **Dinnertime:** When you're done hiking the beach, refuel with delectable food; you'll find everything from burritos to bouillabaisse.

★ **Romance:** Here you can end almost every day with a perfect sunset.

★ **Wildlife:** Watch for migrating whales, sunbathing sea lions and huge Roosevelt elk with majestic antlers.

1 The Sonoma Coast. As you enter Sonoma County from the south on Highway 1, you pass first through gently rolling pastureland. North of Bodega Bay dramatic shoreline scenery takes over. The road snakes up, down, and around sheer cliffs and steep inclines—some without guardrails—where cows seem to cling precariously. Stunning vistas (or cottony fog) and hairpin turns make for an exhilarating drive.

2 The Mendocino Coast. The timber industry gave birth to most of the small towns along this stretch of coastline. Although tourism now drives the economy, the region has retained much of its old-fashioned charm. The beauty of the landscape, of course, has not changed.

3 Redwood Country. There's a different state of mind in Humboldt County. Here, instead of spas, there are old-time hotels. Instead of wineries, there are breweries. The landscape is primarily thick redwood forest; the interior mountains get snow in winter and sizzle in summer while the coast sits covered in fog. Until as late as 1924, there was no road north of Willits; the coastal towns were reachable only by sea. That legacy is apparent in the communities of today: Eureka and Arcata, both former ports, are sizeable, but otherwise towns are tiny and nestled in the woods, and people have an independent spirit that recalls the original homesteaders. Coming from the south, Garberville is a good place to stop for picnic provisions and stretch your legs.

4 Redwood National and State Parks. For a pristine encounter with giant redwoods, make the trek to these coastal parks where even casual visitors have easy access to the trees.

Smith River
199
nt St. George
escent City
101
Klamath
ods National
& State Parks **4**
Orick
Patrick's Point
State Park
Trinidad
cKinleyville
3 Arcata
Willow Creek
Arcata Bay
Eureka
299
ooldt Bay
Fortuna
rndale
Hydesville
ape
docino
Hayfork
36
Rio
Dell
Point
orda
Humboldt
Redwoods
State Park
Garberville
Richardson Grove
State Park
Leggett
Laytonville
Fort Bragg
101
Mendocino
Willits
Little River
20
Albion
2 Elk
128 Ukiah
20
Point Arena
Lighthouse
Lucerne
Point Arena
Kelseyville
Clearlake
Gualala
Cloverdale
Lower Lake
Stewarts
Point
Healdsburg
1 Calistoga
Jenner
101 Saint Helena
Occidental Santa Rosa
Sebastopol 29
Bodega Bay
Napa
Peraluma
Sonoma
Inverness Novato
Vallejo
Point Reyes 1 Concord
National Seashore Richmond 80
Bolinas Berkeley
Marin Headlands Oakland
San Francisco
Daly City

0   30 mi
0   30 km

GETTING
ORIENTED

It's all but impossible to
explore the Northern
California coast without a
car. Indeed, you wouldn't
want to—driving here is half
the fun. The main road is
Highway 1, two lanes that
twist and turn (sometimes
180 degrees) up cliffs and
down through valleys. Towns
appear every so often, but
this is mostly a land of green
pasture, dense forest, and
natural, undeveloped coastline. ■TIP➔ Pace yourself:
Most drivers stop frequently
to appreciate the views (and
you can't drive faster than
20–40 mph on many portions
of the highway), so don't plan
to drive too far in one day.

7

Updated
by Christine
Vovakes

The spectacular coastline between Marin County and the Oregon border defies expectations. The landscape is defined by the Pacific Ocean, but instead of boardwalks and bikinis there are ragged cliffs and pounding waves—and the sunbathers are mostly sea lions. Instead of strip malls and freeways, you'll find a single-lane road that follows a fickle shoreline. Although the towns along the way vary from deluxe spa retreat to hippie hideaway, all are reliably sleepy—and that's exactly why many Californians, especially those from the Bay Area, escape here to enjoy nature unspoiled by the agitations of daily life.

This stretch of Highway 1 is made up of numerous little worlds, each different from the next. From Point Reyes toward Bodega Bay, the land spreads out into green, rolling pastures and sandy beaches. The road climbs higher and higher as it heads north through Sonoma County, and in Mendocino County the coastline follows the ins and outs of lush valleys where rivers pour down from the forests and into the ocean. At Humboldt County the highway heads inland to the redwoods, and then returns to the shoreline at the tidal flats surrounding the ports of Eureka and Arcata. Heading north to the Oregon border, the coast is increasingly wild and lined with giant redwood trees.

PLANNING

WHEN TO GO
The North Coast is a year-round destination, though when you go determines what you will see. The migration of the Pacific gray whales is a wintertime phenomenon, which lasts roughly from mid-December to early April. Wildflowers follow the winter rain, as early as January in southern areas through June and July farther north. Summer is the

high season for tourists, but spring, fall, and even winter are arguably better times to visit when the pace is slower, towns are quieter, and lodging is cheaper.

The coastal climate is similar to San Francisco's, although winter nights are colder than in the city. In July and August thick fog can drop temperatures to the high 50s, but fear not! You need only drive inland to find temperatures that are often 20 degrees higher.

GETTING HERE AND AROUND
AIR TRAVEL
The only North Coast airport with commercial air service, Arcata/Eureka Airport (ACV) receives United Express flights. The airport is in McKinleyville, which is 16 miles from Eureka. A taxi to Eureka costs about $50 and takes roughly 25 minutes. Door-to-door airport shuttles cost $20 to Arcata and Trinidad, $24 to Eureka, and $50 to Ferndale. All prices are for the first person, and go up $5 for each additional person.

Airport Contact Arcata/Eureka Airport ⊠ 3561 Boeing Ave., McKinleyville ☎ 707/839–5401.

Shuttle Contact Door to Door Airport Shuttle ☎ 888/338–5497, 707/839–4186 ⊕ www.doortodoorairporter.com.

BUS TRAVEL
Greyhound buses travel along U.S. 101 from San Francisco to Garberville, Eureka, and Arcata. Humboldt Transit Authority connects Eureka, Arcata, and Trinidad.

Bus Contacts Greyhound ☎ 800/231–2222 ⊕ www.greyhound.com.
Humboldt Transit Authority ☎ 707/443–0826 ⊕ www.hta.org.

CAR TRAVEL
Although U.S. 101 has excellent services, long stretches separate towns along Highway 1, and services are even fewer and farther between on the smaller roads. ■TIP➔ If you're running low on fuel and see a gas station, stop for a refill. Twisting Highway 1 is the scenic route to Mendocino from San Francisco, but the fastest one is U.S. 101 north to Highway 128 west (from Cloverdale) to Highway 1 north. The quickest route to the far North Coast is a straight shot up U.S. 101, which runs inland until Eureka. Weather sometimes forces closure of parts of Highway 1, but it's rare.

Road Conditions Caltrans ☎ 800/427–7623 ⊕ www.dot.ca.gov.

RESTAURANTS
A few restaurants with national reputations, plus several more of regional note, entice palates on the North Coast. Even the smallest cafés take advantage of the abundant fresh seafood and locally grown vegetables and herbs. Attire is usually informal, though at pricier establishments dressy casual is the norm. Most kitchens close at 8 or 8:30 and few places serve past 9:30. Many restaurants close for a winter break in January or early February.

7

HOTELS

Restored Victorians, rustic lodges, country inns, and vintage motels are among the accommodations available here. Few have air-conditioning (the ocean breezes make it unnecessary), and many have no phones or TVs in the rooms. Although several towns have only one or two places to spend the night, some of these lodgings are destinations in themselves. Budget accommodations are rare, but in winter you're likely to find reduced rates and nearly empty inns and B&Bs. In summer and on the weekends, though, make bed-and-breakfast reservations as far ahead as possible—rooms at the best inns often sell out months in advance. *Hotel reviews have been shortened. For full information, visit Fodors.com.*

WHAT IT COSTS				
	$	**$$**	**$$$**	**$$$$**
Restaurants	under $16	$16–$22	$23–$30	over $30
Hotels	under $121	$121–$175	$176–$250	over $250

Restaurant prices are the average cost of a main course at dinner or, if dinner is not served, at lunch, excluding sales tax of 7.5–9%. Hotel prices are the lowest cost of a standard double room in high season, excluding service charges and 8%–11% tax.

VISITOR INFORMATION

Contacts Humboldt County Convention and Visitors Bureau ⊠ *1034 2nd St., Eureka* ☎ *707/443–5097, 800/346–3482* ⊕ *www.redwoods.info.* **Mendocino Coast Chamber of Commerce** ⊠ *217 S. Main St., Fort Bragg* ☎ *707/961–6300* ⊕ *www.mendocinocoast.com.* **Redwood Coast Chamber: Sonoma to Mendocino** ☎ *707/884–1080, 800/778–5252* ⊕ *www.redwoodcoastchamber.com.* **Sonoma County Tourism** ☎ *707/522–5800, 800/576–6662* ⊕ *www.sonomacounty.com.* **Visit Mendocino County** ⊠ *345 N. Franklin St., Ft. Bragg* ☎ *707/964–9010, 866/466–3636* ⊕ *www.visitmendocino.com.*

THE SONOMA COAST

BODEGA BAY

23 miles west of Santa Rosa.

From the busy harbor here, commercial boats pursue fish and Dungeness crab. There's nothing quaint about this working town without a center—it's just a string of businesses along several miles of Highway 1. But some tourists still come to see where Alfred Hitchcock shot *The Birds* in 1962. The Tides Wharf complex, an important location used for the movie, has been expanded and remodeled several times and is no longer recognizable. But a few miles inland, in Bodega, you can find Potter Schoolhouse, which is now a private residence.

GETTING HERE AND AROUND

To reach Bodega Bay, exit U.S. 101 at Santa Rosa and take Highway 12 west (it's called Bodega Highway west of Sebastopol) 23 miles to the coast. A scenic alternative is to take U.S. 101's East Washington Street/Central Petaluma exit and follow signs west to Bodega Bay; just after you merge onto Highway 1, you'll pass through down-home Valley Ford. Mendocino Transit Authority (⊕ *www.mendocinotransit.org*) Route 95 buses connect Bodega Bay with coastal towns and Santa Rosa.

BEACHES

Fodor's Choice ★ **Sonoma Coast State Park.** The park's gorgeous sandy coves stretch for 17 miles from Bodega Head to 4 miles north of Jenner. **Bodega Head** is an especially popular perch for whale-watchers, though if you're lucky you'll catch sight of migrating whales from any of the beaches. **Rock Point, Duncan's Landing,** and **Wright's Beach,** clustered at about the halfway mark, have picnic areas, as do several other spots. Rogue waves have swept people off the rocks at Duncan's Landing, so don't stray past signs warning you away. Relatively calmer **Shell Beach,** about 2 miles north, is known for beachcombing, tide pooling, and fishing. About 2½ miles north of Shell Beach, near the mouth of the Russian River at Jenner, a long road leads from the highway to **Goat Rock.** Harbor seals lounge at the long beach here; pupping season is from March through August. Bring binoculars and walk north from the parking lot to view the seals. During summer lifeguards are on duty at some beaches, but strong rip currents and heavy surf keep most would-be swimmers on shore. Wright's Beach and Bodega Dunes have developed campsites. **Amenities:** parking; toilets. **Best for:** solitude; sunset; walking. ⊠ *Park Headquarters/Salmon Creek Ranger Station, 3095 Hwy. 1, 2 miles north of Bodega Bay* ☎ *707/865–2391* ⊕ *www.parks.gov* ◻ *$8 per vehicle* ⊙ *Daily 8 am–sunset (some beach hrs may be curtailed because of budget cuts).*

WHERE TO EAT AND STAY

$$
SEAFOOD

✕ **Sandpiper Restaurant.** A local favorite, this friendly café on the marina does a good job for a fair price. Peruse the board for the day's fresh catch or order a menu regular such as crab stew or steak and prawns; clam chowder is the house specialty. Breakfast is served on summer weekends. $ *Average main: $22* ⊠ *1400 N. Hwy. 1* ☎ *707/875–2278.*

$$$
HOTEL

▦ **Bodega Bay Lodge.** Looking out to the ocean across a wetland, a group of shingle-and-river-rock buildings houses Bodega Bay's finest accommodations. **Pros:** most rooms have fireplaces and patios; variety of pampering treatments; ocean views. **Cons:** on the highway. $ *Rooms from: $239* ⊠ *103 Coast Hwy. 1* ☎ *707/875–3525, 888/875–2250* ⊕ *www. bodegabaylodge.com* ⬩ *78 rooms, 5 suites* ⦿ *No meals.*

$
HOTEL

▦ **Bodega Harbor Inn.** As humble as can be, this is one of the few places on this stretch of the coast with rooms for less than $100 a night. **Pros:** budget choice; rooms for larger groups. **Cons:** an older facility. $ *Rooms from: $85* ⊠ *1345 Bodega Ave.* ☎ *707/875–3594* ⊕ *www. bodegaharborinn.com* ⬩ *14 rooms, 2 suites* ⦿ *No meals.*

The Sonoma and Mendocino Coasts

Richardson Grove State Park
Leggett
Westport
Laytonville
MacKerricher State Park
Fort Bragg
Noyo
Mendocino Coast Botanical Gardens
Caspar
Pine Grove
Mendocino
Little River
Albion
Willits
101
20
Calpella
Ukiah
Elk
Navarro
Philo
Lucerne
Manchester
Anderson Valley
Boonville
253
Lakeport
Clear Lake
20
Point Arena
Point Arena Lighthouse
Point Arena
128
Yorkville
Hopland
Kelseyville
Clearlake
29
Lower Lak
Anchor Bay
Gualala
Sea Ranch
Cloverdale
Geyserville
Middletowr
Stewarts Point
128
29
Kruse Rhododendron Reserve
ALEXANDER VALLEY
Healdsburg
Calistog
NAPA V
Salt Point State Park
Fort Ross State Hist. Park
Fort Ross
Guerneville
101
Santa Rosa
Saint Helena
Jenner
116
Occidental
Salmon Creek
Freestone
Sebastopol
SONOMA VALLEY
Bodega Bay
Valley Ford
Bodega Bay
Dillon Beach
Tomales Point
Tomales
Petaluma
Sonoma
Pacific Coast Highway
Point Reyes National Seashore
Tomales Bay
Marshall
Inverness
Point Reyes Station
Olema
Novato
Point Reyes Lighthouse
Point Reyes
Drakes Bay
101
Audubon Canyon Ranch
Bolinas
San Rafael
Stinson Beach
Mt. Tamalpais
Marin
Mt. Tamalpais State Park
Muir Woods Nat'l. Mon.
1
Marin Headlands
San Francisco
PACIFIC OCEAN
FARALLON ISLANDS
0 15 mi
0 15 km
Daly City
280

SPORTS AND THE OUTDOORS
GOLF
The Links at Bodega Harbour. Robert Trent Jones II designed this Scottish-style, incredibly scenic, and fairly challenging 18-hole oceanfront course. Rates include a golf cart. ⊠ *21301 Heron Dr.* ☎ *707/875–3538, 866/905–4657* ⊕ *www.bodegaharbourgolf.com* 🖃 *$60 for weekdays; $90 for weekends* 🏌 *18 holes, 6290 yards, par 70.*

HORSEBACK RIDING
Horse N Around Trail Rides. Saddle up at this ranch for guided horseback trail rides, some along the beach. Reservations are required. ⊠ *2660 N. Hwy. 1* ☎ *707/875–8849* ⊕ *www.horsenaroundtrailrides.com.*

WHALE-WATCHING
Bodega Bay Sportfishing. This outfitter charters ocean-fishing boats, rents equipment, and conducts whale-watching trips from mid-winter through spring. ⊠ *1410 B Bay Flat Rd.* ☎ *707/875–3344* ⊕ *www. bodegabaysportfishing.com.*

OCCIDENTAL

14 miles northeast of Bodega Bay.

A village surrounded by redwood forests, orchards, and vineyards, Occidental is a former logging hub with a bohemian vibe. The 19th-century downtown offers a top-notch B&B, good food, and a handful of art galleries and boutiques. On your way, you'll pass through the neighboring town of Freestone, which has a popular bakery and an excellent winery.

GETTING HERE AND AROUND
To reach Occidental, take Highway 12 (Bodega Highway) east 5 miles from Highway 1. Take a left onto Bohemian Highway, where you'll find Freestone; after another 3½ miles you'll be in Occidental. From U.S. 101 north or south take Highway 12 west from Santa Rosa about 13 miles, then head north on Bohemian Highway about 3½ miles to the village.

EXPLORING
Fodor's Choice ★ **Joseph Phelps Freestone Vineyards Guest Center.** The renowned Napa Valley winery's western Sonoma outpost is a good place to learn about biodynamic growing techniques while tasting crisp Chardonnays and earthy Pinot Noirs. Phelps wines have always garnered praise for their expression of *terroir* (the land), and the ones made here have a composed, ascetic quality that perfectly mirrors the rugged Sonoma Coast. You can almost taste the vines sending out long roots to find nutrients in the rocky, mineral-laden soil. If prompted, your pourer may regale you with descriptions of biodynamic strategies that involve timing vineyard activities to the waxing or waning moon and compost preparations that incorporate yarrow, stinging nettle, and other herbs. Sonoma Coast wines predominate on the tasting list—the estate-grown Pinot Noir is a standout—but there's nearly always a Napa Valley selection also. ⊠ *12747 El Camino Bodega, at Bohemian Hwy.* ☎ *707/874–1010* ⊕ *www.josephphelps.com* 🖃 *Tastings $10–$15* ☉ *Daily 11–5.*

WHERE TO EAT AND STAY

$ ✕ **Wild Flour Bread.** The sticky buns at Wild Flour are legendary in west-
BAKERY ern Sonoma, as are the mouthwatering rye bread and sock-it-to-me
scones in flavors like double chocolate, espresso, and hazelnut. There's
a long table inside, but most people enjoy their baked goods on the
benches outside. ■ TIP➔ On weekends after 1 pm, the most popular
items start running out. ⑤ *Average main: $5* ✉ *140 Bohemian Hwy., at
El Camino Bodega, Freestone* ☎ *707/874–2938* ⊕ *www.wildflourbread.
com* ▭ *No credit cards* ⊗ *Closed Tues.–Thurs. No dinner.*

$$$ ▦ **The Inn at Occidental.** Quilts, folk art, and original paintings and
B&B/INN photographs fill this colorful and friendly inn. **Pros:** whimsical decor;
most rooms have private decks and jetted tubs; friendly. **Cons:** not for
those with minimalist tastes; not for kids. ⑤ *Rooms from: $249* ✉ *3657
Church St.* ☎ *707/874–1047, 800/522–6324* ⊕ *www.innatoccidental.
com* ⇲ *13 rooms, 3 suites, 1 cottage* ¶○¶ *Breakfast.*

SHOPPING

SPA

Osmosis Day Spa Sanctuary. The signature treatment at this locally popu-
lar spa is a traditional Japanese detoxifying bath. You'll slip into a deep
redwood tub filled with damp cedar shavings and rice bran that are
naturally heated to 140°F by the action of enzymes. Attendants bury
you up to the neck and throughout the 20-minute bath session bring sips
of water and place cool cloths on your forehead. After a shower, you
can lie down and listen to brain-balancing music through headphones
or have a massage, perhaps in one of the creek-side pagodas. Facials
and other treatments are also available. Reservations are recommended.
✉ *209 Bohemian Hwy., Freestone* ☎ *707/823–8231* ⊕ *www.osmosis.
com* ▦ *Treatments $99–$299* ⊗ *Daily 9–9* ⇲ *$99 90-min Signature
Cedar Enzyme Bath & Wrap; $219 2½-hr Rejuvenation package; $299
2½-hr Bath as Medicine package; $139 75-min massage. Services: Aro-
matherapy, body wraps, facials, massage.*

FORT ROSS STATE HISTORIC PARK

22 miles north of Bodega Bay.

With its reconstructed Russian Orthodox chapel, stockade, and officers'
barracks, Fort Ross looks much the way it did after the Russians made
it their major California coastal outpost in 1812. An excellent museum
documents the fort's history.

GETTING HERE AND AROUND

From Santa Rosa, head west on Highway 116 about 31 miles to Jenner,
then north 12 miles on Highway 1 to the park entrance. The Mendocino
Transit Authority (⊕ *www.mendocinotransit.org*) Route 95 bus pro-
vides service between Fort Ross and other coastal towns.

EXPLORING

FAMILY **Fort Ross State Historic Park.** Established in 1812, Fort Ross became Rus-
sia's major outpost in California, meant to produce crops and other sup-
plies for northerly fur-trading operations. The Russians brought Aleut
sea-otter hunters down from Alaska. By 1841 the area was depleted of

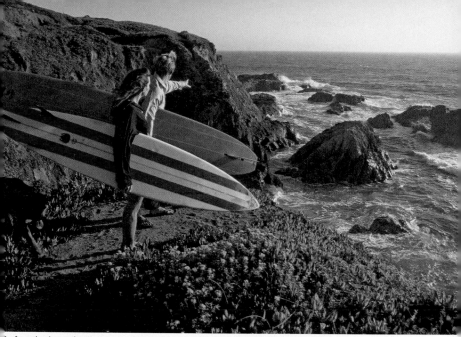

Surfers check out the waves near Bodega Bay on the Sonoma Coast.

seals and otters, and the Russians sold their post to John Sutter, later of gold-rush fame. After a local Anglo rebellion against the Mexicans, the land fell under U.S. domain, becoming part of California in 1850. The state park service has reconstructed Fort Ross, including its Russian Orthodox chapel, a redwood stockade, the officers' barracks, and a blockhouse. The excellent museum here documents the history of the fort and this part of the North Coast. ⊠ *19005 Hwy. 1* ☎ *707/847–3286* ⊕ *www.parks.ca.gov* ⊠ *$8 per vehicle* ☉ *Weekends 10–4:30* ☞ *No dogs allowed past parking lot and picnic area.*

SALT POINT STATE PARK

6 miles north of Fort Ross.

Enjoy dramatic views, forested acres, and a rocky, rugged shoreline along Highway 1's 5-mile route through this park. With 20 miles of hiking trails and a variety of picnicking, horseback riding, scuba diving, and fishing opportunities, you'll want to stay a while. At Fisk Mill Cove you'll see where centuries of wind and rain erosion have carved unusual honeycomb patterns in the sandstone called "tafonis."

GETTING HERE AND AROUND

Exit U.S. 101 in Santa Rosa and travel west on Highway 116 about 31 miles to Jenner, then north 18 miles on Highway 1 to reach the park. Mendocino Transit Authority (⊕ *www.mendocinotransit.org*) Route 95 buses stop at Salt Point and connect with other North Coast towns.

EXPLORING

Salt Point State Park. For 5 miles, Highway 1 winds through this park, 6,000 acres of forest, meadows, and rocky shoreline. Heading north, the first park entrance (on the right) leads to forest hiking trails and several campgrounds. The next entrance—the park's main road—winds through meadows and along the wave-splashed coastline. This is also the route to the visitor center and Gerstle Cove, a favorite spot for abalone divers and sunbathing seals. Next along the highway is Stump Beach Cove, with picnic tables, toilets, and a ¼-mile walk to the sandy beach. The park's final entrance is at Fisk Mill Cove, where centuries of wind and rain erosion have carved unusual honeycomb patterns in the sandstone called "tafonis." A five-minute walk uphill from the parking lot leads to a dramatic view of Sentinel Rock, an excellent spot for sunsets.

Just up the highway, narrow, unpaved Kruse Ranch Road leads to the **Kruse Rhododendron State Reserve**, where each May thousands of rhododendrons bloom within a quiet forest of redwoods and tan oaks. ⊠ 25050 Hwy. 1 ☎ 707/847–3221, 707/865–2391 ⊕ www.parks.ca.gov ⊡ $8 per vehicle ☉ Daily sunrise–sunset; some sections closed in winter, call ahead.

THE MENDOCINO COAST

GUALALA

16 miles north of Salt Point State Park.

This former lumber port on the Gualala River has become a headquarters for exploring the coast. The busiest town on Highway 1 between Bodega Bay and Mendocino, it has all the basic services plus some galleries and gift shops.

GETTING HERE AND AROUND

From San Francisco, take U.S. 101 to the East Washington Street/Central Petaluma exit and follow signs west through Valley Ford (you're on Highway 1 by this point) to Bodega Bay. From there, continue north on Highway 1. From Ukiah, exit U.S. 101 at Highway 253, driving southwest to Boonville/Highway 128. From Boonville, turn west on Mountain View Road, which winds 24 miles to Highway 1; from there, drive south 18½ miles. Mendocino Transit Authority (⊕ www.mendocinotransit.org) Routes 75 and 95 buses connect Gualala with coastal and inland towns.

EXPLORING

Gualala Point Regional Park. This 195-acre park has a long, sandy beach and picnic areas, and is an excellent whale-watching spot from December through April. Opposite the beach, along the Gualala River estuary, two-dozen campsites are shaded by redwoods. Dogs must be on a leash at all times throughout the park. ■TIP→ Watch out for unpredictable sleeper waves which are common along the North Coast. ⊠ 42401 Hwy. 1, 1 mile south of Gualala ☎ 707/785–2377 ⊕ www.sonoma-county.org/parks/pk_glala.htm ⊡ $7 per vehicle (day use) ☉ Daily 8 am–sunset.

WHERE TO EAT AND STAY

$$$$
AMERICAN

✕ St. Orres. Resembling a traditional Russian dacha with two onion-dome towers, this intriguing lodge stands on 42 acres of redwood forest and meadow. In one of the towers is a spectacular atrium dining room. Here, locally farmed and foraged ingredients appear in dishes such as garlic flan with black chanterelles and rack of venison medallions with wild huckleberries. The prix-fixe menu ($45) includes soup and salad but no appetizer or dessert (available à la carte). A fine brunch is served on weekends. ⑤ *Average main: $48* ✉ *36601 Hwy. 1, 3 miles north of Gualala* ☎ *707/884–3303* ⊕ *www.saintorres. com* ⚑ *Reservations essential* ⊘ *Closed Tues. and Wed Dec.–May. No lunch weekdays.*

$$$
HOTEL
Fodor's Choice
★

⛬ Mar Vista Cottages. Escape to nature and retro-charm at these refurbished, gadget-free 1930s cottages, where your daily activities will include snipping flowers for a bouquet, harvesting a bounty of vegetables for dinner from the organic garden and greenhouse, finding a basket of freshly-laid eggs at your door every morning, roaming open meadows with resident goats and chickens, and soaking in views of the blustery coastline. **Pros:** commune-with-nature solitude, peaceful retreat. **Cons:** no other businesses within walking distance. ⑤ *Rooms from: $185* ✉ *35101 S. Hwy 1, 5 miles north of Gualala* ☎ *707/884–3522, 877/855–3522* ⊕ *www.marvistamendocino.com* ⚑ *8 1-bedroom cottages, 4 2-bedroom cottages* ⦿ *No meals.*

$$
HOTEL

⛬ Seacliff on the Bluff. Wedged in front of a small shopping center, this motel is not much to look at—the interiors are motel standard—but you'll spend your time here staring at the Pacific panorama since all rooms have ocean views. **Pros:** budget choice; great views. **Cons:** limited dining options nearby. ⑤ *Rooms from: $140* ✉ *39140 S. Hwy. 1* ☎ *707/884–1213, 800/400–5053* ⊕ *www.seacliffmotel.com* ⚑ *16 rooms* ⦿ *No meals.*

POINT ARENA

14 miles north of Gualala.

Occupied by an eclectic mix of long-time locals and long-haired surfers, this former timber town on Highway 1 is part New Age, part rowdy—and always laid-back. The one road going west out of downtown will lead you to the harbor, where fishing boats unload sea urchins and salmon and there's almost always someone riding the waves.

GETTING HERE AND AROUND

To reach Point Arena from Santa Rosa, drive north on U.S. 101, exit at Cloverdale, and follow Highway 128 northwest 28 miles to Boonville. From Boonville take winding Mountain View Road west 25 miles to Highway 1. Point Arena is 4 miles south. From points north, exit U.S. 101 at Ukiah, take Highway 253 southwest to Boonville and follow Mountain View Road west to Highway 1 south. Mendocino Transit Authority (⊕ *www.mendocinotransit.org*) Routes 75 and 95 buses stop in Point Arena.

EXPLORING

Point Arena Lighthouse. For an outstanding view of the ocean and, in winter, migrating whales, take the marked road off Highway 1 north of town to the 115-foot lighthouse. It's possible to stay out here, in one of four rental units ($$), all of which have full kitchens. (On weekends there's a two-night minimum.) ⊠ *45500 Lighthouse Rd., off Hwy. 1* 🕾 *707/882–2809, 877/725–4448* ⊕ *www.pointarenalighthouse.com* 🎫 *Tour $7.50* ⊙ *Late May–early Sept. daily 10–4:30, early Sept.–late May daily 10–3:30.*

BEACHES

Manchester State Park. Before slipping into the sea, the northernmost segment of the San Andreas Fault cuts through this park beloved by locals for its 5 miles of sandy, usually empty shoreline and trails that wind through dunes and wetlands. Hiking, bird-watching, and beach strolling are the popular activities here. There's steelhead fishing most of the year at Brush and Alder creeks, and beautiful coastal wildflowers bloom in early spring. Tundra swans winter in this area, and migrating whales are often spotted close to shore. Swimming and water sports are too dangerous because of the strong undertow. Dogs are not allowed on the beach. **Amenities:** parking. **Best for:** solitude; sunset; walking. ⊠ *Park entrance, 44500 Kinney La., off Hwy. 1, ½ mile north of Manchester* 🕾 *707/937–5804* ⊕ *www.parks.ca.gov* ⊙ *Some reduced services and hrs due to budget cutbacks; call ahead.*

WHERE TO EAT

$

CAFÉ

✕ **Arena Market and Café.** The simple café at this all-organic grocery store serves up hot soups, fine sandwiches and has an ample salad bar. The market, which specializes in food from local farms, sells cheese, bread, and other picnic items. ⑤ *Average main: $8* ⊠ *185 Main St.* 🕾 *707/882–3663* ⊕ *www.arenaorganics.org* ⊙ *Mon.–Sat. 7–7; Sun. 8–6.*

$

CAFÉ

✕ **Franny's Cup and Saucer.** Aided by her mother, Barbara, a former pastry chef at Chez Panisse, Franny turns out baked goods that are sophisticated and inventive. Morning favorites include scones and sweet pastries as well as savory twists. Specialty cakes are dazzling concoctions such as Champagne cake layered with raspberries and lemon curd, or rich chocolate almond tortes spread with marzipan and berry preserves and iced with dark chocolate ganache. More familiar options at this delightful spot include fruit tarts and strawberry-apricot crisps, plus a mouth-watering assortment of cookies, candy, jams, and jellies. ⑤ *Average main: $5* ⊠ *213 Main St.* 🕾 *707/882–2500* ⊕ *www.frannyscupandsaucer.com* ▱ *No credit cards* ⊙ *Closed Sun.–Tues. No dinner.*

ANDERSON VALLEY

28 miles east of Elk.

At the town of Albion, Highway 128 leads southeast into the Anderson Valley, where warm summer weather lures those weary of the persistent coastal fog. Most of the first 13 miles wind through redwood forest along the Navarro River, then the road opens up to reveal farms and vineyards. While the community here is anchored in ranching, in the past few decades a progressive, gourmet-minded counterculture has taken root and that is what defines most visitors' experiences. In the towns of Philo and Boonville, you'll find B&Bs with classic Victorian style as well as small eateries.

Anderson Valley is best known to outsiders for its wineries. Tasting rooms here are more low-key than their counterparts in Napa; most are in farmhouses, and you're as likely to hear reggae as classical music as you sip. That said, Anderson Valley wineries produce world-class wines, particularly Pinot Noirs and Gewürztraminers, whose grapes thrive in the moderate coastal climate. Many wineries straddle Highway 128, mostly in Navarro and Philo with a few east of Boonville.

GETTING HERE AND AROUND

From the coast, pick up Highway 128 at Albion. From inland points south, take Highway 128 northwest from U.S. 101 at Cloverdale. From inland points north, exit U.S. 101 in Ukiah and take Highway 253 southwest 17 miles to Boonville. Mendocino Transit Authority (⊕ *www.mendocinotransit.org*) Route 75 buses serve the Anderson Valley between the coast and Ukiah.

EXPLORING

TOP ATTRACTIONS

Navarro River Redwoods State Park. Described by locals as the "11-mile-long redwood tunnel to the sea," this park that straddles Highway 128 is great for walks amid second-growth redwoods and for summer swimming in the gentle Navarro River. There's also fishing, canoeing, and kayaking in the late winter and spring, when the river is higher. The two campgrounds (one on the river "beach") are quiet and clean. ⊠ *Hwy. 128, 2 miles east of Hwy. 1, Navarro* ☎ *707/937–5804* ⊕ *www. parks.ca.gov.*

Navarro Vineyards. A visit to this family-run winery is a classic Anderson Valley experience. Make time if you can for a vineyard tour—the guides draw from years of hands-on experience to explain every aspect of production, from sustainable farming techniques to the choices made in aging and blending. Best known for Alsatian varietals such as Gewürztraminer and Riesling, Navarro also makes Chardonnay, Pinot Noir, and other wines. The tasting room sells cheese and charcuterie for picnickers. ⊠ *5601 Hwy. 128, Philo* ☎ *707/895–3686* ⊕ *www. navarrowine.com* 🍷 *Tasting free* ⊗ *Apr.–Oct. daily 9–6; Nov.–Mar. daily 9–5; tour daily at 10:30 and 3 by appointment.*

Roederer Estate. The Anderson Valley is particularly hospitable to Pinot Noir and Chardonnay grapes, the two varietals used to create Roederer's well-regarded sparkling wines. The view from the patio here is splendid. ⊠ *4501 Hwy. 128, Philo* ☎ *707/895–2288* ⊕ *www.roedererestate.com* 🍷 *Tasting $6* ⊗ *Tasting room daily 11–5.*

WORTH NOTING

Greenwood Ridge Vineyards. White Riesling is the specialty of this winery that also makes Pinot Noir, Syrah, and other wines. You can picnic here at tables on an island in the middle of a pond. ⊠ *5501 Hwy. 128, Philo* ☎ *707/895–2002* ⊕ *www.greenwoodridge.com* 🍷 *Tasting $5* ⊗ *Daily 10–5.*

7

Husch Vineyards. Anderson Valley's oldest winery, known for white wines and its reasonably priced Pinot Noir, has a cozy tasting room next to sheep pastures and picnic tables under a grapevine-covered arbor. ✉ *4400 Hwy. 128, Philo* ☎ *800/554–8724* ⊕ *www.huschvineyards.com* 🍷 *Tasting free* ⊗ *Daily 10–5.*

WHERE TO EAT AND STAY

$ ✕ **The Boonville General Store.** The café menu here is nothing surprising,
CAFÉ but the exacting attention paid to ingredients elevates each dish above the ordinary. Sandwiches are served on fresh-baked bread, and the beet salad comes with roasted pecans and local blue cheese. Breakfast options include granola and pastries, made in-house. ⑤ *Average main: $11* ✉ *14077A Hwy. 128, Boonville* ☎ *707/895–9477* ⊗ *No dinner.*

$$$$ ✕ **Table 128.** The restaurant at the Boonville Hotel takes small-town
AMERICAN dining into the 21st century. Proprietor Johnny Schmitt and his kitchen
Fodor's Choice staff prepare one prix-fixe meal per night ($40 for three courses, $50
★ for four) and serve it family-style, with platters of food brought to the table to be shared. Expect an expertly grilled or roasted entrée (such as prosciutto wrapped halibut, flank steak, or slow roasted lamb), a sophisticated side dish (radicchio with polenta; curried cauliflower soup), and don't forget dessert (linzer torte with Chantilly cream; local blackberry tart). This is essentially home cooking done at a high level, and despite the limited menu—posted a few days in advance on the restaurant's website—most diners will leave satisfied. ⑤ *Average main: $45* ✉ *14050 Hwy. 128, Boonville* ☎ *707/895–2210* ⊕ *www.boonvillehotel. com* ⊗ *No lunch; closed Mon.–Thurs. Nov.–Apr; closed Tues. and Wed. May–mid-June; closed Tues. mid-June–Oct.*

$$$ 🛏 **Boonville Hotel.** From the street this looks like a standard small-town
HOTEL hotel, but once you cross the threshold you start picking up on the laid-back sophistication that makes the entire Anderson Valley so appealing. **Pros:** stylish but homey; beautiful gardens and grounds. **Cons:** friendly but straightforward service—don't expect to be pampered; two-night stay required most weekends. ⑤ *Rooms from: $185* ✉ *14050 Hwy. 128, Boonville* ☎ *707/895–2210* ⊕ *www.boonvillehotel.com* 🛏 *8 rooms, 7 cottages* ⦿ *Breakfast.*

$$$ 🛏 **The Philo Apple Farm.** Set in an orchard of organic, heirloom apples,
HOTEL the three cottages and one guest room here are tasteful, inviting, and
Fodor's Choice inspired by the surrounding landscape. **Pros:** country charm; a unique
★ back-to-nature, off-the-grid experience. **Cons:** occasionally hot in summer. ⑤ *Rooms from: $200* ✉ *18501 Greenwood Rd., Philo* ☎ *707/895–2333* ⊕ *www.philoapplefarm.com* 🛏 *1 room, 3 cottages* ⦿ *Breakfast.*

LITTLE RIVER

14 miles north of Elk.

The town of Little River is not much more than a post office and a convenience store; Albion, its neighbor to the south, is even smaller. Along this winding portion of Highway 1 though, you'll find numerous inns and restaurants, all of them quiet and situated to take advantage of the breathtaking ocean views.

You'll find excellent vintages and great places to taste wine in the Anderson Valley—but it's much more laid-back than Napa.

GETTING HERE AND AROUND

From inland points south, exit U.S. 101 at Cloverdale and follow Highway 128 northwest about 56 miles to Highway 1, then head north 7 miles. From points north, exit U.S. 101 in Ukiah at Highway 253 and follow it west 17 miles to Boonville, where you'll pick up Highway 128 and drive northwest to Highway 1. Mendocino Transit Authority (⊕ *www.mendocinotransit.org*) Route 60 buses serve the area.

EXPLORING

Van Damme State Park. Best known for its beach, this park is a prime abalone diving spot. Upland trails lead through lush riparian habitat and the bizarre **Pygmy Forest,** where acidic soil and poor drainage have produced mature cypress and pine trees that are no taller than a person. The visitor center has displays on ocean life and the historical significance of the redwood lumber industry along the coast. ⊠ *Little River Park Rd., off Hwy. 1* ☎ *707/937–5804* ⊕ *www.parks.ca.gov.*

WHERE TO EAT AND STAY

$$$

FRENCH

Fodor's Choice

★

✕ **Ledford House.** The only thing separating this bluff-top wood-and-glass restaurant from the Pacific Ocean is a great view. Entrées evoke the flavors of southern France and include hearty bistro dishes—stews, cassoulets, and pastas—and large portions of grilled meats and freshly caught fish (though the restaurant also is vegetarian friendly). The long bar, with its unobstructed water view, is a scenic spot for a sunset aperitif. ⑤ *Average main: $24* ⊠ *3000 N. Hwy. 1, Albion* ☎ *707/937–0282* ⊕ *www.ledfordhouse.com* ☉ *Closed Mon. and Tues. and mid-Feb.–mid-Mar. No lunch.*

$$$ ⌐ **Albion River Inn.** Contemporary New England–style cottages at this
B&B/INN inn overlook the dramatic bridge and seascape where the Albion River
empties into the Pacific. **Pros:** great views; great bathtubs. **Cons:** newer
buildings aren't as quaint as they could be. $ *Rooms from: $195*
⌂ *3790 N. Hwy. 1, Albion* ☎ *707/937–1919, 800/479–7944* ⊕ *www.
albionriverinn.com* ⌐ *18 rooms, 4 cottages* ⎮○⎮ *Breakfast.*

MENDOCINO

3 miles north of Little River.

Many of Mendocino's original settlers came from the Northeast and
built houses in the New England style. Thanks to the logging boom,
the town flourished for most of the second half of the 19th century. As
the timber industry declined, many residents left, but the town's setting
was too beautiful to be ignored. Artists and craftspeople began flocking
here in the 1950s, and Elia Kazan chose Mendocino as the backdrop
for his 1955 film adaptation of John Steinbeck's *East of Eden,* starring
James Dean. As the arts community thrived, restaurants, cafés, and inns
sprang up. Today, the small downtown area consists almost entirely of
places to eat and shop.

GETTING HERE AND AROUND
From U.S. 101, exit at Cloverdale and follow Highway 128 northwest
about 56 miles and Highway 1 north 10 miles. You can also exit at Wil-
lits and drive west on Highway 20 about 33 miles to Highway 1, then
south 8 miles. Mendocino Transit Authority (⊕ *www.mendocinotransit.
org*) Route 60 buses serve the area.

EXPLORING
Ford House. The restored Ford House, built in 1854, serves as the visi-
tor center for Mendocino Headlands State Park and the town. The
house has a scale model of Mendocino as it looked in 1890, when it
had 34 water towers and a 12-seat public outhouse. From the museum,
you can head out on a 3-mile trail across the spectacular seaside cliffs
that border the town. ⌂ *735 Main St., west of Lansing St.* ☎ *707/937–
5397* ⊕ *mendoparks.org/mendocino-headlands-state-park-ford-house-
museum* ⌐ *$2* ⊗ *Daily 11–4.*

Kelley House Museum. An 1861 structure holds this museum, whose
artifacts include Victorian-era furniture and historical photographs of
Mendocino coast's logging days. ⌂ *45007 Albion St.* ☎ *707/937–5791*
⊕ *www.kelleyhousemuseum.org* ⌐ *$2* ⊗ *Late May–early Sept., Thurs.–
Tues. 11–3; early Sept.–late May, Fri.–Mon. 11–3.*

Mendocino Art Center. The center has an extensive program of workshops,
mounts exhibits in its galleries, and is the home of the Mendocino
Theatre Company. Artists from several states paint and sell their work
during the center's plein air festival the second week of September.
⌂ *45200 Little Lake St.* ☎ *707/937–5818, 800/653–3328* ⊕ *www.
mendocinoartcenter.org.*

The North Coast is famous for its locally caught Dungeness crab; be sure to try some during your visit.

WHERE TO EAT AND STAY

$$$
AMERICAN
✕ **Cafe Beaujolais.** The yellow Victorian cottage that houses this popular restaurant is surrounded by a garden of heirloom and exotic plantings. A commitment to the freshest possible organic and local ingredients guides the chef here. The menu is eclectic and ever-evolving, but often includes free-range fowl, line-caught fish, and Niman Ranch beef. The bakery turns out several delicious varieties of bread from a wood-fired oven. $ *Average main: $29* ⊠ *961 Ukiah St.* ☎ *707/937–5614* ⊕ *www. cafebeaujolais.com* ⊗ *No lunch Mon. and Tues.*

$$$$
B&B/INN
Fodor's Choice
★
🛏 **Brewery Gulch Inn.** The feel is modern yet tasteful at this smallish inn—furnishings are redwood and leather, beds are plush, and two rooms have whirlpool tubs with views. **Pros:** stylish; peaceful with ocean views; wine hour and buffet included in room rate. **Cons:** must drive to town. $ *Rooms from: $295* ⊠ *9401 N. Hwy. 1, 1 mile south of Mendocino* ☎ *707/937–4752, 800/578–4454* ⊕ *www.brewerygulchinn.com* ⊷ *10 rooms, 1 suite* ⦿ *Breakfast.*

$$
B&B/INN
Fodor's Choice
★
🛏 **Glendeven Inn Medocino.** If Mendocino is the New England village of the West Coast, then Glendeven is the local country manor with sea views. **Pros:** great ocean views; elegant; romantic. **Cons:** not within walking distance of town; on the main drag. $ *Rooms from: $165* ⊠ *8205 N. Hwy. 1* ☎ *707/937–0083, 800/822–4536* ⊕ *www.glendeven. com* ⊷ *6 rooms, 4 suites* ⦿ *Breakfast.*

$$
B&B/INN
🛏 **MacCallum House.** Set on two flower-filled acres in the middle of town, this inn is a perfect mix of Victorian charm and modern luxury. **Pros:** excellent breakfast; great central location. **Cons:** new luxury suites on a separate property are less charming. $ *Rooms from: $159* ⊠ *45020*

Albion St. ☎ *707/937–0289, 800/609–0492* ⊕ *www.maccallumhouse.com* ⊅ *19 rooms, 9 suites, 7 cottages* ⊙| *Breakfast.*

THE ARTS
THEATER
Mendocino Theatre Company. Dedicated to producing plays of substance and excitement, this well-established company mounts a repertoire that ranges all over the contemporary map, including works by Pulitzer Prize winners and local playwrights. ⊠ *Mendocino Art Center, 45200 Little Lake St.* ☎ *707/937–4477* ⊕ *www.mendocinotheatre.org.*

SPORTS AND THE OUTDOORS
Catch-A-Canoe and Bicycles Too. Rent kayaks and regular and outrigger canoes here, as well as mountain and suspension bicycles. Book a variety of tours that explore Big River and its estuary, some by moonlight. ⊠ *Stanford Inn by the Sea, Comptche-Ukiah Rd., east of Hwy. 1* ☎ *707/937–0273* ⊕ *www.catchacanoe.com* ⊠ *From $65.*

FORT BRAGG

10 miles north of Mendocino.

Fort Bragg is a working-class town that many feel is the most authentic place on the coast; it's certainly less expensive than its neighbors to the south. The declining timber industry has been steadily replaced by booming tourism, but the city maintains a local feel since most people who work at the area hotels and restaurants also live here, as do many artists. A stroll down Franklin Street (one block east of Highway 1) takes you past numerous bookstores, antiques shops, and boutiques.

GETTING HERE AND AROUND
From U.S. 101 at Willits follow Highway 20 west about 33 miles to Highway 1 and drive north 2 miles. Mendocino Transit Authority (⊕ *www.mendocinotransit.org*) Route 60 buses serve the town and region.

EXPLORING
Fodor'sChoice ★   **Mendocino Coast Botanical Gardens.** Something beautiful is always abloom in these marvelous gardens. Along 3½ miles of trails, including pathways with ocean views and observation points for whale-watching, lie a splendid profusion of flowers. The rhododendrons are at their peak from April through June; the dahlias begin their spectacular show in August and last until October. Even in winter, the heather and camellias add more than a splash of color. The main trails are wheelchair accessible. ⊠ *18220 N. Hwy. 1, 2 miles south of Fort Bragg* ☎ *707/964–4352* ⊕ *www.gardenbythesea.org* ⊠ *$14* ⊙ *Mar.–Oct., daily 9–5; Nov.–Feb., daily 9–4.*

Museum in the Triangle Tattoo Parlor. At the top of a steep staircase, this two-room museum pays homage to Fort Bragg's rough-and-tumble past with memorabilia that includes early 20th-century Burmese tattooing instruments, pictures of astonishing tattoos from around the world, and a small shrine to sword-swallowing sideshow king Captain Don Leslie. ⊠ *356-B N. Main St.* ☎ *707/964–8814* ⊕ *www.triangletattoo.com* ⊠ *Free* ⊙ *Daily noon–6.*

FAMILY **The Skunk Train.** In the 1920s, a fume-spewing gas-powered train car shuttled passengers along a rail line dating from the logging days of the 1880s. Nicknamed the Skunk Train, it traversed redwood forests inaccessible to automobiles. A reproduction train now travels the same route, making a 3½–4 hour round-trip trek between Fort Bragg and the town of Northspur, 21 miles inland. The schedule varies depending on the season and in summer includes evening barbecue excursions and wine parties. ⊠ *Foot of Laurel St., west of Main St.* ☎ *707/964–6371, 866/457–5865* ⊕ *www.skunktrain.com* ⧉ *$54–$74.*

BEACHES

Glass Beach. The ocean isn't visible from most of Fort Bragg, but a gravel path on Elm Street three blocks west of Main Street leads to wild coastline where you can walk for miles along the bluffs. The sandy coves nearest the road are called Glass Beach because here lies more sea glass than you've likely ever seen in one place (this area formerly served as the city dump, and the surf pulverized the trash into beautiful treasures). You can gaze at the dazzling colors, but don't take any glass with you; it's now against the law. No swimming at this beach either, for safety's sake. **Amenities:** parking; toilets. **Best for:** sunset; walking. ⊠ *Elm St. and Old Haul Rd.* ⊕ *www.parks.ca.gov.*

MacKerricher State Park. This park begins at Glass Beach and stretches north for 9 miles, beginning with rocky headlands that taper into dunes and sandy beaches. The headland is a good place for whale-watching from December to mid-April. Fishing at Lake Cleone (a freshwater lake stocked with trout), canoeing, hiking, tidepooling, jogging, bicycling, beachcombing, camping, and harbor seal watching at Laguna Point are among the popular activities, many of which are accessible to the mobility-impaired. Rangers, who lead nature hikes in summer, discourage swimming in the treacherous surf and remind those on shore to be vigilant for rogue waves and to never turn their backs on the sea. Dogs must be leashed. **Amenities:** parking; toilets. **Best for:** solitude; sunset; walking. ⊠ *Hwy. 1, 3 miles north of Fort Bragg* ☎ *707/937–5804* ⊕ *www.parks.ca.gov* ⧉ *$8 per vehicle.*

WHERE TO EAT AND STAY

$$ ✕ **Mendo Bistro.** Everything on this menu is made from scratch, including the bread, pastas, and charcuterie. Though the chef doesn't tout it, his ingredients are nearly all organic, many of them local. In season, the roasted whole crab with three dipping sauces is sensational. A wide selection of pastas includes something for everyone—or, if not, there's the DIY menu: select your protein (beef, chicken, tofu), method of cooking, and sauce. This is a good place for upscale family dining. ⑤ *Average main: $22* ⊠ *301 N. Main St.* ☎ *707/964–4974* ⊕ *www.mendobistro. com* ⊗ *No lunch.*

$ ✕ **Piaci Pub and Pizzeria.** The seats are stools and your elbows might bang a neighbor's, but nobody seems to mind at this cozy spot that's hands down the area's most popular casual restaurant. The food is simple, mostly pizza and calzones, but everything is carefully prepared and comes out tasty. The well-chosen beers served here receive the same respect the wines do: the chalkboard list notes the origin,

7

brewmaster, and alcohol content. Dogs and their owners are welcome at the tables outside. Cash only. ⑤ *Average main: $14* ⊠ *120 W. Redwood Ave.* ☎ *707/961–1133* ⊕ *www.piacipizza.com* ⊟ *No credit cards* ⊘ *No lunch Sun.*

$ 🖬 **Surf and Sand Lodge.** As its name implies, this hotel sits practically
HOTEL   on the beach; pathways lead from the property down to the rockstrewn shore. **Pros:** beach location; gorgeous sunsets. **Cons:** motel style; no restaurants close by. ⑤ *Rooms from: $119* ⊠ *1131 N. Main St.* ☎ *707/964–9383, 800/964–0184* ⊕ *www.surfsandlodge.com* ⇘ *30 rooms* ⦿ *No meals.*

$$$ 🖬 **Weller House Inn.** It's hard to believe that this house was abandoned
B&B/INN   and slated for demolition when it was purchased in 1994 and then carefully restored into the loveliest Victorian in Fort Bragg. **Pros:** handcrafted details; radiant heat in the wood floors; friendly innkeepers. **Cons:** some may find it too old-fashioned. ⑤ *Rooms from: $210* ⊠ *524 Stewart St.* ☎ *707/964–4415* ⊕ *www.wellerhouse.com* ⇘ *9 rooms* ⦿ *Breakfast.*

SPORTS AND THE OUTDOORS
HORSEBACK RIDING
Ricochet Ridge Ranch. Come here for private and group trail rides through redwood forest and on the beach. ⊠ *24201 N. Hwy. 1* ☎ *707/964–7669, 888/873–5777* ⊕ *www.horse-vacation.com* ☞ *From $50.*

WHALE-WATCHING
All Aboard Adventures. Captain Tim of All Aboard operates fishing excursions year-round and whale-watching trips from late December through April. ⊠ *Noyo Harbor, 32410 N. Harbor Dr.* ☎ *707/964–1881* ⊕ *www. allaboardadventures.com* ☞ *From $35.*

REDWOOD COUNTRY

HUMBOLDT REDWOODS STATE PARK

20 miles north of Garberville, 43 miles south of Eureka.

Conservationists banded together a century ago as the Save the Redwoods League and scored a key victory when a memorial grove was dedicated in 1921. That grove is now part of Humboldt Redwoods State Park, which these days has grown to nearly 53,000 acres, about a third of which are filled with untouched old-growth coast redwoods.

GETTING HERE AND AROUND
Access the park right off U.S. 101. *(See Bus Travel, at the beginning of this chapter, for Humboldt County public transportation information.)*

EXPLORING
FAMILY   **Avenue of the Giants.** Some of the tallest trees on Earth tower over this
Fodor'sChoice   magnificent 32-mile stretch of two-lane blacktop, also known as High-
★   way 254, that follows the south fork of the Eel River through Humboldt Redwoods State Park. The highway runs more or less parallel to U.S. 101 from Phillipsville in the south to the town of Pepperwood in the north. A brochure available at either end of the highway or

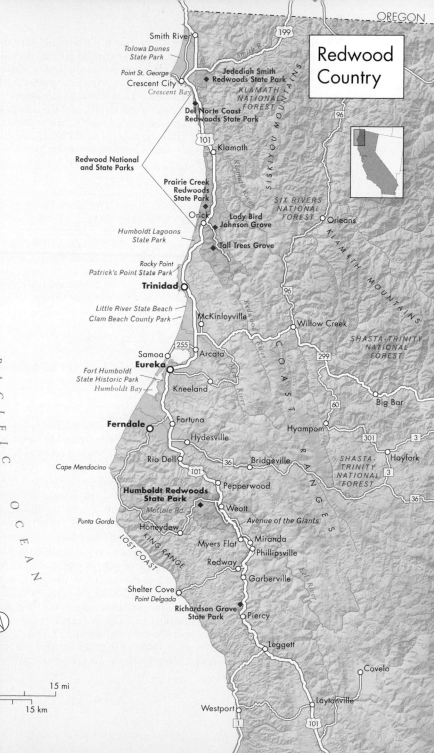

the **visitor center,** 2 miles south of Weott, contains a self-guided tour, with short and long hikes through various redwood groves. A trail at **Founders Grove** passes by several impressive trees, among them the fallen 362-foot-long Dyerville Giant, whose root base points skyward 35 feet. The tree can be reached via a short trail that begins 4 miles north of the visitor center. About 6 miles north of the center lies **Rockefeller Forest.** The largest remaining old-growth coast redwood forest, it contains 40 of the 100 tallest trees in the world. ⊠ *Humboldt Redwoods State Park Visitor Center, Hwy. 254, Weott* ☎ *707/946–2263* ⊕ *www.parks.ca.gov* ▭ *Free; $8 day-use fee for Williams Grove* ⊙ *Visitor center: Apr.–Sept., daily 9–5; Oct.–Mar., daily 10–4.*

FERNDALE

35 miles northwest of Weott; 57 miles northwest of Garberville.

Though gift shops and ice-cream stores comprise a fair share of the businesses here, Ferndale remains a fully functioning small town. There's a butcher, a small grocery, and a local saloon (the westernmost in the contiguous United States), and descendants of the Portuguese and Scandinavian dairy farmers who settled this town continue to raise dairy cows in the surrounding pastures. Ferndale is best known for its colorful Victorian architecture; many shops carry a self-guided tour map that highlights the town's most interesting historical buildings.

GETTING HERE AND AROUND

Ferndale is about 19 miles south of Eureka. Exit U.S. 101 at Highway 211 and follow it southwest 5 miles. There is no public transit service to Ferndale.

EXPLORING

Eel River Delta Tours. Bruce Slocum's engaging two-hour boat trips examine the wildlife and history of the Eel River's estuary and salt marsh. ⊠ *285 Morgan Slough Rd.* ☎ *707/786–4902 leave message for call back* ▭ *From $25.*

Ferndale Historic Cemetery. The worn, lovely gravestones at this cemetery on Ferndale's east side provide insight into the hard, often short lives of the European immigrants who cultivated this area in the mid-18th century. From the top of the hill here you can view the town, the surrounding farms, and the ocean. ⊠ *Bluff St. and Craig St.*

Ferndale Museum. The main building of this museum exhibits Victoriana and historical photographs and has a display of an old-style barbershop and another of Wiyot Indian baskets. In the annex are a horse-drawn buggy, a re-created blacksmith's shop, and antique farming, fishing, and dairy equipment. Don't miss the historic Bosch-Omori seismograph, installed in 1933 in Ferndale; it's still checked daily for recordings of earthquake activity. ⊠ *515 Shaw Ave.* ☎ *707/786–4466* ⊕ *www.ferndale-museum.org* ▭ *$1* ⊙ *June–Sept., Tues.–Sat. 11–4, Sun. 1–4; Oct.–Dec. and Feb.–May, Wed.–Sat. 11–4, Sun. 1–4; closed Jan.*

WHERE TO STAY

$$
B&B/INN

▥ **Gingerbread Mansion.** A dazzler that rivals San Francisco's "painted ladies," this Victorian mansion has detailed exterior spindle work, turrets, and gables. **Pros:** elegant; relaxing; friendly. **Cons:** some may find it gaudy. ⑤ *Rooms from: $150* ⊠ *400 Berding St.* ☎ *707/786–4000, 855/786–4001* ⊕ *www.thegingerbreadmansion.com* ⇨ *7 rooms, 4 suites* ⅠⓄⅠ *Breakfast.*

EUREKA

19 miles north of Ferndale; 67 miles north of Garberville.

With a population of 27,191, Eureka is the North Coast's largest city. Over the past century, it has cycled through several periods of boom and bust—first with mining and later with timber and fishing—but these days tourism helps keep the local economy afloat. The town's nearly 100 Victorian buildings have inspired some to dub it "the Williamsburg of the West." Shops draw people to the renovated downtown, and a walking pier extends into the harbor.

GETTING HERE AND AROUND

U.S. 101 travels through Eureka. From Redding and Interstate 5, travel west along Highway 299 about 138 miles to U.S. 101; Eureka is 9 miles south. Eureka Transit (⊕ *www.eurekatransit.org*) buses serve the town and connect with regional transit.

EXPLORING

Blue Ox Millworks. This woodshop is among a handful in the country specializing in Victorian-era architecture, but what makes it truly unique is that its craftspeople use antique tools to do the work. The most modern tool here is a 1948 band saw. Lucky for curious craftspeople and history buffs, the shop doubles as a dusty historical park. Visitors can watch craftsmen use printing presses, lathes, and even a mill that pares down whole redwood logs into the ornate fixtures for Victorians like those around town. The museum is less interesting on Saturday, when most craftspeople take the day off. ⊠ *1 X St.* ☎ *707/444–3437, 800/248–4259* ⊕ *www.blueoxmill.com* ⊡ *$10* ⊙ *Weekdays 9–5, Sat. 9–4; Dec.–Mar., closed Sat.*

Clarke Historical Museum. The Native American Wing of this museum contains a beautiful collection of northwestern California basketry. Artifacts from Eureka's Victorian, logging, and maritime eras fill the rest of the space. ⊠ *240 E St.* ☎ *707/443–1947* ⊕ *www.clarkemuseum. org* ⊡ *$3* ⊙ *Wed.–Sat. 11–4.*

Eureka Chamber of Commerce Visitor Center. The center has maps of self-guided driving tours of Eureka's Victorian architecture, and you can learn about organized tours. ⊠ *2112 Broadway* ☎ *707/442–3738* ⊕ *www.eurekachamber.com* ⊙ *Mon.–Fri. 8:30–5, Sat. 10–3; Sept.–May, closed Sat.*

FAMILY **Fort Humboldt State Historic Park.** The structure that gives this park its name was built in response to conflicts between white settlers and Native Americans. It no longer stands, but on its grounds are some reconstructed buildings, fort and logging museums, and old logging locomotives. ⊠ *3431 Fort Ave.* ☎ *707/445–6547* ⊕ *www.parks.ca.gov* ☞ *Free* ⊙ *Daily 8–5.*

QUICK BITES

Lost Coast Brewery & Cafe. This bustling microbrewery is the best place in town to relax with a pint of ale or porter. Soups, salads, and light meals are served for lunch and dinner. ⊠ *617 4th St.* ☎ *707/445–4480* ⊕ *www.lostcoast.com.*

WHERE TO EAT AND STAY

$$$
AMERICAN
Fodor'sChoice
★

✕ **Restaurant 301.** Eureka's most elegant restaurant, situated in the Carter House, uses ingredients selected from the farmers' market, local cheese makers and ranchers, and the on-site gardens. Dishes are prepared with a delicate hand and a sensuous imagination. There's always a fresh seafood offering, and you can dine à la carte or choose from two prix-fixe menus (five courses, $62; eight courses, $92). The restaurant has earned high praise for its comprehensive wine selection. $ *Average main: $28* ⊠ *301 L St.* ☎ *707/444–8062, 800/404–1390* ⊕ *carterhouse.com* ⊙ *No lunch.*

$$
AMERICAN
FAMILY

✕ **Samoa Cookhouse.** Waiters at this former cafeteria for local mill workers deliver family-style bowls—whatever is being served at the meal you've arrived for—to long, communal tables. For breakfast that means eggs, sausage, biscuits and gravy, and the like. Lunch and dinner usually feature soup, potatoes, salad, and pie, plus daily-changing entrées such as pot roast and pork loin. A museum in the back pays homage to logging culture, but the entire place is a tribute to the rough-and-tumble life and hard work that tamed this wild land. Dieters and vegetarians should look elsewhere for sustenance. $ *Average main: $16* ⊠ *908 Vance Ave., near Cookhouse Rd., Samoa* ☎ *707/442–1659* ⊕ *www.samoacookhouse.net.*

$
HOTEL
Fodor'sChoice
★

🏨 **Abigail's Elegant Victorian Mansion.** Innkeepers Doug and Lily Vieyra have devoted themselves to honoring this National Historic Landmark by decorating it with authentic, Victorian-era opulence; and indeed, it seems that every square inch of the home—once owned by the town's millionaire real-estate sultan—is covered in brocade, antique wallpaper, or redwood paneling, and from every possible surface hangs a painting with gilt frame, or a historical costume. **Pros:** unique; lots of character; delightful innkeepers. **Cons:** downtown is not within walking distance. $ *Rooms from: $115* ⊠ *1406 C St.* ☎ *707/444–3144* ⊕ *www.eureka-california.com* ⤸ *4 rooms, 2 with shared bath* ¶⊙¶ *No meals.*

$$$
HOTEL
Fodor'sChoice
★

🏨 **Carter House.** Owner Mark Carter says he trains his staff always to say yes; whether it's breakfast in bed or an in-room massage, someone here will get you what you want. **Pros:** elegant; every detail in place; excellent dining at Restaurant 301; bar off lobby. **Cons:** kids are allowed, but it's best suited for grown-ups. $ *Rooms from: $179* ⊠ *301 L St.* ☎ *707/444–8062, 800/404–1390* ⊕ *carterhouse.com* ⤸ *22 rooms, 8 suites, 2 cottages* ¶⊙¶ *Breakfast.*

SHOPPING

Eureka has several art galleries and numerous antiques stores in the district running from C to I streets between 2nd and 3rd streets.

ART GALLERY

First Street Gallery. Run by Humboldt State University, this is the best spot for contemporary art by local and regional artists, with some national and international representation. ⊠ *422 1st St.* ☎ *707/443–6363* ⊕ *www.humboldt.edu/first.*

BOOKS

Eureka Books. Along with classics and bestsellers, this bibliophile's haven has an exceptional collection of used books on all topics. ⊠ *426 2nd St.* ☎ *707/444–9593* ⊕ *www.eurekabooksellers.com.*

SPORTS AND THE OUTDOORS

WHALE-WATCHING

Humboats Kayak Adventures. Kayak rentals and lessons are available here, along with group kayaking tours, including whale-watching trips ($75, December–June) that get you close enough for good photos of migrating gray whales and resident humpback whales. ⊠ *Dock A, Woodley Island Marina* ☎ *707/443–5157* ⊕ *www.humboats.com* ⊠ *From $50.*

TRINIDAD

7

21 miles north of Eureka.

Trinidad got its name from the Spanish mariners who entered the bay on Trinity Sunday, June 9, 1775. The town became a principal trading post for the mining camps along the Klamath and Trinity rivers. Mining and whaling have faded from the scene, and now Trinidad is a quiet and genuinely charming community with ample sights and activities to entertain low-key visitors.

GETTING HERE AND AROUND

Trinidad sits right off U.S. 101. To reach the town from Interstate 5, head west from Redding on Highway 299 and turn north on U.S. 101 north of Arcata. Redwood Transit System (⊕ *www.redwoodtransit. org*) provides bus service between Trinidad, Eureka, and nearby towns.

EXPLORING

Patrick's Point State Park. On a forested plateau almost 200 feet above the surf, the park has stunning views of the Pacific, great whale- and sea lion–watching, picnic areas, bike paths, and hiking trails through old-growth spruce forest. There are also tidal pools at Agate Beach, a re-created Yurok Indian village, and a small museum with natural-history exhibits. Because the park is far from major tourist hubs, there are few visitors (most are local surfers)—it's sublimely quiet here. Three campgrounds amid spruce and alder trees have all amenities except RV hookups. Reservations are recommended in summer. Dogs are not allowed on trails or the beach. ⊠ *U.S. 101, 5 miles north of Trinidad* ☎ *707/677–3570* ⊕ *www.parks.ca.gov* ⊠ *$8 per vehicle.*

BEACHES

FAMILY **Clam Beach County Park and Little River State Beach.** Together these make a park that stretches for several miles south of Trinidad. The sandy beach here is exceptionally wide, perfect for kids who need to get out of the car and burn off some energy. Beachcombing and clamming are favored activities, as well as savoring fabulous sunsets. The two parks share day-use facilities. **Amenities:** parking; toilets. **Best for:** solitude; sunset; walking. ⊠ *Clam Beach Dr. & U.S. 101, 6 miles south of Trinidad* ☎ *707/445–7651* ⊕ *www.parks.ca.gov* ◔ *5 am–midnight.*

WHERE TO EAT AND STAY

$ ✕ **Katy's Smokehouse.** This tiny operation has been doing things the
SEAFOOD   same way since the 1940s, curing day-boat, line-caught fish with its original smokers. Albacore jerky, smoked scallops, and salmon cured with brown sugar are popular. Buy bread and drinks in town and walk to the waterside for fine alfresco snacking. Ⓢ *Average main: $10* ⊠ *740 Edwards St.* ☎ *707/677–0151* ⊕ *www.katyssmokehouse. com* ◔ *No dinner.*

$$$ ✕ **Larrupin' Cafe.** Set in a two-story house on a quiet country road north
AMERICAN   of town, this restaurant—locally considered one of the best places to eat on the North Coast—is often thronged with people enjoying fresh seafood, Cornish game hen, or mesquite-grilled ribs. The garden setting and candlelight stir thoughts of romance. Ⓢ *Average main: $29* ⊠ *1658 Patrick's Point Dr.* ☎ *707/677–0230* ⊕ *www.larrupin.com* ◔ *No lunch.*

$$$$ ▓ **Trinidad Bay Bed and Breakfast Inn.** Staying at this small Cape Cod-
B&B/INN   style inn perched above Trinidad Bay is like spending the weekend at a friend's vacation house. **Pros:** great location above bay; lots of light. **Cons:** if all rooms are full, the main house can feel a bit crowded. Ⓢ *Rooms from: $260* ⊠ *560 Edwards St., Box 849* ☎ *707/677–0840* ⊕ *www.trinidadbaybnb.com* ⤳ *4 rooms* ⦿| *Breakfast.*

$$$$ ▓ **Turtle Rocks Oceanfront Inn.** This comfortable inn has the best view in
B&B/INN   Trinidad, and the builders have made the most of it, adding private, glassed-in decks to each room so that guests can fully enjoy the ocean and sunning sea lions. **Pros:** great ocean views; comfy king beds. **Cons:** no businesses within walking distance. Ⓢ *Rooms from: $295* ⊠ *3392 Patrick's Point Dr., 4½ miles north of town* ☎ *707/677–3707* ⊕ *www. turtlerocksinn.com* ⤳ *5 rooms, 1 suite* ⦿| *Breakfast.*

REDWOOD NATIONAL PARK

WELCOME TO REDWOOD NATIONAL PARK

TOP REASONS TO GO

★ **Giant trees:** These mature coastal redwoods are the tallest trees in the world.

★ **Hiking to the sea:** The park's trails wind through majestic redwood groves, and many connect to the Coastal Trail running along the western edge of the park.

★ **Rare wildlife:** Mighty Roosevelt elk favor the park's flat prairie and open lands; seldom-seen black bears roam the backcountry; trout and salmon leap through streams; and Pacific gray whales swim along the coast during their biannual migrations.

★ **Stepping back in time:** Hike Fern Canyon Trail and explore a prehistoric scene of lush vegetation and giant ferns.

★ **Cheeps, not beeps:** Amid the majestic redwoods you're out of range for cell-phone service—and in range for the soothing sounds of warblers and burbling creeks.

1 Del Norte Coast Redwoods State Park. The rugged terrain of this far northwest corner of California combines stretches of treacherous surf, steep cliffs, and forested ridges. On a clear day it's postcard-perfect; with fog, it's mysteriously mesmerizing.

2 Jedediah Smith Redwoods State Park. Gargantuan old-growth redwoods dominate the scenery here. The Smith River cuts through canyons and splits across boulders, carrying salmon to the inland creeks where they spawn.

3 Prairie Creek Redwoods State Park. The forests here give way to spacious, grassy plains where abundant wildlife thrives. Roosevelt elk are a common sight in the meadows and down to Gold Bluffs Beach.

4 Orick Area. The highlight of the southern portion of Redwood National and State Parks is the Tall Trees Grove. It's difficult to reach and requires a special pass, but it's worth the hassle—this section has the tallest coast redwood trees, with a new record holder discovered in 2006.

CALIFORNIA

GETTING ORIENTED

U.S. 101 weaves through the southern portion of the park, skirts around the center, and then slips back through redwoods in the north and on to Crescent City. Kuchel Visitor Center, Prairie Creek Redwoods State Park and Visitor Center, Tall Trees Grove, Fern Canyon, and Lady Bird Johnson Grove are all in the park's southern section. In the park's central section, where the Klamath River Overlook is the dominant feature, the narrow, mostly graveled Coastal Drive loop yields ocean vistas. To the north you'll find Mill Creek Trail, Enderts Beach, and Crescent Beach Overlook in Del Norte Coast Redwoods State Park as well as Jedediah Smith Redwoods State Park, Stout Grove, Little Bald Hills, and Simpson-Reed Grove.

8

Updated
by Christine
Vovakes

Soaring to more than 300 feet, the coastal redwoods that give this park its name are miracles of efficiency— some have survived hundreds of years (a few live for more than 2,000 years). These massive trees glean nutrients from the rich alluvial flats at their feet and from the moisture and nitrogen trapped in their uneven canopy. Their huge, thick-barked trunks can hold thousands of gallons of water, reservoirs that have helped them withstand centuries of firestorms.

REDWOOD PLANNER

WHEN TO GO

Campers and hikers flock to the park from mid-June to early September. Crowds disappear in winter, but you'll have to contend with frequent rains and nasty potholes on side roads. Temperatures fluctuate widely throughout the park: the foggy coastal lowland is much cooler than the higher-altitude interior.

The average annual rainfall here is 90 to 100 inches, and during dry summer months thick fog rolling in from the Pacific veils the forests.

GETTING HERE AND AROUND

CAR TRAVEL

U.S. 101 runs north–south along the park, and Highway 199 cuts east–west through its northern portion. Access routes off 101 include Bald Hills Road, Davison Road, Newton B. Drury Scenic Parkway, Coastal Drive loop, Requa Road, and Enderts Beach Road. From 199 take South Fork Road to Howland Hill Road. Many of the park's roads aren't paved, and winter rains can turn them into obstacle courses or close them completely. Motorhomes/RVs and trailers aren't permitted on some routes. ■TIP➔ Park rangers say don't rely solely on GPS; closely consult park maps, available at the visitor information centers.

PARK ESSENTIALS
PARK FEES AND PERMITS

Admission to Redwood National Park is free. There's an $8 day-use fee to enter one or all of Redwood's state parks; for camping at these state parks it's an additional $35. To visit Tall Trees Grove, you must get a free permit at the Kuchel Information Center in Orick. Permits also are needed to camp in all designated backcountry camps.

PARK HOURS

The park is open year-round, 24 hours a day.

VISITOR INFORMATION
PARK CONTACT INFORMATION

Redwood National and State Parks ✉ *1111 2nd St., Crescent City* ☎ *707/465–7335* ⊕ *www.nps.gov/redw.*

VISITOR CENTERS

Crescent City Information Center. As the park's headquarters, this center is the main information stop if you're approaching the redwoods from the north. A gift shop and picnic area are here. ✉ *1111 Second St., near K St., off U.S. 101, Crescent City* ☎ *707/465–7335* ⊕ *www.nps.gov/redw* ☉ *Mid-May–mid-Oct., daily 9–6; mid-Oct.–mid-May, daily 9–4.*

Hiouchi Information Center. Located in Jedediah Smith Redwoods State Park, 2 miles west of Hiouchi and 9 miles east of Crescent City off Highway 199, this center has a bookstore, film, and exhibits about the flora and fauna in the park. It's also a starting point for seasonal ranger programs. ✉ *Hwy. 199* ☎ *707/458–3294, 707/465–7335* ⊕ *www.nps. gov/redw* ☉ *Late May–early Sept., daily 9–6.*

Jedediah Smith Visitor Center. Located off Highway 199, this center has information about ranger-led walks and evening campfire programs in the summer in Jedediah Smith Redwoods State Park. Also here are nature and history exhibits, a gift shop, and a picnic area. ✉ *Off Hwy. 199, Hiouchi* ☎ *707/458–3496, 707/465-7335* ⊕ *www.parks.ca.gov* ☉ *Late May–early-Sept., daily 10–6; closed early Sept.–late-May.*

Fodor's Choice ★ **Prairie Creek Visitor Center.** Housed in a redwood lodge, this center has wildlife displays and a massive stone fireplace that was built in 1933. Several trailheads begin here. Stretch your legs with an easy stroll along Revelation Trail, a short loop behind the lodge. Pick up information about summer programs in Prairie Creek Redwoods State Park. There's a nature museum, gift shop, picnic area, and exhibits on flora and fauna. ■TIP→ **Roosevelt elk often roam in the vast field adjacent to the center.** ✉ *Off southern end of Newton B. Drury Scenic Pkwy., Orick* ☎ *707/488–2039* ⊕ *www.parks.ca.gov* ☉ *Mid-May–mid-Oct., daily 9–5; mid-Oct.–mid-May, daily 9–4.*

Thomas H. Kuchel Visitor Center. If you're approaching the park from the south end, stop here to get brochures, advice, and a free permit to drive up the access road to Tall Trees Grove. Whale-watchers find the deck of the visitor center an excellent observation point, and bird-watchers enjoy the nearby Freshwater Lagoon, a popular layover for migrating waterfowl. Many of the exhibits here are hands-on and kid-friendly. ✉ *Off U.S. 101, Orick* ☎ *707/465–7765* ⊕ *www.nps.gov/redw* ☉ *Mid-May–mid-Oct., daily 9–5; mid-Oct.–mid-May, daily 9–4.*

8

Plants and Wildlife in Redwood

Coast redwoods, the world's tallest trees (a new record holder, topping out at 379 feet, was found within the park in 2006) grow in the moist, temperate climate of California's North Coast. These ancient giants thrive in an environment that exists in only a few hundred coastal miles along the Pacific Ocean. They commonly live 600 years—though some have been around for 2,000 years.

A healthy redwood forest is diverse and includes Douglas firs, western hemlocks, tan oaks, and madrone trees. The complex soils of the forest floor support a verdant profusion of ferns, mosses, and fungi, along with numerous shrubs and berry bushes. In spring, California rhododendron bloom throughout the forest, providing a dazzling purple and pink contrast to the dense greenery.

Redwood National and State Parks hold 45% of all California's old-growth redwood forests. Of the original 3,125 square miles (2 million acres) in the Redwoods Historic Range, only 4% remain following the logging that began in 1850; 1% is privately owned and managed, and 3% is on public land.

In the park's backcountry, you might spot mountain lions, black bears, black-tailed deer, river otters, beavers, and minks. Roosevelt elk roam the flatlands, and the rivers and streams teem with salmon and trout. Gray whales, seals, and sea lions cavort near the coastline. And thanks to the area's location along the Pacific Flyway, more than 400 species of birds have been recorded in the park.

EXPLORING

SCENIC DRIVES

Coastal Drive. This 8-mile, narrow and mostly unpaved road is closed to trailers and RVs and takes about one hour to drive. The slow pace alongside stands of redwoods offers close-up views of the Klamath River and expansive panoramas of the Pacific. From here you'll find access to the Flint Ridge section of the Coastal Trail. Recurring landslides have closed sections of the original road; this loop is all that remains. ⊠ *On U.S. 101, 1 mile south of Klamath ✛ Take the Klamath Beach Rd. exit and follow signs to Coastal Dr.*

SCENIC STOPS

Crescent Beach Overlook. The scenery here includes ocean views and, in the distance, Crescent City and its working harbor; in balmy weather this is a great place for a picnic. From the overlook you can spot migrating gray whales going south November through December and returning north February through April. ⊠ *Off Enderts Beach Rd., 2 miles south of Crescent City.*

Fodor's Choice **Fern Canyon.** Enter another world and be surrounded by 30-foot canyon walls covered with sword, maidenhair, and five-finger ferns. Allow
★

an hour to explore the ¼-mile-long vertical garden along a 0.7-mile loop. From the north end of Gold Bluffs Beach it's an easy walk, although you'll have to wade across a small stream several times (in addition to driving across streams on the way to the parking area). But the lush surroundings are otherworldly, and worth a visit when creeks aren't running too high. Be aware that motorhomes/RVs and all trailers are prohibited here. ⊠ *Davison Rd., off U.S. 101, 10 miles northwest of Prairie Creek Visitor Center, Orick* ⊕ *www.nps.gov/redw.*

Lady Bird Johnson Grove. This section of the park was dedicated by, and named for, the former first lady. A 1-mile nature loop follows an old logging road through a mature redwood forest. Allow 45 minutes to complete the trail. ⊠ *1 mile north of Orick off U.S. 101 onto Bald Hills Rd., Orick* ✛ *Turn onto Bald Hills Rd. for 2½ miles to trailhead* ⊕ *www.nps.gov/redw.*

Tall Trees Grove. From the Kuchel Visitor Center, you can get a free permit to make the steep 14-mile drive (the last 6½ miles, on Tall Trees Access Road, are unpaved) to the grove's trailhead (trailers and RVs not allowed). Access to the popular grove is first-come, first-served, and a maximum of 50 permits are handed out each day. ⊠ *On U.S. 101, 1 mile north of Orick* ✛ *Turn right at Bald Hills Rd. and follow signs about 6½ miles to access road, then 6½ miles, unpaved, to trailhead.*

SPORTS AND THE OUTDOORS

HIKING

MODERATE

Coastal Trail. Although this easy-to-difficult trail runs along most of the park's length, smaller sections—of varying degrees of difficulty—are accessible via frequent, well-marked trailheads. The moderate-to-difficult DeMartin section leads past 6 miles of old growth redwoods and through prairie. If you're up for a real workout, you'll be well rewarded with the brutally difficult but stunning Flint Ridge section, a 4.5-mile stretch of steep grades and numerous switchbacks that leads past redwoods and Marshall Pond. The moderate 5.5-mile-long Klamath section, which connects the Wilson Creek picnic area with Hidden Beach tidepools and up to the Klamath Overlook, provides coastal views and whale-watching opportunities. *Moderate.* ⊠ *Shares Flint Ridge trailhead, at Douglas Bridge parking area, north end of Coastal Dr., Klamath.*

KAYAKING

With many miles of often-shallow rivers and streams in the area, kayaking is a popular pastime in the park.

OUTFITTERS

Humboats Kayak Adventures. Kayak rental and lessons are available here, along with a variety of group kayak tours, including full-moon and sunset tours and popular whale-watching trips (October–June) that

Best Campgrounds in Redwood

Within a 30-minute drive of Redwood National and State Parks there are nearly 60 public and private camping facilities. None of the four primitive areas in Redwood—DeMartin, Flint Ridge, Little Bald Hills, and Nickel Creek—is a drive-in site. You will need to get a free permit from any visitor center except Prairie Creek before camping in these campgrounds, and along Redwood Creek in the backcountry. Bring your own water, since drinking water isn't available in any of these sites. These campgrounds, plus Gold Bluffs Beach, are first-come, first-served.

If you'd rather drive than hike in, Redwood has four developed campgrounds—Elk Prairie, Gold Bluffs Beach, Jedediah Smith, and Mill Creek—that are within the state-park boundaries. None has RV hookups, and some length restrictions apply. Fees are $35 in state park campgrounds. For details and reservations, call ☎ 800/444–7275 or check ⊕ www.reserveamerica.com.

Elk Prairie Campground. Roosevelt elk frequent this popular campground adjacent to a prairie and old-growth redwoods. ⊠ On Newton B. Drury Scenic Pkwy., 6 miles north of Orick in Prairie Creek Redwoods State Park ☎ 800/444–7275.

Gold Bluffs Beach Campground. You can camp in tents or RVs right on the beach at this Prairie Creek Redwoods State Park campground near Fern Canyon. ⊠ At end of Davison Rd., 5 miles south of Prairie Creek Visitor Center off U.S. 101 ☎ 707/465–7335.

Jedediah Smith Campground. This is one of the few places to camp—in tents or RVs—within groves of old-growth redwood forest. ⊠ 8 miles east of Crescent City on Hwy. 199 ☎ 800/444–7275.

Mill Creek Campground. Mill Creek is the largest of the state-park campgrounds. ⊠ East of U.S. 101, 7 miles southeast of Crescent City ☎ 800/444–7275.

Nickel Creek Campground. An easy hike gets you to this primitive site, which is near tide pools and has great ocean views. ⊠ On Coastal Trail ½ mile from end of Enderts Beach Rd. ☎ 707/465–7335.

get you close enough for photos of migrating gray whales and resident humpback whales. ⊠ Dock A, Woodley Island Marina, Eureka ☎ 707/443–5157 ⊕ www.humboats.com.

WHALE-WATCHING

Good vantage points for whale-watching include Crescent Beach Overlook, the Kuchel Visitor Center in Orick, points along the Coastal Trail, and the Klamath River Overlook. Late November through January are the best months to see their southward migrations; February through April they return and generally pass closer to shore.

THE SOUTHERN SIERRA

Around Sequoia, Kings Canyon,
and Yosemite National Parks

Visit Fodors.com for advice, updates, and bookings

WELCOME TO THE SOUTHERN SIERRA

TOP REASONS TO GO

★ **Strap 'em on:** Whether you walk the paved loops in the national parks or head off the beaten path into the backcountry, a hike through groves and meadows or alongside streams and waterfalls will allow you to see, smell, and feel nature up close.

★ **Down you go:** Famous for its incredible snowpack—some of the deepest in the North American continent—the Sierra Nevada has something for every winter-sports fan.

★ **Live it up:** Mammoth Lakes is eastern California's most exciting resort area.

★ **Pamper yourself:** Tucked in the hills south of Oakhurst, the elegant Château du Sureau will make you feel as if you've stepped into a fairy tale.

★ **Go with the flow:** Three Rivers, the gateway to Sequoia National Park, is the launching pad for white-water trips down the Kaweah River.

1 South of Yosemite National Park. Several gateway towns to the south and west of Yosemite National Park, most within an hour's drive of Yosemite Valley, have food, lodging, and other services.

2 Mammoth Lakes. A jewel in the vast Eastern Sierra Nevada, the Mammoth Lakes area lies just east of the Sierra crest, on the backside of Yosemite and the Ansel Adams Wilderness. It's a place of rugged beauty, where giant sawtooth mountains drop into the vast deserts of the Great Basin. In winter, 11,053-foot-high Mammoth Mountain offers the finest skiing and snowboarding in California—sometimes as late as June or even July. Once the snows melt, Mammoth transforms itself into a warm-weather playground, with fishing, mountain biking, golfing, hiking, and horseback riding. Nine deep-blue lakes are spread throughout the Mammoth Lakes Basin, and another 100 lakes dot the surrounding countryside.

3 East of Yosemite National Park. The area to the east of Yosemite National Park includes some ruggedly handsome, albeit desolate, terrain, most notably around Mono Lake. The area is best visited by car, as distances are great and public transportation is negligible. U.S. 395 is the main north–south road on the eastern side of the Sierra Nevada, at the western edge of the Great Basin. It's one of California's most beautiful highways; plan to snap pictures at roadside pullouts.

GETTING ORIENTED

The transition between the Central Valley and the rugged Southern Sierra may be the most dramatic in California sightseeing; as you head into the mountains, your temptation to stop the car and gawk will increase with every foot gained in elevation. Although you should spend most of your time here in the national parks, be sure to check out some of the mountain towns on the parks' fringes—in addition to being great places to stock up on supplies, they have worthy attractions, restaurants, and lodging options.

9

4 South of Sequoia and Kings Canyon: Three Rivers. Scenic Three Rivers is the main gateway for Sequoia and Kings Canyon National Parks.

Updated by Cheryl Crabtree

The Southern Sierra's granite peaks and giant sequoias bedazzle heart and soul so completely that for many visitors the experience surpasses that at more famous urban attractions. Most of the Sierra's wonders lie within national parks accessed most easily via the gateway towns surrounding them—Oakhurst, Fish Camp, and Lee Vining for Yosemite, and Three Rivers for Sequoia and Kings Canyon. Lee Vining also provides entrée to deep-blue Mono Lake, a much-photographed attraction. The megaresort Mammoth Lakes, meanwhile, lures skiers and snowboarders in winter and hikers and mountain bikers in summer.

Outside the national parks, the Southern Sierra's pristine lakes and rolling hills—not to mention the region's laid-back small towns—offer year-round opportunities for rest and relaxation. Or not. In winter, the thrill of the slopes (and their relative isolation, especially compared to busy Lake Tahoe) draws a hearty breed of outdoor enthusiast. In summer, a hike through groves and meadows or alongside streams and waterfalls allows you to see, smell, and feel nature up close. Whether you're taking it easy, though, or braving the elements, you're in for a treat.

PLANNING

GETTING HERE AND AROUND
AIR TRAVEL
Three main airports provide access to the Southern Sierra: Fresno Yosemite International (FAT), on the western side, and, on the eastern side, Mammoth-Yosemite (MMH), 6 miles east of Mammoth Lakes, and Reno–Tahoe (RNO), 130 miles north of Mammoth Lakes via U.S. 395. Alaska, Alaska, Allegiant, American, Delta, Frontier, United, and

a few other carriers serve Fresno and Reno. Alaska and United serve Mammoth Lakes.

Airports Fresno Yosemite International Airport ✉ *5175 E. Clinton Ave., Fresno* ☎ *559/621–4500, 800/244–2359* ⊕ *www.flyfresno.org.* **Mammoth Yosemite Airport** ✉ *1200 Airport Rd., Mammoth Lakes* ☎ *760/934–2712, 888/466–2666* ⊕ *www.visitmammoth.com.* **Reno–Tahoe International Airport** ✉ *2001 E. Plumb La., Reno, Nevada* ☎ *775/328–6400* ⊕ *www.renoairport.com.*

BUS TRAVEL

Greyhound serves Fresno, Madera, and other Central Valley towns west of the Sierra. Madera County Connection buses travel between Madera and Oakhurst. Eastern Sierra Transit Authority buses serve Mammoth Lakes and other eastern Sierra towns. *YARTS* (Yosemite Area Regional Transportation System) *connects Yosemite National Park with surrounding towns; this is a good option during summer, when parking there is difficult.*

Bus Contacts Eastern Sierra Transit Authority ☎ *760/872–1901* ⊕ *www.estransit.com.* **Greyhound** ☎ *800/231–2222* ⊕ *www.greyhound.com.* **Madera County Connection** ✉ *Madera* ☎ *559/661 7433* ⊕ *www.maderactc. com/pubtrans.html.* **YARTS** (*Yosemite Area Regional Transportation System*). ☎ *877/989–2787* ⊕ *www.yarts.com.*

CAR TRAVEL

From San Francisco, heading east on Interstate 80 to 580 to 205E is the most efficient connecting route to Interstate 5 and Highway 99, which straddle the western side of the Sierra Nevada. From Los Angeles, head north on Interstate 5 and Highway 99. To best reach the eastern side from the Bay Area, take Interstate 80 to U.S. 395, then head south. To get to Mammoth Lakes in summer and early fall you can travel via Highway 120 (to U.S. 395 south) through the Yosemite high country (Tioga Pass is closed from November to April). In winter, the quickest route from the San Francisco Bay Area is Interstate 80 to U.S. 50 to Highway 207 (also known as the Kingsbury Grade, just east of South Lake Tahoe) to U.S. 395 south. From Los Angeles, take Interstate 5 to Highway 14 to U.S. 395 and head north. All routes take about seven hours. ■**TIP→** Watch your gas gauge. Gas stations are few and far between in the Sierra, so fill your tank when you can. If you're traveling between October and May, heavy snow may cover mountain roads. Carry tire chains, know how to put them on (on Interstate 80 and U.S. 50 you can pay a chain installer $35 to do it for you, but on other routes you'll have to do it yourself), and always check road conditions before you leave.

Travel Reports Caltrans Current Highway Conditions ☎ *800/427–7623* ⊕ *www.dot.ca.gov.*

TRAIN TRAVEL

Amtrak San Joaquin trains stop daily in Bakersfield, Hanford, Fresno, and Merced, where you can connect with local transit.

Amtrak ☎ *800/872–7245* ⊕ *www.amtrak.com.*

TOUR OPERATORS

Mammoth All Weather Shuttle. In summer, multilingual guides drive vans and SUVs on regular tours from Mammoth Lakes to Yosemite; north to June Lake, Mono Lake, and Bodie Ghost Town; and around the Mammoth Lakes region. MAW also provides charter shuttles to Los Angeles, Reno, and Las Vegas airports—very useful when flights at Mammoth Yosemite Airport are cancelled due to inclement weather. Custom itineraries are possible as well. ⊠ *Mammoth Lakes* ☎ *760/709–2927* ⊕ *www.mawshuttle.com.*

VISITOR INFORMATION

Mammoth Lakes Tourism ⊠ *Mammoth Lakes* ☎ *760/934–2712, 888/466–2666* ⊕ *www.visitmammoth.com.* **Mono County Tourism** ⊠ *Mammoth Lakes* ☎ *800/845–7922* ⊕ *monocounty.org.*

RESTAURANTS

Most small towns in the Sierra Nevada have at least one restaurant; with few exceptions, dress is casual. You'll most likely be spending a lot of time in the car while you're exploring the area, so pick up snacks and drinks to keep with you. With picnic supplies on hand, you'll be able to enjoy an impromptu meal under giant trees or in one of the eastern Sierra towns' municipal parks.

HOTELS

For visits to the Sierra Nevada's western side, book your hotel in advance—especially in summer—or you may wind up in the Central Valley, far from the action. Booking in advance is less crucial for travel to the Eastern Sierra, except in Mammoth Lakes. In either area, keep in mind that rural and rustic does not always mean inexpensive. *Hotel reviews have been shortened. For full information, visit Fodors.com.*

Hotel Contacts Mammoth Reservations ⊠ *Mammoth Lakes* ☎ *800/223–3032* ⊕ *www.mammothreservations.com.*

WHAT IT COSTS			
$	**$$**	**$$$**	**$$$$**
Restaurants	under $16	$16–$22	$23–$30	over $30
Hotels	under $121	$121–$175	$176–$250	over $250

Restaurant prices are the average cost of a main course at dinner or, if dinner is not served, at lunch. Hotel prices are the lowest cost of a standard double room in high season.

SOUTH OF YOSEMITE NATIONAL PARK

People heading to Yosemite National Park, especially those interested in seeing the giant redwoods on the park's south side, pass through Oakhurst and Fish Camp on Highway 41.

OAKHURST

40 miles north of Fresno on Hwy. 41.

Motels, restaurants, gas stations, and small businesses line Highway 41 in Oakhurst, the last sizeable community before Yosemite—the southern entrance is 23 miles north of town—and a good spot to find provisions. Continue north on Highway 41 to get to Yosemite. Three miles north of town on Highway 41, then 6 miles east, lies honky-tonk Bass Lake, a popular spot in summer with motorboaters, Jet Skiers, and families looking to cool off in the reservoir.

GETTING HERE AND AROUND

At the junction of highways 41 and 49, Oakhurst is about an hour's drive north of Fresno. It's the southern gateway to Yosemite, so many people fly into Fresno and rent a car to get here and beyond. The town has no public transportation of consequence.

ESSENTIALS

Visitor Information Yosemite Sierra Visitors Bureau ☎ 559/683–4636 ⊕ *www.yosemitethisyear.com.*

WHERE TO EAT

$$$$
EUROPEAN
Fodor'sChoice
★

✕ **Erna's Elderberry House.** Erna Kubin-Clanin, the grande dame of Château du Sureau, created this culinary oasis, stunning for its understated elegance, gorgeous setting, and impeccable service. Red walls and wood beams accent the dining room's high ceilings, and arched windows reflect the glow of candles. The seasonal six-course prix-fixe dinner ($95) can be paired with superb wines, with every course delivered in perfect synchronicity by the elite waitstaff. ■TIP➔ Diners can also order à la carte, and a short bar menu is served in the former wine cellar. ⑤ *Average main: $38* ⌧ *Château du Sureau, 48688 Victoria La., off Hwy. 41* ☎ *559/683–6800* ⊕ *www.elderberryhouse.com* ⌔ *Reservations essential* ⊘ *No lunch Mon.–Sat.*

WHERE TO STAY

$$
HOTEL
FAMILY

▦ **Best Western Yosemite Gateway Inn.** Oakhurst's best motel has carefully tended landscaping and rooms with attractive colonial-style furniture and slightly kitschy hand-painted wall murals of Yosemite. **Pros:** close to Yosemite's southern entrance and Wawona area; clean; indoor and outdoor swimming pools; comfortable. **Cons:** some rooms on the small side; Internet connection can be slow. ⑤ *Rooms from: $150* ⌧ *40530 Hwy. 41, Oakhurst* ☎ *888/256–8042, 559/683–2378* ⊕ *www.yosemitegatewayinn.com* ⌁ *133 rooms, 16 suites.*

$$$$
RESORT
Fodor'sChoice
★

▦ **Château du Sureau.** You'll feel pampered from the moment you drive through the wrought-iron gates of this fairy-tale castle. **Pros:** luxurious; great views. **Cons:** expensive; if you're not really into spas, it might not be worth your while. ⑤ *Rooms from: $385* ⌧ *48688*

9

Victoria La., Oakhurst ☎ *559/683–6860* ⊕ *www.chateausureau.com* ☞ *10 rooms, 1 villa* ⦿*Breakfast.*

$$
B&B/INN

⊞ **Homestead Cottages.** Set on 160 acres of rolling hills that once held a Miwok village, these cottages (the largest sleeps six) have gas fireplaces, fully equipped kitchens, and queen-size beds. **Pros:** remote location; quiet setting; friendly owners. **Cons:** might be too quiet for some. $ *Rooms from: $169* ⊠ *41110 Rd. 600, 2½ miles off Hwy. 49, Ahwahnee* ☎ *559/683–0495* ⊕ *www.homesteadcottages.com* ☞ *6 cottages.*

FISH CAMP

57 miles north of Fresno and 4 miles south of Yosemite National Park's south entrance.

As you climb in elevation along Highway 41 northbound, you see nothing but trees until you get to the small settlement of Fish Camp, where there's a post office and general store, but no gasoline (for gas, head 10 miles north to Wawona, in the park, or 17 miles south to Oakhurst).

GETTING HERE AND AROUND

Arrive here by car via Highway 41, from Yosemite National Park a few miles to the north, or from Oakhurst (and, farther down the road, Fresno) to the south. Unless you're on foot or a bicycle, a car is your only option.

EXPLORING

FAMILY   **Yosemite Mountain Sugar Pine Railroad.** Travel back to a time when powerful steam locomotives hauled massive log trains through the Sierra. This 4-mile, narrow-gauge railroad excursion takes you near Yosemite's south gate; there's also a moonlight special, with dinner and entertainment ($55). Take Highway 41 south from Yosemite about 8 miles to the departure point. ⊠ *56001 Hwy. 41, Fish Camp* ☎ *559/683–7273* ⊕ *www.ymsprr.com* ⊡ *$21* ⊗ *May–Sept., daily; Apr. and Oct., weekends and selected weekdays.*

WHERE TO STAY

$$$
B&B/INN

⊞ **Narrow Gauge Inn.** The well-tended rooms at this family-owned property have balconies with great views of the surrounding woods and mountains. **Pros:** close to Yosemite's south entrance; nicely appointed rooms; wonderful balconies. **Cons:** rooms can be a bit dark; dining options are limited, especially for vegetarians. $ *Rooms from: $209* ⊠ *48571 Hwy. 41, Fish Camp* ☎ *559/683–7720, 888/644–9050* ⊕ *www.narrowgaugeinn.com* ☞ *26 rooms* ⦿*Breakfast.*

$$$$
HOTEL

⊞ **Tenaya Lodge.** One of the region's largest hotels, Tenaya Lodge is ideal for people who enjoy wilderness treks by day but prefer creature comforts at night. **Pros:** rustic setting with modern comforts; good off-season deals; very close to Yosemite National Park. **Cons:** so big it can seem impersonal; pricey during summer. $ *Rooms from: $295* ⊠ *1122 Hwy. 41, Fish Camp* ☎ *559/683–6555, 888/514–2167* ⊕ *www.tenayalodge.com* ☞ *244 rooms, 6 suites* ⦿*No meals.*

MAMMOTH LAKES

30 miles south of the eastern edge of Yosemite National Park.

International real-estate developers joined forces with Mammoth Mountain Ski Area to transform the once sleepy town of Mammoth Lakes (elevation 7,800 feet) into an upscale ski destination. The Village at Mammoth has been a focus of recent attention—relatively sophisticated dining and lodging options have been added, and there is a busy schedule of concerts and events. The "downtown" area of Old Mammoth Road is experiencing a renaissance, as tired motels and restaurants have undergone multimillion-dollar transformations under new owners. It's also the home of the hoppin' Mammoth Rock 'n' Bowl, a two-story activity, dining, and entertainment complex. Winter is high season at Mammoth; in summer, the room rates drop.

GETTING HERE AND AROUND

The best way to get to Mammoth Lakes is by car. The town is a couple of miles west of U.S. 395. Highway 203 heads west from U.S. 395, becoming Main Street as it passes through the town of Mammoth Lakes, and later Minaret Road (which makes a right turn) as it continues westward to the Mammoth Mountain Ski Area and Devils Postpile National Monument. In summer, YARTS (Yosemite Area Regional Transportation System ⊕ *www.yarts.com*) provides once-a-day public-transit service between Mammoth Lakes and Yosemite Valley. The shuttle buses of Eastern Sierra Transit Authority (☎ *800/922–1930* ⊕ *www.estransit.com*) serve Mammoth Lakes and nearby tourist sites.

ESSENTIALS

Visitor Information Mammoth Lakes Visitor Center ⊠ *Welcome Center, 2510 Main St., near Sawmill Cutoff Rd.* ☎ *760/934–2712, 888/466–2666* ⊕ *www.visitmammoth.com.*

9

EXPLORING

TOP ATTRACTIONS

Fodor's Choice
★

Devils Postpile National Monument. West of Mammoth Lakes lies this formation of smooth, vertical basalt columns sculpted by volcanic and glacial forces. A short, steep trail winds to the top of the 60-foot cliff for a bird's-eye view of the columns. A 2-mile hike past Devils Postpile leads to the monument's second scenic wonder, **Rainbow Falls,** where a branch of the San Joaquin River plunges more than 100 feet over a lava ledge. When the water hits the pool below, sunlight turns the resulting mist into a spray of color. Scenic picnic spots dot the banks of the river. ■TIP→ **Follow Highway 203 west to Mammoth Mountain Ski Area to board the shuttle bus to the monument, which day-use visitors must take from mid-June to early September.** ⊠ *13 miles southwest of Mammoth Lakes off Minaret Rd. (Hwy. 203)* ☎ *760/934–2289, 760/872–1901 shuttle* ⊕ *www.nps.gov/depo* 🖅 *$7 per person* ☉ *Shuttle daily mid-June–early Oct.*

Fodor's Choice
★
Mammoth Lakes Basin. Mammoth's seven main lakes are popular for fishing and boating in summer, and a network of multi-use paths connects them to the North Village. First comes Twin Lakes, at the far end of which is Twin Falls, where water cascades 300 feet over a shelf of volcanic rock. Also popular are Lake Mary, the largest lake in the basin; Lake Mamie; and Lake George. ■**TIP→ Horseshoe Lake is the only lake in which you can swim.** ⊠ *Lake Mary Rd., off Hwy. 203, southwest of town.*

Mammoth Rock 'n' Bowl. The biggest attraction in town apart from the ski slopes, Mammoth Rock 'n' Bowl offers one-stop recreation, entertainment, and dining for all ages along with sweeping views of the Sherwin Mountains. The sprawling, two-story complex opened in spring 2014. Downstairs are 12 bowling lanes, a band stage and dance floor, Ping-Pong and foosball tables, dartboards, and a casual bar-restaurant ($$) serving burgers, pizzas, and small plates. The upstairs floor has three golf simulators, a pro shop, and Mammoth Rock Brasserie ($$$), an upscale dining room and lounge. ■**TIP→ If the weather's nice, sit on the outdoor patio or the upstairs deck and soak in the unobstructed vistas.** ⊠ *3029 Chateau Rd.* ☎ *760/934–4200* ⊕ *mammothrocknbowl. com* 🖃 *Bowling: weekends and evenings $7 per game per person + $3 shoe rental, weekdays $5 per game per person + $3 shoe rental* ⊙ *Daily 9–midnight.*

FAMILY
Fodor's Choice
★
Panorama Gondola. Even if you don't ski, ride the gondola to see Mammoth Mountain, the aptly named dormant volcano that gives Mammoth Lakes its name. Gondolas serve skiers in winter and mountain bikers and sightseers in summer. The high-speed, eight-passenger gondolas whisk you from the chalet to the summit, where you can read about the area's volcanic history and take in top-of-the-world views. Standing high above the tree line, you can look west 150 miles across the state to the Coast Range; to the east are the highest peaks of Nevada and the Great Basin beyond. You won't find a better view of the Sierra High Country without climbing. Remember, though, that the air is thin at the 11,053-foot summit; carry water, and don't overexert yourself. The boarding area is at the Main Lodge. ⊠ *Off Minaret Rd. (Hwy. 203), west of village center* ☎ *760/934–2571* 🖃 *$25* ⊙ *July 4–Oct., daily 9–4:30; Nov.–July 3, daily 8:30–4.*

WORTH NOTING

Minaret Vista. The glacier-carved sawtooth spires of the Minarets, the remains of an ancient lava flow, are best viewed from the Minaret Vista. ⊠ *Off Hwy. 203, 1¼ mile west of Mammoth Mountain Ski Area.*

Village at Mammoth. This huge complex of shops, restaurants, and luxury accommodations is the town's tourist center and the venue for many special events—check the website for the weekly schedule. The complex is also the transfer hub for the free public transit system, with fixed routes throughout the Mammoth Lakes area. The free village gondola starts here and travels up the mountain to Canyon Lodge and back. Unless you're staying in the village and have access to the on-site lots, parking can be very difficult here, if not impossible. ■**TIP→ If you must drive, try your luck getting a space in the public lot across the street**

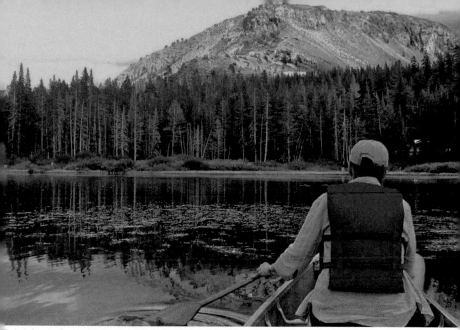

Twin Lakes, in the Mammoth Lakes region, is a great place to unwind.

on Minaret Road; as a compromise, you could drive to the park-and-ride lot at Old Mammoth and Tavern roads and ride a free shuttle bus to and from the Village. ✉ *100 Canyon Blvd.* ☎ *760/924–1575* ⊕ *villageatmammoth.com.*

WHERE TO EAT

$
WINE BAR
✕ **Bleu Handcrafted Foods.** Handcrafted artisanal cheeses and meats, wine and beer tastings, bread baked on-site, and specialty meats and seafood draw patrons to Bleu, a combination market and wine bar. Chef-owner Brandon Brocia and his wife, Theresa, cure their own salumi and prepare daily specials such as duck confit, pastas, and tapenades. Bleu, open daily from 11 to 8, also sells fine foods from California, the U.S., and Europe. Tastings can include cheeses, charcuterie, pâté, and olives, along with flights of beer, wine, or Port. ■ **TIP →** You can order a gourmet box lunch to take hiking or skiing. ⑤ *Average main: $11* ✉ *3325 Main St., Unit C* ☎ *760/914–2538* ⊕ *www.bleufoods.com.*

$$$
STEAKHOUSE
FAMILY
✕ **The Mogul.** A local longtime favorite, the Mogul is the place to go for straightforward steaks—top sirloin, New York, filet mignon, and porterhouse. The only catch is that the waiters cook them, and the results vary depending on their experience. But generally you can't go wrong, and kids love the experience. The knotty-pine walls lend a woodsy touch and suggest Mammoth Mountain before all the development. ■ **TIP →** For vegetarians and other lettuce lovers, there's an extensive salad bar—all you can eat, with hot bread included. ⑤ *Average main: $24* ✉ *1528 Tavern Rd., off Old Mammoth Rd., Mammoth Lakes* ☎ *760/934–3039* ⊕ *www.themogul.com* ⊙ *No lunch.*

$$$ ✕ **Petra's Bistro & Wine Bar.** The ambience at Petra's—quiet, dark, and
AMERICAN warm (there's a great fireplace)—complements its seductive meat and
seafood entrées and smart selection of mostly California-made wines.
The service is top-notch. With its pub grub, whiskies, and craft beers
and ales, the downstairs Clocktower Cellar bar provides a lively, if
sometimes rowdy, alternative. ⑤ *Average main: $28* ⊠ *Alpenhof Lodge,
6080 Minaret Rd.* ☎ *760/934–3500* ⊕ *www.petrasbistro.com* ⌾ *Reservations essential* ⊘ *Closed Mon. No lunch.*

$$$$ ✕ **Restaurant at Convict Lake.** The lake, named for an 1871 gunfight
AMERICAN between local vigilantes and six escaped prisoners, is one of the most
spectacular spots in the eastern Sierra, and the food here lives up to
the view. The chef's specialties include beef Wellington, rack of lamb,
and pan-seared local trout, all beautifully prepared. The woodsy room
has a vaulted knotty-pine ceiling and a copper-chimney fireplace that
roars on cold nights. Natural light abounds in the daytime, but if
it's summer opt for a table outdoors under the white-barked aspens.
Service is exceptional, as is the wine list, with reasonably priced European and California varietals. ⑤ *Average main: $32* ⊠ *Convict Lake
Rd. off U.S. 395, 4 miles south of Mammoth Lakes* ☎ *760/934–3803*
⊕ *www.convictlake.com* ⌾ *Reservations essential* ⊘ *No lunch early
Sept.–mid-June.*

$$ ✕ **Side Door Café.** Half wine bar, half café, this is a laid-back spot for
WINE BAR an easy lunch or a long afternoon. The Side Door serves grilled panini,
sweet and savory crepes, and espresso. At the wine bar, order cheese
plates and charcuterie platters, designed to pair with the 25 wines (fewer
in summertime) available by the glass. If you're lucky, a winemaker
will show up and hold court at the bar. ⑤ *Average main: $18* ⊠ *Village
at Mammoth, 100 Canyon Blvd., Unit 229* ☎ *760/934–5200* ⊕ *www.
sidedoormammoth.com.*

$$ ✕ **The Stove.** Down-to-earth, folksy cooking is the hallmark of this
AMERICAN casual place—the kind to chow down at before or after a long car
ride. New owners have freshened up the menu but have kept the comfort-food tradition alive with prime-rib hash and strawberry waffles,
fried chicken, meat loaf, and other items. Breakfast is served all day;
chicken and waffles are among the mainstays. Save room for the house-made pie, baked daily. The dining room here is cozy, with gingham
curtains and dark-wood booths, and the service is friendly. Reservations are accepted for dinner only. ⑤ *Average main: $16* ⊠ *644 Old
Mammoth Rd.* ☎ *760/934–2821* ⊕ *www.thestoverestaurantmammoth.
com* ⌾ *Reservations not accepted* ⊘ *No dinner occasionally during off-season months; call for hrs.*

$$ ✕ **Toomey's.** After 16 years at the helm of Lee Vining's popular Whoa
MODERN   Nellie Deli, chef Matt Toomey started this restaurant just steps from
AMERICAN the Village Gondola. A passionate baseball fan, Toomey designed
FAMILY   the casual space to resemble a dugout and decorated it with baseball
memorabilia. At breakfast, don't miss the coconut mascarpone pancakes. After a day on the slopes you can relax over lobster taquitos,
giant chicken wings with homemade ranch dressing, fish tacos, and
Angus beef sliders. Favorite lunch and dinner entrées include buffalo
meat loaf, seafood jambalaya, a New Zealand elk rack chop, and

Caesar salad topped with grilled steak. Save room for homemade, organic, gluten-free pie and other desserts. ■TIP→ If you're in a real hurry, place your order by phone, and someone will deliver your meal curbside to your car. ⑤ *Average main: $20* ⊠ *6085 Minaret Rd., at the Village* ☎ *760/924–4408* ⊕ *www.toomeyscatering.com.*

WHERE TO STAY

$ · **Alpenhof Lodge.** The owners of Alpenhof lucked out when developers
B&B/INN · built the Village at Mammoth across the street from their mom-and-pop motel, which remains a simple lodging offering basic comforts and a few niceties such as the attractive pine furniture. **Pros:** convenient for skiers; reasonable rates. **Cons:** some bathrooms on the small side; rooms above the pub can be noisy. ⑤ *Rooms from: $109* ⊠ *6080 Minaret Rd., Box 1157* ☎ *760/934–6330, 800/828–0371* ⊕ *www.alpenhof-lodge. com* ⤵ *54 rooms, 3 cabins* ⏐⊙⏐ *Breakfast.*

$$ · **Cinnamon Bear Inn Bed and Breakfast.** In a business district off Main
B&B/INN · Street, this bed-and-breakfast feels more like a small motel, with nicely decorated rooms, many with four-poster beds. **Pros:** comparatively quiet; affordable; friendly. **Cons:** a bit tricky to find; limited parking. ⑤ *Rooms from: $129* ⊠ *113 Center St.* ☎ *760/934–2873, 800/845– 2873* ⊕ *www.cinnamonbearinn.com* ⤵ *22 rooms* ⏐⊙⏐ *Breakfast.*

$$$ · **Double Eagle Resort and Spa.** You won't find a better spa retreat in
RESORT · the eastern Sierra than this one under lofty pine peaks on the June Lake Loop. **Pros:** pretty setting; generous breakfast; spectacular indoor pool; 1½ mile from June Mountain Ski Area. **Cons:** expensive; remote. ⑤ *Rooms from: $229* ⊠ *5587 Hwy. 158, Box 736, June Lake* ⊕ *www. doubleeagle.com* ⤵ *17 2-bedroom cabins, 16 rooms, 1 3 bedroom house* ⏐⊙⏐ *No meals.*

$$ · **Juniper Springs Resort.** Tops for slope-side comfort, these condomin-
RESORT · ium-style units have full kitchens and ski-in ski-out access to the mountain. **Pros:** bargain during summer; direct access to the slopes; good views. **Cons:** no nightlife within walking distance; no air-conditioning. ⑤ *Rooms from: $159* ⊠ *4000 Meridian Blvd.* ☎ *760/924–1102, 800/626–6684* ⊕ *www.mammothmountain.com* ⤵ *10 studios, 99 1-bedrooms, 92 2-bedrooms, 3 3-bedrooms* ⏐⊙⏐ *No meals.*

$$ · **Mammoth Mountain Inn.** If you want to be within walking distance of the
RESORT · Mammoth Mountain Main Lodge, this is the place. **Pros:** great location; big rooms; a traditional place to stay. **Cons:** can be crowded in ski season. ⑤ *Rooms from: $134* ⊠ *1 Minaret Rd.* ☎ *760/934–2581, 800/626–6684* ⊕ *www.mammothmountain.com* ⤵ *124 rooms, 91 condos.*

$$ · **Sierra Nevada Resort.** A full-service resort in the heart of Old Mam-
RESORT · moth, the Sierra Nevada has it all: three restaurants, four bars, a dedicated spa facility, on-site ski and snowboard rentals, a pool and Jacuzzi, miniature golf, and room and suite options in three buildings. **Pros:** many on-site amenities; walk to restaurants on property or downtown area. **Cons:** must drive or ride a bus to the slopes; thin walls in some rooms. ⑤ *Rooms from: $149* ⊠ *164 Old Mammoth Rd.* ☎ *760/934– 2515, 800/824–5132* 🖷 *760/934–7319* ⊕ *thesierranevadaresort.com* ⤵ *143 rooms, 6 townhomes* ⏐⊙⏐ *No meals.*

9

$$$
RESORT
Fodor's Choice
★

▤ **Tamarack Lodge Resort & Lakefront Restaurant.** On the edge of the John Muir Wilderness Area, where cross-country ski trails loop through the woods, this 1924 lodge looks like something out of a snow globe. **Pros:** rustic; eco-sensitive; many nearby outdoor activities. **Cons:** pricey; shared bathrooms for some main lodge rooms. $ *Rooms from: $218* ⊠ *Lake Mary Rd., off Hwy. 203* ☎ *760/934–2442, 800/626–6684* ⊕ *www.tamaracklodge.com* ⤴ *11 rooms, 35 cabins* ⦿ *No meals.*

$$$
RESORT

▤ **The Village Lodge.** With their exposed timbers and peaked roofs, these four-story condo buildings at the epicenter of Mammoth's dining and nightlife scene pay homage to alpine style. **Pros:** central location; clean; big rooms; good restaurants nearby. **Cons:** pricey; can be noisy outside. $ *Rooms from: $239* ⊠ *1111 Forest Trail* ☎ *760/934–1982, 800/626–6684* ⊕ *www.mammothmountain.com* ⤴ *277 units* ⦿ *No meals.*

$$$$
RESORT

▤ **Westin Monache Resort.** On a hill just steps from the Village at Mammoth, the Westin provides full-service comfort and amenities close to restaurants, entertainment, and free public transportation to all Mammoth Lakes destinations. **Pros:** upscale amenities; prime location; free gondola across the street to the slopes. **Cons:** long, steep stairway down to village; added resort fee. $ *Rooms from: $349* ⊠ *50 Hillside Dr.* ☎ *760/934–0400, 888/627–8154 reservations* 🖷 *760/934–4686* ⊕ *www.westinmammoth.com* ⤴ *109 rooms, 121 suites* ⦿ *No meals.*

SPORTS AND THE OUTDOORS

BIKING

Mammoth Mountain Bike Park. The park opens when the snow melts, usually by July, and has 100-plus miles of single-track trails—from mellow to super-challenging. Chairlifts and shuttles provide trail access, and rentals are available. ⊠ *Mammoth Mountain Ski Area* ☎ *760/934–0677, 800/626-6684* ⊕ *www.mammothmountain.com* ▥ *$47 day pass.*

FISHING

The fishing season runs from the last Saturday in April until the end of October. Crowley Lake is the top trout-fishing spot in the area; Convict Lake, June Lake, and the lakes of the Mammoth Basin are other prime spots. One of the best trout rivers is the San Joaquin, near Devils Postpile. Hot Creek, a designated Wild Trout Stream, is renowned for fly-fishing (catch-and-release only).

Kittredge Sports. This outfit rents rods and reels and also conducts guided trips. ⊠ *3218 Main St., at Forest Trail* ☎ *760/934–7566* ⊕ *www.kittredgesports.com.*

Sierra Drifters Guide Service. To maximize your time on the water, get tips from local anglers, or better yet, book a guided fishing trip, contact Sierra Drifters. ☎ *760/935–4250* ⊕ *www.sierradrifters.com.*

HIKING

Hiking in Mammoth is stellar, especially along the trails that wind through alpine scenery around the Lakes Basin. Carry lots of water; and remember, the air is thin at 8,000-plus feet.

U.S. Forest Service Ranger Station. Stop at the ranger station, just east of the town of Mammoth Lakes, for an area trail map and permits for backpacking in wilderness areas. ⊠ *2510 Main St., Hwy. 203* ☎ *760/924–5500* ⊕ *www.fs.usda.gov/main/inyo.*

HORSEBACK RIDING

Stables around Mammoth are typically open from June through September.

Mammoth Lakes Pack Outfit. This company runs day and overnight horseback trips and will shuttle you to the high country. ⊠ *Lake Mary Rd., between Twin Lakes and Lake Mary* ☎ *888/475–8747* ⊕ *www. mammothpack.com.*

McGee Creek Pack Station. These folks customize pack trips or will shuttle you to camp alone. ⊠ *2990 McGee Creek Rd., Crowley Lake* ☎ *760/935–4324 summer, 760/878–2207, 800/854–7407* ⊕ *www. mcgeecreekpackstation.com.*

SKIING

In winter, check the On the Snow website or call the Snow Report for information about Mammoth weather conditions.

FAMILY **June Mountain Ski Area.** In their rush to Mammoth Mountain, most people overlook June Mountain, a compact, low-key resort 20 miles to the north. Snowboarders especially dig it. Three beginner-to-intermediate terrain areas—the Silverado Fun Zone, Mambo Playground, and Bucky's Adventure—are for both skiers and boarders. There's rarely a line for the lifts here: if you must ski on a weekend and want to avoid the crowds, this is the place to come. In a storm, June is better protected from wind and blowing snow than Mammoth is. (If it starts to storm, you can use your Mammoth ticket at June.) Expect all the usual services, including a rental-and-repair shop, a ski school, and a sports shop. There's food, too, but the options are better at Mammoth. Lift tickets cost $72, with discounts for multiple days. ■TIP➔ Kids 12 and under ski and ride free, making this is a great choice for families. ⊠ *3819 Hwy. 158, off June Lake Loop, June Lake* ☎ *760/648–7733, 888/586–3686* ⊕ *www.junemountain.com* ⚲ *35 trails on 1,400 acres, rated 35% beginner, 45% intermediate, 20% advanced. Longest run 2 miles, base 7,545 feet, summit 10,190 feet. Lifts: 7.*

Fodor'sChoice **Mammoth Mountain Ski Area.** One of the West's largest and best ski areas,
★ Mammoth has more than 3,500 acres of skiable terrain and a 3,100-foot vertical drop. The views from the 11,053-foot summit are some of the most stunning in the Sierra. Below, you'll find a 6½-mile-wide swath of groomed boulevards and canyons, as well as pockets of tree-skiing and a dozen vast bowls. Snowboarders are everywhere on the slopes; there are three outstanding freestyle terrain parks of varying technical difficulty, with jumps, rails, tabletops, and giant super pipes—this is the location of several international snowboarding competitions, and, in summer, mountain-bike ones. Mammoth's season begins in November and often lingers into May. Lift tickets start at $79. Lessons and equipment are available, and there's a children's ski and snowboard school. Mammoth runs free shuttle-bus routes around town and to the ski area, and the Village Gondola runs from the Village complex

9

to Canyon Lodge. But only overnight guests are allowed to park at the Village for more than a few hours. ⚠ The main lodge is dark and dated, unsuited in almost every way for the crush of ski season. Within a decade, it's likely to be replaced. ✉ *Minaret Rd., west of Mammoth Lakes* ☎ *760/934–2571, 800/626–6684, 760/934–0687 shuttle* ⊕ *www. mammothmountain.com* ☞ *150 trails on 3,500 acres, rated 25% beginner, 40% intermediate, 20% advanced, 15% expert. Longest run 3 miles, base 7,953 feet, summit 11,053 feet. Lifts: 28, including 11 high-speed and 3 gondolas.*

Tamarack Cross Country Ski Center. Trails at the center, adjacent to Tamarack Lodge, meander around several lakes. Rentals are available. The all-day inclusive rate is $55. ✉ *Lake Mary Rd., off Hwy. 203* ☎ *760/934–5293, 760/934–2442* ⊕ *tamaracklodge.com.*

SKI RENTALS AND RESOURCES

Fodor's Choice
★

Black Tie Ski Rentals. Skiers and snowboarders love this rental outfit whose staffers will deliver and custom-fit equipment for free. They also offer slope-side assistance. ☎ *760/934–7009* ⊕ *mammoth.black tieskis.com.*

Footloose. When the U.S. Ski Team visits Mammoth and needs boot adjustments, everyone heads to Footloose, the best place in town—and possibly all California—for ski-boot rentals and sales, as well as custom insoles. ✉ *3043 Main St., at Mammoth Rd.* ☎ *760/934–2400* ⊕ *www. footloosesports.com.*

Kittredge Sports. Advanced skiers should consider this outfit, which has been around since the 1960s. ✉ *3218 Main St.* ☎ *760/934–7566* ⊕ *www.kittredgesports.com.*

Mammoth Sporting Goods. This company rents good skis for intermediates and sells equipment, clothing, and accessories. ✉ *452 Old Mammoth Rd.* ☎ *760/934–3239* ⊕ *www.mammothoutdoorsports.com.*

OntheSnow.com. This website provides ski and weather reports. ⊕ *www. onthesnow.com/california/mammoth-mountain-ski-area/skireport.html.*

Snow Report. For information on winter conditions around Mammoth, call the Snow Report. ☎ *760/934–7669, 888/766–9778.*

EAST OF YOSEMITE NATIONAL PARK

Most people enter Yosemite National Park from the west, having driven out from the Bay Area or Los Angeles. The eastern entrance on Tioga Pass Road (Highway 120), however, provides stunning, sweeping views of the High Sierra. Gray rocks shine in the bright sun, with scattered, small vegetation sprinkled about the mountainside. To drive from Lee Vining to Tuolumne Meadows is an unforgettable experience, but keep in mind the road tends to be closed for at least seven months of the year.

LEE VINING

20 miles east of Tuolumne Meadows via Hwy. 120 to U.S. 395; 30 miles north of Mammoth Lakes on U.S. 395.

Tiny Lee Vining is known primarily as the eastern gateway to Yosemite National Park (summer only) and the location of vast and desolate Mono Lake. Pick up supplies at the general store year-round, or stop here for lunch or dinner before or after a drive through the high country. In winter the town is all but deserted, except for the ice climbers who come to scale frozen waterfalls. To try your hand at ice climbing, contact Doug Nidever (☎ 760/937–6922 ⊕ *www.themountainguide. com*), aka the Mountain Guide.

GETTING HERE AND AROUND
Lee Vining is on U.S. 395, just north of the road's intersection with Highway 120 and on the south side of Mono Lake. In summer, Yosemite Area Regional Transportation System (YARTS ⊕ *www.yarts.com*) can get you here from Yosemite Valley, but you'll need a car to explore the area.

ESSENTIALS
Visitor Information Lee Vining Chamber of Commerce ☎ 760/647–6629 ⊕ www.leevining.com. **Mono Basin National Forest Scenic Area Visitor Center** ✉ *Visitor Center Dr., off U.S. 395, 1 mile north of Hwy. 120* ☎ *760/647–3044* ⊕ *www.monolake.org/visit/vc* ⊙ *Mid-May–mid-Oct., daily 8–5; early Apr.–mid-May and mid-Oct.–Nov., Thurs.–Mon. 9–4:30.*

EXPLORING
Fodor's Choice ★ **Mono Lake.** Since the 1940s Los Angeles has diverted water from this lake, exposing striking towers of tufa, or calcium carbonate. Court victories by environmentalists have meant fewer diversions, and the lake is rising again. Although to see the lake from U.S. 395 is stunning, make time to walk about South Tufa, whose parking lot is 5 miles east of U.S. 395 off Highway 120. There in summer you can join the naturalist-guided **South Tufa Walk,** which lasts about 1½ hours. The sensational **Scenic Area Visitor Center,** off U.S. 395, is open daily (8–5) from mid-May through mid-October; hours vary at other times, and it's closed in winter. The center's hilltop and sweeping views of Mono Lake, along with its interactive exhibits inside, make this one of California's best visitor centers. Rangers and naturalists lead walking tours of the tufa daily in summer and on weekends (sometimes on cross-country skis) in winter. In town at U.S. 395 and 3rd Street, the **Mono Lake Committee Information Center & Bookstore,** open 9 to 5 daily, has more information about this beautiful area. ✉ *Hwy. 120, east of Lee Vining, Lee Vining* ☎ *760/647–3044 visitor center, 760/647–6595 Mono Lake Committee Information Center* ⊕ *www.monolake.org*

June Lake Loop. Heading south from Lee Vining, U.S. 395 intersects the June Lake Loop. This gorgeous 17-mile drive follows an old glacial canyon past Grant, June, Gull, and other lakes before reconnecting with U.S. 395 on its way to Mammoth Lakes. ■TIP➔ The loop is especially colorful in fall. ✉ *Hwy. 158 W.*

EN ROUTE

9

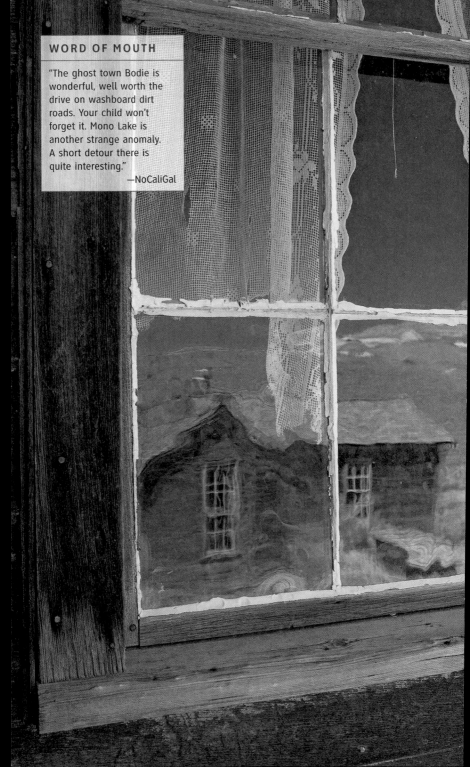

WHERE TO EAT AND STAY

$ AMERICAN ✕ **Tioga Gas Mart & Whoa Nelli Deli.** This might be the only gas station in the United States that serves craft beers and lobster taquitos, but its appeal goes way beyond novelty. Everything on the inventive menu is well executed, from the succulent fish tacos with mango salsa to a generous portion of barbecued ribs served with a slightly sweet huckleberry glaze.■**TIP→** Order at the counter and grab a seat inside, or, better yet, sit at one of the picnic tables on the lawn outside, which have a distant view of Mono Lake. $ *Average main: $15* ⊠ *Hwy. 120 and U.S. 395* ☎ *760/647–1088* ⊕ *www.whoanelliedeli.com* ☯ *Closed early Nov.–late Apr.*

$ B&B/INN ⛺ **Lake View Lodge.** Enormous rooms and lovely landscaping, which includes several shaded sitting areas, set this motel apart from its competitors in town. **Pros:** attractive; clean; friendly staff. **Cons:** could use updating. $ *Rooms from: $89* ⊠ *51285 U.S. 395* ☎ *760/647–6543, 800/990–6614* ⊕ *www.lakeviewlodgeyosemite.com* ⇥ *76 rooms, 12 cottages.*

BODIE STATE HISTORIC PARK

23 miles northeast of Lee Vining via U.S. 395 to Hwy. 270.

The historic town of Bridgeport is the gateway to Bodie State Historic Park, and the only supply center for miles around. The scenery is spectacular, with craggy, snowcapped peaks looming over vast prairies. Tiny and for tourist purposes worth nothing more than a place to sleep and eat, Bridgeport's claim to fame is that most of the 1947 film-noir classic *Out of the Past,* starring Robert Mitchum in his prime as a private eye whose past catches up with him, was filmed here. In winter, much of Bridgeport shuts down.

GETTING HERE AND AROUND

A car is the best way to reach this area. About 15 miles north of Lee Vining (7 miles south of Bridgeport), look for signs for the ghost town, another 13 miles east via Highway 270. The last 3 miles are unpaved. A snowmobile might be necessary to reach Bodie in winter.

EXPLORING

Fodor's Choice ★ **Bodie Ghost Town.** The mining village of Rattlesnake Gulch, abandoned mine shafts, and the remains of a small Chinatown are among the sights at this fascinating ghost town. The town boomed from about 1878 to 1881, but by the late 1940s all its residents had departed. A state park was established here in 1962, with a mandate to preserve everything in a state of "arrested decay." Evidence of Bodie's wild past survives at an excellent museum, and you can tour an old stamp mill where ore was crushed into fine powder to extract gold and silver. The town is 23 miles from Lee Vining, north on U.S. 395, then east on Highway 270; the last 3 miles are unpaved. Snow may close Highway 270 from late fall through early spring. No food, drink, or lodging is available in Bodie. ⊠ *Main and Green Sts.* ☎ *760/647–6445* ⊕ *www.parks.ca.gov/ bodie* ⛉ *$5* ☯ *Mid-May–Oct., daily 9–6; Nov.–mid-May, daily 9–3.*

9

SOUTH OF SEQUOIA AND KINGS CANYON: THREE RIVERS

Numerous towns and cities tout themselves as "gateways" to Sequoia and Kings Canyon national parks, but one that merits the distinction is frisky Three Rivers, a foothills hamlet along the Kaweah River. Close to Sequoia National Park's Ash Mountain and Lookout Point entrances, Three Rivers is a good spot to find a room when park lodgings are full. Either because Three Rivers residents appreciate their idyllic setting or because they know that tourists are their bread and butter, you'll find them almost uniformly pleasant and eager to share tips about the best spots for "Sierra surfing" the Kaweah's smooth, moss-covered rocks or where to find the best cell phone reception (it's off to the cemetery for Verizon customers).

GETTING HERE AND AROUND

Driving is the easiest way to get to and around long and slender Three Rivers, which straddles a long stretch of Highway 198. From late May to early September, the Sequoia Shuttle (☏ 877/404–6473 ⊕ www.ci.visalia. ca.us) connects Three Rivers to Visalia and Sequoia National Park.

WHERE TO EAT AND STAY

$$$
AMERICAN
✕ **Gateway Restaurant and Lodge.** The view's the main draw at this raucous roadhouse that overlooks the roaring Kaweah River as it plunges out of the high country. Taking seriously its role as its town's only true fine-dining establishment, the Gateway serves everything from panfried trout to osso buco to shrimp in Thai chili sauce. Some menu items are pricey, but you can also order a pizza or a Kobe beef or salmon burger. In general, the simpler the preparation is, the better the result. Dinner reservations are essential on summer weekends. $ *Average main: $29* ⊠ *45978 Sierra Dr., Three Rivers* ☏ *559/561–4133* ⊕ *www.gateway-sequoia.com* ⊙ *No breakfast weekdays Nov.–March.*

$$
B&B/INN
⛅ **Buckeye Tree Lodge.** Every room at this two-story motel has a patio facing a sun-dappled grassy lawn, right on the banks of the Kaweah River. **Pros:** near the park entrance; fantastic river views; friendly staff; kitchenette in some rooms. **Cons:** can fill up quickly in the summer; could use a little updating. $ *Rooms from: $134* ⊠ *46000 Sierra Dr., Hwy. 198, Three Rivers* ☏ *559/561–5900* ⊕ *www.buckeyetree.com* ⤵ *11 rooms* ⁑⊙⁑ *Breakfast* ⌁ *2-night minimum on summer weekends.*

SPORTS AND THE OUTDOORS

RAFTING

Kaweah White Water Adventures. Owner Frank Root's outfit offers three Kaweah River trips: a two-hour excursion (good for families) through Class III rapids, a longer paddle through Class IV rapids, and an extended trip (typically Class IV and V rapids). ⊠ *40443 Sierra Dr.* ☏ *559/740–8251, 800/229–8658* ⊕ *www.kaweah-whitewater.com* ⌁ *$50–$140 per person.*

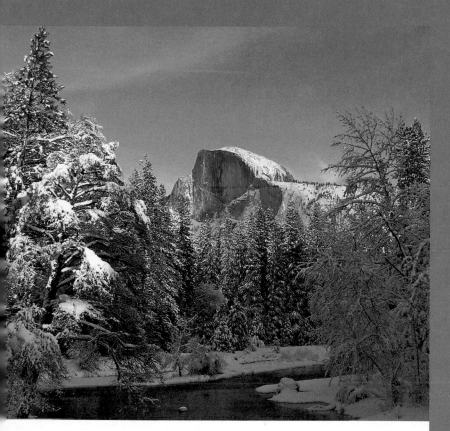

YOSEMITE
NATIONAL PARK

Visit Fodors.com for advice, updates, and bookings

WELCOME TO
YOSEMITE NATIONAL PARK

TOP REASONS
TO GO

★ **Wet and wild:** An easy stroll brings you to the base of Lower Yosemite Falls, where roaring springtime waters make for misty lens caps and lasting memories.

★ **Tunnel vision:** Approaching Yosemite Valley, Wawona Road passes through a mountainside and emerges before one of the park's most heart-stopping vistas.

★ **Inhale the beauty:** Pause to smell the light, pristine air as you travel about the High Sierra's Tioga Pass and Tuolumne Meadows, where 10,000-foot granite peaks just might take your breath away.

★ **Walk away:** Leave the crowds behind—but do bring along a buddy—and take a hike somewhere along Yosemite's 800 miles of trails.

★ **Powder your nose:** Winter's hush floats into Yosemite on snowflakes. Lift your face to the sky and listen to the trees.

1 Yosemite Valley. At an elevation of 4,000 feet, in roughly the center of the park, beats Yosemite's heart. This is where you'll find the park's most famous sights and biggest crowds.

2 Wawona and Mariposa Grove. The park's southern tip holds Wawona, with its grand old hotel and pioneer history center, and the Mariposa Grove of Big Trees, filled with giant sequoias. These are closest to the South Entrance, 35 miles (a one-hour drive) south of Yosemite Village.

3 Tuolumne Meadows. The highlight of east-central Yosemite is this wildflower-strewn valley with hiking trails, nestled among sharp, rocky peaks. It's a 1½-hour drive northeast of Yosemite Valley along Tioga Road (closed mid-October–late May).

4 Hetch Hetchy. The most remote, least visited part of Yosemite accessible by automobile, this glacial valley is dominated by a reservoir and veined with wilderness trails. It's near the park's western boundary, about a half-hour drive north of the Big Oak Flat Entrance.

CALIFORNIA

GETTING ORIENTED

Yosemite is so large that you can think of it as five parks. Yosemite Valley, famous for waterfalls and cliffs, and Wawona, where the giant sequoias stand, are open all year. Hetch Hetchy, home of less-used backcountry trails, is most accessible from late spring through early fall. The subalpine high country, Tuolumne Meadows, is open for summer hiking and camping; in winter it's accessible via cross-country skis or snowshoes. Badger Pass Ski Area is open in winter only. Most visitors spend their time along the park's southwestern border, between Wawona and Big Oak Flat Entrance; a bit farther east in Yosemite Valley and Badger Pass Ski Area; and along the east–west corridor of Tioga Road, which spans the park north of Yosemite Valley and bisects Tuolumne Meadows.

10

Updated by
Sharron Wood

By merely standing in Yosemite Valley and turning in a circle, you can see more natural wonders in a minute than you could in a full day pretty much anywhere else. Half Dome, Yosemite Falls, El Capitan, Bridalveil Fall, Sentinel Dome, the Merced River, white-flowering dogwood trees, maybe even bears ripping into the bark of fallen trees or sticking their snouts into beehives—it's all in Yosemite Valley.

In the mid-1800s, when tourists were arriving to the area, the valley's special geologic qualities and the giant sequoias of Mariposa Grove 30 miles to the south so impressed a group of influential Californians that they persuaded President Abraham Lincoln to grant those two areas to the state for protection. On October 1, 1890—thanks largely to lobbying efforts by naturalist John Muir and Robert Underwood Johnson, the editor of *Century Magazine*—Congress set aside 1,500 square miles for Yosemite National Park.

YOSEMITE PLANNER

WHEN TO GO

During extremely busy periods—such as July 4—you will experience delays at the entrance gates. For smaller crowds, visit midweek. Or come mid-April through Memorial Day or mid-September through October, when the park is a bit less busy and the days usually are sunny and clear.

Summer rainfall is rare. In winter, heavy snows occasionally cause road closures, and tire chains or four-wheel drive may be required on the roads that remain open. The road to Glacier Point beyond the turnoff for Badger Pass is closed after the first major snowfall; Tioga Road is closed from late October through May or mid-June. Mariposa Grove Road is typically closed for a shorter period in winter.

GETTING HERE AND AROUND
BUS TRAVEL

Once you're in Yosemite you can take advantage of the free shuttle buses, which operate on low emissions, have 21 stops, and run from 7 am to 10 pm year-round. Buses run about every 10 minutes in summer, a bit less frequently in winter. A separate (but also free) summer-only shuttle runs out to El Capitan. Also in summer, you can pay to take the morning "hikers' bus" from Yosemite Valley to Tuolumne or the bus up to Glacier Point. Bus service from Wawona is geared for people who are staying there and want to spend the day in Yosemite Valley. Free and frequent shuttles transport people between the Wawona Hotel and Mariposa Grove. During the snow season, buses run regularly between Yosemite Valley and Badger Pass Ski Area.

CAR TRAVEL

Roughly 200 miles from San Francisco, 300 miles from Los Angeles, and 500 miles from Las Vegas, Yosemite takes a while to reach—and its many sites and attractions merit much more time than what rangers say is the average visit: four hours. Most people arrive via automobile or tour bus, but public transportation (courtesy of Amtrak and the regional YARTS bus system) also can get you to the valley efficiently.

Of the park's four entrances, Arch Rock is the closest to Yosemite Valley. The road that goes through it, Route 140 from Merced and Mariposa, is a scenic western approach that snakes alongside the boulder-packed Merced River. Route 41, through Wawona, is the way to come from Los Angeles (or Fresno, if you've flown in and rented a car). Route 120, through Crane Flat, is the most direct route from San Francisco. The only way in from the east is Tioga Road, which may be the best route in terms of scenery—though due to snow accumulation it's open for a frustratingly short amount of time each year (typically early June through mid-October).

There are few gas stations within Yosemite (Crane Flat, Tuolumne Meadows, and Wawona; none in the valley), so fuel up before you reach the park. From late fall until early spring, the weather is especially unpredictable, and driving can be treacherous. You should carry chains.

PARK ESSENTIALS
PARK FEES AND PERMITS

The admission fee, valid for seven days, is $20 per vehicle or $10 per individual.

If you plan to camp in the backcountry or climb Half Dome, you must have a wilderness permit. Availability of permits depends upon trailhead quotas. It's best to make a reservation, especially if you will be visiting May through September. You can reserve two days to 24 weeks in advance by phone, mail, or fax (⊠ *Box 545, Yosemite, CA 95389* ☎ *209/372–0740* 🖷 *209/372–0739*); you'll pay $5 per person plus $5 per reservation if and when your reservations are confirmed. Requests must include your name, address, daytime phone, the number of people in your party, trip date, alternative dates, starting and ending trailheads, and a brief itinerary. Without a reservation, you may still get a free permit on a first-come, first-served basis at wilderness permit offices at Big

10

Plants and Wildlife in Yosemite

Dense stands of incense cedar and Douglas fir—as well as ponderosa, Jeffrey, lodgepole, and sugar pines—cover much of the park, but the stellar standout, quite literally, is the *Sequoiadendron giganteum*, the giant sequoia. Sequoias grow only along the west slope of the Sierra Nevada between 4,500 and 7,000 feet in elevation. Starting from a seed the size of a rolled-oat flake, each of these ancient monuments assumes remarkable proportions in adulthood; you can see them in the Mariposa Grove of Big Trees. In late May the valley's dogwood trees bloom with white, starlike flowers. Wildflowers, such as black-eyed Susan, bull thistle, cow parsnip, lupine, and meadow goldenrod, peak in June in the valley and in July at higher elevations.

The most visible animals in the park—aside from the omnipresent western gray squirrel, which fearlessly attempt to steal your food at every campground and picnic site—are the mule deer. Though sightings of bighorn sheep are infrequent in the park itself, you can sometimes see them on the eastern side of the Sierra Crest, just off Route 120 in Lee Vining Canyon. You may also see the American black bear, which often has a brown, cinnamon, or blond coat. The Sierra Nevada is home to thousands of bears, and you should take all necessary precautions to keep yourself—and the bears—safe. Bears that acquire a taste for human food can become very aggressive and destructive and often must be destroyed by rangers, so store all your food and even scented toiletries in the bear lockers located at many campgrounds and trailheads, or use bear-resistant canisters if you'll be hiking in the backcountry.

Watch for the blue Steller's jay along trails, near public buildings, and in campgrounds, and look for golden eagles soaring over Tioga Road.

Oak Flat, Hetch Hetchy, Tuolumne Meadows, Wawona, the Wilderness Center in Yosemite Village, and Yosemite Valley in summer. From fall to spring, visit the Valley Visitor Center.

PARK HOURS

The park is open 24/7 year-round. All entrances are open at all hours, except for Hetch Hetchy Entrance, which is open roughly dawn to dusk. Yosemite is in the Pacific time zone.

TOURS

Fodor's Choice ★ **Ansel Adams Photo Walks.** Photography enthusiasts shouldn't miss these 90-minute guided camera walks offered four mornings (Mon., Tues., Thurs., and Sat.) each week by professional photographers. All are free, but participation is limited to 15 people. Meeting points vary, and advance reservations are essential. ☎ 209/372–4413 ⊕ www.anseladams.com ✉ Free.

FAMILY **Wee Wild Ones.** Designed for kids under 7, this 45-minute program includes animal-theme games, songs, stories, and crafts. The event is held outdoors before the regular Yosemite Lodge or Curry Village evening programs in summer and fall; it moves to the Ahwahnee's big fireplace in winter and spring. All children must be accompanied by an adult. ☎ 209/372–1240 ⊕ www.yosemitepark.com ✉ Free.

VISITOR INFORMATION

PARK CONTACT INFORMATION

Yosemite National Park ☎ *209/372–0200* ⊕ *www.nps.gov/yose.*

VISITOR CENTERS

Le Conte Memorial Lodge. This small but striking National Historic Landmark, with its granite walls and steeply pitched shingle roof, is Yosemite's first permanent public information center. Step inside to see the cathedral-like interior, which contains a library and environmental exhibits. To find out about evening programs, check the kiosk out front. ⊠ *Southside Dr., about ½ mile west of Curry Village* ⊕ *www.nps.gov/ yose* ⊗ *May–Sept., Wed.–Sun. 10–4.*

Valley Visitor Center. Learn about Yosemite Valley's geology, vegetation, and human inhabitants at this visitor center, which is also staffed with helpful rangers and contains a bookstore with a wide selection of books and maps. Don't leave without watching *Spirit of Yosemite*, a 23-minute introductory film that runs every half hour in the theater behind the visitor center. ⊠ *Yosemite Village* ☎ *209/372–0299* ⊕ *www.nps.gov/yose* ⊗ *Late May–early Sept., daily 9–7:30; early Sept.–late May, daily 9–5.*

EXPLORING

HISTORIC SITES

Ahwahneechee Village. This solemn smattering of structures, accessed by a short loop trail behind the Yosemite Valley Visitor Center, is a look at what American Indian life might have been like in the 1870s. One interpretive sign points out that the Miwok people referred to the 19th-century newcomers as "Yohemite" or "Yohometuk," which have been translated as meaning, "some of them are killers." ⊠ *Northside Dr., Yosemite Village* ⊠ *Free* ⊗ *Daily sunrise–sunset.*

Pioneer Yosemite History Center. Some of Yosemite's first structures—those not occupied by American Indians, that is—were relocated here in the 1950s and 1960s. You can spend a pleasurable and informative half-hour walking about them and reading the signs, perhaps springing for a self-guided-tour pamphlet (50¢) to further enhance the history lesson. Weekends and some weekdays in the summer, costumed docents conduct free blacksmithing and "wet-plate" photography demonstrations, and for a small fee you can take a stagecoach ride. ⊠ *Rte. 41, Wawona* ☎ *209/375–9531, 209/379–2646* ⊠ *Free* ⊗ *Building interiors: mid-June–Labor Day, Wed. 2–5, Thurs.–Sun. 10–1 and 2–5.*

SCENIC STOPS

El Capitan. Rising 3,593 feet—more than 350 stories—above the valley, El Capitan is the largest exposed-granite monolith in the world. Since 1958, people have been climbing its entire face, including the famous "nose." You can spot adventurers with your binoculars by scanning the smooth and nearly vertical cliff for specks of color. ⊠ *Off Northside Dr., about 4 miles west of the Valley Visitor Center.*

10

Yosemite's Valley Floor

KEY

Ranger Station	
Campground	
Picnic Area	
Restaurant	
Lodge	
Trailhead	
Restrooms	
Scenic Viewpoint	
Walking/Hiking Trails	– – –
John Muir Trail	– · – ·
Bicycle Path	· · · · ·
Valley Floor	

Half Dome
8,836 ft

Liberty Cap

Mist Trail

Nevada Fall

Emerald Pools

Foolbridge

Vernal Fall

Mist Trail

Clark Point

John Muir Trail

Panorama Cliff

Grizzly Peak

Sierra Point

Illilouette Gorge

Happy Isles Bridge

John Muir Trail

Nature Center at Happy Isles

Panorama Trail

Glacier Point
7,214 ft

Glacier Point Road

Pohono Trail

Road open only to bicycles and Shuttlebuses

Upper Pines

Clarks Bridge

North Pines

Lower Pines

CURRY VILLAGE

Curry Village Store

Road open only to bicycles and Shuttlebuses

Four Mile Trail

Staircase Falls

Moran Point

Union Point

Four Mile Trail

Sentinel Fall

Sentinel Rock

Mirror Lake

Washington Column

Royal Arches

Royal Arch Cascade

bicycle path

The Ahwahnee Hotel

Medical Clinic

Village Store

Auto Repair

bicycle path

Housekeeping Camp

Le Conte Memorial Lodge

Chapel

YOSEMITE VILLAGE

Ahwahneechee Village

Yosemite Museum

Ansel Adams Gallery

Wilderness Office

P.O.

Valley Visitor Center

Yosemite Lodge

Yosemite Fall

Lower Yosemite Fall

Road open only to bicycles and Shuttlebuses

Merced River

bicycle path

1/2 mi

1/2 km

0

Fodor's Choice
★

Glacier Point. If you lack the time, desire, or stamina to hike more than 3,200 feet up to Glacier Point from the Yosemite Valley floor, you can drive here—or take a bus from the valley—for a bird's-eye view. You are likely to encounter a lot of day-trippers on the short, paved trail that leads from the parking lot to the main overlook. Take a moment to veer off a few yards to the Geology Hut, which succinctly explains and illustrates what the valley looked like 10 million, 3 million, and 20,000 years ago. ⊠ *Glacier Point Rd., 16 miles northeast of Rte. 41* ☎ *209/372–1240.*

Fodor's Choice
★

Half Dome. Visitors' eyes are continually drawn to this remarkable granite formation that tops out at more than 4,700 feet above the valley floor. Despite its name, the dome is actually about three-quarters intact. You can hike to the top of Half Dome on an 8.5-mile (one-way) trail whose last 400 feet must be ascended while holding onto a steel cable. Permits are required (and checked on the trail), and available only by lottery. Visit ⊕ *www.recreation.gov* well in advance of your trip for details. Back down in the valley, see Half Dome reflected in the Merced River by heading to Sentinel Bridge just before sundown. The brilliant orange light on Half Dome is a stunning sight.

Hetch Hetchy Reservoir. When Congress approved the O'Shaughnessy Dam in 1913, pragmatism triumphed over aestheticism. Some 2.5 million residents of the San Francisco Bay Area continue to get their water from this 117-billion-gallon reservoir. Although spirited efforts are being made to restore the Hetch Hetchy Valley to its former, pristine glory, three-quarters of San Francisco voters in 2012 ultimately opposed a measure to even consider draining the reservoir. Eight miles long, the reservoir is Yosemite's largest body of water, and one that can be seen up close from several trails. ⊠ *Hetch Hetchy Rd., about 15 miles north of the Big Oak Flat entrance station.*

Fodor's Choice
★

Mariposa Grove of Big Trees. Of Yosemite's three sequoia groves—the others being Merced and Tuolumne, both near Crane Flat well to the north—Mariposa is by far the largest and easiest to walk around. Grizzly Giant, whose base measures 96 feet around, has been estimated to be one of the largest in the world. Perhaps more astoundingly, it's about 2,700 years old. Up the hill, you'll find many more sequoias, a small museum, and fewer people. Summer weekends are especially crowded here. Consider taking the free shuttle from Wawona. ⊠ *Rte. 41, 2 miles north of the South Entrance station.*

10

Tuolumne Meadows. The largest subalpine meadow in the Sierra (at 8,600 feet) is a popular way station for backpack trips along the Pacific Crest and John Muir trails. The setting is not as dramatic as Yosemite Valley, 56 miles away, but the almost perfectly flat basin, about 2½ miles long, is intriguing, and in July it's resplendent with wildflowers. The most popular day hike is up Lembert Dome, atop which you'll have breathtaking views of the basin below. Keep in mind that Tioga Road rarely opens before June and usually closes by mid-October. ⊠ *Tioga Rd. (Rte. 120), about 8 miles west of the Tioga Pass entrance station.*

"This is us taking a break before conquering the top of Lembert Dome, while enjoying the beautiful view over Yosemite's high country." —photo by Rebalyn, Fodors.com member

WATERFALLS

Yosemite's waterfalls are at their most spectacular in May and June. When the snow starts to melt (usually peaking in May), streaming snow-melt spills down to meet the Merced River. By summer's end, some falls, including the mighty Yosemite Falls, trickle or dry up. Their flow increases in late fall, and in winter they may be hung dramatically with ice. Even in drier months, the waterfalls can be breathtaking. If you choose to hike any of the trails to or up the falls, be sure to wear shoes with no-slip soles; the rocks can be extremely slick. Stay on trails at all times.

■TIP→ Visit the park during a full moon and you can stroll without a flashlight and still make out the ribbons of falling water, as well as silhouettes of the giant granite monoliths.

Bridalveil Fall. This 620-foot waterfall is often diverted dozens of feet one way or the other by the breeze. It is the first marvelous site you will see up close when you drive into Yosemite Valley. ⊠ *Yosemite Valley, access from parking area off Wawona Rd.*

Nevada Fall. Climb Mist Trail from Happy Isles for an up close view of this 594-foot cascading beauty. If you don't want to hike (the trail's final approach is quite taxing), you can see it—albeit distantly—from Glacier Point. ⚠ Stay safely on the trail, as people sometimes die when they climb over the railing and onto the slippery rocks. ⊠ *Yosemite Valley, access via Mist Trail from Nature Center at Happy Isles.*

Ribbon Fall. At 1,612 feet, this is the highest single fall in North America. It's also the first waterfall to dry up in summer; the rainwater and melted snow that create the slender fall evaporate quickly at this height. Look just west of El Capitan for the best view of the fall from the base of Bridalveil Fall. ⊠ *Yosemite Valley, west of El Capitan Meadow.*

Vernal Fall. Fern-covered black rocks frame this 317-foot fall, and rainbows play in the spray at its base. You can get a distant view from Glacier Point, or hike to see it close up. You'll get wet, but the view is worth it. ⊠ *Yosemite Valley, access via Mist Trail from Nature Center at Happy Isles.*

Fodor's Choice ★ **Yosemite Falls.** Actually three falls, they together constitute the highest waterfall in North America and the fifth highest in the world. The water from the top descends a total of 2,425 feet, and when the falls run hard, you can hear them thunder across the valley. If they dry up—that sometimes happens in late summer—the valley seems naked without the wavering tower of spray. ■TIP➔ **If you hike the mile-long loop trail (partially paved) to the base of the Lower Falls in May, prepare to get wet.** You can get a good full-length view of the falls from the lawn of Yosemite Chapel, off Southside Drive. ⊠ *Yosemite Valley, access from Yosemite Lodge or trail parking area.*

EDUCATIONAL OFFERINGS

CLASSES AND SEMINARS

Art Classes. Professional artists conduct workshops in watercolor, etching, drawing, and other mediums. Bring your own materials or purchase the basics at the Art Activity Center, next to the Village Store. Children under 13 must be accompanied by an adult. ⊠ *Art Activity Center, Yosemite Village* ☏ *209/372–1442* ⊕ *www.yosemitepark.com* 🖾 *Free* ⊙ *Early Apr.–early Oct., Mon.–Sat. 10–2.*

Yosemite Outdoor Adventures. Naturalists, scientists, and park rangers lead multihour to multiday educational outings on topics from woodpeckers to fire management to pastel painting. Most sessions take place spring through fall, but a few focus on winter phenomena. ⊠ *Various locations* ☏ *209/379–2321* ⊕ *www.yosemitepark.com* 🖾 *$82–$465.*

RANGER PROGRAMS

Junior Ranger Program. Children ages 7 to 13 can participate in the informal, self-guided Junior Ranger program. A park activity handbook ($4) is available at the Valley Visitor Center or the Nature Center at Happy Isles. Once kids complete the book, rangers present them with a certificate and a badge. ⊠ *Yosemite Valley Visitor Center or the Nature Center at Happy Isles* ☏ *209/372–0299.*

Ranger-Led Programs. Rangers lead entertaining walks and give informative talks several times a day from spring to fall. The schedule is more limited in winter, but most days you can find a program somewhere in the park. In the evenings at Yosemite Lodge and Curry Village, lectures, slide shows, and documentary films present unique perspectives on Yosemite. On summer weekends, Camp Curry and Tuolumne Meadows Campground host sing-along campfire programs. Schedules and locations are posted on bulletin boards throughout the park as well as in the indispensable *Yosemite Guide,* which is distributed to visitors as they arrive at the park. ⊕ *www.yosemitepark.com.*

10

SPORTS AND THE OUTDOORS

BIKING

One enjoyable way to see Yosemite Valley is to ride a bike beneath its lofty granite monoliths. The eastern valley has 12 miles of paved, flat bicycle paths across meadows and through woods, with bike racks at convenient stopping points. For a greater challenge but at no small risk, you can ride on 196 miles of paved park roads—but bicycles are not allowed on hiking trails or in the backcountry. Kids under 18 must wear a helmet.

TOURS AND OUTFITTERS

Yosemite bike rentals. You can arrange for rentals from Yosemite Lodge and Curry Village bike stands. Bikes with child trailers, baby-jogger strollers, and wheelchairs are also available. The cost for bikes is $11.50 per hour, or $31.50 per day. ⊠ *Yosemite Lodge or Curry Village* ☎ *209/372–1208* ⊕ *www.yosemitepark.com* ☉ *Apr.–Oct.*

BIRD-WATCHING

More than 250 bird species have been spotted in the park, including the sage sparrow, pygmy owl, blue grouse, and mountain bluebird. Park rangers lead free bird-watching walks in Yosemite Valley a few days each week in summer; check at a visitor center or information station for times and locations. Binoculars sometimes are available for loan.

HIKING

TOURS AND OUTFITTERS

Wilderness Center. This facility provides free wilderness permits, which are required for overnight camping (advance reservations are available for $5 per person plus $5 per reservation and are highly recommended for popular trailheads in summer and on weekends). The staff here also provide maps and advice to hikers heading into the backcountry, as well as rent bear-resistant canisters, which are required if you don't have your own. ☎ *209/372–0308.*

Yosemite Mountaineering School and Guide Service. From April to November, Yosemite Mountaineering School and Guide Service leads two-hour to full-day treks, as well as backpacking and overnight excursions. Reservations are recommended. ⊠ *Yosemite Mountain Shop, Curry Village* ☎ *209/372–8344.*

EASY

Yosemite Falls Trail. This is the highest waterfall in North America. The upper fall (1,430 feet), the middle cascades (675 feet), and the lower fall (320 feet) combine for a total of 2,425 feet and, when viewed from the valley, appear as a single waterfall. The 0.25-mile trail leads from the parking lot to the base of the falls. Upper Yosemite Fall Trail, a strenuous 3½-mile climb rising 2,700 feet, takes you above the top of the falls. Lower trail: *Easy.* Upper trail: *Difficult.* ⊠ *Trailhead off Camp 4, north of Northside Dr.*

GOOD READS

■ *The Photographer's Guide to Yosemite*, by Michael Frye, is an insider's guide to the park, with maps for shutterbugs looking to capture perfect images.

■ John Muir penned his observations of the park he long advocated for in *The Yosemite*.

■ *Yosemite and the High Sierra*, edited by Andrea G. Stillman and John Szarkowski, features beautiful reproductions of landmark photographs by Ansel Adams,

accompanied by excerpts from the photographer's journals written when Adams traveled in Yosemite National Park in the early 20th century.

■ An insightful collection of essays accompanies the museum-quality artworks in *Yosemite: Art of an American Icon*, by Amy Scott.

■ Perfect for budding botanists, *Sierra Nevada Wildflowers*, by Karen Wiese, identifies more than 230 kinds of flora growing in the Sierra Nevada region.

MODERATE

Mist Trail. Except for Lower Yosemite Falls, more visitors take this trail (or portions of it) than any other in the park. The trek up to and back from Vernal Fall is 3 miles. Add another 4 miles total by continuing up to 594-foot Nevada Fall; the trail becomes quite steep and slippery in its final stages. The elevation gain to Vernal Fall is 1,000 feet, and to Nevada Fall an additional 1,000 feet. Merced River tumbles down both falls on its way to a tranquil flow through the Valley. *Moderate.* ⊠ *Trailhead at Happy Isles.*

Fodor's Choice ★ **Panorama Trail.** Few hikes come with the visual punch that this 8.5-mile trail provides. The star attraction is Half Dome, visible from many intriguing angles, but you also see three waterfalls up close and walk through a manzanita grove. Before you begin, look down on Yosemite Valley from Glacier Point, a special experience in itself. △ If you start after taking the last bus from the valley floor to Glacier Point, you might run out of daylight before you finish. *Moderate.* ⊠ *Trailhead at Glacier Point.*

DIFFICULT

Fodor's Choice ★ **John Muir Trail to Half Dome.** Ardent and courageous trekkers continue on from Nevada Fall to the top of Half Dome. Some hikers attempt this entire 10- to 12-hour, 16.75-mile round-trip trek in one day; if you're planning to do this, remember that the 4,800-foot elevation gain and the 8,842-foot altitude will cause shortness of breath. Another option is to hike to a campground in Little Yosemite Valley near the top of Nevada Fall the first day, then climb to the top of Half Dome and hike out the next day. Get your wilderness permit (required for a one-day hike to Half Dome, too) at least a month in advance. Be sure to wear hiking boots and bring gloves. The last pitch up the back of Half Dome is very steep—the only way to climb this sheer rock face is to pull yourself up using the steel cable handrails, which are in place only from late spring to early fall. Those who brave the ascent will be rewarded with an unbeatable view of Yosemite Valley below and the high country beyond. △ Only 300 hikers per day are allowed atop Half Dome, and they all must have permits,

10

which are distributed by lottery, one in the spring before the season starts and another two days before the climb. Contact ⊕ www.recreation.gov for details. *Difficult.* ✉ *Trailhead at Happy Isles.*

HORSEBACK RIDING

Reservations for guided trail rides must be made in advance at the hotel tour desks or by phone. Scenic trail rides range from two hours to a half day; four- and six-day High Sierra saddle trips are also available.

TOURS AND OUTFITTERS

Tuolumne Meadows Stables. Tuolumne Meadows Stables runs two- and four-hour trips that start at $64, as well as four- to six-day camping treks on mules that start at $1,018. Reservations are mandatory. ✉ *Off Tioga Rd., 2 miles east of Tuolumne Meadows Visitor Center* ☎ *209/372–8427* ⊕ *www.yosemitepark.com.*

Wawona Stables. Two- and five-hour rides start at $64. Reservations are recommended. ✉ *Rte. 41, Wawona* ☎ *209/375–6502.*

Yosemite Valley Stables. You can tour the valley on two-hour and four-hour rides starting from the Yosemite Valley Stables. Reservations are strongly recommended for the trips, which start at $64. ✉ *At entrance to North Pines Campground, 100 yards northeast of Curry Village* ☎ *209/372–8348* ⊕ *www.yosemitepark.com.*

RAFTING

Rafting is permitted only on designated areas of the Middle and South Forks of the Merced River. Check with the Valley Visitor Center for closures and other restrictions.

OUTFITTERS

Curry Village raft stand. The per-person rental fee ($30) at Curry Village raft stand covers the four- to six-person raft, two paddles, and life jackets, plus a return shuttle at the end of your trip. ✉ *South side of Southside Dr., Curry Village* ☎ *209/372–4386* ⊕ *www.yosemitepark. com* 🎟 *$30* ⊘ *Late May–July.*

ROCK CLIMBING

Fodor'sChoice
★
The granite canyon walls of Yosemite Valley are world-renowned for rock climbing. El Capitan, with its 3,593-foot vertical face, is the most famous, but there are many other options here for all skill levels.

TOURS AND OUTFITTERS

Yosemite Mountaineering School and Guide Service. The one-day basic lesson at Yosemite Mountaineering School and Guide Service includes some bouldering and rappelling, and three or four 60-foot climbs. Climbers must be at least 10 years old and in reasonably good physical condition. Intermediate and advanced classes include instruction in first aid, anchor building, multipitch climbing, summer snow climbing, and big-wall climbing. There's a Nordic program in the winter. ✉ *Yosemite Mountain Shop, Curry Village* ☎ *209/372–8344* ⊕ *www.yosemitepark. com* 🎟 *Starting at $148* ⊘ *Apr.–Nov.*

Waterfalls in Yosemite Valley are especially famous for their heart-stopping drops over sheer granite cliffs. At peak times, hydrologists estimate that almost 135,000 gallons of water tumble down Yosemite Falls' triple cascade every minute.

WINTER SPORTS

ICE-SKATING

Curry Village Ice Rink. Winter visitors have skated at this outdoor rink for decades, and there's no mystery why: it's a kick to glide across the ice while soaking up views of Half Dome and Glacier Point. ⊠ *South side of Southside Dr., Curry Village* ☎ *209/372–8319* 🎫 *$9.75 per session, $4 skate rental* ☾ *Mid-Nov.–mid-Mar. afternoons and evenings daily, morning sessions weekends (hrs vary).*

SKIING AND SNOWSHOEING

Badger Pass Ski Area. California's first ski resort has five lifts and 10 downhill runs, as well as 90 miles of groomed cross-country trails. Free shuttle buses from Yosemite Valley operate between December and the end of March, weather permitting. Lift tickets are $47, downhill equipment rents for $36, and snowboard rental with boots is $37.50. ⊠ *Badger Pass Rd., off Glacier Point Rd., 18 miles from Yosemite Valley* ☎ *209/372–8430.*

Yosemite Ski School. The gentle slopes of Badger Pass make Yosemite Ski School an ideal spot for children and beginners to learn downhill skiing or snowboarding for as little as $45.50 for a group lesson. ☎ *209/372–8430* ⊕ *www.yosemitepark.com.*

Yosemite Cross-Country Ski School. The highlight of Yosemite's cross-country skiing center is a 21-mile loop from Badger Pass to Glacier Point. You can rent cross-country skis for $25 per day at the Cross-Country Ski School, which also rents snowshoes ($24 per day) and telemarking equipment ($29.50). ☎ *209/372–8444* ⊕ *www.yosemitepark.com.*

Yosemite Mountaineering School. This branch of the Yosemite Mountaineering School, open at the Badger Pass Ski Area during ski season only, conducts snowshoeing, cross-country skiing, telemarking, and skate-skiing classes starting at $35.50. ⊠ *Badger Pass Ski Area* ☎ *209/372–8344* ⊕ *www.yosemitepark.com.*

WHERE TO EAT

In addition to the dining options listed here, you'll find fast-food grills and cafeterias, plus temporary snack bars, hamburger stands, and pizza joints lining park roads in summer. Many dining facilities in the park are open summer only.

WHAT IT COSTS				
	$	$$	$$$	$$$$
Restaurants	under 12	$13–$20	$21–$30	over $30
Hotels	under $100	$101–$150	$151–$200	over $200

Restaurant prices are the average cost of a main course at dinner or, if dinner is not served, at lunch. Hotel prices are the lowest cost of a standard double room in high season, excluding taxes and service charges.

$$$$
EUROPEAN
Fodor'sChoice
★

✕**Ahwahnee Hotel Dining Room.** Rave reviews about the dining room's appearance are fully justified—it features towering windows, a 34-foot-high ceiling with interlaced sugar-pine beams, and massive chandeliers. Although many continue to applaud the food, others have reported that they sense a dip in the quality of both the service and what is being served. Diners must spend a lot of money here, so perhaps that inflates the expectations and amplifies the disappointments. In any event, the lavish $43 Sunday brunch is a popular way to experience the grand room. Reservations are always advised, and the attire is "resort casual." ⑤ *Average main: $35* ✉ *Ahwahnee Hotel, Ahwahnee Rd., about ¾ mile east of Yosemite Valley Visitor Center, Yosemite Village* ☎ *209/372–1489* ⊕ *www.yosemitepark.com* ⚱ *Reservations essential.*

$$$
AMERICAN
Fodor'sChoice
★

✕**Mountain Room.** Though good, the food becomes secondary when you see Yosemite Falls through this dining room's wall of windows—almost every table has a view. The chef makes a point of using locally sourced, organic ingredients whenever possible, so you can be assured of fresh vegetables to accompany the hearty main courses, such as steaks and seafood, as well as vegetarian and even vegan options. The Mountain Room Lounge, a few steps away in the Yosemite Lodge complex, has about 10 beers on tap. Weather permitting, take your drink out onto the small back patio. ⑤ *Average main: $23* ✉ *Yosemite Lodge, Northside Dr. about ¾ mile west of the visitor center, Yosemite Village* ☎ *209/372–1281* ⊕ *www.yosemitepark.com* ☾ *No lunch.*

$
FAST FOOD

✕**Tuolumne Meadows Grill.** Serving continuously throughout the day until 5 or 6, this fast-food eatery cooks up basic breakfast, lunch, and snacks. It's possible that ice cream tastes better at this altitude. Stop in for a quick meal before exploring the meadows. ⑤ *Average main: $8* ✉ *Tioga Rd. (Rte. 120), 1½ miles east of Tuolumne Meadows Visitor Center* ☎ *209/372–8426* ☾ *Closed Oct.–Memorial Day.*

$$
AMERICAN

✕**Tuolumne Meadows Lodge.** At the back of a small building that contains the lodge's front desk and small gift shop, this restaurant serves a menu of hearty American fare at breakfast and dinner. The decor is ultrawoodsy, with dark-wood walls, red-and-white-checkered tablecloths, and a handful of communal tables, which give it the feeling of an old-fashioned summer camp. The menu is small, often featuring a few meat and seafood dishes and one pasta or other special, including a vegetarian choice. If you have any dietary restrictions, let the front desk know in advance and the cooks will not let you down. Order box lunches from here for before hikes. ⑤ *Average main: $20* ✉ *Tioga Rd. (Rte. 120)* ☎ *209/372–8413* ⊕ *www.yosemitepark.com* ⚱ *Reservations essential* ☾ *Closed late Sept.–mid-June. No lunch.*

$$$
AMERICAN

✕**Wawona Hotel Dining Room.** Watch deer graze on the meadow while you dine in the romantic, candlelit dining room of the whitewashed Wawona Hotel, which dates from the late 1800s. The American-style cuisine favors fresh ingredients and flavors; trout and flatiron steaks are menu staples. There's also a brunch on some Sunday holidays, like Mother's Day and Easter, and a barbecue on the lawn Saturday evenings in summer. ⑤ *Average main: $27* ✉ *Wawona Hotel, Rte. 41, Wawona* ☎ *209/559–4935* ⚱ *Reservations essential* ☾ *Closed Dec.–Mar.*

10

PICNIC AREAS

Considering how large the park is and how many visitors come here—some 4 million people every year, most of them just for the day—it is somewhat surprising that Yosemite has so few formal picnic areas, though in many places you can find a smooth rock to sit on and enjoy breathtaking views along with your lunch. The convenience stores all sell picnic supplies, and prepackaged sandwiches and salads are widely available. Those options can come in especially handy during the middle of the day, when you might not want to spend precious daylight hours in such a spectacular setting sitting in a restaurant for a formal meal.

> **LODGING TIP**
>
> Reserve your room or cabin in Yosemite as far in advance as possible. You can make a reservation up to a year before your arrival (within minutes after the reservation office makes a date available, the Ahwahnee, Yosemite Lodge, and Wawona Hotel often sell out their weekends, holiday periods, and all days between May and September).

WHERE TO STAY

Hotel reviews have been shortened. For full information, visit Fodors. com.

$$$$
HOTEL
Fodor's Choice
★

Ahwahnee Hotel. A National Historic Landmark, the hotel is constructed of sugar-pine logs and features American Indian design motifs; public spaces are enlivened with art deco flourishes, oriental rugs, and elaborate iron- and woodwork. **Pros:** best lodge in Yosemite; helpful concierge. **Cons:** expensive rates; some reports that service has slipped in recent years. $ *Rooms from: $471* ⊠ *Ahwahnee Rd., about ¾ miles east of Yosemite Valley Visitor Center, Yosemite Village* ☎ *801/559–4884* ⊕ *www.yosemitepark.com* ↝ *99 lodge rooms, 4 suites, 24 cottage rooms* ⦿ *No meals.*

$$
HOTEL

Curry Village. Opened in 1899 as a place for budget-conscious travelers, Curry Village has plain accommodations: standard motel rooms, simple cabins with either private or shared baths, and tent cabins with shared baths. **Pros:** close to many activities; family-friendly atmosphere. **Cons:** not that economical after a recent price surge; can be crowded; sometimes a bit noisy. $ *Rooms from: $124* ⊠ *South side of Southside Dr.* ☎ *801/559–4884* ⊕ *www.yosemitepark.com* ↝ *18 rooms, 389 cabins* ⦿ *No meals.*

$$
HOTEL

Wawona Hotel. This 1879 National Historic Landmark at Yosemite's southern end is an old-fashioned New England–style estate, with whitewashed buildings, wraparound verandahs, and pleasant, no-frills rooms decorated with period pieces. **Pros:** lovely building; peaceful atmosphere. **Cons:** few modern amenities, such as phones and TVs; an hour's drive from Yosemite Valley. $ *Rooms from: $159* ⊠ *Rte. 41, Wawona* ☎ *801/559–4884* ⊕ *www.yosemitepark.com* ↝ *104 rooms, 50 with bath* ⊙ *Closed Dec.–Mar., except Dec. 20–Jan. 2* ⦿ *No meals.*

CLOSE UP

Best Campgrounds in Yosemite

If you are going to concentrate solely on valley sites and activities, you should endeavor to stay in one of the "Pines" campgrounds, which are clustered near Curry Village and within an easy stroll from that busy complex's many facilities. For a more primitive and quiet experience, and to be near many backcountry hikes, try one of the Tioga Road campgrounds.

National Park Service Reservations Office. Reservations are required at many of Yosemite's campgrounds, especially in summer; you can book a site up to five months in advance, starting on the 15th of the month. Unless otherwise noted, book your site through the central National Park Service Reservations Office. If you don't have reservations when you arrive, many sites, especially those outside Yosemite Valley, are available on a first-come, first-served basis. ☎ 877/436–7275 ⊕ www.recreation. gov ☉ Daily 7–7.

Bridalveil Creek. This campground sits among lodgepole pines at 7,200 feet, above the valley on Glacier Point Road. From here, you can easily drive to Glacier Point's magnificent valley views. ⊠ From Rte. 41 in Wawona, go north to Glacier Point Rd. and turn right; entrance to campground is 25 miles ahead on right side.

Camp 4. Formerly known as Sunny-side Walk-In, and extremely popular with rock climbers, who don't mind that a total of six are assigned to each campsite, no matter how many are in your group, this is the only valley campground available on a first-come, first-served basis. ⊠ Base of Yosemite Falls Trail, just west of Yosemite Lodge on Northside Dr., Yosemite Village.

Housekeeping Camp. Composed of three concrete walls and covered with two layers of canvas, each unit has an open-ended fourth side that can be closed off with a heavy white canvas curtain. You can rent "bedpacks," consisting of blankets, sheets, and other comforts. ⊠ South-side Dr., ½ mile west of Curry Village.

Porcupine Flat. Sixteen miles west of Tuolumne Meadows, this campground sits at 8,100 feet. If you want to be in the high country, this is a good bet. ⊠ Rte. 120, 16 miles west of Tuolumne Meadows.

Tuolumne Meadows. In a wooded area at 8,600 feet, just south of its namesake meadow, this is one of the most spectacular and sought-after campgrounds in Yosemite. ⊠ Rte. 120, 46 miles east of Big Oak Flat entrance station.

Upper Pines. This is one of the valley's largest campgrounds and the closest one to the trailheads. Expect large crowds in the summer—and little privacy. ⊠ At east end of valley, near Curry Village.

Wawona. Near the Mariposa Grove, just downstream from a popular fishing spot, this year-round campground has larger, less densely packed sites than campgrounds in the valley. ⊠ Rte. 41, 1 mile north of Wawona.

White Wolf. Set in the beautiful high country at 8,000 feet, this is a prime spot for hikers from early July to mid-September. ⊠ Tioga Rd., 15 miles east of Big Oak Flat entrance.

10

$$
HOTEL
⊞ **White Wolf Lodge.** Set in a subalpine meadow, the rustic accommodations at White Wolf Lodge make it an excellent base camp for hiking the backcountry. **Pros:** quiet location; near some of Yosemite's most beautiful, less crowded hikes; good restaurant. **Cons:** far from the valley. $ *Rooms from: $124* ✉ *Off Tioga Rd. (Rte. 120), 25 miles west of Tuolumne Meadows and 15 miles east of Crane Flat* ☎ *801/559–4884* ⌁ *24 tent cabins, 4 cabins* ☉ *Closed mid-Sept.–mid-June* ⎟◯⎟ *No meals.*

$$$
HOTEL
⊞ **Yosemite Lodge at the Falls.** This 1915 lodge near Yosemite Falls more closely resembles a 1960s resort with its numerous two-story structures tucked beneath the trees, and it doesn't help that the brown buildings are surrounded by large parking lots. **Pros:** centrally located; dependably clean rooms; lots of tours leave from out front. **Cons:** can feel impersonal; appearance is a little dated; prices recently skyrocketed. $ *Rooms from: $199* ✉ *Northside Dr., about ¾ mile west of the visitor center, Yosemite Village* ☎ *801/559–4884* ⊕ *www.yosemitepark.com* ⌁ *245 rooms* ⎟◯⎟ *No meals.*

SEQUOIA AND KINGS CANYON NATIONAL PARKS

WELCOME TO SEQUOIA AND KINGS CANYON NATIONAL PARKS

TOP REASONS TO GO

★ **Gentle giants:** You'll feel small—in a good way—walking among some of the world's largest living things in Sequoia's Giant Forest and Kings Canyon's Grant Grove.

★ **Because it's there:** You can't even glimpse it from the main part of Sequoia, but the sight of majestic Mt. Whitney is worth the trek to the eastern face of the High Sierra.

★ **Underground exploration:** Far older even than the giant sequoias, the gleaming limestone formations in Crystal Cave will draw you along dark, marble passages.

★ **A grander-than-Grand Canyon:** Drive the twisting Kings Canyon Scenic Byway down into the jagged, granite Kings River Canyon, deeper in parts than the Grand Canyon.

★ **Regal solitude:** To spend a day or two hiking in a subalpine world of your own, pick one of the 11 trailheads at Mineral King.

1 **Giant Forest–Lodgepole Village.** The most heavily visited area of Sequoia lies at the base of the "thumb" portion of Kings Canyon National Park and contains major sights such as Giant Forest, General Sherman Tree, Crystal Cave, and Moro Rock.

2 **Grant Grove Village–Redwood Canyon.** The "thumb" of Kings Canyon National Park is its busiest section, where Grant Grove, General Grant Tree, Panoramic Point, and Big Stump are the main attractions.

3 **Cedar Grove.** The drive through the high-country portion of Kings Canyon National Park to Cedar Grove Village, on the canyon floor, reveals magnificent granite formations of varied hues. Rock meets river in breathtaking fashion a few miles beyond Cedar Grove in Zumwalt Meadow.

4 **Mineral King.** In the southeast section of Sequoia, the highest road-accessible part of the park is a good place to hike, camp, and soak up the unspoiled grandeur of the Sierra Nevada.

5 **Mount Whitney.** The highest peak in the Lower 48 stands on the eastern edge of Sequoia; to get there from Giant Forest you must either backpack eight days through the mountains or drive nearly 400 miles around the park to its other side.

CALIFORNIA

GETTING ORIENTED

The two parks comprise 865,964 acres (1,353 square miles), mostly on the western flank of the Sierra. A map of the adjacent parks looks vaguely like a mitten, with the palm of Sequoia National Park south of the north-pointing, skinny thumb and long fingers of Kings Canyon National Park. Between the western thumb and eastern fingers, north of Sequoia, lies part of Sequoia National Forest, which includes Giant Sequoia National Monument.

0 — 5 mi
0 — 5 km

McClure Meadow

LE CONTE DIVIDE

Le Conte Canyon

John Muir Trail

Bench Lake

MONARCH DIVIDE

Woods Creek Trail

Kings Canyon Scenic Byway

3

KINGS CANYON

Cedar Grove

Visitor Center

Roads End Permit Station

Rae Lakes

Charlotte Lake

Roaring River

KINGS-KERN DIVIDE

Table Mountain 13,630 ft

Tyndall Creek

Whitney Portal

tony Creek village

Wuksachi Village

Lodgepole Village

Visitor Center

stal ve

General Sherman Tree

Bearpaw Meadow

Crabtree

John Muir Trail

5

Mount Whitney 14,491 ft

t Forest seum

Moro Rock

eye Flat sho

Visitor Center

Mount Kaweah 13,802 ft

Mount Guyot 12,300 ft

Rock Creek

Mountain rance

Lookout Point Entrance

Little Five Lakes

4

Mineral King

Cold Springs

KERN CANYON

Hockett Meadows

h Fork

Sheep Mountain 10,050 ft

Kern Canyon

Updated by
Daniel Mangin

Although *Sequoiadendron giganteum* is the formal name for the redwoods that grow here, everyone outside the classroom calls them sequoias, big trees, or Sierra redwoods. Their monstrously thick trunks and branches, remarkably shallow root systems, and neck-craning heights are almost impossible to believe, as is the fact they can live for more than 2,500 years. Many of these towering marvels are in the Giant Forest stretch of Generals Highway, which connects Sequoia and Kings Canyon national parks.

Next to or a few miles off the 43-mile Generals Highway are most of Sequoia National Park's main attractions and Grant Grove Village, the orientation hub for Kings Canyon National Park. The two parks share a boundary that runs from the Central Valley in the west, where the Sierra Nevada foothills begin, to the range's dramatic eastern ridges. Kings Canyon has two portions: the smaller is shaped like a bent finger and encompasses Grant Grove Village and Redwood Mountain Grove (the two parks' largest concentration of sequoias), and the larger is home to stunning Kings River Canyon, whose vast, unspoiled peaks and valleys are a backpacker's dream. Sequoia is in one piece and includes Mt. Whitney, the highest point in the Lower 48 states (although it is impossible to see from the western part of the park and is a chore to ascend from either side).

SEQUOIA AND KINGS CANYON PLANNER

WHEN TO GO

The best times to visit are late spring and early fall, when temperatures are moderate and crowds thin. Summertime can draw hordes of tourists to see the giant sequoias, and the few, narrow roads mean congestion at peak holiday times. If you must visit in summer, go during the week. By contrast, in wintertime you may feel as though you have the parks all to yourself. But because of heavy snows, sections of the main park roads can be closed without warning, and low-hanging clouds can move in and obscure mountains and valleys for days. From mid-November to late April, check road and weather conditions before venturing out.

GETTING HERE AND AROUND

CAR TRAVEL

Sequoia is 36 miles east of Visalia on Route 198; Grant Grove Village in Kings Canyon is 56 miles east of Fresno on Route 180. There is no automobile entrance on the eastern side of the Sierra. Routes 180 and 198 are connected by Generals Highway, a paved two-lane road that sometimes sees delays at peak times due to ongoing improvements. The road is extremely narrow and steep from Route 198 to Giant Forest, so keep an eye on your engine temperature gauge, as the incline and congestion can cause vehicles to overheat; to avoid overheated brakes, use low gears on downgrades.

If you are traveling in an RV or with a trailer, study the restrictions on these vehicles. Do not travel beyond Potwisha Campground on Route 198 with an RV longer than 22 feet; take straighter, easier Route 180 instead. Maximum vehicle length on Generals Highway is 40 feet, or 50 feet combined length for vehicles with trailers.

Generals Highway between Lodgepole and Grant Grove is sometimes closed by snow. The Mineral King Road from Route 198 into southern Sequoia National Park is closed 2 miles below Atwell Mill either on November 1 or after the first heavy snow. The Buckeye Flat–Middle Fork Trailhead Road is closed from mid-October to mid-April when the Buckeye Flat Campground closes. The lower Crystal Cave Road is closed when the cave closes in November. Its upper 2 miles, as well as the Panoramic Point and Moro Rock–Crescent Meadow roads, close with the first heavy snow. Because of the danger of rockfall, the portion of Kings Canyon Scenic Byway east of Grant Grove closes in winter. For current road and weather conditions, call ☏ 559/565–3341.

■TIP➜ Snowstorms are common from late October through April. Unless you have a four-wheel-drive vehicle with snow tires, you should carry chains and know how to install them.

PARK ESSENTIALS

PARK FEES AND PERMITS

The admission fee is $20 per vehicle and $10 for those who enter by bus, on foot, bicycle, motorcycle, or horse; it is valid for seven days in both parks. U.S. residents over the age of 62 pay $10 for a lifetime pass, and permanently disabled U.S. residents are admitted free.

If you plan to camp in the backcountry, you need a permit, which costs $15 for hikers or $30 for stock users (e.g., horseback riders). One permit covers the group. Availability of permits depends upon trailhead quotas. Reservations are accepted by mail or fax for a $15 processing fee, beginning March 1, and must be made at least 14 days in advance (☏ 559/565–3766). Without a reservation, you may still get a permit on a first-come, first-served basis starting at 1 pm the day before you plan to hike. For more information on backcountry camping or travel with pack animals (horses, mules, burros, or llamas), contact the Wilderness Permit Office (☏ 530/565–3761).

PARK HOURS

The parks are open 24/7 year-round. They are in the Pacific time zone.

VISITOR INFORMATION

NATIONAL PARK SERVICE

Sequoia and Kings Canyon National Parks ✉ *47050 Generals Hwy. (Rte. 198), Three Rivers* ☎ *559/565–3341* ⊕ *www.nps.gov/seki/planyourvisit/things2know.htm.*

SEQUOIA VISITOR CENTERS

Foothills Visitor Center. Exhibits here focus on the foothills and resource issues facing the parks. You can pick up books, maps, and a list of ranger-led walks, and get wilderness permits. ✉ *47050 Generals Hwy. (Rte. 198), 1 mile north of Ash Mountain entrance* ☎ *559/565–4212* ☾ *Daily 8–4:30.*

Lodgepole Visitor Center. Along with exhibits on the area's history, geology, and wildlife, the center screens an outstanding 22-minute film about bears. You can buy books, maps, and tickets to cave tours and the Wolverton barbecue here. ✉ *Generals Hwy. (Rte. 198), 21 miles north of Ash Mountain entrance* ☎ *559/565–4436* ☾ *Late May–early Sept., daily 7–7; days and hrs vary Apr.–late May and early Sept.–Dec. Closed Jan.–Mar.* ☞ *Shuttle: Giant Forest or Wuksachi-Lodgepole-Dorst.*

KINGS CANYON VISITOR CENTERS

Cedar Grove Visitor Center. Off the main road and behind the Sentinel Campground, this small ranger station has books and maps, plus information about hikes and other activities. ✉ *Kings Canyon Scenic Byway, 30 miles east of Rte. 180/198 junction* ☎ *559/565–3793* ☾ *Late May–early Sept., Tues.–Sun. 9–5.*

Kings Canyon Park Visitor Center. The center's 15-minute film and various exhibits provide an overview of the park's canyon, sequoias, and human history. Books, maps, and weather advice are dispensed here, as are (if available) free wilderness permits. ✉ *Grant Grove Village, Generals Hwy. (Rte. 198), 3 miles northeast of Rte. 180, Big Stump entrance* ☎ *559/565–4307* ☾ *Mid-May–early Sept., daily 8–5; hrs vary rest of year.*

WHAT IT COSTS			
$	**$$**	**$$$**	**$$$$**
Restaurants	under 12	$13–$20	$21–$30	over $30
Hotels	under $100	$101–$150	$151–$200	over $200

Restaurant prices are the average cost of a main course at dinner or, if dinner is not served, at lunch. Hotel prices are the lowest cost of a standard double room in high season, excluding taxes and service charges.

Western Sequoia and Kings Canyon National Park

Yucca Point

180

Boyden Cavern

Kings Canyon Scenic Byway

Grizzly Falls

South Fork Kings River

Lewis Creek Trail

Sheep Creek

Cedar Grove Visitor Center

CONVERSE BASIN GROVE

Hume Lake

KINGS CANYON NATIONAL PARK

General Grant Tree

zalea

Sunset

Crystal Springs

Kings Canyon Park Visitor Center

15

180

TO AT HAVEN

Big Stump Entrance

Redwood Mountain Overlook

Kings Canyon Overlook

Eshom

REDWOOD CANYON

Montecito Sequoia Lodge

Generals Highway

Stony Creek

SILLIMAN CREST

Stony Creek Village

Dorst Creek

Twin Lakes Trail

Wuksachi Village

Lodgepole Visitor Center and Village

Wolverton

Crystal Cave

Pinewood

General Sherman Tree

Kaweah River

Yucca Creek

Colony Mill Trail

Giant Forest Museum

Tharps Log

High Sierra Trail

CRESCENT MEADOW

Tunnel Log

Moro Rock

ASH PEAKS

North Fork Kaweah River

Hospital Rock

Potwisha

Buckeye Flat

Crystal Cave

SEQUOIA NATIONAL PARK

Foothills Visitor Center

Generals Highway

Ash Mountain Entrance

TO MINERAL KING AREA

Atwell Mill

3 mi

3 km

Kaweah River

198

Mineral King Rd

Three Rivers

Lake Kaweah

Lookout Point Entrance

SEQUOIA NATIONAL PARK

EXPLORING

SCENIC DRIVES

Fodor'sChoice   **Generals Highway.** One of California's most scenic drives, this 43-mile
★   road is the main asphalt artery between Sequoia and Kings Canyon
national parks. Some portions are also signed as Route 180, others
as Route 198. Named after the landmark Grant and Sherman trees
that leave so many visitors awestruck, Generals Highway runs from
Sequoia's Foothills Visitor Center north to Kings Canyon's Grant Grove
Village. Along the way, it passes the turnoff to Crystal Cave, the Giant
Forest Museum, Lodgepole Village, and other popular attractions. The
lower portion, from Hospital Rock to the Giant Forest, is especially
steep and winding. If your vehicle is 22 feet or longer, avoid that stretch
by entering the parks via Route 180 (from Fresno) rather than Route
198 (from Visalia or Three Rivers). ■TIP→ Take your time on this
road—there's a lot to see, and wildlife can scamper across at any time.

SCENIC STOPS

Sequoia National Park is all about the trees, and to understand the scale
of these giants you must walk among them. But there is much more to
the park than the trees. Try to access one of the vista points that provide
a panoramic view over the forested mountains. Generals Highway (on
Routes 198 and 180) will be your route to most of the park's sights. A
few short spur roads lead from the highway to some sights, and Mineral
King Road branches off Route 198 to enter the park at Lookout Point,
winding east from there to park's the southernmost section.

Crescent Meadow. A sea of ferns signals your arrival at what John Muir
called the "gem of the Sierra." Walk around for an hour or two and you
might decide that the Scotland-born naturalist was exaggerating a wee
bit, but the verdant meadow is quite pleasant and you just might see a
bear. ■TIP→ Wildflowers bloom here throughout the summer. ⊠ *End
of Moro Rock–Crescent Meadow Rd., 2.6 miles east off Generals Hwy.*
⎯ *Shuttle: Moro Rock–Crescent Meadow.*

Fodor'sChoice   **Crystal Cave.** One of more than 200 caves in Sequoia and Kings Canyon,
★   Crystal Cave is composed largely of marble, the result of limestone
being hardened under heat and pressure. It contains several eye-popping
formations. There used to be more, but some were damaged or oblit-
erated by early-20th-century dynamite blasting. You can only see the
cave on a tour. The Daily Tour ($15), a great overview, takes about 50
minutes. To immerse yourself in the cave experience—at times you'll be
crawling on your belly—book the exhilarating Wild Cave Tour ($130).
■TIP→ Purchase Daily Tour tickets at either the Foothills or Lodgepole
visitor center; they're not sold at the cave itself. ⊠ *Crystal Cave Rd.,
off Generals Hwy.* ☎ *559/565–3759* ⊕ *www.sequoiahistory.org* ⎙ *$15*
⊙ *Mid-May–Nov., daily 10–4.*

Fodor'sChoice   **General Sherman Tree.** The 274.9-foot-tall General Sherman is one of the
★   world's tallest and oldest sequoias, and it ranks no. 1 in volume, adding the equivalent of a 60-foot-tall tree every year to its approximately

CLOSE UP

Plants and Wildlife in Sequoia and Kings Canyon   11

The parks can be divided into three distinct zones. In the west (1,500–4,500 feet) are the rolling, lower elevation foothills, covered with shrubby chaparral vegetation or golden grasslands dotted with oaks. Chamise, red-barked manzanita, and the occasional yucca plant grow here. Fields of white popcorn flower cover the hillsides in spring, and the yellow fiddleneck flourishes. In summer, intense heat and absence of rain cause the hills to turn golden brown. Wildlife includes the California ground squirrel, noisy blue-and-gray scrub jay, black bears, coyotes, skunks, and gray fox.

At middle elevation (5,000–9,000 feet), where the giant sequoia belt resides, rock formations mix with meadows and huge stands of evergreens—red and white fir,

incense cedar, and ponderosa pines, to name a few. Wildflowers like yellow blazing star and red Indian paintbrush bloom in spring and summer. Mule deer, golden-mantled ground squirrels, Steller's jays, mule deer, and black bears (most active in fall) inhabit the area, as does the chickaree.

The high alpine section of the parks is extremely rugged, with a string of rocky peaks reaching above 13,000 feet to Mt. Whitney's 14,494 feet. Fierce weather and scarcity of soil make vegetation and wildlife sparse. Foxtail and whitebark pines have gnarled and twisted trunks, the result of high wind, heavy snowfall, and freezing temperatures. In summer you can see yellow-bellied marmots, pikas, weasels, mountain chickadees, and Clark's nutcrackers.

52,500 cubic feet of mass. The tree doesn't grow taller, though—it's dead at the top. A short, wheelchair-accessible trail leads to the tree from Generals Highway, but the main trail (0.5 mile) winds down from a parking lot off Wolverton Road. ■TIP→ The walk back up the main trail is steep, but benches along the way provide rest for the short of breath. ⊠ *Wolverton Rd., off Generals Hwy. (Rte. 198)* ☞ *Shuttle: Giant Forest or Wolverton–Sherman Tree.*

Mineral King Area. A subalpine valley of fir, pine, and sequoia trees, Mineral King sits at 7,800 feet at the end of a steep, winding road (⇨ *Scenic Drives, above*). This is the highest point to which you can drive in the park. ⊠ *Mineral King Rd., 25 miles east of Generals Hwy. (Rte. 198).*

Fodor's Choice ★ **Moro Rock.** Sequoia National Park's best non-tree attraction offers panoramic views to those fit and determined enough to mount its 350 or so steps. In a case where the journey rivals the destination, Moro's stone stairway is so impressive in its twisty inventiveness that it's on the National Register of Historic Places. The rock's 6,725-foot summit overlooks the Middle Fork Canyon, sculpted by the Kaweah River and approaching the depth of Arizona's Grand Canyon, although smoggy, hazy air often compromises the view. ⊠ *Moro Rock–Crescent Meadow Rd., 2 miles east off Generals Hwy. (Rte. 198) to parking area* ☞ *Shuttle: Moro Rock–Crescent Meadow.*

Tunnel Log. This 275-foot tree fell in 1937, and soon a 17-foot-wide, 8-foot-high hole was cut through it for vehicular passage (not to mention the irresistible photograph) that continues today. Large vehicles take the nearby bypass. ⊠ *Moro Rock–Crescent Meadow Rd., 2 miles east of Generals Hwy. (Rte. 198)* ☞ *Shuttle: Moro Rock–Crescent Meadow.*

EDUCATIONAL OFFERINGS

PROGRAMS AND SEMINARS

Evening Programs. Film and slide shows and evening campfire lectures about Sequoia and Kings Canyon take place often during the summer. The Wonders of the Night Sky programs celebrate the often-stunning views of the heavens experienced at both parks. ☎ *559/565–3341* ⊕ *www.sequoiahistory.org/snhacalendar.asp* ⊘ *Locations and hrs vary.*

Free Nature Programs. Almost any summer day, half-hour to 1½-hour ranger talks and walks explore subjects such as the life of the sequoia, the geology of the park, and the habits of bears. Giant Forest, Lodgepole Visitor Center, Wuksachi Village, and Dorst Creek Campground are frequent starting points. Check bulletin boards throughout the park for the week's offerings.

Seminars. Expert naturalists lead seminars on a range of topics, including birds, wildflowers, geology, botany, photography, park history, backpacking, and pathfinding. Reservations are recommended. Information about times and prices is available at the visitor centers or through the Sequoia Natural History Association. ☎ *559/565–3759* ⊕ *www.sequoiahistory.org.*

TOURS

Fodor'sChoice ★ **Sequoia Field Institute.** The Sequoia Natural History Association's highly regarded educational division conducts single-day and multiday "EdVenture" tours that include backpacking hikes, natural-history walks, and kayaking excursions. ⊠ *47050 Generals Hwy., Unit 10, Three Rivers* ☎ *559/565–4251* ⊕ *www.sequoiahistory.org.*

Sequoia Sightseeing Tours. This operator's friendly, knowledgeable guides conduct interpretive sightseeing tours in a 10-passenger van. Reservations are essential. The company also offers private tours of Kings Canyon. ⊠ *Three Rivers* ☎ *559/561–4489* ⊕ *www.sequoiatours.com* ⊡ *$65 half-day tour, $88 full-day tour.*

SPORTS AND THE OUTDOORS

The best way to see Sequoia is to take a hike. Unless you do so, you'll miss out on the up-close grandeur of mist wafting between deeply scored, red-orange tree trunks bigger than you've ever seen. If it's winter, put on some snowshoes or cross-country skis and plunge into the snow-swaddled woodland. There are not too many other outdoor options: no off-road driving is allowed in the parks, and no special provisions have been made for bicycles. Boating, rafting, and snowmobiling are also prohibited.

BIRD-WATCHING

More than 200 species of birds inhabit Sequoia and Kings Canyon national parks. Not seen in most parts of the United States, the white-headed woodpecker and the pileated woodpecker are common in most

Mt. Whitney

At 14,494 feet, Mt. Whitney is the highest point in the contiguous United States and the crown jewel of Sequoia National Park's wild eastern side. The peak looms high above the tiny, high-mountain desert community of Lone Pine, where numerous Hollywood Westerns have been filmed. The high mountain ranges, arid landscape, and scrubby brush of the eastern Sierra are beautiful in their vastness and austerity.

Despite the mountain's scale, you can't see it from the more traveled west side of the park because it is hidden behind the Great Western Divide. The only way to access Mt. Whitney from the main part of the park is to circumnavigate the Sierra Nevada via a 10-hour, nearly 400-mile drive outside the park. No road ascends the peak; the best vantage point from which to catch a glimpse of the mountain is at the end of Whitney Portal Road. The 13 miles of winding road leads from U.S. 395 at Lone Pine to the trailhead for the hiking route to the top of the mountain. Whitney Portal Road is closed in winter.

mid-elevation areas here. There are also many hawks and owls, including the renowned spotted owl. Species are diverse in both parks due to the changes in elevation, and range from warblers, kingbirds, thrushes, and sparrows in the foothills to goshawk, blue grouse, red-breasted nuthatch, and brown creeper at the highest elevations. Ranger-led bird-watching tours are held on a sporadic basis. Call the park's main information number to find out more about these tours. The Sequoia Natural History Association (☎ 559/565–3759 ⊕ www.sequoiahistory.org) also has information about bird-watching in the southern Sierra.

CROSS-COUNTRY SKIING

Wuksachi Lodge. Rent skis here. Depending on snowfall amounts, instruction may also be available. Reservations are recommended. Marked trails cut through Giant Forest, about 5 miles south of the lodge. ⊠ Off Generals Hwy. (Rte. 198), 2 miles north of Lodgepole ☎ 559/565–4070 ⊘ Nov.–May (unless no snow), daily 9–4 ⊂ Shuttle: Wuksachi-Lodgepole-Dorst.

HIKING

The best way to see the park is to hike it. Carry a hiking map and plenty of water. Visitor center gift shops sell maps and trail books and pamphlets. Check with rangers for current trail conditions, and be aware of rapidly changing weather. As a rule of thumb, plan on covering about a mile per hour.

EASY

Fodor's Choice ★ **Congress Trail.** This 2-mile trail, arguably the best hike in the parks in terms of natural beauty, is a paved loop that begins near General Sherman Tree. You'll get close-up views of more big trees here than on any other Sequoia hike. Watch for the clusters known as the House and Senate. The President Tree, also on the trail, supplanted the General Grant Tree in 2012 as the world's second largest in volume (behind the General Sherman). ■TIP→ An offshoot of the Congress Trail leads to

Crescent Meadow, where in summer you can catch a free shuttle back to the Sherman parking lot. *Easy.* ✉ *Trailhead off Generals Hwy. (Rte. 198), 2 miles north of Giant Forest* ☞ *Shuttle: Giant Forest.*

Crescent Meadow Trails. A 1.8-mile trail loops around lush Crescent Meadow past Tharp's Log, a cabin built from a fire-hollowed sequoia. ■ **TIP➜** Brilliant wildflowers bloom here in midsummer. *Easy.* ✉ *Trailhead at the end of Moro Rock–Crescent Meadow Rd., 2.6 miles east off Generals Hwy. (Rte. 198)* ☞ *Shuttle: Moro Rock–Crescent Meadow.*

MODERATE

Tokopah Falls Trail. This trail with a 500-foot elevation gain follows the Marble Fork of the Kaweah River for 1.75 miles one way and dead-ends below the impressive granite cliffs and cascading waterfall of Tokopah Canyon. The trail passes through a mixed-conifer forest. It takes 2½ to 4 hours to make the round-trip journey. *Moderate.* ✉ *Trailhead off Generals Hwy. (Rte. 198), ¼ mile north of Lodgepole Campground* ☞ *Shuttle: Lodgepole-Wuksachi-Dorst.*

DIFFICULT

Mineral King Trails. Many trails to the high country begin at Mineral King. Two popular day hikes are Eagle Lake (6.8 miles round-trip) and Timber Gap. (4.4 miles round-trip) ■ **TIP➜** At the Mineral King Ranger Station (☎ 559/565–3768) you can pick up maps and check about conditions. *Difficult.* ✉ *Trailheads at end of Mineral King Rd., 25 miles east of Generals Hwy. (Rte. 198).*

HORSEBACK RIDING

TOURS AND OUTFITTERS

Grant Grove Stables. Grant Grove Stables (⇨ *Horseback Riding in Kings Canyon National Park*) isn't too far from parts of Sequoia National Park and is perfect for short rides. ⊕ *www.visitsequoia.com/grant-grove-stables.aspx.*

Horse Corral Pack Station. One- and two-hour trips through Sequoia are available for beginning and advanced riders. ✉ *Big Meadow Rd., 12 miles east of Generals Hwy. (Rte. 198) between Sequoia and Kings Canyon national parks* ☎ 559/565–3404 in summer, 559/564–6429 year-round ✉ *$40–$75* ⊙ *May–Sept.*

KINGS CANYON NATIONAL PARK

EXPLORING

SCENIC DRIVES

Kings Canyon Scenic Byway. The 30-mile stretch of Route 180 between Grant Grove Village and Zumwalt Meadow delivers eye-popping scenery—granite cliffs, a roaring river, waterfalls, and Kings River Canyon itself—much of which you can experience at vista points or on easy walks. The canyon comes into view about 10 miles east of the village at **Junction View.** Five miles beyond at **Yucca Point,** the canyon is thousands of feet deeper than the more famous Grand Canyon. **Canyon View,** a special spot 1 mile east of the Cedar Grove Village turnoff, showcases evidence of the area's glacial history. Here, perhaps more than anywhere else, you'll understand why John Muir compared Kings Canyon vistas with those in Yosemite. ■TIP➜ Driving the byway takes about an hour each way without stops.

HISTORIC SITES

Fallen Monarch. This toppled sequoia's hollow base was used in the second half of the 19th century as a home for settlers, a saloon, and even to stable U.S. Cavalry horses. As you walk through it (assuming entry is permitted, which is not always possible), notice how little the wood has decayed, and imagine yourself tucked safely inside, sheltered from a storm or protected from the searing heat. ⊠ *Grant Grove Trail, 1 mile north of Kings Canyon Park Visitor Center.*

SCENIC STOPS

General Grant Tree. President Coolidge proclaimed this to be "the nation's Christmas tree," and 30 years later President Eisenhower designated it as a living shrine to all Americans who have died in wars. Bigger at its base than the General Sherman Tree, it tapers more quickly. It's estimated to be the world's third-largest sequoia by volume. ■TIP➜ A spur trail winds behind the tree, where scars from a long-ago fire remain visible. ⊠ *Trailhead 1 mile north of Grant Grove Visitor Center.*

Redwood Mountain Sequoia Grove. One of the world's largest sequoia groves, Redwood contains within its 2,078 acres nearly 2,200 sequoias whose diameters exceed 10 feet. Your can view the grove from afar at an overlook or hike 6 to 10 miles down into the richest regions, which include two of the world's 25 heaviest trees. ⊠ *Drive 5 miles south of Grant Grove on Generals Hwy. (Rte. 198), then turn right at Quail Flat; follow it 1½ miles to the Redwood Canyon trailhead ✛ From Grant Grove, drive south on Generals Hwy. (Rte. 198) 5 miles, turn right (west) at sign for Redwood Canyon, and follow road 2 miles to Redwood Canyon trailhead.*

SPORTS AND THE OUTDOORS

The siren song of beauty, challenge, and relative solitude (by national parks standards) draws hard-core outdoors enthusiasts to the Kings River Canyon and the backcountry of the park's eastern section. Backpacking, rock-climbing, and extreme-kayaking opportunities abound, but the park also has day hikes for all ability levels. Winter brings sledding, skiing, and snowshoeing fun. No off-road driving or biking is allowed in the park, and snowmobiling is also prohibited.

CROSS-COUNTRY SKIING

Roads to Grant Grove are accessible even during heavy snowfall, making the trails here a good choice over Sequoia's Giant Forest when harsh weather hits.

HIKING

You can enjoy many of Kings Canyon's sights from your car, but the giant gorge of the Kings River Canyon and the sweeping vistas of some of the highest mountains in the United States are best seen on foot. Carry a hiking map—available at any visitor center—and plenty of water. Check with rangers for current trail conditions, and be aware of rapidly changing weather. Except for one trail to Mt. Whitney, permits are not required for day hikes.

Roads End Permit Station. You can obtain wilderness permits, maps, and information about the backcountry at this station, where bear canisters, a must for campers, can be rented or purchased. When the station is closed, complete a self-service permit form. ⊠ *Eastern end of Kings Canyon Scenic Byway, 6 miles east of Cedar Grove Visitor Center* ⊙ *Mid-May–Sept., daily 7–4.*

EASY

Fodor'sChoice
★

Zumwalt Meadow Trail. Rangers say this is the best (and most popular) day hike in the Cedar Grove area. Just 1.5 miles long, it offers three visual treats: the South Fork of the Kings River, the lush meadow, and the high granite walls above, including those of Grand Sentinel and North Dome. *Easy.* ⊠ *Trailhead 4½ miles east of Cedar Grove Village turnoff from Kings Canyon Scenic Byway.*

MODERATE

Big Baldy. This hike climbs 600 feet and 2 miles up to the 8,209-feet summit of Big Baldy. Your reward is the view of Redwood Canyon. Round-trip the hike is 4 miles. *Moderate.* ⊠ *Trailhead 8 miles south of Grant Grove on Generals Hwy. (Rte. 198).*

Redwood Canyon Trails. Two main trails lead into Redwood Canyon Grove, the world's largest sequoia grove. The 6.5-mile **Hart Tree and Fallen Goliath Loop** passes by a 19th-century logging site, pristine Hart Meadow, and the hollowed-out Tunnel Tree before accessing a side trail to the grove's largest sequoia, the 277.9-foot-tall Hart Tree. The 6.4-mile **Sugar Bowl Loop** provides views of Redwood Mountain and Big Baldy before winding down into its namesake, a thick grove of mature and young sequoias. *Moderate.* ⊠ *Trail begins off Quail Flat. Drive 5 miles south of Grant Grove on Generals Hwy. (Rte. 198), then turn right at Quail Flat; follow it 1½ miles to the Redwood Canyon trailhead.*

DIFFICULT

Hotel Creek Trail. For gorgeous canyon views, take this trail from Cedar Grove up a series of switchbacks until it splits. Follow the route left through chaparral to the forested ridge and rocky outcrop known as Cedar Grove Overlook, where you can see the Kings River Canyon stretching below. This strenuous 5-mile round-trip hike gains 1,200 feet and takes three to four hours to complete. *Difficult.* ⊠ *Trailhead at Cedar Grove Pack Station, 1 mile east of Cedar Grove Village.*

HORSEBACK RIDING

One-day destinations by horseback out of Cedar Grove include Mist Falls and Upper Bubb's Creek. In the backcountry, many equestrians head for Volcanic Lakes or Granite Basin, ascending trails that reach elevations of 10,000 feet. Costs per person range from $35 for a one-hour guided ride to around $250 per day for fully guided trips for which the packers do all the cooking and camp chores.

TOURS AND OUTFITTERS

Cedar Grove Pack Station. Take a day or overnight trip along the Kings River Canyon with Cedar Grove Pack Station. Popular routes include the Rae Lakes Loop and Monarch Divide. ⊠ *Kings Canyon Scenic Byway, 1 mile east of Cedar Grove Village* ☎ *559/565–3464* ✉ *Call for prices* ☾ *Late May–early Sept.*

Grant Grove Stables. A one- or two-hour trip through Grant Grove leaving from the stables provides a taste of horseback riding in Kings Canyon. ⊠ *Rte. 180, ½ mile north of Grant Grove Visitor Center* ☎ *559/335–9292 mid-June–Sept.* ✉ *$45–$70* ☾ *June–Labor Day, daily 8–6.*

SLEDDING AND SNOWSHOEING

In winter, Kings Canyon has a few great places to play in the snow. Sleds, inner tubes, and platters are allowed at both the Azalea Campground area on Grant Tree Road, ¼ mile north of Grant Grove Visitor Center, and at the Big Stump picnic area, 2 miles north of the lower Route 180 entrance to the park.

Snowshoeing is good around Grant Grove, where you can take naturalist-guided snowshoe walks on Saturdays and holidays from mid-December through mid-March as conditions permit. For a small donation, you can rent snowshoes at the Grant Grove Visitor Center for the guided walks. Grant Grove Market rents sleds and snowshoes.

Hiking in the Sierra Mountains is a thrilling experience, putting you amid some of the world's highest trees.

WHERE TO EAT

SEQUOIA

$
CAFÉ

✕ **Lodgepole Market and Snack Bar.** The choices here run the gamut from simple to very simple, with the three counters only a few strides apart in a central eating complex. For hot food, venture into the snack bar. The deli sells prepackaged salads, sandwiches, and wraps along with ice cream scooped from tubs. You'll find other prepackaged foods in the market. ⑤ *Average main: $6* ✉ *Next to Lodgepole Visitor Center* ☎ *559/565–3301* ⊘ *Closed late Sept.–mid-Apr.*

$$$
MODERN
AMERICAN

✕ **The Peaks.** Huge windows run the length of the Wuksachi Lodge's high-ceilinged dining room, and a large fireplace on the far wall warms both body and soul. The diverse dinner menu—by far the best at both parks—includes items such as venison medallions, grilled pork tenderloin, and pan-seared mountain trout. The menu might also include pastas, a vegan burger or other vegan dish, and ratatouille. The wine selection is serviceable but lacks imagination. Breakfast and lunch are also served. ⑤ *Average main: $24* ✉ *Wuksachi Village* ☎ *559/565–4070* ⊕ *www. visitsequoia.com/the-peaks-restaurant.aspx* ⚑ *Reservations essential.*

$$$
BARBECUE

✕ **Wolverton Barbecue.** Weather permitting, diners congregate nightly on a wooden porch that looks directly out onto a small but strikingly verdant meadow. In addition to the predictable meats such as ribs and chicken, the all-you-can-eat buffet has sides that include baked beans, corn on the cob, and potato salad. Following the meal, listen to a ranger talk and clear your throat for a campfire sing-along. Purchase tickets at Lodgepole Market, Wuksachi Lodge, or Wolverton Recreation Area's office. $ *Average main: $24* ⊠ *Wolverton Rd., 1½ miles northeast off Generals Hwy. (Rte. 198)* ☎ *559/565–4070* ⊘ *Closed early Sept.–mid-June. No lunch.*

KINGS CANYON

$ ✕ **Cedar Grove Restaurant.** The menu here is surprisingly extensive,
AMERICAN with dinner entrées such as pasta, pork chops, trout, and steak. For breakfast, try the biscuits and gravy, French toast, pancakes, or cold cereal. Burgers (including vegetarian patties) and hot dogs dominate the lunch choices. Outside, a patio dining area overlooks the Kings River. $ *Average main: $14* ⊠ *Cedar Grove Village* ☎ *559/565–0100* ⊘ *Closed Oct.–May.*

$$ ✕ **Grant Grove Restaurant.** In a no-frills, open room, this restaurant offers
AMERICAN utterly standard American fare such as pancakes for breakfast or hot sandwiches and chicken for later meals. Take-out service is available year-round, and during the summer, there's also a pizza parlor. $ *Average main: $17* ⊠ *Grant Grove Village* ☎ *559/335–5500.*

WHERE TO STAY

Hotel reviews have been shortened. For full information, visit Fodors.com.

SEQUOIA

$$$ ⛭ **Wuksachi Lodge.** The striking cedar-and-stone main building here is
HOTEL a fine example of how a structure can blend effectively with lovely
Fodor's Choice mountain scenery. **Pros:** best place to stay in the parks; lots of wildlife.
★ **Cons:** rooms can be small; main lodge is a few-minutes' walk from guest rooms. $ *Rooms from: $185* ⊠ *64740 Wuksachi Way, Wuksachi Village* ☎ *559/565–4070, 888/252–5757* ⊕ *www.visitsequoia.com* ⊅ *102 rooms* ⦿| *No meals.*

KINGS CANYON

$$$ ⛭ **John Muir Lodge.** This modern, timber-sided lodge occupies a wooded
HOTEL area in the hills above Grant Grove Village. **Pros:** open year-round; common room stays warm; lodge is far enough from the main road to be quiet. **Cons:** check-in is down in the village. $ *Rooms from: $184* ⊠ *Kings Canyon Scenic Byway, ¼ mile north of Grant Grove Village* ☎ *877/522–6966* ⊕ *www.visitsequoia.com/kings-canyon.aspx* ⊅ *36 rooms* ⦿| *No meals.*

SACRAMENTO AND THE GOLD COUNTRY

WELCOME TO SACRAMENTO AND THE GOLD COUNTRY

TOP REASONS TO GO

★ **Gold Rush:** Marshall Gold Discovery State Park and Hangtown's Gold Bug & Mine conjure up California's mid-19th century boom.

★ **State Capital:** Easygoing Sacramento offers sights like the Capitol and historic Old Sacramento along with a sophisticated dining scene.

★ **Bon appetit:** Sacramento is home to the California state fair in July and several ethnic food festivals. Nevada City and environs are known for summer mountain-music festivals and Victorian and Cornish winter-holiday celebrations.

★ **Wine Tasting:** With bucolic scenery and friendly tasting rooms, the Gold Country's Shenandoah Valley has become an acclaimed wine-making region, specializing in Zinfindel.

★ **Sequoias and Caverns:** Calaveras Big Trees State Park is filled with giant sequoias, and Moaning Cavern's main chamber is big enough to hold the Statue of Liberty.

1 **Sacramento and Nearby.** The gateway to the Gold Country, the seat of state government, and an agricultural hub, Sacramento plays many important contemporary roles. About 2.5 million people live in the metropolitan area, which offers up more sunshine and lower prices than coastal California.

2 **The Gold Country— South.** South of its junction with U.S. 50, Highway 49 traces in asphalt the famed Mother Lode. The peppy former gold-rush towns strung along the road have for the most part been restored and made presentable to visitors with an interest in one of the most frenzied episodes of American history.

3 **The Gold Country— North.** Highway 49 north of Placerville links the towns of Coloma, Auburn, Grass Valley, and Nevada City. Most are gentrified versions of once-rowdy mining camps, vestiges of which remain in roadside museums, old mining structures, and restored homes now serving as inns.

12

GETTING ORIENTED

The Gold Country is a largely laid-back destination popular with those seeking a reasonably priced escape from Southern California and the Bay Area. Sacramento, Davis, and Woodland are in an enormous valley just east of the Sierra Nevada range. Foothill communities Nevada City, Placerville, and Sutter Creek were products of the gold rush and remain popular stopovers with travelers en route to Lake Tahoe.

Updated by
Jenie Skoy

The Gold Country is one of California's less expensive destinations, a region of the Sierra Nevada foothills that's filled with natural and cultural pleasures. Visitors come to Nevada City, Auburn, Coloma, Sutter Creek, and Columbia not only to relive the past but also to explore art galleries, shop for antiques, and stay at friendly, atmospheric inns. Spring brings wildflowers, and in fall the hills are colored by bright red berries and changing leaves. Because it offers plenty of outdoor diversions, the Gold Country is a great place to take kids.

Old Sacramento's museums provide a good introduction to the region's considerable history, but the Gold Country's heart lies along Highway 49, which winds the approximately 300-mile north–south length of the historic mining area. The highway—often a twisting, hilly—two-lane road, begs for a convertible with the top down.

A new era dawned for California when James Marshall turned up a gold nugget in the tailrace of a sawmill he was constructing along the American River. On January 24, 1848, Mexico and the United States were still wrestling for ownership of what would become the Golden State. Marshall's discovery helped compel the United States to tighten its grip on the region, and prospectors from all over the world soon came to seek their fortunes in the Mother Lode.

As gold fever seized the nation, California's population of 15,000 swelled to 265,000 within three years. The mostly young, male adventurers who arrived in search of gold—the forty-niners—became part of a culture that discarded many of the button-down conventions of the eastern states. It was also a violent time. Yankee prospectors chased Mexican miners off their claims, and California's leaders initiated a plan to exterminate the local Native American population. Bounties were paid and private militias were hired to wipe out the Native Americans or sell them into slavery. California was to be dominated by the Anglo.

The gold-rush boom lasted scarcely 20 years, but it changed California forever, producing 546 mining towns, of which fewer than 250 remain. The hills of the Gold Country were alive, not only with prospecting and mining but also with business, the arts, gambling, and a fair share of crime. Opera houses went up alongside brothels, and the California State Capitol, in Sacramento, was built partly with the gold dug out of the hills.

The mild climate and rich soil in and around Sacramento Valley are responsible for the region's current riches: fresh and bountiful food and high-quality wines. Gold Country restaurants and wineries continue to earn national acclaim, and they're without the high prices of the Bay Area and Sonoma and Napa wine regions. There's a growing local craft beer scene, too.

PLANNING

WHEN TO GO
The Gold Country is most pleasant in spring, when the wildflowers are in bloom, and in fall. Summers can be hot: temperatures of 100°F are fairly common. Sacramento winters tend to be cool with occasionally foggy or rainy days; many Sacramentans drive to the foothills (or the coast) for a dose of winter sunshine. Throughout the year Gold Country towns stage community and ethnic celebrations. In December many towns are decked out for Christmas.

GETTING HERE AND AROUND
AIR TRAVEL
Sacramento International Airport (SMF) is served by Aeromexico, Alaska/Horizon, American, Delta, Hawaiian, JetBlue, Southwest, United, and Volaris. A private taxi from the airport to Downtown Sacramento costs about $40; the Super Shuttle fare is $25. Public buses (⇨ *Bus and Light-Rail Travel*) are also an option.

Contacts Sacramento International Airport ✉ *6900 Airport Blvd., 12 miles northwest of downtown off I-5, Sacramento* ☎ *916/929–5411* ⊕ *www.sacramento.aero/smf.* **Super Shuttle** ☎ *800/258–3826* ⊕ *www.supershuttle.com.*

BUS AND LIGHT-RAIL TRAVEL
Greyhound serves Sacramento from San Francisco and Los Angeles. Sacramento Regional Transit serves the capital area with buses and light-rail vehicles. Yolobus public buses Nos. 42A and 42B connect SMF airport and Downtown Sacramento, West Sacramento, Davis, and Woodland.

Contacts Greyhound ☎ *800/231–2222* ⊕ *www.greyhound.com.* **Sacramento Regional Transit** ☎ *916/321–2877* ⊕ *www.sacrt.com.* **Yolobus** ☎ *530/666–2837, 916/371–2877* ⊕ *www.yolobus.com.*

CAR TRAVEL
Interstate 5 (north–south) and Interstate 80 (east–west) are the two main routes into and out of Sacramento. From Sacramento, three highways fan out toward the east, all intersecting with historic Highway 49: Interstate 80 heads northeast 34 miles to Auburn; U.S. 50 goes east

The Gold Country

40 miles to Placerville; and Highway 16 angles southeast 45 miles to Plymouth. Highway 49 is an excellent two-lane road that winds and climbs through the foothills and valleys, linking the principal Gold Country towns. Traveling by car is the only practical way to explore the Gold Country.

12

TRAIN TRAVEL

One of the most authentic ways to relive the Old West is traveling via train. On the Amtrak California Zephyr, you can ride the same route traveled by prospectors in the late 1800s. Docents from the Sacramento Railroad Museum ride the route from Sacramento to Reno daily, and are available to answer questions. The route into the Sierra Nevadas is memorable, especially if you book a sleeper car. Amtrak trains serves Sacramento and Davis from San Jose, Oakland, and Emeryville (Amtrak buses transport passengers from San Francisco's Ferry Building to Emeryville). The trip takes 2½ hours. Amtrak also runs trains and connecting motor coaches from the Central Valley.

Contacts Amtrak ☎ *800/872-7245* ⊕ *www.amtrak.com.*

RESTAURANTS

American, Italian, and Mexican are common Gold Country fare, but chefs also prepare ambitious European, French, and contemporary regional cuisine that mixes California ingredients with international preparations. Grass Valley's meat- and vegetable-stuffed *pasties,* introduced by 19th-century gold miners from Cornwall, are one of the region's more unusual treats.

HOTELS

Sacramento has plenty of full-service hotels, budget motels, and small inns. Larger towns along Highway 49—among them Auburn, Grass Valley, and Jackson—have chain motels and inns. Many Gold Country bed-and-breakfasts occupy former mansions, miners' cabins, and other historic buildings. *Hotel reviews have been shortened. For full information, visit Fodors.com.*

Contacts Amador Council of Tourism ✉ *115 Valley View Way, Sutter Creek* ☎ *209/267-9249, 877/868-7262* ⊕ *www.touramador.com.* **California Association of Bed & Breakfast Inns** ☎ *800/373-9251* ⊕ *www.cabbi.com/region/ Sierra-Foothills.* **Gold Country Inns of Tuolumne County** ⊕ *www.goldbnbs.com.*

VISITOR INFORMATION

Contacts Amador County Chamber of Commerce & Visitors Bureau ✉ *115 Main St., Jackson* ☎ *209/223-0350* ⊕ *www.amadorcountychamber.com.* **El Dorado County Visitors Authority** ✉ *542 Main St., Placerville* ☎ *530/621-5885, 800/457-6279* ⊕ *visit-eldorado.com.* **Grass Valley/Nevada County Chamber of Commerce** ✉ *128 E. Main St., Grass Valley* ☎ *530/273-4667, 800/655-4667* ⊕ *www.grassvalleychamber.com.* **Yosemite/Mariposa County Tourism Bureau** ✉ *5158 Hwy. 140, Mariposa* ☎ *209/742-4567* ⊕ *www. mariposachamber.org.* **Tuolumne County Visitors Bureau** ✉ *542 W. Stockton Rd., Sonora* ☎ *209/533-4420, 800/446-1333* ⊕ *www.yosemitegoldcountry.com.*

WHAT IT COSTS				
	$	$$	$$$	$$$$
Restaurants	under $16	$16–$22	$23–$30	over $30
Hotels	under $121	$121–$175	$176–$250	over $250

Restaurant prices are the average cost of a main course at dinner or, if dinner is not served, at lunch, excluding sales tax. Hotel prices are the lowest cost of a standard double room in high season, excluding taxes.

SACRAMENTO AND NEARBY

California's capital is an ethnically diverse city, with sizable Mexican, Hmong, and Ukrainian populations, among many others.

SACRAMENTO

87 miles northeast of San Francisco; 384 miles north of Los Angeles.

All around the Golden State's seat of government you'll experience echoes of the gold-rush days, most notably in Old Sacramento, whose wooden sidewalks and horse-drawn carriages on cobblestone streets lend the waterfront district a 19th-century feel. The California State Railroad Museum and other venues hold artifacts of state and national significance, and historic buildings house shops and restaurants. River cruises and train rides are fun family diversions for an hour or two.

Due east of Old Sacramento is Downtown, where landmarks include the Capitol building and the surrounding Capitol Park. The convention center is also here. The area is a little uneven economically, but some of the boarded-up storefronts have begun to enjoy some revitalization in recent years.

Farther east, starting at about 15th Street, lies the city's most interesting neighborhood, Midtown, a mix of genteel Victorian edifices, ultramodern lofts, and innovative restaurants and cozy wine bars. The neighborhood springs to life on the second Saturday evening of the month, when art galleries hold open houses and the sidewalks are packed. A few intersections are jumping most evenings when the weather's good; they include the corner of 20th and L streets in what's known as Lavender Heights, the center of the city's gay and lesbian community.

GETTING HERE AND AROUND

Most people drive to Sacramento and get around by car. Yellow Cab is a reliable company.

Bus Travel Sacramento Regional Transit buses and light-rail vehicles serve the area. The No. 30 DASH shuttle bus links Old Sacramento, Midtown, and Sutter's Fort.

Car Travel Assuming that traffic is not a factor (though it often is), Sacramento is a 90-minute drive from San Francisco and a seven-hour drive from Los Angeles. Parking garages serve Old Sacramento and other tourist spots; on-street parking Downtown can be difficult to find.

ESSENTIALS

Transportation Contacts Sacramento Regional Transit ☎ 916/321–2877 ⊕ www.sacrt.com. Yellow Cab Co. of Sacramento ☎ 916/444–2222 ⊕ www.yellowcabsacramento.com.

Visitor Information Old Sacramento Visitor Information Center ✉ 1002 2nd St. ☎ 916/442–7644 ⊕ www.discovergold.org ⊙ Daily 10–5. Sacramento Convention and Visitors Bureau ✉ 1608 I St. ☎ 916/808–7777 ⊕ www.visitsacramento.com.

EXPLORING
TOP ATTRACTIONS

American River Bicycle Trail. The Jedediah Smith Memorial Trail, as it's formally called, runs for 32 miles from Old Sacramento to Beals Point in Folsom. Walk or ride a bit of it and you'll see why local cyclists and pedestrians adore its scenic lanes, if not always each other: confrontations do occur between humorless speeders and meandering gawkers. Enjoy great views of the American River and the bluffs overlooking it. ■ TIP→ Bring lunch or a snack. Pretty parks and picnic areas dot the trail.

California Automobile Museum. More than 150 vintage automobiles— including Model Ts, Hudsons, Studebakers, Pontiacs, and other bygone makes and models—are on display at this museum that pays tribute to automotive history and car culture. Check out a replica of Henry Ford's 1896 Quadracycle and a 1920s roadside café and garage exhibit. The docents are ready to explain everything you see. The museum is near Downtown and Old Sacramento, with ample free parking. ⊠ *2200 Front St., Downtown* 📷 *916/442–6802* ⊕ *www.calautomuseum.org* ⌧ *$8* ☉ *Daily 10–6.*

FAMILY **California State Railroad Museum.** Near what was the terminus of the transcontinental and Sacramento Valley railroads, this 100,000-square-foot museum is a recreation of the original train station and roundhouse. There are 21 locomotives and railroad cars on display along with dozens of other exhibits. You can walk through a post-office car and peer into cubbyholes and canvas mailbags, enter a sleeping car that simulates the swaying on the roadbed and the flashing lights of a passing town at night, or glimpse inside the first-class dining car. The room containing the gold "Last Spike," one of two cast in 1869 to commemorate the completion of the transcontinental railroad, is quietly compelling. Kids have lots of fun at this museum, especially in the play area upstairs. ■TIP→ You can visit an original roundhouse, not just a replica, at Railtown 1897 in Jamestown, near Sonora. ⊠ *125 I St., at 2nd St., Old Sacramento* 📷 *916/445–6645* ⊕ *www.csrmf.org* ⌧ *$10* ☉ *Daily 10–5.*

Capitol. The lacy plasterwork of the Capitol's 120-foot-high rotunda has the complexity and colors of a Fabergé egg. Underneath the gilded dome are marble floors, glittering chandeliers, monumental staircases, reproductions of century-old state offices, and legislative chambers decorated in the style of the 1890s (the Capitol was built in 1869). Guides conduct tours of the building and the 40-acre Capitol Park, which contains a rose garden, a fragrant display of camellias (Sacramento's city flower), and the California Vietnam Veterans Memorial. ■TIP→ Wander the Capitol's botanical grounds to glimpse the diverse collection of trees, shrubs, and flowers, including some 1,200 trees from around the world. The original Deodar Cedars on the west side date back to 1872. ⊠ *Capitol Mall and 10th St., Downtown* 📷 *916/324–0333* ⊕ *www.statecapitolmuseum.com* ⌧ *Free* ☉ *Daily 9–5; tours hourly 9–4.*

Fodor's Choice **Crocker Art Museum.** Established in 1885, this esteemed art museum contains one of the finest collections of Californian art in the nation—two highlights include *Sunday Morning in the Mines* (1872), a large canvas by Charles Christian Nahl depicting the original mining industry, and the magnificent *Great Canyon of the Sierra, Yosemite* (1871), by Thomas Hill. The Crocker has exceptional holdings of master drawings as well as an impressive collection of international ceramics and works from Europe, Asia, and Africa. A huge contemporary wing was added in 2010 and regularly hosts outstanding traveling exhibitions. On view in 2015 are works by Toulouse-Lautrec, William S. Rice, David Ligare, and Armin Hansen. ⊠ *216 O St., at 3rd St., Downtown* 📷 *916/808–7000* ⊕ *www.crockerartmuseum.org* ⌧ *$10* ☉ *Tues., Wed., and Fri.–Sun. 10–5; Thurs. 10–9.*

Governor's Mansion. This 15-room Italianate mansion was built in 1877 and used by the state's chief executives from the early 1900s until 1967, when Ronald Reagan vacated it in favor of an upscale modern residence. Many of the interior decorations were ordered from the Huntington, Hopkins & Co. Hardware Store, one of whose partners, Albert Gallatin, was the original occupant. Each of the seven marble fireplaces has a petticoat mirror that ladies strolled past to see if their slips were showing. ⊠ *1526 H St., at 16th St., Midtown* ☎ *916/323–3047* ⊕ *www. parks.ca.gov* ▨ *$5* ⊙ *Wed.–Sun.10–5; tours hourly until 4.*

12

WORTH NOTING

FAMILY **California Museum.** Some of the exhibits at this celebration of all things California are high-tech and interactive, but there are also scores of archival drawers that you can pull out to see the real artifacts of history and culture—from the California State Constitution to surfing magazines. Board a 1949 cross-country bus to view a video on immigration, visit a Chinese herb shop maintained by a holographic proprietor, or find familiar names inducted into the annually expanded California Hall of Fame. The museum's café is open on weekdays until 2:30 pm. ⊠ *1020 O St., at 11th St., Downtown* ☎ *916/653–7524* ⊕ *www. californiamuseum.org* ▨ *$9* ⊙ *Tues.–Sat. 10–5, Sun. noon–5.*

FAMILY **Central Pacific Railroad Passenger Station.** At this reconstructed 1876 depot there's rolling stock to admire, a typical waiting room, and a small restaurant. Part of the year a train departs from the freight depot, south of the passenger station, making a 40-minute out-and-back trip between the Sacramento River and, less interestingly, Interstate 5. ⊠ *930 Front St., at J St., Old Sacramento* ☎ *916/445–6645* ▨ *Station $4 (free with same-day ticket from state railroad museum); train rides $10* ⊙ *Train rides: Apr.–Sept., weekends 11–5, Oct.–Dec., call for hrs.*

State Indian Museum. Among the interesting displays at this museum near Sutter's Fort is one about Ishi, the last Yahi Indian to emerge from the mountains, in 1911. Ishi provided anthropologists with insight into his people's traditions and culture. Arts-and-crafts exhibits, a demonstration village, and an evocative 10-minute video also explore the lives and history of California's native peoples. ⊠ *2618 K St., at 27th St.* ☎ *916/324–0971* ⊕ *www.parks.ca.gov* ▨ *$3* ⊙ *Daily 10–5.*

FAMILY **Sutter's Fort.** German-born Swiss immigrant John Augustus Sutter founded Sacramento's earliest Euro-American settlement in 1839. Audio speakers give information at each stop along a self-guided tour that includes a blacksmith's shop, bakery, prison, living quarters, and livestock areas. Costumed docents sometimes reenact fort life, demonstrating crafts, food preparation, and firearms maintenance. ⊠ *2701 L St., at 27th St., Midtown* ☎ *916/445–4422* ⊕ *www.parks.ca.gov* ▨ *$5 most days, $7 on interpretive program days* ⊙ *Mon.–Sun. 10–5.*

WHERE TO EAT

$$$
ITALIAN
odor's Choice
★

✕ **Biba.** Owner Biba Caggiano is a nationally recognized authority on Italian cuisine, having written numerous cookbooks, several of which are sold here in her inviting restaurant. The Capitol crowd flocks here for exceptional renditions of lasagna with Bolognese sauce, classic Milanese-style veal osso buco with saffron-risotto cakes, and pan-roasted halibut topped with a light caper-lemon-butter sauce. For dessert, try delicious *zuccotto Florentino* (a layer of rum-soaked cake with chocolate ganache crowned with a mountain of whipped cream, and bites

The California State Railroad Museum is North America's most popular railroad museum.

of hazelnuts, almonds, and chocolate. A pianist adds to the upscale ambience nightly. ⑤ *Average main: $28* ✉ *2801 Capitol Ave., at 28th St., Midtown* ☎ *916/455–2422* ⊕ *www.biba-restaurant.com* ⌕ *Reservations essential* ⊘ *Closed Sun. No lunch Mon. or Sat.*

$$$
MODERN
AMERICAN
✕ **Ella.** With fresh white calla lilies on the tables, ivory linen curtains, and distressed-wood shutters installed across the ceiling, this swank restaurant and bar near the Capitol building is artfully designed and thoroughly modern—a nice fit for the stellar California-French farm-to-table cuisine served within. The menu changes seasonally, but typical are the steak tartare with garlic popovers and a farm egg, seared local sturgeon with caul fat, grilled endive, and romanesco sauce, and wood-fired pork chop with root vegetables. The impeccable waitstaff works with Ninja-like precision, paying close attention to every detail. ⑤ *Average main: $30* ✉ *1131 K St., Downtown* ☎ *916/443–3772* ⊕ *www. elladiningroomandbar.com.*

$$$$
AMERICAN
Fodor's Choice
★
✕ **The Firehouse.** Long celebrated by locals and foodies as one of the city's top restaurants, this historic eatery has a full bar, breezy courtyard seating, and creative American cooking, such as char-grilled spring rack of lamb served with roasted French fingerling potatoes and baby artichoke and fava bean succotash. Visitors who can afford to treat themselves to a fine and leisurely meal can do no better in Old Sacramento—although they might also opt for the less-pricey **Ten 22.** Located a block away and under the same ownership as the Firehouse, it serves pizza and other fancified comfort food. ⑤ *Average main: $36* ✉ *1112 2nd St., at L St., Old Sacramento* ☎ *916/442–4772* ⊕ *www.firehouseoldsac.com* ⊘ *No lunch Sat.*

12

$$ **✕ Hook & Ladder Manufacturing Company.** Youthful and hip, with found-
MODERN art decorative elements and exposed vents, this historic former fire sta-
AMERICAN tion is a favorite stop for creative cocktails, craft beers, and creative
gastropub fare. Lighter dishes include pizza with gooey burrata cheese
and fresh tomatoes, house-made sausages with assorted chutneys and
mustards, and and seared-ahi *bahn mi* sliders. There's more complex
fare, too, such as bacon-wrapped pork tenderloin with gnocchi and
smoked tomato, and roasted-pumpkin risotto with mascarpone. A
refined drink list includes rotating local wine and beers on tap. $ *Av-
erage main: $18* ✉ *1630 S. St., Midtown* ☎ *916/442–4885* ⊕ *www.
hookandladder916.com.*

$$ **✕ Magpie Cafe.** This hip Midtown eatery with a casual vibe takes its food
AMERICAN quite seriously: nearly all the produce is sourced locally, and menus are
Fodor's Choice printed each day reflecting availability from local farms. The array of
★ small-batch farmstead cheeses, all from California, is mouthwatering
(especially the Point Reyes Blue, drizzled with honey).
Recent offerings have included roasted chicken for two with a chervil-
ginger green sauce, and—at lunch—a smoked-trout and Meyer lemon
sandwich with dill, capers, and cream cheese. Be sure to choose a couple
of the perfectly braised or roasted side vegetable dishes, perhaps asparagus with green-garlic oil, or pan-seared creamy polenta with sage. If you
make it here for brunch, consider the savory bread pudding with bacon,
chipotle-cheddar, and chives. The pub next door can get loud after 9,
so arrive before if aiming for a relaxed dinner. $ *Average main: $21*
✉ *1409 R St., No.102, Midtown* ☎ *916/452–7594* ⊕ *www.magpiecafe.
com* ◷ *No dinner Sun.*

$$ **✕ Rio City Café.** Contemporary and seasonal Mediterranean and Califor-
AMERICAN nian cuisine, and huge floor-to-ceiling windows and an outdoor deck
overlooking the river are the attractions of this popular restaurant that's
designed to resemble a vintage steamship warehouse. Consider din-
ing here for lunch or brunch, when you can enjoy the beautiful water
views. The food is unfussy and consistently good—burgers with rose-
mary fries, Baja-style fish tacos with pineapple-papaya salsa, Dungeness
crab and shrimp Louie salad. The big draw here, however, is the ambi-
ence. $ *Average main: $18* ✉ *1110 Front St., at L St., Old Sacramento*
☎ *916/442–8226* ⊕ *www.riocitycafe.com.*

$$$ **✕ The Waterboy.** Rural French cooking with locally sourced, high-
ECLECTIC quality (often organic) ingredients are the hallmark of this upscale
Fodor's Choice but refreshingly unfussy Midtown restaurant that's as appealing for
★ a casual meal with friends as it is for a drawn-out romantic dinner
for two. The artisan cheese and antipasto plates are appealing starters
for sharing, as is a standout chicken-liver crostini with fennel, frisée,
apple, and caramelized shallots. Among the mains, try the braised
Niman Ranch pork cheeks with green garlic *jus*, or pan-seared day-
boat scallops with a celery root–sunchoke–bacon hash and a Meyer
lemon–brown butter sauce. $ *Average main: $27* ✉ *2000 Capitol Ave.,
at 20th St., Midtown* ☎ *916/498–9891* ⊕ *www.waterboyrestaurant.
com* ◷ *No lunch weekends.*

WHERE TO STAY

$$$
B&B/INN

☷ **Amber House Bed & Breakfast Inn.** About a mile from the Capitol, this B&B has rooms in a 1905 Craftsman-style home and an 1895 Dutch colonial–revival home. **Pros:** Midtown location; attentive service. **Cons:** freeway access isn't easy. $ *Rooms from: $179* ✉ *1315 22nd St., Midtown* ☏ *916/444–8085, 800/755–6526* ⊕ *www.amberhouse.com* ⤴ *10 rooms* ⫶⃝| *Breakfast.*

$$$
HOTEL
Fodor's Choice
★

☷ **Citizen Hotel.** This boutique hotel built within the historic 1926 Cal Western Life building is dapper and refined, with marble stairs, striped wallpaper, and plush velvet chairs, lending the place a Roaring Twenties charm. **Pros:** hip, sophisticated decor; smooth and solicitous service; terrific restaurant and bar. **Cons:** rooms near elevator can be noisy. $ *Rooms from: $189* ✉ *926 J St., Downtown* ☏ *916/447–2700* ⊕ *www.jdvhotels.com* ⤴ *175 rooms, 23 suites* ⫶⃝| *Breakfast.*

$$
HOTEL

☷ **Delta King.** For the opportunity to sleep in one of Sacramento's most unusual and historic relics, book a stay in this riverboat that's been gloriously restored. **Pros:** exudes old-world charm; steps from historic Old Town shopping and dining. **Cons:** slanted floors can feel a bit jarring; rooms are a bit cramped. $ *Rooms from: $165* ✉ *1000 Front St., Old Sacramento* ☏ *916/444–5464, 800/825–5464* ⊕ *www.deltaking. com* ⤴ *44 rooms* ⫶⃝| *Breakfast.*

$$$
HOTEL

☷ **Hyatt Regency Sacramento.** With a marble-and-glass lobby and luxurious rooms, this hotel across from the Capitol and adjacent to the convention center is arguably Sacramento's finest. **Pros:** beautiful Capitol Park is across the street; some rooms have small balconies. **Cons:** nearby streets can feel a little dodgy at night; somewhat impersonal. $ *Rooms from: $195* ✉ *1209 L St., Downtown* ☏ *916/443–1234, 800/633–7313* ⊕ *www.hyatt.com* ⤴ *500 rooms, 24 suites* ⫶⃝| *No meals.*

NIGHTLIFE AND THE ARTS
NIGHTLIFE

Blue Cue. A billiard lounge known for its selection of single-malt scotches, the Blue Cue is upstairs from the popular Mexican restaurant Centro. Wednesday night's trivia contest is a spirited event. ✉ *1004 28th St., at J St., Midtown* ☏ *916/441–6810* ⊕ *www.bluecue.com.*

Dive Bar. Live "mermaids" and "mermen" swim in a massive tank above the bar at this lively Downtown nightspot known for its extensive list of craft cocktails and local beers. ✉ *1016 K St, Downtown* ☏ *916/737–5999* ⊕ *divebarsacramento.com.*

Fox and Goose. This casual pub with live music serves fish-and-chips, Cornish pasties, and other traditional items—plus vegetarian/vegan fare—on weekdays until 9:30. ✉ *1001 R St., at 10th St., Downtown* ☏ *916/443–8825* ⊕ *www.foxandgoose.com.*

Harlow's. This sceney restaurant draws a young-ish crowd to its art deco bar-nightclub for live music after 9 pm. ✉ *2708 J St., at 27th St., Midtown* ☏ *916/441–4693* ⊕ *www.harlows.com.*

Streets of London Pub. A favorite among Anglophiles, Streets is open after midnight every night. Darts and TV soccer, anyone? ✉ *1804 J St., at 18th St., Midtown* ☏ *916/498–1388* ⊕ *streetsoflondon.net.*

12

THE ARTS

California Musical Theatre. This group presents Broadway shows at the Sacramento Community Center Theater and the summer Music Circus offerings (think *Oklahoma, Annie*) at the theater-in-the-round Wells Fargo Pavilion. ⊠ *1419 H St., at 14th St., Downtown* ☎ *916/557–1999* ⊕ *www.calmt.com.*

Crest Theatre. It's worth peeking inside the Crest even if you don't catch a show there, just to see the swirling and flambouyant art deco design in the foyer. It's a beloved venue for classic and art-house films, along with concerts and other cultural events. ⊠ *1013 K St., at 10th St., Downtown* ☎ *916/442–7378* ⊕ *www.thecrest.com.*

Sacramento Box Office. Tickets to major comedy, music, theater, and other cultural and sports events are sold through this online vendor. ☎ *888/583–6046* ⊕ *sacramentoboxoffice.com.*

SHOPPING

Greater Sacramento is filled with familiar shops. To try something new, wander through Midtown, especially J, K, and L streets between 16th and 26th streets.

Westfield Galleria at Roseville. The Sacramento region's largest shopping complex is a sprawling, heavily trafficked collection of chain stores and restaurants. It's always jumping. ⊠ *1151 Galleria Blvd., north of Sacramento off I–80 Exit 105A, Roseville* ⊕ *www.westfield.com/galleriaatroseville.*

WOODLAND

20 miles northwest of Sacramento.

In its heyday, Woodland was among California's wealthiest cities. Established by gold seekers and entrepreneurs, it later became an agricultural gold mine. The legacy of the old land barons lives on in the restored Victorian and Craftsman architecture downtown; the best examples are south of Main Street on College, Elm, 1st, and 2nd streets. The town's top attraction is the splendid Heidrick Ag History Center.

GETTING HERE AND AROUND

Yolobus (⊕ *www.yolobus.com*) serves downtown Woodland from Sacramento, but it's far more practical to drive here via Interstate 5.

ESSENTIALS

Visitor Information Woodland Chamber of Commerce ⊠ *307 1st St., at Dead Cat Alley* ☎ *530/662–7327* ⊕ *www.woodlandchamber.org.*

EXPLORING

FAMILY **Heidrick Ag History Center Tractor & Truck Museum.** This gigantic space provides a marvelous overview of the entire history of motorized agricultural vehicles. Souped-up and shiny, the antique threshers, harvesters, combines, tractors, and proto-tractors on display here look ready to service the farms of their eras all over again. And there's more. A separate wing surveys the evolution of the truck, with an emphasis on ones used for farm work. ⊠ *1962 Hays La., off County Rd. 102* ☎ *530/666–9700* ⊕ *www.aghistory.org* ⬛ *$8* ☉ *Mid-Mar.–early Nov. Wed.–Sun. 10–5; early Nov.–mid-Mar. 10–4.*

Woodland Opera House. This 1896 structure hosted minstrel shows, John Philip Sousa's marching band, and early vaudeville acts before closing for six decades (a sad saga that involved a penny-pinching Hershey's chocolate heir). Now restored, it hosts plays, musicals, and concerts. If the box office is open, ask for a backstage tour or a peek at the auditorium. ⊠ *340 2nd St.* ☎ *530/666–9617* ⊕ *www.woodlandoperahouse. org* ⊗ *Tours: Tues. 1–4 or by appointment.*

WHERE TO EAT

$$

AMERICAN

✕ **Mojo's Kitchen428.** Woodland's dining scene turned a shade greener when Mojo's opened with restored furnishings reportedly rescued from other businesses. The steaks, lamb shanks, and turkey potpies all have their adherents, but if you're not into meat you'll find salmon and other seafood on the menu, along with vegetarian and even a few vegan items. There's a popular brunch on weekends. A friendly, stylish place, Mojo's rewards customers for also adopting green practices: ride a bike here, and you'll receive 10% off your bill. ⑤ *Average main: $20* ⊠ *428 1st St., off Main St.* ☎ *530/661–0428* ⊕ *www. mojoskitchen428.com.*

DAVIS

10 miles west of Sacramento.

Davis began as a rich agricultural area and remains one, but it doesn't feel like a cow town. It's home to the University of California at Davis, whose students hang at downtown cafés, galleries, and bookstores (most of the action takes place between 1st and 4th and C and G streets), lending the city a vaguely cosmopolitan feel.

GETTING HERE AND AROUND

Most people arrive here by car via Interstate 80. In a pinch, you can get here via Yolobus (⊕ *www.yolobus.com*) from Sacramento. Downtown is walkable. Touring by bicycle is also a popular option—Davis is mostly flat.

ESSENTIALS

Visitor Information Davis Chamber of Commerce ⊠ *640 3rd St.* ☎ *530/756–5160* ⊕ *www.davischamber.com.*

EXPLORING

University of California, Davis. A top research university, UC Davis educates many of the Wine Country's vintners and grape growers. Campus tours depart from Buehler Alumni and Visitors Center. On a tour or not, worthy stops include the **Arboretum** (⊕ *arboretum.ucdavis.edu*)—this is a major agricultural school, and it shows—and the **Mondavi Center for the Performing Arts** (⊕ *www.mondaviarts.org*), a striking modern glass structure that presents top-tier artists. ⊠ *Visitor Center, Alumni La.* ☎ *530/752–8111* ⊕ *visit.ucdavis.edu* ⊗ *Visitor Center, weekdays 8–5, Sat. 10–2; campus tours, Sat. at 11:30.*

THE GOLD COUNTRY—SOUTH

This hilly region has an old-timey vibe. It's rich with antiques shops, quaint coffee shops, and delightfully appointed Victorian B&Bs.

PLACERVILLE

12

44 miles east of Sacramento.

It's hard to imagine now, but in 1849 about 4,000 miners staked out every gully and hillside in Placerville, turning the town into a rip-roaring camp of log cabins, tents, and clapboard houses. The area was then known as Hangtown, a graphic allusion to the nature of frontier justice. It took on the name Placerville in 1854 and became an important supply center for the miners. (*Placer* is defined roughly as valuable minerals found in riverbeds or lakes.) Mark Hopkins, Philip Armour, and John Studebaker were among the industrialists who got their starts here. Today, Placerville ranks among the hippest towns in the region, its Main Street abuzz with indie shops, coffeehouses, and wine bars, many of them inside rehabbed historic buildings.

GETTING HERE AND AROUND

You'll need a car to get to and around Placerville; it's a 45-minute drive from Sacramento via U.S. 50.

EXPLORING

FAMILY **Apple Hill.** During the fall harvest season (September through December), the members of the Apple Hill Growers Association open their orchards and vineyards for apple and berry picking, picnicking, and wine and cider tasting. Start your tour at High Hill Ranch, where there are fishing ponds for kids (they'll clean and pack the fish for you). Nibble on apple doughnuts or buy jewelry from local crafters. Stop at Larsen Apple Barn, a legacy farm. Family-favored Kid's Inc. serves apples pie and empanadas, and you can sample Cabernet and Bordeaux-style blends at Grace Patriot Wines, and fresh-pressed juices at Barsotti. Stop at Wofford Acres Vineyard just to see a dramatic view of the American River canyon below. ⚠ Traffic on weekends is often backed up, so take the Camino exit or go during the week to avoid the crowds (although kid-centric events are on weekends). ⊠ *About 5 miles east of Hwy. 49; take Camino exit from U.S. 50* ☎ *530/644–7692* ⊕ *www.applehill.com.*

FAMILY **Hangtown's Gold Bug Park & Mine.** Take a self-guided tour of this fully lighted mine shaft owned by the City of Placerville. The worthwhile audio tour (included) makes clear what you're seeing. ■TIP➔ A shaded stream runs through the park, and there are picnic facilities. ⊠ *2635 Goldbug La., off Bedford Ave., 1 mile off U.S. 50* ☎ *530/642–5207* ⊕ *www.goldbugpark.org* ⊠ *$5* ☉ *Apr.–Oct., daily 10–4; Nov.–Mar., weekends noon–4.*

WHERE TO EAT AND STAY

$ ╳ **The Cozmic Cafe.** Crowds come for healthful wraps, burritos, sand-
VEGETARIAN wiches, salads, and the like, plus breakfast (served anytime), smoothies, and espresso drinks. Portions are big, prices are low, and the ambience is distinctive. The eatery is in the 1859 Pearson's Soda Works

Building and extends back into the side of a mountain, into what used to be a mineshaft. The live music here is among the best in the foothills, and an upstairs pub beckons with local wines and microbrews. $ *Average main: $9* ✉ *594 Main St.* ☎ *530/642–8481* ⊕ *www.ourcoz. com* ⊘ *Closed Mon.*

$$$
B&B/INN
Fodor's Choice
★

Eden Vale Inn. Hand-crafted by the owners, this lavish but rustic B&B occupies a converted turn-of-the-20th-century hay barn, the centerpiece of which is a 27-foot slate fireplace that rises to a sloping roof of timber beams. **Pros:** rooms are exceptionally plush; the patio and grounds are stunning; plenty of places outside for kids to run. **Cons:** fairly expensive for the area. $ *Rooms from: $200* ✉ *1780 Springvale Rd* ☎ *530/621-0901* ⊕ *www. edenvaleinn.com* ↝ *5 rooms, 2 suites* �‖ *Breakfast.*

$$
B&B/INN

Seasons Bed & Breakfast. One of Placerville's oldest homes has been transformed into a lovely and relaxing oasis. **Pros:** quiet setting; short walk to downtown; attentive hosts; great breakfasts. **Cons:** B&B environment not for everyone. $ *Rooms from: $135* ✉ *2934 Bedford Ave.* ☎ *530/626-4420* ⊕ *www.theseasons.net* ↝ *1 room, 2 suites, 1 cottage* �‖ *Breakfast.*

SHENANDOAH VALLEY

20 miles south of Placerville.

The most concentrated Gold Country wine-touring area lies in the hills of the Shenandoah Valley, east of Plymouth. Robust Zinfandel is the primary grape grown here, but vineyards here produce plenty of other varietals, from Rhône blends to Italian Barberas and Sangioveses. Most wineries are open for tastings at least on weekend afternoons, and some of the top ones are open daily; several have shaded picnic areas. ■ TIP→ This region is gaining steam as a less-congested alternative to the Napa Valley.

GETTING HERE AND AROUND
Reach the Shenandoah Valley by turning east on Fiddletown Road in Plymouth, between Placerville and Sutter Creek, and then north on Plymouth-Shenandoah Road. You will need a car to explore the valley and its vineyards.

EXPLORING
Shenandoah Vineyards. A plummy Barbera and an almost chocolaty Zinfandel top this winery's repertoire, but for a contrast you can also try a startlingly crisp Sauvignon Blanc. The Tempranillo is also good. An adjacent gallery sells contemporary art, pottery, photographs, and souvenirs. ■ TIP→ Shenandoah is affiliated with the nearby Sobon Estate Winery, which has an engaging on-site museum about the area. ✉ *12300 Steiner Rd.* ☎ *209/245-4455* ⊕ *www.sobonwine.com* ⌑ *Tasting $5* ⊘ *Daily 10–5.*

12

Terre Rouge and Easton Wines. The winery of Bill and Jane Easton has two labels with two different wine-making styles: Terre Rouge focuses on Rhône-style wines, while Easton covers old-vine Zinfandel and Barbera. The winery has had good results with inky, soft Syrahs and Enigma, a Rhône-style white blend of Marsanne, Viognier, and Roussane. ■**TIP→** You can picnic on the shaded patio here and there's a pétanque court nearby. ✉ *10801 Dickson Rd.* ☎ *209/245–4277* ⊕ *www.terrerougewines.com* ✇ *Tasting $5* ☉ *Nov.–Aug., Thurs.–Mon. 11–4; Sept.–Oct., daily 11–4.*

Vino Noceto. This winery is an example of the benefits of focusing mostly on one varietal—in this case Sangiovese—and doing it well. Owners Suzy and Jim Gullett produce their Sangioveses in several different styles, from light and fruity to rich and heavy. They also produce small lots of wines from other varietals. ✉ *11011 Shenandoah Rd., at Dickson Rd.* ☎ *209/245–6556* ⊕ *www.noceto.com* ✇ *Tasting free* ☉ *Weekdays 11–4, weekends 11–5.*

WHERE TO EAT

$$$$
MODERN
AMERICAN
Fodor's Choice
★

✕ **Taste.** A serendipitous find on the dusty streets of tiny Plymouth, Taste serves eclectic modern dishes made from fresh local fare. Phyllo-wrapped mushroom "cigars" or pan-seared scallops served with golden-beet risotto, kumquat, mint, fennel, and orange butter. Toss in tahini-grilled cauliflower with red wine–braised carrots and turnip greens, and even the vegetarians leave happy. ■**TIP→** Gold Country wine making can be hit or miss, but with several sommeliers on staff, this is a terrific place to find out which producers are worth seeking out. There's also a great beer list. $ *Average main: $32* ✉ *9402 Main St.* ☎ *209/245–3463* ⊕ *www.restauranttaste.com* ☉ *Closed Tues. and Wed. No lunch weekdays.*

AMADOR CITY

6 miles south of Plymouth.

The history of tiny Amador City mirrors the boom-bust-boom cycle of many Gold Country towns. With an output of $42 million in gold, its Keystone Mine was one of the most productive in the Mother Lode. After all the gold was extracted, the miners cleared out, and the area suffered. Amador City now derives its wealth from tourists, who come to browse through its antiques and specialty shops, most of them on or just off Highway 49.

GETTING HERE AND AROUND

Park where you can along Old Highway 49 (a bypass diverts Highway 49 traffic around Sutter Creek and Amador City), and walk around.

WHERE TO STAY

$$
B&B/INN

🛏 **Imperial Hotel.** The whimsically decorated mock-Victorian rooms at this 1879 hotel give a modern twist to the excesses of the era. **Pros:** comfortable; good restaurant and bar; tiny-town charm. **Cons:** no nightlife. $ *Rooms from: $135* ✉ *14202 Old Hwy. 49* ☎ *209/267–9172* ⊕ *www. imperialamador.com* ⤷ *6 rooms, 3 suites* ⦿*◯*❘ *Breakfast.*

SUTTER CREEK

2 miles south of Amador City.

Sutter Creek is a charming conglomeration of balconied buildings, Victorian homes, and neo–New England structures. The stores on Main Street (formerly part of Highway 49, which was rerouted) are worth visiting for works by the many local artists and craftspeople.

GETTING HERE AND AROUND

Arrive here by car on Highway 49. There's no public transit, but downtown is walkable. The visitor center organizes walking tours.

ESSENTIALS

Information Sutter Creek Visitor Center ✉ *71A Main St.* ☎ *209/267–1344* ⊕ *www.suttercreek.org.*

EXPLORING

Monteverde Store Museum. This store, opened 1896, is a relic from the past: its final owner walked out more than four decades ago and never returned. These days you can peruse what he left behind, including typical wares from a century ago, an elaborate antique scale, and a chair-encircled potbellied stove. ✉ *3 Randolph St.* ☎ *209/267–0493* ☉ *Thurs.–Mon. if volunteers available, hrs vary.*

WHERE TO EAT AND STAY

$$
AMERICAN
✕ **Susan's Place.** Fresh produce, prompt and attentive service, and a lovely patio (especially so on warm summer evenings) distinguish this local favorite a half-block off the main drag. The serving of wine is a big deal here; there's even a "mystery wine" option that leaves the bottle (or glass) choice up to the owner. Try the eggplant and Portobello mushrooms on grilled panini bread. ⑤ *Average main: $20* ✉ *15 Eureka St.* ☎ *209/267–0945* ⊕ *www.susansplace.com* ☉ *Closed Mon.–Wed.*

$$
B&B/INN
🖼 **Eureka Street Inn.** The lead- and stained-glass windows and the original redwood paneling, wainscoting, and beams—and, oh yes, those gas-log fireplaces in most rooms—lend the Eureka Street Inn a cozy feel. **Pros:** quiet location; lovely porch; engaging owners. **Cons:** only four rooms. ⑤ *Rooms from: $145* ✉ *55 Eureka St.* ☎ *209/267–5500, 800/399–2389* ⊕ *www.eurekastreetinn.com* ⊡ *4 rooms* ⦿ *Breakfast.*

$$$
B&B/INN
🖼 **The Foxes Inn of Sutter Creek.** The rooms in this 1857 white-clapboard house are handsome, with high ceilings, antique beds, and armoires; five have gas fireplaces. **Pros:** lovely inside and out; friendly owners. **Cons:** pricey. ⑤ *Rooms from: $200* ✉ *77 Main St.* ☎ *209/267–5882, 800/987–3344* ⊕ *www.foxesinn.com* ⊡ *5 rooms, 2 suites* ⦿ *Breakfast.*

$$
B&B/INN
🖼 **Grey Gables Inn.** Charming yet modern, this inn brings a touch of the English countryside to the Gold Country; the rooms, named after British poets, have gas-log fireplaces. **Pros:** English feel; tasteful interiors. **Cons:** hovers over main road; not much to do in town after dark. ⑤ *Rooms from: $163* ✉ *161 Hanford St.* ☎ *209/267–1039, 800/473–9422* ⊕ *www.greygables.com* ⊡ *8 rooms* ⦿ *Breakfast.*

$
HOTEL
🖼 **Sutter Creek Days Inn.** If you're on a budget, this hotel is a good choice; the rooms have coffeemakers, and most have queen-size beds. **Pros:** affordable; convenient; clean. **Cons:** can feel a bit impersonal. ⑤ *Rooms from: $84* ✉ *271 Hanford St.* ☎ *209/267–9177* ⊕ *www.daysinn.com/suttercreek* ⊡ *52 rooms* ⦿ *Breakfast.*

Continued on page 500

EUREKA! CALIFORNIA'S GOLD RUSH

When James W. Marshall burst into John Sutter's Mill on January 24, 1848, carrying flecks of gold in his hat, the millwright unleashed the glittering California gold rush with these immortal words:

"Boys, I believe I've found a gold mine!"

Before it was over, drowsy San Francisco had become the boomtown of the Golden West, Columbia's mines alone yielded $87,000,000, and California's Mother Lode—a vein of gold-bearing quartz that stretched 150 miles across the Sierra Nevada foothills—had been nearly tapped dry. Even though the gold rush soon became the gold bust, today you can still strike it rich by visiting the historic sites where it all happened.

Journey down the Gold Country Highway—a serpentine, nearly 300-mi-long two-lane route appropriately numbered 49—to find pure vacation treasure: fascinating mother lode towns, rip-roaring mining camps, and historic strike sites. In fact, in Placerville—as the former Hangtown, this spot saw so much new money and crime that outlaws were hanged in pairs—you can still pan the streams. And after you've seen the sights, the prospects remain just as golden: the entire region is a trove of gorgeous wineries, fun eateries, and Victorian-era hotels.

by: Reed Parsell and Robert I.C. Fisher

ALL THAT GLITTERED: '49ER FEVER

From imagination springs adventure, and perhaps no event in the 19th century provoked more wild adventures than the California gold rush of 1848 to 1855.

James Marshall   1856 U.S. quarter   John Sutter

GOLD IN THEM THAR HILLS California's golden lava was discovered purely by accident. Upon finding his cattle ranch had gone to ruin while he was away fighting in the Mexican-American War, New Jersey native James W. Marshall decided to build a sawmill, with John Sutter, outside the town of Coloma, 40 miles upstream of Sutter's Fort on the American River. To better power the mill, he had a wider siphon created to divert the river water and, one morning, spotted golden flakes in the trench. Rich fur magnate Sutter tried to keep the mother strike quiet, but his own staff soon decamped to pan the streams and the secret was out. The gold rush's impact was so profound that, practically overnight, it catapulted San Francisco into one of the nation's—and the world's—wealthiest cities.

BROTHER, CAN YOU SPARE AN INGOT? After Marshall, 37 at the time, saw his fledgling mill abandoned by workers who went to pan the streams, he left Coloma for almost a decade. During the 1860s he made some money as a vintner there—a dicey profession for a reported alcoholic. Eventually Marshall's wine business dried up, and he returned to prospecting in the 1870s. But without success. For six years starting in 1872, the state Legislature gave him a small pension as an acknowledgment of his gold rush importance, but for the last years of his life he was

practically penniless. He died on Aug. 10, 1885, at age 74.w

THE GOLD CRUSH Before the gold rush ended, in 1855, it is estimated that it drew 300,000 people—Americans, Europeans, and Chinese—to the Sierra Nevada foothills to seek their fortune. Sadly, accidents, disease, and skirmishes with Native Americans took their toll on both the prospectors and the environment. In addition, the gold lust of '49er fever left more than a thousand murders in its wake (not counting the infamous "suspended" sentences meted out at Hangtown).

BOOM TO BUST

Jan. 24, 1848: James W. Marshall spies specks of bright rock in the streambed at his sawmill's site; Sutter certifies they are gold.

May, 1848: California's coastal communities empty out as prospectors flock to the hills to join the "forty-eighters."

Aug. 19, 1848: The *New York Herald* is the first East Coast newspaper to report a gold rush in California.

Oct. 13, 1849: California's state constitution is approved in Monterey. The state's new motto becomes "Eureka!"

1855: The California gold rush effectively ends, as digging for the precious mineral becomes increasingly difficult, and large corporations monopolize mining operations.

DID YOU KNOW?

You can still pan the streams, but any shiny stuff will usually be worthless iron pyrite. Here a young prospector tries his hand at Marshall Gold Discovery State Park.

GOING FOR THE GOLD

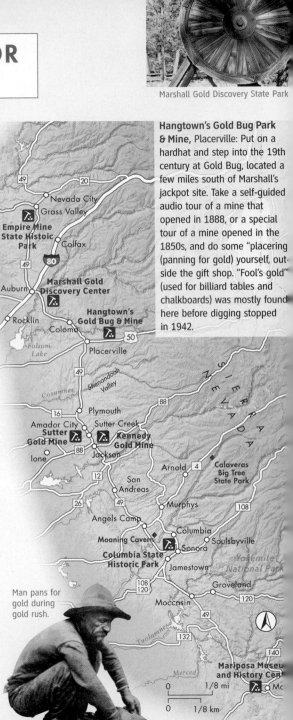

Marshall Gold Discovery State Park

If you want to go prospecting for the best sightseeing treasures in Gold Country, just follow this map.

Coloma

Empire Mine State Historic Park, Grass Valley: During the century that it was operating, Empire Mine produced some 5.6 million ounces of gold. More than 350 miles of tunnels were dug, most under water. Operations ceased in 1956, but today visitors to the 800-acre park can go on 50-minute guided tours of the mines and enjoy great hiking trails and picnic spots.

Marshall Gold Discovery State Historic Park, Coloma: Here's where it all began—a can't-miss gold rush site. See the stone cairn that marks the spot of James Marshall's discovery, the huge statue of him that rests on his grave site, and visit—together with crowds of schoolchildren—the updated museum, and more.

Hangtown's Gold Bug Park & Mine, Placerville: Put on a hardhat and step into the 19th century at Gold Bug, located a few miles south of Marshall's jackpot site. Take a self-guided audio tour of a mine that opened in 1888, or a special tour of a mine opened in the 1850s, and do some "placering (panning for gold) yourself, outside the gift shop. "Fool's gold" (used for billiard tables and chalkboards) was mostly found here before digging stopped in 1942.

Man pans for gold during gold rush.

Sutter Gold Mine: Between Amador City and Sutter Creek off Highway 49, this is the place to see how the so-called "Forty-Niner" individual prospectors were succeeded by large, deep-pocket mining companies. One-hour tours, offered daily April through most of October, take visitors deep into a hard-rock mine, where they can see ore veins that contain gold and learn the basics of hydraulic extraction.

Kennedy Gold Mine, Jackson: At 5,912 feet below ground, this is one of the world's deepest mines. Its head frame is one of the most dominant man-made sights along Highway 49's 295 miles. In operation from 1880 until World War II, the mine produced tens of millions of dollars of gold. One-hour tours, offered weekends and holidays from March through October, include a look inside the stately Mine Office.

Columbia State Historic Park. Just north of Sonora, this is the best extant example of a gold rush-era town as it appeared in the mid-19th century. During its "golden" years, Columbia yielded more than $85 million in gold. Since World War II, the town has been restored. Fandango halls, Wells Fargo stage coaches, and a costumed staff bring a working 1850's mining town to life again.

Gold dollars

Mariposa Museum and History Center, Mariposa: Find all sorts of mining equipment, including a five-stamp ore mill, at this modest museum in the gold rush region's southernmost area. Also here is the fascinating California State Mining and Mineral Museum, home to a famous 13-pound golden nugget.

A PROSPECTING PRIMER

Grab any non-Teflon-coated pan with sloping sides and head up to "them thar hills." Find a stream—preferably one containing black sand—you can stoop beside, and then:

■ Scoop out sediment to fill your pan.

■ Add water, then gently shake the pan sideways, back and forth. This allows any gold to settle at the bottom.

■ Pick out and toss away any larger rocks.

■ Keep adding water, keep shaking the pan, and slowly pour the loosened waste gravel over the rim of the pan, making sure not to upend the pan while doing so.

■ If you're left with gold, yell "Eureka!" then put it in a glass container. Your findings may not make you rich, but will entitle you to bragging rights for as long as you keep the gold handy to show friends.

■**TIP→** If you'd rather not pan on your own, plenty of attractions and museums in the Gold Country will let you try your hand at prospecting. See listings in this chapter for more details on these historic sites.

JACKSON

8 miles south of Sutter Creek.

Jackson wasn't the Gold Country's rowdiest town, but the party lasted longer here than most anywhere else: "girls' dormitories" (aka brothels) and nickel slot machines flourished until the mid-1950s. Jackson also had the world's deepest and richest gold mines, the Kennedy and the Argonaut, which together produced $70 million in gold. Most of the miners who worked the lode were of Serbian or Italian origin, and they gave the town a European character that persists to this day. Jackson has pioneer cemeteries whose headstones tell the stories of local Serbian and Italian families. The city's official website (⊕ *ci.jackson.ca.us;* click on "Visitor Center") has great cemetery and walking-tour maps; there are some interesting shops downtown.

GETTING HERE AND AROUND

Arrive by car on Highway 49. You can walk to downtown sights but otherwise will need a car.

EXPLORING

Fodor'sChoice **Preston Castle.** History buffs and ghost hunters regularly make the trip to
★ this fantastically creepy building that was built to house troubled youth in 1894. Having fallen into a state of disrepair, the building is slowly undergoing a full renovation, and tours are available by appointment and on certain Saturdays throughout the year (it's best to call ahead to confirm schedule). The dramatic Romanesque-revival structure has appeared on TV's *Ghost Hunters,* and during tours of this 156-room building you'll learn all sorts of spine-tingling tales, including one about a student murdering a housekeeper and then rolling her up in a carpet. ⊠ *909 Palm Dr., 12 miles west of Jackson via Hwys. 88 and 104, Ione* ☎ *209/256–3623* ⊕ *www.prestoncastle.com* ⊠ *$10* ⊗ *1st, 2nd, and 3rd Sat. of month, 10–1; or by appointment.*

St. Sava Serbian Orthodox Church. The terraced cemetery on the grounds of the handsome church is an impressive sight. ⊠ *724 N. Main St.*

WHERE TO EAT AND STAY

$ ✕ **Mel and Faye's Diner.** A local hangout famous for its "Moo Burger"—
AMERICAN so big it still makes cow sounds, presumably—the diner is run by its namesakes' son, who has added slightly more sophisticated fare for breakfast, lunch, and dinner. ⑤ *Average main: $10* ⊠ *31 Main St.* ☎ *209/223–0853* ⊕ *melandfayesdiner.com* ⊗ *Closed Tues.*

$ ⊞ **Hotel Leger.** Home to a still convivial old saloon that was one of the
HOTEL rowdiest miners' haunts back in the day, this atmospheric 1851 inn, which is about 8 miles south of Jackson, is inhabited today by friendly ghosts. **Pros:** friendly and accomodating proprietors; rich in history; reasonably priced. **Con:** bathrooms are private but some are located across the hall; thin walls and creaky floorboards. ⑤ *Rooms from: $95* ⊠ *8304 Main St., Mokelumme Hill* ☎ *209/286–1401* ⊕ *www.hotelleger. com* ⇆ *7 rooms, 6 suites* ⦿ *No meals.*

ANGELS CAMP

12

20 miles south of Jackson.

Angels Camp is famous chiefly for its May jumping-frog contest, based on Mark Twain's short story "The Celebrated Jumping Frog of Calaveras County." The writer reputedly heard the story of the jumping frog from Ross Coon, proprietor of Angels Hotel, which has been in operation since 1856. It's a favorite destination these days among outdoor adventurers, who love exploring the subterranean caverns, and fishing for salmon, trout, and bass in the area's crystal clear rivers and lakes.

GETTING HERE AND AROUND

Angels Camp is at the intersection of Highway 49 and Highway 4. You'll need a car to get here and around.

EXPLORING

Angels Camp Museum. Gold-rush relics are on display here: photos, rocks, petrified wood, blacksmith and mining equipment, even a horse-drawn hearse. The carriage house out back holds 31 carriages and impressive mineral specimens. ⊠ *753 S. Main St.* ☎ *209/736–2963* ⊕ *www. angelscampmuseumfoundation.org* 🎟 *$5* ⊗ *Thurs.–Mon. 10–4.*

FAMILY **California Cavern.** A ½-mile subterranean trail winds through large chambers and past underground streams and lakes. There aren't many steps to climb, but it's a strenuous walk with some narrow passageways and steep spots. The caverns, at a constant 55°F, contain crystalline formations not found elsewhere, and the 80-minute guided tour explains local history and geology. ⊠ *Cave City Rd., 9 miles east of San Andreas on Mountain Ranch Rd., then about 3 miles on Cave City Rd.* ☎ *209/736–2708* ⊕ *www.caverntours.com* 🎟 *$14.95* ⊗ *Mar. and Apr., daily 10–4; May–Oct., daily 10–5; Nov.–Feb. weekends 10–4; hrs can vary, call to confirm.*

FAMILY **Moaning Cavern.** There's no better way than to see what life was like
Fodor'sChoice underground for prospectors than to descend into the belly of the
★ land. This fascinating tour let's you wander down a chasm into the wonder of an ancient limestone cave. Take the 235-step spiral staircase built in 1922 into this vast cavern. More intrepid explorers can rappel into the chamber—ropes and instruction are provided. Otherwise, the only way inside is via the 45-minute tour, during which you'll see giant (and still growing) stalactites and stalagmites and an archaeological site that holds some of the oldest human remains yet found in America. Outside there are three zip lines, starting at $44 per person. ⊠ *5350 Moaning Cave Rd., off Parrots Ferry Rd., about 2 miles south of Vallecito* ☎ *209/736–2708* ⊕ *www.caverntours.com* 🎟 *$14.95* ⊗ *May–Oct., daily 9–6; Nov.–Apr., weekdays 10–5, weekends 9–5; hrs can vary, call to confirm.*

MURPHYS

10 miles northeast of Angels Camp.

Murphys is the Gold Country's most compact, orderly town, with enough shops and restaurants to keep families busy for at least a half-day, and more than 20 tasting rooms within walking distance. A well-preserved town of white-picket fences, Victorian houses, and interesting shops, it exhibits an upscale vibe. Horatio Alger and Ulysses S. Grant came through here, staying at what's now called the Murphys Historic Hotel & Lodge when they, along with many other 19th-century tourists, came to investigate the giant sequoia groves in nearby Calaveras Big Trees State Park.

12

GETTING HERE AND AROUND

Murphys is 10 miles northeast of Highway 49 on Highway 4. You'll need to drive here. Parking can be difficult on summer weekends.

EXPLORING

Calaveras Big Tree State Park. The park protects hundreds of the largest and rarest living things on the planet—magnificent giant sequoia redwood trees. Some are 3,000 years old, 90 feet around at the base, and 250 feet tall. There are campgrounds and picnic areas; swimming, wading, fishing, and sunbathing on the Stanislaus River are popular in summer. Enjoy the "three senses" trail, designated for the blind, with interpretive signs in Braille that guide visitors to touch the bark and encourage children to slow down and enjoy the forest in a more sensory way. ⌧ *Off Hwy. 4, 15 miles northeast of Murphys, 4 miles northeast of Arnold, Angels Camp* ☎ *209/795–2334* ⊕ *www.parks.ca.gov* ⌧ *$10 per vehicle* ☉ *Park: daily sunrise–sunset. Visitor center: May–Oct., daily 10–4; Nov.–Apr., weekends 9–5.*

Ironstone Vineyards. Tours here take in spectacular gardens and underground tunnels cooled by a waterfall, and include the automated performance of a restored silent-movie-era pipe organ. On display near the tasting room is a 44-pound specimen of crystalline gold. The winery, known for Merlot, Cabernet Sauvignon, and Cabernet Franc, hosts concerts and other events. Its deli has picnic items. ■**TIP➜** Ironstone is worth a visit even if you don't drink wine. ⌧ *1894 6 Mile Rd.* ⊹ *From Jones St. in town, head south on Scott St.* ☎ *209/728–1251* ⊕ *www. ironstonevineyards.com* ⌧ *Tastings $3–$6* ☉ *Daily 10–5; open until 6 in summer.*

WHERE TO EAT AND STAY

$$
AMERICAN
✕ **Grounds.** Light entrées, grilled vegetables, chicken, seafood, and steak are the specialties at this bustling bistro and coffee shop with a good wine list. Sandwiches, salads, and homemade soups are served for lunch. The crowd is friendly and the service attentive. ⑤ *Average main: $20* ⌧ *402 Main St.* ☎ *209/728–8663* ⊕ *www.groundsrestaurant.com.*

$
HOTEL
🔲 **Murphys Historic Hotel & Lodge.** This 1855 stone hotel, whose register has seen the signatures of Mark Twain and the bandit Black Bart, figured in a Bret Harte short story. **Pros:** historical ambience; great bar; downtown location. **Cons:** dated; creaky. ⑤ *Rooms from: $109* ⌧ *457 Main St.* ☎ *209/728–3444, 800/532–7684* ⊕ *www.murphyshotel.com* ⤴ *29 rooms, 20 with bath* ⦿︎ *No meals.*

COLUMBIA

14 miles south of Angels Camp.

Columbia is the gateway for Columbia State Historic Park, one of the Gold Country's most visited sites. The historic Fallon House Theater is a great place for families to participate in living history activities like candle dipping and soap making on weekends. There are several inviting spots for a picnic in the area.

GETTING HERE AND AROUND

The only way to get here is by car, via either Highway 4 (the northern route) or Highway 49 (the southern) from Angels Camp.

EXPLORING

FAMILY

Fodor's Choice

★

Columbia State Historic Park. Columbia comes as close to a gold-rush town in its heyday as any site in the Gold Country. Usually, you can ride a stagecoach, pan for gold, and watch a blacksmith working at an anvil. Street musicians perform in summer. Restored or reconstructed buildings include a Wells Fargo Express office, a Masonic temple, an old-fashioned candy store, saloons, a firehouse, churches, a school, and a newspaper office. At times, all are staffed to simulate a working 1850s town. The park also includes the must-stop, **Historic Fallon House Theater,** where Broadway-quality shows are performed Wednesday through Sunday—Mark Twain once performed in this gorgeous Victorian structure. The town's two 19th-century historic lodgings, the Fallon Hotel ($) and City Hotel ($–$$) perch you in the past; to reserve a hotel or cottage go to ⊕ *www.reserveamerica.com.* ⊠ *11255 Jackson St.* ☎ *209/588–9128* ⊕ *www.parks.ca.gov/columbia* 🎟 *Free* ⊘ *Daily 9–5.*

SONORA

4 miles south of Columbia.

Miners from Mexico founded Sonora and made it the biggest town in the Mother Lode. Following a period of racial and ethnic strife, the Mexican settlers moved on, and Yankees built the commercial city visible today. Sonora's historic downtown section sits atop the Big Bonanza Mine, one of the richest in the state. Another mine, on the site of nearby Sonora High School, yielded 990 pounds of gold in a single week in 1879. Reminders of the gold rush are everywhere in Sonora, in prim Victorian houses, typical Sierra-stone storefronts, and awning-shaded sidewalks. Reality intrudes beyond the town's historic heart, with strip malls, shopping centers, and modern motels.

GETTING HERE AND AROUND

Arrive in Sonora by car via Highway 49 (if coming from Columbia, drive south on Parrots Ferry Road). Parking can be difficult on the busy main drag, Washington Street (Highway 49).

EXPLORING

Tuolumne County Museum and History Center. The small museum occupies a historic gold rush–era building that served as a jail until 1960. Vintage firearms and paraphernalia, gold specimens, and MiWuk baskets are among the many artifacts on display. ✉ *158 W. Bradford St.* ☎ *209/532–1317* ⊕ *www.tchistory.org* 🎫 *Free* ⊙ *Weekdays 10–4, Sat. 10–3:30* ⊙ *Closed Sun.*

WHERE TO EAT AND STAY

$ ✕ **Diamondback Grill and Wine Bar.** The bright decor and refined atmo-
AMERICAN sphere suggest more ambitious fare, but burgers are what this place is about. Locals crowd the tables, especially after 6 pm, for the ground-meat patties, beer-battered onion rings, veggie burger, and fine wines. ⑤ *Average main: $11* ✉ *93 S. Washington St.* ☎ *209/532–6661* ⊕ *www.thediamondbackgrill.com* ⊙ *Closed Sun.*

$$ 🛏 **Barretta Gardens Bed and Breakfast Inn.** This inn is perfect for a roman-
B&B/INN tic getaway, with elegant Victorian rooms varying in size, all furnished with period pieces. **Pros:** lovely grounds; yummy breakfasts; romantic. **Cons:** only seven rooms. ⑤ *Rooms from: $159* ✉ *700 S. Barretta St.* ☎ *209/532–6039, 800/206–3333* ⊕ *www.barrettagardens.com* ⇆ *7 rooms* ⑩ *Breakfast.*

JAMESTOWN

4 miles south of Sonora.

Compact Jamestown supplies a touristy view of gold rush–era life. Shops in brightly colored buildings along Main Street sell antiques and gift items. You can try your hand at panning for gold here or explore a bit of railroad history.

GETTING HERE AND AROUND

Jamestown lies at the intersection of north–south Highway 49 and east–west Highway 108. You'll need a car to tour here.

EXPLORING

FAMILY **Gold Prospecting Adventures.** You'll get a real feel (sort of) for the life of a prospector on the three-hour gold-panning excursions led by this outfit's congenial, steeped-in-history tour guides. You might even strike gold at the Jimtown Mine. ✉ *18170 Main St.* ☎ *209/984–4653, 800/596–0009* ⊕ *www.goldprospecting.com* ☞ *Call for hrs and fees.*

Fodor's Choice **Railtown 1897.** A must for rail enthusiasts and families with kids, this
★ is one of the most intact early roundhouses (maintenance facilities) in North America. You can hop aboard a steam train for a 40-minute journey—bring along the family dog if you'd like. The docents entertain guests with tales about the history of locomotion. Listen to the origi-nal rotor and pulleys in the engine house and take in the smell of axle grease. Walk through a genteel passenger car with dusty-green velvet seats and ornate metalwork, where Grace Kelly and Gary Cooper filmed a scene in the epic Western *High Noon.* You can also climb onto a his-toric train to see where the fireman once shoveled coal into the tender. ✉ *5th Ave. and Reservoir Rd.* ☎ *209/984–3953* ⊕ *www.railtown1897. org* 🎫 *Roundhouse tour $5; train ride $15* ⊙ *Apr.–Oct., daily 9:30–4:30; Nov.–Mar., daily 10–3; train ride, weekends Apr.–Oct. (additional holiday rides are offered some weekends in late Nov. and Dec.).*

WHERE TO STAY

$ ⚏ **Black Oak Casino Resort.** About 12 miles east of Jamestown off High-
RESORT   way 108, this flashy, contemporary property appeals heavily to casino
FAMILY   gamers, but it's also just a nice place to stay with well-outfitted rooms
(comfy bedding, down pillows, and alarm clocks with MP3 players) and
a central Gold Country location. **Pros:** clean and spacious rooms; plenty
of diversions on hand for both kids and adults. **Cons:** must go through
smokey casino to reach bowling alley and restaurants; there's nothing quaint or historic about this place. $ *Rooms from: $109* ✉ *19400
Tuolumne Rd. N, Tuolumne* ☎ *209/928–9300* ⊕ *www.blackoakcasino.
com* ⟿ *148 rooms* ❧○❘ *No meals.*

$$ ⚏ **McCaffrey House Bed and Breakfast Inn.** Remoteness is one of McCaf-
B&B/INN   frey's appeals—it's about 20 miles east of Jamestown on Highway 108
in the mountain community of Twain Harte. **Pros:** large rooms; wonder-
ful nearby hiking; romantically remote. **Cons:** remote. $ *Rooms from:
$169* ✉ *23251 Hwy. 108* ☎ *209/586–0757, 888/586–0757* ⊕ *www.
mccaffreyhouse.com* ⟿ *8 rooms* ❧○❘ *Breakfast.*

$$ ⚏ **National Hotel.** The National has been in business since 1859, and
HOTEL   its furnishings—brass beds, regal comforters, and lace curtains—are
authentic but not overly embellished. **Pros:** historic feel; great brunches.
Cons: not much happens in town after dark. $ *Rooms from: $140*
✉ *18183 Main St.* ☎ *209/984–3446, 800/894–3446 in CA* ⊕ *www.
national-hotel.com* ⟿ *9 rooms* ❧○❘ *Breakfast.*

THE GOLD COUNTRY—NORTH

Gold has had a significant presence along this northern stretch of Highway 49, whose highlights include the bucolic Empire State Historic
Park and Coloma, where the discovery of a few nuggets triggered the
gold rush.

COLOMA

8 miles northwest of Placerville.

The California gold rush started in Coloma. "My eye was caught with
the glimpse of something shining in the bottom of the ditch," James
Marshall recalled. Marshall himself never found any more "color," as
gold came to be called.

GETTING HERE AND AROUND

A car is the only practical way to get to Coloma, via Highway 49. Once
parked, you can walk to all the worthwhile sights.

EXPLORING

FAMILY   **Marshall Gold Discovery State Historic Park.** Most of Coloma lies within
the historic park. Though crowded with tourists in summer, Coloma
hardly resembles the mob scene it was in 1849, when 2,000 prospectors
staked out claims along the streambed. The town's population grew to
4,000, supporting seven hotels, three banks, and many stores and businesses. But when reserves of the precious metal dwindled, prospectors
left as quickly as they had come. A working reproduction of an 1840s
mill lies near the spot where James Marshall first saw gold. A trail

leads to a modest sign (considering the impact) marking his discovery. ■**TIP→** Take a stroll up the surrounding hills for sublime views. ✉ *310 Back St., off Hwy. 49* ☎ *530/622–3470* ⊕ *www.parks.ca.gov* 🔢 *$8 per vehicle* ☉ *Park: daily 8–sunset. Museum: Mar.–Oct., Tues.–Sat. 10–4; Nov.–Feb., daily 10–3.*

12

WHERE TO STAY

$$
B&B/INN
🏨 **Coloma Country Inn.** Four of the rooms at this B&B on 2½ acres in the state historic park are inside an 1850s farmhouse, and two suites with kitchenettes occupy the carriage house. **Pros:** convenient to the park; quiet; leisurely ambience. **Cons:** no nightlife. ⑤ *Rooms from: $135* ✉ *345 High St.* ☎ *530/622–6919* ⊕ *www.colomacountryinn.com* 🛏 *4 rooms, 2 suites* ⑩ *Breakfast.*

AUBURN

18 miles northwest of Coloma; 34 miles northeast of Sacramento.

Auburn is the Gold Country town most accessible to travelers on Interstate 80. An important transportation center during the gold rush, downtown Auburn has a small Old Town district with narrow climbing streets, cobblestone lanes, wooden sidewalks, and many original buildings. ■**TIP→** Fresh produce, flowers, baked goods, and gifts are for sale at the farmers' market, held on Saturday morning year-round.

GETTING HERE AND AROUND

Amtrak serves Auburn, though most visitors arrive by car on Highway 49 or Interstate 80. Once downtown, you can tour on foot.

EXPLORING

Bernhard Museum Complex. Party like it's 1889 at this space whose main structure opened in 1851 as the Traveler's Rest Hotel and for 100 years was the residence of the Bernhard family. The congenial docents, dressed in Victorian garb, describe the family's history and 19th-century life in Auburn. ✉ *291 Auburn–Folsom Rd.* ☎ *530/889–6500* 🔢 *Free* ☉ *Tues.–Sun. 11–4.*

FAMILY **Gold Country Museum.** You'll get a feel for life in the mines at this museum whose highlights include a re-created mine tunnel, a gold-panning stream, and a reproduction saloon. ✉ *1273 High St.* ☎ *530/889–6500* 🔢 *Free to museum, $3 to pan for gold* ☉ *Tues.–Sun. 11–4.*

Placer County Courthouse. Auburn's standout structure is the Placer County Courthouse. The classic gold-dome building houses the Placer County Museum, which documents the area's history—Native American, railroad, agricultural, and mining—from the early 1700s to 1900. ✉ *101 Maple St.* ☎ *530/889–6500* 🔢 *Free* ☉ *Daily 10–4.*

WHERE TO EAT AND STAY

$
AMERICAN
✕ **Awful Annie's.** Big patio umbrellas (and outdoor heaters when necessary) allow patrons to take in the Old Town view from this popular spot for lunch or breakfast—one specialty is a chili omelet. A second Annie's is at 490 G Street in nearby Lincoln. ⑤ *Average main: $10* ✉ *160 Sacramento St.* ☎ *530/888–9857* ⊕ *www.awfulannies.com* ☉ *No dinner.*

$$$
MODERN
AMERICAN
Fodor's Choice
★

✕ **Carpe Vino.** Chef Eric Alexander is known for his hearty and imaginative French-inspired dishes—sophisticated fare presented in a nonchalant, almost effortless way, as if ingredients rolled right from the farm basket onto your plate. Consider purple and yellow beets in olive oil with fans of sliced fennel stalks and creamy panna cotta, roasted bone marrow, duck-fat fries, and brothy mussels steamed with lemon and chilis. This gem is tucked into an old downtown saloon and mine with a handsome old bar. Note the extensive and varied wine list. ⑤ *Average main: $28* ✉ *1568 Lincoln Way* ☎ *530/823–0320* ⊕ *www. carpevinoauburn.com* ⊘ *Closed Mon.*

$$
HOTEL

🏨 **Holiday Inn Auburn Hotel.** Above the freeway across from Old Town, this hotel has a welcoming lobby and chain-standard but nice rooms. **Pros:** convenient; clean; books available on loan. **Cons:** noise in rooms near parking lot. ⑤ *Rooms from: $127* ✉ *120 Grass Valley Hwy.* ☎ *530/887–8787, 800/814–8787* ⊕ *www.auburnhi.com* ⟿ *96 rooms, 6 suites* ⑩ *Breakfast.*

GRASS VALLEY

24 miles north of Auburn.

More than half of California's total gold production was extracted from mines around Grass Valley, including the Empire Mine, which, along with the North Star Mining Museum, is among the Gold Country's most fascinating attractions.

GETTING HERE AND AROUND

You'll need a car to get here. Take Highway 20 east from Interstate 5 or west from Interstate 80. Highway 49 is the north–south route into town. Gold Country Stage vehicles (☎ *530/477–0103* ⊘ *Weekdays 7–6*) serve some attractions. Expect to wait, though.

EXPLORING

FAMILY **Empire Mine State Historic Park.** Relive the days of gold, grit, and glory, when this mine was one of the biggest and most prosperous hard-rock gold mines in North America. Visit Bourn Cottage with its exquisite woodwork, lovely fountains, and stunning gardens. On a tour, you can walk into a mineshaft and peer into into dark, deep recesses—you can almost imagine what it felt like to work this vast operation. An estimated 5.8 million ounces of gold were extracted from the mine's 367 miles of underground passages during its lifetime. Dressed-up docents portraying colorful characters who shaped Northern California's history share stories about the period. The grounds have picnic tables and gentle trails—perfect for a family outing. ✉ *10791 E. Empire St.* ☎ *530/273–8522* ⊕ *www.parks.ca.gov* 🎟 *$7* ⊘ *Daily 10–5.*

Holbrooke Hotel. The recently refurnished landmark hotel ($$), built in 1851, hosted entertainer Lola Montez and writer Mark Twain as well as Ulysses S. Grant and other U.S. presidents. The restaurant-saloon ($$) is one of the oldest operating west of the Mississippi. ✉ *212 W. Main St.* ☎ *530/273–1353, 800/933–7077* ⊕ *www.holbrooke.com.*

FAMILY **North Star Mining Museum.** Housed in a former powerhouse, the museum displays the 32-foot-high Pelton Water Wheel, said to be the largest ever

Almost 6 million ounces of gold were extracted from the Empire Mine.

built. It was used to power mining operations and was a forerunner of the modern turbines that generate hydroelectricity. Hands-on displays are geared to children. You can picnic nearby. ✉ *10933 Allison Ranch Rd.* ☎ *530/273–4255* ⊕ *www.nevadacountyhistory.org* 🖆 *Donation requested* ☉ *May–mid-Oct., Tues.–Sun. 11–5.*

WHERE TO EAT AND STAY

$ ✗ **Cousin Jack Pasties.** Meat- and vegetable-stuffed pasties are a taste
BRITISH of the region's history, having come across the Atlantic with Cornish miners and their families in the mid-19th century. The flaky crusts practically melt in your mouth. A simple food stand, Jack's is nonetheless a local landmark. ⑤ *Average main: $8* ✉ *100 S. Auburn St.* ☎ *530/272–9230* ▭ *No credit cards.*

$$ ✗ **Villa Venezia Restaurant.** Pasta and seafood are the specialties served
ITALIAN up in a cozy, warm Victorian building with an intimate patio area. The appetizers and salads very nearly outshine the outstanding main dishes. ⑤ *Average main: $22* ✉ *124 Bank St.* ☎ *530/273–3555* ⊕ *www.villavenezia.info* ☉ *No lunch Sat.–Thurs.*

NEVADA CITY

4 miles north of Grass Valley.

Nevada City, once known as the Queen City of the Northern Mines, is the most appealing of the northern Mother Lode towns. The iron-shutter brick buildings that line the narrow downtown streets contain antiques shops, galleries, boutiques, B&Bs, restaurants, and a winery. Horse-drawn carriage tours add to the romance, as do gas street lamps.

At one point in the 1850s, Nevada City had a population of nearly 10,000—enough to support much cultural activity. Today, about 3,100 people live here.

GETTING HERE AND AROUND

You'll need a car to get here. Take Highway 20 east from Interstate 5 or west from Interstate 80. Highway 49 is the north–south route into town. Gold Country Stage vehicles (☎ 530/477–0103 ☉ Weekdays 7–6) serve some attractions.

ESSENTIALS

Visitor Information Nevada City Chamber of Commerce ⊠ 132 Main St. ☎ 530/265-2692 ⊕ www.nevadacitychamber.com.

EXPLORING

Firehouse No. 1. With its gingerbread-trim bell tower, Firehouse No. 1 is one of the Gold Country's most distinctive buildings. A museum, it houses gold-rush artifacts and the altar from a Chinese joss house (temple). ⊠ 214 Main St. ☎ 530/265–5468 ⊒ Donation suggested ☉ May–Nov., Tue.–Sun. 1–4.

Nevada City Winery. Watch wine being created while you sip at this winery whose tasting room overlooks the production area. Syrah and Zinfandel are among the strengths here. ⊠ Miners Foundry Garage, 321 Spring St., at Bridge St. ☎ 530/265–9463, 800/203–9463 ⊕ www. ncwinery.com ⊒ Tasting and tour free ☉ Sun.–Thurs. noon–5, Fri. and Sat. noon–6; tour on Sat. at 1:30.

WHERE TO EAT AND STAY

$$$
ECLECTIC
✕ **Friar Tuck's.** Popular Friar Tuck's specializes in creative, interactive fondues and has an extensive menu of seafood, steaks, and pasta dishes, too. The sparkling interior has a late-19th century ambience—it's one of Nevada City's best indoor spaces. ⑤ Average main: $25 ⊠ 111 N. Pine St. ☎ 530/265–9093 ⊕ friartucks.com ☉ No lunch.

$
AMERICAN
✕ **South Pine Cafe.** Locals flock here, especially for brunch. Lobster and beef are on the menu, but the real attention-grabbers are vegetarian entrées and side dishes, such as breakfast potatoes and apple-ginger muffins. There's a branch in Grass Valley at 102 North Richardson Street. ⑤ Average main: $11 ⊠ 110 S. Pine St. ☎ 530/265–0260 ⊕ www. southpinecafe.com ☉ No dinner.

$$
B&B/INN
Fodor's Choice
★
🛏 **Red Castle Historic Lodgings.** Antique furnishings and Oriental rugs decorate the rooms of this 1857 Gothic-revival mansion, a fine option for those who appreciate the finer points of Victorian design. **Pros:** friendly owners; spectacular food; fascinating architecture. **Cons:** the walk uphill from downtown is a workout. ⑤ Rooms from: $155 ⊠ 109 Prospect St. ☎ 530/265–5135, 800/761–4766 ⊕ www.redcastleinn.com ⤳ 4 rooms, 3 suites ⑩ Breakfast.

LAKE TAHOE

With Reno, Nevada

WELCOME TO LAKE TAHOE

TOP REASONS TO GO

★ **The lake:** Blue, deep, and alpine pure, Lake Tahoe is far and away the main reason to visit this high Sierra paradise.

★ **Skiing:** Daring black-diamond runs or baby-bunny bumps—whether you're an expert, a beginner, or somewhere in between, there are many slopes to suit your skills at the numerous Tahoe-area ski parks.

★ **The great outdoors:** A ring of national forests and recreation areas linked by miles of trails makes Tahoe excellent for nature lovers.

★ **Dinner with a view:** You can picnic lakeside at state parks or dine in restaurants perched along the shore.

★ **A date with lady luck:** Whether you want to roll dice, play the slots, or hope the blackjack dealer goes bust before you do, you'll find round-the-clock gambling at the casinos on the Nevada side of the lake and in Reno.

1 California Side. With the exception of Stateline, Nevada—which, aside from its casino-hotel towers, seems almost indistinguishable from South Lake Tahoe, California—the California side is more developed than the Nevada side. Here you can find both commercial enterprises—restaurants, motels, lodges, resorts, residential subdivisions—and public-access facilities, such as historic sites, parks, campgrounds, marinas, and beaches.

2 Nevada Side. You don't need a highway sign to know when you've crossed from California into Nevada: the flashing lights and elaborate marquees of casinos announce legal gambling in garish hues. But you'll find more here than tables and slot machines. Reno, the Biggest Little City in the World, has a vibrant art scene and a serene downtown RiverWalk. And when you really need to get away from the chip-toting crowds, you can hike through pristine wilderness at Lake Tahoe–Nevada State Park, or hit the slopes near Incline Village.

GETTING ORIENTED

In the northern section of the Sierra Nevada mountain range, the Lake Tahoe area covers portions of four national forests, several state parks, and rugged wilderness areas with names like Desolation and Granite Chief. Lake Tahoe, the star attraction, straddles California and Nevada and is one of the world's largest, clearest, and deepest alpine lakes. The region's proximity to the Bay Area and Sacramento to the west and Reno to the east draws thrill seekers during ski season and again in summer when water sports, camping, and hiking are the dominant activities.

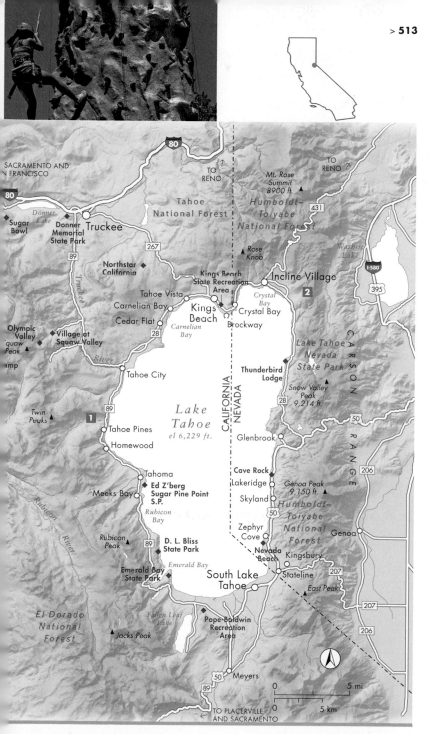

13

2

1

SACRAMENTO AND
N FRANCISCO

80

Donner
Lake

Sugar
Bowl

Donner
Memorial
State Park

Truckee

Northstar
California

89

267

Tahoe
National Forest

TO
RENO

Mt. Rose
Summit
8900 ft.

Humboldt-
Toiyabe
National Forest

431

Rose
Knob

Washoe
Lake

I-580

395

Kings Beach
State Recreation
Area

Incline Village

Tahoe Vista

Carnelian Bay

Cedar Flat

28

Kings
Beach

Crystal Bay

Crystal
Bay

Brockway

Carnelian
Bay

Olympic
Valley
quaw
Peak

Village at
Squaw Valley

mp

Truckee River

Tahoe City

Twin
Peaks

89

1

Tahoe Pines

Homewood

Lake
Tahoe
el 6,229 ft.

CALIFORNIA
NEVADA

Thunderbird
Lodge

Lake Tahoe
Nevada
State Park

Snow Valley
Peak
9,214 ft.

28

Glenbrook

CARSON RANGE

50

Tahoma

Ed Z'berg
Sugar Pine Point
S.P.

Meeks Bay

Rubicon
Bay

Rubicon River

Rubicon
Peak

89

D. L. Bliss
State Park

Cave Rock

Lakeridge

Skyland

Genoa Peak
9,150 ft.

Humboldt-
Toiyabe
National
Forest

206

Genoa

50

Emerald Bay
State Park

Emerald Bay

Zephyr
Cove

Nevada Beach

South Lake
Tahoe

Kingsbury

Stateline

207

El Dorado
National
Forest

Fallen Leaf
Lake

Jacks Peak

Pope-Baldwin
Recreation
Area

East Peak

207

206

50

Meyers

89

TO PLACERVILLE
AND SACRAMENTO

N

0   5 mi

0   5 km

Updated
by Christine
Vovakes

Whether you swim, fish, sail, or simply rest on its shores, you'll be wowed by the overwhelming beauty of Lake Tahoe, the largest alpine lake in North America. Famous for its cobalt-blue water and surrounding snowcapped peaks, Lake Tahoe straddles the state line between California and Nevada. The border gives this popular Sierra Nevada resort region a split personality. About half its visitors are intent on low-key sightseeing, hiking, camping, and boating. The rest head directly to the Nevada side, where bargain dining, big-name entertainment, and the lure of a jackpot draw them into the glittering casinos.

To explore the lake area and get a feel for its many differing communities drive the 72-mile road that follows the shore through wooded flatlands and past beaches, climbing to vistas on the rugged southwest side of the lake and passing through busy commercial developments and casinos on its northeastern and southeastern edges. Another option is to actually go out *on* the 22-mile-long, 12-mile-wide lake on a sightseeing cruise or kayaking trip.

The lake, the communities around it, the state parks, national forests, and protected tracts of wilderness are the region's main draws, but other nearby destinations are gaining in popularity. Truckee, with an Old West feel and innovative restaurants, entices visitors looking for a relaxed pace and easy access to Tahoe's north shore and Olympic Valley ski parks. And today Reno, once known only for its casinos, attracts tourists with its buzzing arts scene, revitalized downtown riverfront, and campus events at the University of Nevada.

PLANNING

WHEN TO GO

A sapphire blue lake shimmering deep in the center of an ice white wonderland—that's Tahoe in winter. But those blankets of snow mean lots of storms that often close roads and force chain requirements on the interstate. In summer the roads are open, but the lake and lodgings are clogged with visitors seeking respite from valley heat. If you don't ski, the best times to visit are early fall—September and October—and late spring. The crowds thin, prices dip, and you can count on Tahoe being beautiful.

Most Lake Tahoe accommodations, restaurants, and even a handful of parks are open year-round, but many visitor centers, mansions, state parks, and beaches are closed from October through May. During those months, winter-sports enthusiasts swamp Tahoe's downhill resorts and cross-country centers, North America's largest concentration of skiing facilities. In summer it's cooler here than in the scorched Sierra Nevada foothills, the clean mountain air is bracingly crisp, and the surface temperature of Lake Tahoe is an invigorating 65°F to 70°F (compared with 40°F to 50°F in winter). This is also the time, however, when it may seem as if every tourist at the lake—100,000 on peak weekends—is in a car on the main road circling the shoreline (especially on Highway 89, just south of Tahoe City; on Highway 28, east of Tahoe City; and on U.S. 50 in South Lake Tahoe). Christmas week and July 4th are the busiest times, and prices go through the roof; plan accordingly.

GETTING HERE AND AROUND

AIR TRAVEL

The nearest airport to Lake Tahoe is Reno–Tahoe International Airport (RNO), in Reno, 50 miles northeast of the closest point on the lake. Airlines serving RNO include Alaska, Allegiant Air, American, Delta, Southwest, and United. Except for Allegiant Air, these airlines plus Aeromexico, Hawaiian, and JetBlue serve Sacramento International Airport (SMF), 112 miles from South Lake Tahoe. North Lake Tahoe Express runs buses ($45 one-way, $85 round-trip) between RNO and towns on the lake's western and northern shores, plus Incline Village, Truckee, Squaw Valley, and Northstar. South Tahoe Express runs buses ($29.75 one-way, $53 round-trip) between Reno–Tahoe Airport and resort hotels in the South Lake Tahoe area.

Airport Contacts Reno–Tahoe International Airport ✉ 2001 E. Plumb La., off U.S. 395/I–580, at Reno-Tahoe International Airport Exit, Reno, Nevada ☎ 775/328–6400 ⊕ www.renoairport.com. **Sacramento International Airport** ✉ 6900 Airport Blvd., 12 miles northwest of downtown off I-5, Sacramento ☎ 916/929–5411 ⊕ www.sacramento.aero/smf.

Transfer Contacts North Lake Tahoe Express ☎ 866/216–5222 ⊕ www.northlaketahoeexpress.com. **South Tahoe Express** ☎ 775/325–8944, 866/898–2463 ⊕ www.southtahoeexpress.com.

BUS TRAVEL

Greyhound stops in San Francisco, Sacramento, Truckee, and Reno. BlueGO ($2 per ride) provides year-round local service in South Lake Tahoe. On the north shore, Tahoe Area Regional Transit (TART; $1.75) operates buses between Tahoma and Incline Village and runs shuttles to Truckee. RTC RIDE buses ($2) serve the Reno area. All local rides require exact change.

In winter, BlueGO provides free ski shuttle service from South Lake Tahoe hotels and resorts to various Heavenly Mountain ski lodge locations. Most of the major ski resorts offer shuttle service to nearby lodging.

Bus Contacts Greyhound ☎ 800/231–2222 ⊕ www.greyhound.com. **BlueGO** ☎ 530/541–7149 ⊕ www.tahoetransportation.org/southtahoe. **RTC RIDE** ☎ 775/348–7433 ⊕ www.rtcwashoe.com. **Tahoe Area Regional Transit (TART)** ☎ 530/550–1212, 800/736–6365 ⊕ www.placer.ca.gov/departments/works/transit/tart.

CAR TRAVEL

Lake Tahoe is 198 miles northeast of San Francisco, a drive of less than four hours in good weather and light traffic—if possible avoid heavy weekend traffic, particularly leaving the San Francisco area for Tahoe on Friday afternoon and returning on Sunday afternoon. The major route is Interstate 80, which cuts through the Sierra Nevada about 14 miles north of the lake. From there Highway 89 and Highway 267 reach the west and north shores, respectively.

U.S. 50 is the more direct route to the south shore, a two-hour drive from Sacramento. From Reno you can get to the north shore by heading south on U.S. 395/Interstate 580 for 10 miles, then west on Highway 431 for 25 miles. For the south shore, head south on U.S. 395/Interstate 580 through Carson City, and then turn west on U.S. 50 (56 miles total).

The scenic 72-mile highway around the lake is marked Highway 89 on the southwest and west shores, Highway 28 on the north and northeast shores, and U.S. 50 on the east and southeast. Sections of Highway 89 sometimes close during snowy periods, usually at Emerald Bay because of avalanche danger, which makes it impossible to complete the circular drive around the lake. Interstate 80, U.S. 50, and U.S. 395/Interstate 580 are all-weather highways, but there may be delays while snow is cleared during major storms.

Interstate 80 is a four-lane freeway; much of U.S. 50 is only two lanes with no center divider. Carry tire chains from October through May, or rent a four-wheel-drive vehicle. Most rental agencies do not allow tire chains to be used on their vehicles; ask when you book.

Contacts California Highway Patrol ☎ 530/577–1001 South Lake Tahoe ⊕ www.chp.ca.gov. **Caltrans Current Highway Conditions** ☎ 800/427–7623 ⊕ www.dot.ca.gov. **Nevada Department of Transportation Road Information** ☎ 877/687–6237 ⊕ nvroads.com. **Nevada Highway Patrol** ☎ 775/687–5300 ⊕ nhp.nv.gov.

TRAIN TRAVEL

Amtrak's cross-country rail service makes stops in Truckee and Reno. Amtrak also operates several buses daily between Reno and Sacramento to connect with coastal train routes.

Train Contact Amtrak ☎ *800/872–7245* ⊕ *www.amtrak.com.*

OUTDOORS AND BACKCOUNTRY TIPS

If you're planning to spend any time outdoors around Lake Tahoe, whether hiking, climbing, skiing, or camping, be aware that weather conditions can change quickly in the Sierra. To avoid hypothermia, always bring a pocket-size, fold-up rain poncho (available in all sporting-goods stores) to keep you dry. Wear long pants and a hat. Carry plenty of water. Because you'll likely be walking on granite, wear sturdy, closed-toe hiking boots, with soles that grip rock. If you're going into the backcountry, bring a signaling device (such as a mirror), emergency whistle, compass, map, energy bars, and water purifier. When heading out alone, tell someone where you're going and when you plan to return.

If you plan to ski, be aware of resort elevations. In the event of a winter storm, determine the snow level before you choose the resort you'll ski. Often the level can be as high as 7,000 feet, which means rain at some resorts' base areas but snow at others.

BackCountry, in Truckee, operates an excellent website with current information about how and where to (and where not to) ski, mountain bike, and hike in the backcountry around Tahoe. The store also stocks everything from crampons to transceivers. For storm information, check the National Weather Service's website; for ski conditions, visit ⊕ *onthesnow.com.* For reservations at campgrounds in California state parks, contact Reserve America. If you plan to camp in the backcountry of the national forests, you'll need to purchase a wilderness permit, which you can pick up at the forest service office or at a ranger station at any forest entrance. If you plan to ski the backcountry, check the U.S. Forest Service's recorded information for conditions.

Contacts and Information BackCountry ⊠ *11400 Donner Pass Rd., at Meadow Way, Truckee* ☎ *530/582–0909 Truckee* ⊕ *www.thebackcountry. net.* **National Weather Service** ⊕ *www.wrh.noaa.gov/rev.* **OntheSnow. com** ⊕ *www.onthesnow.com/california/skireport.html.* **Reserve America** ☎ *800/444–7275* ⊕ *www.reserveamerica.com.* **U.S. Forest Service** ⊠ *Office, 35 College Dr., South Lake Tahoe* ☎ *530/543–2600 general information, 530/587–3558 backcountry recording* ⊕ *www.fs.usda.gov/ltbmu.*

TOURS

Lake Tahoe Balloons. Take a hot-air balloon flight over the lake from mid-may through mid-October with this experienced company. The experience begins shortly after sunrise and takes four hours total, including a traditional champagne toast at journey's end. ⊠ *Tahoe Keys Marina, South Lake Tahoe* ☎ *530/544–1221, 800/872–9294* ⊕ *www. laketahoeballoons.com* ⌑ *From $295.*

MS *Dixie II*. The 520-passenger *MS Dixie II*, a stern-wheeler, sails year-round from Zephyr Cove to Emerald Bay on sightseeing and dinner cruises. ⊠ *Zephyr Cove Marina, 760 U.S. Hwy. 50, near Church*

St., Zephyr Cove, Nevada ☎ *775/589–4906, 800/238–2463* ⊕ *www. zephyrcove.com/cruises* ✉ *From $49.*

Sierra Cloud. From May to September, the *Sierra Cloud*, a 41-passenger catamaran, departs from the Hyatt Regency beach at Incline Village and cruises the north shore area. ⊠ *Hyatt Regency Lake Tahoe, 111 Country Club Dr., Incline Village* ☎ *775/831–4386* ⊕ *www.awsincline. com* ✉ *From $65.*

Tahoe Queen. The 312-passenger *Tahoe Queen*, a partially glass-bottomed paddle wheeler, departs from South Lake Tahoe daily for 2½-hour sightseeing cruises year-round by reservation and 3-hour dinner-dance cruises daily from late spring to early fall (weekly the rest of the year). Fares range from $49 to $75. ⊠ *Ski Run Marina, 900 Ski Run Blvd., off U.S. 50, South Lake Tahoe* ☎ *530/543–6191, 800/238–2463* ⊕ *www.zephyrcove.com/cruises* ✉ *From $47.*

Tahoe Boat Cruises. From April to October, this company offers various boating experiences. The *Woodwind II*, a 50-passenger catamaran, sails from Zephyr Cove on regular and Champagne cruises. The company's *Safari Rose*, an 80-foot-long wooden motor yacht, departs from Tahoe Keys Marina for half-day cruises around the lake. From late May to mid-October, their classic wooden boat, the *Tahoe*, takes passengers on an east shore cruise with a walking tour of Thunderbird Lodge historic site. ⊠ *Zephyr Cove Resort, 760 U.S. Hwy. 50, near Church St., Zephyr Cove* ☎ *775/588–1881, 888/867–6394* ⊕ *www.tahoecruises. com* ✉ *From $34.*

RESTAURANTS

On weekends and in high season, expect a long wait at the more popular restaurants. And expect to pay resort prices almost everywhere. Some restaurants are only open six out of 12 months a year; during the "shoulder seasons" (from April to May and September to November), some places may close temporarily or limit their hours, so call ahead. Also, check local papers for deals and discounts during this time, especially two-for-one coupons. Many casinos use their restaurants to attract gamblers. Marquees often tout "$8.99 prime rib dinners" or "$2.99 breakfast specials." Some of these meals are downright lousy and they are usually available only in the coffee shops and buffets, but at those prices, it's hard to complain. The finer restaurants in casinos deliver pricier food, as well as reasonable service and a bit of atmosphere. Unless otherwise noted, even the most expensive area restaurants welcome customers in casual clothes.

HOTELS

Quiet inns on the water, suburban-style strip motels, casino hotels, slope-side ski lodges, and house and condo rentals throughout the area constitute the lodging choices at Tahoe. The crowds come in summer and during ski season; reserve as far in advance as possible, especially for holiday periods when prices skyrocket. Spring and fall give you a little more leeway and lower—sometimes significantly lower, especially at casino hotels—rates. Check hotel websites for the best deals.

Head to South Lake Tahoe for the most activities and the widest range of lodging options. Heavenly Village in the heart of town has an ice rink, cinema, shops, fine-dining restaurants, and simple cafés, plus a gondola that will whisk you up to the ski park. Walk two blocks south from downtown, and you can hit the casinos.

Tahoe City, on the west shore, has a small-town atmosphere and is accessible to several nearby ski resorts. A few miles northwest of the lake, Squaw Valley USA has its own self-contained upscale village, an aerial tram to the slopes, and numerous outdoor activities once the snow melts.

Looking for a taste of old Tahoe? The north shore with its woodsy backdrop is your best bet, with Carnelian Bay and Tahoe Vista on the California side. And across the Nevada border are casino resorts where Hollywood's glamour-stars once romped. *Hotel reviews have been shortened. For full information, visit Fodors.com.*

13

WHAT IT COSTS				
	$	**$$**	**$$$**	**$$$$**
Restaurants	under $16	$16–$22	$23–$30	over $30
Hotels	under $121	$121–$175	$176–$250	over $250

Restaurant prices are the average cost of a main course at dinner or, if dinner is not served, at lunch. Hotel prices are the lowest cost of a standard double room in high season.

SKIING AND SNOWBOARDING

The mountains around Lake Tahoe are bombarded by blizzards throughout most winters and sometimes in fall and spring; 10- to 12-foot bases are common. Indeed, the Sierras often have the deepest snowpack on the continent, but because of the relatively mild temperatures over the Pacific, falling snow can be very heavy and wet—it's nicknamed "Sierra Cement" for a reason. The upside is that you can sometimes ski and board as late as May (snowboarding is permitted at all Tahoe ski areas). The major resorts get extremely crowded on weekends. If you're going to ski on a Saturday, arrive early and quit early. Avoid moving with the masses: eat at 11 am or 1:30 pm, not noon. Also consider visiting the ski areas with few high-speed lifts or limited lodging and real estate at their bases: Alpine Meadows, Sugar Bowl, Homewood, Mt. Rose, Sierra-at-Tahoe, Diamond Peak, and Kirkwood. And to find out the true ski conditions, talk to waiters and bartenders—most of them are ski bums.

The Lake Tahoe area is also a great destination for Nordic skiers. "Skinny" (i.e., cross-country) skiing at the resorts can be costly, but you get the benefits of machine grooming and trail preparation. If it's bargain Nordic you're after, take advantage of thousands of acres of public forest and parkland trails.

VISITOR INFORMATION

Contacts Lake Tahoe Visitors Authority ✉ *169 U.S. Hwy. 50, Stateline, Nevada* ☎ *775/588–5900, 800/288–2463* ⊕ *tahoesouth.com.* **U.S. Forest Service** ☎ *530/587–3558 backcountry recording* ⊕ *www.fs.usda.gov/tahoe.*

THE CALIFORNIA SIDE

The most hotels, restaurants, ski resorts, and state parks are on the California side of the lake, but you'll also encounter the most congestion and developed areas.

SOUTH LAKE TAHOE

50 miles south of Reno, 198 miles northeast of San Francisco.

The city of South Lake Tahoe's raison d'être is tourism: the casinos of adjacent Stateline, Nevada; the ski slopes at Heavenly Mountain; the beaches, docks, bike trails, and campgrounds all around the south shore; and the backcountry of Eldorado National Forest and Desolation Wilderness. The main road into town, however, shows less attractive features: older motels, strip malls, and low-rise prefab-looking buildings that line both sides of U.S. 50. Though there are plenty of places to stay, we haven't recommended many because they're not top choices. The small city's saving grace is its convenient location and bevy of services, as well as its gorgeous lake views.

GETTING HERE AND AROUND

The main route into and through South Lake Tahoe is U.S. 50; signs say "Lake Tahoe Boulevard" in town. Arrive by car or, if coming from Reno Airport, take the South Tahoe Express bus. BlueGO operates daily bus service in the south shore area year-round, plus a ski shuttle from the large hotels to Heavenly Ski Resort in the winter.

ESSENTIALS

Visitor Information Lake Tahoe Visitors Authority ⊠ *Visitor Center, 169 U.S. Hwy. 50, at Kingsbury Grade, Stateline, Nevada* ☎ *775/588–5900, 800/288–2463* ⊕ *tahoesouth.com* ⊠ *Visitor Center, 3066 Lake Tahoe Blvd., at San Francisco Ave.* ☎ *530/541–5255* ⊕ *tahoesouth.com.*

EXPLORING

FAMILY

Fodor'sChoice

★

Heavenly Gondola. Whether you ski or not, you'll appreciate the impressive view of Lake Tahoe from the Heavenly Gondola. Its eight-passenger cars travel from the middle of town 2.4 miles up the mountain in 15 minutes. When the weather's fine, you can take one of three hikes around the mountaintop and then have lunch at Tamarack Lodge. Heavenly also offers day care for children. ⊠ *4080 Lake Tahoe Blvd.* ☎ *775/586–7000, 800/432–8365* ⊕ *www.skiheavenly.com* ⊠ *$45* ☉ *Summer, daily 10–5; winter, weekdays 9–4, weekends 8:30–4.*

Heavenly Village. The centerpiece of South Lake Tahoe's efforts to reinvent itself and provide a focal point for tourism, this complex at the base of the gondola has restaurants, some good shopping, a cinema, an arcade for kids, and the Heavenly Village Outdoor Ice Rink. ⊠ *1001 Heavenly Village Way, at U.S. 50* ⊕ *www.theshopsatheavenly.com.*

WHERE TO EAT

$

ECLECTIC

✕ **Blue Angel Café.** A favorite of locals, who fill the dozen or so wooden tables, this cozy spot with Wi-Fi serves basic sandwiches and salads along with internationally inspired dishes like chipotle shrimp tacos and Thai curry. On cold days warm up with wine or an espresso in front of the fireplace. ⑤ *Average main: $13* ✉ *1132 Ski Run Blvd., at Larch Ave.* ☎ *530/544–6544* ⊕ *www.theblueangelcafe.com.*

$
MEXICAN

✕ **The Cantina.** A casual Tahoe favorite, the Cantina serves traditional Mexican dishes—huge burritos, enchiladas, and rellenos—as well as stylized Southwestern fare such as smoked-chicken polenta with grilled vegetables, and crab cakes in jalapeño cream sauce. The bartenders make great margaritas and serve 30 different kinds of beer. ⑤ *Average main: $13* ✉ *765 Emerald Bay Rd., Hwy. 89, at 10th St.* ☎ *530/544–1233* ⊕ *www.cantinatahoe.com* ⌖ *Reservations not accepted.*

$$$$
ECLECTIC
Fodor's Choice
★

✕ **Evan's American Gourmet Cafe.** Its excellent service, world-class food, and superb wine list make this the top choice for high-end dining in South Lake. Inside a converted cabin, the restaurant serves creative American cuisine that includes catch-of-the-day seafood offerings and meat dishes such as rack of lamb marinated with rosemary and garlic and served with raspberry demi-glace. Some diners find the table spacing a tad close. Evan's is intimate, to be sure, but the food always pleases. ⑤ *Average main: $32* ✉ *536 Emerald Bay Rd., Hwy. 89, at 15th St.* ☎ *530/542–1990* ⊕ *evanstahoe.com* ☾ *No lunch.*

$$$
SEAFOOD

✕ **Fresh Ketch.** Fish is the specialty at this dockside restaurant, where you can look out at the yachts in the Tahoe Keys marina. The upstairs dining room serves full dinners (no lunch) that feature fresh seafood and meats. The menu downstairs in the lively fireside seafood bar, beginning with lunch, is lighter and more eclectic, with reasonably priced hot and cold appetizers, salads, and sandwiches served through dinner. Have a hankering for something sweet? Stop by for dessert only and enjoy the view. There's live entertainment on Tuesday, Thursday, and Friday nights year-round, and on Saturday in summer. ⑤ *Average main: $23* ✉ *2435 Venice Dr., off Tahoe Keys Blvd.* ☎ *530/541–5683* ⊕ *thefreshketch.com.*

$$
ECLECTIC

✕ **Freshies.** When you've had your fill of junk food, come here for delicious, healthful meals prepared with an "earth-friendly" attitude and commitment. Specialties include seafood and vegetarian dishes, but good grilled meats are always available, such as teriyaki steak and Hawaiian spare ribs with grilled pineapple. Freshies is in a minimall, and can be loud and crowded—try to snag a spot on the upstairs lake-view deck. ⑤ *Average main: $16* ✉ *Lakeview Plaza, 3330 Lake Tahoe Blvd., at Fremont Ave.* ☎ *530/542–3630* ⊕ *www.freshiestahoe.com* ⌖ *Reservations not accepted* ☾ *Closed Nov. until weekend after Thanksgiving.*

$$$$
ASIAN

✕ **Kalani's.** Fresh-off-the-plane seafood gets delivered from the Honolulu fish market to Heavenly Village's sexiest (and priciest) restaurant. The sleek, white-tablecloth dining room is decked out with carved bamboo, a burnt-orange color palette, and a modern-glass sculpture, all of which complement contemporary Pacific Rim specialties such as melt-from-the-bone baby back pork ribs with sesame-garlic soy sauce. Sushi selections with inventive rolls and sashimi combos, plus less expensive vegetarian dishes, add depth to the menu. ⑤ *Average main: $34* ✉ *1001 Heavenly Village Way, #26, at U.S. 50* ☎ *530/544–6100* ⊕ *www.kalanis.com* ☾ *No lunch weekdays in winter.*

$
THAI

✕ **Orchid's Thai.** If you're hungry for Thai, stop here for good food at reasonable prices served in an attractive dining room. Tucked into a tiny mall, the restaurant isn't fantastic, but it's reliably good, and when every place in town is booked, this is a great backup. Carry outs are welcome. $ *Average main: $12* ⊠ *2180 Lake Tahoe Blvd., at 3rd St.* ☎ *530/544–5541* ⊘ *No lunch Sun.*

$ ╳ **Red Hut Café.** A vintage-1959 Tahoe diner, all chrome and red plastic,
AMERICAN the Red Hut is a tiny place with a wildly popular breakfast menu: huge omelets; banana, pecan, and coconut waffles; and other tasty vittles. A second South Lake branch has a soda fountain and is the only one that serves dinner. There's a third location in Stateline. $ *Average main: $9* ⊠ *2723 Lake Tahoe Blvd., near Blue Lake Ave.* ☎ *530/541–9024* ⊕ *www.redhutcafe.com* ⌕ *Reservations not accepted* ⊘ *No dinner* $ *Average main: $9* ⊠ *3660 Lake Tahoe Blvd., at Ski Run Blvd.* ☎ *530/544–1595* ⊕ *www.redhutcafe.com* $ *Average main: $9* ⊠ *229 Kingsbury Grade, off U.S. 50, Stateline, Nevada* ☎ *775/588–7488* ⊕ *www.redhutcafe.com* ⊘ *No dinner.*

$$ ╳ **Scusa! Italian Ristorante.** This longtime favorite turns out big plates
ITALIAN of veal scallopine, chicken piccata, and garlicky linguine with clams—straightforward Italian-American food (and lots of it), served in an intimate dining room warmed by a crackling fire on many nights. There's an outdoor patio that's open in warm weather. $ *Average main: $20* ⊠ *2543 Lake Tahoe Blvd., at Sierra Blvd.* ☎ *530/542–0100* ⊕ *www. scusalaketahoe.com* ⊘ *No lunch.*

WHERE TO STAY

$$$ ⊞ **Black Bear Inn Bed and Breakfast.** The rooms and cabins at South Lake
B&B/INN Tahoe's most luxurious inn feature 19th-century American antiques,
Fodor'sChoice fine art, and fireplaces; cabins also have kitchenettes. **Pros:** intimate;
★ serene, woodsy grounds; within walking distance of good restaurants. **Cons:** not appropriate for children under 16; pricey. $ *Rooms from: $225* ⊠ *1202 Ski Run Blvd.* ☎ *530/544–4451, 877/232–7466* ⊕ *www. tahoeblackbear.com* ⊃ *5 rooms, 4 cabins* ⦿ *Breakfast.*

$$ ⊞ **Forest Suites Resort.** The location of this resort is excellent—5½ acres
HOTEL bordering a forest, right behind the Heavenly Village, a half block from the casinos, and adjacent to a supermarket, cinema, and shops. **Pros:** as close to the city center as pricier hotels; good bet for families. **Cons:** an older facility with some rooms still being updated. $ *Rooms from: $147* ⊠ *1 Lake Pkwy.* ☎ *530/541–6655, 800/822–5950* ⊕ *www.forestsuites. com* ⊃ *17 rooms, 102 suites* ⦿ *Breakfast.*

$$$ ⊞ **Inn by the Lake.** Across the road from a beach, this "inn" is essen-
HOTEL tially a high-end motel, with spacious, spotless rooms and suites. **Pros:** great value; stellar service; short drive from Heavenly Mountain. **Cons:** on busy Lake Tahoe Boulevard. $ *Rooms from: $180* ⊠ *3300 Lake Tahoe Blvd., at Fremont Ave.* ☎ *530/542–0330, 800/877–1466* ⊕ *www.innbythelake.com* ⊃ *90 rooms, 10 suites* ⦿ *No meals.*

$$ ⊞ **Marriott's Grand Residence and Timber Lodge.** You can't beat the loca-
RESORT tion of these two gigantic, modern condominium complexes right at the base of Heavenly Gondola, smack in the center of town. **Pros:** central location; great for families; near excellent restaurants. **Cons:** can be jam-packed on weekends. $ *Rooms from: $175* ⊠ *1001 Heavenly Village Way* ☎ *530/542–8400 Marriott's Grand Residence, 800/845–5279, 530/542–6600 Marriott's Timber Lodge* ⊕ *www.marriott.com* ⊃ *431 condos* ⦿ *No meals.*

Continued on page 530

TAHOE A LAKE FOR ALL SEASONS

by Christine Vovakes

Best known for its excellent skiing, Lake Tahoe is a year-round resort and outdoor sports destination. All kinds of activities are available, from snowboarding some of the best runs in North America and gliding silently along the lakeshore on cross-country skis in winter, to mountain biking through lush forests and puttering around the alpine lake in a classic yacht in summer. Whatever you do—and whenever you visit—the sapphire lake is at the center of it all, pulling you out of your posh resort or rustic cabin rental like a giant blue magnet. There are many ways to enjoy and experience Lake Tahoe, but here are some of our favorites.

(top) Heavenly Mountain Resort, (bottom) Sand Harbor Beach.

WINTER WONDERLAND

Home to a host of world-famous Sierra resorts, Tahoe is a premier ski destination. Add sledding, ice skating, cross-country skiing, and jingly sleigh rides under the stars to the mix, and you begin to get a glimpse of Tahoe's cold-weather potential.

DOWNHILL SKIING AND SNOWBOARDING

Even if you've never made it off the bunny hill before, you should definitely hit the slopes here at least once. The Lake Tahoe region has the deepest snowpack in North America, and you can ski from Thanksgiving until it melts—which is sometimes July.

One of the top-rated resorts in the country, Olympic Valley's **Squaw Valley USA** hosted the 1960 Winter Olympics that put Tahoe on the map. A great classic resort is **Sugar Bowl,** where you can revel in a bit of Disney nostalgia while you swoop down the slopes. Walt helped start the resort, which opened in 1939 and had Tahoe's first chair lift.

Even if you're not hitting the slopes at South Lake Tahoe's **Heavenly Mountain,** be sure to take a ride on their **Heavenly Gondola** so you can take in awe-inspiring views of the frozen circle of white ice that rings the brilliant lake.

(top) Skiing in Lake Tahoe,. (above left) Cross-country skiing, (above right) Snow boarding at Heavenly Mountain.

SKI RESORT	LOCATION	TRAILS	ACRES	BEGIN.	INTER.	ADV./EXP.
CALIFORNIA						
Alpine Meadows	Tahoe City	100	2,400	25%	40%	35%
Heavenly Mountain	South Lake Tahoe	97	4,800	20%	45%	35%
Homewood Mountain	Homewood	64	1,260	15%	50%	35%
Kirkwood	Kirkwood	81	2,300	15%	50%	35%
Northstar California	Truckee	97	3,170	13%	60%	27%
Sierra-at-Tahoe	South Lake Tahoe	46	2,000	25%	50%	25%
Squaw Valley USA	Olympic Valley	170	3,600	25%	45%	30%
Sugar Bowl	Truckee	102	1,650	17%	45%	38%
NEVADA						
Diamond Peak	Incline Village	30	655	18%	46%	36%
Mt. Rose Ski Tahoe	Incline Village	61	1,200	20%	30%	50%

CROSS-COUNTRY SKIING

Downhill skiing may get all the glory here, but Lake Tahoe is also a premier cross-country (or Nordic) skiing destination. "Skinny" skiers basically have two options: pony up the cash to ski the groomed trails at a resort, or hit the more rugged (but cheaper—or free) public forest and parkland trails.

Beautiful **Royal Gorge** is the country's largest cross-country ski resort. Other resorts with good skinny skiing include **Kirkwood, Squaw Valley USA, Tahoe Donner,** and **Northstar California.** Private operators **Spooner Lake Cross Country** and **Hope Valley Cross Country** will also have you shushing through pristine powder in no time.

For bargain Nordic on public trails, head to **Sugar Pine Point State Park.** Other good low-cost cross-country skiing locations include **Donner Memorial State Park, Lake Tahoe—Nevada State Park,** and **Tahoe Meadows** near Incline Village.

CAUTION⚠ Cross-country skiing is relaxing and provides a great cardiovascular workout—but it's also quite strenuous. If it's your first time out or you're not in great shape, start out slow.

SLEDDING AND TUBING

Kirkwood, Squaw Valley USA, Boreal, Soda Springs, and many other Tahoe resorts have areas where you can barrel down hills on inflatable tubes. Some good non-resort sledding spots are **Tahoe National Forest** and **Tahoe Meadows,** near Incline Village.

ICE SKATING

Want to work on your triple lutz? You can skate seasonally at **Heavenly Village Outdoor Ice Rink,** or year-round at the **South Tahoe Ice Arena.** Other great gliding spots include **Squaw Valley USA's Olympic Ice Pavilion.**

WARMING UP

To defrost your ski-stiff limbs, take a dip in a resort's heated pool, de-stress in a hotel spa...or enjoy a brandy by the fire at a cozy restaurant. Our favorite places to warm up and imbibe include Graham's of Squaw Valley and Soule Domain, near Crystal Bay.

13

IN FOCUS TAHOE: A LAKE FOR ALL SEASONS

Lake Tahoe
Outdoor Activities

FROSTY CATCH

Too cold to fish? Nonsense. South Lake's Tahoe Sport Fishing runs charters year-round with crews that will clean and package your catch.

IN THE WARM CALIFORNIA SUN

Summer in Tahoe means diving into pure alpine waters, hiking a mountain trail with stunning lake views, or kayaking on glorious Emerald Bay. From tennis to golf to fishing, you can fill every waking moment with outdoor activity—or just stretch out on a sunny lakeside beach with a good book and a cool drink.

HIKING

The lake is surrounded by protected parkland, offering countless opportunities to take jaunts through the woods or rambles along lakeside trails.

One of the most unique hiking experiences in Tahoe is at Heavenly Mountain Resorts, where the **Heavenly Gondola** runs up to three nice trails. When you're done enjoying sky-high views of the lake, grab lunch at the nearby Tamarack Lodge.

Another out-of-the-ordinary option is a romantic moonlit trek. **Camp Richardson** has lots of trails and a long curve of lake to catch the moonlight.

In **Eldorado National Forest and Desolation Wilderness,** you can hike a small portion of the famous Pacific Crest Trail and branch off to discover beautiful backcountry lakes. Nearby **Eagle Falls** has stunning views of Emerald Bay.

One of Tahoe's best hikes is a 4½-mi trail at **D.L. Bliss State Park;** it has lovely views of the lake and leads to bizarre **Vikingsholm** (*see box on next page*).

Other great places to hike in Lake Tahoe include **Sugar Pines Point State Park, Olympic Valley's Granite Chief Wilderness, Squaw Valley USA's High Camp, Donner Memorial State Park,** and **Lake Tahoe—Nevada State Park.**

You can pick up hiking maps at the **U.S. Forest Service** office at the **Lake Tahoe Visitor Center.**

HIT THE BEACH

Lake Tahoe has some gorgeous lakeside sunbathing terrain; get to perennial favorite **Kings Beach State Recreation Area** early to snag a choice spot. Or, if you never want to be far from the water, reserve one of the prime beachside spots at **D.L. Bliss State Park Campground.**

(left) Fannette Island in Emerald Bay. (right) A young man leaps off a cliff into Lake Tahoe.

MOUNTAIN BIKING AND CYCLING

You don't need to be preparing for the Tour de France to join the biking fun. While there are myriad rugged mountain biking trails to choose from, the region is also blessed with many flat trails.

Truly intrepid cyclists take the lift up **Northstar California** and hit the resort's 100 mi of trails. Another good option is **Sugar Pine Point State Park,** where you can hop on a 10-mi trail to Tahoe City.

Tahoe Sports in South Lake Tahoe is a good place for bike rentals and tips for planning your trip. **Cyclepaths Mountain Bikes Adventures** in Truckee leads guided mountain biking tours, and **Flume Trail Bikes** on the Nevada side of the lake, near Glenbrook, rents bikes and operates a bike shuttle to popular trails.

LAKE TOURS AND KAYAKING

One of the best ways to experience the lake is by getting out on the water.

The **Tahoe Queen** is a huge glass-bottomed paddle-wheel boat that offers sightseeing cruises and dinner-dance cruises. The **Sierra Cloud, MS Dixie II,** and **Woodwind II** also ply the lake, offering a variety of enjoyable cruises. *(See Tour Options in the Planner section of this chapter for contact info.)*

Another enjoyable option is taking a throwback wooden cruiser from Tahoe Keys Marina in South Lake Tahoe to tour **Thunderbird Lodge,** the meticulously crafted stone mansion built in 1936 by socialite George Whittell.

For a more personal experience, rent a kayak and glide across **Emerald Bay.** **Kayak Tahoe** in South Lake Tahoe will have you paddling in no time.

VIKINGS?

As you kayak around Tahoe, you'll see many natural wonders…and a few manmade ones as well. One of the most impressive and strangest is **Vikingsholm**, a grand 1929 estate that looks like an ancient Viking castle. You can see it from **Emerald Bay** (which, appropriately, resembles a fjord), or hike to it via a steep one-mile trail.

(left top) Biking along the shore. (left bottom) Kayaking. (right) Steamboat cruise.

$$
RESORT
⚑ **Sorensen's Resort.** Escape civilization by staying in a log cabin at this woodsy 165-acre resort within the Eldorado National Forest, 20 minutes south of town. **Pros:** gorgeous, rustic setting. **Cons:** nearest nightlife is 20 miles away. $ *Rooms from: $135* ✉ *14255 Hwy. 88, Hope Valley* ☎ *530/694–2203, 800/423–9949* ⊕ *www.sorensens resort.com* ⥥ *2 rooms with shared bath, 29 cabins, 5 houses* ⦿ *No meals.*

NIGHTLIFE

Most of the area's nightlife is concentrated in the casinos over the border in Stateline. To avoid slot machines and blinking lights, try the California-side nightspots in and near Heavenly Village. The Marriott Timber Lodge bars are always dependable.

BARS

Mc P's Irish Pub & Grill. You can hear live bands—rock, jazz, blues, alternative—on most nights at Mc P's, across the street from the Heavenly Gondola. ✉ *4093 Lake Tahoe Blvd., near Friday Ave.* ☎ *530/542–4435* ⊕ *www.mcpspubtahoe.com.*

SPORTS AND THE OUTDOORS

FISHING

Tahoe Sport Fishing. One of the area's largest and oldest fishing-charter services offers morning and afternoon trips. Outings include all necessary gear and bait, and the crew cleans and packages your catch. ✉ *900 Ski Run Blvd., off U.S. 50* ☎ *530/541–5448, 800/696–7797 in CA* ⊕ *www.tahoesportfishing.com* ⥥ *From $90.*

GOLF

Lake Tahoe Golf Course. Set in a meadow with mountain views, this public championship course was designed by William Bell. The Upper Truckee River comes into play on several holes. The twilight rate ($29) starts at 4 pm. ✉ *2500 Emerald Bay Rd, Hwy. 89/U.S. 50* ☎ *530/577–0788* ⊕ *www.laketahoegc.com* ⥥ *$65 for weekdays, $85 for weekends; $20 for golf cart* ⛳ *18 holes, 6741 yards, par 71.*

HIKING

The south shore is a great jumping-off point for day treks into nearby Eldorado National Forest and Desolation Wilderness.

Desolation Wilderness. Trails within the 63,960-acre wilderness lead to gorgeous backcountry lakes and mountain peaks. It's called Desolation Wilderness for a reason, so bring a topographic map and compass, and carry water and food. In summer, you can access this area by boarding a boat taxi (⥥ *$12 one-way*) at **Echo Chalet** (✉ *9900 Echo Lakes Rd., off U.S. 50* ☎ *530/659–7207* ⊕ *www.echochalet.com*) and crossing Echo Lake. The Pacific Crest Trail also traverses Desolation Wilderness. ✉ *El Dorado National Forest Information Center* ☎ *530/644–6048* ⊕ *www. fs.usda.gov/eldorado.*

Pacific Crest Trail. Hike a couple of miles on this famous mountain trail that stretches from Mexico to Canada. ⊠ *Echo Summit, about 12 miles southwest of South Lake Tahoe off U.S. 50* ☏ *916/285–1846, 888/728– 7245* ⊕ *www.pcta.org.*

ICE-SKATING

FAMILY **Heavenly Village Outdoor Ice Rink.** If you're here in winter, practice your jumps and turns at this rink between the gondola and the cinema. ⊠ *1001 Heavenly Village Way* ☏ *530/542–4230* ⊕ *www.theshopsatheavenly. com* ⊠ *$20; skate rental available* ⊗ *Nov.–Mar., Mon.–Fri, noon–8; Sat.–Sun.10–8, weather permitting.*

South Tahoe Ice Arena. For year-round fun, head to this city-operated, NHL regulation–size indoor rink where you can rent equipment and sign up for lessons. In the evening the lights are turned low and a disco ball lights up the ice. ⊠ *1176 Rufus Allen Blvd.* ☏ *530/542–6056* ⊕ *tahoearena.com* ⊠ *$15; includes skate rental* ⊗ *Daily, hrs vary.*

KAYAKING

Kayak Tahoe. Sign up for lessons and excursions (to the south shore, Emerald Bay, and Sand Harbor), offered from May through September. You can also rent a kayak and paddle solo on the lake. ⊠ *Timber Cove Marina, 3411 Lake Tahoe Blvd., at Balbijou Rd.* ☏ *530/544–2011* ⊕ *www.kayaktahoe.com* ⊠ *From $40.*

MOUNTAIN BIKING

Tahoe Sports Ltd. You can rent road and mountain bikes and get tips on where to ride from the friendly staff at this full-service sports store. ⊠ *Tahoe Crescent V Shopping Center, 4000 Lake Tahoe Blvd.* ☏ *530/542–4000* ⊕ *www.tahoesportsltd.com.*

SKIING

If you don't want to pay the high cost of rental equipment at the resorts, you'll find reasonable prices and expert advice at Tahoe Sports Ltd. (⇨ *Mountain Biking, above).*

Fodor's Choice ★ **Heavenly Mountain Resort.** Straddling two states, vast Heavenly Mountain Resort—composed of nine peaks, two valleys, and four base-lodge areas, along with the largest snowmaking system in the western United States—has terrain for every skier. Beginners can choose wide, well-groomed trails, accessed from the California Lodge or the gondola from downtown South Lake Tahoe; kids have short and gentle runs in the Enchanted Forest area all to themselves. The Sky Express high-speed quad chair whisks intermediate and advanced skiers to the summit for wide cruisers or steep tree-skiing. Mott and Killebrew canyons draw experts to the Nevada side for steep chutes and thick-timber slopes. For snowboarders and tricksters, there are five different terrain parks.

The ski school is big and offers everything from learn-to-ski packages to canyon-adventure tours. Call about ski and boarding camps. Skiing lessons are available for children ages four and up; there's day care for infants older than six weeks. ⊠ *Ski Run Blvd., off U.S. 50* ☏ *775/586–7000, 800/432–8365* ⊕ *www.skiheavenly.com* ⊙ *97 trails on 4,800 acres, rated 20% beginner, 45% intermediate, 35% expert. Longest run 5½ miles, base 6,540 feet, summit 10,067 feet. Lifts: 30, including 1 aerial tram, 1 gondola, 2 high-speed 6-passenger lifts, and 8 high-speed quads.*

13

Hope Valley Cross Country. Operating from a yurt at Pickett's Junction, Hope Valley provides lessons and equipment rentals to prepare you for cross-country skiing and snow-shoeing. The outfit has 60 miles of trails through Humboldt–Toiyabe National Forest, 10 of which are groomed. ⊠ *Hwy. 88, at Hwy. 89, Hope Valley* ☎ *530/721–2015* ⊕ *www.hopevalleyoutdoors.com.*

Kirkwood Ski Resort. Thirty-six miles south of Lake Tahoe, Kirkwood is the hard-core skiers' and boarders' favorite south-shore mountain, known for its craggy gulp-and-go chutes, sweeping cornices, steep-aspect glade skiing, and high base elevation. But there's also fantastic terrain for newbies and intermediates down wide-open bowls, through wooded gullies, and along rolling tree-lined trails. Tricksters can show off in two terrain parks on jumps, wall rides, rails, and a half-pipe, all visible from the base area. The mountain gets hammered with more than 600 inches of snow annually, and often has the most in all of North America. If you're into out-of-bounds skiing, check out Expedition Kirkwood, a backcountry-skills program that teaches basic safety awareness. Kirkwood is also the only Tahoe resort to offer Cat-skiing. If you're into cross-country, the resort has 80 km (50 miles) of superb groomed-track skiing, with skating lanes, instruction, and rentals. Nonskiers can snowshoe, snow-skate, and go dogsledding or snow-tubing. The children's ski school has programs for ages three to 12. ⊠ *1501 Kirkwood Meadows Dr., off Hwy. 88, 14 miles west of Hwy. 89, Kirkwood, Kirkwood* ☎ *800/967–7500 information, 209/258–7248 cross-country, 209/258–7293 lodging information, 877/547–5966 snow phone* ⊕ *www.kirkwood.com* ☞ *81 trails on 2,300 acres, rated 15% beginner, 50% intermediate, 20% advanced, 15% expert. Longest run 2½ miles, base 7,800 feet, summit 9,800 feet. Lifts: 15, including 2 high-speed quads.*

Sierra-at-Tahoe. Often overlooked by skiers and boarders rushing to Heavenly or Kirkwood, Sierra-at-Tahoe has meticulously groomed intermediate slopes, some of the best tree-skiing in California, and gated backcountry access. Extremely popular with snowboarders, Sierra also has six terrain parks, including a super-pipe with 17-foot walls. For nonskiers there's a snow-tubing hill. Sierra has a low-key atmosphere that's great for families. Kids and beginners take the slow routes in the Mellow Yellow Zone. ⊠ *1111 Sierra-at-Tahoe Rd., 12 miles from South Lake Tahoe off U.S. 50, past Echo Summit, Twin Bridges* ☎ *530/659–7453 information, 530/659–7475 snow phone* ⊕ *www.sierraattahoe.com* ☞ *46 trails on 2,000 acres, rated 25% beginner, 50% intermediate, 25% advanced. Longest run 2½ miles, base 6,640 feet, summit 8,852 feet. Lifts: 14, including 3 high-speed quads.*

POPE-BALDWIN RECREATION AREA

5 miles west of South Lake Tahoe.

To the west of downtown South Lake Tahoe, U.S. 50 and Highway 89 come together, forming an intersection nicknamed "the Y." If you head northwest on Highway 89, also called Emerald Bay Road, and follow the lakefront, commercial development gives way to national forests and state parks. One of these is Pope-Baldwin Recreation Area.

GETTING HERE AND AROUND

The entrance to the Pope-Baldwin Recreation Area is on the east side of Emerald Bay Road. The area is closed to vehicles in winter, but you can cross-country ski here.

EXPLORING

Tallac Historic Site. At this site, you can stroll or picnic lakeside, and then explore three historic estates. The **Pope House** is the magnificently restored 1894 mansion of George S. Pope, who made his money in shipping and lumber and played host to the business and cultural elite of 1920s America. The **Baldwin Museum** is in the estate that once belonged to entrepreneur "Lucky" Baldwin; today it houses a collection of family memorabilia and Washoe Indian artifacts. The **Valhalla** (⊕ *valhallatahoe.com*), with a spectacular floor-to-ceiling stone fireplace, belonged to Walter Heller. Its Grand Hall and a lakeside boathouse, refurbished as a theater, host summertime concerts, plays, and cultural activities. Docents conduct tours of the Pope House in summer; call for tour times. In winter you can cross-country ski around the site. ☒ *Hwy. 89* ☎ *530/541–5227 late May–Oct., 530/543–2600 year-round* ⊕ *tahoeheritage.org* ☞ *Free, Pope House tour $8* ☉ *Grounds: daily sunrise–sunset. Pope House and Baldwin Museum: late May–late Sept., call for hrs.*

FAMILY **Taylor Creek Visitor Center.** At this center operated by the U.S. Forest Service, you can visit the site of a Washoe Indian settlement; walk self-guided trails through meadow, marsh, and forest; and inspect the Stream Profile Chamber, an underground display with windows right into Taylor Creek. In fall you may see spawning kokanee salmon digging their nests. In summer Forest Service naturalists organize discovery walks and evening programs. ☒ *Hwy. 89, 3 miles north of junction with U.S. 50* ☎ *530/543–2674 late May–Oct., 530/543–2600 year-round* ⊕ *www.fs.usda.gov/recarea/ltbmu/recarea/?recid=11785* ☞ *Free* ☉ *Late May–late Sept., 10–4; call for Oct. hrs.*

Fjord-like Emerald Bay is quite possibly the prettiest part of Lake Tahoe.

EMERALD BAY STATE PARK

4 miles west of Pope-Baldwin Recreation Area.

You can hike, bike, swim, camp, scuba dive, kayak, or tour a lookalike Viking castle at this state park. Or you can simply enjoy the most popular tourist stop on Lake Tahoe's circular drive: the high cliff overlooking Emerald Bay, famed for its jewel-like shape and color.

GETTING HERE AND AROUND

The entrance to Emerald Bay State Park is on the east side of a narrow, twisting section of Highway 89. Caution is the keyword for both drivers and pedestrians. The park is closed to vehicles in winter.

EXPLORING

Fodor's Choice ★ **Emerald Bay.** A massive glacier millions of years ago carved this 3-mile-long and 1-mile-wide fjordlike inlet. Famed for its jewel-like shape and colors, the bay surrounds Fannette, Tahoe's only island. Highway 89 curves high above the lake through Emerald Bay State Park; from the Emerald Bay lookout, the centerpiece of the park, you can survey the whole scene. This is one of the don't-miss views of Lake Tahoe. The light is best in mid- to late morning, when the bay's colors really pop. ⊠ *Hwy. 89, 20 miles south of Tahoe City* ☎ *530/525–7232* ⊕ *www. parks.ca.gov* ✉ *$10 parking fee.*

Vikingsholm. This 38-room estate was completed in 1929. The original owner, Lora Knight, had this precise copy of a 1,200-year-old Viking castle built out of materials native to the area. She furnished it with Scandinavian antiques and hired artisans to build period reproductions. The sod roof sprouts wildflowers each spring. There are picnic tables nearby and a gray-sand beach for strolling. A steep 1-mile-long trail from the Emerald Bay lookout leads down to Vikingsholm, and the hike back up is hard (especially if you're not yet acclimated to the elevation), although there are benches and stone culverts to rest on. At the 150-foot peak of Fannette Island are the ruins of a stone structure known as the Tea House, built in 1928 so that Knight's guests could have a place to enjoy afternoon refreshments after a motorboat ride. The island is off-limits from February through mid-June to protect nesting Canada geese. The rest of the year it's open for day use. ⊠ *Hwy. 89* ☎ *530/541–6498 summer, 530/525–7232 year-round* ⊕ *www.vikingsholm.com* ⊡ *Day-use parking fee $10; mansion tour $10* ☉ *Late May–Sept., daily 10:30–4.*

13

SPORTS AND THE OUTDOORS
HIKING
Eagle Falls. To reach these falls, leave your car in the parking lot of the Eagle Falls picnic area (near Vikingsholm; arrive early for a good spot), and walk up the short but fairly steep canyon nearby. You'll have a brilliant panorama of Emerald Bay from this spot near the boundary of Desolation Wilderness. For a strenuous full-day hike, continue 5 miles, past Eagle Lake, to Upper and Middle Velma Lakes. Pick up trail maps at Taylor Creek Visitor Center in summer, or year-round at the main U.S. Forest Service Office in South Lake Tahoe, at 35 College Drive. ⊠ *Hwy. 89, South Lake Tahoe.*

D.L. BLISS STATE PARK

3 miles north of Emerald Bay State Park, 17 miles south of Tahoe City.

This park shares six miles of shoreline with adjacent Emerald Bay State Park and has two white-sand beaches. Hike the Rubicon Trail for stunning views of the lake.

GETTING HERE AND AROUND
The entrance to D.L. Bliss State Park is on the east side of Highway 89 just north of Emerald Bay. No vehicles are allowed in when the park is closed for the season.

EXPLORING
D.L. Bliss State Park. This park takes its name from Duane LeRoy Bliss, a 19th-century lumber magnate. At one time Bliss owned nearly 75% of Tahoe's lakefront, along with local steamboats, railroads, and banks. The park shares 6 miles of shoreline with Emerald Bay State Park; combined the two parks cover 1,830 acres, 744 of which the Bliss family donated to the state. At the north end of Bliss is Rubicon Point, which overlooks one of the lake's deepest spots. Short trails lead to an old lighthouse and Balancing Rock, which weighs 250,000 pounds and balances on a fist of granite. The 4.5-mile Rubicon Trail—one of Tahoe's premier hikes—leads to Vikingsholm and provides stunning lake views. Two white-sand beaches front some of Tahoe's warmest water. ⊠ *Hwy. 89* ☎ *530/525–3345, 800/777–0369* ⊕ *www.parks.ca.gov* ⊡ *$8 per vehicle, day use* ☉ *Late May–Sept., daily sunrise–sunset.*

ED Z'BERG SUGAR PINE POINT STATE PARK

8 miles north of D. L. Bliss State Park, 10 miles south of Tahoe City.

Visitors love to hike, swim, and fish here in the summer, but this park is also popular in winter, when a small campground remains open. Eleven miles of cross-country ski and snowshoe trails allow beginners and experienced enthusiasts alike to whoosh through pine forests and glide past the lake.

GETTING HERE AND AROUND

The entrance to Sugar Pine Point is on the east side of Highway 89, about a mile south of Tahoma. A bike trail links Tahoe City to the park.

EXPLORING

Hellman-Ehrman Mansion. The main attraction at Sugar Pine Point State Park is Ehrman Mansion, a 1903 stone-and-shingle summer home furnished in period style. In its day it was the height of modernity, with a refrigerator, an elevator, and an electric stove. Also in the park are a trapper's log cabin from the mid-19th century, a nature preserve with wildlife exhibits, a lighthouse, the start of the 10-mile biking trail to Tahoe City, and an extensive system of hiking and cross-country skiing trails. If you're feeling less ambitious, you can relax on the sun-dappled lawn behind the mansion and gaze out at the lake. ⊠ *Hwy. 89* 🕾 *530/525–7982 mansion in season, 530/525–7232 year-round* ⊕ *www.parks.ca.gov* 🖃 *$10 per vehicle, day use; mansion tour $10* ☉ *Mansion: late May–Aug., daily 10–3; call for Sept. hrs.*

Ed Z'Berg Sugar Pine Point State Park. Named for a state lawmaker who sponsored key conservation legislation, Lake Tahoe's largest state park has 2,000 acres of dense forests and nearly 2 miles of shore frontage. A popular spot during snow season, Sugar Pine provides 11 miles of cross-country trails and winter camping on a first-come, first-served basis. Rangers lead full-moon snowshoe tours from January to March. ⊠ *Hwy. 89, 1 mile south of Tahoma* 🕾 *530/525–7982* ⊕ *www.parks. ca.gov.*

TAHOMA

1 mile north of Ed Z'berg Sugar Pine Point State Park, 23 miles south of Truckee.

With its rustic waterfront vacation cottages, Tahoma exemplifies life on the lake in its quiet early days before bright-lights casinos and huge crowds proliferated. In 1960 Tahoma was host of the Olympic Nordic-skiing competitions. Today there's little to do here except stroll by the lake and listen to the wind in the trees, making it a favorite home base for mellow families and nature buffs.

GETTING HERE AND AROUND

Approach Tahoma by car on Highway 89, called West Lake Boulevard in this section. From the northern and western communities, take a TART bus to Tahoma. A bike trail links Tahoe City to Tahoma.

WHERE TO STAY

$$
B&B/INN

Tahoma Meadows B&B Cottages. It's hard to beat this serene property for atmosphere and woodsy charm; it's a great retreat for families and couples. **Pros:** lovely setting; good choice for families; close to Homewood ski resort. **Cons:** far from the casinos. $ *Rooms from: $159* ⊠ *6821 W. Lake Blvd.* ☎ *530/525–1553, 866/525–1553* ⊕ *www. tahomameadows.com* ⊅ *16 cabins* ⦿ *Breakfast.*

SPORTS AND THE OUTDOORS

SKIING

Homewood Mountain Resort. Schuss down these slopes for fantastic views—the mountain rises across the road from the Tahoe shoreline. This small, usually uncrowded resort is the favorite area of locals on a snowy day, because you can find lots of untracked powder. It's also the most protected and least windy Tahoe ski area during a storm; when every other resort's lifts are on wind hold, you can almost always count on Homewood's to be open. There's only one high-speed chairlift, but there are rarely any lines, and the ticket prices are some of the cheapest around—kids 5 to 12 ski for $24, and those four and under are free. The resort may look small as you drive by, but most of it isn't visible from the road. ⊠ *5145 W. Lake Blvd., Hwy. 89, 6 miles south of Tahoe City, Homewood* ☎ *530/525–2992 information, 530/525–2900 snow phone* ⊕ *www.skihomewood.com* ⊅ *64 trails on 1,260 acres, rated 15% beginner, 50% intermediate, and 35% advanced. Longest run 2 miles, base 6,230 feet, summit 7,880 feet. Lifts: 4 chairlifts, 4 surface lifts.*

13

TAHOE CITY

9 miles north of Tahoma, 14 miles south of Truckee.

Tahoe City is the only lakeside town with a charming downtown area good for strolling and window-shopping. Stores and restaurants are all within walking distance of the Outlet Gates, where water is spilled into the Truckee River to control the surface level of the lake. You can spot giant trout in the river from Fanny Bridge, so-called for the views of the backsides of sightseers leaning over the railing.

GETTING HERE AND AROUND

Tahoe City is at the junction of Highway 28, also called North Lake Boulevard, and Highway 89 where it turns northwest toward Squaw Valley and Truckee. TART buses serve the communities along the north and west shores, and connects them to Truckee.

ESSENTIALS

Visitor Information North Lake Tahoe Resort Association ☎ *530/583–3494, 888/434–1262* ⊕ *www.gotahoenorth.com.*

EXPLORING

Gatekeeper's Museum. This museum preserves a little-known part of the region's history. Between 1910 and 1968 the gatekeeper who lived on this site was responsible for monitoring the level of the lake, using a hand-turned winch system (still used today) to keep the water at the correct level. Also on this site, the fantastic Marion Steinbach Indian

Basket Museum displays 800 baskets from 85 tribes. ⊠ *130 W. Lake Blvd.* ☎ *530/583–1762* ⊕ *www.northtahoemuseums.org* ⌨ *$5* ☉ *Late June–Sept., Wed.–Mon. 10–5; Oct.–late June., Fri. and Sat. 10–4.*

Watson Cabin Living Museum. In the middle of Tahoe City sits a 1909 log cabin built by Robert M. Watson and his son. Now a museum, it's filled with century-old furnishings and many reproductions. Docents are available to answer questions and will lead tours if you call ahead. ⊠ *560 N. Lake Blvd.* ☎ *530/583–8717, 530/583–1762* ⊕ *www.northtahoemuseums. org* ⌨ *$2* ☉ *Late May–early Sept., Thurs.–Mon. 10–5.*

WHERE TO EAT

$$$

AMERICAN

✕ **Christy Hill.** Huge windows give diners here some of the best lake views in Tahoe. The menu features solid Euro–Cal preparations of fresh seafood, filet of beef, or vegetarian dishes. The extensive wine list and exceptionally good desserts earn accolades, as do the gracious service and casual vibe. If the weather is balmy, have dinner on the deck. In any season, this is a romantic choice for lake gazing and wine sipping. $ *Average main: $27* ⊠ *115 Grove St., at N. Lake Blvd.* ☎ *530/583–8551* ⊕ *www.christyhill.com* ☉ *No lunch.*

$

AMERICAN

✕ **Fire Sign Café.** Watch the road carefully or you'll miss this great little diner two miles south of Tahoe City on Highway 89. There's often a wait for breakfast and lunch, but it's worth it. The pastries are made from scratch, the salmon is smoked in-house, the salsa is hand cut, and there's real maple syrup for the many types of pancakes and waffles. Leave room for dessert; a fruit cobbler is almost always on the menu. $ *Average main: $10* ⊠ *1785 W. Lake Blvd., at Fountain Ave.* ☎ *530/583–0871* ⊕ *www.firesigncafe.com* ⌦ *Reservations not accepted* ☉ *No dinner.*

$

AMERICAN

✕ **Syd's Bagelry & Espresso.** For breakfast bagels and pastries and lunchtime salads and sandwiches, locals head to Syd's, which brews good coffee and provides free Wi-Fi, too. Want the skinny on Tahoe City? Talk to Dean, the affable owner. $ *Average main: $8* ⊠ *550 N. Lake Tahoe Blvd., at Grove St.* ☎ *530/583–2666* ☉ *No dinner.*

$$$

ECLECTIC

Fodor'sChoice

★

✕ **Wolfdale's.** Consistent, inspired cuisine makes Wolfdale's one of the top restaurants on the lake. Seafood is the specialty on the changing menu; the imaginative entrées merge Asian and European cooking (drawing on the chef-owner's training in Japan) and lean toward the light and healthful, rather than the heavy and overdone. Everything from teriyaki glaze to smoked fish is made in-house. Request a window table, and book early enough to see the lake view from the elegantly simple dining room. $ *Average main: $28* ⊠ *640 N. Lake Blvd., near Grove St.* ☎ *530/583–5700* ⊕ *www.wolfdales.com* ☉ *Closed Tues. No lunch.*

WHERE TO STAY

$$

B&B/INN

⛫ **Cottage Inn.** Avoid the crowds by staying in one of these charming circa-1938 log cottages under the towering pines on the lake's west shore. **Pros:** romantic, woodsy setting; each room has a fireplace; full breakfast. **Cons:** no kids under 12. $ *Rooms from: $160* ⊠ *1690 W. Lake Blvd., Box 66* ☎ *530/581–4073, 800/581–4073* ⊕ *www. thecottageinn.com* ⇌ *22 rooms* ⦿ *Breakfast.*

$$$$
HOTEL
Fodor's Choice
★

Sunnyside Steakhouse and Lodge. The views are superb at this pretty little lodge right on the lake, three miles south of Tahoe City. **Pros:** complimentary Continental breakfast and afternoon tea; most rooms have balconies overlooking the lake. **Cons:** can be pricey for families. $ *Rooms from: $265* ✉ *1850 W. Lake Blvd., Box 5969* ☎ *530/583–7200, 800/822–2754* ⊕ *www.sunnysideresort.com* ⟿ *18 rooms, 5 suites* ❍| *Breakfast.*

SPORTS AND THE OUTDOORS

GOLF

Tahoe City Golf Course. This 9-hole course, which opened in 1917, gives golfers views of Lake Tahoe. Rent a cart for $10. ■**TIP**→ All greens break toward the lake. ✉ *251 N. Lake Blvd.* ☎ *530/583–1516* ☞ *$30 for 9 holes; $50 for 18* ⅃. *18 holes, 5261 yards, par 66.*

RAFTING

FAMILY **Truckee River Rafting.** In summer you can take a self-guided raft trip down a gentle 5-mile stretch of the Truckee River. This outfitter will shuttle you back to Tahoe City at the end of your two- to three-hour trip. On a warm day, this makes a great family outing. ✉ *175 River Rd., near W. Lake Blvd.* ☎ *530/583–1111* ⊕ *www.truckeeriverrafting. com* ☞ *From $28.*

SKIING

Fodor's Choice
★

Alpine Meadows Ski Area. With 450 inches of snow annually, Alpine has some of Tahoe's most reliable conditions. It's usually one of the first areas to open in November and one of the last to close in May or June. Alpine isn't the place for show-offs; instead, you'll find down-to-earth alpine fetishists. The two peaks here are well suited to intermediate skiers, with a number of runs for experts only. Snowboarders and hot-dog skiers will find a terrain park with a super-pipe, rails, and tabletops, as well as a boarder-cross course. Alpine is a great place to learn to ski and has a ski school that coaches those with physical and mental disabilities. On Saturday, because of the limited parking, there's more acreage per person than at other resorts. Lift tickets are good at neighboring Squaw Valley; a free shuttle runs all day between the two ski parks. ✉ *2600 Alpine Meadows Rd., off Hwy. 89, 6 miles northwest of Tahoe City and 13 miles south of Truckee* ☎ *530/583–4232, 800/403–0206, 530/452–4356 snow phone* ⊕ *www.skialpine. com* ⟿ *100 trails on 2,400 acres, rated 25% beginner, 40% intermediate, 35% advanced. Longest run 2½ miles, base 6,835 feet, summit 8,637 feet. Lifts: 13, including 1 high-speed 6-passenger lift and 2 high-speed quads.*

Tahoe Dave's Skis and Boards. You can rent skis, boards, and snowshoes at this shop, which has the area's best selection of downhill rental equipment. ✉ *590 N. Lake Blvd.* ☎ *530/583–6415* ⊕ *www. tahoedaves.com.*

13

OLYMPIC VALLEY

7 miles north of Tahoe City to Squaw Valley Road; 8½ miles south of Truckee.

Olympic Valley got its name in 1960, when Squaw Valley USA, the ski resort here, hosted the Winter Olympics. Snow sports remain the primary activity, but once summer comes, you can hike into the adjacent Granite Chief Wilderness, explore wildflower-studded alpine meadows, or lie by a swimming pool in one of the Sierra's prettiest valleys.

GETTING HERE AND AROUND

Squaw Valley Road, the only way into Olympic Valley, branches west off Highway 89 about 8 miles south of Truckee. TART connects the Squaw Valley ski area with the communities along the north and west shores, and Truckee, with year-round public transportation. Squaw Valley Ski Resort provides a free shuttle to many stops in those same areas.

EXPLORING

High Camp. You can ride the Squaw Valley Aerial Tram to this activity hub, which at 8,200 feet commands superb views of Lake Tahoe and the surrounding mountains. In summer, go for a sunset hike, sit by the pool, or have a cocktail and watch the sunset. In winter, you can ski, ice-skate, snow-tube or go for a full-moon hike. There's also a restaurant, a lounge, and a small Olympic museum. Pick up trail maps at the tram building. ⊠ *Aerial Tram Bldg., Squaw Valley* ☎ *800/403–0206* ⊕ *squaw.com/the-village* ⊠ *Aerial Tram, $29* ⊘ *Daily; call for hrs.*

FAMILY **Village at Squaw Valley.** The centerpiece of Olympic Valley is a pedestrian mall at the base of several four-story ersatz Bavarian stone-and-timber buildings, where you'll find restaurants, high-end condo rentals, boutiques, and cafés. ⊠ *1750 Village East Rd.* ☎ *530/584–1000, 800/403–0206 information, 800/731–8021 condo reservations* ⊕ *squaw.com/the-village.*

WHERE TO EAT

$$ ✕ **Fireside Pizza Company.** Adults might opt for the signature pear and
PIZZA Gorgonzola pizza at this modern Italian restaurant, but most kids
FAMILY clamor for the house favorite: an Italian-sausage-and-pepperoni combo with a bubbly blend of four cheeses. Salads and pasta dishes round out the menu at this family-friendly spot. Ⓢ *Average main: $16* ⊠ *The Village at Squaw Valley, 1985 Squaw Valley Rd., #25* ☎ *530/584–6150* ⊕ *firesidepizza.com.*

$$$ ✕ **Graham's of Squaw Valley.** Sit by a floor-to-ceiling river-rock hearth
ECLECTIC under a knotty-pine peaked ceiling in the intimate dining room in the Christy Inn Lodge. The southern European–inspired menu changes often, but expect hearty entrées such as grilled beef tenderloin with wild mushroom sauce, along with lighter-fare small plates like quail with fig demi-glace. You can also stop in at the fireside bar for appetizers and wine from Graham's highly regarded wine list. Ⓢ *Average main: $30* ⊠ *1650 Squaw Valley Rd.* ☎ *530/581–0454* ⊘ *Closed Mon. No lunch.*

$$ ✕ **Mamasake.** The hip sushi spot at Squaw serves stylized presentations.
JAPANESE On some evenings you can sit at the bar and watch extreme-skiing movies, many of them filmed right outside the window. From 3 to 5 enjoy the afternoon special: a spicy-tuna or salmon hand roll and a can of Bud

quaw Valley USA has runs for skiers of all ability levels—from beginner trails to cliff drops for experts.

for five bucks. $ *Average main: $16* ✉ *1850 Village South Rd., No. 52, off Squaw Valley Rd.* ☎ *530/584–0110* ⊕ *mamasake.com.*

$$$$
AMERICAN
Fodor's Choice
★

✕ **PlumpJack Café.** The best restaurant in the entire Tahoe Basin is the epitome of discreet chic for serious foodies. The menu changes seasonally, but look for filet mignon "Oscar" with Dungeness crab, crispy sweetbreads, and inventive vegetarian dishes. Rather than complicated, heavy sauces, the chef uses simple reductions to complement a dish. The result: clean, dynamic flavors. The wine list is exceptional for its variety and reasonable prices. A less expensive but equally adventurous menu, including lunch, is served at the bar. $ *Average main: $34* ✉ *1920 Squaw Valley Rd.* ☎ *530/583–1578, 800/323–7666* ⊕ *www. plumpjackcafe.com* ⚓ *Reservations essential.*

WHERE TO STAY

$$$$
HOTEL
Fodor's Choice
★

🛏 **PlumpJack Squaw Valley Inn.** Stylish and luxurious, this two-story, cedar-sided inn has a snappy, sophisticated look and laid-back sensibility, perfect for the Bay Area cognoscenti who flock here on weekends. **Pros:** small; intimate; lots of attention to details. **Cons:** not the best choice for families with small children. $ *Rooms from: $255* ✉ *1920 Squaw Valley Rd.* ☎ *530/583–1576, 800/323–7666* ⊕ *www. plumpjacksquawvalleyinn.com* ⇨ *56 rooms, 8 suites* ¶◎¶ *Breakfast.*

$$$$
RESORT

🛏 **Resort at Squaw Creek.** This multi-facility Squaw Valley resort offers a plethora of year-round activities. **Pros:** every conceivable amenity; private chairlift to Squaw Valley USA for ski-in, ski-out. **Cons:** large and pricey. $ *Rooms from: $259* ✉ *400 Squaw Creek Rd.* ☎ *530/583–6300, 800/327–3353* ⊕ *www.squawcreek.com* ⇨ *205 rooms, 200 suites* ¶◎¶ *No meals.*

$$$
HOTEL

The Village at Squaw Valley USA. Right at the base of the slopes, at the center point of Olympic Valley, the Village's condominiums (from studio to three bedrooms) come complete with gas fireplaces, daily maid service, and heated slate-tile bathroom and kitchen floors. **Pros:** family-friendly; near Village restaurants and shops. **Cons:** claustrophobia-inducing crowds on weekends. ⑤ *Rooms from: $199* ✉ *1750 Village East Rd.* ☎ *530/584–1000, 888/259–1428* ⊕ *www.squaw.com/the-village/lodging* ⇨ *198 suites* ⦿ *No meals.*

SPORTS AND THE OUTDOORS

GOLF

Resort at Squaw Creek Golf Course. For beautiful views of Squaw Valley's surrounding peaks, play this narrow, challenging championship course designed by Robert Trent Jones Jr. Rates start at $98 with midrange twilight fees beginning at noon for $78; the lowest rate, $60, starts at 3 pm. All fees include a golf cart plus valet parking. ✉ *400 Squaw Creek Rd.* ☎ *530/583–6300, 530/581–6637 pro shop* ⊕ *www.squawcreek.com* ⛳ *$98* ⛳ *18 holes, 6931 yards, par 71.*

ICE-SKATING

FAMILY **Olympic Ice Pavilion.** Ice-skate here from late November to early March. A ride up the mountain in the Aerial Tram costs $29, plus $12 for skate rental and one hour of skate time. End your outing in the hot tub ($14). In summer, the pavilion converts into a roller-skating rink. Year-round, you get fabulous views of the lake and the Sierra Nevada. ✉ *1960 Squaw Valley Rd., High Camp, Squaw Valley* ☎ *800/403–0206* ⊕ *squaw.com/things-to-do/high-camp/ice-skating.*

MINIATURE GOLF

FAMILY **Squaw Valley Adventure Center.** Next to the Olympic Village Lodge, on the far side of the creek, this seasonal activities center has an 18-hole miniature golf course, a ropes course, and sometimes a bungee trampoline, a blast for kids. ✉ *1960 Squaw Valley Rd.* ☎ *530/581–7563* ⊕ *www.squawadventure.com.*

ROCK CLIMBING

Headwall Climbing Wall. Before you rappel down a granite monolith, hone your skills at this challenging wall at the base of the Aerial Tram. ✉ *Squaw Valley Adventure Center, 1960 Squaw Valley Rd.* ☎ *530/581–7563* ⊕ *www.squawadventure.com.*

SKIING

Resort at Squaw Creek. Cross-country skiers enjoy looping through the valley's giant alpine meadow. The resort rents ski equipment and provides trail maps. ✉ *400 Squaw Creek Rd.* ☎ *530/583–6300, 530/581–6637 pro shop* ⊕ *www.squawcreek.com.*

Fodor'sChoice ★ **Squaw Valley USA.** Known for some of the toughest skiing in the Tahoe area, this park was the centerpiece of the 1960 Winter Olympics. Today it's the definitive North Tahoe ski resort and among the top-three megaresorts in California (the other two are Heavenly and Mammoth). Although Squaw has changed significantly since the Olympics, the skiing is still world-class and extends across vast bowls stretched between six peaks. Experts often head directly to the untamed terrain of the infamous KT-22 face, which has bumps, cliffs, and gulp-and-go chutes, or to the nearly vertical Palisades, where many famous extreme-skiing films have been shot. Fret not, beginners and intermediates: you have plenty of wide-open, groomed trails at High Camp (which sits at the *top* of the mountain) and around the more challenging Snow King Peak. Snowboarders and show-off skiers can tear up the six fantastic terrain parks, which include a giant super-pipe. Ski passes are good at neighboring Alpine Meadows; free shuttles run all day between the two ski parks. ⊠ *1960 Squaw Valley Rd., off Hwy. 89, 7 miles northwest of Tahoe City* ☎ *800/731–8021 lodging reservations, 530/452–4355 snow phone, 800/403–0206 information* ⊕ *squaw.com* ⟿ *170 trails on 3,600 acres, rated 25% beginner, 45% intermediate, 30% advanced. Longest run 3.2 miles, base 6,200 feet, summit 9,050 feet. Lifts: 29, including a gondola-style funitel, a tram, 7 high-speed chairs, and 15 fixed-grip chairs and 5 surface lifts.*

Tahoe Dave's Skis and Boards. If you don't want to pay resort prices, you can rent and tune downhill skis and snowboards at this shop. ⊠ *3039 Hwy. 89, at Squaw Valley Rd.* ☎ *530/583–5665* ⊕ *www.tahoedaves.com.*

TRUCKEE

13 miles northwest of Kings Beach, 14 miles north of Tahoe City.

Formerly a decrepit railroad town in the mountains, Truckee is now the trendy first stop for many Tahoe visitors. The town was officially established around 1863, and by 1868 it had gone from a stagecoach station to a major stopover for trains bound for the Pacific via the new transcontinental railroad. Freight trains and Amtrak's California Zephyr still stop every day at the depot right in the middle of town. Stop inside the depot for a walking-tour map of historic Truckee. Across from the station, where Old West facades line the main drag, you'll find galleries, gift shops, boutiques, old-fashioned diners, and several remarkably good restaurants. Look for outlet stores, strip malls, and discount skiwear shops along Donner Pass Road, north of the freeway. Because of its location on Interstate 80, Truckee is a favorite stopover for people traveling from the San Francisco Bay Area to the north shore of Lake Tahoe, Reno, and points east.

GETTING HERE AND AROUND

Truckee is just off Interstate 80 between highways 89 and 267. Greyhound and Amtrak stop here, Enterprise and Hertz provide car rentals, and TART buses serve Truckee and north shore communities.

ESSENTIALS

Visitor Information Truckee Donner Chamber of Commerce and the California Welcome Center ⊠ *Amtrak depot, 10065 Donner Pass Rd., near Spring St.* ☎ *530/587–8808 chamber of commerce, 866/443–2027 welcome center* ⊕ *www.truckee.com.*

EXPLORING

Donner Memorial State Park and Emigrant Trail Museum. The park and museum commemorate the Donner Party, westward-bound pioneers—about 90; historians debate the exact number—who became trapped in the Sierra in the winter of 1846–47 in snow 22 feet deep. Barely more than half the pioneers survived, some by resorting to cannibalism. The Emigrant Trail Museum details the Donner Party's plight, and other displays explain railroad development through the Sierra. In the park, you can picnic, hike, camp, and go boating, fishing, and waterskiing in summer; winter brings cross-country skiing and snowshoeing on groomed trails. Slated for a 2015 debut, a new High Sierra Crossing Museum will contain exhibits about the Donner Party, regional Native Americans, and railroad and transportation development through Donner Pass. ⊠ *12593 Donner Pass Rd., off I–80, 2 miles west of Truckee* ☎ *530/582–7892 museum, 800/444–7275 camping reservations* ⊕ *www.parks.ca.gov* ⊇ *$8 parking, day use* ☉ *Museum daily 10–5.*

OFF THE BEATEN PATH

Tahoe National Forest. Draped along the Sierra Nevada Crest north of Lake Tahoe, the national forest offers abundant outdoor recreation: hiking, picnicking, and camping in summer, and snowshoeing, skiing, and sledding over some of the deepest snowpack in the West in winter. ⊠ *Truckee ranger station, 10811 Stockrest Springs Rd.* ☎ *530/587–3558 Truckee ranger station, 530/265–4531 forest headquarters* ⊕ *www.fs.usda.gov/tahoe.*

WHERE TO EAT

$$$
ECLECTIC
Fodor'sChoice
★

✕ **Cottonwood Restaurant & Bar.** Perched above town on the site of North America's first chairlift, this restaurant is an institution. The bar is decked out with old wooden skis, sleds, skates, and photos of Truckee's early days. The ambitious menu includes everything from grilled steak to baby back ribs with Cajun spices to butternut-squash enchiladas—plus fresh-baked breads and desserts. But people come here mainly for the atmosphere and hilltop views. ⑤ *Average main: $24* ⊠ *10142 Rue Hilltop Rd., off Brockway Rd., ¼ mile south of downtown* ☎ *530/587–5711* ⊕ *www.cottonwoodrestaurant.com* ☉ *No lunch.*

$$$
ASIAN

✕ **Dragonfly.** Flavors are bold and zingy at this Cal-Asian spot, where every dish is well executed and stylishly presented. Southeast Asian cooking inspires most dishes, which you can savor in the bright, contemporary dining rooms—one for sushi—or, when the weather's nice, an outdoor terrace overlooking the busy street scene and the train depot. Lunch is a bargain, and there are many choices for vegetarians. Look for the staircase: the restaurant is on the second floor. ⑤ *Average main: $26* ⊠ *10118 Donner Pass Rd., near Spring St.* ☎ *530/587–0557* ⊕ *www.dragonflycuisine.com.*

$$
AMERICAN

✕ **FiftyFifty Brewing Company.** In this Truckee brewpub, warm red tones and comfy booths, plus a pint of the Donner Party porter, will take the nip out of a cold day on the slopes. The menu includes salads, burgers, and the house specialty, a pulled-pork sandwich, plus barbecued ribs and pan-seared salmon. Their inventive pizzas are popular anytime. There's a full bar along with the brews, and lots of après-ski action. ⑤ *Average main: $21* ⊠ *11197 Brockway Rd.* ☎ *530/587–2337* ⊕ *www.fiftyfiftybrewing.com.*

$$$
ECLECTIC

✕ **Moody's Bistro Bar & Beats.** Head here for contemporary-Cal cuisine in a sexy dining room with pumpkin-color walls, burgundy velvet banquettes, and art deco fixtures. The earthy, sure-handed cooking features organically grown ingredients: look for ahi *poke*, snazzy pizzas bubbling-hot from a brick oven, braised lamb shanks, pan-roasted wild game, fresh seafood, and organic beef. Lunch fare is lighter. In summer dine alfresco surrounded by flowers. From Thursday through Saturday there's music in the borderline-raucous bar that gets packed with Truckee's bon vivants. ⑤ *Average main: $23* ✉ *10007 Bridge St., at Donner Pass Rd.* ☎ *530/587–8688* ⊕ *moodysbistro.com.*

WHERE TO STAY

$$$
HOTEL
🏨 **Cedar House Sport Hotel.** The clean, spare lines of the Cedar House's wooden exterior evoke a modern European feel, while energy-saving heating, cooling, and lighting systems emphasize the owners' commitment to sustainability. **Pros:** environmentally friendly; comfortable; hip. **Cons:** some bathrooms on the small side. ⑤ *Rooms from: $190* ✉ *10918 Brockway Rd.* ☎ *530/582–5655, 866/582–5655* ⊕ *www.cedarhousesporthotel.com* ⤳ *40 rooms* ⑩ *Breakfast.*

$$$
RESORT
🏨 **Northstar California Resort.** The area's most complete destination resort entices families with its sports activities and concentration of restaurants, shops, and accommodations. **Pros:** array of lodging types; on-site shuttle; several dining options in Northstar Village. **Cons:** family accommodations are very pricey. ⑤ *Rooms from: $249* ✉ *100 Northstar Dr., off Hwy. 267, 6 miles southeast of Truckee* ☎ *530/562–1010, 800/466–6784* ⊕ *www.northstarcalifornia.com* ⤳ *250 units* ⑩ *No meals.*

$$$$
RESORT
🏨 **Ritz-Carlton Highlands Court, Lake Tahoe.** Nestled midmountain on the Northstar ski resort, the plush accommodations of the Ritz-Carlton have floor-to-ceiling windows for maximum views, along with fireplaces, cozy robes, and down comforters. **Pros:** superb service; gorgeous setting. **Cons:** prices as breathtaking as the views; must go off-site for golf and tennis. ⑤ *Rooms from: $569* ✉ *13031 Ritz-Carlton Highlands Court* ☎ *530/562–3000, 800/241–3333* ⊕ *www.ritzcarlton.com/laketahoe* ⤳ *153 rooms, 17 suites* ⑩ *No meals.*

$$
B&B/INN
🏨 **River Street Inn.** On the banks of the Truckee River, this 1885 wood-and-stone inn has uncluttered, comfortable rooms that are simply decorated, with attractive, country-style wooden furniture and extras like flat-screen TVs. **Pros:** nice rooms; good value. **Cons:** parking is a half-block from inn. ⑤ *Rooms from: $145* ✉ *10009 E. River St.* ☎ *530/550–9290* ⊕ *www.riverstreetinntruckee.com* ⤳ *11 rooms* ⑩ *Breakfast.*

SPORTS AND THE OUTDOORS

GOLF

Coyote Moon Golf Course. With towering pine trees lining the fairways and no houses to spoil the view, this course is as beautiful as it is challenging. Fees include a shared cart; the greens fee drops at 1 pm and dips again at 3. ✉ *10685 Northwoods Blvd., off Donner Pass Rd.* ☎ *530/587–0886* ⊕ *www.coyotemoongolf.com* ⛳ *$155* ⛳ *18 holes, 7177 yards, par 72* ☼ *Closed late fall–late spring.*

Northstar. The front nine holes here are open-links style, while the challenging back nine move through tight, tree-lined fairways. Fees include a shared cart. Twilight rates begin at 1 pm. You can play nine holes for $45; special teen rates encourage family outings. The restaurant serves breakfast and lunch only. ✉ *168 Basque Dr., off Northstar Dr., west off Hwy. 267* ☎ *530/562–3290 pro-shop* ⊕ *www.northstarcalifornia.com/info/summer/golf.asp* ⛳ *$70* ⛳ *18 holes, 6781 yards, par 72.*

Old Greenwood. Beautiful mountain and forest views add to the pleasure of a round played at north Lake Tahoe's only Jack Nicklaus Signature Golf Course. The regular fees are high, but there's a $75 twilight rate beginning at 4 pm. ✉ *12915 Fairway Dr., off Overland Trail Rd., off I–80, Exit 190* ☎ *530/550–7010* ⊕ *www.golfintahoe.com/old_ greenwood* ☜ *$200* 🏌 *18 holes, 7518 yards, par 72.*

MOUNTAIN BIKING

Northstar California. In summer you can rent a bike and ride the lifts ($46, ages 13 and up) to the mountain-biking park for 100 miles of challenging terrain. The season extends from mid-June through September with varying hours. ✉ *Northstar Dr., off Hwy. 267* ☎ *530/562–1010* ⊕ *www.northstarcalifornia.com/info/summer/biking.asp.*

Cyclepaths Mountain Bike Adventures. This combination full-service bike shop and bike-adventure outfitter offers instruction in mountain biking, guided tours, tips for self-guided bike touring, bike repairs, and books and maps on the area. ✉ *10095 W. River St., by Bridge St.* ☎ *530/582–1890* ⊕ *www.cyclepaths.net.*

SKIING

Several smaller resorts around Truckee offer access to the Sierra's slopes for less than half the price of the big resorts. Though you'll sacrifice vertical rise, acreage, and high-speed lifts, you can ski or ride and still have money left over for room and board. These are great places for first-timers and families with kids learning to ski.

Boreal Mountain Resort. These slopes have 480 skiable acres and 500 vertical feet of terrain visible from the freeway. Lift-served snow-tubing and night skiing go until 9. ✉ *19749 Boreal Ridge Rd., at I–80, Boreal/Castle Peak exit, Soda Springs* ☎ *530/426–3666* ⊕ *www. rideboreal.com.*

Donner Ski Ranch. This ski park has 505 acres and 750 vertical feet. A popular area with kids in this small, family-friendly park is the Tubing Hill. Riders whisk down the slope in a huge inflated inner tube and then go back to the top on a moving carpet. ✉ *19320 Donner Pass Rd., Norden* ☎ *530/426–3635* ⊕ *www.donnerskiranch.com.*

Fodor's Choice ★ **Northstar California.** With two tree-lined, northeast-facing, wind-protected bowls, this park is the ideal place in a storm, and just may be the best all-around family ski resort at Tahoe. Hotshot experts unfairly call the mountain "Flatstar," but the meticulous grooming and long cruisers make it an intermediate skier's paradise. Boarders are especially welcome, with awesome terrain parks, including a 420-foot-long superpipe, a half-pipe, rails and boxes, and lots of kickers. Experts can ski the steeps and bumps off Lookout Mountain, where there's rarely a line for the high-speed quad. Northstar-at-Tahoe's cross-country center has 35 km (22 miles) of groomed trails, including double-set tracks and skating lanes. The school has programs for skiers ages three and up, and day care is available for tots two and older. The mountain gets packed on busy weekends, but when there's room on the slopes, Northstar is loads of fun. ✉ *5001 Northstar Dr.* ☎ *530/562–1010 information, 800/466–6784 lodging, 530/562–1330 snow phone* ⊕ *www.northstarcalifornia. com* ☞ *97 trails on 3,170 acres, rated 13% beginner, 60% intermediate,*

27% advanced. Longest run 1.4 miles, base 6,330 feet, summit 8,610 feet. Lifts: 20, including 2 gondolas and 7 high-speed quads.

Royal Gorge. If you love to cross-country, don't miss Royal Gorge, which serves up 200 km (124 miles) of track for all abilities, 75 trails on a whopping 6,000 acres, a ski school, and eight warming huts. Two trailside cafés and two lodges round out the facilities. Because the complex sits right on the Sierra Crest, the views are drop-dead gorgeous. ⊠ *9411 Pahatsi Dr., off I–80, Soda Springs/Norden exit, Soda Springs* ☎ *530/426–3871* ⊕ *www.royalgorge.com.*

Soda Springs. Along with 200 acres and 652 vertical feet, this ski park also has lift-served snow-tubing. ⊠ *10244 Soda Springs Rd., I–80 Soda Springs exit, Soda Springs* ☎ *530/426–3901* ⊕ *www.skisodasprings.com.*

Fodor's Choice ★ **Sugar Bowl Ski Resort.** Opened in 1939 by Walt Disney, this is the oldest—and one of the best—resorts at Tahoe. Atop Donner Summit, it receives an incredible 500 inches of snowfall annually. Four peaks are connected by 1,650 acres of skiable terrain, with everything from gentle groomed corduroy to wide-open bowls to vertical rocky chutes and outstanding tree skiing. Snowboarders can hit two terrain parks with numerous boxes, rails, and jumps. Because it's more compact than some of the area's megaresorts, there's a gentility here that distinguishes Sugar Bowl from its competitors, making this a great place for families and a low-pressure, low-key place to learn to ski. It's not huge, but there's some very challenging terrain (experts: head to the Palisades). There's limited lodging at the base area. ⊠ *629 Sugar Bowl Rd., off Donner Pass Rd., 3 miles east of I–80 Soda Springs/Norden exit, 10 miles west of Truckee, Norden* ☎ *530/426–9000 information and lodging reservations, 530/426–1111 snow phone, 866/843–2695 lodging referral* ⊕ *www.sugarbowl.com* ☞ *102 trails on 1,650 acres, rated 17% beginner, 45% intermediate, 38% advanced. Longest run 3 miles, base 6,883 feet, summit 8,383 feet. Lifts: 13, including 5 high-speed quads.*

Tahoe Dave's. You can save money by renting skis and boards at this shop, which has the area's best selection and also repairs and tunes equipment. ⊠ *10200 Donner Pass Rd., near Spring St.* ☎ *530/582–0900* ⊕ *www.tahoedaves.com.*

Tahoe Donner. Just north of Truckee, this park covers 120 acres and 600 vertical feet; the cross-country center includes 51 trails on 100 km (62 miles) of groomed tracks on 4,800 acres, with night skiing on Wednesday in January and February. ⊠ *11603 Snowpeak Way* ☎ *530/587–9444* ⊕ *www.tahoedonner.com.*

ARNELIAN BAY TO KINGS BEACH

5–10 miles northeast of Tahoe City.

The small lakeside commercial districts of Carnelian Bay and Tahoe Vista service the thousand or so locals who live in the area year-round and the thousands more who have summer residences or launch their boats here. Kings Beach, the last town heading east on Highway 28 before the Nevada border, is to Crystal Bay what South Lake Tahoe is to Stateline: a bustling town full of basic motels and rental condos, restaurants, and shops, used by the hordes of hopefuls who pass through on their way to the casinos.

GETTING HERE AND AROUND

To reach Kings Beach and Carnelian Bay from the California side, take Highway 89 north to Highway 28 north and then east. From the Nevada side, follow Highway 28 north and then west. TART provides public transportation in this area.

BEACHES

FAMILY **Kings Beach State Recreation Area.** The 28-acre Kings Beach State Recreation Area, one of the largest such areas on the lake, is open year-round. The 700-foot-long sandy beach gets crowded in summer with people swimming, sunbathing, Jet Skiing, riding in paddleboats, spiking volleyballs, and tossing Frisbees. If you're going to spend the day, come early enough to snag a table in the picnic area; there's also a good playground. **Amenities:** food and drink; parking (fee); toilets; water sports. **Best for:** sunrise; swimming; windsurfing. ⊠ *8318 N. Lake Blvd., Hwy. 28, Kings Beach* ☎ *530/546–7248* ⊕ *www.parks.ca.gov* ⊡ *$8 parking fee.*

WHERE TO EAT AND STAY

$$$ ✕ **Gar Woods Grill and Pier.** The view's the thing at this lakeside stalwart,
ECLECTIC   where you can watch the sun shimmer on the water through the dining room's plate-glass windows or from the heated outdoor deck. Grilled steak and fish are menu mainstays, but be sure to try specialties like crab chilis rellenos and chipotle chicken salad. At all hours in season, the bar gets packed with boaters who pull up to the restaurant's private pier. ⑤ *Average main: $29* ⊠ *5000 N. Lake Blvd., Hwy. 28, Carnelian Bay* ☎ *530/546–3366* ⊕ *www.garwoods.com.*

$$$ ✕ **Spindleshanks American Bistro and Wine Bar.** This restaurant, which relo-
AMERICAN   cated in 2014 to the Old Brockway Golf Course, serves mostly classic American cooking—ribs, steaks, and seafood updated with adventurous sauces—as well as house-made ravioli. Savor a drink from the full bar or choose a wine from the extensive list while you enjoy views of Lake Tahoe or the historic greens, where Bing Crosby hosted his first golf tournament in 1934. ⑤ *Average main: $23* ⊠ *400 Brassie Ave., at Hwy. 267 & N. Lake Tahoe Blvd., Tahoe Vista* ☎ *530/546–2191* ⊕ *www. spindleshankstahoe.com* ☽ *No lunch except in summer.*

$ 🏨 **Ferrari's Crown Resort.** Great for families with kids, the family-
HOTEL   owned and-operated Ferrari's has straightforward motel rooms in
FAMILY   a resort setting. **Pros:** family-friendly; lakeside location. **Cons:** older facility. ⑤ *Rooms from: $105* ⊠ *8200 N. Lake Blvd., Kings Beach* ☎ *530/546–3388, 800/645–2260* ⊕ *www.tahoecrown.com* ⇗ *72 rooms* ⑩ *Breakfast.*

$$$$ 🏨 **Shore House.** The lovingly tended, knotty-pine-paneled guest rooms
B&B/INN   at this lakefront B&B in Tahoe Vista beautifully and simply capture the woodsy spirit of Tahoe, but without overdoing the pinecone motif. **Pros:** waterfront honeymoon cottage; massage appointments available. **Cons:** not a good choice for children. ⑤ *Rooms from: $276* ⊠ *7170 N. Lake Blvd., Tahoe Vista* ☎ *530/546–7270, 800/207–5160* ⊕ *www. shorehouselaketahoe.com* ⇗ *8 rooms, 1 cottage* ⑩ *Breakfast.*

THE NEVADA SIDE

The difference on the Nevada side of the lake is, of course, gambling, with all its repercussions.

CRYSTAL BAY

1 mile east of Kings Beach, 30 miles north of South Lake Tahoe.

Right at the Nevada border, Crystal Bay features a cluster of casinos, a few spunky ones with personality and some smaller ones that locals tend to favor. There's not much lodging; the largest property, the Cal-Neva Resort, Spa and Casino that Frank Sinatra owned, is, as of this writing, undergoing a multimillion-dollar remodel. Look for it to reopen with great hoopla in 2015. For now, one of Tahoe's best restaurants, Soule Domain, is reason enough for a stop in Crystal Bay.

13

GETTING HERE AND AROUND

From the California side, reach Crystal Bay via Highway 89 or 267 to Highway 28. TART serves the communities along the north and west shores.

WHERE TO EAT

$$$
ECLECTIC

✕ **Soule Domain.** Rough-hewn wood beams, a vaulted wood ceiling, and, in winter, a roaring fireplace lend high romance to this cozy 1927 pine-log cabin next to the Tahoe Biltmore. Chef-owner Charlie Soule's specialties include curried almond chicken, fresh sea scallops poached in Champagne with a kiwi and mango cream sauce, and a vegan sauté with ginger, jalapeños, and tofu. If you're looking for a place with a sterling menu where you can hold hands by candlelight, this is it. $ *Average main: $27* ⊠ *9983 Cove St., ½ block up Stateline Rd. off Hwy. 28, Kings Beach* ☎ *530/546–7529* ⊕ *www.souledomain. com* ☾ *No lunch.*

NIGHTLIFE

CASINOS

Crystal Bay Club. Known for its classic steak and lobster dinner, the restaurant in this casino has a distinctive open-truss ceiling. With entertainment in two venues, and accomodations in its historic 10-room Border House ($$$) next to the club, this refurbished casino tempts tourists to linger on Tahoe's north shore. ⊠ *14 Hwy. 28, near Stateline Rd.* ☎ *775/833–6333* ⊕ *www.crystalbaycasino.com.*

Tahoe Biltmore. A daily happy hour keeps this old favorite hopping, along with dinner specials in Bilty's Brew & Q restaurant, and inexpensive breakfasts in their café. Expect simple accommodations ($–$$) in the casino's hotel. The circular Tahoe Biltmore sign is a 1962 "Googie-style" architectural riff off the Seattle Space Neeedle, which debuted the same year. ⊠ *5 Hwy. 28, at Stateline Rd.* ☎ *800/245–8667* ⊕ *www. tahoebiltmore.com.*

INCLINE VILLAGE

3 miles east of Crystal Bay.

Incline Village dates to the early 1960s when an Oklahoma developer bought 10,000 acres north of Lake Tahoe. His idea was to sketch out a plan for a town without a central commercial district, hoping to prevent congestion and to preserve the area's natural beauty. One-acre lakeshore lots originally fetched $12,000 to $15,000; today you couldn't buy the same land for less than several million.

GETTING HERE AND AROUND

From the California side, reach Incline Village via Highway 89 or 267 to Highway 28. From South Lake Tahoe, take U.S. 50 north to Highway 28 north. TART serves the communities along Lake Tahoe's north and west shores from Incline Village to Tahoma.

ESSENTIALS

Visitor Information Lake Tahoe Incline Village/Crystal Bay Visitors Bureau ⊠ *969 Tahoe Blvd.* ☎ *775/832–1606, 800/468–2463* ⊕ *www.gotahoenorth.com.*

EXPLORING

Lakeshore Drive. Take this beautiful drive to see some of the most expensive real estate in Nevada. The route is discreetly marked: to find it, start at the Hyatt hotel and drive westward along the lake.

Fodor'sChoice **Thunderbird Lodge.** George Whittell, a San Francisco socialite who once
★ owned 40,000 acres of property along the lake, built this lodge in 1936. You can tour the mansion and the grounds by reservation only, and though it's pricey to do so, you'll be rewarded with a rare glimpse of a time when only the very wealthy had homes at Tahoe. The lodge is accessible via a bus from the Incline Village Visitors Bureau, a catamaran from the Hyatt in Incline Village ($110), or a 1950 wooden cruiser from Tahoe Keys Marina in South Lake Tahoe, which includes Continental breakfast and lunch ($135). ⊠ *5000 Nevada 28* ☎ *775/832–8750 lodge info, 800/468–2463 reservations, 775/588–1881, 888/867–6394 Tahoe Keys boat, 775/831–4386 Hyatt Incline catamaran* ⊕ *thunderbirdtahoe.org/tours* 🖃 *$39 bus tour, $110 & 135 for boat tours* ☉ *May–Oct., Tues.–Sat., call for tour times.*

BEACHES

Lake Tahoe–Nevada State Park and Sand Harbor Beach. Protecting much of the lake's eastern shore from development, this park comprises several sections that stretch from Incline Village to Zephyr Cove. Beaches and trails provide access to a wilder side of the lake, whether you're into cross-country skiing, hiking, or just relaxing at a picnic. With a gently sloping beach for lounging, crystal clear water for swimming and snorkeling, and a picnic area shaded by cedars and pines, **Sand Harbor Beach** is so popular that it sometimes fills to capacity by 11 am on summer weekends. Boaters have two launch ramps. A handicap-accessible nature trail has interpretive signs and beautiful lake views. Pets are not allowed. **Amenities:** food and drink; parking ($12 mid-Apr.–mid-Oct., $7 rest of the year); toilets; water sports. **Best for:** snorkeling; sunset; swimming; walking. ⊠ *Sand Harbor Beach, Hwy. 28, 3 miles south of Incline Village* ☎ *775/831–0494* ⊕ *parks.nv.gov/parks/sand-harbor.*

WHERE TO EAT AND STAY

$$$
ECLECTIC

✗ **Fredrick's Fusion Bistro.** Copper-top tables lend a chic look to the dining room at this intimate bistro. The menu consists of a mélange of European and Asian dishes, most of them prepared with organic produce and free-range meats. Try the braised short ribs, roasted duck with caramel-pecan glaze, or the deliciously fresh sushi rolls. ■TIP➔ On cold nights ask for a table by the fire. $ *Average main: $24* ✉ *907 Tahoe Blvd., at Village Blvd.* ☎ *775/832–3007* ⊕ *fredricksbistro.com* ۵ *Closed Sun. and Mon. No lunch.*

$$$
FRENCH
Fodor's Choice
★

✗ **Le Bistro.** Incline Village's hidden gem serves expertly prepared French-country cuisine in a relaxed, romantic dining room. The chef-owner makes everything himself, using organically grown ingredients. Expect such dishes as pâté de campagne, escargot, herb-crusted roast lamb and fresh fish. Try the five-course prix-fixe menu ($54), which can be paired with award-winning wines. Service is gracious and attentive. ■TIP➔ This restaurant is hard to find, so ask for directions when you book. $ *Average main: $30* ✉ *120 Country Club Dr., No. 29, off Lakeshore Blvd.* ☎ *775/831–0800* ⊕ *www.lebistrorestaurant.net* ۵ *Closed Sun. and Mon. No lunch.*

$
SOUTHERN

✗ **T's Rotisserie.** There's nothing fancy about T's (it looks like a small snack bar), but the mesquite-grilled chicken and tri-tip steaks are delicious and inexpensive—a rare combination in pricey Incline Village. It's mainly a take-out spot; seating is limited. $ *Average main: $9* ✉ *901 Tahoe Blvd., at Village Blvd.* ☎ *775/831–2832* ▭ *No credit cards.*

$$$$
RESORT

⌂ **Hyatt Regency Lake Tahoe.** A full-service destination resort on 26 acres of prime lakefront property, the Hyatt has a range of luxurious accommodations, from tower-hotel rooms to lakeside cottages. **Pros:** incredible views; low-key casino. **Cons:** pricey (especially for families). $ *Rooms from: $359* ✉ *111 Country Club Dr.* ☎ *775/832–1234, 888/899–5019* ⊕ *www.laketahoe.hyatt.com* ⇆ *386 rooms, 36 suites* ⍾ *No meals.*

SPORTS AND THE OUTDOORS
GOLF

Incline Championship. Robert Trent Jones Sr. designed this challenging course of tightly cut, tree-lined fairways laced with water hazards that demand accuracy as well as distance skills. Greens fee includes a cart, except the 4:30 pm Super Twilight rate of $3 per hole (cart $25). ✉ *955 Fairway Blvd., at Northwood Blvd., north off Hwy. 28* ☎ *866/925–4653 reservations, 775/832–1146 pro shop* ⊕ *www.inclinegolf.com* ⛳ *$179* ⛳ *18 holes, 7106 yards, par 72.*

Incline Mountain. Robert Trent Jones Jr. designed this executive (shorter) course that requires accuracy more than distance skills. The greens fee includes a cart. ✉ *690 Wilson Way, at Golfer's Pass, south off Hwy. 431* ☎ *866/925–4653 reservations, 775/832–1150 pro shop* ⊕ *www.inclinegolf.com* ⛳ *$65 for weekdays, $75 for weekends* ⛳ *18 holes, 3519 yards, par 58.*

Get to Sand Harbor Beach in Lake Tahoe–Nevada State Park early; the park sometimes fills to capacity before lunchtime in summer.

MOUNTAIN BIKING

Flume Trail Bikes. You can rent bikes and get helpful tips from this company, which also operates a bike shuttle to popular trailheads. Ask about the secluded backcountry rental cabins for overnight rides. ⊠ *1115 Tunnel Creek Rd., at Ponderosa Ranch Rd., off Hwy. 28* ☎ *775/298–2501* ⊕ *www.flumetrailtahoe.com.*

SKIING

Diamond Peak. A fun family mood prevails at Diamond Peak, which has affordable rates and many special programs. Snowmaking covers 75% of the mountain, and runs are groomed nightly. The ride up the 1-mile Crystal Express rewards you with fantastic views. Diamond Peak is less crowded than Tahoe's larger ski parks and provides free shuttles to nearby lodgings. A great place for beginners and intermediates, it's appropriately priced for families. Though there are some steep-aspect black-diamond runs, advanced skiers may find the acreage too limited. For snowboarders there's a small terrain park. ⊠ *1210 Ski Way, off Country Club Dr.* ☎ *775/832–1177* ⊕ *www.diamondpeak.com* ☞ *30 trails on 655 acres, rated 18% beginner, 46% intermediate, 36% advanced. Longest run 2½ miles, base 6,700 feet, summit 8,540 feet. Lifts: 7, including 1 high-speed quad and a surface lift.*

Mt. Rose Ski Tahoe. At this park, ski some of Tahoe's highest slopes and take in bird's-eye views of Reno, the lake, and Carson Valley. Though more compact than the bigger Tahoe resorts, Mt. Rose has the area's highest base elevation and consequently the driest snow. The mountain has a wide variety of terrain. The most challenging is the Chutes, 200 acres of gulp-and-go advanced-to-expert vertical. Intermediates can choose steep groomers or mellow, wide-open boulevards. Beginners have their own corner of the mountain, with gentle, wide slopes. Boarders and tricksters have three terrain parks to choose from, on opposite sides of the mountain, allowing them to follow the sun as it tracks across the resort. The

> ### TAHOE TESSIE
>
> Local lore claims this huge sea monster slithers around Lake Tahoe. Skeptics laugh, but true believers keep their eyes peeled for surprise sightings.

13

mountain gets hit hard in storms; check conditions before heading up during inclement weather or on a windy day. ✉ *22222 Mt. Rose Hwy., Hwy. 431, 11 miles north of Incline Village, Reno ☎ 775/849–0704, 800/754–7673 ⊕ www.skirose.com ✆ 61 trails on 1,200 acres, rated 20% beginner, 30% intermediate, 40% advanced, 10% expert. Longest run 2½ miles, base 8,260 feet, summit 9,700 feet. Lifts: 8, including 2 high-speed 6-passenger lifts.*

Tahoe Meadows Snowplay Area. This is the most popular area near the north shore for noncommercial cross-country skiing, sledding, tubing, snowshoeing, and snowmobiling. ✉ *Off Hwy. 431, between Incline Village and Mt. Rose.*

ZEPHYR COVE

22 miles south of Incline Village.

The largest settlement between Incline Village and the Stateline area is Zephyr Cove, a tiny resort. It has a beach, marina, campground, picnic area, coffee shop in a log lodge, rustic cabins, and nearby riding stables.

GETTING HERE AND AROUND

From the north shore communities, reach Zephyr Cove by following Highway 28 along the eastern side of the lake. From South Lake Tahoe, take U.S. 50 north and then west. Public transportation isn't available in Zephyr Cove.

EXPLORING

Cave Rock. Near Zephyr Cove, this 75 feet of solid stone at the southern end of Lake Tahoe–Nevada State Park is the throat of an extinct volcano. Tahoe Tessie, the lake's version of the Loch Ness monster, is reputed to live in a cavern below the impressive outcropping. Cave Rock towers over a parking lot, a lakefront picnic ground, and a boat launch. The views are some of the best on the lake; this is a good spot to stop and take a picture. But this area is a sacred burial site for the Washoe Indians, and climbing up to the cave, or through it, is prohibited. ✉ *U.S. 50, 4 miles north of Zephyr Cove ☎ 775/831–0494.*

WHERE TO STAY

$$$

RENTAL

FAMILY

☒ **Zephyr Cove Resort.** Beneath towering pines at the lake's edge stand 28 cozy, modern vacation cabins with peaked knotty-pine ceilings. **Pros:** family-friendly. **Cons:** lodge rooms are basic; can be noisy. ⑤ *Rooms from: $199 ✉ 760 U.S. 50, 4 miles north of Stateline ☎ 775/589–4907, 800/238–2463 ⊕ www.zephyrcove.com ✆ 28 cabins; 4 lodge rooms* ⫯⊙⫯ *No meals.*

STATELINE

5 miles south of Zephyr Cove.

Stateline is the archetypal Nevada border town. Its four high-rise casinos are as vertical and contained as the commercial district of South Lake Tahoe, on the California side, is horizontal and sprawling. And Stateline is as relentlessly indoors-oriented as the rest of the lake is focused on the outdoors. This strip is where you'll find the most concentrated action at Lake Tahoe: restaurants (including typical casino buffets), showrooms with famous headliners and razzle-dazzle revues, tower-hotel rooms and suites, and 24-hour casinos.

GETTING HERE AND AROUND

From South Lake Tahoe take U.S. 50 north across the Nevada border to reach Stateline and its casinos. If coming from Reno's airport, take U.S. 395/Interstate 580 south to Carson City, and then head west on U.S. 50 to the lake and head south. Or take the South Tahoe Express bus. BlueGO operates daily bus service in the south shore area year-round, plus a ski shuttle from the large hotels to Heavenly in the winter.

BEACHES

Nevada Beach. Although less than a mile long, this is the widest beach on the lake and especially good for swimming (many Tahoe beaches are rocky). You can boat and fish here, and there are picnic tables, barbecue grills, and a campground beneath the pines. This is the best place to watch the July 4th or Labor Day fireworks, but most of the summer the subdued atmosphere attracts families and those seeking a less-touristy spot. **Amenities:** parking ($7 fee), water sports, toilets. **Best for:** sunrise, swimming, walking. ⊠ *Elk Point Rd., off U.S. 50, 3 miles north of Stateline* ☎ *530/543–2600* ⊕ *www.fs.usda.gov/ltbmu* ☉ *Open daily late May–Oct.* ☞ *No pets.*

WHERE TO EAT AND STAY

$$$

FRENCH

Fodor's Choice

★

✕ **Mirabelle.** Don't be put off by this restaurant's nondescript exterior. Inside there's an airy dining room with creamy yellow walls and white tablecloths. Enticing scents drift from the kitchen, where the Alsatian-born chef-owner, Camille Schwartz, prepares everything from puff pastry to meringues to homemade bread. Specialties include sautéed veal sweetbreads, garlicky escargot, and rack of lamb with fresh thyme. There's always a fresh fish entrée, plus a $31.50 prix-fixe "epicurean menu." Ⓢ *Average main: $27* ⊠ *290 Kingsbury Grade, off U.S. 50* ☎ *775/586–1007* ⊕ *www.mirabelletahoe.com* ☉ *Closed Mon. No lunch.*

$

HOTEL

🏨 **Harrah's Tahoe Hotel/Casino.** The hotel's major selling point is that every room has two full bathrooms, a boon if you're traveling with family. **Pros:** central location; great midweek values. **Cons:** can get noisy. Ⓢ *Rooms from: $109* ⊠ *15 U.S. 50, at Stateline Ave.* ☎ *775/588–6611, 800/427–7247* ⊕ *www.harrahslaketahoe.com* ➴ *470 rooms, 62 suites* ⦅❂⦆ *No meals.*

$

HOTEL

🏨 **Harveys Resort Hotel/Casino.** This resort began as a cabin in 1944, and now it's Tahoe's largest casino-hotel; premium rooms have custom furnishings, oversize marble baths, minibars, and good lake views. **Pros:** hip entertainment; just a few blocks north of the Heavenly Gondola.

Cons: can get loud at night. ⑤ *Rooms from: $79* ⊠ *18 U.S. 50, at State-line Ave.* ☎ *775/588–2411, 800/648–3361* ⊕ *www.harveystahoe.com* ↝ *742 rooms, 36 suites* ⏏ *No meals.*

NIGHTLIFE

Each of the major casinos has its own showroom, featuring everything from comedy to magic acts to sexy floor shows to Broadway musicals.

DANCE CLUBS

Peek. You can dance the night away with top-notch DJs, and often hear live performances, at this club that emulates a Vegas vibe. ⊠ *Harrah's Lake Tahoe, 15 U.S. 50* ☎ *775/588–6611 information, 775/586–6705 Peek reservations* ⊕ *www.caesars.com/peek.*

LIVE MUSIC

Harveys Outdoor Summer Concert Series. Harveys Lake Tahoe books outdoor concerts on weekends in summer with headliners such as the Zac Brown Band, Journey, and Bruno Mars. ⊠ *18 U.S. 50* ☎ *775/588–2411* ⊕ *www.harveystahoe.com/shows.html.*

South Shore Room. Classic acts like the Temptations and legendary reggae band the Wailers play Harrah's big showroom, along with tribute shows for groups such as the Beatles and Bruce Springsteen and the E Street Band. ⊠ *Harrah's Lake Tahoe, 15 U.S. 50* ☎ *775/586–6244 tickets, 775/588–6611* ⊕ *www.harrahslaketahoe.com/shows.html.*

SPORTS AND THE OUTDOORS

GOLF

Edgewood Tahoe. Golfers of all skill levels enjoy this scenic lakeside course that has four sets of tees, offering a variety of course lengths. The greens fee includes an optional cart. ⊠ *100 Lake Pkwy., at U.S. 50* ☎ *775/588–3566, 866/761–4653* ⊕ *www.edgewood-tahoe.com* ▱ *$220 for weekdays, $240 for weekends* ⚑ *18 holes, 7543 yards, par 72.*

RENO

32 miles east of Truckee, 38 miles northeast of Incline Village.

Established in 1859 as a trading station at a bridge over the Truckee River, Reno grew along with the silver mines of nearby Virginia City and the transcontinental railroad that chugged through town. Train officials named it in 1868, but gambling—legalized in 1931—put Reno on the map. This is still a gambling town, with most of the casinos crowded into five square blocks downtown, but a thriving university scene and outdoor activities also attract tourists.

Parts of downtown are sketchy, but things are changing. Several defunct casinos are being converted into condominiums, and the riverfront is being reconceived. The town now touts family-friendly activities like kayaking on the Truckee, and new shops and excellent restaurants have sprung up outside the hotels. Temperatures year-round in this high-mountain-desert climate are warmer than at Tahoe, though it rarely gets as hot here as in Sacramento and the Central Valley, making strolling around town a pleasure.

GETTING HERE AND AROUND
Interstate 80 bisects Reno east–west, U.S. 395 north–south (south of town the road is signed U.S. 395/Interstate 580). Greyhound and Amtrak stop here, and several airlines fly into Reno-Tahoe International Airport. RTC Ride provides bus service in the greater Reno area.

> ### RENO'S RIVERWALK
>
> Stroll along the Truckee River and check out the art galleries, cinema, specialty shops, theater, and restaurants that line this lively refurbished section of town near Reno's casino district.

ESSENTIALS
Bus Contact RTC Ride ⊠ *Transit Center, E. 4th and Lake Sts.* ☎ *775/348–7433* ⊕ *rtcwashoe.com.*

Visitor Information Reno-Sparks Convention and Visitors Authority ⊠ *4001 S. Virginia St.* ☎ *775/827–7650, 800/367–7366* ⊕ *www.visitrenotahoe.com.*

EXPLORING
TOP ATTRACTIONS

FAMILY **National Automobile Museum.** Antique and classic automobiles, including an Elvis Presley Cadillac, a Mercury coupe driven by James Dean in the movie *Rebel Without a Cause,* and the experimental and still futuristic-looking 1938 Phantom Corsair, are all on display at this museum. ⊠ *10 S. Lake St., at Mill St.* ☎ *775/333–9300* ⊕ *www.automuseum.org* ≊ *$10* ☉ *Mon.–Sat. 9:30–5:30, Sun. 10–4.*

Nevada Museum of Art. A dramatic four-level structure designed by Will Bruder houses this splendid museum's collection, which focuses on themes such as the Sierra Nevada/Great Basin and altered-landcape photography. The building's exterior torqued walls are sided with a black zinc-based material that has been fabricated to resemble textures found in the Black Rock Desert. Inside the building, a staircase installed within the central atrium is lit by skylights and suspended by a single beam attached to the atrium ceiling; visitors can climb 55 feet to the fourth-floor, rooftop landing. ⊠ *160 W. Liberty St., and Hill St.* ☎ *775/329–3333* ⊕ *www.nevadaart.org* ≊ *$10* ☉ *Wed. and Fri.–Sun. 10–6, Thurs. 10–8.*

Fodor's Choice **Riverwalk District.** The makeover of Reno's waterfront has transformed
★ this formerly dilapidated area into the toast of the town. The Riverwalk itself is a half-mile promenade on the north side of the Truckee River, which flows around lovely Wingfield Park, where outdoor festivals and other events take place. On the third Saturday of each month, local merchants host a **Wine Walk** between 2 and 5. For $20, you receive a wine glass and can sample fine wines at participating shops, bars, restaurants, and galleries. In July look for stellar outdoor art, opera, dance, and kids' performances as part of the month-long **Artown festival** (⊕ *renoisartown.com*), presented mostly in Wingfield Park. Also at Wingfield is the **Truckee River Whitewater Park.** With activities for all skill levels, it's become a major attraction for water-sports enthusiasts. ⊠ *Riverwalk, north side of Truckee River between Lake and Ralston Sts.* ⊕ *renoriver.org.*

WORTH NOTING

FAMILY **Fleischmann Planetarium.** Digital star shows provide the glittering lights inside this facility. The shows aim to make learning about astronomy entertaining for kids and adults. ⊠ *University of Nevada, 1664 N. Virginia St., near E. 15th St.* ☎ *775/784–4811 recorded information, 775/784–4812 office* ⊕ *www.planetarium.unr.nevada.edu* ⬜ *Exhibits free, films and star shows $7* ⊙ *Mon.–Thurs. noon–7; Fri. noon–9; Sat. 10–9; Sun. 10–7.*

WHERE TO EAT

$$$ ✕ **4th St. Bistro.** For deliciously simple, smart cooking, head to this
AMERICAN charming little bistro on the edge of town. The chef-owner uses organic
Fodor's Choice produce and meats in her soulful preparation of dishes like Cabernet-
★ braised lamb shanks with white beans, spinach, and black olive gremolata. Ochre-color sponge-painted walls, tablecloths from Provence, and a roaring fireplace in winter warm the dining room. $ *Average main: $30* ⊠ *3065 W. 4th St.* ☎ *775/323–3200* ⊕ *www.4thstbistro.com* ⊙ *Closed Sun. and Mon. No lunch.*

$ ✕ **Bangkok Cuisine.** To eat well but not break the bank, come to this
THAI busy Thai restaurant and sample the delicious soups, salads, stir-fries, and curries. $ *Average main: $12* ⊠ *55 Mt. Rose St., at S. Virginia St.* ☎ *775/322–0299* ⊕ *thaifoodreno.com* ⊙ *No lunch Sun.*

$$$ ✕ **Beaujolais Bistro.** Across from the Truckee River, this Reno favorite
FRENCH serves earthy, country-style French food with zero pretension—classics
Fodor's Choice like beef bourguignon, escargots, steak frites béarnaise, and braised
★ lamb shoulder. Wood floors, large windows, and brick walls with a fireplace create a welcoming and intimate atmosphere. Diners who want a more casual experience can dine at the long bar. Less expensive small plates as well as an inventive cocktail menu are also offered. $ *Average main: $28* ⊠ *753 Riverside Dr.* ☎ *775/323–2227* ⊕ *www. beaujolaisbistro.com* ⊙ *No lunch. Closed Mon.*

$ ✕ **Chocolate Bar.** Part café, part cocktail bar, this hip little spot close to
CAFÉ the river makes truffles, chocolate fondue, fabulous fruity cocktails, hot chocolate, gourmet small plates, and entrees, all served at a long wooden bar or at several tables and leather banquettes. Chocolate Bar is open late each night for those craving dessert, a chocolate cocktail, or a simple, unadorned cognac. $ *Average main: $15* ⊠ *95 N. Sierra St., at W. 1st St.* ☎ *775/337–1122* ⊕ *thechocbar.com.*

WHERE TO STAY

$ ⌂ **Harrah's Reno.** Of the big-name casino hotels in downtown Reno,
HOTEL double-towered Harrah's is still the best, with no surprises. **Pros:** sets the standard for downtown Reno; great online midweek rates. **Cons:** huge property. $ *Rooms from: $67* ⊠ *219 N. Center St., at E. 2nd St.* ☎ *775/786–3232, 800/427–7247* ⊕ *www.harrahsreno.com* ⬌ *876 rooms, 52 suites* |⊙| *No meals.*

$ ⌂ **Peppermill Reno.** A few miles removed from downtown's flashy main
HOTEL drag, this property sets a new standard for luxury in Reno; its 600 baroque suites in the Tuscan Tower have plush king-size beds, marble bathrooms, and European soaking tubs. **Pros:** luxurious rooms; casino decor; good coffee shop. **Cons:** deluge of neon may be off-putting to some. $ *Rooms from: $99* ⊠ *2707 S. Virginia St., at Peppermill La.*

13

☎ *775/826–2121, 866/821–9996* ⊕ *www.peppermillreno.com* ⇝ *915 rooms, 720 suites* ⊺◯⊦ *No meals.*

NIGHTLIFE
CASINOS

FAMILY **Circus Circus.** Families with kids head to this casino, where a midway above the floor has clowns, games, fun-house mirrors, and circus acts. ⊠ *500 N. Sierra St., at W. 5th St.* ☎ *775/329–0711, 800/648–5010* ⊕ *www.circusreno.com.*

Eldorado. Action-packed, with lots of slots and popular bar-top video poker, this casino also has good coffee-shop and food-court fare. Don't miss the Fountain of Fortune with its massive Florentine-inspired sculptures. ⊠ *345 N. Virginia St., at W. 4th St.* ☎ *775/786–5700, 800/879–8879* ⊕ *www.eldoradoreno.com.*

Harrah's Reno. Occupying two city blocks, this landmark property has a sprawling casino and an outdoor promenade. ⊠ *219 N. Center St., at E. 2nd St.* ☎ *775/786–3232, 800/427–7247* ⊕ *www.harrahsreno.com.*

Peppermill. A few miles from downtown, this casino is known for its excellent restaurants and neon-bright gambling areas. The Fireside cocktail lounge is a blast. ⊠ *2707 S. Virginia St., at Peppermill La.* ☎ *775/826–2121, 866/821–9996* ⊕ *www.peppermillreno.com.*

Silver Legacy. A 120-foot-tall mining rig and video poker games draw gamblers to this razzle-dazzle casino. ⊠ *407 N. Virginia St., at W. 4th St.* ☎ *775/329–4777, 800/687–8733* ⊕ *www.silverlegacyreno.com.*

THE FAR NORTH

With Lake Shasta, Mt. Shasta, and
Lassen Volcanic National Park

Visit Fodors.com for advice, updates, and bookings

WELCOME TO THE FAR NORTH

TOP REASONS TO GO

★ **Mother Nature's wonders:** California's Far North has more rivers, streams, lakes, forests, and mountains than you'll ever have time to explore.

★ **Rock and roll:** With two volcanoes to entice you—Lassen and Shasta—you can learn firsthand what happens when a mountain blows its top.

★ **Fantastic fishing:** Whether you like casting from a riverbank or letting your line bob beside a boat, you'll find fabulous fishing in all the northern counties.

★ **Cool hops:** On a hot day there's nothing quite as inviting as a visit to Chico's world-famous Sierra Nevada Brewery. Take the tour and then savor a chilled glass on tap at the adjacent brewpub.

★ **Shasta:** Wonderful in all its forms: lake, dam, river, mountain, forest, and town.

1 **From Chico to Mt Shasta.** The Far North is bisected, south to north, by Interstate 5, which passes through several historic towns and state parks, as well as miles of mountainous terrain. Halfway to the Oregon border is Lake Shasta, a favorite recreation destination, and farther north stands the spectacular snowy peak of Mt. Shasta.

2 **The Backcountry.** East of Interstate 5, the Far North's main corridor, dozens of scenic two-lane roads crisscross the wilderness, leading to dramatic mountain peaks and fascinating natural wonders. Small towns settled in the second half of the 19th century seem frozen in time, except that they are well equipped with tourist amenities.

GETTING ORIENTED

The Far North is a vast area that stretches from the upper reaches of the Sacramento Valley north to the Oregon border and east to Nevada. The region includes all or part of eight counties with sparsely populated rural farming and mountain communities, as well as thriving small cities in the valley. Much of the landscape was shaped by two volcanoes—Mt. Shasta and Mt. Lassen—that draw amateur geologists, weekend hikers, and avid mountain climbers to their rugged terrain. An intricate network of high mountain watersheds feeds lakes large and small, plus streams and rivers that course through several forests.

14

Updated
by Christine
Vovakes

The Far North's soaring mountain peaks, trail-filled national forests, alpine lakes, and wild rivers teeming with trout make it the perfect destination for outdoor enthusiasts, including hikers, cyclists, kayakers, and bird-watchers. You won't find many hot nightspots or cultural enclaves in this region, but you will find crowd-free national and state parks, crystal clear mountain streams, superlative hiking and fishing, plus small towns worth exploring. And the spectacular landscapes of Lassen Volcanic National Park and Mt. Shasta are sure to impress.

The wondrous landscape of California's northeastern corner, relatively unmarred by development, congestion, and traffic, is the product of volcanic activity. At the southern end of the Cascade Range, Lassen Volcanic National Park is the best place to witness the Far North's fascinating geology. Beyond the sulfur vents and bubbling mud pots, the park owes much of its beauty to 10,457-foot Mt. Lassen and 50 wilderness lakes.

The most enduring image of the region, though, is Mt. Shasta, whose 14,179-foot snowcapped peak beckons outdoor adventurers of all kinds. There are many versions of Shasta to enjoy—the mountain, the lake, the river, the town, the dam, and the forest—all named after the Native Americans known as the Shatasla, or Sastise, who once inhabited the region.

PLANNING

WHEN TO GO

Heat scorches the valley in summer. Temperatures above 110°F are common, but the mountains provide cool respite. Fall throughout the Far North is beautiful, rivaled only by spring, when wildflowers and almond orchards bloom and mountain creeks fed by the snowmelt splash through the forests. Winter is usually temperate in the valley, but cold and snowy in high country. A few favorite tourist attractions are closed in winter.

GETTING HERE AND AROUND

AIR TRAVEL

For the cheapest fares, fly into Sacramento and then rent a car—you'll need one anyway—and drive north. Chico and Redding, both served by United Express, have small airports. Neither has shuttle service, but you can take a taxi for about $32 to downtown Redding or $21 to downtown Chico.

Air Contacts Redding Municipal Airport ⊠ *6751 Woodrum Circle, off Airport Rd., Redding* ☎ *530/224–4320* ⊕ *www.ci.redding.ca.us/transeng/airports/rma.htm.*

Ground Transportation Taxi Service, Chico ☎ *530/893–4444, 530/898–1776.* **Taxi Service, Redding** ☎ *530/246–0577, 530/222–1234.*

BUS TRAVEL

Greyhound buses stop in Chico, Red Bluff, Redding, and Weed. Various transit authorities provide local bus transportation *(see individual town listings for details)*, though few tourists avail themselves of it.

Bus Contact Greyhound ☎ *800/231–2222* ⊕ *www.greyhound.com.*

CAR TRAVEL

Interstate 5 runs up the center of California through Red Bluff and Redding. Chico is east of Interstate 5 on Highway 32. Lassen Volcanic National Park can be reached by Highway 36 from Red Bluff or (except in winter) Highway 44 from Redding. Highway 299 connects Weaverville, Redding and Alturas. U.S. 395 leads from Susanville to Alturas. Highway 89 will take you from Mt. Shasta to Quincy. Highway 36 links Chester and Susanville. Check weather reports and carry detailed maps, warm clothing, and tire chains whenever you head into mountainous terrain in winter.

Road Conditions Caltrans Current Highway Conditions ☎ *800/427–7623* ⊕ *www.dot.ca.gov.*

TRAIN TRAVEL

Amtrak serves Chico, Redding, and Dunsmuir.

Train Contacts Amtrak ☎ *800/872–7245* ⊕ *www.amtrak.com.*

RESTAURANTS

Redding, the urban center of the Far North, and college-town Chico have the greatest selection of restaurants. Cafés and simple eateries are the rule in the smaller towns, though trendy, innovative restaurants have been popping up. Dress is always informal.

HOTELS

Aside from the large chain hotels and motels in Redding and Chico, most accommodations in the Far North blend rustic appeal, simplicity, and coziness. Rooms in Redding, Chico, and Red Bluff usually are booked solid only during popular local events. Wilderness resorts close in fall and reopen after the snow season ends in May. For summer holiday weekends in towns such as Mt. Shasta, Dunsmuir, and

14

Chester, and at camping sites within state or national parks, make lodging reservations well in advance. *Hotel reviews have been shortened. For full information, visit Fodors.com.*

B&B Info California Association of Boutique & Breakfast Inns ☎ *800/373–9251* ⊕ *www.cabbi.com/region/Mount-Shasta.*

WHAT IT COSTS			
$	**$$**	**$$$**	**$$$$**
Restaurants	under $16	$16–$22	$23–$30	over $30

	$	$$	$$$	$$$$
Restaurants	under $16	$16–$22	$23–$30	over $30
Hotels	under $121	$121–$175	$176–$250	over $250

Restaurant prices are the average cost of a main course at dinner or, if dinner is not served, at lunch. Hotel prices are the lowest cost of a standard double room in high season.

VISITOR INFORMATION

Contacts Lassen County Chamber of Commerce ✉ *75 N. Weatherlow St., Susanville* ☎ *530/257–4323* ⊕ *lassencountychamber.com.* **Shasta Cascade Wonderland Association** ✉ *1699 Hwy. 273, Anderson* ☎ *530/365–7500, 800/474–2782* ⊕ *www.shastacascade.com.* **Visit Siskiyou** ☎ *800/926–4865 Mt. Shasta Chamber of Commerce* ⊕ *visitsiskiyou.org.*

FROM CHICO TO MT. SHASTA

From the blooming almond orchards of the fertile Sacramento River valley, through the forested mountains and to the dominating peak of a dormant volcano, this section of the Far North entices tourists in all seasons.

CHICO

180 miles from San Francisco, east on I–80, north on I–505 to I–5, and east on Hwy. 32; 86 miles north of Sacramento on Hwy. 99.

Chico (which is Spanish for "small") lies in the Sacramento Valley and offers a welcome break from the monotony of Interstate 5. The Chico campus of California State University, the scores of local artisans, and the area's agriculture (primarily almond orchards) all influence the culture here. Chico's true claim to fame, however, is the popular Sierra Nevada Brewery, which keeps beer drinkers across the country happy with its distinctive brews.

GETTING HERE AND AROUND

Both Highway 99, coming north from Sacramento or south off Interstate 5 at Red Bluff, and Highway 32, going east off Interstate 5 at Orland, intersect Chico. Amtrak and Greyhound stop here, and United Express flies into the Chico airport. Butte Regional Transit's B-Line buses serve Chico and nearby towns. Anchored by a robust university scene, the downtown neighborhoods are great for walking.

ESSENTIALS

Bus Contact B-Line ☎ *530/342–0221, 800/822–8145* ⊕ *www.blinetransit.com.*

Visitor Information Chico Chamber of Commerce ⊠ *441 Main St., Ste. 150, near E. 5th St.* ☎ *530/891–5556, 800/852–8570* ⊕ *www.chicochamber.com.*

EXPLORING

Bidwell Mansion State Historic Park. Built between 1865 and 1868 by General John Bidwell, the founder of Chico, this mansion was designed by Henry W. Cleaveland, a San Francisco architect. Bidwell and his wife welcomed many distinguished guests to their distinctive pink Italianate home, including President Rutherford B. Hayes, naturalist John Muir, suffragist Susan B. Anthony, and General William T. Sherman. A one-hour tour takes you through most of the mansion's 26 rooms. Credit cards are not accepted. ⊠ *525 The Esplanade, at Memorial Way* ☎ *530/895–6144* ⊕ *www.parks.ca.gov/parkindex* ⊡ *$6* ⊙ *Mon. noon–5, weekends 11–5; last tour at 4* ⊙ *Closed Tues.–Fri.*

Bidwell Park. The sprawling 3,670-acre Bidwell Park is a community green space straddling Big Chico Creek, where scenes from *Gone With the Wind* and the 1938 version of *Robin Hood* (starring Errol Flynn) were filmed. The region's recreational hub, it includes a golf course, swimming areas, and biking, hiking, horseback riding, and in-line skating trails. One of the largest city-run parks in the country, Bidwell starts as a slender strip downtown and expands eastward 11 miles toward the Sierra foothills. Chico Creek Nature Center serves as the official information site for Bidwell Park. ⊠ *1968 E. 8th St., off Hwy. 99* ☎ *530/896–7800 Chico Public Works Dept., 530/891–4671 Chico Creek Nature Center* ⊕ *www.bidwellpark.org.*

Sierra Nevada Brewing Company. This pioneer of the microbrewery movement still has a hands-on approach to beer making. Tour the brew house and see how the beer is produced—from the sorting of hops through fermentation and bottling. You can also visit the gift shop and enjoy a hearty lunch or dinner in the brewpub where tastings are available (for a fee). ⊠ *1075 E. 20th St., at Sierra Nevada St.* ☎ *530/345–2739 Brew Pub, 530/899-4776 Tours* ⊕ *www.sierranevada.com* ⊡ *Free* ⊙ *Tours daily, call for times.*

WHERE TO EAT AND STAY

$$$
STEAKHOUSE

✕ **5th Street Steakhouse.** Hand-cut steak is the star in this refurbished early 1900s building, the place to come when you're craving red meat and a huge baked potato. Exposed redbrick walls warm the small dining area. A long mahogany bar catches the overflow crowds that jam the place on weekends. Lunch is served on Fridays only. No reservations for parties smaller than six persons are accepted on Fridays and Saturdays. ⑤ *Average main: $29* ⊠ *345 W. 5th St., at Normal Ave.* ☎ *530/891–6328* ⊕ *www.5thstreetsteakhouse.com* ⊙ *No lunch Sat.–Thurs.*

$
AMERICAN

✕ **Madison Bear Garden.** This downtown favorite two blocks south of the Chico State campus is a great spot for checking out the vibrant college scene while enjoying a burger and a brew. ⑤ *Average main: $8* ⊠ *316 W. 2nd St., at Salem St.* ☎ *530/891–1639* ⊕ *www.madisonbeargarden.com.*

$$$
MEDITERRANEAN

✕ **Red Tavern.** With its burgundy carpet, white linen tablecloths, and mellow lighting, this is one of Chico's coziest restaurants. The Mediterranean-influenced menu, inspired by fresh local produce, changes seasonally. There's a great California wine list, and a full bar. $ *Average main: $23* ⊠ *1250 The Esplanade, at E. 3rd Ave.* ☎ *530/894–3463* ⊕ *www.redtavern.com* ☾ *No dinner Sun., no lunch Mon.–Sat.*

$$ ⟐ **Hotel Diamond.** Crystal chandeliers and gleaming wood floors and
HOTEL banisters elegantly welcome guests into the foyer of this restored gem in downtown Chico near the university. **Pros:** refined; great location; breakfast voucher included in room rate. **Cons:** not a good choice for families. $ *Rooms from: $139* ⊠ *220 W. 4th St., near Broadway* ☎ *530/893–3100, 866/993–3100* ⊕ *hoteldiamondchico.com* ⤥ *39 rooms, 4 suites* ⦿ *Breakfast.*

SHOPPING

Made in Chico. This establishment sells locally made goods, including pottery, olives, almonds, and Woof and Poof creations—whimsical home-decor items, such as stuffed Santas, elves, animals, and pillows. ⊠ *127 W. 3rd St., between Main St. and Broadway* ☎ *530/894–7009* ⊕ *www.madeinchicostore.com.*

Needham Studios. Beautiful custom-made etched, stained, and beveled glass is created at Needham Studios. ⊠ *237 Broadway, at 3rd St.* ☎ *530/345–4718* ⊕ *www.needhamstudios.com.*

RED BLUFF

41 miles north of Chico on Hwy 99.

Historic Red Bluff is a gateway to Lassen Volcanic National Park. Established in the mid-19th century as a shipping center on the Sacramento River, and named for the color of its soil, the town is filled with dozens of restored Victorians. It's a great home base for outdoor adventures in the area.

GETTING HERE AND AROUND

Access Red Bluff via exits off Interstate 5, or by driving north on Highway 99. Highway 36 is a long, twisting road that begins near the Pacific Coast and goes to Red Bluff, then east to the towns near Lassen Volcanic National Park. Greyhound buses stop here and also provide connecting service to Amtrak. TRAX (Tehama Rural Area Express) serves Red Bluff and neighboring towns.

ESSENTIALS

Bus Information TRAX ☎ *530/385–2877* ⊕ *www.taketrax.com.*

Visitor Information Red Bluff–Tehama County Chamber of Commerce ⊠ *100 Main St., at Rio St.* ☎ *530/527–6220* ⊕ *www.redbluffchamber.com.*

EXPLORING

William B. Ide Adobe State Historic Park. Named for the first and only president of the short-lived California Republic of 1846, William B. Ide Adobe State Historic Park is on an oak-lined bank of the Sacramento River. The Bear Flag Party proclaimed California a sovereign nation, separate from Mexican rule, and the republic existed for 22 days before it was taken over by the United States. The republic's flag has survived, with minor refinements, as California's state flag. The park's main attraction is an adobe home built in the 1850s and outfitted with period furnishings. ⊠ *21659 Adobe Rd., at Park Pl.* ☎ *530/529–8599* ⊕ *www.parks.ca.gov/?page_id=458* ⊠ *$6 per vehicle* ⊙ *Park and picnic facilities, adobe home, and historic sites Fri.–Sun. 10–4.*

RED BLUFF ROUND-UP

Check out old-time rodeo at its best during the Red Bluff Round-Up. Held the third weekend of April, this annual event attracts some of the best cowboys in the country. For more information, visit ⊕ *redbluffroundup.com.*

WHERE TO EAT AND STAY

$$
STEAKHOUSE

✕ **Green Barn Steakhouse.** You're likely to find cowboys sporting Stetsons and spurs feasting on sizzling porterhouse, baby back ribs, and prime rib at Red Bluff's premier steak house. For lighter fare, there's rainbow trout or clam fettuccine. Don't miss the bread pudding with rum sauce. The lounge is usually hopping, especially when there's an event at the nearby rodeo grounds. ⑤ *Average main: $19* ⊠ *5 Chestnut Ave., at Antelope Blvd.* ☎ *530/527–3161* ⚄ *Reservations not accepted* ⊙ *Closed Sun.*

$

HOTEL

⛺ **Sportsman Lodge.** On-site owners keep this small motel neat and inviting, with practical amenities like refrigerators, microwaves, cable TV, and free Wi-Fi. **Pros:** spacious rooms; helpful owners; pet-friendly. **Cons:** an older facility. ⑤ *Rooms from: $62* ⊠ *768 Antelope Blvd., near Trinity Ave.* ☎ *530/527-2888* ⊕ *www.redbluffsportsmanlodge. com* ⇥ *19* ⊙ *No meals.*

REDDING

32 miles north of Red Bluff on I–5.

As the largest city in the Far North, Redding is an ideal headquarters for exploring the surrounding countryside.

GETTING HERE AND AROUND

Reach Redding from exits off Interstate 5 or via Highway 299, which originates near coastal Eureka and crosses Weaverville and Redding before heading northeast to Burney and Alturas. Highway 44 stretches from Susanville past Lassen Park's north entrance before ending in Redding. United Express serves the Redding airport. Amtrak and Greyhound make stops here.

ESSENTIALS

Bus Information Redding Area Bus Authority ☎ *530/241–2877* ⊕ *www.rabaride.com.*

Visitor Information Redding Convention and Visitors Bureau ⊠ *2334 Washington Ave., Ste. B* ☎ *530/225–4100, 800/874–7562* ⊕ *www.visitredding.com.*

EXPLORING

FAMILY

Fodor's Choice

★

Turtle Bay Exploration Park. This park features walking trails, an arboretum and botanical gardens, and lots of interactive exhibits for kids, including a gold-panning area and the seasonal butterfly exhibit. The main draw is the stunning **Sundial Bridge,** which links the Sacramento River Trail and the park's arboretum and gardens. Access to the bridge and arboretum is free, but there's a fee for the museum. ⊠ *844 Sundial*

14

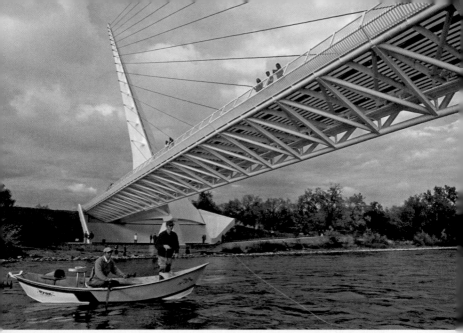

Anglers fish under Santiago Calatrava's striking Sundial Bridge next to Turtle Bay Exploration Park.

Bridge Dr., off Hwy. 44 ☎ *530/243–8850, 800/887–8532* ⊕ *www.turtlebay.org* ✉ *Museum $14* ◔ *May–early Sept., Mon.–Sat. 9–5, Sun. 10–5; early Sept.–Apr., Wed.–Sat. 9–4, Sun. 10–4.*

WHERE TO EAT AND STAY

$$$
STEAKHOUSE
✕ **Jack's Grill.** Famous for its 16-ounce steaks, this popular bar and steak house also serves shrimp and chicken. A town favorite, the place is usually jam-packed and noisy. The bar serves great martinis. ⑤ *Average main: $26* ✉ *1743 California St., near Sacramento St.* ☎ *530/241–9705* ⊕ *www.jacksgrillredding.com* ◔ *Closed Sun. No lunch.*

$
AMERICAN
✕ **Klassique Kafe.** Two sisters run this small, bustling restaurant that caters to locals looking for simple but hearty breakfast and lunch fare. The hot luncheon specials served daily might include butter beans and ham with corn bread, or chicken and dumplings. ⑤ *Average main: $9* ✉ *2427 Athens Ave., at Locust St.* ☎ *530/244–4939* ◔ *Closed Sat. & Sun. No dinner.*

$$$
ITALIAN
✕ **Nello's Place.** Fine Italian dining and romantic ambience go hand-in-hand at Nello's Place, one of Redding's best restaurants. You'll find a varied selection of veal, chicken, beef, and pasta dishes mixed with lighter fish and vegetarian fare. For special presentations, order a Caesar salad prepared tableside for two, and bananas flambé for dessert. There's a full bar in addition to an extensinve wine list. ⑤ *Average main: $24* ✉ *3055 Bechelli Ln., near Hartnell Ave.* ☎ *530/223-1636* ⊕ *nellosrestaurant.net* ◔ *No lunch. Closed Mon.*

$
HOTEL
🛏 **The Red Lion.** Close to Redding's convention center and regional recreation sites, this hotel is a top choice for both business and vacation travelers. **Pros:** family-friendly; close to a major shopping and dining

area. **Cons:** on a noisy street. $ *Rooms from: $119* ✉ *1830 Hilltop Dr., Hwy. 44/299 exit off I-5* ☎ *530/221–8700, 800/733–5466* ⊕ *www. redlion.com* ⤳ *192 rooms, 2 suites* ⦿ *No meals.*

SPORTS AND THE OUTDOORS
FISHING
Fly Shop. This store sells fishing licenses and has information about guides, conditions, and fishing packages. ✉ *4140 Churn Creek Rd., at Denton Way* ☎ *530/222–3555* ⊕ *www.flyshop.com.*

WEAVERVILLE

46 miles west of Redding on Hwy. 299.

A man known only as Weaver struck gold here in 1849, and the fledgling community that developed at the base of the Trinity Alps was named after him. With its impressive downtown historic district, today Weaverville is a popular headquarters for family vacations and biking, hiking, fishing, and gold-panning excursions.

GETTING HERE AND AROUND
Highway 299 becomes Main Street down the center of Weaverville. Take the highway either east from the Pacific Coast or west from Redding. Highway 36 from Red Bluff to Highway 3 heading north leads to Weaverville. Trinity Transit provides minimal local bus service plus a line that links Weaverville to Interstate 5 at Redding.

EXPLORING
Trinity County Courthouse. Built in 1856 as a store, office building, and hotel, Trinity County Courthouse was converted to county use in 1865. The Apollo Saloon, in the basement, became the county jail. It's the oldest courthouse still in use in California. ✉ *Court and Main Sts.*

Trinity County Hal Goodyear Historical Park. For a vivid sense of Weaverville's past, visit the Trinity County Hal Goodyear Historical Park, especially its **Jake Jackson Memorial Museum,** which has a blacksmith shop and a stamp mill (where ore is crushed) from the 1890s that is still in use. Also here are the original jail cells of the Trinity County Courthouse. ✉ *780 Main St., at Bartlett La.* ☎ *530/623–5211* ⊕ *trinity museum.org* ☉ *Jan.–Mar., Wed. and Sat. 11–4; Apr. and Oct., daily 11–4; May–Sept., daily 10–5; Nov. and Dec., Wed.–Sat. 11–4.*

Fodor's Choice ★ **Weaverville Joss House.** Weaverville's main attraction is the Joss House, a Taoist temple built in 1874 and called Won Lim Miao ("the temple of the forest beneath the clouds") by Chinese miners. The oldest continuously used Chinese temple in California, it attracts worshippers from around the world. With its golden altar, antique weaponry, and carved wooden canopies, the Joss House is a piece of California history that can best be appreciated on a guided 30-minute tour. The original temple building and many of its furnishings—some of which came from China—were lost to fire in 1873, but members of the local Chinese community soon rebuilt it. ✉ *630 Main St., at Oregon St.* ☎ *530/623–5284* ⊕ *www.parks.ca.gov/parkindex* ⬛ *Museum free; guided tour $4* ☉ *Thurs., Sat.–Sun. 10–5; last tour at 4.*

14

WHERE TO EAT AND STAY

$ ✕**La Casita.** A traditional selection of Mexican food is on the menu
MEXICAN here, including quesadillas (try the version with roasted chili peppers),
tostadas, enchiladas, tacos, and tamales. Many dishes are available
without meat. Open from late morning through dinner, this casual spot
is great for a midafternoon snack. $ *Average main: $9* ✉ *570 Main St.*
☎ *530/623–5797* ☉ *Closed Sun.*

$$ ✕**La Grange Café.** In two brick buildings dating from the 1850s (they're
AMERICAN among the oldest edifices in town), this eatery serves beef, buffalo, and
other game meats, pasta, fresh fish, and farmers' market vegetables
when they're available. There's a full premium bar, and the wine list
is extensive. $ *Average main: $20* ✉ *520 Main St.* ☎ *530/623–5325*
☉ *Hours vary in winter.*

$ ▦**Red Hill Motel.** This 1940s-era property is popular with anglers, who
HOTEL appreciate the outdoor fish-cleaning area on the premises. **Pros:** close to
popular bass fishing sites; inexpensive. **Cons:** older facility; some rooms
need sprucing up. $ *Rooms from: $53* ✉ *50 Red Hill Rd., off Main St./
Hwy. 299* ☎ *530/623–4331* ⊕ *www.redhillresorts.com* ⬧ *4 rooms, 6
cabins, 2 duplexes* �‖ *No meals.*

SPORTS AND THE OUTDOORS

Fly Stretch. Below the Lewiston Dam, east of Weaverville on Highway
299, is the Fly Stretch of the Trinity River, an excellent fly-fishing area.

Pine Cove Boat Ramp. This ramp on Lewiston Lake provides fishing
access for those with disabilities—decks here are built over prime trout-
fishing waters.

Weaverville Ranger Station. Check here for maps and information
about hiking trails in the Trinity Alps Wilderness. ✉ *360 Main St.*
☎ *530/623–2121.*

LAKE SHASTA AREA

12 miles north of Redding on I–5.

When you think of the Lake Shasta Area, picture water, wilderness,
dazzling stalagmites—and a fabulous man-made project in the midst
of it all.

GETTING HERE AND AROUND

Interstate 5 north of Redding is the main link to the entire Lake Shasta
area. Get to the dam by passing through the tiny city of Shasta Lake.
There is no local bus service.

ESSENTIALS

Shasta Cascade Wonderland Association. Stop in the association's visitor
center in the Anderson outlet mall off I-5 between Red Bluff and Red-
ding, or check the website for special events taking place during your
visit to California's northernmost counties. A weekly fishing report
informs anglers about stream closures and which spots are yielding the
best catches. ✉ *1699 Hwy. 273, Anderson* ☎ *530/365–7500, 800/474–
2782* ⊕ *www.shastacascade.com.*

EXPLORING

Lake Shasta. Numerous types of fish inhabit the lake, including rainbow trout, salmon, bass, brown trout, and the humble catfish. The lake region also has the largest nesting population of bald eagles in California. You can rent fishing boats, ski boats, sailboats, canoes, paddleboats, Jet Skis, and windsurfing boards at one of the many marinas and resorts along the 370-mile shoreline. ⊠ *Shasta Lake.*

Fodor'sChoice ★ **Lake Shasta Caverns.** Stalagmites, stalactites, flowstone deposits, and crystals entice visitors to the Lake Shasta Caverns. To see this impressive spectacle, you must take the two-hour tour, which includes a catamaran ride across the McCloud arm of Lake Shasta and a bus ride up North Grey Rocks Mountain to the cavern entrance. The caverns are 58°F year-round, making them a cool retreat on a hot summer day. The most awe-inspiring of the limestone rock formations is the glistening Cathedral Room, which appears to be gilded. A gift shop is open from 8 to 4:30. ⊠ *20359 Shasta Caverns Rd., off I–5, 17 miles north of Redding, Lakehead* ☎ *530/238–2341, 800/795–2283* ⊕ *lakeshastacaverns.com* ⊡ *$24* ☺ *June–Aug., tours on the half hour, daily 9–4; Apr., May, and Sept., tours on the hour, daily 9–3; Oct.–Mar., tours at 10, noon, and 2.*

Shasta Dam. This is the second-largest concrete dam in the United States (only Grand Coulee in Washington is bigger). The visitor center has computerized photographic tours of the dam construction, video presentations, fact sheets, and historical displays. Hour-long guided tours inside the dam and its powerhouse leave from the center. ⊠ *16349 Shasta Dam Blvd., off Lake Blvd., Shasta Lake* ☎ *530/275–4463* ⊕ *www.usbr.gov/mp/ncao* ⊡ *Free* ☺ *Visitor center, daily 8–5; call for tour times.*

WHERE TO EAT

$$ SEAFOOD **✕Tail o' the Whale.** As its name suggests, this restaurant has a nautical theme. You can enjoy a panoramic view of Lake Shasta here while you savor house specials like charbroiled salmon, prime rib with prawns, and pasta dishes. This is a favorite spot for boaters, who anchor at a courtesy dock while they're dining. ⑤ *Average main: $20* ⊠ *10300 Bridge Bay Rd., Bridge Bay exit off I–5, Redding* ☎ *530/275–3021* ☺ *No dinner Mon.–Wed. in winter.*

SPORTS AND THE OUTDOORS

FISHING

The Fishen Hole. A couple of miles from the lake, this bait-and-tackle shop sells fishing licenses and provides information about conditions. ⊠ *3844 Shasta Dam Blvd., at Red Bluff Ave., Shasta Lake* ☎ *530/275–4123.*

HOUSEBOATING

Houseboats here come in all sizes except small. As a rule, rentals are outfitted with cooking utensils, dishes, and most of the equipment you'll need—you supply the food and the linens. When you rent a houseboat, you receive a short course in how to maneuver your launch before you set out. You can fish, swim, sunbathe on the flat roof, or sit on the deck and watch the world go by. The shoreline of Lake Shasta is beautifully ragged, with countless inlets; it's not hard to find privacy. Expect to

14

spend a minimum of $350 a day for a craft that sleeps six. A three-day, two-night minimum is customary. Prices are often lower during the off-season (September through May). Bridge Bay Resort rents houseboats, fishing boats, ski boats, and patio boats. Shasta Cascade offers general information.

Bridge Bay Resort. This resort offers modest lakeside lodging, a restaurant, boat and Jet Ski rentals, and a full service marina. If you want to sleep on the lake rather than beside it, rent one of the houseboats that come in sizes large enough to accomodate up to a dozen people. ✉ *10300 Bridge Bay Rd., Redding* ☎ *800/752–9669, 530/275–3021* ⊕ *www.sevencrown.com/lakes/lake_shasta/bridge_bay/index.htm.*

DUNSMUIR

10 miles south of Mt. Shasta on I–5.

Surrounded by towering forests and boasting world-class fly-fishing in the Upper Sacramento River, tiny Dunsmuir was named for a 19th-century Scottish coal baron who offered to build a fountain if the town was renamed in his honor. Another major attraction is the Railroad Park Resort, where you can spend the night in restored cabooses.

GETTING HERE AND AROUND
Reach Dunsmuir via exits off Interstate 5 at the north and south ends of town. When snow hasn't closed the route, you can take Highway 89 from the Lassen Park area toward Burney then northeast to Interstate 5 at Mt. Shasta. From there it's a 10-mile drive south to Dunsmuir. Amtrak stops here; Greyhound stops in Weed, 20 miles north. On weekdays, STAGE buses serve Dunsmuir.

ESSENTIALS
Bus Information STAGE ☎ *530/842–8295* ⊕ *www.co.siskiyou.ca.us/GS/ stageschedule.aspx.*

Visitor Information Dunsmuir Chamber of Commerce ✉ *5915 Dunsmuir Ave., Ste. 100* ☎ *530/235–2177* ⊕ *dunsmuir.com.*

EXPLORING
Fodor's Choice **Castle Crags State Park.** Named for its 6,000-foot glacier-polished crags,
★   which were formed by volcanic activity centuries ago, this park offers fishing in Castle Creek, hiking in the backcountry, and a view of Mt. Shasta. The crags draw climbers and hikers from around the world. The 4,350-acre park has 28 miles of hiking trails, including a 2.75-mile access trail to **Castle Crags Wilderness,** part of the **Shasta-Trinity National Forest.** There are excellent trails at lower altitudes. Camping is allowed in winter on a first-come, first-served basis. ✉ *6 miles south of Dunsmuir, Castella/Castle Crags exit off I–5* ☎ *530/235–2684* ⊕ *www. parks.ca.gov/parkindex* ✍ *$8 per vehicle, day use.*

WHERE TO EAT AND STAY
$$ ✕ **Café Maddalena.** The chef here gained experience working in top
MEDITERRANEAN   San Francisco restaurants before moving north to prepare adventurous Mediterranean fare with a French influence. Selections change seasonally but always feature a vegetarian dish, along with entrées

such as Genovese seafood stew, and lamb shoulder with cassoulet. Wines from Spain, Italy, and France complement the meals. Ask about the daily prix fixe menu. ⑤ *Average main: $21* ✉ *5801 Sacramento Ave.* ☎ *530/235–2725* ⊕ *www.cafemaddalena.com* ⊗ *Closed Mon.–Wed. and Jan.–mid-Feb. No lunch.*

FINE FISHING

The upper Sacramento River near Dunsmuir is consistently rated one of the best fishing spots in the country. Check with the chamber of commerce for local fishing guides.

$ ▨ **Railroad Park Resort.** The antique cabooses here were collected over
HOTEL more than three decades and have been converted into cozy motel
FAMILY rooms in honor of Dunsmuir's railroad legacy. **Pros:** gorgeous setting; kitschy fun. **Cons:** cabooses can feel cramped. ⑤ *Rooms from: $115* ✉ *100 Railroad Park Rd.* ☎ *530/235–4440* ⊕ *www.rrpark.com* ⇆ *23 cabooses, 4 cabins* ⦿ *No meals.*

MT. SHASTA

34 miles north of Lake Shasta on I–5.

While a snow-covered dormant volcano is the area's dazzling draw, the town of Mt. Shasta charms visitors with its small shops, friendly residents and beautiful scenery in all seasons.

GETTING HERE AND AROUND

Three exits off Interstate 5 lead to the town of Mt. Shasta. When snow hasn't closed the route, you can take Highway 89 from the Lassen Park area toward Burney then northeast to Mt. Shasta. The ski park is off Highway 89. Greyhound stops at Weed, 10 miles north; Amtrak stops at Dunsmuir, 10 miles south. There's no local bus system.

ESSENTIALS

Visitor Information Mt. Shasta Chamber of Commerce and Visitors Bureau ✉ *300 Pine St., at W. Lake St., Mt. Shasta* ☎ *530/926–4865, 800/926–4865* ⊕ *mtshastachamber.com.*

EXPLORING

Fodor'sChoice **Mt. Shasta.** The crown jewel of the 2.5-million-acre Shasta-Trinity
★ National Forest, Mt. Shasta, a 14,179-foot-high dormant volcano, is a mecca for day hikers. It's especially enticing in spring, when fragrant Shasta lilies and other flowers adorn the rocky slopes. A paved road, the Everitt Memorial Highway, reaches only as far as the timberline; the final 6,000 feet are a tough climb of rubble, ice, and snow (the summit is perpetually ice packed). Only a hardy few are qualified to make the trek to the top.

The town of Mt. Shasta has real character and some fine restaurants. Lovers of the outdoors and backcountry skiers abound, and they are more than willing to offer advice on the most beautiful spots in the region, which include out-of-the-way swimming holes, dozens of high mountain lakes, and a challenging 18-hole golf course with 360 degrees of spectacular views. ⊕ *mtshastachamber.com.*

WHERE TO EAT AND STAY

$
CAFÉ
✕ **Seven Suns Coffee and Cafe.** A favorite gathering spot for locals, this small coffee shop serves specialty wraps for breakfast and lunch, plus soup and salad selections. Pastries, made daily, include muffins and scones, and blackberry fruit bars in season. If the weather's nice, grab a seat on the patio. ⑤ *Average main: $9* ⌧ *1011 S. Mt. Shasta Blvd., at Holly St.* ☎ *530/926–9701* ⊕ *www.mtshastacoffee.com.*

$$
HOTEL
⛉ **Best Western Tree House Motor Inn.** The clean, standard rooms at this motel less than a mile from downtown Mt. Shasta are decorated with natural-wood furnishings. **Pros:** close to ski park; lobby's roaring fireplace is a big plus on winter days. **Cons:** not all lodging buildings have elevators. ⑤ *Rooms from: $170* ⌧ *111 Morgan Way* ☎ *530/926–3101, 800/545–7164* ⊕ *www.bestwestern.com* ⌁ *98 rooms, 7 suites* ⧉ *Breakfast.*

$$
RENTAL
⛉ **Mount Shasta Resort.** Private chalets are nestled among tall pine trees along the shore of Lake Siskiyou, all with gas-log fireplaces and full kitchens. **Pros:** romantic woodsy setting; some pet-friendly rooms for extra fee. **Cons:** kids may get bored. ⑤ *Rooms from: $159* ⌧ *1000 Siskiyou Lake Blvd.* ☎ *530/926–3030, 800/958–3363* ⊕ *www.mountshastaresort.com* ⌁ *65 units* ⧉ *No meals.*

SPORTS AND THE OUTDOORS

GOLF

Mount Shasta Resort. At a bit under 6,100 yards, the Mount Shasta Resort golf course isn't long, but it's beautiful and challenging, with narrow, tree-lined fairways and natural alpine terrain. Carts rent for $15; fabulous views are free. ⌧ *1000 Siskiyou Lake Blvd.* ☎ *530/926–3052* ⊕ *www.mountshastaresort.com* ⌑ *$45 weekdays, $60 weekends* ⟘ *18 holes, 6035 yards, par 70.*

HIKING

Mt. Shasta Forest Service Ranger Station. Check in here for current trail conditions and avalanche reports. ⌧ *204 W. Alma St., at Pine St.* ☎ *530/926–4511, 530/926–9613 avalanche conditions.*

MOUNTAIN CLIMBING

Fifth Season Mountaineering Shop. This shop rents bicycles and skiing and climbing equipment, and operates a recorded 24-hour climber-skier report. ⌧ *300 N. Mt. Shasta Blvd.* ☎ *530/926–3606, 530/926–5555 ski phone* ⊕ *www.thefifthseason.com.*

Shasta Mountain Guides. These guides lead hiking, climbing, and ski-touring groups to the summit of Mt. Shasta. ☎ *530/926–3117* ⊕ *shasta guides.com.*

SKIING

FAMILY **Mt. Shasta Board & Ski Park.** On the southeast flank of Mt. Shasta, this ski park has three triple-chair lifts and two surface lifts on 425 skiable acres. Three-quarters of the trails are for beginning or intermediate skiers. The area's vertical drop is 1,435 feet, with a top elevation of 6,890 feet. The longest of the 32 trails is 1.75 miles. A package for beginners, available through the ski school, includes a lift ticket, ski rental, and a lesson. The school also runs ski and snowboard programs for children. There's night skiing for those who want to see the moon rise as they schuss. The base lodge has a simple café, a ski shop, and a ski-snowboard rental shop. ⊠ *Hwy. 89 exit east from I–5, south of Mt. Shasta* ☎ *530/926–8610, 800/754–7427* ⊕ *www.skipark.com* ☯ *Winter ski season schedule: Sun.–Wed. 9–4, Thurs.–Sat. 9–9.*

Mt. Shasta Nordic Center. This center, run by a nonprofit, maintains 15 miles of groomed cross-country ski trails. ⊠ *Ski Park Hwy., off Hwy. 89 (take I–5's McCloud exit)* ☎ *530/926–2142* ⊕ *mtshastanordic.org.*

THE BACKCOUNTRY

The Far North's primitive, rugged backcountry is arguably full of more natural wonders than any other region in California.

14

MCARTHUR–BURNEY FALLS MEMORIAL STATE PARK

Hwy. 89, 52 miles southeast of Mt. Shasta and 41 miles north of Lassen Volcanic National Park.

One of the most spectacular sights in the Far North is Burney Falls, where countless ribbon-like streams pour from moss-covered crevices. You have to travel forested back roads to reach this gem, but the park's beauty is well worth the trek.

GETTING HERE AND AROUND

To see some stunning falls, head east off Interstate 5 on Highway 89 at Mt. Shasta. The drive is 52 miles. From Interstate 5 in Redding, head east 55 miles on Highway 299 to connect with Highway 89; follow signs 6 miles to the park. From Alturas, head west on Highway 299 for about 86 miles and hook up with Highway 89.

EXPLORING

FAMILY
Fodor's Choice
★

McArthur–Burney Falls Memorial State Park. Just inside the park's southern boundary, Burney Creek wells up from the ground and divides into two falls that cascade over a 129-foot cliff into a pool below. Countless ribbonlike streams pour from hidden moss-covered crevices; resident bald eagles are frequently seen soaring overhead. You can walk a self-guided nature trail that descends to the foot of the falls, which Theodore Roosevelt—according to legend—called "the eighth wonder of the world." On warm days, swim at Lake Britton; lounge on the beach; rent motorboats, paddleboats, and canoes; or relax at one of the campsites or picnic areas. The camp store is open from late April to the end of October. ⊠ *24898 Hwy. 89, 6 miles north of Hwy. 299, Burney* ☎ *530/335–2777* ⊕ *www.parks.ca.gov/parkindex* ⊠ *$8 per vehicle, day use.*

ALTURAS

86 miles northeast of McArthur–Burney Falls Memorial State Park on Hwy. 299.

Alturas is the county seat and largest town in Modoc County. The Dorris family arrived in the area in 1874, built Dorris Bridge over the Pit River, and later opened a small wayside stop for travelers. As in the past, travelers today come to see eagles and other wildlife, the Modoc National Forest, and active geothermal areas.

GETTING HERE AND AROUND

To get to Alturas from Susanville take Main Street/Highway 36 south for about 4 miles; turn left at U.S. 395 and stay on that highway for 99 miles. From Redding, take the Lake Blvd./299E exit off Interstate 5, head east and stay on Highway 299 for 140 miles. Sage Stage buses serve Alturas from Redding and Susanville.

ESSENTIALS

Bus Information Modoc County Sage Stage ☎ 530/233-6410 ⊕ www.sagestage.com.

Visitor Information Alturas Chamber of Commerce ⊠ 600 S. Main St. ☎ 530/233-4434 ⊕ www.alturaschamber.org.

EXPLORING

Modoc National Forest. Encompassing 1.6 million acres, Modoc National Forest protects 300 species of wildlife, including Rocky Mountain elk, wild horses, mule deer, and pronghorn antelope. In spring and fall, watch for migratory waterfowl as they make their way along the Pacific Flyway above the forest. Hiking trails lead to Petroglyph Point, one of the largest panels of rock art in the United States. ⊠ *Park Headquarters, 225 W. 8th St.* ☎ *530/233-5811* ⊕ *www.fs.usda.gov/modoc.*

Modoc National Wildlife Refuge. The 7,021-acre Modoc National Wildlife Refuge was established in 1961 to protect migratory waterfowl. You might see Canada geese, sandhill cranes, mallards, teal, wigeon, pintail, white pelicans, cormorants, and snowy egrets. The refuge is open for hiking, bird-watching, and photography, but one area is set aside for hunters. Regulations vary according to season. ⊠ *5364 County Rd. 115, U.S. 395, 1½ miles south of Alturas, left on Rd. 56, then right on Rd. 115* ☎ *530/233-3572* ⊕ *www.fws.gov/refuge/modoc* ⊠ *Free* ☉ *Daily dawn–dusk.*

WHERE TO EAT

$$
SPANISH ✕ **Brass Rail.** Prix-fixe dinners at this authentic Basque restaurant include wine, homemade bread, soup, salad, side dishes, coffee, and ice cream. Steak, lamb chops, fried chicken, shrimp, and scallops are among the best entrée selections. A lounge with a full bar adjoins the dining area. ⑤ *Average main: $21* ⊠ *395 Lake View Dr.* ☎ *530/233-2906* ☉ *Closed Mon.*

SUSANVILLE

104 miles south of Alturas via U.S. 395; 65 miles east of Lassen Volcanic National Park via Highway 36.

Susanville, established as a trading post in 1854, tells the tale of its rich history through murals painted on buildings in the historic uptown area. You can take a self-guided tour around the original buildings and stop for a bite at one of the restaurants now housed within them. If you'd rather work up a sweat, you can hit the Bizz Johnson Trail and Eagle Lake recreation areas just outside town.

GETTING HERE AND AROUND

U.S. 395 connects Susanville and Alturas, about a 100-mile trip. From Red Bluff, take Interstate 5's Highway 36E/Fairgrounds exit and drive east for about 3 miles; turn left at Highway 36E and continue through the mountains for 103 miles. Lassen Rural Bus serves Susanville Monday through Saturday, and surrounding areas on weekdays only.

ESSENTIALS

Bus Information Lassen Rural Bus ☎ 530/252–7433 ⊕ www.lassentransportation.com/a/Lassen-Rural-Bus-LRB.php.

Visitor Information Lassen County Chamber of Commerce ⊠ 75 N. Weatherlow St., off Main St. ☎ 530/257–4323 ⊕ lassencountychamber.com.

EXPLORING

Bizz Johnson Trail. This trail follows a defunct line of the Southern Pacific Railroad for 25 miles. Known to locals as the Bizz, the trail is open for hikers, walkers, mountain bikers, horseback riders, and cross-country skiers. It skirts the Susan River through a scenic landscape of canyons, bridges, and forests abundant with wildlife. ⊠ Trailhead, old railroad depot, 601 Richmond Rd., near N. Railroad Ave. ☎ 530/257–0456 ⊕ www.blm.gov/ca/st/en/fo/eaglelake/bizztrail.html ☜ Free.

Eagle Lake. Anglers travel great distances to fish the waters of this large lake where the trout is prized for its size and fighting ability. Surrounded by high desert to the north and alpine forests to the south, Eagle Lake is also popular for picnicking, hiking, boating, waterskiing and windsurfing, and bird-watching—ospreys, pelicans, and many other waterfowl visit the lake. On land you might see mule deer, small mammals, and even pronghorn antelope—and be sure to watch for bald-eagle nesting sites. ⊠ 16 miles north of Susanville, Eagle Lake Rd. off Hwy. 139 ☎ 530/257–0456 for Eagle Lake Recreation Area, 530/825–3454 for Eagle Lake Marina ⊕ www.blm.gov/ca/st/en/fo/eaglelake.html.

WHERE TO EAT AND STAY

$ ✕ **Mazatlan Grill.** The sauces are prepared on-site in this friendly, family-
MEXICAN   run restaurant and lounge, which serves lunch and dinner daily. The dining room is simple and tidy, with comfortable upholstered booths. The extensive menu offers authentic, inexpensive Mexican fare ranging from fajitas and enchiladas to a vegetarian burrito. $ Average main: $10 ⊠ 1535 Main St., at Park St. ☎ 530/257–1800.

$ ☷ **High Country Inn.** Rooms are spacious in this colonial-style motel on
HOTEL   the eastern edge of town. **Pros:** great mountain views; heated pool. **Cons:** lots of traffic in the area. $ Rooms from: $87 ⊠ 3015 Riverside Dr., at Main St. ☎ 530/257–3450, 866/454–4566 ⊕ www.high-country-inn.com ☜ 66 rooms ⏐◎⏐ Breakfast.

Lassen Volcanic National Park

Butte Lake

Cinder Cone

Prospect Peak
8,338 ft.

PAINTED DUNES

FANTASTIC LAVA BEDS

Ash Butte

Snag Lake

Fairfield Peak

Crater Butte

Juniper Lake

Horseshoe Lake

GRASSY SWALE

Pacific Crest Trail

Warner Valley

CORRAL MEADOW

Hat Mt.

Summit Lake North
Summit Lake South

DERSCH MEADOWS

READING PEAK

Devil's Kitchen

DEVASTATED AREA

Bumpass Hell

Kings Creek

TWIN MEADOWS

CHAOS CRAGS

Lassen Peak
10,457 ft.

89

Sulphur Works

Kohm Yah-mah-nee
Visitor Center

Manzanita Lake

Ranger Station

Entrance Station

89

TO REDDING

44

Entrance Station

TO RED BLUFF
AND CHICO

BLUE LAKE CANYON

44

TO CHESTER
AND SUSANVILLE

1/2 mi

1/2 km

0

0

LASSEN VOLCANIC NATIONAL PARK

45 miles east of Redding on Hwy. 44; 48 miles east of Red Bluff on Hwy. 36.

Fissures and fumaroles burble and belch as reminders of Lassen Peak's dramatic eruption a century ago. Four different types of volcanoes form part of this park's fascinating geothermal landscape.

GETTING HERE AND AROUND

Whether coming from the west or the east, reach the park's southern entrance via Highway 36E, and turn onto Highway 89 for a short drive to the park. The northwest entrance is reached via Highway 44 from Redding and Susanville. No buses serve the area.

EXPLORING

Fodor's Choice **Lassen Scenic Byway.** This 185-mile scenic drive begins in Chester and ★ loops through the forests, volcanic peaks, geothermal springs, and lava fields of Lassen National Forest and Lassen Volcanic National Park, providing for an all-day excursion into dramatic wilderness. From Chester, take Route 36 west to Route 89 north through the park, then Route 44 east to Route 36 west back to Chester. Parts of the road are inaccessible in winter. ⊠ *Lassen Volcanic National Park* ☎ *800/427–7623 CA Highway info service, 530/595-4480 Lassen Park visitor center* ⊕ *www.nps.gov/lavo.*

Fodor's Choice **Lassen Volcanic National Park.** A dormant plug dome, Lassen Peak is ★ the focus of Lassen Volcanic National Park's 165.6 square miles of distinctive landscape. The peak began erupting in May 1914, sending pumice, rock, and snow thundering down the mountain and gas and hot ash billowing into the atmosphere. Lassen's most spectacular outburst occurred in 1915 when it blew a cloud of ash some 7 miles into the stratosphere. The resulting mudflow destroyed vegetation for miles in some directions; the evidence is still visible today, especially in the Devastated Area. The volcano finally came to rest in 1921. Today, fumaroles, mud pots, lakes, and bubbling hot springs create a fascinating but dangerous landscape that can be viewed throughout the park, especially via a hiked descent into Bumpass Hell. Because of its significance as a volcanic landscape, Lassen became a national park in 1916. Several volcanoes—the largest of which is now Lassen Peak—have been active in the area for roughly 600,000 years. The four types of volcanoes found in the world are represented in the park, including shield (Prospect Peak), plug dome (Lassen Peak), cinder cone (Cinder Cone), and composite (Brokeoff Volcano). Lassen Park Road (the continuation of Highway 89 within the park) and 150 miles of hiking trails provide access to many of these volcanic wonders. ■**TIP➔** Caution is key here: heed signs that warn visitors to stay on the trails and railed boardwalks to avoid falling into boiling water or through dangerous thin-crusted areas of the park. Although the park is closed to cars in winter, it's usually open to intrepid cross-country skiers and snowshoers. ⊕ *www.nps.gov/lavo* ▦ *$10 per car, $5 per person if not in a car.*

FAMILY **Sulphur Works Thermal Area.** Proof of Lassen Peak's volatility becomes evident shortly after you enter the park at the southwest entrance. Sidewalks skirt boiling springs and sulphur-emitting steam vents. This area is usually the last site to close because of snow. ⊠ *Lassen Park Rd., 1 mile from the southwest entrance ranger station, Lassen Volcanic National Park* ⊕ *www.nps.gov/lavo.*

14

WHERE TO STAY

$$$$ **Drakesbad Guest Ranch.** With propane furnaces and kerosene lamps,
B&B/INN everything about this century-old property harkens back to a simpler time. **Pros:** a true back-to-nature experience; great for family adventures. **Cons:** accessible only via a partially paved road leading out of Chester. $ *Rooms from: $338* ⊠ *End of Warner Valley Rd., Chester* ☎ *866/999–0914* ⊕ *www.drakesbad.com* ⟿ *19 rooms* ⊗ *Closed mid Oct.–early June* ¶⊙| *All meals.*

SPORTS AND THE OUTDOORS
HIKING

Fodor'sChoice **Bumpass Hell Trail.** Boiling springs, steam vents, and mud pots highlight
★ this 3-mile round-trip hike. Expect the loop to take about two hours. During the first mile of the hike there's a gradual climb of 500 feet before a steep 300-foot descent to the basin. You'll encounter rocky patches, so wear hiking boots. ⚠ Stay on trails and boardwalks near the thermal areas, as what appears to be firm ground may be only a thin crust over scalding mud. *Moderate.* ⊠ *Trailhead at end of paved parking area off Lassen Park Rd., 6 miles from the southwest entrance ranger station, Lassen Volcanic National Park* ⊕ *www.nps.gov/lavo.*

Fodor'sChoice **Lassen Peak Hike.** This trail winds 2½ miles to the mountaintop. It's a
★ tough climb—2,000 feet uphill on a steady, steep grade—but the reward is a spectacular view. At the peak you can see into the rim and view the entire park (and much of California's far north). Bring sunscreen, water, and a jacket since it's often windy and much cooler at the summit. ■TIP➔ A multiyear restoration project means that all or part of the trail will be open only a few times during the year, so call ahead. Depending on funding, trail work is expected to be completed by the end of 2015. ⊠ *Trailhead past a paved parking area off Lassen Park Rd., 7 miles north of the southwest entrance ranger station, Lassen Volcanic National Park* ☎ *530/595–4480* ⊕ *www.nps.gov/lavo.*

CHESTER

36 miles west of Susanville on Hwy 36.

The population of this small town on Lake Almanor swells from 2,500 to nearly 5,000 in summer as tourists come to visit. Chester serves as a gateway to Lassen Volcanic National Park.

GETTING HERE AND AROUND

Chester is on Highway 36E. When snow doesn't close Highway 89, the main road through Lassen Park, visitors can take Highway 44 from Redding to Highway 89 through the park and to Highway 36E and onto Chester and Lake Almanor. Plumas County Transit connects Chester to the Quincy area.

ESSENTIALS

Bus Information Plumas County Transit ☎ *530/283–2538* ⊕ *www.plumastransit.com.*

Visitor Information Lake Almanor Area Chamber of Commerce and Visitors Bureau ⊠ *289 #7 Main St., near Stone Ave.* ☎ *530/258–2426* ⊕ *www.lakealmanorarea.com.*

EXPLORING

Lake Almanor. This lake's 52 miles of forested shoreline are popular with campers, swimmers, water-skiers, and anglers. At an elevation of 4,500 feet, the lake warms to above 70°F for about eight weeks in summer. ⊠ *Off Hwys. 89 and 36* ☎ *530/258–2426* ⊕ *www.lakealmanorarea.com.*

WHERE TO EAT AND STAY

$

AMERICAN

✕**Kopper Kettle Cafe.** Locals return again and again to this tidy restaurant that serves home-cooked lunches and dinners. Head here for breakfast whenever you've got a hankering for scrambled eggs or biscuits and gravy. ⑤ *Average main: $14* ⊠ *243 Main St., at Myrtle St.* ☎ *530/258–2698.*

$$

HOTEL

Best Western Rose Quartz Inn. Down the road from Lake Almanor and close to Lassen Volcanic National Park, this small-town inn balances traditional decor and up-to-the-minute amenities like Wi-Fi. **Pros:** near national park; within easy walking distance of town's restaurants. **Cons:** standard rooms on the pricey side. ⑤ *Rooms from: $130* ⊠ *306 Main St.* ☎ *530/258–2002, 888/571–4885* ⊕ *bestwesterncalifornia.com/chester-hotels* ⟳ *51 rooms* ⦿| *Breakfast.*

$$

B&B/INN

Fodor's Choice

★

Bidwell House. Some guest rooms at this 1901 ranch house have wood-burning stoves, claw-foot tubs, and antique furnishings; a separate cottage with a kitchen sleeps six. **Pros:** unique decor in each room; beautiful wooded setting; near Lake Almanor. **Cons:** not ideal for kids. ⑤ *Rooms from: $125* ⊠ *1 Main St.* ☎ *530/258–3338* ⊕ *www.bidwellhouse.com* ⟳ *14 rooms, 2 with shared bath* ⦿| *Breakfast.*

QUINCY

67 miles southwest of Susanville via Hwys. 36 and 89.

A center for mining and logging in the 1850s, Quincy is nestled against the western slope of the Sierra Nevada. The county seat and largest community in Plumas County, the town is rich in historic buildings that have been the focus of preservation and restoration efforts. The four-story courthouse on Main Street, one of several stops on a self-guided tour, was built in 1921 with marble posts and staircases. The arts are thriving in Quincy, too: catch a play or a bluegrass performance at the Town Hall Theatre.

Lassen Volcanic National Park's King Creek Falls Hike, which takes you through forests and meadows dotted with wildflowers, is a good hike for nature photographers.

GETTING HERE AND AROUND

Quincy is on Highway 70 and is accessible from all directions via mountain roads. Highway 70 goes through the Feather River Canyon to Highway 149, then Highway 99 to Chico and Red Bluff, a 198-mile trip. From Quincy, Highway 70 connects to Highway 89 and then to Highway 36E toward Susanville in the east, or westward toward Chester and Lassen Park. Plumas County Transit serves Chester and Quincy. Lassen Rural Bus connects Quincy and Susanville.

ESSENTIALS

Bus Information Lassen Rural Bus ☎ *530/252–7433*
⊕ *www.lassentransportation.com/a/Lassen-Rural-Bus-LRB.php.*
Plumas County Transit ☎ *530/283–2538* ⊕ *www.plumastransit.com.*

Visitor Information Quincy Chamber of Commerce ✉ *336 W. Main St., inside Plumas Bank* ☎ *530/283–0188* ⊕ *www.quincychamber.com.*

EXPLORING

Bucks Lake Recreation Area. The main recreational attraction in central Plumas County is 17 miles southwest of Quincy at elevation 5,200 feet. During warm months the lake's 17-mile shoreline, two marinas, and eight campgrounds attract anglers and water-sports enthusiasts. Trails through the tall pines beckon hikers and horseback riders. In winter much of the area remains open for snowmobiling and cross-country skiing. ✉ *Bucks Lake Rd.* ☎ *530/283–0188* ⊕ *www.plumascounty.org/Communities/BucksLake.htm.*

Plumas County Museum. The cultural, home arts, and industrial history displays at the Plumas County Museum contain artifacts dating to the

1850s. Highlights include collections of Maidu Indian basketry, pioneer weapons, and rooms depicting life in the early logging and mining days of Plumas County. Out in the Exhibit Yard are a working blacksmith shop, a restored goldminer's cabin, and a railroad exhibit. ⊠ *500 Jackson St., at Coburn St.* ☎ *530/283–6320* ⊕ *www.plumasmuseum.org* ⊠ *$2* ☉ *Tues.–Sat. 10–4.*

Plumas National Forest. Plumas County is known for its wide-open spaces, and the 1.2-million-acre Plumas National Forest, with its high alpine lakes and crystal clear woodland streams, is a beautiful example. Hundreds of campsites are maintained in the forest, and picnic areas and hiking trails abound. You can enter the forest along highways 70 and 89. ⊠ *U.S. Forest Service, 159 Lawrence St., near W. Main St.* ☎ *530/283–2050* ⊕ *www.fs.usda.gov/plumas* ☉ *Office weekdays 8–4:30.*

WHERE TO EAT AND STAY

$$ ✕ **Sweet Lorraine's.** Hearty fare served in this casual, bustling restaurant in Quincy's historic downtown area includes meaty dishes like
AMERICAN St. Louis–style ribs as well as vegetarian options and lighter items; there's also a good selection of wines. If the weather is mild, dine alfresco on the patio. Counter seating is fast and friendly. ⑤ *Average main: $17* ⊠ *384 Main St., at Harbison Ave.* ☎ *530/283–5300* ☉ *Closed Sun. and Mon.*

$ ⌂ **Ada's Place.** This place is actually four uniquely beautiful cottages,
RENTAL secluded on a quiet street one block from the county courthouse and
Fodor's Choice downtown Quincy. **Pros:** on-site owners' meticulous upkeep. **Cons:** not
★ a good choice for children. ⑤ *Rooms from: $100* ⊠ *562 Jackson St., near Court St.* ☎ *530/283–1954, 877/234–2327* ⊕ *www.adasplace.com* ⌐ *4 cottages* ⦿ *No meals.*

$ ⌂ **Lariat Lodge.** This small, single-story motel two miles east of down-
HOTEL town is a quiet haven surrounded by views of the Plumas National Forest. **Pros:** inexpensive rooms; lovely setting. **Cons:** older facility. ⑤ *Rooms from: $70* ⊠ *2370 E. Main St.* ☎ *530/283–1000, 800/999–7199* 🖷 *530/283–2164* ⌐ *19 rooms* ⦿ *No meals.*

TRAVEL SMART NORTHERN CALIFORNIA

GETTING HERE AND AROUND

Wherever you plan to go in Northern California, getting there will likely involve driving, even if you fly. Major airports are usually far from main attractions. (In San Francisco, it's a 30-minute-plus trip between any Bay Area airport and downtown.) Northern California's major airport hub is SFO in San Francisco, but satellite airports can be found around most major cities. When booking flights, it pays to check these locations, as you may find more convenient times and a better location in relation to your hotel. Most small cities have their own commercial airports, with connecting flights to larger cities—but service may be extremely limited, and it may be cheaper to rent a car and drive from San Francisco.

FROM SAN FRANCISCO TO:	BY AIR	BY CAR
San Jose		1 hr
Monterey	45 mins	2 hrs
Los Angeles	1 hr 30 mins	5 hrs 40 mins
Portland, OR	1 hr 50 mins	10 hrs
Mendocino		3 hrs
Yosemite NP/ Fresno	1 hr	3 hrs 30 mins
Lake Tahoe/ Reno	1 hr	3 hrs 30 mins

▮ AIR TRAVEL

Flying time to California is about 5½ hours from New York and 4 hours from Chicago. Travel from London to either Los Angeles or San Francisco is 11 hours and from Sydney approximately 15½. Flying between San Francisco and Los Angeles takes about 90 minutes.

AIRPORTS

California's gateways are Los Angeles International Airport (LAX), San Francisco International Airport (SFO), San Diego International Airport (SAN),

Sacramento International Airport (SMF), and San Jose International Airport (SJC). Oakland International Airport (OAK) is another option in the Bay Area, and other Los Angeles airports include Long Beach (LGB), Bob Hope Airport (BUR), LA/Ontario (ONT), and John Wayne Airport (SNA).

Airport Information Bob Hope Airport ✉ Burbank ☎ 818/840–8840 ⊕ www. burbankairport.com. **John Wayne Airport** ☎ 949/252–5200 ⊕ www.ocair.com. **LA/ Ontario International Airport** ☎ 909/937–2700 ⊕ www.flyontario.com. **Long Beach Airport** ☎ 562/570–2600 ⊕ www.lgb.org. **Los Angeles International Airport** ☎ 310/646–5252 ⊕ www.lawa.org/lax. **Oakland International Airport** ☎ 510/563–3300 ⊕ www. flyoakland.com. **Sacramento International Airport** ☎ 916/929–5411 ⊕ www.sacramento. aero/smf. **San Diego International Airport** ☎ 619/400–2404 ⊕ www.san.org. **San Francisco International Airport** ☎ 650/821–8211, 800/435–9736 ⊕ www.flysfo.com. **San Jose International Airport** ☎ 408/392–3600 ⊕ www.flysanjose.com.

FLIGHTS

United, with hubs in San Francisco and Los Angeles, has the greatest number of flights into and within California. But most national and many international airlines fly to the state. Southwest Airlines and United Airlines connect smaller cities within California, often from satellite airports near major cities.

Airline Contacts Air Canada ☎ 888/247–2262 ⊕ www.aircanada.com. **Alaska Airlines/ Horizon Air** ☎ 800/252–7522 ⊕ www. alaskaair.com. **American Airlines** ☎ 800/433–7300 ⊕ www.aa.com. **British Airways** ☎ 800/247–9297 ⊕ www.britishairways. com. **Cathay Pacific** ☎ 800/233–2742 ⊕ www.cathaypacific.com. **Delta Airlines** ☎ 800/221–1212 for U.S. reservations, 800/241–4141 for international reservations ⊕ www.delta.com. **Frontier Airlines** ☎ 800/432–1359 ⊕ www.flyfrontier.com. **Japan**

Air Lines ☎ 800/525–3663 ⊕ www.jal.com.
JetBlue ☎ 800/538–2583 ⊕ www.jetblue.
com. **Qantas** ☎ 800/227–4500 ⊕ www.qantas.
com.au. **Southwest Airlines** ☎ 800/435–
9792 ⊕ www.southwest.com. **Spirit Airlines**
☎ 801/401–2200 ⊕ www.spirit.com. **United
Airlines** ☎ 800/864–8331 for U.S. reservations, 800/538–2929 for international
reservations ⊕ www.united.com. **US Airways**
☎ 800/428–4322 for U.S. and Canada reservations, 800/622–1015 for international reservations ⊕ www.usairways.com.

▌ BOAT TRAVEL

CRUISES

A number of major cruise lines offer trips
that begin or end in California. Most voy-
ages sail north along the Pacific Coast to
Alaska or south to Mexico. California
cruise ports include San Francisco, Los
Angeles, and San Diego.

Cruise Lines Carnival Cruise Line
☎ 305/599–2600, 800/227–6482 ⊕ www.
carnival.com. **Celebrity Cruises** ☎ 800/647–
2251, 800/437–3111 ⊕ www.celebritycruises.
com. **Crystal Cruises** ☎ 310/785–9300,
888/722–0021 ⊕ www.crystalcruises.com.
Disney Cruise Line ☎ 800/951–3532
⊕ disneycruiseline.com. **Holland America
Line** ☎ 206/281–3535, 877/932–4259 ⊕ www.
hollandamerica.com. **Norwegian Cruise Line**
☎ 305/436–4000, 866/234–7350 ⊕ www.
ncl.com. **Princess Cruises** ☎ 661/753–0000,
800/774–6237 ⊕ www.princess.com. **Regent
Seven Seas Cruises** ☎ 954/776–6123,
877/505–5370 ⊕ www.rssc.com. **Royal
Caribbean International** ☎ 305/539–6000,
866/562–7625 ⊕ www.royalcaribbean.
com. **Silversea Cruises** ☎ 954/522–4477,
877/276–6816 ⊕ www.silversea.com.

BUS TRAVEL

Greyhound is the major bus carrier in California. Regional bus service is available
in metropolitan areas.

Bus Information Greyhound ☎ 800/231–
2222 ⊕ www.greyhound.com.

▌ CAR TRAVEL

There are two basic north–south routes
in California: Interstate 5 runs inland
most of the way from the Oregon border to the Mexican border; and U.S. 101
hugs the coast for part of the route from
Oregon to Mexico. A slower but much
more scenic option is to take California
State Route 1, also referred to as Highway
1 and the Pacific Coast Highway, which
winds along much of the California coast
and provides an occasionally hair-raising,
but breathtaking, ride.

From north to south, the state's east–west
interstates are Interstate 80, Interstate 15,
Interstate 10, and Interstate 8. Much of
California is mountainous, and you may
encounter winding roads, frequently cliff-
side, and steep mountain grades. In winter, roads crossing the Sierra from east to
west may close at any time due to weather.
Also in winter, Interstate 5 north of Los
Angeles closes during snowstorms.

The flying and driving times in the
accompanying chart represent best-case
scenario estimates, but know that the
infamous California traffic jam can occur
at any time.

GASOLINE

Gasoline prices in California vary widely,
depending on location, oil company,
and whether you buy it at a full-service
or self-serve pump. It's less expensive to
buy fuel in the southern part of the state
than in the north. If you're planning to
travel near Nevada, you can sometimes
save a bit by purchasing gas over the border. Gas stations are plentiful throughout
the state. Most stay open late (24 hours
along major highways and in big cities),
except in rural areas, where Sunday hours
are limited and where you may drive long
stretches without a chance to refuel.

FROM SAN FRANCISCO TO:	ROUTE	DISTANCE
San Jose	U.S. 101	50 miles
Monterey	U.S. 101 to Hwy. 156 to Hwy. 1	120 miles
Los Angeles	U.S. 101 to Hwy. 156 to I-5	382 miles
Portland, OR	I-80 to I-505 to I-5	635 miles
Mendocino	Hwy. 1	174 miles
Yosemite NP	I-80 to I-580 to I-205 to Hwy. 120 east	184 miles
Lake Tahoe/ Reno	I-80	220 miles

ROAD CONDITIONS

Rainy weather can make driving along the coast or in the mountains treacherous. Some of the smaller routes over mountain ranges and in the deserts are prone to flash flooding. When the rains are severe, coastal Highway 1 can quickly become a slippery nightmare, buffeted by strong winds and obstructed by falling debris from the cliffs above. When the weather is particularly bad, Highway 1 may be closed due to mud and rock slides.

Many smaller roads over the Sierra Nevada are closed in winter, and if it's snowing, tire chains may be required on routes that are open, most notably those to Yosemite and Lake Tahoe. From October through April, if it's raining along the coast, it's usually snowing at higher elevations. Consider renting a four-wheel-drive vehicle, or purchase chains before you get to the mountains. (Chains or cables generally cost $30 to $70, depending on tire size; cables are easier to attach than chains, but chains are more durable.) If you delay and purchase them in the vicinity of the chain-control area, the cost may double. Be aware that most rental-car companies prohibit chain installation on their vehicles. If you choose

to risk it and do not tighten them properly, they may snap—your insurance likely will not cover any resulting damage. Uniformed chain installers on Interstate 80 and U.S. 50 will apply them at the checkpoint for about $40 or take them off for less than that. Chain installers are independent business people, not highway employees, and set their own fees. They are not allowed to sell or rent chains. On smaller roads, you're on your own. Always carry extra clothing, blankets, water, and food when driving to the mountains in the winter, and keep your gas tank full to prevent the fuel line from freezing.

Road Conditions Caltrans Current Highway Conditions ☏ *800/427-7623* ⊕ *www.dot.ca.gov.*

Weather Conditions National Weather Service ☏ *707/443-6484 northernmost California, 831/656-1725 San Francisco Bay area and central California, 775/673-8100 Reno, Lake Tahoe, and northern Sierra, 805/988-6610 Los Angeles area, 858/675-8700 San Diego area, 916/979-3051 Sacramento area* ⊕ *www.weather.gov.*

ROADSIDE EMERGENCIES

Dial 911 to report accidents and to reach the police, the California Highway Patrol (CHP), or the fire department. On some rural highways and on most interstates, look for emergency phones on the side of the road.

RULES OF THE ROAD

All passengers must wear seat belts at all times. It is illegal to leave a child six years of age or younger unattended in a motor vehicle. A child must be secured in a federally approved child passenger restraint system and ride in the back seat until at least eight years of age or until the child is at least 4 feet 9 inches tall. Children who are eight but don't meet the height requirement must ride in a booster seat or a car seat. Unless indicated, right turns are allowed at red lights after you've come to a full stop. Left turns between two one-way streets are allowed at red lights after you've come to a full stop.

Drivers with a blood-alcohol level higher than 0.08 who are stopped by police are subject to arrest, and those under 21 convicted of driving with a level of 0.01 or more can have their driving privileges revoked for a year. California's drunk-driving laws are extremely tough—violators may have their licenses immediately suspended, pay hefty fines, and spend the night in jail.

The speed limit on many interstate highways is 70 mph; unlimited-access roads are usually 55 mph. In cities, freeway speed limits are between 55 mph and 65 mph. Many city routes have commuter lanes during rush hour.

You must turn on your headlights whenever weather conditions require the use of windshield wipers.

Those 18 and older must use a hands-free device for their mobile phones while driving; those under 18 may not use mobile phones or wireless devices while driving. Texting on a wireless device is illegal for all drivers. Smoking in a vehicle where a minor is present is an infraction. For more information refer to the Department of Motor Vehicles driver's handbook at ⊕ *www.dmv.ca.gov.*

CAR RENTAL

When you reserve a car, ask about cancellation penalties, taxes, drop-off charges (if you're planning to pick up the car in one city and leave it in another), and surcharges (for being under or over a certain age, for additional drivers, or for driving across state or country borders or beyond a specific distance from your point of rental). All of these things can add substantially to your costs. Request car seats and extras such as GPS when you book.

Rates are sometimes—but not always—better if you book in advance or reserve through a rental agency's website. There are other reasons to book ahead, though: for popular destinations, during busy times of the year, or to ensure that you get certain types of cars (vans, SUVs, exotic sports cars).

■**TIP→** Make sure that a confirmed reservation guarantees you a car. Agencies sometimes overbook, particularly for busy weekends and holiday periods.

A car is essential in most parts of California, though in compact San Francisco it's better to use public transportation to avoid parking headaches.

Rates statewide for the least expensive vehicle begin as low as $30 a day, usually on weekends, and less than $200 a week (though they increase rapidly from here, especially in some of the larger metropolitan areas). This does not include additional fees or the tax on car rentals, which is 8.75% in San Francisco. Be sure to shop around—you can get a decent deal by shopping the major car rental companies' websites. Also, rates are sometimes lower in San Diego; compare prices by city before you book, and ask about "drop charges" if you plan to return the vehicle in a city other than the one where you rented it. If you pick up at an airport, there may also be a facility charge of as much as $12 per rental, plus higher tax rates; ask when you book.

In California, you must have a valid driver's license and be 21 to rent a car; rates may be higher if you're under 25. Some agencies will not rent to those under 25; check when you book. Non-U.S. residents must have a license with text that is in the Roman alphabet that is valid for the entire rental period. Though it need not be entirely written in English, it must have English letters that clearly identify it as a driver's license. In addition, most companies also require an international license; check in advance.

If you dream of driving down the coast with the top down consider renting a specialty vehicle. Agencies that specialize in convertibles and sport-utility vehicles will often arrange airport delivery in larger cities. Unlike most of the major agencies, the following companies guarantee the car class that you book.

Specialty Car Agencies Enterprise Exotic Car Rentals ☎ 800/400-8412, 866/458-9227 *locations in San Francisco, Los Angeles, and other Southern California locations* ⊕ *exotic-cars.enterprise.com*. Beverly Hills Rent a Car ☎ 800/479-5996 *San Francisco and several locations in Los Angeles, 310/274-6969* ⊕ *www.bhrentacar.com*. Midway Car Rental ☎ 866/717-6802 *several locations in Los Angeles and Southern California* ⊕ *www.midwaycarrental.com*.

Major Rental Agencies
Alamo ☎ 800/462-5266 ⊕ *www.alamo.com*.
Avis ☎ 800/331-1212 ⊕ *www.avis.com*.
Budget ☎ 800/527-0700 ⊕ *www.budget.com*.
Hertz ☎ 800/654-3131 ⊕ *www.hertz.com*.
National Car Rental ☎ 877/222-9058 ⊕ *www.nationalcar.com*.

▌ TRAIN TRAVEL

One of the most beautiful train trips in the country, Amtrak's *Coast Starlight* begins in Los Angeles and hugs the Pacific Coast to San Luis Obispo before it turns inland for the rest of its journey to Portland and Seattle. The *California Zephyr* travels from Chicago to Oakland via Denver; the *Pacific Surfliner* connects San Diego and San Luis Obispo via Los Angeles and Santa Barbara with multiple departures daily; and the *Sunset Limited* runs from Los Angeles to New Orleans via Arizona, New Mexico, and Texas.

Information Amtrak ☎ 800/872-7245 ⊕ *www.amtrak.com*.

ESSENTIALS

■ ACCOMMODATIONS

The lodgings we review are the top choices in each price category. ⇨ *For an expanded review of each property, please see* ⊕ *www.fodors.com.* We don't specify whether the facilities cost extra; when pricing accommodations, ask what's included and what costs extra. ⇨ *For price information, see the planner in each chapter.*

Most hotels require you to give your credit-card details before they will confirm your reservation. If you don't feel comfortable emailing this information, ask if you can fax it or call and give details over the phone. However you book, get confirmation in writing and have a copy of it handy when you check in.

Be sure you understand the hotel's cancellation policy. Some places allow you to cancel without any kind of penalty—even if you prepaid to secure a discounted rate—if you cancel at least 24 hours in advance. Others require you to cancel a week in advance or penalize you the cost of one night. Small inns and B&Bs are most likely to require you to cancel far in advance. Most hotels allow children under a certain age to stay in their parents' room at no extra charge, but others charge for them as extra adults; find out the cutoff age for discounts.

Many B&Bs are entirely nonsmoking, and hotels and motels are decreasing their inventory of smoking rooms; if you require one, ask when you book if any are available.

BED-AND-BREAKFASTS

California has more than 1,000 bed-and-breakfasts. You'll find everything from simple homestays to lavish luxury lodgings, many in historic hotels and homes. The California Association of Boutique and Breakfast Inns has about 300 member properties that you can locate and book through its website.

Reservation Services Bed & Breakfast.com ☎ 512/322–2710, 800/462–2632 ⊕ *www. bedandbreakfast.com.* **Bed & Breakfast Inns Online** ☎ 800/215–7365 ⊕ *www.bbonline. com.* **BnB Finder.com** ☎ 212/480–0414, 888/547–8226 ⊕ *www.bnbfinder.com.* **California Association of Boutique and Breakfast Inns** ☎ 800/373–9251 ⊕ *www.cabbi.com.*

■ COMMUNICATIONS

INTERNET

Internet access is widely available in urban areas, but it's usually more difficult to get online in the state's rural areas. Most hotels offer some kind of connection—usually broadband or Wi-Fi. Many hotels charge a daily fee (about $10) for Internet access. Cybercafés are located throughout California.

■ EATING OUT

California has led the pack in bringing natural and organic foods to the forefront of American cooking. Though rooted in European cuisine, California cooking sometimes has strong Asian and Latin influences. Wherever you go, you're likely to find that dishes are made with fresh produce and other local ingredients.

The restaurants we list are the cream of the crop in each price category. ⇨ *For price information, see the planner in each chapter.*

CUTTING COSTS

■ TIP➔ If you're on a budget, take advantage of the "small plates" craze sweeping California by ordering several appetizer-size portions and having a glass of wine at the bar, rather than having a full meal. Also, the better grocery and specialty-food stores have grab-and-go sections, with prepared foods on par with restaurant cooking, perfect for picnicking (remember, it infrequently rains between May and October). At resort areas in the off-season (such as Lake Tahoe in October and May), you can often find two-for-one dinner specials at upper-end restaurants; check coupon apps or local papers or with visitor bureaus.

RESERVATIONS AND DRESS

Regardless of where you are, it's a good idea to make a reservation if you can. We only mention reservations specifically when they are essential (there's no other way you'll ever get a table) or when they are not accepted. For popular restaurants, book as far ahead as you can (often 30 days), and reconfirm as soon as you arrive. (Large parties should always call ahead to check the reservations policy.) We mention dress only when men are required to wear a jacket or a jacket and tie.

Online reservation services make it easy to book a table before you even leave home. OpenTable covers many California cities.

Contacts OpenTable ⊕ *www.opentable.com.*

WINES, BEER, AND SPIRITS

Throughout the state, most famously in the Napa and Sonoma valleys, you can visit wineries, many of which have tasting rooms and offer tours. Microbreweries are an emerging trend in the state's cities and in some rural areas in northern California. The legal drinking age is 21.

▌ HEALTH

Smoking is illegal in all California bars and restaurants, including on outdoor dining patios in some cities. If you have an existing medical condition that may require emergency treatment, be aware that many rural and mountain communities have only daytime clinics, not hospitals with 24-hour emergency rooms.

Outdoor sports are a huge draw in California's moderate climate but caution, especially in unfamiliar areas, is key. Drownings occur each year because beach lovers don't heed warnings about high surfs with their deadly rogue waves. Do not fly within 24 hours of scuba diving.

▌ HOURS OF OPERATION

Banks in California are typically open weekdays from 9 to 6 and Saturday morning; most are closed on Sunday and most holidays. Smaller shops usually operate from 10 to 6, with larger stores remaining open until 8 or later. Hours vary for museums, historical sites, and state parks, and many are closed one or more days a week, or for extended periods during off-season months. It's a good idea to check before you visit a tourist site.

▌ MONEY

San Francisco tends to be an expensive city to visit, and rates at coastal resorts are almost as high. Hotel rates average $150 to $250 a night (though you can find cheaper places), and dinners at even moderately priced restaurants often cost $20 to $40 per person. Costs in the Gold Country and the Far North are considerably less—many fine Gold Country bed-and-breakfasts charge around $100 a night, and some motels in the Far North charge $70 to $90.

CREDIT CARDS

It's a good idea to inform your credit-card company before you travel. Otherwise, unusual activity might prompt the company to put a hold on your card—not a good thing halfway through your trip. Record all your credit-card numbers—as well as the phone numbers to call if your cards are lost or stolen—in a safe place, so you're prepared should something go wrong. Both MasterCard and Visa have general numbers you can call (collect if you're abroad) if your card is lost or not working.

Reporting Lost Cards American Express
☎ 800/992–3404 in U.S., 715/343–7977 collect from abroad ⊕ www.americanexpress.com. **Discover** ☎ 800/347–2683 in U.S., 801/902–3100 collect from abroad ⊕ www.discover.com. **Diners Club** ☎ 800/234–6377 in U.S., 514/877–1577 collect from abroad ⊕ www.dinersclub.com. **MasterCard** ☎ 800/627–8372 in U.S., 636/722–7111 collect from abroad ⊕ www.mastercard.com. **Visa** ☎ 800/847–2911 in U.S., 303/967–1096 collect from abroad ⊕ www.visa.com.

▌ SAFETY

California is a safe place to visit, as long as you take the usual precautions. In large cities ask the concierge or desk clerk to point out areas on your map that you should avoid. Lock valuables in a hotel safe when you're not using them. (Some hotels have in-room safes large enough to hold a laptop computer.) Keep an eye on your handbag when you're out in public. Security is high (but mostly invisible) at theme parks and resorts.

▌ TAXES

Sales tax in the state of California is 8.25% but local taxes vary and may be as much as an additional 1.5%. Sales tax applies to all purchases except for food bought in a grocery store; food consumed in a restaurant is taxed but take-out food is not. Hotel taxes vary widely by region, from about 8% to 15.5%.

▌ TIME

California is in the Pacific time zone. Pacific daylight time (PDT) is in effect from mid-March through early November; the rest of the year the clock is set to Pacific standard time (PST).

▌ TIPPING

Most service workers in California are fairly well paid compared to those in the rest of the country, and extravagant tipping is not the rule here. Exceptions include wealthy enclaves such as San Francisco as well as the most expensive resort areas.

TIPPING GUIDELINES FOR CALIFORNIA	
Bartender	$1 per drink, or 10%–15% of tab per round of drinks
Bellhop	$1–$5 per bag, depending on the level of the hotel
Hotel Concierge	$5 or more, if he/she performs a service for you
Hotel Doorman	$1–$2 if he/she helps you get a cab
Valet Parking Attendant	$2–$5 when you get your car
Hotel Maid	$2–$3 per person, per day; more in high-end hotels
Waiter	15%–20% (20%–25% is standard in upscale restaurants); nothing additional if a service charge is added to the bill
Skycap at Airport	$1–$3 per bag
Hotel Room-Service Waiter	15%–20% per delivery, even if a service charge was added since that fee goes to the hotel, not the waiter
Taxi Driver	15%–20%, but round up the fare to the next dollar amount
Tour Guide	15% of the cost of the tour, more depending on quality

▌ TOURS

Guided tours are a good option when you don't want to do it all yourself. You travel along with a group (sometimes large, sometimes small), stay in prebooked hotels, eat with your fellow travelers (the cost of meals is sometimes included in the price of your tour, sometimes not), and follow a schedule.

But not all guided tours are an if-it's-Tuesday-this-must-be-Yosemite experience. A knowledgeable guide can take you places that you might never discover on your own, and you may be pushed to see more than you would have otherwise. Tours aren't for everyone, but they can be just the thing for trips to places where making travel arrangements is difficult or time-consuming.

Whenever you book a guided tour, find out what's included and what isn't. A "land-only" tour includes all your travel (by bus, in most cases) in the destination, but not necessarily your flights to and from or even within it. Also, in most cases prices in tour brochures don't include fees and taxes. And remember that you'll be expected to tip your guide (in cash) at the end of the tour.

SPECIAL-INTEREST TOURS

BIKING

Bicycling is a popular way to see the California countryside, and commercial tours are available throughout the state. Most three- to five-day trips are all-inclusive— you'll stay in delightful country inns, dine at good regional restaurants, and follow experienced guides. The Northern California Wine Country, with its flat valley roads, is one of the most popular destinations. When booking, ask about level of difficulty, as nearly every trip will involve some hill work. Tours fill up early, so book well in advance.

■ TIP→ Most airlines accommodate bikes as luggage, provided they're dismantled and boxed.

Napa and Sonoma Valley Bike Tours. Single-day bike tours through beautiful Napa and Sonoma wine country offer a casual pace and frequent winery stops. ✉ *6500 Washington St., Yountville* ☎ *707/251–8687 Napa tours, 707/996–2453 Sonoma tours* ⊕ *www.napavalleybiketours.com* 🖃 *From $99.*

Bicycle Adventures. Based in Washington state, this outfitter plans all the meal, lodging and travel details of multi-day bike trips through some of California's most engaging scenery, including the redwoods, wine country, and the North Coast. ✉ *29700 S.E. High Point Way, Issaquah, Washington* ☎ *800/443–6060, 425/250–5540* ⊕ *www.bicycleadventures. com.*

■ VISITOR INFORMATION

The California Travel and Tourism Commission's website takes you to each region of California, with digital visitor guides in multiple languages, driving tours, maps, welcome center locations, information on local tours, links to bed-and-breakfasts, and a complete booking center. It also links you—via the Destinations menu—to the websites of city and regional tourism offices and attractions. ⇨ *For the numbers and websites of regional and city visitor bureaus and chambers of commerce see the "Planning" sections in each chapter.*

Contacts California Travel and Tourism Commission ✉ *Sacramento* ☎ *916/444–4429 CA Tourism Commission office, 800/862–2543 brochures and information* ⊕ *www. visitcalifornia.com.*

INDEX

S

Photo Credits

Front cover: Nick Elias [Description: Carneros, Napa Valley]. 1, Yuen Kwan, Fodors.com member. 2, Bryan Brazil/Shutterstock 5, Heavenly Mountain Resort. Chapter 1: Experience California: 8-9, Jay Anderson, Fodors.com member. 11, Helio San Miguel. 12 (top), Clinton Steeds/Flickr. 12 (bottom), Jose Vigano, Fodors.com member. 13, comfortablynirm, Fodors.com member. 15, vathomp, Fodors.com member. 16, Robert Holmes. 17 (left), sd_foodies, Fodors.com member. 17 (right), Lisa M. Hamilton. 18 (left), Christophe Testi/iStockphoto. 18 (top right), Corbis. 18 (bottom right), Warren H. White. 19 (top left), Alan A. Tobey/iStockphoto. 19 (bottom left), Janet Fullwood. 19 (right), Aaron Kohr/iStockphoto. 20, Warren H. White. 21, Thomas Kranzel/Venture Media. 22, Andrew Zarivny/iStockphoto. 25, Robert Holmes. 26 (top), Janine Bolliger/iStockphoto. 26 (bottom), Lise Gagne/iStockphoto. 27, iStockphoto. 28 (top), Evan Meyer/ iStockphoto. 28 (center), Lise Gagne/iStockphoto. 28 (bottom left), iStockphoto. 28 (bottom right), Lise Gagne iStockphoto. 29, Tom Baker/Shutterstock. 30 (left), SuperStock/age fotostock. 30 (top right), CURAphotography/Shutterstock. 30 (bottom right), Michael Almond/iStockphoto. 31 (top), iStockphoto. 31(bottom), Lise Gagne/iStockphoto. 32 (top), Ross Stapleton-Gray/iStockphoto. 32 (center), Jay Spooner/iStockphoto. 32 (bottom),nTebNad/Shutterstock. 33 (top), Jay Spooner/iStockphoto. 33 (bottom), Lise Gagne/iStockphoto. 34, John Elk III/Alamy. Chapter 2: The Central Coast: 35, TweetieV, Fodors.com member. 36, Stephen Walls/iStockphoto. 37 (top), Bart Everett/iStockphoto. 37 (bottom), Robert Holmes. 38, David M. Schrader/Shutterstock. 48, S. Greg Panosian/iStockphoto. 49, Ruben G. Mendoza. 50 (top), Richard Wong/www.rwongphoto.com/Alamy. 50 (bottom), Ruben G. Mendoza. 51 (top left), Witold Skrypczak/Alamy. 51 (top right), S. Greg Panosian/iStockphoto. 51 (bottom), Janet Fullwood. 52 (top left), GIPhotoStock Z/Alamy. 52 (top right), Craig Lovell/Eagle Visions Photography/Alamy. 52 (bottom) and 53 (top), S. Greg Panosian/iStockphoto. 53 (bottom), Eugene Zelenko/wikipedia.org. 59, David M. Schrader/Shutterstock. 67, Doreen Miller, Fodors.com member. 78, Robert Holmes. 96-97, Valhalla Design & Conquer, Fodors.com member. Chapter 3: The Monterey Bay Area: 101, mellifluous, Fodors.com member. 102, Janet Fullwood. 103 (top), vittorio sciosia/age fotostock. 103 (bottom). Jeff Greenberg/age fotostock. 104, Brent Reeves/Shutterstock. 111, Robert Holmes. 120, Holger Mette/iStockphoto. 127, laurel stewart/iStockphoto. Chapter 4: San Francisco: 151-154,160, Brett Shoaf/Artistic Visuals Photography. 166 (top), Arnold Genthe. 166 (bottom), Library of Congress Prints and Photographs Division. 167 (left), Sandor Balatoni/SFCVB. 167 (right), Detroit Publishing Company Collection, Photography Collection, Miriam and Ira D. Wallach Division of Art, Prints and Photographs, The New York Public Library, Astor, Lenox and Tilden Foundation. 168, Brett Shoaf/Artistic Visuals Photography. 169 (top), Gary Soup/Flickr. 169 (bottom), Albert Cheng/Shutterstock. 170 (top), Sheryl Schindler/SFCVB. 170 (center), Ronen/Shutterstock. 170 (bottom), Robert Holmes. 179, travelstock44/Alamy. 181, Brett Shoaf/Artistic Visuals Photography. 182, San Francisco Municipal Railway Historical Archives. 187, Lewis Sommer/SFCVB. 197, Robert Holmes. 207, aprillilacs, Fodors.com member. 211, Rafael Ramirez Lee/iStockphoto. 216, yummyporky/Flickr. 217 (top and bottom), Lisa M. Hamilton. 244, Rough Guides/Alamy. 251, Robert Holmes. Chapter 5: The Bay Area: 255 and 256, Robert Holmes. 257, Jyeshern Cheng/iStockphoto. 258, Brett Shoaf/Artistic Visuals Photography. 262, Caro/Alamy. 269, 277, 287, Robert Holmes. 295, Robert Holmes. 299, Mark Rasmussen/iStockphoto. 303, S. Greg Panosian/iStockphoto. Chapter 6: The Wine Country: 307, Robert Holmes. 308, iStockphoto. 309, Robert Holmes. 310, Warren H. White. 316, Robert Holmes. 317 (top), kevin miller/iStockphoto. 317 (bottom), Far Niente+Dolce+Nickel & Nickel. 318 (top and bottom) Robert Holmes. 319 (top) Domaine Carneros. 319 (bottom), star5112/Flickr. 320 (top left), Rubicon Estate. 320 (top right and bottom) and 321 (top and bottom), Robert Holmes. 322 (top), Philippe Roy/Alamy. 322 (center), Agence Images/Alamy. 322 (bottom), Cephas Picture Library/Alamy. 323 (top), Napa Valley Conference Bureau. 323 (second and third from top), Wild Horse Winery (Forrest L. Doud). 323 (fourth from top), Napa Valley Conference Bureau. 323 (fifth from top), Panther Creek Cellars (Ron Kaplan). 323 (sixth from top), Clos du Val (Marvin Collins). 323 (seventh from top), Panther Creek Cellars (Ron Kaplan). 323 (bottom), Warren H. White. 325, courtesy of the di Rosa Collection. 328, Robert Holmes. 337, Far Niente+Dolce+Nickel & Nickel. 339, Terry Joanis/Frog's Leap. 347, Chuck Honek/Schramsberg Vineyard. 351, Castello di Amorosa. 361, 364, 370-371, and 374, Robert Holmes. Chapter 7: The North Coast: 381, Thomas Barrat/Shutterstock. 382 (all), Robert Holmes 383 (top), Russ Bishop/age fotostock. 383 (bottom), Robert Holmes. 384, Janet Fullwood. 391, 397, and 399, Robert Holmes. Chapter 8: Redwood National Park: 409, iStockphoto. 410 (top), Michael Schweppe/wikipedia.org. 410 (center), Agnieszka Szymczak/iStockphoto. 410 (bottom), Natalia Bratslavsky/Shutterstock. 412, WellyWelly/Shutterstock. Chapter 9: The Southern Sierra: 417, Randall Pugh, Fodors.com member. 418, Craig Cozart/iStockphoto. 419 (top), David T Gomez/iStockphoto. 419 (bottom left and bottom right), Robert Holmes. 420, christinea78, Fodors.com member. 427, moonjazz/Flickr. 434, Douglas

Atmore/iStockphoto. Chapter 10: Yosemite National Park: 437, Sarah P. Corley, Fodors.com member. 438, Yosemite Concession Services. 439 (top), Andy Z./Shutterstock. 439 (bottom), Greg Epperson/age fotostock. 440, Doug Lemke/Shutterstock. 446, Rebalyn, Fodors.com member. 451, Nathan Jaskowiak/Shutterstock. Chapter 11: Sequoia and Kings Canyon National Parks: 457 and 458, Robert Holmes. 459 (top), Greg Epperson/age fotostock. 459 (bottom) and 460, Robert Holmes. 467, urosr/Shutterstock. 473, Robert Holmes. Chapter 12: Sacramento and the Gold Country: 475 and 477 (top and bottom), Robert Holmes. 478, Andy Z./Shutterstock. 486, Marcin Wichary/Flickr. 495, Image Asset Management/age fotostock. 496 (left and right), wikipedia.org. 496 (center), Charles Danek. 497, Ambient Images Inc./Alamy. 498 (top), Trailmix.Net/Flickr. 498 (center), oger jones/Flickr. 498 (bottom), L. C. McClure/wikipedia.org. 499 (top left), Russ Bishop/age fotostock. 499 (top center), vera bogaerts/iStockphoto. 499 (top right and bottom left), Walter Bibikow/age fotostock. 499 (bottom right), Charles Danek. 502, Janet Fullwood. 509, RickC/Flickr. Chapter 13: Lake Tahoe: 511, Tom Zikas/North Lake Tahoe. 512 (top), Rafael Ramirez Lee/iStockphoto. 512 (bottom) and 513, Janet Fullwood. 514, Jay Spooner/iStockphoto. 523 (top), Heavenly Mountain Resort. 523 (bottom), Jake Foster/iStockphoto. 524 (top), Lake Tahoe Visitors Authority. 524 (bottom left), iStockphoto. 524 (bottom right), Heavenly Mountain Resort. 527 and 528 (left), Andrew Zarivny/iStockphoto. 528 (right), Harry Thomas/iStockphoto. 529 (top left), Joy Strotz/Shutterstock. 529 (bottom left), iStockphoto. 529 (right), Jennifer Stone/Shutterstock. 534, Jay Spooner/iStockphoto. 541, Tom O'Neill. 552, Christopher Russell/iStockphoto. Chapter 14: The Far North: 559, NPS. 560, Robert Holmes. 561 (top), Andy Z./Shutterstock. 561 (bottom), NPS. 562, ThreadedThoughts/Flickr. 568, Robert Holmes. 577, kathycsus/Flickr. 583, NPS. Back cover (from left to right): Celso Diniz/Shutterstock; Dan Harmeson/iStockphoto; Robert Holmes. Spine: S. Greg Panosian/iStockphoto.

About Our Writers: All photos are courtesy of the writers except for the following: Michele Bigley, courtesy of Tony Belko; Cheryl Crabtree, courtesy of Bryn Berg; Denise Leto, courtesy of Kevin Finney; Daniel Mangin, courtesy of J. Rodby; Christine Vovakes, courtesy of Michael Vovakes; Bobbi Zane, courtesy of Leena Hanonnen.

ABOUT OUR WRITERS

Michele Bigley spends most of her days exploring California with her two sons and husband. When not hunting for sand dollars in Santa Cruz, hiking through redwood groves, or munching on tacos in San Francisco, she writes articles, books, iPhone apps, and essays about her travels. Michele updated the San Francisco chapter.

Native Californian **Cheryl Crabtree**—who updated the Central Coast, Monterey Bay, and Southern Sierra chapters—has worked as a freelance writer since 1987. Cheryl is editor of *Montecito Magazine*. Her articles have appeared in many regional and national publications, including US Airways in-flight magazine and *Santa Barbara Seasons*, and annual visitor magazines in Santa Barbara, Ventura, and Pismo Beach. She also authors regional travel apps for mobile devices and co-authors two California winery books.

Longtime Fodor's writer, editor, and contributor to our San Francisco chapter, **Denise M. Leto** roams the city out of sheer love for SF, peeking down overgrown alleyways and exploring tucked-away corners from the Tenderloin to the Richmond, often with her three homeschooled kids in tow.

Daniel Mangin returned to California, where he's maintained a home for three decades, after two stints at the Fodor's editorial offices in New York City, the second one as the Editorial Director of Fodors.com and the Compass American Guides. While at Compass he was the series editor for the California Wine Country guide and commissioned the Oregon Wine Country and Washington Wine Country guides. With several dozen wineries less than a half-hour's drive from home, he often

finds himself transported as if by magic to a tasting room bar, communing with a sophisticated Cabernet or savoring the finish of a smooth Pinot Noir. For this edition, Daniel updated our Wine Country and Sequoia and Kings Canyon National Park chapters.

Jenie Skoy is a travel writer who has contributed to AOL Travel, *Sunset, USA Today,* and many others. When she's not writing about travel or food, she teaches college-level writing in Salt Lake City, Utah. For this edition, she updated the Sacramento and the Gold Country chapter.

Freelance writer **Christine Vovakes**—who updated the North Coast, Lake Tahoe, Far North, the Redwoods, and Travel Smart chapters—has contributed to *Fodor's California* since 2004. Her travel articles and photographs have appeared in many publications, including *The Washington Post, The Christian Science Monitor, The Sacramento Bee,* and the *San Francisco Chronicle.*

Sharron Wood has contributed to dozens of Fodor's travel guides, writing about everything from hiking in the high Sierra to hitting the nightclubs in San Francisco. She also writes about San Francisco restaurants, edits cookbooks, or shakes up cocktails for a houseful of friends in San Francisco. She updated the Yosemite chapter for this edition.

Bobbi Zane—who updated Experience Northern California—grew up in Southern California. She now lives in historic Julian in San Diego County. Her articles on Palm Springs have appeared in the *Orange County Register* and *Westways* magazine. She has also contributed to *Escape to Nature Without Roughing It.*